The Heart & Soul of Change

Mark A. Hubble   Barry L. Duncan   Scott D. Miller

The Heart & Soul of Change

What Works in Therapy

American Psychological Association
Washington, DC

Published by
American Psychological Association
750 First Street, NE
Washington, DC 20002

Copies may be ordered from
APA Order Department
P.O. Box 92984
Washington, DC 20090-2984

In the United Kingdom and Europe, copies may be ordered from
American Psychological Association
3 Henrietta Street
Covent Garden
London WC2E 8LU
England

Typeset in Meridien by Harlowe Typography, Inc., Cottage City, MD

Printer: Braun-Brumfield Inc., Ann Arbor, MI
Jacket designer: Design Concepts, San Diego, CA
Technical/production editor: Tanya Y. Alexander

Library of Congress Cataloging-in-Publication Data
The heart and soul of change : what works in therapy / Mark A. Hubble,
    Barry L. Duncan, and Scott D. Miller, editors.
        p. cm.
    Includes bibliographical references and index.
    ISBN 1-55798-557-X (case : alk. paper)
    1. Psychiatry—Differential therapeutics. 2. Psychotherapy.
    3. Strategic therapy. I. Hubble, Mark L., 1951–xxxx. II. Duncan,
    Barry L. III. Miller, Scott D.
    RC480.52.H43   1999
    616.89'14—dc21   96-27729
                                                            CIP

British Library Cataloguing-in-Publication Data
A CIP record is available from the British Library.

Printed in the United States of America
First edition

*Dedicated
to
Saul Rosenzweig*

Contents

III

SPECIAL APPLICATIONS OF THE COMMON FACTORS

IV

IMPLICATIONS OF THE COMMON FACTORS FOR REIMBURSEMENT POLICY AND PRACTICE

Contributors

Timothy Anderson, PhD, is an assistant professor in the Department of Psychology at Ohio University. Dr. Anderson researches psychotherapy training, assessment issues in psychotherapy research, and basic interpersonal processes in therapeutic relationships. He completed a postdoctoral fellowship in clinical psychology at Vanderbilt University with Hans Strupp.

Ted P. Asay, PhD, is a clinical psychologist in private practice in Dallas, Texas, and a research associate at the Timberlawn Psychiatric Research Foundation. Dr. Asay received his doctoral degree in clinical psychology from Brigham Young University and later completed a postdoctoral fellowship in clinical psychology at Timberlawn Psychiatric Hospital. He has served in several leadership positions in local and state professional associations and has written and presented on treatment outcome.

Alexandra Bachelor, PhD, joined the faculty of Laval University in Quebec, Canada, in 1984, after several years in private practice. Currently, as professor of psychology, Dr. Bachelor is involved in clinical training and supervision and also teaches qualitative research methodology. Over the past years, her research interests have focused on the therapeutic relationship and related topics, with special interest in the therapy participant's perspective.

Adrian J. Blow is a native of South Africa and a doctoral candidate in the Marriage and Family Therapy program at Purdue University. His main interests include the process of therapy and what factors bring about change in people's lives. He has written on the role of self-agency in therapy.

Arthur C. Bohart, PhD, received his doctoral degree in clinical psychology and is currently professor of psychology at California State University, Dominguez Hills. Dr. Bohart is a Fellow of the American Psychological Association (APA), the author of a number of professional articles, and the coeditor (with Leslie Greenberg) of *Empathy Reconsidered: New Directions in Psychotherapy* (APA, 1997). He is coauthor of the upcoming book *How Clients Make Therapy Work: The Process of Active Self-Healing* (APA, 1999).

Jeb Brown, PhD, is director of the Clinical Informatics Program for Human Affairs International, Inc. Dr. Brown received his doctorate from Duke University and is a licensed psychologist with more than 20 years of experience in a variety of clinical and managed care environments.

Jennifer S. Cheavens received her bachelor of science degree summa cum laude from James Madison University in 1994. She began her graduate work in the Clinical Psychology Program at the University of Kansas in 1996 and has taught undergraduate psychology courses in this setting. Cheavens has published articles and chapters on hope theory and is interested in exploring the role of hope in facilitating the coping process.

Ronald J. Chenail, PhD, is dean of the School of Social and Systemic Studies and associate professor in the Department of Family Therapy at Nova Southeastern University in Fort Lauderdale. He is editor of the online journal, *The Qualitative Report,* and serves on the editorial boards of *Qualitative Inquiry* and *Contemporary Family Therapy.* His books include *Medical Discourse and Systemic Frames of Comprehension, Practicing Therapy* (with Anne Rambo and Tony Heath), *The Talk of the Clinic* (with G. H. Morris), and *New Careers for Therapists* (with Jan Chenail).

Mitchell H. Dickey, PhD, received his doctorate in clinical psychology from Yale University. Dr. Dickey has taught at two family therapy programs—Purdue University and Southern Connecticut State University. His research interests focus on improving the quality of care (process and outcome) for children and families in community-based agencies. As a Fellow in the Health Policy Program in Yale University's Department of Epidemiology and Public Health, Dr. Dickey is studying how managed care has affected family involvement on a child inpatient unit. He has been doing clinical work with families since 1982, when he coordinated an outpatient department at a small community health agency in Ohio.

Sandra Dreis, LCSW, graduated with her master's degree in social work from the University of Utah in 1978. Her clinical background includes a 2-year internship at the Veterans Affairs Hospital in Salt Lake City, 2 years with a county mental health intensive treatment unit, 11 years with a private nonprofit child welfare agency (which she managed for the past 6 years). Dreis has served a wide variety of populations and has been involved with the Utah legislature and chairing a variety of committees, including Title XX for Salt Lake County. Dreis joined the staff of Human Affairs International (HAI) in 1991 as a care manager. She has worked at HAI in an assortment of roles that eventually led to her early and continued involvement with the Clinical Informatics Program.

Roger P. Greenberg, PhD, is professor and head of the Division of Clinical Psychology in the Department of Psychiatry and Behavioral Science at the State University of New York Science Center in Syracuse. He also has an active private practice. His more than 160 publications include several books (coauthored or coedited with Seymour Fisher): *The Scientific Credibility of Freud's Theories and Therapy* (1985, selected by both the National Library Association and *Psychology Today* as 1 of the 10 best books in the Behavioral Sciences), *The Limits of Biological Treatments for Psychological Distress: Comparisons with Psychotherapy and Placebo* (1989), *Freud Scientifically Reappraised: Testing the Theories and Therapy* (1996), and *From Placebo to Panacea: Putting Psychiatric Drugs to the Test* (1997).

Adam Horvath, PhD, was born in Budapest, Hungary, and has been living in Canada since 1956. Dr. Horvath is currently associate professor in the Counseling Psychology program and an associate of the Psychology Department at Simon Fraser University. He is also in private practice, counseling couples, families, and individuals since 1970. Since 1980, Dr. Horvath has been interested in the interpersonal aspects of counseling and therapy. This interest led to a variety of research projects, including the development of The Working Alliance Inventory, intensive longitudinal case studies, investigations of the relationship in a variety of counseling and therapeutic environments, and his currently ongoing program of research on the alliance. He has published over 25 articles and chapters and edited a book on the therapeutic relationship. Dr. Horvath is currently principal investigator of an ongoing research program exploring critical events in couples counseling.

Michael J. Lambert, PhD, is a professor in the Department of Psychology at Brigham Young University, where he teaches in the doctoral training program. Dr. Lambert is currently associate editor of the *Journal of Consulting and Clinical Psychology* and on the editorial board of numerous scientific journals. Dr. Lambert has also served as a consultant to the National Institute for Mental Health and many behavioral health insurance companies evaluating and developing outcome measures for clinical trials in psychotherapy. He is coauthor of the Outcome Questionnaire and Youth Outcome Questionnaire (measures of patient change used in private practice and managed care settings), and coauthored *Assessing Outcome in Clinical Practice* (Allyn & Bacon, 1996).

Kirk M. Lunnen received his bachelor's degree in psychology from Brigham Young University and his master's degree in clinical psychology from Ohio University. He is currently a clinical psychology resident at Wright–Patterson Air Force Base in Dayton, Ohio in pursuit of his doctoral degree. His research interests include psychotherapy process and outcome, instrument development, and the assessment and treatment of depression.

Paul V. Maione, PhD, is an adjunct professor in the School of Social and Systemic Studies at Nova Southeastern University and the clinical director of the Atrium Family Center in Fort Lauderdale, Florida. Maione recently completed a clinical qualitative research project on family therapy with adolescents incarcerated in adult jails and he has published several articles on qualitative research in family therapy.

Scott T. Michael received his bachelor of science degree, cum laude, in psychology from Santa Clara University in 1992. Thereafter, he worked as a substance abuse counselor for 3 years at the Bay Area Addiction Research and Treatment Clinic on the edge of the Tenderloin in San Fransisco. In the fall of 1996, Michael began his graduate studies in the Clinical Psychology Program at the University of Kansas, where he has focused his interests on hope as a common factor in psycotherapy outcome, as well as the role of sharing and disclosing personal narrative as a process facilitating hope and coping. Michael has authored several publications dealing with various aspects of hope theory.

John J. Murphy, PhD, is an assistant professor of Psychology and Counseling at the University of Central Arkansas. Dr. Murphy has extensive experience applying a common factors approach to school problems and other issues affecting children, adolescents, and families. He has published numerous articles and chapters on practical, cooperative approaches to resolving school problems, including two recent books, *Solution-Focused Counseling in Middle and High Schools* (American Counseling Association, 1997) and, with Barry L. Duncan, *Brief Intervention for School Problems* (Guilford Press, 1997). Dr. Murphy has worked in public schools as a psychologist, teacher, and administrator. He frequently presents training workshops to school counselors, psychologists, social workers, and teachers throughout the United States. Dr. Murphy is the winner of the American Counseling Association's 1998 "Writer of the Year" Award.

David K. Nace, MD, is vice president and chief medical officer, Clinical Policies and Programs, of Human Affairs International, Inc. Dr. Nace earned his bachelor's degree (magna cum laude) in chemistry and biology from the Philadelphia College of Pharmacy and Science and his doctor of medicine degree from the University of Pittsburgh. Dr. Nace is board certified with multiple subspecialty certifications and has considerable experience in directing behavioral healthcare programs in a variety of settings. Dr. Nace is the author of a number of original papers, articles, and book reviews. He often presents at key industry conferences and is frequently consulted by government and various professional industry groups. He is also very active in the American Psychiatric Association and the American Managed Behavioral Healthcare Association.

Benjamin M. Ogles, PhD, received his doctoral degree from Brigham Young University in 1990, after completing a predoctoral clinical internship at Indiana University Medical School. He is currently an associate professor in the Department of Psychology at Ohio University. Dr. Ogles is a coauthor of *Assessing Outcome in Clinical Practice* (Allyn & Bacon, 1996).

James O. Prochaska, PhD, is director of the Cancer Prevention Research Consortium and professor of clinical and health psychology at the University of Rhode Island. He is the author of over 100 publications, including three books, *Changing for Good, Systems of Psychotherapy: A Transtheoretical Analysis,* and *The Transtheoretical Approach: Crossing Traditional Boundaries of Psychotherapy.* Dr. Prochaska has won numerous awards, including one of the Top Five Most Cited Authors in Psychology from the American Psychological Society and an Honorary Chair of Medicine from the University of Birmingham, England. He is frequently an invited speaker at regional, national, and international meetings and conferences.

Albert W. Scovern, PhD, received his doctoral degree in clinical psychology in 1980 from the University of South Carolina following an internship at Duke University Medical Center. Subsequently, he completed a research fellowship at Duke's Center for the Study of Aging and Adult Development and a 2-year postdoctoral fellowship at Menninger in Topeka, Kansas. Dr. Scovern has both a clinical and research background in the areas of behavioral and psychosomatic medicine, with special emphasis on psychological treatments for chronic pain and headache. He has also coauthored several articles dealing with behavioral aspects of diabetes and diabetes management. Formerly director of Harding Hospital's Outpatient Diagnostic and Psychotherapy Service, he is partner and founder of Northeast Psychology Associates (NPA), a private practice group of clinical psychologists. Dr. Scovern currently teaches in NPA's Postgraduate Clinical Training Program.

C. R. Snyder, PhD, received his doctoral degree in clinical psychology from Vanderbilt University in 1971, and in 1972, was a fellow in medical psychology at the Langley Porter Neuropsychiatric Institute, University of California, San Francisco. Since 1972, Dr. Snyder has been in the Department of Psychology at the University of Kansas, Lawrence, where he has been the director of the Graduate Training Program in Clinical Psychology since 1975. He has received awards for his research and teaching at Kansas, with the unique honor of being selected as the outstanding professor at both the undergraduate (the Hope Award) and graduate (the Byrd Award and Kemper Fellow) levels. An advocate of the interface between social and clinical psychology, Dr. Snyder has been the editor of the *Journal of Social and Clinical Psychology* since 1988. He has published books on the process of distancing oneself from negative outcomes (*Excuses: Masquerades in Search of Grace,* 1983; *Coping With Negative Life Events,* 1987; and *Self-Handicapping: The Paradox That Isn't,* 1990) and the process of attaching oneself to positive outcomes (*Uniqueness: The Human Pursuit of Difference,* 1980; *Hope: You Can Get There From Here,* 1994; and *Hope for the Journey: Helping Children Through Good Times and Bad,* 1997). Dr. Snyder has been elected to fellow status in Divisions 2, 8, 12, and 38 of the American Psychological Association.

Douglas H. Sprenkle, PhD, is professor of Marriage and Family Therapy (MFT) at Purdue University and for nine years was the Director of the Doctoral Program in MFT at the same institution. He is a former editor of the *Journal of Marital and Family Therapy.* Dr. Sprenkle has authored and edited five books including the recently published *Family Therapy Research: A Handbook of Methods* (with Sidney Moon) and *The Family Therapy Sourcebook* (2nd ed., with Fred Piercy and Joseph Wetchler). He has served on the Commission on Accreditation for and Family Therapy Education and was given the Significant Contribution to Family Therapy Award by the American Association for Marriage and Family Therapy for both his scholarly and professional contributions to the field.

Karen Tallman has masters' degrees in both clinical psychology and statistics and measurement. She is currently completing work on a doctorate in educational psychology at the University of

Southern California, Los Angeles. Her research includes qualitative and quantitative investigations into motivational systems. She is developing and validating an instrument assessing beliefs about personality change and their impact on performance in clinical psychology, education, and business. She is coauthor of the upcoming book for the American Psychological Association titled *How Clients Make Therapy Work: The Process of Active Self-Healing (1999).*

John C. Norcross, PhD

Foreword

Let's confront the unpleasant reality and say it out loud: The rivalrous warfare among theoretical orientations in psychotherapy has impeded scientific advances and hindered the development of effective treatments. In the dogma-eat-dogma environment of "schoolism," clinicians traditionally operated from within their own particular theoretical frameworks, often to the point of being oblivious to alternative conceptualizations and potentially superior interventions. Although this ideological cold war may have been a necessary developmental stage, its day has come and passed. The era of rapprochement is upon us.

Yet, the features that ostensibly distinguish psychotherapies from each other still receive special emphasis in the pluralistic, competitive American society. Therapy developers, like Madison Avenue advertisers, continue to market their systems as both novel and superior—all in the absence of empirical evidence. As Marvin Goldfried (1980) lamented, far too often in psychotherapy we speak of "who is correct" rather than "what is correct."[1] The result, Jerome Frank (1973) argued in his classic *Persuasion and Healing*,[2] is that little glory has been accorded the identification of shared or common components. Purportedly new and unique psychotherapies are advanced weekly at the expense of the fundamentals of effective treatment.

---

[1]Goldfried, M. R. (1980). Toward the delineation of therapeutic change principles. *American Psychologist, 35,* 991–999.

[2]Frank, J. (1973). *Persuasion and healing* (2nd ed.). Baltimore: Johns Hopkins University Press.

An appreciable portion, probably the majority, of psychotherapy outcome is attributable to common factors. The massive evidence supporting this conclusion has been largely dismissed in professional circles. Such evidence threatens the "bonfire of the vanities," as the editors characterize it, and our theoretical narcissism, as I prefer to call it.

In this context, Drs. Hubble, Duncan, and Miller manifest considerable courage and admirable foresight in compiling this superb volume, aptly titled *The Heart and Soul of Change*, that summarizes what the evidence tells us actually works in psychotherapy, as opposed to what theories posit should work. They expertly systematize and concretize the role of the common factors across the helping professions. The 14 chapters of this book convincingly demonstrate how these commonalities powerfully operate in any behavioral change enterprise, including individual therapy, medicine, pharmacotherapy, family therapy, and in the schools.

The aim of common factors is to determine the core ingredients that different therapies share, with the eventual goal of creating more parsimonious and efficacious treatments based on those commonalities. Although different terms are applied to the phenomenon—active ingredients, therapeutic commonalities, curative factors, effective principles, and the appalling phrase, "nonspecific factors"—the clinical and empirical conviction is that commonalities are more important in accounting for therapy success than the unique factors that differentiate them. In specifying what is common across disparate orientations, we are also probably specifying what works best among them.

This position is easily misconstrued with such classic refrains as "anything goes" or "technique doesn't matter." The contributors and editors carefully but forcefully distance themselves from such substantive misrepresentations.

The contributors concur that more than commonalities are evident across the therapies: There are unique or specific factors attributable to different therapies as well. One of the seminal achievements of psychotherapy research, as Asay and Lambert note in chapter 2, is the demonstration of the differential effectiveness of psychotherapies with specific disorders (e.g., behavior therapy for child conduct disorders, conjoint therapy for marital conflict, and cognitive therapy for panic disorder). Psychotherapies are also differentially effective with clients at different stages of change, as Prochaska notes in chapter 8, and with clients of different personalities and goals, as other contributors note. Effective clinicians will thus implement those factors common across therapies while capitalizing on the contributions of specific techniques.

Put another way, the thoughtful synthesis of common *and* specific factors will probably be most effective for clients and most congenial to practitioners. Integration will gradually occur by combining fundamental similarities and useful differences across the schools, treasuring our sameness while capitalizing on our differences.

Hubble, Duncan, and Miller assert in their preface that one of the principal objectives of the volume is to specify how psychotherapy informed by common factors can be operationalized in practice. All the authors were encouraged to address what our knowledge of common factors means specifically for conducting psychotherapy. Or providing service, or, in the title of the editors' closing chapter, "Directing Attention to What Works." This constitutes the central challenge to all psychotherapies, common factors and otherwise, in today's mental health marketplace or, perhaps more accurately, jungle place.

We must operationalize specific therapist and client behaviors associated with common factors for purposes of education and research. One cannot function nonspecifically in therapy or training. To encourage a supervisee to "cultivate hope" or to "enhance expectations" is as well intentioned but probably as inefficacious as advising patients to "just relax." The reader will be rewarded with reasonably concrete and specific suggestions for improving treatment outcomes in every chapter and particularly in the splendid final chapter.

Early efforts to catalog or distill common factors have suffered from narrow views of the common factors themselves. Several years ago Lisa Grencavage and I conducted a review of 50 publications to discern commonalities among proposed therapeutic commonalities—commonalities squared, so to speak. We discovered that several authors proposed only a single common factor and that most authors focused on a single domain, be it client characteristic, therapist quality, treatment structure, or the therapeutic relationship. No such simplistic formulations will be proposed in this book. The contributors in this engaging dialogue offer transtheoretical and inclusive views of a complex process. Common factors are not located solely in the therapist, but also in the client; not solely in the intratherapy alliance, but also in the broader environmental context (including managed care); not solely in formal treatment, but also as part of clients' self-change.

The Heart and Soul of Change transcends the therapy wars and advances a mature peace in which effective psychotherapy and suffering clients are the victors. Let's say that out loud, too: The victors should be effective psychotherapy and our clients, not rivalrous theories of psychotherapy.

Preface

Five years ago, we got together at the annual Family Therapy Network Symposium in Washington, DC. All of us were presenting at the conference and were impressed with the wide range of theories, therapies, models, and approaches being promoted. The experience, far from uplifting, however, led to much discussion about the status of the field and, more important, the future of the profession. We were very alarmed that at a time when special interest groups, outside agencies, and insurance entities are scrutinizing therapy, so many disagreements continue about what makes therapy work and whose is better. If our own house was in such disorder, we worried that our survival could hardly be assured in the increasingly unfriendly environment professional therapy now finds itself. In harsher terms, a field that sees models and therapies fall in and out of favor with the capriciousness observed in the fashion industry demands little respect.

No longer comfortable merely sitting on the sidelines and watching the steady parade of therapies, we decided to turn to the clinical and research literature for answers on what matters for effective treatment. The results of our efforts resulted in two books (Duncan, Hubble, & Miller, 1997b; Miller, Duncan, & Hubble, 1997), many articles (Duncan, Hubble, & Miller, 1997a, 1997c; Duncan, Hubble, & Rusk, 1994; Hubble, 1993, 1995; Hubble, Miller, & Duncan, in press; Miller, 1994; Miller, Hubble, & Duncan, 1995, 1997), and several book chapters (Duncan, Hubble, Miller, & Coleman, 1998; Duncan, Miller, & Hubble, 1998a,

1998b). In all, we found that the effectiveness of therapies resides not in the many variables that ostensibly distinguish one approach from another. Instead, it is principally found in the factors that all therapies share in common.

On reviewing the literature, we also ran across many people who have contributed to our understanding of the pantheoretical or common factors of therapy. Both influenced and inspired by their efforts, we chose as our next project a book that would bring some of these leading clinicians and researchers together. In effect, we wanted to create another forum where the important findings bearing on the common factors could be presented and evaluated. To our delight, the contributors, when invited, enthusiastically agreed to be part of this work and put their full support behind it. The American Psychological Association and especially our editors, Margaret Schlegel and Ted Baroody, seeing the timeliness and value of this undertaking, agreed to publish it.

Understanding that the now famous *Handbook of Psychotherapy and Behavior Change* had made its last appearance in its fourth edition (Bergin & Garfield, 1994), we conceived this new volume, *The Heart and Soul of Change*, to serve as a handbook for the common factors. It would accomplish two purposes. First, to the common factors, we wanted to bring the coverage of research seen in past editions of the *Handbook of Psychotherapy and Behavior Change*. Second, we hoped to emphasize how a therapy informed by the common factors might be operationalized in actual practice. Thus, the present volume seeks to reflect the best of both worlds, empirical investigation and day-to-day clinical work.

As we noted in our book *Escape from Babel: A Unifying Language for Psychotherapy Practice* (Miller, Duncan, & Hubble, 1997), the ideas we have written about depend heavily on others. In particular, we acknowledge the many researchers in the fields of psychotherapy outcome and process and social psychology. We are indebted to all of the researchers and therapists whose work we have read and cited. Our contributors deserve a special, heartfelt thanks. They made this book a reality.

Appreciation also goes to other researchers and clinicians whose pioneering work on the common curative elements in psychotherapy has greatly influenced our own work. Though not exhaustive, we want to recognize Jerome Frank, Lewis Wolberg, Carl Rogers, Sol Garfield, Ken Howard, and C. H. Patterson. We also want to mention a number of people whose work, supervision, and support has nurtured and enriched our personal and professional lives. These include Lynn Johnson, Hal Miller, John Walter, Jeffrey Zeig, Larry Hopwood, Karen Donahey, Karen Adler, John Weakland, Doug Buchanan,

Charles Gelso, Andy Solovey, and Sue Van Allen. Barry would like extend thanks to the faculty of the Department of Family Therapy at Nova Southeastern University: Pat Cole, Margo Weiss, Lee Shilts, Anne Rambo, and especially Chris Burnett, Douglas Flemons, and Shelley Green, for both providing a collaborative context for scholarship, and for their ongoing commitment to quality teaching and training of our students. Barry is also appreciative of the unending enthusiasm of the students, too many to mention, in the Department of Family Therapy. We are indebted to Jeff Blyth for his invaluable library assistance. Last, a special thanks goes to Jean Hubble, Medical Director of the Parkinson's Disease Center of Excellence at the Ohio State University Hospitals. Without these many researchers, mentors, and friends, this book would not have been possible.

References

Bergin, A. E., & Garfield, S. L. (Eds.). (1994). *Handbook of psychotherapy and behavior change* (4th ed.). New York: Wiley.

Duncan, B. L., Hubble, M. A., & Miller, S. D. (1997a). Doing the impossible. *Professional Counselor, 12*(3), 45–50

Duncan, B. L., Hubble, M. A., & Miller, S. D. (1997b). *Psychotherapy with "impossible" cases: The efficient treatment of therapy veterans.* New York: Norton.

Duncan, B. L. Hubble, M. A., & Miller, S. D. (1997c). Stepping off the throne. *The Family Therapy Networker, 21*(4), 22–31, 33.

Duncan, B., Hubble, M., Miller, S., & Coleman, S. (1998). Escaping the lost world of impossibility: Honoring clients' language, motivation, and theories of change. In M. A. Hoyt (Ed.), *The handbook of constructive therapies* (pp. 293–313). San Francisco: Jossey-Bass.

Duncan, B. L., Hubble, M. A., & Rusk, G. (1994). To intervene or not to intervene? That is not the question. *Journal of Systemic Therapies, 13*(4), 22–30.

Duncan, B., Miller, S., & Hubble, M. (1998a). Some therapies are more equal than others. In W. H. Matthews & J. Edgette (Eds.), *Current thinking and research in brief therapy: Solutions, strategies, narratives* (pp. 203–227). New York: Brunner/Mazel.

Duncan, B. L., Miller, S. D., & Hubble, M. A. (1998b). Uncommonly common therapy. In W. H. Matthews & J. Edgette (Eds.), *Current thinking and research in brief therapy: Solutions, strategies, narratives* (pp. 231–235). New York: Brunner/Mazel.

Hubble, M. A. (1993). Therapy research: The bonfire of the uncertainties. *The Family Psychologist: Bulletin of the Division of Family Psychology (43), 9*(2), 14–16.

Hubble, M. A. (1995). The integration of therapy: There is nothing new under the sun [Review of *Handbook of psychotherapy integration* edited by J. C. Norcross & M. R. Goldfried and *Metaframeworks: Transcending the models of family therapy*, by D. C. Breulin, R. C. Schwartz, & B. M. Mac Kune-Karrer]. *Journal of Systemic Therapies, 14*(1), 69–75.

Hubble, M. A., Miller, S. D., & Duncan, B. L. (in press). S.W.A.T.: "Special" words and tactics for critical situations. *Crisis Intervention and Time-Limited Treatment.*

Miller, S. D. (1994). The solution conspiracy: A mystery in three installments. *Journal of Systemic Therapies, 13*(1), 18–37.

Miller, S. D., Duncan, B. L., & Hubble, M. A. (1997). *Escape from Babel: Toward a unifying language for psychotherapy practice.* New York: Norton.

Miller, S. D., Hubble, M. A., & Duncan, B. L. (1995). No more bells and whistles. *The Family Therapy Networker, 19*(2), 52–58, 62–63.

Miller, S. D., Hubble, M. A., & Duncan, B. L. (1997). Counseling for a change. *Professional Counselor, 12*(1), 15–16, 52–53.

Mark A. Hubble, Barry L. Duncan, and Scott D. Miller

Introduction | 1

To follow knowledge like a sinking star,
Beyond the upmost bound of human thought . . .
To strive, to seek, to find, and not to yield.

—TENNYSON, *Ulysses*

 s this book was being prepared, British psychologist Hans Eysenck died. Eysenck, the great gadfly to the advocates of therapy, slammed the mental health professions for their ineffectiveness during the 1950s and 1960s. Through his analyses of outcome research, he claimed that approximately two thirds of all clients, bearing a diagnosis of neurosis, substantially improved within 2 years of entering therapy. He also claimed that an equal proportion of clients, also labeled *neurotic*, improved within a comparable period without therapy (Bergin & Lambert, 1978). This inauspicious, unfavorable assessment ignited a firestorm of debate and long put the mental health professions on the defensive.

The uncertainties loosed on the clinical and counseling disciplines by Eysenck and like-minded critics have now been set aside. Therapy works (Asay & Lambert, Chap. 2, this volume; Lambert, 1992; Lambert & Bergin, 1994). More than 40 years of outcome research make clear that therapists are not witch doctors, snake oil peddlers, or overachieving do-gooders (Hubble, 1993; Miller, Duncan, & Hubble, 1997, Miller, Hubble, & Duncan, 1995). Study after study, meta-analyses, and scholarly reviews have legitimized psychologically based or informed interventions.

Regarding at least its general efficacy, few believe that therapy need be put to the test any longer.

The good news of therapy's usefulness has been accompanied by an unprecedented expansion in the number of mental health practitioners. This boom amounts nearly to a 275% increase in professional therapists since the mid-1980s (Miller, Hubble, & Duncan, 1996). Consumers can currently choose among psychiatrists, psychologists, psychoanalysts, Jungian analysts, social workers, licensed professional counselors, family therapists, marriage and family counselors, psychiatric nurses, pastoral counselors, alcoholism and addiction counselors, and others advertising their services under an assortment of job titles and descriptions. Observers both in and out of the helping professions (e.g., Austad, 1996; Barker, 1982; Coontz, 1992; Katz & Liu, 1991; Sykes, 1993; Zeig & Munion, 1990; Zilbergeld, 1983) offer rich and provocative commentary on the reasons for the growth of the therapy industry, but many agree it has little to do with a real decline in the overall mental health of the American public.

With so many therapists to choose from, the economic and political consequences could not be escaped. The inevitable competition for jobs, prestige, and influence markedly spiraled (Spivack, 1984). In response, the various professions promote a psychological and social agenda in which they render the world their oyster (Hubble & Duncan, 1993). In short, aggressive efforts are pursued to convert every aspect of living into a problem amenable to therapy (see Barker, 1982). This helps explain, in part, why the number of categories of the American Psychiatric Association's *Diagnostic and Statistical Manual of Mental Disorders* (*DSM*) jumped from 66 in the first edition to 286, in the fourth (American Psychiatric Association, 1952, 1994). Renowned psychiatrist Jerome Frank's (1973) ironic observation is apparently being borne out—psychotherapy may be the only treatment that creates the illness it treats.

Competition has also promoted proliferation of other sorts. Among professions, notably between psychiatry and psychology, loud, incessant, and even hateful arguments are heard. The basic theme is that we in X profession are better equipped to minister to the psychological needs of the citizenry than you in Y profession. So-called biological or organic psychiatrists insist, for instance, that psychopharmacotherapy, a practice licensed to them, holds the answer to the many sufferings visited on people. Some psychologists, ready to accept that claim, press hard for prescription privileges. Of course, whether this achieves the parity to which these clinicians aspire remains open. Moreover, owing to the problems with drug therapy—carefully discussed by Roger Greenberg in chapter 10 of this volume—the desired victory, if won, may be decidedly hollow. In any event, for all the rancor and partisan posturing, none of the participants "clearly demonstrate a consistent superiority in efficacy over all other groups" (Garfield & Bergin, 1994, p. 5).

The proliferation of claims and counterclaims of exceptional abilities among the mental health disciplines perhaps has only been exceeded by the propagation of different models of therapy. Dating from the 1960s, the number of psychotherapy approaches and theories has grown approximately 600% (Miller et al., 1996) . Although the actual figures vary among observers, it is estimated there are now more than 200 therapy models. Techniques, associated with the various models exceed 400 (Garfield & Bergin, 1994). Based on projections available to him at the time, veteran therapy researcher Sol Garfield (1987) said, "I am inclined to predict that sometime in the next century there will be one form of psychotherapy for every adult in the Western World!" (p. 98). Similar to the turf wars witnessed between professions, the quarrels between the clinicians promoting these models have been acrimonious and unrelenting. The proponents vigorously defend their therapies, emphasizing the singular curative powers of their theories and methods (Miller et al., 1997).

To those who greet these many numbers of therapy approaches and schemes with indifference or a "more is better," cheerful acceptance, the proverbial rude awakening may be imminent. In years past, the professions could spin off as many therapies as they wanted or dared. Consistent with the precedent established by advocates of classical psychoanalysis, the enthusiastic testimonials of their leaders were used to justify treatment protocols. Recognition, if only by the avant garde, was almost certain and payment by the client or insurance company would be made. However, an environment once hospitable to direct analysis, primal screams, protracted hospitalizations, body manipulations of every kind, and past-life regressions has turned hostile. Consumers are better informed. Managed mental health care companies already regulate dosage (frequency and number of sessions), mode of therapy (individual, group, marital, or family), and setting (inpatient and outpatient). Management of treatment philosophy and technique also is gaining ground. A law positing the relationship between theories and their patronage is holding true: *The tolerance for theoretical allegiance is in direct proportion to the money available to support it* (Hubble & O'Hanlon, 1992, emphasis added).

In the wake of these developments and to ensure their continued viability in the market, professional groups are rushing to establish empirically validated treatments (EVTs). Psychiatrists, arguably better positioned because of their historical hegemony in health care and more cooperative attitude with third-party payers, have prepared and distributed practice guidelines targeting specific treatments for specific disorders. Psychologists, fearing that as they did with the *DSM*, they will have to use procedures defined for them by their rivals, are jumping on the EVT bandwagon. EVTs are being extolled as the rallying point, a "common cause" for a clinical profession fighting exclusion (Nathan, 1997, p. 10).

The issue of how consumers, the recipients of our assistance, fare in the midst of these internecine squabbles and changes in service delivery enters tangentially. All the professions passionately proclaim their concern for the welfare of their clientele and wish to preserve consumers' rights to free choice among mental health providers. Yet it does not take a hard-boiled cynic to realize that, when the bottom-line financial and factional interests of the professional guilds are at stake, other considerations come forward. As Abraham Lincoln once said, "Moral principle is a looser bond than pecuniary interest."

At this point, before we are described as traitors to our profession, grumbling malcontents, "on the fringe," or empathically removed from the interests of day-to-day practitioners, other developments even more alarming than the reimbursement revolution are emerging. Specifically, the mental health field has become the target of mass-market books, articles, and newspaper and television exposés (e.g., Kaminer, 1992; Sharkey, 1994). In these reports, clinicians are often accused of greed, fraud, incompetence, ethical violations, and extreme susceptivity to every oddball fad that streaks through the popular culture. The inpatient, for-profit scandal and controversy over false memories have given a strong impetus to these writings and news stories.

The net effect of these indictments is that serious questions have been raised about the right of therapists to practice any form of treatment that has not withstood rigorous empirical or scientific scrutiny. Several interest groups outside the field are lobbying for legislation that would altogether exclude third-party payment for procedures that have not been stringently documented as both safe and effective. Most practicing clinicians, trying with ever more difficulty to do their jobs and do them well, are not likely to be included in these evaluations (Miller et al., 1997). In effect, control of one's professional destiny may be slipping further into the hands not only of insurance entities, but also of legislators and governmental policy makers.

Despite the tsunami of forces threatening to sweep away therapists' livelihoods and deeply felt commitment to helping, clinicians want to know what works. The natural question is, What do we know? What guidelines exist for helping us navigate the difficult terrain of clinical practice? Do EVTs provide the answer or do they represent just another round in the perennial boxing match between and within the mental health professions?

The "Bonfire of the Vanities"

Seek facts and classify them and you will be the workmen of science. Conceive or accept theories and you will be their politicians.

    —NICHOLAS MAURICE ARTHUS (1862–1945), *De l'Anaphylaxie a l'immunité*

The great tragedy of Science—the slaying of a beautiful hypothesis by an ugly fact.

    —THOMAS HENRY HUXLEY, *"Biogenesis and Abiogenesis," (1870)*

Although the mental health professions can rightly claim they have arrived—to the degree we know clinical services do make a difference in the lives of our clientele—we remain strangely adrift. The apparent contradiction is resolved when it is recognized that we have yet to agree on what enables our work to work. In short, if therapy is a mighty engine that helps convey clients to places they want to go, what provides the power? This question is central both to our identity and survival as we enter the next millennium (Miller & Hubble, 1995).

The search for what works has contributed to the explosion of therapy models described above. With Freud, modern psychotherapy was born. Yet before he barely left a mark on the professional landscape, others rose to propose alternatives to his theory and methods. Setting aside discussion of the divisive, emotional tensions at play in Freud's small group of followers (Bennet, 1962; Flegenheimer, 1982; Grosskurth, 1991; Hannah, 1976), Jung, Adler, Rank, and Ferenczi broke ranks. The former disciples proclaimed their theoretical differences, if not independence, promoting their own versions of mental life and therapy. Since those days, the divisions have multiplied. New schools of therapy arrive with the regularity of the Book-of-the-Month Club's main selection. Many claim to be the corrective for all that came before. In addition, most profess to have the inside line on human motivation, the causes of psychological dysfunction, and the best remedies.

Once therapists broke the early taboo against observing and researching therapy, they turned to proving empirically that their therapies were the best. A generation of investigators ushered in the age of comparative clinical trials. Winners and losers were to be had. As Bergin and Lambert (1978) described this time, "Presumably, the one shown to be most effective will prove that position to be correct and will serve as a demonstration that the 'losers' should be persuaded to give up their views " (p. 162). Thus, behavior, psychoanalytic, client-centered or humanistic, rational–emotive, cognitive, time-limited, time-unlimited, and other therapies were pitted against each other in a great battle of the brands.

Nonetheless, all this sound and fury produced an unexpected "bonfire of the vanities." Hubris and the pursuit of dominance flared as the results of these studies mounted. Put another way, reiterating Huxley's epigram introducing this section, science slew a beautiful hypothesis with an ugly fact.

As it turned out, the underlying premise of the comparative studies, that one (or more) therapy would prove superior to others, received virtually no support (Norcross & Newman, 1992). Besides the occasional significant finding for a particular therapy, the critical mass of data revealed no differences in effectiveness among the various treatments for psychological distress. This finding of no difference was cleverly tagged the dodo bird verdict (Luborsky, Singer, & Luborsky, 1975). Borrowed from *Alice in Wonderland* it says, "Everyone has won and so all must have prizes." Now, more than 20 years later and after many attempts to dismiss or overturn it, the dodo bird verdict still stands. Therapy works, but our understanding of what works in therapy is unlikely to be found in the insular explanations and a posteriori reasoning adopted by the different theoretical orientations.

Enter the Common Factors

There is no new thing under the sun.
—BIBLE, Ecclesiastes 1:9

Left with "little evidence to recommend the use of one type [of therapy] over another in the treatment of specific problems" (Norcross & Newman, 1992, p. 9), psychotherapy observers and researchers redirected their attention. A less provincial or *metaview* of therapy was adopted (e.g., Garfield, 1992). Breaking with the tradition of saying, "mine's better," efforts were made to identify the pantheoretical elements that made the various treatments effective. The organizing question became, if therapies work, but it has nothing to do with their bells and whistles, what are the common therapeutic factors?

Interestingly enough, this formulation is not new. The possibility that therapies have more in common than less was broached more than 60 years ago. In 1936, Saul Rosenzweig (to whom this book is dedicated) writing in the *Journal of Orthopsychiatry*, suggested that the effectiveness of different therapy approaches had more to do with their common elements than with the theoretical tenets on which they were based (Goldfried & Newman, 1992, p. 48). Luborsky (1995) says that Rosenzweig's article "deserves a laurel in recognition of its being the first systematic presentation of the idea that common factors across diverse forms of psychotherapy are so omnipresent that comparative treatment studies *should* show nonsignificant differences in outcomes" (p. 106, italics in original). Without any way of knowing, Rosenzweig anticipated the recent interest in the therapeutic alliance as a critical pantheoretical factor (discussed in chap. 5, this volume, by Bachelor and Horvath). In particular, he mentioned that one of the most common factors across therapies was the relationship between the client and clinician. He also noted that all of the therapies of his day involved a system of explanation.

If Rosenzweig wrote the first note of the call to the common factors, Johns Hopkins University's Jerome Frank composed an entire symphony. In all three editions of *Persuasion and Healing: A Comparative Study of Psychotherapy* (1961, 1973; Frank & Frank, 1991), Frank placed therapy within the larger family of projects designed to bring about healing. He (with his psychiatrist daughter, Julia, in the last edition) looked for the threads joining such different activities as traditional psychotherapy, group and family therapies, inpatient treatment, drug therapy, medicine, religiomagical healing in nonindustrialized societies, cults, and revivals.

In their analysis, Frank and Frank (1991) concluded that therapy in its various forms should be thought of as "a single entity." They proposed the following analogy:

> Two such apparently different psychotherapies as psychoanalysis and systematic desensitization could be like penicillin and digitalis—totally different pharmacological agents suitable for totally different conditions. On the other hand, the active therapeutic ingredient of both could be the same analogous to two aspirin-containing compounds marketed under different names. We believe the second alternative is closer to the truth (p. 39).

They also identified four features shared by all effective therapies: (a) "an emotionally charged, confiding relationship with a helping person," (b) "a healing setting," (c) "a rationale, conceptual scheme, or myth that provides a plausible explanation for the patient's symtoms and prescribes a ritual or procedure for resolving them," and (d) "a ritual or procedure that requires the active participation of both patient and therapist and that is believed by both to be the means of restoring the patient's health" (pp. 40–43).

Weinberger (1995) observed that after 1980, an outpouring of writing began to appear on the common factors. Until that time, Frank's work stood virtually alone. Now, a flood of "views on and lists of common factors" may be found; Weinberger noted, too, that a positive relationship exists between year of publication and the number of common factors proposals offered (pp. 44–45).

At this stage in the field's understanding of common factors, an up-to-date compilation and critical review of all the many diverse proposals would be welcome. However desirable, such an undertaking is not attempted in this chapter, nor is it a purpose established for the book. Instead, we offer a plan in this volume for organizing and understanding common factors, including their clinical implications, that provides the following benefits. First, it offers the advantages of both economy and flexibility. Second, it weighs the relative importance of the common factors on the basis of their estimated contribution to treatment outcomes. Third, it gives a direction for future investigations into the relationship between common factors and effective therapy.

The Big Four

What can be done with fewer means is done in vain with many.
　　—WILLIAM OF OCKHAM (1300?–1349?)

Less is more.
　　—ROBERT BROWNING, "Andrea Del Sarto," *Men and Women (1855),*
　　78. *Maxim of Ludwig Mies van der Rohe*

In 1992, Brigham Young University's Michael Lambert proposed four therapeutic factors—extratherapeutic, common factors, expectancy or placebo, and techniques—as the principal elements accounting for improvement in clients. Although not derived from a strict statistical analysis, he wrote that they embody what empirical studies suggest about psychotherapy outcome. Lambert added that the research base for this interpretation of the factors was extensive; spanned decades; dealt with a large number of adult disorders and a variety of research designs, including naturalistic observations, epidemiological studies, comparative clinical trials, and experimental analogues (pp. 96–98).

Inspired by this specification of a "big four," the editors of this volume turned to the literature with the purpose of selecting the major components or ingredients of therapy that provided the best bridge between the various schools (see the Preface). The result of this effort builds on Lambert's earlier work and, more important, significantly broadens the base of what has traditionally been called the common factors (i.e., "nonspecific factors"; Duncan, Hubble, & Miller, 1997; Duncan, Solovey, & Rusk, 1992; Miller et al., 1997; Miller et al., 1995). Although they are discussed thoroughly in the following chapters, the four factors are summarized below.

CLIENT/EXTRATHERAPEUTIC FACTORS

Without a client, therapy does not exist. These factors, unquestionably the most common and powerful of the common factors in therapy, are part of the client or the client's life circumstances that aid in recovery despite the client's formal participation in therapy. They consist of the client's strengths, supportive elements in the environment, and even chance events. In short, they are what clients bring to the therapy room and what influences their lives outside it. As examples of these factors, persistence, faith, a supportive grandmother, membership in a religious community, sense of personal responsibility, a new job, a good day at the tracks, a crisis successfully managed all may be included (Duncan et al., 1997). Lambert (1992) estimated that the client/extratherapeutic factors account for 40% of outcome variance. This hefty percentage represents a departure from convention, considering, as Tallman and Bohart indicate in chapter 4 of this volume, most of what is written about therapy celebrates the contribution of the therapist, therapist's model, or technique.

RELATIONSHIP FACTORS

The next class of factors weighs in with 30% of the successful outcome variance (Lambert, 1992) and largely coincides with what has been typically called the common factors in the literature. These represent a wide range of relationship-mediated variables found among therapies no matter the therapist's theoretical persuasion. Caring, empathy, warmth, acceptance, mutual affirmation, and encouragement of risk taking and mastery are but a few. Except what the client brings to therapy, these variables are probably responsible for most of the gains resulting from psychotherapy interventions (Lambert & Bergin, 1994). True to the position of Rosenzweig (1936) and Frank and Frank (1991), investigators have recently expended much time and energy in researching the therapeutic alliance as one of the more important relationship factors. Therapist-provided variables, especially the core conditions popularized by Carl Rogers, also have been closely examined.

PLACEBO, HOPE, AND EXPECTANCY

Following extratherapeutic and relationship factors are placebo, hope, and expectancy. Lambert (1992) put their contribution to psychotherapy outcome at 15%. In part, this class of therapeutic factors refers to the portion of improvement deriving from clients' knowledge of being treated and assessment of the credibility of the therapy's rationale and related techniques. Expectancy parallels Frank and Frank's (1991) idea that in successful therapies both client and therapist believe in the restorative power of the treatment's procedures or rituals. These curative effects therefore are not thought to derive specifically from a given treatment procedure; they come from the positive and hopeful expectations that accompany the use and implementation of the method.

MODEL/TECHNIQUE FACTORS

Models and techniques are the last of the four factors. Like expectancy, Lambert (1992) suggested that they account for 15% of improvement in therapy. In a narrow sense, model/technique factors may be regarded as beliefs and procedures unique to specific treatments. The miracle question in solution-focused brief therapy, the use of the genogram in Bowen-oriented family therapy, hypnosis, systematic desensitization, biofeedback, transference interpretations, and the respective theoretical premises attending these practices are exemplary.

In concert with Frank and Frank (1991), the editors of this volume interpret model/techniques factors more broadly as therapeutic or healing rituals (see Hubble, Duncan, & Miller, chap. 14, this volume; Miller et al., 1997). They include a rationale, offer an explanation for the client's difficulties, and establish strategies or procedures to follow for resolving them. Depending on the clinician's theoretical orientation, different content is emphasized. Nevertheless, most therapeutic methods or tactics share the common quality of preparing clients to take some action to help themselves. In particular, therapists expect their clients to do something different—to develop new understandings, feel different emotions, face fears, or alter old patterns of behavior (Hubble, 1993; Miller et al., 1997).

Staying With What Works

Whoever acquires knowledge and does not practice it resembles him who ploughs his land and leaves it unsown.

—SA'DI, *Gulistan (1258)*

Unless revolutionary new findings emerge, a prospect in which we place little faith, we maintain that our knowledge of what makes therapy effective is already in the hands of mental health professionals. We know what works. More than 40 years of research points the way toward the defining role of common factors. As for EVTs, the latest manifestation of touting powerful main effects for specialized and preferred therapies, a step forward into the past is being made. It is a practice with faint support (see Ogles, Anderson, & Lunnen, chapter 7, this volume). At the same time, the historical and continuing courtesy extended to theoretical proliferation suggests a place in which both assertions, "The world is round" and "the world is flat," receive equal respect. This civility that extends forbearance to all in the end gives consideration to none.

Focusing on what unites the different therapies has the best promise of not only helping practicing clinicians do their job more effectively but also ensuring that mental health professions continue to have a viable role in health care. Unfortunately, except the dedicated efforts of some of the field's integrationists (e.g., Bergin & Garfield, 1994; Norcross & Goldfried, 1992), the leadership for such an undertaking is not likely to be found within the various schools of therapy or at the highest levels of the professional organizations. Invoking the popular saying, the ship is sinking and all the gurus seem able to do is argue over which way to arrange the deck chairs.

In time, if current fashions continue (i.e., trumpeting one therapy as better than the rest or parroting the activities of whatever profession currently has the favor of third-party payers), the continued diminution of professional therapy looks assured. Unless clinicians come together, they may find themselves sharing the same status as the real dodo bird of Mauritius and Réunion—extinct. There is no doubt. Staying with whatever has not worked in the past does not promise to bring security in the future. Accordingly, the purpose of this book is to reverse the slide toward greater divisiveness and present the state of therapy's data and knowledge. In short, it is time to articulate clearly the effective elements of therapy, all therapy.

A Position Statement

If a man will kick a fact out of the window, when he comes back he finds it again in the chimney corner.

—RALPH WALDO EMERSON, *Journals (1842)*

If fact is defined as a straightforward presentation of what is now known, then this work is factual. It aims to explain what enables psychotherapy and practices in certain related fields to achieve their results. For this reason, we have attempted to put to rest the customary equivocation found in the writings of therapy researchers and clinicians. The profession has labored under the conventions of "it seems," "it appears," "it also could be" when describing therapy and its processes. Further, the discussion sections of research articles habitually bow to the need for further research; in effect, often trivializing whatever was found or not found in the report at hand. It is no wonder practicing clinicians do not read research. It is easy to derive the impression that nobody wants to say, "This is it. This is fact as close as we can come to it now, and here's what to do."

The facts contributing to the longstanding schism between practice and research are legion (see Goldfried, 1993). What is even more compelling and troubling are the results. The recurrent finding that theories and their associated technical operations do not significantly contribute to outcome is very important news. It deserves much more notice. This discovery holds implications for professional specialization, the training and licensure of therapists, continuing education, reimbursement, research, clinical work, and above all, the public welfare (see the last section of chapter 14, this volume). Accordingly, as unpopular as it may be among the separate therapy schools, the stand taken in this work is that the common factors require the helping professions' utmost attention. We are in complete agreement with Sol Garfield (1991), who said that to overlook their significance is to limit our understanding of the therapeutic process and the possibility of improving our therapeutic effectiveness and efficiency. If this position puts this book outside the mainstream of current professional discourse, we welcome the chance to be outliers. The weight of the extant empirical literature suggests that to do less is to be out of step with the facts.

Overview of the Book

The Heart and Soul of Change: What Works in Therapy is intended to be a cross-over work. It is designed for academicians, students, and line practitioners. Influenced by the excellent example of past editions of *The Handbook of Psychotherapy and Behavior Change* (Bergin & Garfield, 1971, 1994; Garfield & Bergin, 1978, 1986), this book strives for thoroughness in its coverage of the common factors. Mindful, too, of the gap between the domains of research and practice, the authors were asked to specify the day-to-day implications of the findings they review. In particular, all were invited to address these questions: "If this is what the research says, then what does this mean specifically for conducting therapy or providing service?" and "Now that we know this, what should we do?" The result provides a useful and provocative blend of research reporting and practical recommendations. Readers will also see that each chapter ends with three questions from the editors and the contributors' responses. Requesting further reflection or exposition, the questions provide the authors an opportunity to discuss candidly the implications and major issues raised in their chapters.

The book is divided into four parts. The first section gives a broad overview of the support for the common factors—the empirical case from both quantitative and qualitative perspectives. Part II describes, in order, each of the four common factors identified earlier—client/ extratherapeutic factors; relationship factors; placebo, hope, and expectancy; model/technique factors—and the research evidence for them. The fifth chapter of this section details an empirically based, transtheoretical model of how people change in natural and therapeutic settings. In the four chapters of Part III, the role of common factors is reviewed in medicine, drug therapy, marriage and family therapy, and school and educational settings. The authors show the pervasive influence of common factors and sample areas of practice usually omitted in most discussions of these variables. Part IV examines the implications of the common factors findings. The first chapter of this section looks at reimbursement issues. The second chapter revisits both practice implications and the client's contribution to therapy. It also looks to the future of therapy.

Although the presentation of common factors in *The Heart and Soul of Change* builds between sections, each chapter also stands on its own. Therefore, readers can feel comfortable selecting chapters in an order of their own choosing. A brief description of each chapter follows.

EMPIRICAL FOUNDATION

Asay and Lambert begin chapter 2 with a brief survey of the quantitative evidence establishing the effectiveness of therapy. From there, they turn their attention to the four principal factors accounting for improvement in therapy: client/extratherapeutic, relationship, placebo, hope and expectancy, and models/techniques. Research supporting the contribution of each of these factors is sampled and major findings highlighted. Drawing on the results from psychotherapy outcome research and particularly the literature on the common factors, the authors conclude their chapter with a thoughtful and valuable list of recommendations for clinical practice.

Chapter 3 surveys the literature on qualitative research into psychotherapeutic processes. Authors Maione and Chenail introduce the reader to qualitative research and explore why such approaches to inquiry are uniquely suited to the study of psychotherapy. In this review, the authors describe what these studies tell us about the practice of psychotherapy and how their results contribute to the work on identifying common factors contributing to change in clinical interactions.

COMMON FACTORS

In chapter 4, Tallman and Bohart suggest that the client is the most potent common factor in therapy (more important than theoretical orientation or techniques) and that this is an explanation for the dodo bird verdict—that different therapies all work about equally well. Clients' own generative, self-healing capacities allow them to take what different therapies have to offer and use them to self-heal. This capacity, moreover, surpasses differences in therapeutic procedures and techniques. The evidence for clients' self-healing capacities is reviewed, including findings on spontaneous recovery and the effectiveness of approaches such as computer therapy, journaling, and self-help materials. Effective therapy provides a safe setting, information and skills, and an extended "workspace" for thinking through problems and experimenting with potential solutions.

The therapeutic relationship lies at the very heart of psychotherapy. In chapter 5, authors Bachelor and Horvath present an array of clinically relevant information on this crucial topic. After providing an overview of the history of the relationship in therapy, including current thinking, they summarize some of the latest research conclusions. These include the importance of the therapeutic relationship across a variety of therapies and broad range of presenting complaints, the significance of the initial therapy sessions for the development of a positive client–therapist alliance, and notable differences between clients' and therapists' notions of a positive relationship. The authors then examine more closely the factors that contribute to the establishment of a positive alliance, beginning with the therapist's interventions and facilitative attitudes. Bachelor's research results are presented suggesting the importance of taking into account clients' differential responsivity and then intervening accordingly. The client's role in contributing to a productive relationship is then discussed, followed by a look at the therapist–client interactional field. Next, the authors address possible deteriorations of the relationship, examining attitudes and behaviors in the participants that could lead to serious misunderstandings and ruptures. Finally, the influence of various preexisting characteristics of clients and therapists is reviewed. Throughout the chapter, attention is given to the practical implications of research findings, and a concluding section offers a useful summary of current knowledge about the therapeutic relationship.

Snyder and his colleagues in chapter 6 present the latest research data and theoretical formulations regarding the role of hope and expectancy in successful psychotherapy. The authors identify the two critical ingredients for enabling clients to emerge from the depths of discouragement and take charge of their lives. Unique in their own right, these factors can be empowered in the clinical work of therapists practicing in any theoretical orientation.

Although chapter 7, at first glance, might seem out of place in a book about the common factors, authors Ogles, Andersen, and Lunnen critically examine the role that psychotherapy models play in treatment outcome. Their thoughtful and comprehensive review of 40 years of research will not win favor among those who continue to advocate forcefully various brands of treatment. Rather than conceding victory to the common factors camp, however, the researchers propose an alternative vision for future psychotherapy theory and research.

In chapter 8, Prochaska offers a nontraditional perspective for approaching the question of the influence of common factors. Arguing that studying people in therapy is insufficient for understanding the common pathways to change, he reviews his research on how people change, period. This work, resulting in the transtheoretical model, shows that change occurs in stages over time and that the person's stage of change determines which therapeutic approach to use. Prochaska sees that the future of therapy lies in being able to manage entire populations presenting with costly conditions (e.g., alcohol abuse, anxiety disorders, depression, and smoking). To do this, in part, a shift is needed from using specific therapeutic strategies varying across different therapies to common pathways and processes integrated from approaches once considered incompatible.

SPECIAL APPLICATIONS OF THE COMMON FACTORS

Independent of medical technique, what is it about the doctor–patient interaction that is ameliorative in medical practice? What psychological factors do physician and patient bring to their appointments that affect treatment outcomes? These and other questions, Scovern poses in chapter 9, an examination of the influential role of common factors in medical practice. Finding that medicine has overemphasized the technical and procedural aspects of its work, this chapter convincingly places psychological and psychophysiological factors present in all medical treatment on an equal par. To optimize treatment outcomes, proposals for the arrangement of health care systems and the conduct of individual medical practice are offered.

At a time when psychiatric drug therapy is prescribed for an increasing number of complaints, empirical findings demonstrate that the reports of effectiveness are being overstated and variables other than the psychoactive properties of the medications may account for a significant portion of the outcomes. In chapter 10, Greenberg provides a cogent summary of this body of research. He explains how common psychosocial factors operate in drug therapy and act to undermine confidence in the enthusiastic claims of drug companies and their promoters.

In chapter 11, Sprenkle, Blow, and Dickey relate that because of its history as a maverick discipline, marriage and family therapists have tended to emphasize differences rather than commonalities. The field's early charismatic leaders built "schools" that were not only "oppositionally defiant" to the prevailing zeitgeist of individual psychotherapy but also to each other. Most marriage and family therapists have ignored the common factors literature and have blithely assumed, despite the dearth of evidence to support this conclusion, that their school-specific techniques were the major factor in the success of their work. This chapter focuses on those factors, not related to specific techniques, that contribute to outcomes and demonstrates that most of the common factors from the individual literature are probably powerfully at work in marriage and family treatments as well. The unique common factors in marriage and family therapy are also highlighted. Finally, the authors discuss the implications of a common factors approach for training and research in marriage and family therapy.

School practitioners, like psychotherapists, are in the business of change, says John Murphy in chapter 12. Efforts to bring about school-related change range from concerns regarding individual students to changes involving an entire school district. Drawing from research on common factors in psychotherapy, this chapter examines school-based change with an eye toward discovering essential elements of effective change across a variety of school contexts. Research on what works to promote change in psychotherapy and schools is integrated into the 5-E Method, a collaborative common factors approach to school-based change. The 5-E Method is illustrated by a case example involving a small group of high school students.

IMPLICATIONS OF COMMON FACTORS FOR REIMBURSEMENT POLICY AND PRACTICE

Brown, Dreis, and Nace offer readers a rare glimpse into the dynamics of managed care from a privileged position inside one of the nation's largest managed behavioral health care organizations. With extensive research, they document the effectiveness of the common factors over other variables traditionally used to determine appropriateness and need for treatment (e.g., diagnosis, professional discipline, treatment type, etc.). Readers walk away from chapter 13 completely up-to-date with the current trends and fully prepared to address future challenges in the psychotherapy marketplace.

The last chapter of *The Heart and Soul of Change* is directed to three tasks. First, a distillation of the implications for direct practice is offered. Specifically, what may be done to promote the therapeutic action of the common factors is given further emphasis. Second, the part clients play in therapy is revisited. Traditionally cast in a supporting or ancillary role in the drama of therapy, their contributions to the therapy are reinterpreted. Here, the case is made that working within and accommodating the clients' "theory of change" is integral to their participation and to a good outcome. Finally, speculation into what the future might hold for therapy is made.

References

American Psychiatric Association. (1952). *Diagnostic and statistical manual of mental disorders* (1st ed.). Washington, DC: Author.

American Psychiatric Association. (1994). *Diagnostic and statistical manual of mental disorders* (4th ed.). Washington, DC: Author.

Austad, C. S. (1996). *Is long-term psychotherapy unethical? Toward a social ethic in an era of managed care.* San Francisco: Jossey-Bass.

Barker, R. L. (1982). *The business of psychotherapy.* New York: Columbia University Press.

Bennet, E. A. (1962). *C. G. Jung.* New York: Dutton.

Bergin, A. E., & Garfield, S. L. (Eds.). (1971). *Handbook of psychotherapy and behavior change.* New York: Wiley.

Bergin, A. E., & Garfield, S. L. (Eds.). (1994). *Handbook of psychotherapy and behavior change* (4th ed.). New York: Wiley.

Bergin, A. E., & Lambert, M. J. (1978). The evaluation of therapeutic outcomes. In S. L. Garfield & A. E. Bergin (Eds.), *Handbook of psychotherapy and behavior change* (2nd ed., pp. 139–189). New York: Wiley.

Coontz, S. (1992). *The way we never were.* New York: Basic Books.

Duncan, B. L., Hubble, M. A., & Miller, S. D. (1997). Stepping off the throne. *The Family Therapy Networker, 21*(3), pp. 22–31, 33.

Duncan, B. L., Solovey, A., & Rusk, G. (1992). *Changing the rules: A client-directed approach to therapy.* New York: Guilford Press.

Flegenheimer, W. V. (1982). *Techniques of brief psychotherapy.* New York: Aronson.

Frank, J. D. (1961). *Persuasion and healing: A comparative study of psychotherapy.* Baltimore: Johns Hopkins University Press.

Frank, J. D. (1973). *Persuasion and healing: A comparative study of psychotherapy* (2nd ed.). Baltimore: Johns Hopkins University Press.

Frank, J. D., & Frank, J. B. (1991). *Persuasion and healing: A comparative study of psychotherapy* (3rd ed.). Baltimore: Johns Hopkins.

Garfield, S. L. (1987). Towards a scientifically oriented eclecticism. *Scandinavian Journal of Behaviour Therapy, 16,* 95–109.

Garfield, S. L. (1991). Common and specific factors in psychotherapy. *Journal of Integrative and Eclectic Psychotherapy, 10,* 5–13.

Garfield, S. L. (1992). Eclectic psychotherapy: A common factors approach. In J. C. Norcross & M. R. Goldfried (Eds.), *Handbook of psychotherapy integration* (pp. 169–201). New York: Basic Books.

Garfield, S. L., & Bergin, A. E. (Eds.). (1978). *Handbook of psychotherapy integration* (2nd ed.). New York: Wiley.

Garfield, S. L., & Bergin, A. E. (Eds.). (1986). *Handbook of psychotherapy integration* (3rd ed.). New York: Wiley.

Garfield, S. L., & Bergin, A. E. (1994). Introduction and historical overview. In A. E. Bergin and S. L. Garfield (Eds.), *Handbook of psychotherapy and behavior change* (4th ed., pp. 3–18). New York: Wiley.

Goldfried, M. R. (1993). SB #10: Implications of research for the practicing therapist: An unfulfilled promise? *Clinician's Research Digest, 11.*

Goldfried, M. R., & Newman, C. F. (1992). A history of psychotherapy integration. In J. C. Norcross & M. R. Goldfried (Eds.), *Handbook of psychotherapy integration* (pp. 46–93). New York: Basic Books.

Grosskurth, P. (1991). *The secret ring: Freud's inner circle and the politics of psychoanalysis.* Reading, MA: Addison-Wesley.

Hannah, B. (1976). *Jung: His life and work.* New York: Perigee.

Hubble, M. A. (1993). Therapy research: The bonfire of the uncertainties. *The Family Psychologist: Bulletin of the Division of Family Psychology* (Division 43), *9*(2), 14–16.

Hubble, M. A., & Duncan, B. L. (Speakers). (1993). Reality versus the therapy industry (Cassette Recording No. 713-407). Norcross, GA: Resource Link.

Hubble, M., & O'Hanlon, W. H. (1992). Theory countertransference. *Dulwich Centre Newsletter* (1), 25–30.

Kaminer, W. (1992). *I'm dysfunctional, you're dysfunctional: The recovery movement and other self-help fashions.* Reading, MA: Addison-Wesley.

Katz, S. J., & Liu, A. E. (1991). *The codependency conspiracy.* New York: Warner Books.

Lambert, M. J. (1992). Implications of outcome research for psychotherapy integration. In J. C. Norcross & M. R. Goldfried (Eds.), *Handbook of psychotherapy integration* (pp. 94–129). New York: Basic Books.

Lambert, M. J., & Bergin, A. E. (1994). The effectiveness of psychotherapy. In A. E. Bergin & S. L. Garfield (Eds.), *Handbook of psychotherapy and behavior change* (4th ed., pp. 143–189). New York: Wiley.

Luborsky, L. (1995). Are common factors across different psychotherapies the main explanation for the dodo bird verdict that "Everyone has won so all shall have prizes"? *Clinical Psychology: Science and Practice, 2,* 106–109.

Luborsky, L., Singer, B., & Luborsky, L. (1975). Comparative studies of psychotherapies: Is it true that "Everybody has won and all must have prizes"? *Archives of General Psychiatry, 32,* 995–1008.

Miller, S. D., Duncan, B. L., & Hubble, M. A. (1997). *Escape from Babel: Toward a unifying language for psychotherapy practice.* New York: Norton.

Miller, S. D., & Hubble, M. A. (Speakers). (1995). No model, no method, no guru. (Cassette Recording No. 715-409). Norcross, GA: Resource Link.

Miller, S. D., Hubble, M.A., & Duncan, B. (1995). *No more bells and whistles. The Family Therapy Networker, 19*(2), pp. 52–58, 62–63.

Miller, S. D., Hubble, M. A., & Duncan, B. L. (1996, March). *Psychotherapy is dead, long live psychotherapy.* Workshop presented at the 19th Annual Family Therapy Network Symposium, Washington, DC.

Nathan, P. E. (1997). Fiddling while psychology burns? *Register Report, 23*(2), pp. 1, 4–5, 10.

Norcross, J. C., & Goldfried, M. R. (Eds.). (1992). *Handbook of psychotherapy integration.* New York: Basic Books.

Norcross, J. C., & Newman, C. F. (1992). Psychotherapy integration: Setting the context. In J. C. Norcross & M. R. Goldfried (Eds.), *Handbook of psychotherapy integration* (pp. 3–45). New York: Basic Books.

Rosenzweig, S. (1936). Some implicit common factors in diverse methods in psychotherapy. *Journal of Orthopsychiatry, 6,* 412–415.

Sharkey, J. (1994). *Bedlam: Greed, profiteering, and fraud in a mental health system gone crazy.* New York: St. Martin's Press.

Spivack, J. D. (1984). Animals at the crossroads: A perspective on credentialing in the mental health field. *The Counseling Psychologist, 12,* 175–182.

Sykes, C. J. (1993, Summer). Society of victims. *Current Books,* pp. 86–90.

Weinberger, J. (1995). Common factors aren't so common: The common factors dilemma. *Clinical Psychology: Science and Practice, 2,* 45–69.

Zeig, J. K., & Munion, W. M. (Eds.). (1990). *What is psychotherapy? Contemporary perspectives.* San Francisco: Jossey-Bass.

Zilbergeld, B. (1983). *The shrinking of America: Myths of psychological change.* Boston: Little, Brown.

EMPIRICAL FOUNDATION

Ted P. Asay and Michael J. Lambert

The Empirical Case for the Common Factors in Therapy:
Quantitative Findings

2

With the rise of managed care and the growing emphasis on accountability in health care, it is not surprising to see researchers advocate empirically "validated" psychotherapy (Task Force, 1995), treatment guidelines, and manual-based therapies (Wilson, 1998). However well intended these efforts may be, they scream of scientific or theoretical arrogance (Lambert, 1998) or as Silverman (1996) has suggested, "painting by numbers." Indeed, the conclusions reached here do not offer strong or widespread support for the field's pursuit of model-driven, technical interventions and approaches. On the contrary, much of what is effective in psychotherapy is attributable to pantheoretical or common factors, those shared by many schools of therapy. In this chapter, we first present a sampling of research findings on the general effects of psychotherapy and then direct particular attention directed to research on common factors.

Is Therapy Effective?

Spanning six decades, reviews of psychotherapy outcome research document the empirical evidence supporting the effectiveness of psychotherapy (Bergin, 1971; Bergin & Lambert, 1978; Lambert & Bergin, 1994; Lambert, Shapiro & Bergin, 1986; Meltzoff & Kornreich, 1970; Smith, Glass, & Miller, 1980). These reviews include controlled studies on thousands of patients, hundreds of therapists, a wide range of presenting problems, and highly diverse therapeutic approaches. Assorted and comprehensive measures of change have been used, incorporating perspectives from patients, their families, mental health professionals, and society in general.

These reviews leave little doubt. Therapy is effective. Treated patients fare much better than the untreated. The positive conclusions about the effects of psychotherapy are also supported by more abstract mathematical summaries of the research literature. One mathematical technique, meta-analysis (used to summarize large collections of empirical data), has been successfully used to estimate, in percentages, the size of treatment effects. With meta-analysis, Smith et al. (1980) found that at the end of treatment, the average treated person is better off than 80% of the untreated sample. Later meta-analytic reviews have reported comparable positive treatment effects across a variety of treatments and client problems. A list of meta-analytic reviews of psychotherapy is provided in Table 1. Figure 1 graphically displays the general conclusions from these studies. In short, the evidence supporting outpatient psychotherapy is now well established.

The good news about the effectiveness of therapy is enhanced by data suggesting that the road to recovery is not long. For example, a meta-analysis by Howard and his colleagues (Howard, Kopta, Krause, & Orlinsky, 1986) as well as a session-by-session analysis of patient progress (Kadera, Lambert, & Andrews, 1996) found that about 75% of clients significantly improved after 26 sessions or 6 months of weekly psychotherapy. The investigators also found that, even with as few as 8 to 10 sessions, approximately 50% of clients show clinically significant change. These results are reproduced in Figure 2 for a subset of clients who met criteria for "recovery" (Kadera et al., 1996). The amount of therapy needed to produce effects, moreover, continues to be discussed (Kadera et al., 1996; Kopta, Howard, Lowry, & Beutler, 1994; Shapiro, Barkham, Rees, Hardy, Reynolds, & Startup, 1994; Steenbarger, 1994). More refined and clinically valuable studies are expected. At length, the patterns of change during psychotherapy have been examined, with some research suggesting that different symptom clusters improve at different times during treatment: early restoration of morale, followed by symptomatic improvement, and finally characterological changes.

Besides finding that the road to recovery is short for the majority receiving therapy, researchers have discovered that improvement is sustained. Believing that psychotherapy will forever safeguard a person from psychological disturbance is unwarranted, but many clients who undergo therapy do achieve a healthy adjustment for long periods. To illustrate, in a meta-analytic study of this research literature—concerned with whether follow-up evaluations provide different conclusions than posttreatment evaluations—it was found that treatment

TABLE 1

Meta-Analytic Reviews of Outcome in Anxiety Disorders

Researchers	Diagnosis/treatment	No. of studies	Effect size
Anderson & Lambert (1995)	Mixed	11	0.71
Andrews & Harvey (1981)	Neurotic	81	0.72
Andrews, Guitar, & Howie (1980)	Stuttering	29	1.30
Asay et al. (1984)	Mixed	9	0.82
Balestrieri, Williams, & Wilkinson (1988)	Mixed	11	0.22
Barker, Funk, & Houston (1988)	Mixed	17	1.05
Benton & Schroeder (1990)	Schizophrenia	23	0.76
Blanchard et al. (1980)	Headache	35	40%–80%
Bowers & Clum (1988)	Behavior therapy	39	0.76
Christensen et al. (1980)	Behavior treatment	14	1.16
Crits-Christoph (1992)	Short-term dynamic therapy	11	0.82
Dunn & Schwebel (1995)	Marital therapy	15	0.79
Dush, Hirt, & Schroeder (1983)	Self-statement modification	39	0.74
Engels, Garnefskl, & Diekstra (1993)	Rational emotive	31	1.62
Giblin, Sprenkle, & Sheehan (1985)	Family therapy	85	0.44
Hahlweg & Markman (1988)	Behavioral marital therapy	17	0.95
Hazelrigg, Cooper, & Borduin (1987)	Family therapy	7	0.45
Hill (1987)	Paradoxical treatment	15	0.99
Holroyd (1990)	Migraines/Biofeedback	22	47.3%
Kirsch, Montgomery, & Sapirstein (1995)	Cognitive–behavioral	20	1.23
Laessie, Zoettle, & Pirke (1987)	Bulemia	9	1.14
Landman & Dawes (1982)	Mixed	42	0.90
Lyons & Woods (1991)	Rational emotive therapy	70	0.98
Markus, Lange, & Pettigrew (1990)	Family therapy	10	0.70
Miller & Berman (1983)	Cognitive–behavioral therapy	38	0.83
Nicholson & Berman (1983)	Neurotic	47	0.70
Prout & DeMartino	School-based therapy	33	0.58
Quality Assurance Project (1984)	Schizophrenia	5	0.00
Shaidsh et al. (1993)	Behavioral family therapy	13	0.55
Shadish et al. (1993)	Marital therapy	12	0.87
Shapiro & Shapiro (1982a)	Mixed	143	1.03
Shoham-Salomon & Rosenthal (1987)	Paradoxical treatment	10	0.42
Smith, Glass, & Miller (1980)	Mixed	475	0.85
Svartbert & Stiles (1991)	Short-term dynamic therapy	3	0.14
Wampler (1982)	Marital communication	20	0.43
Weisz et al. (1995)	Child behavioral therapy	197	0.54
Weisz et al. (1987)	Mixed adolescent	108	0.79
Whilebreat & McGown (1994)	Bulemia/cognitive behavioral	9	1.72

continued

TABLE 1 *continued*

Meta-Analytic Reviews of Outcome in Anxiety Disorders

Researchers	Diagnosis/treatment	No. of studies	Effect size
Allen et al. (1989)	Public speaking anxiety	97	0.51
Christensen et al. (1987)	OCD/exposure Tx	5	1.37
Clum, Clum, & Surls (1993)	Panic	28	0.88
Clum (1989)	Panic/behavioral Tx	283	70%
Feske & Chambliss (1995)	Social phobia/exposure	9	0.99
Gould, Otto, & Pollack (1995)	Panic	27	0.68
Hyman et al. (1989)	Relaxation training	48	0.58
Jorm (1989)	Trait anxiety	63	0.53
Mattick et al. (1990)	Agoraphobia	51	1.62
QA Project (1982)	Agoraphobia	25	1.20
QA Project (1985a)	OCD/exposure Tx	38	1.34
QA Project (1985b)	Agoraphobia	19	2.10
Von Balkom et al. (1994)	OCD/behavior therapy	45	1.46

FIGURE 1

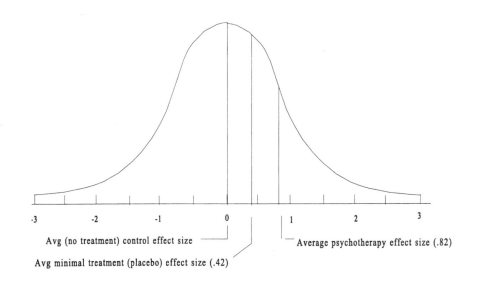

Comparison of placebo and psychotherapy effects in relation to no-treatment control. From Psychotherapy Versus Placebo [Poster presented at the annual meetings of the Western Psychological Association, April 1993, by M. J. Lambert, F. D. Weber, and J. D. Sykes.]

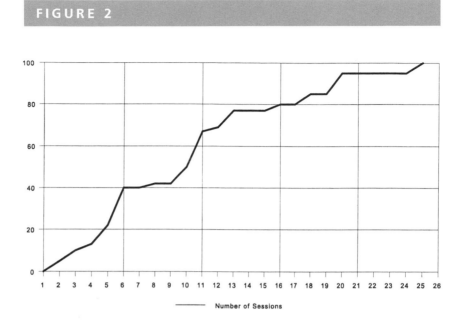

Relation of Percentage Recovered to Number of Sessions Received for 21 Previously Dysfunctional Clients Receiving Psychotherapy. *Note.*   From "How Much Therapy Is Really Enough? A Session-by-Session Analysis of the Psychotherapy Dose–Effect Relationship," by S. W. Kadera, M. J. Lambert, and A. A. Andrews, 1996, *Journal of Psychotherapy: Practice and Research, 5,* p. 10. Copyright 1996 by the American Psychiatric Press. Reprinted with permission.

gains are maintained. Specifically, posttherapy status correlated with follow-up status (Nicholson & Berman, 1983). This review, the most impressive on this topic, is consistent with the conclusion that psychotherapy has lasting effects and that most clients can be expected to maintain their gains over time.

For all that, certain groups of clients may be more vulnerable to relapse, including those with substance abuse problems, eating disorders, recurrent depression, and those diagnosed with personality disorders. A portion of clients will relapse and require additional or extended treatment; yet, the data on the durability of treatment gains should be encouraging to clinicians who are often challenged about the efficacy or long-term effects of their work. Evidence also indicates that the maintenance of treatment effects can be enhanced by efforts directed at this goal in the final therapy sessions. For instance, research findings show that change is more likely to be long lasting in clients who attribute their changes to their own efforts (Lambert & Bergin, 1994).

The Determinants of Treatment Outcomes

That psychotherapy is, in general, effective, efficient, and lasting has been empirically supported time and again. Its legitimacy is confirmed. The next important question is, What leads to positive patient outcomes?

One line of research pertinent to this question has focused on the differential effectiveness between schools of psychotherapy. Several traditional reviews of comparative studies have been conducted (Bergin & Lambert, 1978; Beutler, 1979; Lambert & Bergin, 1994; Rachman & Wilson, 1980), along with more recent investigations using meta-analytic techniques (see Table 2). Most reviews conclude there is little evidence to indicate differences in effectiveness among the various schools of psychotherapy. Although some reviews exist, suggesting superior results for cognitive or behavioral approaches over other therapies, these exceptions have often been explained as methodological artifacts (Lambert & Bergin, 1994).

Two studies illustrate the sort of research in this area. First, in a landmark comparative study, Sloane, Staples, Cristol, Yorkston, and Whipple (1975) compared short-term psychodynamic and behavioral therapy. Ninety outpatients, most presenting with neuroses, were randomly assigned to short-term psychoanalytically oriented psychotherapy, behavior therapy, or a minimal treatment wait-list group. Clients were treated by experienced and respected proponents of their respective approaches. Ratings at 4 months indicated that all three groups had improved significantly on target symptoms and that the two treatment

TABLE 2

Meta-Analytic Reviews of Outcome With Depression

Researchers	Diagnosis/treatment	No. of studies	Effect size
Gaffan et al. (1995)	Depression/cognitive therapy	6	0.72
Dobson (1989)	Depression/cognitive therapy	10	2.15
Nietzel, Russell, Hemmings & Gretter (1987)	Unipolar depression	28	0.71
Quality Assurance Project (1983)	Depression	10	0.65
Robinson, Berman, & Neimeyer (1990)	Depression	29	0.84
Steinbrueck, Maxwell, & Howard (1983)	Depression	56	1.22

Note. References available from the authors on request.

groups had improved much more than the wait-list group. No differences obtained between behavioral therapy and psychotherapy groups on any of the target symptoms. At 8 months, there were no differences among the three groups on any measure of change. Treated patients maintained their gains over time, whereas the wait-list patients eventually reached the improvement levels attained by the patients who had undergone either of the active therapies.

Another important comparative study is the National Institute of Mental Health (NIMH) Collaborative Depression Study. This investigation compared imipramine plus clinical management, cognitive–behavioral therapy, and interpersonal psychotherapy. The three treatments were also contrasted with a drug placebo plus clinical management control group. Results of the comparisons have been extensively reported by Elkin et al. (1989) and Imber et al. (1990). For this reason, the methodology and results of this study are only briefly summarized here.

Two hundred and fifty patients who met the research diagnostic criteria for major depressive disorder were assigned to one of the four treatments. Participants were seen at one of three research sites. The therapists were 28 carefully selected and trained psychologists and psychiatrists who provided a clearly defined treatment, guided by treatment manuals. Each therapist saw between 1 and 11 patients, with the total sample averaging 13 sessions. Outcome measures included symptomatic and adjustment ratings from multiple perspectives. In head-to-head comparisons between interpersonal psychotherapy and cognitive–behavioral therapy, little evidence to support significant differential effectiveness was found. This finding held true for more and less severely disturbed patients.

The general finding of no difference in the outcome of therapy for clients participating in diverse therapies has several alternative explanations. First, different therapies can achieve similar goals through different processes. Second, different outcomes do occur but are not detected by past research strategies. Third, different therapies embody common factors that are curative, though not emphasized by the theory of change central to any one school.

No doubt, different therapies require patients to undergo different experiences and engage in different behaviors. Diverse therapies could be effective for different reasons. Yet we do not know enough about the boundaries of effectiveness for each therapy to address the first alternative and its merits. Neither will the second alternative be examined in detail. Many methodological reasons for failing to detect differences in treatments are suggested. For example, Kazdin and Bass (1989) questioned the value of the majority of past comparative studies on the basis of a "lack of statistical power." There are serious problems, too, in accurately measuring behavioral change (Lambert,

Christensen, & DeJulio, 1983). However, the third alternative, emphasizing the role of common factors in different therapies, is the possibility that has received the most research attention and the one that has the clearest implications for practice. It is not only an interpretation of the comparative outcome literature, but also is based on other research aimed at discovering the active ingredients of psychotherapy. The common factors are considered next.

Research Findings on Common Factors

Common therapeutic factors can be divided into four broad areas: client factors and extratherapeutic events, relationship factors, expectancy and placebo effects, and technique/model factors. Figure 3 provides a graphic display, illustrating our current belief about the degree to which each of these classes of variables contributes to outcome. The findings from research regarding each of these common factors is now discussed.

CLIENT VARIABLES AND EXTRATHERAPEUTIC EVENTS

Although some practitioners, especially the inexperienced, imagine that they or their techniques are the most important factor contributing to outcome, the research literature does not support this contention. On the contrary, outcome is determined to a great degree by the client and outside events—not the therapist. On the basis of his review of the extant literature, Lambert (1992) concluded that as much as 40% of the improvement in psychotherapy clients is attributable to client variables and extratherapeutic influences. The subject of client variables and extratherapeutic events and their relation to outcome could fill a volume. In this context, we mention some of the more important client variables and sample the research on extratherapeutic factors.

When clients come to therapy, they enter with a diverse array of disorders, histories, current stressors, social support networks, and the like. Those client variables that are most important can be organized in many ways. Further, the categories used to describe clients overlap both in their components and presence in a single client. Among the client variables most frequently mentioned are the severity of disturbance (including the number of physical symptoms involved), moti-

FIGURE 3

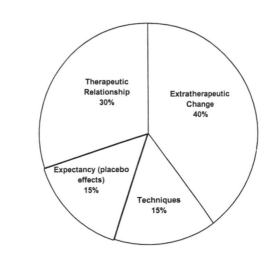

Percentage of Improvement in Psychotherapy Patients as a Function of Therapeutic Factors. Extratherapeutic change: those factors that are a part of the client (e.g., ego strength and other homeostatic mechanisms) and part of the environment (e.g., fortuitous events and social support) that aid in recovery regardless of participation in therapy. Expectancy (placebo effects): that portion of improvement that results from the client's knowledge that he or she is being treated and from the differential credibility of specific treatment techniques and rationale. Techniques: those factors unique to specific therapies (e.g., biofeedback, hypnosis, or systematic desensitization). Therapeutic relationship: includes a host of variables that are found in a variety of therapies regardless of the therapist's theoretical orientation (e.g., empathy, warmth, acceptance, encouragement of risk taking). From *The Handbook of Psychology Integration* by M. J. Lambert, 1992, p. 97. Copyright 1992 by Basic Books. Reprinted with permission.

vation, capacity to relate, ego strength, psychological mindedness, and the ability to identify a focal problem (Lambert & Anderson, 1996; Lambert & Asay, 1984). It is reasonable to conclude that the nature of some problems (e.g., personality disorders, schizophrenia) and the makeup of some clients (e.g., severe abuse in childhood, interpersonal distrust) affect therapy outcome. As an example, a withdrawn, alcoholic client, who is "dragged into therapy" by his or her spouse, possesses poor motivation for therapy, regards mental health professionals with suspicion, and harbors hostility toward others, is not nearly as likely to find relief as the client who is eager to discover how he or she has contributed to a failing marriage and expresses determination to make personal changes.

The importance of client factors in psychotherapy outcome was highlighted in a series of case studies reported by Strupp (1980a, 1980b, 1980c, 1980d). In each study, two patients were seen by the same therapists in time-limited psychotherapy. In each instance, one of the patients was seen as having a successful outcome and the other was considered a treatment failure. The patients were male college students suffering from anxiety, depression, and social withdrawal. Although each therapist was seen as having good interpersonal skills, a different relationship developed with the two patients. In all four cases, the patients who had successful outcomes appeared more willing and able to have a meaningful relationship with the therapist. The patients who did not improve in therapy did not relate well to the therapist and kept the interaction superficial.

In Strupp's analysis, the contributions of the therapist remained relatively constant throughout therapy. Accordingly, the difference in outcome could be attributed to patient factors, such as the nature of the patient's personality makeup, including ego organization, maturity, motivation, and ability to become productively involved in therapy. Commenting on the results of the study, Strupp (1980a) concluded,

> While these findings are congruent with clinical lore, they run counter to the view that "therapist provided conditions" are the necessary and sufficient conditions for therapeutic change. Instead, psychotherapy of the variety under discussion can be beneficial provided the patient is willing and able to avail himself of its essential ingredients. If these preconditions are not met, the experience is bound to be disappointing to the patient as well as the therapist. The fault for such outcomes may lie not with psychotherapy as such but rather with human failure to use it appropriately. (p. 602)

Much of the research on client variables has been summarized elsewhere (see Garfield, 1994). The data suggest that some client variables can change rapidly in psychotherapy (e.g., motivation and expectations for improvement), whereas other client variables are more likely to be immutable in the short run (e.g., personality styles). As already reported, clients who do better in psychotherapy and maintain treatment gains believe that the changes made in therapy were primarily a result of their own efforts.

Other evidence bearing on the role of client or extratherapeutic factors comes from the literature on spontaneous remission. A well-documented finding from research is that a portion of clients improve without formal psychotherapeutic intervention. This phenomenon has been discussed extensively in previous reviews (Bergin & Lambert, 1978; Lambert, 1976; Lambert & Bergin, 1994). The studies examined in these reviews include participants who had minimal treatment, but not extensive psychotherapy, and untreated participants. The median rate for extratherapeutic improvement was 43%, with a range from 18% to 67%.

Several factors may influence the rate of spontaneous improvement. For instance, the length of time that the disorder has persisted; presence of an underlying personality disorder; and the nature, strength, and quality of social supports, especially the marital relationship, affect change (Andrews & Tennant, 1978; Lambert, 1976; Mann, Jenkins, & Belsey, 1981). Differential rates of spontaneous improvement have also been suggested among differing diagnostic groups, with depression having the highest remission rate, followed by anxiety and hysterical, phobic, obsessive–compulsive and hypochrondrical disorders (Schapira, Roth, Kerr, & Gurney, 1972).

The finding that many clients improve without formal psychological intervention highlights the importance of supportive and therapeutic aspects of the natural environment in which clients live and function. In all likelihood, a significant number of people are helped by friends, family, teachers, and clergy who use a variety of supportive and hope instilling techniques. It is interesting that in the study by Howard et al. (1986), the authors estimated that about 15% of clients experience some improvement before the beginning of treatment. Presumably, at least some pretreatment improvement is attributable to clients' reliance on sources of help and support within their environments.

Before ending the discussion of client factors, the influence of self-help literature and self-help groups bears mentioning. These resources often include behavioral, cognitive, and insight-oriented material drawn from a variety of formal psychotherapy systems. Some of this material, such as self-help books, has been shown to reduce symptomatology (Ogles, Lambert, & Craig, 1991). Thus, what is helpful to people—independent of formal psychological intervention—may, in fact, be borrowed from psychological theory and technique. Further examination of client and extratherapeutic factors is found in chapter 4 of this book.

RELATIONSHIP FACTORS

Among the common factors most frequently studied are those focusing on the role of the therapeutic relationship. Empirical findings suggest that relationship factors account for approximately 30% of client improvement (Lambert, 1992). Much of the research on relationship factors began with the client-centered tradition in which certain "necessary and sufficient" conditions for client personality change were identified. These critical or core conditions were conceptualized as accurate empathy, positive regard, nonpossessive warmth, and congruence or genuineness. Most schools of therapy accept the notion that these and related therapist relationship variables are important for significant progress in psychotherapy. In fact, they are considered fundamental in the formation of a working alliance (Lambert, 1983).

Studies showing both positive and equivocal support for the hypothesized relationship between therapist attitudes and outcome are well documented (Gurman, 1977; Howard & Orlinsky, 1986; Lambert, DeJulio, & Stein, 1978; Patterson, 1984). However, strong agreement exists. The therapist–client relationship is critical. Thus, some uncertainty in the research results from findings indicating that client-perceived relationship factors, rather than objective raters' perceptions of the relationship, obtain consistently more positive results. Further, the larger correlations with outcome are often between client process ratings and client self-reports of outcome. One explanation for this may be that clients perceive the therapeutic relationship as more positive than observers and that they are more accurate in their perceptions of the quality of the therapeutic relationship.

In any case, the value of therapist relationship skills has been demonstrated in several studies. For instance, Miller, Taylor, and West (1980) investigated the comparative effectiveness of various behavioral approaches aimed at helping problem drinkers control their alcohol consumption. Although the focus of the study was on the comparative effects of focused versus broad-spectrum behavioral therapy, the authors also collected data on the contribution of therapist empathy to patient outcome. Surprisingly, these authors found a strong relationship between empathy and patient outcome obtained from the 6- to 8-month follow-up interviews used to assess drinking behavior. Therapists' rank on empathy correlated ($r = .82$) with patient outcome, thus accounting for 67% of the variance in the criteria. These results argue for the importance of therapist communicative skills even in behavioral interventions.

In a more recent investigation, Najavits and Strupp (1994) reported on a study in which 16 practicing therapists were identified as "more effective" or "less effective" using time-limited dynamic psychotherapy (TLDP) with outpatients. Therapist effectiveness was determined by patients' outcome scores and length of stay in treatment. Multiple measures of outcome were used and completed by clients, therapists, independent observers, and the therapists' supervisors. Results revealed that more effective therapists showed more positive behavior and fewer negative behaviors than less effective therapists. Positive behaviors included warmth, understanding, and affirmation. Negative behaviors included belittling and blaming, ignoring and negating, attacking and rejecting. Therapists were differentiated almost entirely by nonspecific (relationship) factors rather than specific (technical) factors. On the basis of these findings, the authors suggested that "basic capacities of human relating—warmth, affirmation, and a minimum of attack and blame—may be at the center of effective psychotherapeutic intervention. Theoretically based technical interventions were not nearly as often significant in this study" (p. 121).

In recent years, increasing interest in the therapeutic alliance as an important aspect of the therapist–client relationship has been observed. The therapeutic alliance was first described by Freud (1912, 1913). He underscored both the importance of the analysand's attachment to the psychoanalyst and the psychoanalyst's interest in and "asympathetic understanding" of the patient in the early treatment relationship. Following Freud, the therapeutic alliance was elaborated and revised by many authors (Bowlby, 1988; Fennichel, 1941; Greenson, 1965; Sterba, 1929; Zetzel, 1956).

In an attempt to integrate the various constructs and ideas offered to describe the therapeutic alliance, Gaston (1990) suggested that the following components are measured by some but not all current research rating scales of the alliance: (a) the client's affective relationship to the therapist, (b) the client's capacity to work purposefully in therapy, (c) the therapist's empathic understanding and involvement, and (d) the client–therapist agreement on the goals and tasks of therapy. Bordin (1976, 1989) also identified three components of the therapeutic alliance: tasks, bonds, and goals. Tasks involve the behaviors and processes within the therapy session that constitute the actual work of therapy. Both therapist and client must view these tasks as important and appropriate for a strong therapeutic alliance to exist. The goals of therapy are the agreed on objectives of the therapy process that both parties must endorse and value. Finally, bonds include the positive interpersonal attachments between therapists and clients, shown by mutual trust, confidence, and acceptance.

Most of the empirical work on the therapeutic alliance has been generated by psychodynamic researchers (Gaston, 1990; Horvath & Greenberg, 1994; Horvath & Luborsky, 1993; Horvath & Symonds, 1991; Luborsky, 1994; Luborsky & Auerbach, 1985). Of late, this construct is receiving increasing attention in studies of behavioral therapy (DeRubeis & Feeley, 1991), cognitive therapy (Castonguay, Goldfried, Wiser, Raue, & Hays, 1996; Krupnick et al., 1996), and Gestalt therapy (Horvath & Greenberg, 1989). The alliance is conceived and defined in various ways and has been measured by client ratings, therapist ratings, and judges' ratings (Horvath & Luborsky, 1993). Reviews of the research on therapeutic alliance (Gaston, 1990; Horvath & Greenberg, 1994; Horvath & Luborsky, 1993; Horvath & Symonds, 1991; Lambert, 1992) reveal a positive relationship between therapeutic alliance and outcome, although there are instances when the relationship is small or insignificant. As an example of research on therapeutic alliance, Horvath and Symonds (1991) conducted a meta-analysis of 24 studies in which the relationship between therapeutic alliance and outcome was analyzed. They found an average effect size correlation of .26, suggesting a 26% difference in the rate of therapeutic success attributable to the quality of the alliance.

In the National Institute of Mental Health Treatment of Depression Collaborative Research Program, Krupnick et al. (1996), using a modified version of the Vanderbilt Therapeutic Alliance Scale, investigated the role of the therapeutic alliance in the psychotherapeutic and pharmacological treatment of depressed individuals. Results indicate that the therapeutic alliance had a significant impact on outcome for both psychotherapies and for active and placebo pharmacotherapy. Both early and mean client ratings of alliance were significantly related to treatment outcome. However, therapist contribution to the therapeutic alliance was not significantly related to outcome on any measures. The lack of variability among the carefully selected therapists used in the study was proposed to explain this latter finding. In summarizing the outcomes, the authors concluded, "These results are most consistent with the view that the therapeutic alliance is a common factor across modalities of treatment for depression that is distinguishable from specific technical or pharmacological factors within the treatments" (p. 538).

In yet another study, Castonguay et al. (1996) examined the therapeutic alliance in cognitive therapy. The researchers compared the impact of a treatment variable unique to cognitive therapy (the therapist's focus on distorted cognitions in depressive symptoms) and two variables common with other forms of treatment (therapeutic alliance and client's emotional involvement) on treatment outcome. Subjects were 30 patients with major depressive disorder receiving either cognitive therapy alone or cognitive therapy with medication over a 12-week period. The patients were treated by four experienced therapists who conducted cognitive therapy according to the guidelines of manualized treatment. Outcome was assessed through patient ratings and with independent evaluators.

Results revealed that the two common variables, therapeutic alliance and patient's emotional experiencing, were both related to improvement. At the same time, the variable considered unique to cognitive therapy, linking distorted thoughts and negative emotions, was positively related to depressive symptoms after therapy. Castonguay et al. (1996) suggested that the latter finding was likely attributable to the therapists' attempts to repair strains in the therapeutic alliance by (a) increasing their efforts to persuade the patient to accept the validity of the cognitive therapy rationale or (b) treating alliance strains as manifestations of the patient's distorted thoughts that needed to be challenged.

Beyond the research on client-centered relationship factors and the therapeutic alliance, several other studies have illuminated the importance of the therapist–patient relationship in psychotherapy. For example, Lorr (1965) asked 523 psychotherapy patients to describe their therapists on 65 different statements. A factor analysis of these data identified five factors: understanding, accepting, authoritarian (directive), independence encouraging, and critical hostile. Scores on these descriptive factors were correlated with improvement ratings; patient ratings of understanding and accepting correlated most highly with patient and therapist rated improvement.

The role of relationship factors has also been emphasized in group treatment. Glass and Arnkoff (1988), for instance, examined common and specific factors in patient descriptions and explanations of change. With a presenting complaint of shyness, clients were treated in one of three structured group therapies or an unstructured therapy group. The approach in each group was based on a different theory of change and differed in both content and focus. Notwithstanding theoretical differences, content analysis revealed that, besides specific treatment factors, all groups placed considerable emphasis on group process and relationship factors (e.g., support). The authors suggested that the role of common group process factors was at least as important to the clients as the specific therapy program (p. 437).

As this introductory survey shows, the empirical evidence on the impact of relationship factors in psychotherapy is substantial. These factors play a significant part in psychotherapeutic change and outcome. The role of relationship factors is covered more in depth in chapter 5 in this book.

EXPECTANCY AND PLACEBO EFFECTS

Research on psychotherapy outcome over the past three decades has addressed the importance of expectancy and placebo effects in client change. For example, Lambert (1992) suggested that this factor, which accounts for 15% of the variance in client change, is as important to the change process as technique factors. A pioneer in researching client expectancies and their relationship to outcome is Jerome Frank. In his classic work *Persuasion and Healing*, Frank (1973) argued that the therapeutic enterprise carries the strong expectation that the client will, in fact, be helped. He suggested, too, that an underlying factor unites all the seemingly different approaches to psychotherapy and even other forms of healing, such as the placebo in medicine and various types of religious cures. Namely, people are offered hope that something can be done to help them.

Frank, Gliedman, Imber, Stone, and Nash (1959) produced evidence indicating that the expectations that the client brings into therapy have an important influence on the outcome of therapy. They also found that the greater the felt distress, the greater the likelihood of improvement. More recent research on client expectations has suggested a positive relationship between expectations and improvement, especially in the early phases of treatment (Garfield, 1994).

The role of placebo effects in psychotherapy has also received considerable research attention in studies comparing the effects of a particular type of psychotherapy or psychotherapeutic intervention with a placebo or minimal treatment group and a no-treatment control group. Although placebo effects and the use of placebo controls in psychotherapy research are controversial (Lambert & Bergin, 1994), it is clear from the existing research literature that placebo effects do have an important impact on psychotherapeutic change. For example, Lambert, Weber, and Sykes (1993) summarized studies comparing the effect sizes of psychotherapy, placebo, and no-treatment controls. The results of this summary are depicted in Figure 1 and can be expressed in percentage-improvement rates. Specifically, the average client undergoing a placebo treatment is better off than 66% of the no-treatment controls. On the other hand, the average client undergoing psychotherapy is better off than 79% of the no-treatment controls.

The impact of placebo effects was clearly demonstrated in the NIMH Collaborative Depression Study discussed earlier (Elkin et al., 1989). Of the many comparisons reported in the study, two stood out as particularly pertinent to this discussion. First, in head-to-head comparisons of cognitive behavioral therapy and interpersonal psychotherapy, no significant differences in treatment effects were found. Second, there was little evidence supporting the superiority of the two psychotherapies in contrast to the placebo plus clinical management. Both of the therapies were effective, but placebo plus clinical management patients also improved. While the placebo used in this study was admittedly a potent one, these findings nevertheless support the existing evidence on the impact that placebo and expectancy have in treatment outcome.

Placebo effects look to be less powerful in clients with more severe disorders and in studies where more experienced therapists are used (Barker, Funk, & Houston, 1988). However, placebo, hope, and expectancy factors play an integral enough role in change to deserve careful consideration by therapists interested in maximizing the effects of treatment. Chapter 6 continues discussion of the role of placebo, hope, and expectancy in therapy.

Technique and Model Factors

Although some researchers adhere to the argument for common factors as the principal mediators of change, most research studies have aggressively investigated the role of model-based, technical interventions (Jones, Cumming, & Horowitz, 1988). The enthusiasm for researching the effects of specific schools or interventions exists because of clinicians' allegiance to school-based approaches and because the most suitable control group for past, as well as future studies, is the best alternative treatment. Therefore, specific interventions are often studied in the context of comparative outcome studies. Comparative studies also avoid the ethical and methodological problems in no-treatment, wait-list, and placebo controls, while providing information about the effectiveness of one technique or orientation in relation to others.

For those convinced of the singular abilities of their models and related interventions, the results have been disappointing. Overall, in the many comparative studies completed to date, little evidence to suggest the superiority of one school or technique over another has been obtained. While exceptions occur in the research literature (some of which are discussed below), specific techniques are estimated to account for only about 15% of the improvement in psychotherapy clients (Lambert, 1992).

Examples of Specific Effects

Comparative studies have shown the potent effects of some behavior therapies on certain problems. The treatment of phobic disorders with behavioral techniques incorporating systematic "exposure," has been found highly effective and superior to other forms of intervention. These procedures involve selecting patients with clearly identified fears evoked by specific stimuli. In addition to identifying the evoking stimuli, the patient must be motivated to seek and complete treatment. Exposure also requires the client's willingness to "make contact" with the evoking stimuli until their discomfort subsides (Emmelkamp, 1994; Marks, 1978).

To ameliorate phobic anxiety with exposure, several conditions must be in place. Specifically, the most useful therapeutic strategy, supported by numerous studies, includes the following elements: identify the provoking stimuli, encourage exposure, help the patient remain exposed until the anxiety subsides, and assist the patient in mastering thoughts and feelings linked with the fear-evoking stimuli. The bulk of the evidence suggests that achieving lasting reductions in fears and compulsive rituals is, indeed, a function of exposure.

It is noteworthy that limits to the effectiveness of exposure have been found. Exposure treatments, though effective with agoraphobia, simple phobias, and compulsions, are not as or uniquely effective with social phobias, generalized anxiety disorders, or a combination of these difficulties (Emmelkamp, 1994). Nevertheless, given a circumscribed anxiety-based problem, specific interventions are available that are likely to help the majority of patients.

Additional research suggests that the treatment of panic disorder may be more successful when a cognitive–behavioral intervention is used (Barlow, Craske, Cerny, & Klosko, 1989; Murphy, Cramer, & Lillie, 1984). Barlow et al. (1989) compared relaxation training (RT), imaginal exposure plus cognitive restructuring (E+C), and a combined modality (RT+E+C) versus a wait-list control condition (WL). Differential outcome was evidenced by those patients experiencing panic attacks. Results indicated that 36% of WL, 60% of RT, 85% of E+C, and 87% of the RT+E+C patients were panic free at posttreatment.

Nevertheless, Milrod and Busch's (1996) recent comprehensive review of long-term outcome data for treatments of panic disorder calls for a less sanguine appraisal of Barlow's work. These reviewers concluded, "questions remain as to what is the best type of initial treatment for panic disorder . . . and what types of interventions may be most useful to reduce symptoms in patients whose symptoms are persistent or recurring" (p. 729).

The State of Current Knowledge

Exemplified by the research on exposure, evidence for the effectiveness of specific techniques for particular problems has been gradually accumulating. For this reason, "hope springs eternal"—optimism is expressed that more "treatments of choice" or prescriptive therapies will be found for specific disorders. The preponderance of evidence, however, supports the conclusion that little difference exists between the various schools of therapy in their ability to produce effects. Again, older reviews that analyze studies comparing a wide range of psychotherapies (Bergin & Lambert, 1978; Bergin & Suinn, 1975; Beutler, 1979; Goldstein & Stein, 1976; Kellner, 1975; Meltzoff & Kornreich, 1970) as well as more recent meta-analytic reviews suggest similar conclusions: Typically, there is little or no difference between therapies and techniques.

Curiously, the findings of no difference between treatments go largely unheeded. The debate continues over whether one technique is significantly different from and more effective than another. For example, Hollon and Beck (1986) predicted the continual success and superiority of cognitive therapy as a treatment for depression. In contrast, results from the NIMH Collaborative Depression Study (Elkin et al., 1989), to date the most comprehensive comparative study ever completed, revealed little evidence for the differential effectiveness of cognitive–behavioral therapy and interpersonal psychotherapy with depressed individuals.

Some also anticipate that future research may reveal greater distinctiveness between approaches as the use of therapy manuals becomes more important and more frequently applied. There is, for instance, evidence to suggest that the use of manuals to specify treatment techniques results in objectively discriminable therapist behaviors (Luborsky & DeRubeis, 1984; Rounsaville, O'Malley, Foley, & Weissman, 1988). In addition, the use of treatment manuals (and more experienced therapists) has been shown to reduce the variability in outcome due to the therapist, allowing for more accurate comparisons in comparative outcome studies (Crits-Christoph & Mintz, 1991). The use of and adherence to treatment manuals also helps enhance the effects of specific therapy procedures (Crits-Christoph, 1992).

Yet problems associated with the use of treatment manuals call into question their value in psychotherapy training and research (Strupp & Anderson, 1997). In this regard, Henry, Strupp, Butler, Schacht, and Binder (1993) found that the use of treatment manuals produced negative effects on therapeutic behavior among therapists, including a tendency for therapists to become less approving and supportive, less optimistic, and more authoritarian and defensive.

Owing to the historical and continuing emphasis on specialized models and techniques in graduate and professional training, continuing education seminars, publications, and professional discussions, the impression is easily created that they represent the "big guns" of therapeutic change. That they are not is admittedly frustrating. The often uncertain work of therapy would be simplified if special techniques uniformly exerted powerful main effects for particular complaints. Therapy could then be applied in this manner: "When faced with problem _____, administer technique _____."

At this stage in our understanding of what matters in therapy, the most that can be concluded about the role of techniques is that, like the other common factors, they contribute to positive treatment outcomes. Specific techniques may provide an extra boost to change, depending on the client population. This fact, nonetheless, does not contradict the evidence regarding the significant role of the other common factors—client, relationship, placebo, and expectancy. Rather, it suggests that unique or special variables at times may be important as well (Lambert & Bergin, 1994).

In all, specific techniques and the other common factors are not mutually exclusive as determinants to treatment outcome. As some authors have suggested (Butler & Strupp, 1986), separating specific techniques from common factors is of limited value anyway because techniques can never be offered in a context free of interpersonal meaning. From this perspective, models and their associated techniques are part of a human encounter. They constitute interpersonal events inexorably bound up in the expectations and beliefs of the participants (Lambert & Bergin, 1994). Chapter 7 provides further review and commentary on the part that models and techniques play in therapy.

Implications for Practice and Training

Our brief examination of the empirical research on psychotherapy reveals important and useful findings for clinical work. For the practitioner, the challenge left is to integrate these results into practice. To promote this integration, several conclusions with implications for practice and training are offered. The general implications from psychotherapy outcome research are first discussed and then recommendations arising from research on the common factors are presented.

1. The effects of therapy are positive at treatment termination. Therapists can feel confident that they have something valuable to offer their clients. If clients or others raise questions about the benefits of undergoing treatment, they can be reassured. This knowledge may sustain both therapist and client through any difficult phase that may arise during treatment.

2. The beneficial effects of therapy can be achieved in short periods (5 to 10 sessions) with at least 50% of clients seen in routine clinical practice. For most clients, therapy will be brief. This is not meant to be an endorsement of brief therapy. It is simply a statement of fact. In consequence, therapists need to organize their work to optimize outcomes within a few sessions. Therapists also need to develop and practice intervention methods that assume clients will be in therapy for fewer than 10 sessions.

3. A sizable minority of clients (20% to 30%) requires treatment lasting more than 25 sessions. This group may need alternative interventions or more intensive, multifaceted treatment approaches. Even when intensive efforts are required, clients will improve to a significant degree. Further, clients most likely to fail at brief therapy are those poorly motivated and hostile, who come with a history of poor relationships and expect to be passive recipients of a medical procedure. Therapists need to identify these clients early and attempt to modify their unproductive expectations and behavior.

4. The effects of treatment are lasting for most clients, with follow-up studies suggesting little decline 1 to 2 years after termination. Relapse can be reduced by encouraging and reinforcing the clients'

belief in their ability to cope with the inevitable, temporary setbacks likely to be experienced after therapy.

Therapists also need to adopt methods for enhancing the maintenance of treatment gains. In this respect, facilitating two general beliefs in the client is necessary. First, clients can be encouraged to see the gains they make as a consequence of their own best efforts, rather than of the clinician, medication, or therapy. Second, clients need to know that they are not inoculated against future problems. Without such preparation, when setbacks occur, clients might become demoralized and underrate their newly developed ability to cope. Symptoms can recur without the client interpreting them as evidence of failure.

5. Client outcome is principally determined by client variables and extratherapeutic factors rather than by the therapist or therapy. Clinicians are not yet blessed with the wisdom to know which clients will not profit from therapy, nor do they wish to exhibit the inhumanity of telling them so. Yet certain client characteristics consistently predict better outcomes across studies, types of therapy, and clinical settings. These include indices of severity, chronicity, and complexity of symptoms; motivation; acceptance of personal responsibility for change; and coping styles (Anderson & Lambert, 1995; Safran, Segal, Vallis, Shaw, & Samstag, 1993). Therapists should be familiar with client variables that have been shown to affect outcome and develop the skills to evaluate the suitability of a given client for the intervention offered. In addition, as a supplement to their own psychotherapeutic skills, it behooves the therapist to become familiar with the social support networks and community resources available to their clients and to help them in identifying and using these resources.

6. Outside client and extratherapeutic variables, the best predictors (and possibly causes) of success are clinician–client relationship factors. Therapist relationship skills, such as acceptance, warmth, and empathy are absolutely fundamental in establishing a good therapist–client relationship. They are related to positive outcomes (Lambert & Bergin, 1994). Consequently, keeping a focus on the importance of including these skills or qualities in the therapeutic process is essential for successful treatment. Training in relationship skills is crucial for beginning therapists because they are the foundation on which all other skills and techniques are built.

Reassessing periodically their incorporation and effective use of these skills may also be prudent for more seasoned practitioners. In particular, the increasing influence of managed care, with the accompanying emphasis on symptom reduction, may serve to erode a therapist's capacity to understand and empathize with clients' internal experiencing and, consequently, inhibit their affective expression and processing. This may interfere later with the development of a positive therapist–client relationship or alliance, thus undermining therapeutic effectiveness. It also follows that when therapists become overstressed, fatigued, or "burned out," the first skill that suffers is their ability to empathize with the client and express warmth and understanding. Deterioration in these skills not only reduces therapeutic effectiveness, but also may constitute a "red flag" for the therapist. That is, it may signal the need for clinicians to focus on their personal circumstances and attend to factors that may be impinging on their therapeutic abilities.

The development of a therapeutic or working alliance has been shown to relate positively to outcome (Horvath & Symonds, 1991). Therefore, therapists must engage in behaviors that have been found to facilitate the development of a positive alliance. We have already discussed the value of therapist relationship skills in this process. In addition, the element of collaboration between therapist and client, including the consensual endorsement of therapeutic procedures, has been shown to be an essential part of the development of a strong therapeutic alliance.

We also wish to emphasize the necessity for therapists to avoid communications and behavior that have been shown to be disruptive to the therapist–client relationship. Specifically, behaviors that are critical, attacking, rejecting, blaming, or neglectful have been associated with less effective treatment (Najavits & Strupp, 1994). Therapist sensitivity to the deleterious effects of this type of behavior is critical in avoiding pitfalls that would compromise the therapy. This is especially true in work with certain groups of clients (e.g., those diagnosed with borderline or paranoid personality disorders). In these cases, untoward interpersonal pressures and the vicissitudes of the treatment may tempt the therapist to engage in behavior that is critical, attacking, or abusive.

A final recommendation is for therapists to make weekly assessments of client progress before each session to help the client communicate their psychological status. Simply reviewing with clients their progress in therapy may help to facilitate and solidify treatment gains. Clinicians can accomplish this by creating their own forms, or using formal questionnaires from the literature (see Ogles, Lambert, & Master, 1996).

7. Therapists can contribute to the therapeutic process by enhancing the effects of client expectations and placebo factors in their approach. Positive expectations about treatment include the belief that there is hope for overcoming problems and feeling better. As Frank (1973) pointed out, clients come to therapy because of lost hope or depleted morale. It is more than just being demoralized about having problems—clients have lost hope about being able to solve them. In the early phases of treatment, therapists can instill hope by directly

communicating to clients both their hope for change and reasons for being hopeful. It is assumed that a therapist would not work with the client if she or he felt there was no hope for improvement. Making this assumption explicit and clear for the client is key.

Successful negotiation and acceptance by the therapist and client of the tasks, techniques, or rituals of therapy, as well as the therapist's communication of belief about the efficacy of these tasks, naturally lead to increased morale and hope in the client. One way a therapist can communicate his belief in the value of a particular approach is by monitoring client change either through the client's own report or using a variety of accepted measures and questionnaires (Ogles et al., 1996). Finally, positive outcomes can be enhanced by keeping the treatment focused on the future, particularly on the client's ability to overcome in the future what has happened to them in the past, and by facilitating the client's sense of personal control (See Miller, Duncan, and Hubble, 1997, for a detailed discussion of these factors).

8. Some specific techniques look to be especially helpful with certain symptoms and disorders. Reviews of the psychotherapy outcome literature suggest that specific behavioral techniques have been found efficacious in the treatment of anxiety disorders, particularly circumscribed phobic disorders.

The practicing clinician is well served by reading the research literature and attending to the efforts of the American Psychological Association Task Force on Empirically Validated Treatments for guidelines regarding interactions between outcome and techniques (Task Force, 1995). In addition, many treatment manuals (Barlow, 1993) are available that can be used by the experienced therapist to supplement existing skills. These manuals provide session-by-session steps for assessment of and intervention in specific disorders, ranging from eating disorders to personality disorders.

Certainly, the therapist who intends to offer the highest level of treatment to clients will make every effort to stay abreast of developments and emerging empirical findings. Concurrently, one should remember that serious criticisms have been leveled against the research on "empirically validated treatments" (Silverman, 1996) and the use of treatment manuals (Strupp & Anderson, 1997). Keeping an open mind, but a balanced perspective, in considering the use of treatment manuals and empirically validated treatments will give clinicians more options. It is also helpful to remember that common factors and technical interventions are not mutually exclusive; all therapies use models and techniques. Our hope is that these technically based interventions will not be assumed to be so well established that their application will become mandatory. "Painting-by-numbers" can produce good results with certain clients, but rigid adherence to manuals and guidelines is not a proven way to get the best results.

The current brief review touches the surface of the rich assortment of information available to the practicing clinician on the importance and value of common factors in psychotherapy. As this body of knowledge grows, so will clinicians ability to implement pragmatically and effectively the findings from research on this often overlooked but extremely important aspect of psychotherapeutic change.

Questions From the Editors

1. Bergin and Garfield (1994), in the final chapter of the fourth edition of the Handbook of Psychotherapy and Behavior Change *wrote, "As therapists have depended more upon the client's resources, more change seems to occur" (p. 826). This statement, in concert with your report on the importance of client factors in determining treatment outcomes, suggests a pivotal role for clients' strengths and abilities in fostering therapeutic change. The tradition, however, of most therapeutic schools has been to emphasize psychological weakness, incompetence, and pathology. What practical steps can be taken to enable our clients' resources in day-to-day practice?*

Outcomes, both positive and negative, are largely dependent on what the patient brings to the therapeutic encounter. Whereas psychological assessments and personality theories themselves rely heavily on identifying and labeling what is "wrong" with the patient, therapists of necessity rely heavily on the patient's positive coping mechanisms. Psychodynamic theorists, for example, pay close attention to patient ego strength in making treatment assignment decisions and in guiding in-session behaviors. Behaviorally and cognitively oriented therapists often assign homework, demonstrating their confidence in the patient's ability to self-monitor, recognize patterns, and instigate behavioral changes. Person-centered therapy makes trust in the clients' positive directional tendencies the hallmark of theory and practice. In general, therapists do a good job of enabling clients to call on their own resources in solving problems.

Helping clients to marshal their abilities and resources in the therapeutic enterprise begins with the therapist's attitude about the client's role in the change process. Communicating a belief and hope in the client's ability to change and an optimistic expectation that change will indeed occur is essential, especially in the beginning phases of treatment. Likewise, communicating the expectation that clients will be active participants in the therapeutic process who share responsibility for the type and amount of change implies that they are taken seriously by the therapist and are viewed as competent and capable of change.

The client's sense of efficacy is also enhanced as improvements in functioning are identified and highlighted. This process is facilitated when therapists make a point of actively inquiring about changes that the client may have noticed within sessions and between sessions and how these changes may be related to the client's efforts in therapy. Therapists should also feel free to point out the positive changes and differences that they see in their clients and continue to communicate the expectation that more change is likely to occur. Some therapists have found success in having clients fill out questionnaires or rating scales at the beginning of each session that document client progress. This helps to reinforce the clients' faith in their ability to improve. Finally, keeping in mind that extratherapeutic factors have a significant impact on client change, it is important for therapists to assist clients in becoming aware of and using extratherapeutic resources, including support networks, self-help materials, and community programs that are available to them.

2. When therapy succeeds, the convention is to attribute the positive outcome to the therapy or ministrations of the therapist. In contrast, when therapy goes awry, or at least yields disappointing results, it has been customary to place the failure in the client or the client's personality. As reported in your chapter, Strupp's (1980a, 1980b, 1980c, 1980d) conclusions from his case studies represent this tendency. On the basis of your review of the empirical outcome literature, how much responsibility actually lies with clients or with therapists' difficulty in creating the necessary conditions for the development of the alliance?

The research literature on treatment effects underscores the important role that client factors play in outcome. As we have summarized in this chapter, client variables account for the largest portion of variance in psychotherapeutic change. It follows that what the client brings into the therapy situation is going to have the most influence on what happens in the treatment. However, it is also clear that therapist variables play a critical role in client change and that there is significant variability in therapist's effectiveness.

How therapy proceeds will be determined, to a large extent, by the type of therapeutic relationship or alliance that is formed. Therapists make an important contribution to the alliance and it is probable that the difference between effective and less effective therapists is their ability to form and maintain a therapeutic alliance with the client, particularly in treating more difficult or challenging clients. Therapists who are able to communicate warmth, understanding, and positive feelings toward the client and can facilitate a reasonable dialogue leading to understanding and agreement about therapeutic goals, techniques, and roles will be more likely to effect a positive treatment alliance. It is also important that the therapist be able to respond to negative feelings and expressions from the client about the therapy or the therapist without becoming defensive and resorting to antitherapeutic reactions, such as becoming authoritarian, defensive, critical, rigid, and dogmatic. If handled properly, negative client reactions can ultimately strengthen the therapeutic alliance.

There are usually multiple causes when a workable alliance is not achieved and the treatment is unsuccessful. In many cases the problem may justifiably be laid at the feet of the therapist who is lacking in maturity, skill, or interest, rather than reflexively attributing the failure to the client. Many therapists' behaviors can be linked to negative responses from the client. These include interpretations, passivity, negative confrontations, attempts at humor, mechanical responding, ignoring of patient feelings, and the like. Therapists can always increase the degree to which they attempt to concentrate on the alliance. In training student therapists it is clear that trainees can learn (in a relatively short period of time) how to be attuned to patients' feelings. But it is also clear that they fail routinely and persistently to offer high levels of empathy once they are not monitored. Clients and therapists work together to produce outcomes. When progress is insufficient it makes sense to attribute this failure to ourselves. It does not help to attribute alliance failures to patients because it does not, as readily, lead to changes in our own behaviors, including the need to be flexible in our approach.

Research suggests that the relationship offered by some therapists remains constant across patients (easy and difficult) whereas the quality of the relationship may be much more unstable in other therapists. This finding suggests that there is a sizable subset of therapists who need feedback and work on providing high levels of understanding with the most negative cases.

3. Despite the impressive research support, your position on the common factors is not a popular one. The field remains enamored with psychological theories and technical prowess. What might be done to disseminate information on the role of common factors in effective therapy? And, assuming that the "word gets out," how do you see psychotherapy as a profession changing?

About 70% to 80% of outpatients show significant benefits as a result of a wide range of therapies that use very different techniques. The controversy over causative agents in this behavior change is a natural and healthy phenomena.

Those who are committed to particular theories quite naturally argue for specific techniques and are often in the center of movements to encourage the use of "empirically supported treatments." The American Psychological Association and similar associations that provide accreditation to graduate training programs would do well to make sure that they provide support and encouragement for the development of training modules aimed at fostering relationship skills in addition to empirically supported psychotherapies.

There is no reason for those who are devoted to the development and testing of specific techniques to discount the obvious benefits of common factors and particularly the importance of therapist attitudes of respect, caring, understanding, and concern. By the same token, those of us who are convinced of the primary importance of the therapist, as a person, would be well served by remaining open to the likelihood that specific techniques, when offered within the safety of the therapeutic relationship, will appreciably add to the therapeutic encounter. We are, in fact, excited by efforts that derive their impetus from psychological theories that emphasize technical operations. Psychotherapy will be most effective when it includes high levels of positive attitudes as well as activities that are specific to patient problems.

Changing the emphasis in graduate training toward the development of the therapist as a person who prizes others can only make the enterprise of therapy more valuable, meaningful, and effective. The practice of psychotherapy appears to be moving toward an integrative eclecticism that is fostered by the assumption that there are specific techniques for specific problems. Like Carl Rogers, we believe that the "facts are always friendly." Future research will reveal the degree to which an emphasis on techniques will enhance the outcomes of treatment for the patient.

References

Anderson, E. M., & Lambert M. J. (1995). Short-term dynamically oriented psychothreapy: A review and meta-analysis. *Clinical Psychology Review, 9*, 503–514.

Andrews, J. G., & Tennant, C. (1978). Life event stress and psychiatric illness. *Psychological Medicine, 8*, 545–549.

Barker, S. L., Funk, S. C., & Houston, B. K. (1988). Psychological treatment versus nonspecific factors: A meta-analysis of conditions that engender comparable expectations for improvement. *Clinical Psychology Review, 8*, 579–594.

Barlow, D. H. (1993). *Clinical handbook of psychological disorders* (2nd ed.). New York: Guilford Press.

Barlow, D. H., Craske, M., Cerny, J. A., & Klosko, J. (1989). Behavioral treatment of panic disorder. *Behavior Therapy, 20*, 261–282.

Bergin, A. E. (1971). The evaluation of therapeutic outcomes. In A. E. Bergin & S. L. Garfield (Eds.), *Handbook of psychotherapy and behavior change* (pp. 217–270). New York: Wiley.

Bergin, A. E., & Garfield, S. L. (1994). Overview, trends and future issues. In A. E. Bergin and S. L. Garfield (Eds.), *Handbook of psychotherapy and behavior change* (4th ed., pp. 821–830). New York: Wiley.

Bergin, A. E., & Lambert, M. J. (1978). The evaluation of therapeutic outcomes. In S. L. Garfield & A. E. Bergin (Eds.), *Handbook of psychotherapy and behavior change: An empirical analysis* (2nd ed., pp. 139–189). New York: Wiley.

Bergin, A. E., & Suinn, R. (1975). Individual psychotherapy and behavior therapy. *Annual Review of Psychology, 26,* 509–556.

Beutler, L. E. (1979). Toward specific psychological therapies for specific conditions. *Journal of Consulting and Clinical Psychology, 47,* 882–892.

Bordin, E. S. (1976). The generalizability of the psychoanalytic concept of the working alliance. *Psychotherapy: Theory, Research and Practice, 16,* 252–260.

Bordin, E. S. (1989, April). *Building therapeutic alliances: The base for integration.* Paper presented at the annual meeting of the Society for Exploration of Psychotherapy Integration, Berkeley, CA.

Bowlby, J. (1988). *A secure base: Clinical applications of attachment theory.* London: Routledge & Kegan Paul.

Butler, S. F., & Strupp, H. H. (1986). Specific and non-specific factors in psychotherapy: A problematic paradigm for psychotherapy research. *Psychotherapy, 23,* 30–40.

Castonguay, L. G., Goldfried, M. R., Wiser, S., Raue, P. J., & Hayes, A. M. (1996). Predicting the effect of cognitive therapy for depression: A study of unique and common factors. *Journal of Consulting and Clinical Psychology, 64,* 497–504.

Crits-Christoph, P. (1992). The efficacy of brief dynamic psychotherapy: A meta-analysis. *American Journal of Psychiatry, 149,* 151–158.

Crits-Christoph, P., & Mintz, J. (1991). Implications of therapist effects for the design and analysis of comparative studies of psychotherapies. *Journal of Consulting and Clinical Psychology, 59,* 20–26.

DeRubeis, R. J., & Feeley, M. (1990). Determinants of change in cognitive therapy for depression. *Cognitive Therapy and Research, 14,* 469–482.

Elkin, I., Shea, M. T., Watkins, J. T., Imber, S. D., Stotsky, S. M., Collins, J. F., Glass, D. R., Pilkonis, P. A., Leber, W. R., Docherty, J. P., Fiester, S. J., & Parloff, M. B. (1989). NIMH Treatment of Depression Collaborative Research Program: General effectiveness of treatments. *Archives of General Psychiatry, 46,* 971–983.

Emmelkamp, P. M. G. (1994). Behavior therapy with adults. In A. E. Bergin & S. L. Garfield (Eds.), *Handbook of psychotherapy and behavior change* (4th ed., pp. 379–427). New York: Wiley.

Fennichel, O. (1941). *Problems of psychoanalytic technique.* Albany, NY: The Psychoanalytic Quarterly, Inc.

Frank, J. D. (1973). *Persuasion and healing: A comparative study of psychotherapy.* Baltimore: Johns Hopkins University Press.

Frank, J. D., Gliedman, L. H., Imber, S. D., Stone, A. R., & Nash, E. H., Jr. (1959). Patients expectancies and relearning as factors determining improvement in psychotherapy. *American Journal of Psychiatry, 115,* 961–968.

Freud, S. (1912). The dynamics of transference. *The standard edition of the complete psychological works of Sigmund Freud* (pp. 97–108). London: Hogarth Press.

Freud, S. (1913). On beginning the treatment: Further recommendations on the technique of psychoanalysis. *The standard edition of the complete psychological works of Sigmund Freud.* In J. Strachey (Ed. and Trans., pp. 121–144). London: Hogarth Press.

Garfield, S. L. (1994). Research on client variables in psychotherapy. In S. L. Garfield & A. E. Bergin (Eds.), *Handbook of psychotherapy and behavior change* (4th ed., pp. 190–228). New York: Wiley.

Garfield, S. L., & Bergin, A. E. (Eds.). (1994). *Handbook of psychotherapy and behavior change* (4th ed.). New York: Wiley.

Gaston, L. (1990). The concept of the alliance and its role in psychotherapy: Theoretical and empirical considerations. *Psychotherapy, 27,* 143–153.

Glass, C., & Arnkoff, D. B. (1988). Common and specific factors in client descriptions of and explanations for change. *Journal of Integrative and Eclectic Psychotherapy, 7,* 427–440.

Goldstein, A. P., & Stein, N. (1976). *Prescriptive psychotherapies.* New York: Pergamon.

Greenson, R. (1965). The working alliance and the transference neurosis. *Psychoanalytic Quarterly, 34,* 155–181.

Gurman, A. S. (1977). The patient's perception of the therapeutic relationship. In A. S. Gurman & A. M. Razin (Eds.), *Effective psychotherapy: A handbook of research* (pp. 503–543). New York: Pergamon.

Henry, W. P., Strupp, H. H., Butler, S. F., Schacht, T. E., & Binder, J. L. (1993). Effects of training in time-limited dynamic psychotherapy: Changes in therapists behavior. *Journal of Consulting and Clinical Psychology, 61,* 434–440.

Hollon, S. D., & Beck, A. T. (1986). Cognitive and cognitive–behavioral therapies. In S. L. Garfield & A. E. Bergin (Eds.), *Handbook of psychotherapy and behavior change* (3rd ed., pp. 443–482). New York: Wiley.

Horvath, A. O., & Greenberg, L. S. (1989). Development and validation of the Working Alliance Inventory. *Journal of Counseling Psychology, 36,* 223–233.

Horvath, A. O., & Greenberg, L. S. (Eds.). (1994). *The working alliance: Theory, research, practice.* New York: Wiley.

Horvath, A. O., & Luborsky, L. (1993). The role of the therapeutic alliance in psychotherapy. *Journal of Consulting and Clinical Psychology, 61,* 561–573.

Horvath, A. O., & Symonds, B. D. (1991). Relation between working alliance and outcome in psychotherapy: A meta-analysis. *Journal of Counseling Psychology, 38,* 139–149.

Howard, K. I., Kopta, S. M., Krause, M. S., & Orlinsky, D. E. (1986). The dose–effect relationship in psychotherapy. *American Psychologist, 41,* 159–164.

Howard, K. I., & Orlinsky, P. E. (1986). Process and outcome. In S. C. Garfield & A. E. Bergin (Eds.), *Handbook of psychotherapy and behavior change* (3rd ed., pp. 311–381). New York: Wiley.

Imber, S. D., Pilkonis, P. A., Stotsky, S. M., Elkin, I., Watkins, J. T., Collins, J. F. Shea, M. T., Leber, W. R., & Glass, D. R. (1990). Mode-specific effects among three treatments for depression. *Journal of Consulting and Clinical Psychology, 58,* 352–359.

Jones, E. E., Cumming, J. D., & Horowitz, M. J. (1988). Another look at the nonspecific hypothesis of therapeutic effectiveness. *Journal of Consulting and Clinical Psychology, 56,* 48–55.

Kadera, S. W., Lambert, M. J., & Andrews, A. A. (1996). How much therapy is really enough: A session-by-session analysis of the psychotherapy dose–effect relationship. *Journal of Psychotherapy: Practice and Research, 5,* 1–22.

Kazdin, A. E., & Bass, D. (1989). Power to detect differences between alternative treatments in comparative psychotherapy outcome research. *Journal of Consulting and Clinical Psychology, 57,* 138–147.

Krupnick, J. L., Stotsky, S. M., Simmons, S., Moyer, J., Elkin, I., Watkins, J., & Pilkonis, P. A. (1996). The role of the therapeutic alliance in psychotherapy and pharmacotherapy outcome: Findings in the National Institute Mental Health Treatment of Depression Collaborative Research Program. *Journal of Consulting and Clinical Psychology, 64,* 532–539.

Lambert, M. J. (1976). Spontaneous remission in adult neurotic disorders: A revision and summary. *Psychological Bulletin, 83,* 107–119.

Lambert, M. J. (1983). Introduction to assessment of psychotherapy outcome: Historical perspectives and current issues. In M. J. Lambert, E. R. Christenson, & S. S. DeJulio (Eds.), *The assessment of psychotherapy outcome* (pp. 3–32). New York: Wiley-Interscience.

Lambert, M. J. (1992). Implications of outcome research for psychotherapy integration. In J. C. Norcross & M. R. Goldstein (Eds.), *Handbook of psychotherapy integration* (pp. 94–129). New York: Basic Books.

Lambert, M. J. (1998). Manual-based treatment and clinical practice: Hangman of life or promising development? *Clinical Psychology: Science and Practice, 5,* 391–395.

Lambert, M. J., & Anderson, E. M. (1996). Assessment for the time-limited psychotherapies. *Annual Review of Psychiatry, 15*, 23–47.

Lambert, M. J., & Asay, T. P. (1984). Patient characteristics and their relationship to psychotherapy outcome. In M. Herson, L. Michelson, and A. S. Bellack (Eds.), *Issues in psychotherapy research* (pp. 313–359). New York: Plenum Press.

Lambert, M. J., & Bergin, A. E. (1994). The effectiveness of psychotherapy. In A. E. Bergin & S. L. Garfield (Eds.), *Handbook of psychotherapy and behavior change* (4th ed., pp. 143–189). New York: Wiley.

Lambert, M. J., Christensen, E. R., & DeJulio, S. S. (Eds.). (1983). *The assessment of psychotherapy outcome.* New York: Wiley.

Lambert, M. J., DeJulio, S. S., & Stein, D. M. (1978). Therapist interpersonal skills: Process, outcome, methodological considerations and recommendations for future research. *Psychological Bulletin, 85*, 467–489.

Lambert, M. J., Shapiro, D. A., & Bergin, A. E. (1986). The effectiveness of psychotherapy. In S. L. Garfield & A. E. Bergin (Eds.), *Handbook of psychotherapy and behavior change* (3rd ed., pp. 157–211). New York: Wiley.

Lambert, M. J., Weber, F. D., & Sykes, J. D. (1993, April). Psychotherapy versus placebo. Poster presented at the annual meetings of the Western Psychological Association, Phoenix, AZ.

Lorr, M. (1965). Client perceptions of therapists. *Journal of Consulting Psychology, 29*, 146–149.

Luborsky, L. (1994). Therapeutic alliances as predictors of psychotherapy outcomes: Factors explaining the predictive success. In A. O. Horvath & L. S. Greenberg (Eds.), *The working alliance: Theory, research, and practice* (pp. 38–50). New York: Wiley.

Luborsky, L., & Auerbach, A. (1985). The therapeutic relationship in psycho-dynamic psychotherapy: The research evidence and its meaning for practice. In R. Hales & A. Frances (Eds.), *Psychiatry update annual review* (pp. 550–561). Washington, DC: American Psychiatric Association.

Luborsky, L., & DeRubeis, R. J. (1984). The use of psychotherapy treatment manuals—A small revolution in psychotherapy research style. *Clinical Psychology Review, 4*, 5–14.

Mann, A. H., Jenkins, R., & Belsey, E. (1981). The twelve-month outcome of Patients with neurotic illness in general practice. *Psychological Medicine, 11*, 535–550.

Marks, I. (1978). Behavioral psychotherapy of adult neurosis. In A. E. Bergin & S. L. Garfield (Eds.), *Handbook of psychotherapy and behavior change* (2nd ed., pp. 493–547). New York: Wiley.

Meltzoff, J., & Kornreich, M. (1970). *Research in psychotherapy.* New York: Atherton.

Miller, S. D., Duncan, B. L., & Hubble, M. A. (1997). *Escape from babel: Toward a unifying language for psychotherapy practice.* New York: W. W. Norton.

Miller, W. R., Taylor, C. A., & West, J. C. (1980). Focused versus broad-spectrum behavior therapy for problem drinkers. *Journal of Consulting and Clinical Psychology, 48,* 590–601.

Milrod, B., & Busch, F. (1996). Long-term outcome of panic disorder treatment: A review of the literature. *Journal of Nervous and Mental Disease, 184,* 723–730.

Murphy, P. M., Cramer, D., & Lillie, F. J. (1984). The relationship between curative factors perceived by clients in their psychotherapy and treatment outcome: An exploratory study. *British Journal of Medical Psychology, 57,* 187–197.

Najavits, L. M., & Strupp, H. H. (1994). Differences in the effectiveness of psychodynamic therapists: A process–outcome study. *Psychotherapy, 31,* 114–123.

Nicholson, R. A., & Berman, J. S. (1983). Is follow-up necessary in evaluating psychotherapy? *Psychological Bulletin, 93,* 261–278.

Ogles, B. M., Lambert, M. J., & Craig, D. (1991). A comparison of self-help books for coping with loss: Expectations and attributions. *Journal of Counseling Psychology, 38,* 387–393.

Ogles, B. M., Lambert, M. J., & Master, K. S. (1996) *Assessing outcome in clinical practice.* New York: Allyn & Bacon.

Patterson, C. H. (1984). Empathy, warmth and genuineness in psychotherapy: A review of reviews. *Psychotherapy, 21,* 431–438.

Rachman, S. J., & Wilson, G. T. (1980). *The effects of psychological therapy* (2nd ed.). New York: Pergamon Press.

Rounsaville, B. J., O'Malley, S., Foley, S., & Weissman, M. W. (1988). Role of manual-guided training in the conduct and efficacy of interpersonal psychotherapy for depression. *Journal of Consulting and Clinical Psychology, 51,* 681–688.

Safran, J. C., Segal, Z. V., Vallis, T. M., Shaw, B. F., & Samstag, L. W. (1993). Assessing patient suitability for short-term cognitive therapy with an interpersonal focus. *Cognitive Therapy and Research, 17,* 23–38.

Schapira, K., Roth, M., Kerr, T. A., & Gurney, C. (1972). The prognosis of affective disorders: The differentiation of anxiety states from depressive illnesses. *British Journal of Psychiatry, 12,* 175–181.

Shapiro, D. A., Barkham, M., Rees, A., Hardy, G. E., Reynolds, S., & Startup, M. (1994). Effects of treatment duration and severity of depression on the effectiveness of cognitive–behavioral and psychodynamic–interpersonal psychotherapy. *Journal of Consulting and Clinical Psychology, 62,* 522–534.

Silverman, W. H. (1996). Cookbooks, manuals, and paint-by-numbers: Psychotherapy in the 90's. *Psychotherapy, 33,* 207–215.

Sloan, R. B., Staples, F. R., Cristol, A. H., Yorkston, W. J., & Whipple, K. (1975). *Short-term analytically oriented psychotherapy vs. behavior therapy.* Cambridge, MA: Harvard University Press.

Smith, M. L., Glass, G.V., & Miller, T. I. (1980). *The benefits of psychotherapy.* Baltimore: Johns Hopkins University Press.

Steenbarger, B. N. (1994). Duration and outcome in psychotherapy: An integrative review. *Professional Psychology: Research and Practice, 25,* 111–119.

Sterba, R. F. (1929). The dynamics of the dissolution of the transference resistance. *Psychoanalytic Quarterly, 9,* 363–379.

Strupp, H. H. (1980a.). Success and failure in time-limited psychotherapy. *Archives of General Psychiatry, 37,* 595–603.

Strupp, H. H. (1980b.). Success and failure in time-limited psychotherapy. *Archives of General Psychiatry, 37,* 708–716.

Strupp, H. H. (1980c.). Success and failure in time-limited psychotherapy. *Archives of General Psychiatry, 37,* 831–841.

Strupp, H. H. (1980d.). Success and failure in time-limited psychotherapy. *Archives of General Psychiatry, 37,* 947–954.

Strupp, H. H., & Anderson, T. (1997). On the limitations of therapy manuals. *Clinical Psychology: Science and Practice, 4,* 76–82.

Task Force on Promotion and Dissemination of Psychological Procedures. (1995). Training in and dissemination of empirically-validated therapies. *The Clinical Psychologist, 49,* 3–23.

Wilson, G. T. (1998). Manual-based treatment and clinical practice. *Clinical Psychology: Science and Practice, 5,* 363–375.

Zetzel, E. R. (1956). Current concepts of transference. International *Journal of Psychoanalysis, 37,* 369–376.

Paul V. Maione and Ronald J. Chenail

Qualitative Inquiry in Psychotherapy:

Research on the Common Factors

3

Qualitative research can be perceived in different ways. One way is to see it as a current approach researchers and therapists have incorporated to study psychotherapy and change. Another way is to see qualitative research as a longstanding method clinical researchers and researching clinicians have used to describe and explain therapeutic processes and outcomes. From the "newly arrived perspective," qualitative research is understood as a group of methods borrowed from the social sciences and humanities. These methods have been brought into psychology, social work, and marital and family therapy over the past three decades to provide naturalistic, descriptive, discovery-oriented, interpretive, and quantitative-informing inquires. From the "since-the-beginning point of view," qualitative research is synonymous with the "case-by-case way of knowing" central to most therapists' everyday practice and understanding of therapy, clients, and themselves.

Whichever perspective is more true, qualitative research has emerged as a major influence in contemporary clinical practice and research. This chapter explores the literature on qualitative studies of psychotherapy and relates those findings to the common factors. As described throughout this volume, the common factors are four categories distilled from 40 years of quantitative research on what contributes to effective psychotherapy. These include client, relationship, expectancy, and technique/model factors (Assay & Lambert, chap. 2, this volume).

This chapter begins with a brief discussion of qualitative inquiry in psychotherapy to orient the reader with little exposure to this method of investigation. We then trace the brief history of qualitative research methods in psychotherapy and present a review of what the qualitative literature says about the common factors. Finally, we conclude with the implications of our review for therapists and researchers. Except for some preliminary remarks in the overview on qualitative inquiry, comments on methodology are sparse. Only in instances where such details will be helpful in understanding findings are methodological issues discussed. In describing this body of work, keep in mind that we are interpreting the literature as much as reporting it. The inferences we make are our attempts to relate this material to the study of common factors. Readers are encouraged to make their own interpretations.

Qualitative Inquiry

Qualitative research is a cover term for a group of methodologies dedicated to the description and interpretation of social phenomenon (for a review, see Bogdan & Biklen, 1992; Denzin & Lincoln, 1994; Gilgun, Daly, & Handel, 1992; Glesne & Peshkin, 1992; LeCompte, Millroy, & Preissle, 1992; Leininger, 1985; Lincoln & Guba, 1985). Ethnography (e.g., Fetterman, 1989; Hammersley & Atkinson, 1995; Spradley, 1979), ethnomethodology (e.g., Garfinkel, 1967; Heritage, 1984), discourse analysis (e.g., Brown & Yule, 1983; Potter & Wetherell, 1987; Schiffrin, 1994; Stubbs, 1983), narrative analysis (e.g., Cortazzi, 1993; Polkinghorne, 1988; Riessman, 1993), grounded theory (e.g., Glaser, 1978; Glaser & Strauss, 1967; Strauss, 1987; Strauss & Corbin, 1990), phenomenology (e.g., Moustakas, 1994; Munhall, 1994), frame analysis (e.g., Chenail, 1991; Franklin, 1996; Goffman, 1974); hermeneutics (e.g., Messer, Sass, & Woolfolk, 1988; Packer, 1985; Packer & Addison, 1989), and conversation analysis (e.g., J. Atkinson & Heritage, 1984; Coulthard & Montgomery, 1981; Gale, 1996; Psathas, 1995) are all approaches used by researchers to examine qualitative differences both within and between collected or generated phenomenon.

In general, qualitative studies are discovery oriented (Mahrer, 1988). They are less concerned with quantification and instead "explore the meanings, variations and perceptual experiences of phenomena" (Crabtree & Miller, 1992, p. 6.). Qualitative research or naturalistic inquiry (Kuzel, 1986; Lincoln & Guba, 1985) has no prepackaged designs (W. L. Miller & Crabtree, 1992). Instead, qualitative researchers use a variety of methods, procedures, and analysis techniques "to create unique, question-specific designs that evolve throughout the research process" (Crabtree & Miller, 1992, p. 5).

In going about this work, some qualitative researchers tend to favor traditions, practices, and forms from the humanities and arts, and some lean toward conventions of inquiry from the social and natural sciences (Eisner, 1985, 1991). Those from the artistic camp (e.g., Ellis & Bochner, 1996; Janesick, 1998) emphasize story, performance, interpretation, and sometimes present their work in various literary forms such as biography, autobiography, diaries, and poetry. Those from the scientific tribe (e.g., Creswell, 1994; Miles & Huberman, 1994; Weitzman & Miles, 1995) stress research design, sampling strategies, more traditional views of validity, reliability, and generalizability, compatibility with quantitative approaches, and computer-aided analysis of data.

Researchers using qualitative methodologies attempt to study naturally occurring events from either an insider or an outsider perspective. In the "insider" approach, qualitative researchers go "to the field" (i.e., the setting or place of interest) and interview participants about their lived experiences, carefully observe them in action, or do both. Also, the researchers often become insiders and record their own impressions of being a part of the action. In the "outsider" approach, researchers stay apart from the phenomenon or setting. They collect recordings, study documents, and other artifacts from "the field." They then work to describe or interpret the patterns they "discover" or "construct" through their repeated interactions with the data (Mahrer, 1988).

Qualitative researchers establish credibility for their work by constantly comparing what they learn from previous observations on a site, a group of people, or phenomenon with what they subsequently "see" in later samples from the site, the people, or phenomenon. Each observation of the phenomenon presents an opportunity for researchers to falsify their best story, description, coding, or interpretation of the phenomenon. Also, each visit with the data increases the researchers confidence that their analysis is the best and most fitting account of what they found in the field.

In presenting their work, qualitative researchers must clearly describe their working methods, accounting for the choices they made in constructing their inquiry (Chenail, 1994; Constas, 1992). They describe the setting for their study and how they gained access to the site. In addition, they recount the process of generating and collecting their data, the means for processing and analyzing the data, the ways in which they will re-present their analytical observations, and how they conducted quality controls in their work. During this process, it is important for qualitative researchers to take great care to delineate who they are, what they are attempting to do in their work, and how they participate in their ongoing research endeavors (Wolcott, 1992). Through these self-reflective narratives, qualitative researchers establish their credibility through an accurate and honest accounting of their actions. These method narratives then give the consumers of the research an over the shoulder perspective and a contextual vantage point from which to evaluate and critique the study (see Guba, 1990; Kvale, 1989; Maxwell, 1992; Mishler, 1990; Wolcott, 1990).

Qualitative researchers do not rely on statistics to show their confidence in representations of their field work. Instead, they build confidence in their findings or constructions by attempting to saturate themselves with observations of the phenomenon in question. They continually go to the field or the data set and challenge themselves to come up with the best representation of the patterns they perceive "out there." In presenting these findings to another, qualitative researchers carefully juxtapose their descriptions and interpretations with what is being described or interpreted. As a result, qualitative research publications and presentations are not as condensed or reduced as their quantitative counterparts. Indeed, the heart and soul of a qualitative research paper or talk is displaying the processed data with its accompanying descriptions or interpretations. The validity of these analyses is in the reading and re-reading of the work. Each observer of the interplay between the researchers' words and the phenomenon in focus makes his or her own critique on the fit and coherence of the presentation.

From a qualitative perspective, generalizability is a two-fold process. First, researchers must be confident that how they describe a phenomenon is the best generalization they can make, that is, the most fitting among the variety of ways to discuss a given phenomenon. Second, the consumers of the research must judge whether the work is generalizable and consistent with their perceptual reality. In this way, generalizability is an interactional process; it consists of conversations between the researcher and the researched, and the reader and the text (see B. Atkinson, Heath, & Chenail, 1991).

Qualitative Research in Psychotherapy: An Overview

The presence of qualitative research is often viewed as either a new arrival or a long term and ever-present part of clinical inquiry. In the "since the beginning" story, clinical inquiry is understood as a qualitative process. Therapists work with individual clients and come to know the particularities of that person, couple, or family. The knowledge of the client through the eyes of the therapist becomes the case and each case is described and interpreted by the clinician. The processes and outcomes are dutifully recorded in the case notes by the therapist just as an ethnographer would record details of an encounter in the field notes. How therapists understand clients, therapy, and themselves is constructed in this case-by-case manner. In each encounter with the other or the self, therapists challenge their descriptions, interpretations, and understandings based upon new evidence. This constant comparative approach echoes the grounded theory method so prominent in the qualitative research world.

Because of this similarity in purpose and practice, many therapists realized that qualitative research methods long used by other disciplines could be applied to clinical settings to further understandings of the clinical encounter (e.g., Chenail, 1992; Chenail & Maione, 1997; Crabtree & Miller, 1992; Gale, Chenail, Watson, Wright, & Bell, 1996; Hoshmand, 1989; Maione, 1997; W. L. Miller & Crabtree, 1994; Moon, Dillon, & Sprenkle, 1990). These clinicians also noticed that qualitative approaches were useful in ways that experimental and quantitative methods were not.

This turn toward qualitative methodologies began in the mid to late 1970s but did not really blossom until the 1990s. Through a series of landmark special issues in journals such as the *Journal of Counseling Psychology* (see Polkinghorne,1994) and the *Journal of Marital and Family Therapy* (Moon, Dillon, & Sprenkle, 1990, 1991), qualitative research has been more widely published and accepted. Now, it is difficult to find a clinical journal that has not published at least a handful of qualitative research papers. In the review that follows, we look at the qualitative studies that relate to common factors.

Qualitative Research and Common Factors

CLIENT FACTORS

On the basis of his review of the research findings, Lambert (1992) concluded that as much as 40% of the improvement in psychotherapy clients is attributable to client variables and extratherapeutic influences. These factors are those that are part of the client and his or her environment that aid in recovery separate from the client's participation in therapy. Few qualitative studies have investigated or yield information regarding client factors.

However, Rennie's work (1990, 1992, 1994a, 1994b, 1994c, 1995; Angus & Rennie, 1989) not only has made a great contribution to the study of psychotherapy from a qualitative perspective but also speaks to the client's influence of the therapeutic process. Rennie used inter-personal process recall (IPR) in his work investigating clients' perceptions of the therapy process. He met with clients after a therapy session and replayed an audio or videotape of the session. Clients were then asked "to recall thoughts, images, emotions, and feelings they were experiencing at the moment in the therapy represented in the tape segment just played" (Angus & Rennie, 1989, p. 373).

Rennie also audiotaped the post-therapy interviews and analyzes the transcripts using a form of grounded theory analysis (Glaser, 1978; Glaser & Strauss, 1967; Rennie, Phillips, & Quartaro, 1988). Briefly, in a grounded theory analysis, different phenomena of interest are identified and separated into categories. Data are placed in categories on the basis of their commonalties, and eventually the researcher constructs a scheme of categories stating the relationships between the categories, as well as between the categories and the individual pieces of data.

In one study, Rennie (1994c) used IPR to investigate clients' subjective experience of storytelling. He concluded that storytelling leads to increased self-understanding, feeling, and contact with inner disturbance. On the other hand, he also found that clients may use storytelling to avoid discussing certain problematic issues, struggles and disturbing feelings.

Analyzing clients' experiences of therapy, Rennie (1992) identified "clients' reflexivity" as a major finding of this work. Through his interviews, Rennie found that clients were active in their thinking processes throughout the course of therapy. He defines client reflexivity as "this quality of self-awareness and self-control that is revealed in the respondents' reports and that colligates the categories conceptualized in the grounded analysis . . ." (p. 224) Rennie's work highlights client's active influence of the therapeutic process. Tallman and Bohart (this volume) see Rennie's data as evidence for clients as highly active, thinking, processing, reflective agents during therapy.

Winefield, Chandler, and Bassett (1989) researched a client's use of tag questions (e.g., "It doesn't necessarily follow, *does it*?") in therapy and how such questions affected the therapist's talk. In their study of a complete course of psychotherapy between a male psychiatrist and a female patient, they found that the woman's increased use of tag questions during the course of therapy reflected her growing independence in the sessions. The client became more comfortable involving her therapist in her observations. She felt more confident to ask his opinion on every observation she made on her life and her relationships. This study provides clear evidence that clients, through their conversational patterns, shape how therapists participate in therapy conversations. In this example, the patient felt more confident as therapy continued and spoke to the therapist in a style showing less powerlessness than when therapy began. However, as the authors point out, the use of tag questions implies that clients are dependent on therapists and they look for confirmation for the things they say.

Buttny's (1990, 1993; Buttny & Cohen, 1991; Buttny & Jensen, 1995) work sheds new light on how clients' present their stories or accounts of their problems in therapy. One fascinating finding is how the tasks of "telling, blaming, and accounting" are interwoven in many clients' problem presentations (Buttny, 1993). From this perspective, a client's problem talk should not only be heard as a description of what happened. It should also be heard for clients' opinions on who is to blame for what happened, and whose actions are accountable or justified. Buttny contends that managing such story-telling patterns by clients is a major task for therapists in their clinical work.

Although qualitative investigations of client factors are sparse, not unlike the quantitative literature, there is some evidence for client's active influence and agency in the therapeutic process. In addition, Buttny's research points to the importance of listening to the client's "theory" (see Hubble, Duncan, & Miller, this volume) of who is to blame and should be held accountable in the client's problem presentation.

Therapeutic Relationship

Among the common factors most frequently studied in the quantitative literature are those focusing on the role of the therapeutic relationship. Empirical findings suggest that relationship factors account for approximately 30% of client improvement (Lambert, 1992). By far most qualitative inquiries in psychotherapy have examined and found support for the importance of the therapeutic relationship. Several studies have identified the characteristics of a good therapeutic relationship: therapist empathy (Bischoff & McBride, 1996), being engaged in the therapy process, understanding what was happening, and being understood (Howe, 1996), and therapist characteristics including acceptance, empathy, caring, competence, support, and being personable (Kuehl, Newfield, & Joanning, 1990; McCollum & Trepper, 1995). Howe (1996) describes the goals of these inquiries:

> The aim of the research was to explore with family members
> how they perceived, understood, experienced and felt about
> therapy. The interest was not in whether the presenting problem
> had been "cured" in some objective, measurable sense, but rather
> in whether or not people *felt* they had been helped. (p. 369)

Bachelor (1995) examined clients' perspectives of the therapeutic alliance using accounts provided by clients over different phases of therapy. Using a phenomenological analysis, she identified three different varieties of therapeutic alliances she termed *nurturant, insight-oriented,* and *collaborative.* Bachelor suggests that theoretician-defined alliance variables are not equally relevant for clients and that some crucial features of the perceived working relationship are not accounted for in current alliance theory. She recommends that therapists monitor the clients' idiosyncratic perceptions of the alliance and adjust their relational stance accordingly (see Bachelor & Horvath, this volume).

In a related study, Bachelor (1988) explored the therapeutic relationship by examining the perceptions of clients of the different types of empathy in therapy. She identified four types of client-perceived empathy: cognitive, affective, therapist sharing, and therapist nurturant. Bachelor concluded that empathy is not a global, unidimensional concept, and that therapists should be sensitive to their clients' perceptions of empathy and other therapist provided variables.

Therapist self-disclosure and its impact on clients was studied by Knox, Hess, Petersen, and Hill (1997). They analyzed interviews with clients about therapist self-disclosure and found that helpful disclosures occurred more often when clients discussed important issues, were perceived as intended by therapists to normalize or reassure the clients, and was a disclosure of personal, non-immediate information about the therapists. They concluded that therapist self-disclosures resulted in positive consequences for the clients and improved therapeutic relationships. The results are consistent with Bachelor's findings that some clients find therapist sharing responses as empathic.

Another way the therapeutic relationship has been studied is through exploring misunderstandings in therapy and how clients and therapists work through those issues. For example, Rhodes, Hill, Thompson, and Elliott (1994) used a retrospective recall procedure to analyze both resolved and unresolved misunderstandings. They found that a good relationship and clients' willingness to assert negative feelings about being misunderstood were key factors leading to resolution. In contrast, a poor therapeutic relationship, therapists' unwillingness to discuss or accept clients' assertion of negative reactions, led several clients to discontinue therapy.

Like misunderstandings, another feature of the therapeutic relationship often studied are therapeutic impasses (Diamond & Liddle, 1996; Hill, Nutt-Williams, Heaton, Thompson, & Rhodes, 1996). Hill et al. (1996) conducted posttherapy interviews with and administered questionnaires to therapists who had experienced impasses with clients that terminated therapy. They found that therapists perceived impasses as having a negative impact on both clients and therapists, and in particular, on the therapeutic relationship. These studies point toward openly resolving impasses when they occur with clients.

Some researchers have looked at ways to enhance the therapeutic relationship. For example, Bischoff, McKeel, Moon, and Sprenkle (1996) developed an in-session procedure called the therapist-conducted consultation (TCC) designed to enhance the therapist-client collaborative relationship. During this process, the therapist and client(s) have a conversation on the client's treatment. Therapist and client evaluation of this procedure reflected that it took therapists out of the position of being an expert while allowing clients to become more involved in the process. Therapists reported that asking clients about what was helpful about therapy was valuable feedback for them because it helped them tailor their approach. Therapist-conducted consultation allows therapists and clients to metacommunicate about treatment. Clients are invited to share their perspectives of treatment, discuss whether their goals are being met, and to suggest improvements.

In a similar study designed to enhance the therapeutic relationship and therapy process, Joanides, Brigham, and Joanning (1997) investigated the use of a debriefing technique. Debriefing is a technique where clients are questioned about the therapy process. The authors compared clients' perceptions of their therapist in the role of debriefer versus a third-party debriefer. Results showed fewer differences in client responses when therapists were the debriefer than when a third party was the debriefer. The authors concluded that debriefing enhances therapy by introducing more information into the therapeutic system while fostering a more collaborative therapeutic relationship.

To improve the therapeutic relationship in ongoing therapy, Shilts, Rambo, and Hernandez (1997) used client perspectives about therapy as part of treatment. Working in therapy teams, the authors interviewed clients about the therapy process and used this information to guide future sessions. They make a case for such interviews because they can help the therapist and team develop better ways to accommodate the client's needs, and thus enhance the therapeutic relationship.

In a related study, Shilts, Filippino, and Nau (1994) discuss what they call client-informed supervision to enhance both therapy and the supervisory process. Through a case example they show how therapy, a research interview, and supervisor's comments contribute to client-informed supervision that affects the therapist, the supervisor behind the 1-way mirror, and the therapeutic context. Information gleaned from the research interview was used to improve ongoing therapy as well as the supervisory context. The therapist and supervisor found this information to be invaluable to a successful therapy outcome.

In another attempt to improve the therapeutic relationship, Todd, Joanning, Enders, Mutchler, and Thomas, (1990) used ethnographic interviews with clients to gain a better sense of the family's expectations of therapy during the therapy process. They then used this information to improve ongoing therapy. Including the client's perceptions was again helpful to the therapeutic relationship.

An interesting development from inquiry on client perspectives is investigating the therapeutic value of the research interview itself (Gale, 1992; Gale, Odell, & Nagireddy, 1995; McCollum et al., 1996; McNamee, 1988; Wright, 1990). The posture of most researchers interviewing clients is one of discovery and exploration. Intervention and change is not usually their focus. However, this body of work suggests that researching client's perspectives can have therapeutic benefits sometimes more so than the actual therapy interview.

Qualitative research of the therapeutic relationship reveals a similar story to the quantitative literature. Not only is the relationship an intense focus of inquiry of both traditions, the results yield similar conclusions. Qualitative investigation suggests that client perceptions of the therapeutic relationship are of great importance to the process of therapy and should be actively monitored and incorporated into any chosen theoretical approach. In addition, there is compelling evidence that directly incorporating client feedback, perceptions, and expectations yields favorable dividends regarding the relationship and therefore, for positive outcome.

Techniques/Model Factors

Most research studies in the quantitative realm have aggressively investigated the role of model-based, technical interventions. Despite the massive volume of research generated, specific techniques have been found to account for only about 15% of the improvement in psychotherapy clients (Lambert, 1992). From a qualitative perspective, several studies have explored various therapist techniques and occasionally therapy models. In addition researchers have also studied therapy events and in-session processes.

In an exploration of the therapy process from children's perspectives, Stith, Rosen, McCollum, Coleman, and Herman (1996) used interviews with children who participated in therapy. The authors also interviewed parents and teenagers for their perspectives on their child's participation in therapy. Children 5 to 9 years old enjoyed activities initiated by the therapist and found the personality of the therapist to be important. Support for therapist techniques that initiated activities and actively included children in therapy were reported by respondents as being helpful.

In addition to interviewing techniques to gather information, many qualitative researchers employ communication methodologies to study the patterns of in-therapy conversations. Communication studies are considered a unique subset of qualitative research for several reasons: (a) communication researchers study naturally occurring conversations, (b) these conversations are recorded and transcribed through multiple listenings, (c) communication researchers tend to conduct "micro analytic studies in which they focus on smaller segments of talk in these conversations, (d) predetermined coding systems are not usually employed in their studies, (e) exemplary segments are collected and studied, and (f) communication researchers study not only what is said and the meaning of what is said, but also how speakers accomplish goals with their acts of communication (Chenail & Morris, 1995; Hopper, 1988).

Many communication researchers (e.g., G. Miller, 1987; G. Miller & Silverman, 1995; Stancombe & White, 1997; Viaro & Leonardi, 1983) approach therapeutic technique from the perspective of how therapists help clients with the storytelling process. The focus here is on the question-asking behavior of therapists and on how clients are persuaded to tell their stories in certain ways according to the form and content of therapists' questions.

Viaro and Leonardi (1983) examined how a family therapist in a two-part interview searched for information and then applied this information in the creation of an intervention for the family. They identified a number of information-gathering patterns, called the therapist's "conversational prerogatives," that govern the flow of information in the session. These therapist prerogatives included rights to: decide what topics may be discussed and who may speak at any given time; to cut off other speakers and stop conversations; and to ask questions, summarize, and make organizational glosses (organizational glosses refer to how the conversation is structured). Viaro and Leonardi suggested that these prerogatives are needed to control the flow of information in the session and to have material with which to design interventions.

Stancombe and White (1997) examined a full-length family therapy session. They concentrated on how the therapist guided the family members through the interaction. They pointed out instances where the therapist opened up various topics in the conversation and managed the attribution of blame by the clients. They also noted out how the clients and therapist attempted to control the creation of meaning in the session. Stancome and White concluded that therapy is an act of rhetoric in which client and therapist work to persuade the other of the meaning of clients' actions and thoughts.

Similarly, Miller (1987) examined the therapist's rhetorical role in the construction of family problems in therapy. He examined approximately 300 therapy sessions in a family therapy agency over a 12-month period. Miller found that therapists had a tendency to evoke a "family perspective" to define and remedy client troubles. Problems presented in therapy were treated as being products of the clients' family systems. Clearly the theoretical orientation of the agency influenced both how problems were conceptualized and approached.

Miller and Silverman (1995) compared the ways in which family therapists working in an agency and counselors helping HIV patients employed brief, systemic therapy approaches. They found that both groups took a nonjudgmental approach to their clients. Both emphasized how the clients' personal problems were embedded in the larger social systems like the family. The therapists and counselors used family therapy techniques (such as circular questioning) to get clients to grasp this understanding. The clinicians also used hypothetical questions to encourage their clients to discuss problematic issues and to consider the alternative futures. Another similarity between the groups was that clinicians emphasized the skills of their clients and their abilities to become unstuck and return to a less problematic existence.

A therapist technique receiving much scrutiny in qualitative studies has been "formulations." Formulations are types of talk in which one speaker tells another how he or she is understanding a conversation. For example, a basic formulation is summarizing. Qualitative researchers have taken a close look at how therapists work with the words given to them by their clients (e.g., Aronsson & Cederborg, 1996; Troemel-Ploetz, 1977). Therapists often attempt to change what has been said by reformulating what clients' have uttered. These reformulation techniques are also called restructuring and reframing. Through these behaviors, therapists rework clients' words to produce new meanings and new possibilities in the conversations.

Grossen and Apotheloz (1996) focused on the overt attempts of therapists to reformulate clients' stories. They analyzed sequences of reformulation and found three different levels or ways that therapists intervene using the client's words: the semantic (how the meaning of the situation is changed), the relational (how the relationship between the client and the problem, or between the client and others is changed), and the "facework" (how the client's identity is changed). Facework also involves helping clients to find less pathological ways of constructing their problems.

Similarly, Troemel-Ploetz (1977) examined a family therapy session to show how a series of exchanges between a therapist and a husband restructured the talk in the room. She noted how these exchanges restructured the balance in the relationship between the husband and his wife. As in the Grossen and Apotheloz (1996) study, Troemel-Ploetz found reformulations to contain three properties: syntactic, semantic, and pragmatic or relational. Last, she pointed out that such restructuring behaviors are not unique to family therapy and can be found in other clinical models (see Troemel-Ploetz, 1980, for a Rogerian example).

Last, Aronsson and Cederborg (1996) studied three cases and showed how therapists act as orchestrators of therapy to reformulate problems by setting them in new perspectives between the clients. In their work, they too focused on family therapy sessions and found that their therapists worked to reframe the families' individual-focused problems into family focused formulations. Such a move tended to increase participation of the persons who had been previously the focus of the individualization view of the problem. One interesting feature of this reformulation talk was the use of obliqueness (i.e., impersonal constructions and the use of indefinite pronouns) to avoid taking alignment with any one member of the family (see Peyrot, 1987). This enabled the therapists to work effectively in the multiparty interaction found in family therapy sessions and to create collaborative formulations of the families' problems with the various family members.

Some have challenged the process of formulation. Davis (1986) criticized the way therapists formulate clients' words into problems amenable to therapeutic interventions. In her study of a videotaped initial session, she found that the therapist used a three-step process to transform the client's story. In the first step, the therapist reformulated the client's problem talk by closing down the client's self-narrative, while opening up a therapist's interpretation of the problem. The therapist worked with the client to document this new formulation of the client's situation in the second step. In the third step, the therapist gained consent by persuading the client that this interpretation of the problem provides a method to pursue in therapy. As an example, Davis reports that societal problems can be made into therapy problems because they are more manageable to therapists. She reminds us that therapists deal with problems the way they are trained.

Qualitative researchers have also closely examined a rich variety of therapeutic techniques employed by therapists in their conversations with clients. The qualitative nature of these studies allowed the researchers to explore the nuances of sessions more fully and to concentrate on more subtle changes in therapeutic discourse. Frosh, Burck, Strickland-Clark, and Morgan (1996) examined six full-length family therapy sessions from a discursive and narrative stance. They focused on how the therapist and the family members developed a theme of "managing change and evolving change" in the therapy. They concentrated on the subtle changes encouraged by the therapist as the family gradually shifted their view from change being something managed to something which evolves.

Chenail 's (1993) used recursive frame analysis to examined a full-length family therapy session in which a therapist worked to loosen up the "torqued talk" (repetitive patterns of interaction) of one family. Central to his study was the therapist's handling of the father's "yes, but" talk. In a series of subtle conversational moves such as opening up new topics of conversation while closing down others, the therapist was able to shift the family from an "either/or" dichotomy (i.e., following either one family member's solution or another's) to a "both/and" distinction in which all family members could share in a solution. Chenail shows how the therapist was an active participant in the conversation, channeling the talk toward certain therapeutic outcomes. This is appropriate given his language based perspective on therapy.

In another examination of therapists' closing down clients' talk, Jones and Beach (1995) studied the ways in which therapists responded to unsolicited contributions by family members in therapy. They conceptualized therapy discourse as often containing constrained talk. Constrained talk is repetitive talk that keeps the participants in an interaction stuck. The therapists, according to the authors, attempted to control these interactions. This control allowed therapists to structure therapy talk to both assess family communication patterns and change those patterns found problematic by the families. When family members' talk fell outside of this structure, Jones and Beach found therapists to use a variety of techniques to redirect the talk.

For instance, therapists closed down unsolicited contributions by: turning the talk back to the previous person talking, not responding to the person who made the unsolicited comment, briefly acknowledging the contribution and then continuing with the previous speaker, redirecting focus to another member of the family, and by encouraging family members to collaborate, thereby bringing the conversation back to a more structured pattern. In each occasion, the closing down of the talk allowed the therapist to move the session talk back on a track more in keeping with the therapist's clinical agenda.

Peyrot (1987) studied therapists in a community drug abuse agency who used brief therapy approaches. He found extensive use of a conversational structure he called circumspection. In these conversational moves, therapists used circumspect (i.e., indirect) ways to avoid confrontations and keep clients engaged in therapy. These circumspect techniques employed by the brief therapists contrasted with the usually direct features of this approach. These indirect utterances included proposals (i.e., statements which propose therapeutic matters for client's consideration), suggestions (i.e., a more circumspect way than assertions to present interpretations), and oblique references (i.e., using generic third-person references and indefinite pronouns to state a proposition without claiming that it applied to anyone in the room).

In another study, Peyrot (1995) examined "preliminaries," or the therapists' talk between the elicitation of clients' narratives and the exchanging of therapeutic interventions. He found two distinct types of preliminaries, the conjunctive and disjunctive. Conjunctive transitions were those which flowed naturally out of the surrounding talk and were perceived by the clients as natural transitions in the topics being discussed. Disjunctive transitions were noticeable shifts in the talk and were used to set up succeeding shifts in the conversation. For example, the therapist may note that the forthcoming talk will be a departure from the current talk. Peyrot suggests that moves such as preliminaries enable therapists to manage the interaction in ways that change the repetitive patterns typical of clients' problematic talk.

Madill and Barkham (1997) conducted a discourse analysis of a successful case of brief psychodynamic-interpersonal psychotherapy. They concentrated on how the therapist helped the client to develop her story along three story lines, that of the client as a dutiful daughter, the bad mother, and the damaged child. They also studied how the therapist enabled the client to find new interpretations of her story. Through an understanding of these three themes, the therapist helped the client break out of her bout with depression. By listening carefully, the therapist was able to hear talk about the damaged daughter and by punctuating this, it became a major theme of the therapy and a source of curative insight for the client.

Gale (1991) and Gale and Newfield (1992) researched the procedures used in a complete session by a well-known solution-oriented therapist (see de Shazer, 1991). The therapist's techniques included pursuing a response from clients over many turns, clarifying unclear references, modifying his own assertions, and posing questions to clients and then answering these questions as if he were speaking for the clients. Gale and Newfield found that these techniques allowed the therapist to keep to his model of practice, to control the story elicitation part of the session, and to help the clients to focus on a solution-focused plan for the future. The authors identified therapist behaviors that the therapist himself, on reflection of the findings, was unaware that he performed.

Although there are few qualitative studies that investigate specific therapy models, the solution focused model has been the subject of several studies. Metcalf and Thomas (1994) investigated perceptions of solution-focused therapy (de Shazer, 1991). They interviewed clients and asked questions like, "What was it that occurred in the therapy process that you found most helpful?" To the therapists, for example, they asked "What did you do in the therapy process as the therapist that seemed to help change occur?" (p. 52) According to the authors,

> The influences of change on peoples' lives are as varied as their life experiences. Four out of six couples' descriptions regarding what was helpful in instigating change differed from the therapists' descriptions, while two out of six couples' descriptions were similar to their therapist's. Respondents mentioned listening, amplifying strengths, reinforcing, praising, noticing differences, and questions that pointed out what worked. Therapists described punctuating the experience, showing up, validation, empowering, and finding resources. They also described active participation like positive blame, separating the kids from mom, and helping to figure out goals. (Metcalf & Thomas, 1994, pp. 62–64)

In another analyses of the data, Metcalf, Thomas, Duncan, Miller, and Hubble (1996) closely examined the differences between client and therapists' perceptions. They also explored the differences between the assumptions of solution-focused therapy (de Shazer, 1991) and what the therapists actually did with six cases viewed as successful by both clients and their therapists. Their results suggest that clients attributed favorable results to relationship variables, while therapists tended to credit technique. The study also suggested that therapists were more directive in clients' eyes than solution focused therapy is typically described.

O'Connor, Meakes, Pickering, and Schuman, (1997) conducted ethnographic interviews with eight families regarding their experience of narrative therapy (White & Epston, 1990). They found six major themes: externalizing conversation, developing an alternative story, personal agency, reflecting/consulting teams, building a wider audience, and the helpful and unhelpful aspects of therapy. What clients found helpful included the respect the therapist had for their perceptions and experiences, being listened to, acknowledged, not blamed, and treated like experts on their own family experiences. Unhelpful aspects of therapy included therapy seeming artificial, that it was a slow process, not being able to speak directly with the team, unhelpful feedback and not liking the video taping. It is interesting to note that clients found more relational aspects helpful, as opposed to the specific techniques of narrative therapy.

In another study of narrative therapy, Kogan and Gale (1997) examined a full-length session conducted by a narrative therapist (White & Epston, 1990). They found that the therapist employed five talk practices to "de-center" the therapy conversations (i.e., not having the therapist at the center of the process as an expert) and to encourage co-authoring on the parts of all the participants. These practices were (a) using matching and self-disclosure, (b) reciprocal editing, (c) managing turns to de-objectify, (d) expansion questions, and (e) reversals.

In matching and self-disclosure, the therapist participates fully in the therapy session and in doing so, encourages the others to join in too. Reciprocal editing is a type of formulation in which the summarizing and re-formulation is not only a one-way practice of the therapist. In contrast, Kogan and Gale found that their narrative therapy session contained instances where all members of the session engaged in such activity. Managing turns to de-objectify were defined as attempts on the therapist's part to use conversational turns to involve a person who was mentioned in the previous turn. These moves helped to take the person out of the "object" being talked about and placed him or her into a position of being a person talking also. Reciprocal questions are types of reflexive questions that encourage clients to attempt a shift in context or perspective. They also help to expand the conversation by introducing new language into the interactions between therapist and clients. Finally, reversals involved the therapist taking the role of an objectified person in the process and speaking from that person's perspective. Such a move allowed the therapist to shift the talk from the objectified person and to open up new issues for all to explore.

In addition to techniques and therapy models, change processes in therapy have also been studied. For example, through the use of a questionnaire, Cummings, Hallberg, and Slemon (1994) examined change processes in psychotherapy. After each session, clients completed a questionnaire on what they felt were important events that occurred in the session. The authors identified "consistent change" when the clients reported evidence stable pattern of cognitive, affective, or behavioral improvement.

A second type of change they identified was "interrupted change." They defined this as a change pattern that occurs in the beginning of therapy. This brief surge of improvement is followed by a setback (resistance) with clients reporting the return of the symptom, and increased self-doubt. Finally, the third type of change they identified is "minimal change." Minimal change is a pattern with an initial plateau of no change, then one session of minor change, a long plateau with change occurring, and finally acknowledgment of minor change at the end of counseling. The authors concluded that all three processes can potentially lead to successful outcomes in therapy.

Similar to quantitative research, it seems that therapist techniques and model have received aggressive investigation from a qualitative perspective, revealing a broad range of therapist actions and client responses. The disproportionate percentage of studies examining the therapist mirrors the quantitative literature's benign neglect of client factors, keeping, as Tallman and Bohart (this volume) suggest, the therapist as the hero of the therapeutic encounter. It is interesting to note that two studies of different models (solution-focused and narrative) revealed relationship factors to be more helpful from the client's perspective than model specific techniques.

Multifactor Studies

As previously mentioned, qualitative studies are often exploratory, discovery-oriented inquiries. Researchers analyzing text/talk are not always sure what direction their journey into the data will take. As such, a number of studies have findings that have implications for several of the common factors.

Newfield, Kuehl, Joanning, and Quinn (1990) used an ethnographic approach (Spradley, 1979) to conduct interviews with families in which there was an adolescent abusing drugs. These authors analyzed the talk of interviews using a developmental research sequence (DSR) where "both questions and answers are elicited as much as possible from the informant" (p. 62). They identified four emergent categories or domains. According to the authors, "Domains emerge from the creative interaction between the ethnographer and the traditions of ethnography, the informants being interviewed, and the audience for whom the ethnography is being prepared" (p. 63). The themes that emerged were expectancy factors (expectations and "counseling"), therapists factors (types of "psychos" and "shrinks"), and model factors (individual versus family therapy). These themes are consistent with quantitative findings on the therapy process.

Similarly, Phelps, Friedlander, and Enns (1997) investigated the therapeutic process with clients who had memories of sexual abuse. The authors analyzed transcripts of semi-structured interviews with women who identified themselves as victims of childhood sexual abuse. Consistent with Newfield et al. (1990), respondents identified the therapeutic relationship, therapist characteristics, and specific therapy techniques as significant to the therapy process.

The reflecting team (Andersen, 1991) is a therapeutic procedure often used in family therapy settings where clients get the benefit of hearing the behind-the-scenes discussion of a team of therapists observing their case. Smith and his colleagues (Sells, Smith, Coe, Yoshioka, & Robbins, 1994; Sells, Smith, & Moon, 1996; Smith, Jenkins, & Sells, 1995; Smith, Sells, Alves Pereira, et al. 1995; Smith, Sells, & Clevenger, 1994; Smith, Winton, & Yoshioka, 1992; Smith,

Yoshioka, & Winton, 1993) have been at the forefront of this work. They used qualitative methods to learn more about their use of reflecting team conversations.

In one study, Smith, Sells, Alves Pereira, et al. (1995) used a combination of IPR and ethnographic methods to study couples' perceptions of reflecting team conversations. The authors interviewed couples participating in therapy about what team members had to say during reflecting team conversations. According to clients for reflecting team conversations to be useful certain contextual conditions must be met. The client factor "readiness to listen" was one such condition identified. Other conditions like the presence of trust and the credibility of team members provide support for the therapeutic relationship as a key factor in helpful reflecting team conversations.

Discussion

In reflecting on this body of research, it appears that qualitative inquiries into psychotherapeutic processes and outcomes are growing in frequency and diversity. Although they make limited claims on generalizability in their studies, qualitative researchers make some persuasive, albeit guarded, statements on what they have observed happening in therapy. From our analysis, the following are what we found to be the major points made with respect to the common factors:

1. Qualitative researchers are well on their way to creating a taxonomy of in-session therapist behaviors. From question asking technologies (e.g., Gale, 1991) to reformulations (e.g., Aronsson & Cederborg, 1996), researchers are learning more about how therapists communicate with clients. Although few clinical models have been studied to any great length, the research thus far supports the findings that therapists techniques and models play some role in the change process thus warranting further study. This further study will contribute to our knowledge on basic therapist communicative skills. For example, one technique, circumspection (Peyrot, 1987) was shown to be an effective way for therapists to deliver possibly negative observations to the client. By being indirect, therapists were able to deliver their message without harming the therapeutic alliance.

2. Qualitative researchers have identified a few client factors, mostly concerning how clients present their problems in therapy (e.g., Buttny & Jensen, 1995). This research also reveals how the telling of troubles by clients is more that just the simple sharing of stories. It also affords clients the opportunity to ascribe blame and responsibilities. With the shortage of qualitative studies on client factors, however, it

is premature to discuss exactly what client factors are important for successful therapy and how they impact therapy processes and outcomes. More research is needed on client factors within therapy and factors external to the therapy process.

3. Like many quantitative studies on psychotherapy, the qualitative literature also shows that researchers are intent on learning more about the therapeutic relationship. Studies on the interaction between clients and therapists show the mutual influence each has on the other over the course of therapy (e.g., Knox, Hess, Petersen, & Hill, 1997). Such observations support therapists becoming more observant to the ways they participate in conversations with clients.

4. With respect to the therapeutic relationship, the qualitative literature supports the idea that clients want and appreciate receiving multiple perspectives on their situations from therapists in clinical encounters (Smith, Jenkins, & Sells, 1995). Clients also appreciate therapists who listen carefully and express concerns for their condition (Kuehl et al., 1990). In addition, data from client interviews shows that they want to be more active in the therapeutic process and they share their satisfaction at the opportunity to provide their feedback on therapy. This also supports the observation that when clients and therapists agree on tasks and goals in therapy, clients express a higher level of satisfaction regarding the therapy process.

5. Data indicate that both clients and therapists find it helpful for therapy when there are opportunities to comment on the therapy process (e.g. Shilts et al., 1997). Whether through in-session consults (e.g., Bischoff et al., 1996) or in post-sessions interviews (e.g., Todd et al., 1990), the participants appreciated hearing different perspectives on how each the therapy was proceeding. In some cases, clients found these research interviews to be more therapeutic than therapy (e.g., Gale et al., 1995). This use of in-session interviews support quantitative findings (Lambert, 1992) that when therapists show interest in the client's situation and opinion, they are more likely to find the therapy process satisfying.

6. Qualitative methods are useful for studying in-session change episodes. Although the common factors research does not distinguish in-session processes as a relevant factor for effective outcomes, we view it as a finer distinction of the techniques/model factor. Drawing on a variety of established methodologies, researchers have examined impasses (e.g., Diamond & Liddle, 1996), and goal accomplishments (Buttny & Cohen, 1991). Many research techniques such as discourse activity analysis systems (DAAS; Friedlander, 1984), interpersonal process recall (IPR; Elliott, 1986), recursive dialectical analysis (RDA; Franklin, 1996), comprehensive process analysis (CPA; Elliot, Shapiro, Firth-Cozens, Stiles, & Hardy, 1994), and recursive frame analysis

(RFA; Chenail, 1991) have been developed to help researchers explore these processes in greater detail.

7. More qualitative studies are needed that explore specific therapy models. Contemporary approaches such as reflecting teams (e.g., Andersen, 1991; Smith, Sells, & Clevenger, 1994), narrative therapy (e.g., Kogan & Gale, 1997; White & Epston, 1990), and solution-focused therapy (e.g., de Shazer, 1991; Metcalf & Thomas, 1994) have received the bulk of this scrutiny from researchers. Studies are not usually comparative, and the goal is not necessarily to define effective therapy. Rather, such inquiries are intended to provide rich descriptions of therapy out of which we might discover better ways to conceptualize and carry out therapeutic practices.

8. While many qualitative researchers have focused on the in-session activities of clients and therapists, little attention has been given to extra-therapy factors and conditions that contribute to therapeutic outcomes (see Dallos, Neale, & Strouthos, 1997, for an exception)]. This could easily be remedied by including more broadly focused questions during in-session/post-session interviews conducted with clients. Likewise, adding pre-therapy interviews will assist in gathering more outside-of-therapy information.

9. Future qualitative studies, especially microanalysis of therapy conversations, may offer an explanation as to why, according to common factors research, therapy models contribute little to effective therapy outcomes. By examining the therapist behaviors from various schools of therapy and identifying micro-patterns, we may identify in-room therapist behaviors that are curative but are not emphasized by the theory of change central to a particular school of therapy.

Conclusion

Qualitative researchers have begun to establish themselves as clear voices on the processes and outcomes of psychotherapy and on the stories of clients and therapists. In the coming years, the volume of clinical qualitative research will rise and its relevancy for clinical work will also increase. This development will also include more collaborative efforts between qualitative and quantitative researchers as their appreciation of the differences each other brings to the study of psychotherapy grows. In all of its shapes, qualitative research will continue to help the stakeholders in clinical work—the researchers, the therapists, and the clients, to describe, to interpret, and to discover their understandings of the patterns which make a difference in this process of change.

Questions From the Editors

1. What are the implications of this research for training graduate students?

Graduate students could benefit from learning more about the basics of communication theory and how these concepts can be applied to the study and practice of psychotherapy. There is an inherent gap between the language of therapy models and the actual language of therapy. Distinctions found in the various discourse, language, and communication approaches would help students to bridge this gap more effectively. By becoming more communication conscious, therapists would increase their awareness of the many speech choices they have available to them at any given moment in therapy. In addition, they would develop a more informed "ear" for not only what clients are saying (i.e., the content), but also for how clients are and are not saying things (i.e., the process). They would also have a greater appreciation for the ways in which conversations are managed locally (i.e., from speaker turn to speaker turn and from utterance to utterance) and how both therapists and clients can manipulate the conversations of each other. In doing so, they would be in a better position to evaluate the fit between the theories in their heads and the words in their sessions.

It would also be important for graduate students to learn more about the variety of ways they can engage their clients in therapy. Many of the studies showed that clients greatly appreciated being made more involved in the therapy process. In these cases, the clients were asked about the progress and process of therapy through in-session and post-session interviews and consultations. Incorporating qualitative research interviews into the everyday practice of therapy to allow more client participation and to gain more client feedback on the therapy itself could make the clinical interactions more effective and more satisfying for the clients and therapists alike.

2. How do you account for the neglect of client factors in qualitative research?

It appears from the lack of research on client characteristics that clinicians, both as researchers and practitioners, have a tendency to focus on their work and themselves. It seems natural for these researching therapists to study how they interact with their clients. They wish to test and to improve their clinical skills and models of therapy. In this way, clients' participation appears to be studied as a complementary or reactionary element to the actions taken by the therapists. This "one-way" view of clinical interaction found in the research appears to reflect the therapist-centered practice found in many psychotherapies.

This skewing may also be a result of the trend towards more time-limited models of therapy. By shortening the time given for treatment, therapists may be spending less time on assessment. Less time spent on learning about the clients may lead to less data about the clients and their competencies. Given the tendency for qualitative researchers to study therapy as it naturally occurs, this might explain why so few of these researchers have examined clients and their characteristics.

3. How can qualitative research benefit quantitative research?

Qualitative approaches to research offer social scientists a different way of knowing about the experiential world and particularly psychological phenomena. A qualitative perspective allows researchers to have first-hand experiences with the phenomena they study because the researcher becomes the instrument by which data is collected, organized, analyzed, and interpreted. We encourage quantitative researchers to learn about what qualitative researchers report regarding the phenomena they wish to study. This may help quantitative researchers concentrate their efforts on phenomena that have already been shown to have meaning for therapy participants, and therefore construct hypotheses that are more soundly grounded in sensory experience.

In addition, qualitative research can be employed as a useful tool for post-hoc analysis. When quantitative researchers find that they have not accounted for a significant amount of the variance in a particular study, or they find that other, unforeseen factors have impacted their findings, they can use qualitative methods to verify their speculation. Also, by triangulating qualitative and quantitative methods, researchers can be gain a richer picture of the clinical phenomenon in question. By undertaking more of these multi-method studies, research can benefit from what both traditions have to offer.

References

Andersen, T. (Ed.). (1991). *The reflecting team: Dialogues and dialogues about the dialogues.* New York: W. W. Norton.

Angus, L., & Rennie, D. (1989). Envisioning the representational world: The client's experience of metaphoric expression in psychotherapy. *Psychotherapy, 26*(3), 372–379.

Aronsson, K., & Cederborg, A.-C. (1996). Coming of age in family therapy talk: Perspective setting in multiparty problem formulations. *Discourse Processes, 21*(2), 191–212.

Atkinson, B., Heath, A., & Chenail, R. (1991). Qualitative research and the legitimization of knowledge. *Journal of Marital & Family Therapy, 17*(2), 161–166.

Atkinson, J., & Heritage, J. (Eds.). (1984). *Structures of social action: Studies in conversation analysis.* Cambridge, MA: Cambridge University Press.

Bachelor, A. (1988). How clients perceive therapist empathy: A content analysis of "received" empathy. *Psychotherapy, 25*(2), 227–240.

Bachelor, A. (1995). Clients' perception of the therapeutic alliance: A qualitative analysis. *Journal of Counseling Psychology, 42*(3), 323–337.

Bischoff, R. J., & McBride, A. (1996). Client perceptions of couples and family therapy. *American Journal of Family Therapy, 24*(2), 117–128.

Bischoff, R. J., McKeel, A. J., Moon, S. M., & Sprenkle, D. H. (1996). Therapist-conducted consultation: Using clients as consultants to their own therapy. *Journal of Marital & Family Therapy, 22*(3) 359–379.

Bogdan, R. C., & Biklen, S. K. (1992). *Qualitative research for education: An introduction to theory and methods* (2nd ed.). Boston: Allyn & Bacon.

Brown, G., & Yule, G. (1983). *Discourse analysis.* Cambridge, MA: Cambridge University Press.

Buttny, R. (1990). Blame-accounts sequences in therapy: The negotiation of relational meanings. *Semiotica, 78,* 57–77.

Buttny, R. (1993). Blame-accounts sequences in couples therapy: Accountability for relational problems. In *Social accountability in communication* (pp. 66–84). London: Sage.

Buttny, R., & Cohen, J. R. (1991). The uses of goals in therapy. In K. Tracy (Ed.), *Understanding face-to-face interaction* (pp. 63–78). Hillsdale, NJ: Erlbaum.

Buttny, R., & Jensen, A. D. (1995). Telling problems in an initial family therapy session: The hierarchical organization of problem-talk. In G. H. Morris & R. J. Chenail (Eds.), *The talk of the clinic: Explorations in the analysis of medical and therapeutic discourse* (pp. 19–47). Hillsdale, NJ: Erlbaum.

Chenail, R. J. (1991). *Medical discourse and systemic frames of comprehension.* Norwood, NJ: Ablex.

Chenail, R. J. (1992). A case for clinical qualitative research. *The Qualitative Report* [On-line serial], *1*(4). Available: http://www.nova.edu/ssss/QR/QR1-4/clinqual.html.

Chenail, R. J. (1993). Charting clinical conversations. In A. Rambo, A. Heath, & R. J. Chenail (Eds.), *Practicing therapy: Exercises for growing therapists* (pp. 169–224). New York: Norton.

Chenail, R. J. (1994). Qualitative research and clinical work: "Private-ization" and "public-ation". *The Qualitative Report* [On-line serial], *2*(1). Available: http://www.nova.edu/ssss/QR/BackIssues/QR2-1/private.html.

Chenail, R. J., & Maione, P. (1997). Sensemaking in clinical qualitative research [28 paragraphs]. *The Qualitative Report* [On-line serial], *3*(1). Available: http://www.nova.edu/ssss/QR/QR3-1/sense.html.

Chenail, R. J., & Morris, G. H. (1995). Introduction: The talk of the clinic. In G. H. Morris & R. J. Chenail (Eds.), *The talk of the clinic: Explorations in the analysis of medical and therapeutic discourse* (pp. 1–15). Hillsdale, NJ: Erlbaum.

Constas, M. A. (1992). Qualitative analysis as a public event: The documentation of category development procedures. *American Educational Research Journal, 29,* 253–266.

Cortazzi, M. (1993). *Narrative analysis.* Washington, DC: Falmer Press.

Coulthard, M., & Montgomery, M. (Eds.). (1981). *Studies in discourse analysis.* London: Routledge & Kegan Paul.

Crabtree, B. F., & Miller, W. L. (Eds.). (1992). *Doing qualitative research.* Newbury Park, CA: Sage.

Creswell, J. W. (1994). *Research design: Qualitative & quantitative approaches.* Thousand Oaks, CA: Sage.

Cummings, A. L., Hallberg, E. T., & Slemon, A. G. (1994). Templates of client change in short-term counseling. *Journal of Counseling Psychology, 41*(4), 464–472.

Dallos, R., Neale, A., & Strouthos, M. (1997). Pathways to problems: The evolution of 'pathology'. *Journal of Family Therapy, 19*(4), 369–399.

Davis, K. (1986). The process of problem (re)formulation in psychotherapy. *Sociology of Health & Illness, 8,* 44–74.

Denzin, N., & Lincoln, Y. (Eds.). (1994). *Handbook of qualitative research.* Thousand Oaks, CA: Sage.

de Shazer, S. (1991). *Putting difference to work.* New York: W. W. Norton.

Diamond, G., & Liddle, H. A. (1996). Resolving a therapeutic impasse between parents and adolescents in multidimensional family therapy. *Journal of Consulting & Clinical Psychology, 64*(3), 481–488.

Eisner, E. W. (1985). *The educational imagination: On the design and evaluation of school programs* (2nd ed.). New York: Macmillan.

Eisner, E. W. (1991). *The enlightened eye: Qualitative inquiry and the enhancement of educational practice.* New York: Macmillan.

Elliott, R. (1986). Interpersonal process recall (IPR) as a psychotherapy process research method. In L. Greeneberg & W. Pinsof, (Eds.), *The psychotherapeutic process: A research handbook* (pp. 503–528). New York: Guilford Press.

Elliot, R., Shapiro, D. A., Firth-Cozens, J., Stiles, W. B., & Hardy, G. E. (1994). Comprehensive process analysis of insight events in cognitive–behavioral and psychodynamic–interpersonal psychotherapies. *Journal of Counseling Psychology, 41*(4), 449–463.

Ellis, C., & Bochner, A. P. (1996). *Composing ethnography: Alternative forms of qualitative writing.* Walnut Creek, CA: AltaMira Press.

Fetterman, D. M. (1989). *Ethnography: Step by step.* Newbury Park, CA: Sage.

Franklin, C. (1996). Solution-focused therapy: A marital case study using recursive dialectic analysis. *Journal of Family Psychotherapy, 7*(1), 31–51.

Friedlander, M. L. (1984). Psychotherapy talk as social control. *Psychotherapy, 21*(3), 335–341.

Frosh, S., Burck, C., Strickland-Clark, L., & Morgan, K. (1996). Engaging with change: A process study of family therapy. *Journal of Family Therapy, 18*(2), 141–161.

Gale, J. E. (1991). *Conversation analysis of a marital therapy session: Pursuit of a therapeutic agenda.* Norwood, NJ: Ablex.

Gale, J. E. (1992). When research interviews are more therapeutic than therapy interviews [11 paragraphs]. *The Qualitative Report* [On-line serial], *1*(4). Available: http://www.nova.edu/ssss/QR/QR1-4/gale.html.

Gale, J. E. (1996). Conversation analysis: Studying the construction of therapeutic realities. In D. Sprenkle & S. Moon (Eds.), *Family therapy research: A handbook of methods* (pp. 107–124). New York: Guilford Press.

Gale, J. E., Chenail, R., Watson, W. L., Wright, L. M., & Bell, J. M. (1996). Research and practice: A reflexive and recursive relationship—Three narratives, five voices. *Marriage & Family Review, 24*(3–4), 275–295.

Gale, J. E., & Newfield, N. (1992). A conversation analysis of a solution-focused marital therapy session. *Journal of Marital & Family Therapy, 18*(2), 153–165.

Gale, J. E., Odell, M., & Nagireddy, C. S. (1995). Marital therapy and self-reflexive research: Research and/as intervention. In G. H. Morris & R. J. Chenail (Eds.), *The talk of the clinic: Explorations in the analysis of medical and therapeutic discourse* (pp. 105–129). Hillsdale, NJ: Erlbaum.

Garfinkel, H. (1967). *Studies in ethnomethodology.* Englewood Cliffs, NJ: Prentice Hall.

Gilgun, J. F., Daly, K., & Handel, G. (Eds.). (1992). *Qualitative methods in family research.* Beverly Hills, CA: Sage.

Glaser, B. (1978). *Theoretical sensitivity: Advances in the methodology of grounded theory.* Mill Valley, CA: Sociology Press.

Glaser, B., & Strauss, A. (1967). *The discovery of grounded theory: Strategies for qualitative research.* Chicago: Aldine.

Glesne, C., & Peshkin, A. (1992). *Becoming qualitative researchers: An introduction.* White Plains, NY: Longman.

Goffman, E. (1974). *Frame analysis: An essay of the organization of experience.* Cambridge, MA: Harvard University Press.

Grossen, M., & Apotheloz, D. (1996). Communicating about communication in a therapeutic interview. *Journal of Language & Social Psychology, 15*(2), 101–132.

Guba, E. G. (Ed.). (1990). *The paradigm dialog.* Newbury Park, CA: Sage.

Hammersley, M., & Atkinson, P. (1995). *Ethnography: Principles in practice* (2nd ed.). New York: Routledge.

Heritage, J. (1984). *Garfinkel and ethnomethodology.* Cambridge, England: Polity Press.

Hill, C. E., Nutt-Williams, E., Heaton, K., J., Thompson, B. J., & Rhodes, R. (1996). Therapist retrospective recall impasses in long-term psychotherapy: A qualitative analysis. *Journal of Counseling Psychology, 43*(2), 207–217.

Hopper, R. (1988). Speech, for instance. The exemplar in studies of conversation. *Journal of Language and Social Psychology, 7,* 47–63.

Hoshmand, L. T. (1989). Alternative research paradigms: A review and teaching proposal. *The Counseling Psychologist, 17,* 3–79.

Howe, D. (1996). Client experiences of counselling and treatment interventions: A qualitative study of family views of family therapy. *British Journal of Guidance & Counselling, 24*(3), 367–375.

Janesick, V. J. (1998). *"Stretching" exercises for qualitative researchers.* Thousand Oaks, CA: Sage.

Joanides, C. J., Brigham, L., & Joanning, H. (1997). Co-creating a more cooperative client–therapist relationship through a debriefing process. *American Journal of Family Therapy, 25*(2), 139–150.

Jones, C. M., & Beach, W. A. (1995). Therapists' techniques for responding to unsolicited contributions by family members. In G. H. Morris & R. J. Chenail (Eds.), *The talk of the clinic: Explorations in the analysis of medical and therapeutic discourse* (pp. 49–69). Hillsdale, NJ: Erlbaum.

Knox, S., Hess, S. A., Petersen, D. A., & Hill, C. E. (1997). A qualitative analysis of client perceptions of the effects of helpful therapist self-disclosure in long-term therapy. *Journal of Counseling Psychology, 44*(3), 274–283.

Kogan, S. M., & Gale, J. E. (1997). Decentering therapy: Textual analysis of a narrative therapy session. *Family Process, 36*(2), 101–126.

Kuehl, B. P., Newfield, N. A., & Joanning, H. (1990). A client-based description of family therapy. *Journal of Family Psychology, 3*(3), 310–321.

Kuzel, A. J. (1986). Naturalistic inquiry: An appropriate model for family medicine. *Family Medicine, 18,* 369–374.

Kvale, S. (Ed.), with Enerstvedt, R., Bruhn Jensen, K., Polkinghorne, D., Salner, M., & Tschudi, F. (1989). *Issues of validity in qualitative research.* Lund, Sweden: Studentlitteratur.

Lambert, M. (1992). Psychotherapy outcome research. In J. C. Norcross & M. R. Goldfried (Eds.), *Handbook of psychotherapy integration* (pp. 94–129). New York: Basic Books.

LeCompte, M. D., Millroy, W. L., & Preissle, J. (Eds.). (1992). *The handbook of qualitative research in education.* San Diego, CA: Academic Press.

Leininger, M. M. (Ed.). (1985). *Qualitative research methods in nursing.* Orlando, FL: Grune & Stratton.

Lewis, S. E. (1995). A search for meaning: Making sense of depression. *Journal of Mental Health, 4*(4), 369–382.

Lincoln, Y. S., & Guba, E. G. (1985). *Naturalistic inquiry.* Newbury Park, CA: Sage.

Madill, A., & Barkham, M. (1997). Discourse analysis of a theme in one successful case of brief psychodynamic–interpersonal psychotherapy. *Journal of Counseling Psychology, 44*(2), 232–244.

Mahrer, A. (1988). Discovery-oriented psychotherapy research: Rationale, aims, and methods. *American Psychologist, 43,* 694–702.

Maione, P. V. (1997). Choice points: Creating clinical qualitative research studies [37 paragraphs]. *The Qualitative Report* [On-line serial], *3*(2). Available: http://www.nova.edu/ssss/QR/QR3-2/maione.html.

Maxwell, J. A. (1992). Understanding and validity in qualitative research. *Harvard Educational Review, 62,* 279–300.

McCollum, E. E., & Trepper, T. (1995). "Little by little, pulling me through"—Women's perceptions of successful drug treatment: A qualitative inquiry. *Journal of Family Psychotherapy, 6*(1), 63–81.

McCollum, E. E., Trepper, T. S., Nelson, T. S., McAvoy, P. A., Lewis, R. A., & Wetchler, J. L. (1996). Participating in a couples therapy outcome study: Participants views. *Contemporary Family Therapy: An International Journal, 18*(4), 607–617.

McNamee, S. (1988). Accepting research as social intervention: Implications of a systemic epistemology. *Communications Quarterly, 36,* 50–68.

Messer, S. B., Sass, L. A., & Woolfolk, R. L. (Eds.). (1988). *Hermeneutics and psychological theory: Interpretative perspectives on personality, psychotherapy, and psychopathology.* New Brunswick, NJ: Rutgers University Press.

Metcalf, L., & Thomas, F. (1994). Client and therapist perceptions of solution focused brief therapy: A qualitative analysis. *Journal of Family Psychotherapy, 5*(4), 49–66.

Metcalf, L., Thomas, F., Duncan, L., Miller, S., & Hubble, M. (1996). What works in solution-focused brief therapy: A qualitative analysis of client and therapist perceptions. In S. Miller, M. Hubble, & B. Duncan (Eds.), *Handbook of solution focused brief therapy* (pp. 335–349). San Francisco: Jossey-Bass.

Miles, M. B., & Huberman, A. M. (1994). *Qualitative data analysis: An expanded sourcebook* (2nd ed.). Thousand Oaks, CA: Sage.

Miller, G. (1987). Producing family problems: Organization and uses of the family perspective and rhetoric in family therapy. *Symbolic Interaction, 10*(2), 245–265.

Miller, G., & Silverman, D. (1995). Troubles talk and counseling discourse: A comparative study. *The Sociological Quarterly, 36*(4), 725–747.

Miller, W. L., & Crabtree, B. F. (1994). Clinical research. In N. K. Denzin & Y. S. Lincoln (Eds.), *Handbook of qualitative research* (pp. 340–352). Thousand Oaks, CA: Sage.

Mishler, E. G. (1990). Validation in inquiry-guided research: The role of exemplars in narrative studies. *Harvard Educational Review, 60,* 415–442.

Moon, S. M., Dillon, D. R., & Sprenkle, D. H. (1990). Family therapy and qualitative research. *Journal of Marital & Family Therapy, 16*(4), 357–373.

Moon, S. M., Dillon, D. R., & Sprenkle, D. H. (1991). On balance and synergy: Family therapy and qualitative research revisited. *Journal of Marital & Family Therapy, 17*(2), 173–178.

Moustakas, C. (1994). *Phenomenological research methods.* Thousand Oaks, CA: Sage.

Munhall, P. L. (1994). *Revisioning phenomenology: Nursing and health science research.* New York: National League for Nursing Press.

Newfield, N., Kuehl, B., Joaning, H., & Quinn, W. (1990). A mini ethnography of the family therapy of adolescent drug abuse: The ambiguous experience. *Alcoholism Treatment Quarterly, 7*(2), 57–79.

O'Connor, T. S., Meakes, E., Pickering, M. R., & Schuman, M. (1997). On the right track: Client experience of narrative therapy. *Contemporary Family Therapy, 19*(4), 479–495.

Packer, M. J. (1985). Hermeneutic inquiry in the study of human contact. *American Psychologist, 40*(10), 1081–1093.

Packer, M. J., & Addison, R. B. (Eds.). (1989). *Entering the circle: Hermeneutic investigation in psychology.* Albany, NY: State University of New York Press.

Peyrot, M. (1987). Circumspection in psychotherapy: Structures and strategies of counselor–client interaction. *Semiotica, 65,* 249–268.

Peyrot, M. (1995). Therapeutic preliminaries: Conversational context and process in psychotherapy. *Qualitative Sociology, 18*(3), 311–329.

Phelps, A., Friedlander, M. L., & Enns, C. Z. (1997). Psychotherapy process variables associated with the retrieval of memories of childhood sexual abuse: A qualitative study. *Journal of Counseling Psychology, 44*(3), 321–332.

Polkinghorne, D. E. (1988). *Narrative knowing and the human sciences.* Albany, NY: State University of New York Press.

Polkinghorne, D. E. (1994). Reaction to special section on qualitative research in counseling process and outcome. *Journal of Counseling Psychology, 41*(4), 510–512.

Potter, J., & Wetherell, M. (1987). *Discourse and social psychology: Beyond attitudes and behavior.* London: Sage.

Psathas, G. (1995). *Conversation analysis: The study of talk-in-interaction.* Thousand Oaks, CA: Sage.

Rennie, D. (1990). Toward a representation of the client's experience of the psychotherapy hour. In G. Lietaer, J. Rombauts, & R. Van Balen (Eds.), *Client-centered and experiential therapy in the nineties* (pp. 155–172). Leuven, Belgium: Leuven University Press.

Rennie, D. (1992). Qualitative analysis of the client's experience of psychotherapy: The unfolding of reflexivity. In S. Toukmanian & D. Rennie (Eds.), *Psychotherapy process research: Pragmatic and narrative approaches* (pp. 211–233). Newbury Park, CA: Sage.

Rennie, D. (1994a). Client's accounts of resistance in counseling: A qualitative analysis. *Canadian Journal of Counseling, 28,* 43–57.

Rennie, D. L. (1994b). Clients' deference in psychotherapy. *Journal of Counseling Psychology, 41*(4), 427–437.

Rennie, D. (1994c). Storytelling in psychotherapy: The client's subjective experience. *Psychotherapy, 31*(2), 234–243.

Rennie, D. (1995). Strategic choices in a qualitative approach to psychotherapy research, In L. Hoshmand & J. Martin (Eds.), *Research as praxis: Lessons from programmatic research in therapeutic psychology* (pp. 198–220). New York: Teachers College Press.

Rennie, D., Phillips, J., & Quartaro, G. (1988). Grounded theory: A promising approach to conceptualization in psychology. *Canadian Psychology, 29*(2), 139–150.

Rhodes, R. H., Hill, C. E., Thompson, B. J., & Elliott, R. (1994). Client retrospective recall of resolved and unresolved misunderstanding events. *Journal of Counseling Psychology, 41*(4), 473–483.

Riessman, C. K. (1993). *Narrative analysis.* Newbury Park, CA: Sage.

Schiffrin, D. (1994). *Approaches to discourse.* Oxford, England: Blackwell.

Sells, S. P., Smith, T. E., Coe, M. J., Yoshioka, M., & Robbins, J. (1994). An ethnography of couple and therapist experiences in reflecting team practice. *Journal of Marital & Family Therapy, 20*(3), 247–266.

Sells, S. P., Smith, T. E., & Moon, S. (1996). An ethnographic study of client and therapist perceptions of therapy effectiveness in a university-based training clinic. *Journal of Marital & Family Therapy, 22*(3), 321–342.

Shilts, L., Filippino, C., & Nau, D. S. (1994). Client-informed therapy. *Journal of Systemic Therapies, 13*(4), 39–52.

Shilts, L., Rambo, A., & Hernandez, L. (1997). Clients helping therapists find solutions to their therapy. *Contemporary Family Therapy: An International Journal, 19*(1), 117–132.

Smith, T. E., Jenkins, D., & Sells, S. (1995). Reflecting teams: Voices of diversity. *Journal of Family Psychotherapy, 6*(2), 49–69.

Smith, T. E., Sells, S. P., Alves Pereira, M. G., Todahl, J., & Papagiannis, G. (1995). Pilot process research of reflecting conversations. *Journal of Family Psychotherapy, 6*(3), 71–89.

Smith, T. E., Sells, S., & Clevenger, T. (1994). Ethnographic content analysis of couple and therapist perceptions in a reflecting team setting. *Journal of Marital and Family Therapy, 20,* 267–286.

Smith, T. E., Winton, M., & Yoshioka, M. (1992). A qualitative understanding of reflective-teams: II. Therapists' perspectives. *Contemporary Family Therapy: An International Journal, 14*(5), 419–432.

Smith, T. E., Yoshioka, M., & Winton, M. (1993). A qualitative understanding of reflecting teams: I. Client perspectives. *Journal of Systemic Therapies, 12*(3), 28–43.

Spradley, J. (1979). *The ethnographic interview.* New York: Holt, Rinehart & Winston.

Stancombe, J., & White, S. (1997). Notes on the tenacity of therapeutic presuppositions in process research: Examining the artfulness of blamings in family therapy. *Journal of Family Therapy, 19*(1), 21–41.

Stith, S. M., Rosen, K. H., McCollum, E. E., Coleman, J. U., & Herman, S. A. (1996). The voice of children: Preadolescent children's experiences in family therapy. *Journal of Marital & Family Therapy, 22*(1), 69–86.

Strauss, A. (1987). *Qualitative analysis for social scientists.* Cambridge, England: Cambridge University Press.

Strauss, A., & Corbin, J. (1990). *Basics of qualitative research: Grounded theory procedures and techniques.* Newbury Park, CA: Sage.

Stubbs, M. (1983). *Discourse analysis: The sociolinguistic analysis of natural language.* Chicago: University of Chicago Press.

Todd, T. A., Joanning, H., Enders, L., Mutchler, L., & Thomas, F. (1990). Using ethnographic interviews to create a more cooperative client–therapist relationship. *Journal of Family Psychotherapy, 1*(3), 51–63.

Troemel-Ploetz, S. (1977). "She is just not an open person": A linguistic analysis of a restructuring intervention in family therapy. *Family Process, 16,* 339–352.

Troemel-Ploetz, S. (1980). "I'd come to you for therapy": Interpretation, redefinition and paradox in Rogerian therapy. *Psychotherapy: Theory, Research & Practice, 17*(3), 246–257.

Viaro, M., & Leonardi, P. (1983). Getting and giving information: Analysis of a family-interview strategy. *Family Process, 22,* 27–42.

Weitzman, E. A., & Miles, M. B. (1995). *Computer programs for qualitative data analysis: A software sourcebook.* Thousand Oaks, CA: Sage.

White, M., & Epston, D. (1990). *Narrative means to therapeutic ends.* New York: W. W. Norton.

Winefield, H. R., Chandler, M. A., & Bassett, D. L. (1989). Tag questions and powerfulness: Quantitative and qualitative analyses of a course of psychotherapy. *Language in Society, 18*(1), 77–86.

Wolcott, H. F. (1990). On seeking—and rejecting—validity in qualitative research. In E. W. Eisner & A. Peshkin (Eds.), *Qualitative inquiry in education: The continuing debate* (pp. 121–152). New York: Teachers College Press.

Wolcott, H. F. (1992). Posturing in qualitative research. In M. D. LeCompte, W. L. Millroy, J. & Preissle (Eds.), *The handbook of qualitative research in education* (pp. 3–52). San Diego, CA: Academic Press.

Wright, L. (1990). Research as a family therapy intervention technique. *Contemporary Family Therapy, 12,* 477–484.

II | THE COMMON FACTORS:
Extra-Therapeutic Change,
The Therapeutic Relationship,
Expectancy, and
Therapeutic Technique

Karen Tallman and Arthur C. Bohart

The Client as a Common Factor:
Clients as Self-Healers

4

Until lions have their historians, all tales of hunting will glorify the hunter.

—African proverb.

Our thesis in this chapter is that the client's capacity for self-healing is the most potent common factor in psychotherapy. It is the "engine" that makes therapy work (Bohart & Tallman, 1999; Bohart & Tallman, 1996). Therapy facilitates naturally occurring healing aspects of clients' lives. Therapists function as support systems and resource providers. This view contrasts with most of the literature on psychotherapy. There, the therapist is the "hero" who, with potent techniques and procedures, intervenes in clients' lives and fixes their malfunctioning machinery, be they faulty cognitions, weak and ineffectual egos, primitive defensive structures, conditioned maladaptive behaviors, defective social skills, or poorly working internal self-organizations.

In this chapter we argue that the most parsimonious explanation for the dodo bird verdict is that it is the client, not the therapist or technique, that makes therapy work. After making the empirical case for client centrality in therapeutic change, we then present our model of client generativity and self-healing and discuss its implications for therapy.

The Dodo Bird May Be Extinct Elsewhere but Is Alive and Flourishing in Psychotherapy

In 1975, after a review of psychotherapy outcome studies, Luborsky, Singer, and Luborsky announced the now famous "dodo bird verdict" borrowed from *Alice in Wonderland:* "Everyone has won and all must have prizes." Luborsky et al. cleverly used the "verdict" to illustrate the empirical conclusion that all of the different therapies appeared to be equal in effectiveness. Later, comprehensive reviews drew similar conclusions (e.g., Lambert & Bergin, 1994; Smith, Glass, & Miller, 1980; Stubbs & Bozarth, 1994), and studies comparing different, specific approaches also found no differences in outcome (e.g., Project MATCH Research Group, 1997; Grawe, Caspar, & Ambuhl, 1990; Sloan, Staples, Cristol, Yorkston, & Whipple, 1975). The *Consumer Reports* survey, too, reported no evidence for differential effectiveness of different therapies for any disorder (Seligman, 1995). Moreover, meta-analyses, involving comparisons among different approaches, turned in a finding of no differences (e.g., Elliott, 1996; Robinson, Berman, & Neimeyer, 1990). Finally, the most recent meta-analysis (Wampold et al., 1997), done to answer objections to earlier ones, has once again reconfirmed the dodo bird verdict.

Because of the massive number of outcome studies conducted and the strong motivation of researchers to discount the dodo bird verdict, some studies have uncovered differences between approaches (e.g., Barlow, 1994). Notwithstanding, Wampold (1997) suggested that those few do not exceed the number expected by chance. With the data at hand, he concludes that the dodo bird verdict cannot be overthrown. Furthermore, when meta-analyses account for the allegiance of the investigator, differences favoring one approach over another largely vanish (e.g., Elliott, 1996; Robinson et al., 1990).

Considering that the dodo bird verdict is established on hundreds of studies and continues to be found and re-found, it is surprising that it is not accepted as a fact about psychotherapy. Instead, researchers repeatedly attempt to discount it (e.g., Fisher, 1995). Others, relying on the few studies that do show differences between treatments, claim that the verdict can be rejected (e.g., Barlow, 1994; Task Force on Promotion and Dissemination of Psychological Procedures, 1995).

To overturn the dodo bird verdict, various arguments are leveled. For example, small sample sizes has been offered as an explanation for the no difference finding. In addition, it is said that, if even not statistically significant, the available evidence typically favors cognitive–behavior therapies (Fisher, 1995). That small differences (even if shown to be statistically significant) may possess little psychological consequence is apparently unimportant in staking such a claim (Wampold, 1997). Even if it can be proved that small differences in effectiveness exist (i.e., that they are neither artifacts nor due to chance), we believe what is far more impressive is the conspicuous overlap in outcome between different approaches using widely different methodologies.

The dodo bird verdict is a robust finding worthy of much more respect than it is given. It is curious that accepting it as a real phenomenon is so difficult for the field. If the proverbial shoe were on the other foot—if studies finding differential treatment effects were the rule— it is unlikely that such results would defy acceptance (except, perhaps, by adherents of approaches not "winning"). Bergin and Garfield (1994), reflecting on the current state of this issue, wrote:

> With some exceptions . . . there is massive evidence that psychotherapeutic techniques do not have specific effects; yet there is tremendous resistance to accepting this finding as a legitimate one. Numerous interpretations of the data have been given in order to preserve the idea that technical factors have substantial, unique, and specific effects. The reasons for this are not difficult to surmise. Such pronouncements essentially appear to be rationalizations that attempt to preserve the role of special theories, the status of leaders of such approaches, the technical training programs for therapists, the professional legitimacy of psychotherapy, and the rewards that come to those having supposedly curative powers (p. 822).

THERAPIST AS HERO

Instead of discounting the dodo bird verdict, it may prove more fruitful to discover what it means. Those interested in psychotherapy integration have suggested that common factors cut across different approaches to therapy and make them all equally effective (Arkowitz, 1992; Goldfried & Padawer, 1982). In a conceptual "meta-analysis" of different lists of common factors, Grencavage and Norcross (1990) discovered that the client is rarely mentioned as a therapeutic common factor. The few referrals to clients portray their contribution by (a) hoping it will help, (b) experiencing incongruence in their personalities, and (c) coming to therapy and asking for help. All other common factors were seen as belonging to the therapist and to the process of therapy.

Many common factors listed by Grencavage and Norcross, however, can be viewed as client processes in disguise. For instance, one common factor is "fostering insight and awareness." Here, insight and awareness are depicted as psychological states or events that therapists *bring to* clients. Instead of a therapist-generated event, however, insight is a client process that often occurs to individuals outside of therapy as well. Another example is "acquisition and practice of new behaviors." Again, these are things that clients do, both in and outside of therapy.

This therapist-as-hero writing style is all too common. It emphasizes the all-powerful therapist and his or her mastery of technique as the primary precipitants of change. This is similar to what has been called "professionalcentrism" (e.g., Bickman & Salzer, 1996). The very fact there are more than 400 different approaches to psychotherapy competing for first place gives testimony to therapists' beliefs that it is their efforts, their theories, and their techniques that are responsible for change. Believing this, different therapists go to inordinate lengths to justify the superiority of their theoretical perspectives, and do research to demonstrate the preeminence of their approach in practice.

The privileging of the therapist's contribution in therapy is further exemplified by the tradition of calling what therapists do or say "interventions," and what clients do or say "responses" (e.g., Angus, 1992). For example, if the therapist asks a question, it is an intervention, while if the client asks a question, it is a response. Similarly, a therapist's interpretation is an intervention, while a client's interpretation (insight) is a response to the therapist's intervention.

This is not to say that therapists have not recognized the importance of client active participation. Nearly all approaches recognize the importance of client collaboration to make therapy work. For example, Beck has often described his approach as "collaborative empiricism," suggesting an important role for the client as collaborator.

For all that, in the extant therapy literature, the client is rarely portrayed as an instigator of change. More often, clients are depicted as suffering from lack of insight, weak ego structures, entrenched defensive structures, narcissistic or borderline personality organizations, lack of differentiation, enmeshment, the presence of dysfunctional schema, irrational thinking, unprocessed emotional experience, conditioned dysfunctional reactions, and lack of skills. The therapist is the one who causes change and champions mental health. It is true the client must be an active participant, but it is the therapist's potent interventions that make change occur. If estimates of the relative contributions of therapist and client to change were made, based on reading book after book about therapy, one would probably assign about 70% to the therapist's interventions and interactions, and 30% to the active involvement and participation of the client.

THE CLIENT AS HERO

In contrast, we believe that the primary change agent in therapy is the client. We would reverse the percentages suggested above: 70% of why therapy works goes to the client and 30% to the therapist. Although, as already noted, written accounts of therapy typically glorify the therapist's contributions, many therapists agree. In a poll conducted by Norcross (1986), therapists attributed 67% of the variance in outcome to the client. Lambert (1992) has reported that 40% of the outcome variance is due to extratherapeutic factors, which consist of the client and factors in the client's life; 30% to common therapeutic factors, which primarily consist of relationship factors, or factors that occur through the relationship; 15% to techniques; and 15% to placebo factors. Considering that placebo factors are client factors (client self-healing through hope and belief), and clients contribute at least as much to the therapeutic relationship as does the therapist, Lambert's figures also imply that the client is responsible for 70% or more of the outcome variance.

We believe the dodo bird verdict occurs because the client's abilities to use whatever is offered surpass any differences that might exist in techniques or approaches. The reason that different approaches to psychotherapy work equally well is that they each allow clients the opportunity to work through and resolve their problems. Clients utilize and tailor what each approach provides to address their problems. Even *if* different techniques have different specific effects, clients take these effects, individualize them to their specific purposes, and use them. Thus, for example, a client can use cognitive or interpersonal techniques (Elkin, 1994), or emotional exploration procedures, or empathically based client-centered therapy (Greenberg & Watson, 1998) to move themselves out of depression.

The situation is not unlike exercise. It is as though clients were given a wide range of exercise options and devices with the goal of building their cardiovascular fitness. Despite different approaches or methods, we discover that the active efforts of clients in using the devices lead to functional equivalence of outcomes. In short, what turns out to be most important is how each client uses the device or method, more than the device or method itself.

Clients then are the "magicians" with the special healing powers. Therapists set the stage and serve as assistants who provide the conditions under which this magic can operate. They do not provide the magic, although they may provide means for mobilizing, channeling, and focusing clients' magic.

If this reasoning is sound, then the dodo bird verdict should be found elsewhere in the research literature. That is, if the client is the common denominator of change in the therapeutic process, other examples of the equivalence of outcome finding should readily occur. As we describe next, findings similar to the dodo bird verdict are the rule rather than the exception.

The Dodo Bird Judges Other Races

THERAPIST EXPERIENCE AND TRAINING

If the therapist is the primary agent of change in therapy, then the therapist's experience and training should make a difference. Furthermore, as with electricians and brain surgeons, experience and training should make a *real* difference (Christensen, 1992). Experienced therapists should be much more effective than inexperienced therapists, and more highly trained therapists should be more effective than less trained therapists. On the other hand, if the client is the primary agent of change, then such differences might be less important. Therefore, the functional equivalent of the dodo bird verdict might again be found. That is, little difference in effectiveness between experienced and inexperienced therapists, or between extensively trained therapists and less trained therapists would be obtained.

Studies do conflict, but overall differences in therapist experience have not been found to yield powerful effects. Christensen and Jacobson (1994) cited several reviews finding no evidence of significant differences in effectiveness between professionals and paraprofessionals. Research also has not supported the idea that more experienced therapists are more effective (Christensen & Jacobson, 1994; Lambert & Bergin, 1994).

Strupp and Hadley (1979) found that experienced therapists were no more helpful than a group of untrained college professors selected for their relationship skills. Jacobson (1995) determined that novice graduate students were more effective at doing couples therapy than trained professionals. And Svartberg and Stiles (1991) found, in a meta-analysis of studies on short-term psychodynamic therapy, that inexperienced therapists were more effective than experienced therapists. On the other hand, a recent meta-analysis by Stein and Lambert (1994) did find some evidence of small differences in effectiveness for more well-trained and experienced therapists.

Considered together, it is impressive that these results show little more than small differences in effectiveness between experienced, well-trained practitioners and less experienced nonprofessional therapists. One would not expect differences to be so small if one were comparing trained professionals in other specialties, for example, surgeons or electricians to untrained surgeons or electricians (Christensen, 1992). This does not mean that all therapists are created equal. Evidence exists that some therapists are more helpful than others (Luborsky, McClellan, Woody, O'Brien, & Auerbach 1985; Orlinsky & Howard, 1980). Rather than professional training or experience, it looks as though differences in personal qualities make some therapists more helpful.

PROFESSIONAL INTERVENTION VERSUS SELF-HELP

If clients are the primary agents of change in therapy, then therapists should not always be needed. Self-help material, then, may be as useful as seeing a therapist. In studies that have compared self-help to professionally provided therapy, the dodo bird verdict is again the norm. Meta-analyses by Scogin, Bynum, Stephens, and Calhoun (1990) and by Gould and Clum (1993) found that self-help treatments, such as self-help books, were as effective for a wide range of problems as treatments including therapists.

Additional studies have produced other "dodo bird" findings. No differences have been shown in effectiveness in different self-help books, between conditions where the self-help book is combined with a class, or where it is simply combined with brief phone contacts (Arkowitz, 1997). For example, in a recent study (Arkowitz, 1997) cognitive self-help procedures were taught to depressives in a class. The results were comparable to those obtained from the now classic study of depression, the National Institute of Mental Health (NIMH) Treatment of Depression Collaborative Research Program (Elkin, 1994).

Computer-provided therapy also is as effective as traditional therapy. Selmi, Klein, Greist, Sorrell, and Erdman (1990) found that computer-administered cognitive behavior therapy worked as well as therapist administered therapy for depression. A study at a major Southern California HMO also found that computer-assisted therapy worked as well as therapist-provided therapy (Jacobs, 1995) for a variety of problems.

Self-help books and computer-assisted therapy programs are written by professionals. However, if the clinician is the primary agent of change, it would be unlikely that a self-help book or a computer program would turn out to be as effective as working with a professional. Certainly no surgeon could write a self-help book on surgery that would be as effective as seeing a professional surgeon.

These data are yet another example of the dodo bird verdict. They support the position that it is the client who is the primary change agent, who takes what is offered (a therapist, a self-help book, a computer program), invests it with life, and makes it work. The client is the common factor across helping methods, using whatever resource is available to change.

On the basis of current knowledge, the following conclusions are warranted:

- The dodo bird verdict holds, or mostly holds. Different treatments are not differentially effective for different disorders.
- On the whole, there is little or no difference between therapists that is based on their training or experience, suggesting that specialized expertise on the part of the therapist is not a major contributor to effectiveness.
- Self-help approaches are as effective as professionally provided therapy, and no significant differences between different modalities for providing self-help have been identified.

In all, it is hard to ignore the available research evidence. Indeed, if therapies and therapists were that potent, then there should not be such uniform results across different approaches to therapy, different techniques, differences in training and experience, differences between professionally provided therapy and self-help, and differences in various modalities of providing self-help. The data point to the inevitable conclusion that the primary agent of change, the "engine" of change, is the client.

Where Did All the Therapists Go?
Change Without Professional
Intervention

SELF-EXPRESSION

While the self-help procedures discussed above were designed by professionals, people often use effective self-help procedures without professional guidance. For example, Pennebaker (1990, 1997) has demonstrated that self-expression and self-disclosure are both psychologically and physically beneficial. In one study, college students wrote about a traumatic experience for 15 minutes a day for 4 consecutive days. At a 6-month follow up, it was found that these students, compared with a control group, reduced their visits to the student health center by 50%.

Harvey, Orbuch, Chwalisz, and Garwood (1991) found that giving traumatized individuals a chance to "tell their story" and engage in "account making" is a pathway to healing. In a related finding, Segal and Murray (1994) found that talking into a tape recorder worked about as well as cognitive therapy in helping individuals resolve feelings about traumatic experiences. An early study by Schwitzgabel (1961) showed that paying juvenile delinquents to talk into a tape recorder about their experiences led to meaningful improvements in their behavior, including fewer arrests.

Finally, Burton, Parker, and Wollner (1991) found that breast cancer patients about to undergo surgery, who met in a single 45-minute preoperative interview with their surgeons, had less distress about body image, less anxiety, and less depression. They also were better at a 1-year follow up than control participants who did not have the interview. The surgeons were trained in empathic listening and encouraged patients to express their feelings. No active attempts to intervene therapeutically were used. Further, those patients who had an additional psychotherapeutic intervention showed only a very small gain over the preoperative interview.

These findings show that clients have a considerable capacity to generate their own change. Given the proper structured activity, many can generate change without either active intervention by therapists or the focused guidance of specific techniques in self-help books. Individuals utilize self-healing methods and change without professional intervention.

SELF-GENERATED CHANGE AND SPONTANEOUS RECOVERY

Studies have repeatedly demonstrated what is obvious about human nature: People overcome their problems on their own. For example, many individuals "mature out" of borderline personality disorder (Kroll, 1988) and antisocial, aggressive behavior (Tedeschi & Felson, 1994). Other data shows that many alcoholics recover by themselves (Calahan, 1987; Prochaska, DiClemente, & Norcross, 1992; Robbins, 1979), as do most smokers (Prochaska et al., 1992).

Prochaska and his colleagues have intensively studied how individuals overcome their problems on their own (see Prochaska, this volume). In support of the thesis of this chapter, they assert, "in fact, it can be argued that all change is self-change, and that therapy is simply professionally coached self-change" (Prochaska, Norcross, & DiClemente, 1994, p. 17). Norcross and Aboyoun (1994) note that people who come to therapy are those who have failed in their self-change attempts.

"Spontaneous recovery rates" for various disorders, although quite variable, provide further evidence of clients' capacity to initiate their own change (Bergin & Lambert, 1978). Lambert, Shapiro, and Bergin (1986) have estimated the rate of spontaneous recovery to be approximately 40%. Spontaneous recovery occurs, in part, through individuals accessing resources in their natural environments. For example, Gurin, Veroff, and Feld (1960) found that the majority of individuals faced with problems contacted persons other than mental-health professionals. In general, they were more satisfied with the assistance they received than those who sought help from mental health professionals. Compatible with our view that therapy works by helping clients mobilize their own naturally occurring resources, clients in therapy actually seek more people to talk to outside therapy than those who do not seek therapy (Cross, Sheehan, & Kahn, 1980).

Further support of client-initiated change is found in the phenomena of pretreatment change. Weiner-Davis, de Shazer, and Gingerich (1987) and Lawson (1994) found that 60% or more of clients coming to their first session report improvement in the presenting problem since the appointment was made. Simply scheduling an appointment may help clients mobilize their self-healing capacities. Several studies have also shown that many clients improve after only one therapy session (Rosenbaum, 1994). Even if therapists made a contribution in their single session with these clients, it is clear that clients are doing a significant amount of the work on their own. That single session is only a piece of the overall change effort of the client.

PLACEBO EFFECTS

Placebo effects (see Snyder, this volume) are often treated by medical and psychotherapy researchers as contaminants. It is almost an insult to say that something is merely a "placebo." Yet, as Weil (1995) has pointed out in medicine, placebo effects are powerful and deserve our interest. For instance, Klopfer's (1957) account of a placebo alleviating the symptoms of terminal cancer, is little short of astounding. The power of placebos has repeatedly been observed in psychotherapy research also (Bergin & Lambert, 1978). For example, in the NIMH collaborative study of depression, no significant differences emerged between the placebo and cognitive conditions (Elkin, 1994).

Concerning the placebo effect and psychotherapy, our thesis is similar to Weil's (1995) concept of the active placebo in medicine. Active placebos produce physiologic changes and bodily sensations, but do not do the actual healing. The healing occurs through the patients' self-healing activated by the perceived bodily changes (see Greenberg, this volume, for more on active placebos). Similarly, various techniques used by clinicians, and therapy itself, can be understood as active placebos. Rather than mediating change directly, techniques simply activate the natural healing propensity of the client.

For instance, relaxation procedures have an active effect (e.g., changes in muscle tension and tone, states of awareness). And yet, these alterations, no matter how well they can be produced, reported, and measured, may not be directly involved in helping clients change. Instead, the more active and specific the procedure, the more believable it becomes to clients, thus mobilizing their intrinsic hope, energy, creativity, and self-healing potential. *Personal agency is awakened by technique.* This "active placebo" process may perhaps explain why techniques that evoke strong emotion may be particularly helpful. They more effectively mobilize a client's involvement, commitment, and persistence in the self-change effort.

Once again, we believe that the client accounts for most of the placebo effect. The placebo effect represents the client's personal agency in action. Viewing techniques themselves as active placebos that initiate clients' self-healing processes has received little attention and, consequently, has rarely been controlled for in psychotherapy research. Although we are not suggesting that therapy procedures only contribute as active placebos, the possibility merits strong consideration. The power and consistency of the placebo effect demands that it should no longer be denigrated. Rather than attempting to eliminate its influence, more attention might be paid to understanding its potency in mobilizing and supporting clients' innate, self-curative processes.

THE THERAPEUTIC RELATIONSHIP

So far, we have maintained that the client is the primary agent of change. Many, however, have argued that the relationship between the therapist and client is the primary curative factor. This position posits that even if the therapist's techniques are not curative, the therapist, nevertheless, is still essential. Specifically, the power of the relationship provided by the therapist is viewed as the major healing variable.

Many consider the quality of the therapeutic relationship to be the best predictor of outcome in therapy (Bachelor, 1991; Horvath, 1995; Krupnick et al., 1996; Orlinsky, Grawe, & Parks, 1994). This is true for pharmacological intervention also (Krupnick et al., 1996). Studies have even found that the relationship is more powerful than specific interventions held in high esteem by a particular school, such as cognitive therapy (Burns & Nolen-Hoeksema, 1991; Castonguay, 1993), behavior therapy (W. R. Miller, Taylor, & West, 1980), or psychodynamic therapy (Svartberg & Stiles, 1994). For instance, Svartberg and Stiles (1994) found that the alliance correlated at .48 with outcome, while specific techniques correlated at −.55!

However compelling these findings may be, especially in terms of the relative contributions of technique and the relationship, it remains unclear how the therapeutic relationship is helpful. Several possibilities exist. First, the relationship may be healing because it provides a "corrective emotional experience." The therapist's benign and benevolent listening and intervening is inherently healing—it mends the damage caused by toxic relationships in the client's past. Second, the relationship may heal because it provides an environment in which more appropriate behaviors receive reinforcement. Closely related to the last possibility, the relationship provides new learning opportunities. Clients may learn how to be in a relationship more effectively (Jordan, 1997), without subordinating themselves to others or losing their identity. Fourth, through the relationship, such therapist-provided processes as empathy may mobilize client experiencing or self-structuralization, which in turn are healing (Bohart & Greenberg, 1997).

We do not disagree with these proposed effects of the relationship, yet they are insufficient to explain the therapeutic change process. Not only do client variables account for more of the variance, but also the noted studies of self-help books, the use of computers, and self-expression clearly demonstrate that therapists are frequently not necessary for change to take place. Of course, if the therapist is unnecessary, then the relationship is unnecessary as well.

Therefore, the impact of the relationship must be reinterpreted. Again, all the above effects of the relationship are possible. However, we believe that the relationship is yet another resource which clients utilize to mobilize personal agency and change. In other words, the relationship, while particularly important or useful for many clients, is not in principle different from techniques, self-help books, or computer programs. *It is a resource that facilitates, supports, or focuses clients' self-healing efforts.*

In this respect, the relationship is helpful because it provides a safe, sheltered "space" in which clients can take a deep breath, consider their problems in context, brainstorm with another person, gain perspective, examine their "bad sides," make mistakes, generate new alternatives, re-experience old wounds and problematic issues, think, analyze, recover the strength to re-confront life, and try new behaviors. In all, the relationship provides a supportive structure within which clients' generative, self-healing capacities can optimally operate.

While there is no evidence directly supporting this assertion, there is evidence in accord with it. Findings abound that the client's perceptions of the relationship or alliance, more so than the therapist's, correlate more highly with therapeutic outcome (Horvath, 1995; Orlinsky et al., 1994). If the therapist's expertise in providing ideal relationship conditions were the primary determinant of change, then the opposite would probably be true. However, it is the client's assessment of the alliance that matters more. The client's interpretation of, or perhaps "creation" of, the relationship is most crucial to outcome. Additionally, in a qualitative study of three sessions of therapy, Bohart and Boyd (1997) found that clients in part "created" their own therapists. This constructive process occurred by clients attending to, remembering, and interpreting therapist actions in accordance with their aims and goals in therapy.

The relationship, then, like other therapy-provided components of change, serves as a resource for the client to draw on, construct and tailor as necessary, and use to reach desired goals. The relationship provides the space for client's personal agency to flourish.

SUMMARY

To recap, considerable evidence supports our premise that the client is the major change agent in therapy. We contend (a) it is client self-healing that best accounts for the dodo bird verdict, (b) placebos work by activating clients' agency, and (c) the therapeutic relationship is a resource that clients use like any other, and clients contribute most to that factor as well. Compatible with our view of the potency of client self-healing, Orlinsky et al. (1994) believe that humans have a "powerful endogenous therapeutic system that is part of the psychophysiology of all individuals" (p. 278, quoting Kleinman, 1988, p. 112). Bergin and Garfield (1994) noted,

> Another important observation regarding the client variable is that it is the client more than the therapist who implements the change process . . . Rather than argue over whether or not "therapy works," we could address ourselves to the question of whether or not "the client works!" . . . It is important to rethink the terminology that assumes that "effects" are like Aristotelian impetus causality. As therapists have depended more upon the client's resources, more change seems to occur. (pp. 825–826)

In the next section, we briefly review client factors in psychotherapy relevant to client self-healing.

A Brief Review of Research on Client Factors and Experiences in Psychotherapy

For an extensive review of research on client factors in therapy, the excellent summary chapters by Garfield (1994) and Orlinsky et al. (1994) are recommended. The literature to be reviewed here bears on the proposition that the major engine driving effective therapy is clients' active self-healing. Special attention is given to studies examining clients' participation in and experience of the therapy process.

CLIENT PARTICIPATION

Client Involvement

If clients are first among the dramatis personae in the drama called therapy, then the degree of client participation in therapy should be a major variable in outcome. It is. Along with the alliance, client involvement is the most important variable predicting whether therapy will work. Garfield (1994) cited several studies underscoring its importance and Orlinsky et al. (1994) reported that 69% of the studies they reviewed show that client cooperation (versus resistance) is associated with positive outcomes. Similarly, the client's "role investment" in the therapy has been associated with positive outcome in nearly 70% of the studies completed. Also, client openness versus defensiveness has been found to be associated with outcome in 80% of the studies performed. Finally, the client's "collaborative style" (versus controlling or dependent), is associated with positive outcome in 64% of studies.

Orlinsky et al. (1994) noted that "patients who are cooperative and open . . . are more willing to participate, can more readily absorb the experiences generated by effective therapeutic operations, and thus are more likely to benefit from therapy" (p. 363). They noted, too, that the quality of the patient's participation in therapy stands out as the most important determinant of outcome (p. 361).

Client Motivation and Goals

Because the client's participation is so important, clients' motivation for therapy should play an important role in outcome. Results on this score are conflicting. Garfield (1994) concluded there is no strong evidence that client motivation is associated with outcome, although it may play a role in whether a person enters therapy. On the other hand, Orlinsky et al. (1994) reported that 50% of 28 studies found that client motivation is associated with outcome. Because the odds of obtaining a significant result are 5% or less (if there is no relationship), to get 14 of 28 significant results is beyond what one would expect by chance. Thus, there looks to be a significant but inconsistent relationship between motivation and outcome. Orlinsky et al. added that the significance of motivation increases if it is assessed from the client's perspective. In this case, 80% of the studies found a positive relationship. This is in accord with other data that emphasizes the importance of the client's perspective in general.

In modern personality research, goals have become in many ways the equivalent of motivation (see Cantor & Zirkel, 1990). Goals, therefore, can be viewed as a motivational construct. Many therapists (e.g., de Shazer, 1985; Zilbergeld & Lazarus, 1987) believe that having clear, concrete, and specific goals is motivating.

Defined in this way, the concept of motivation gains significance and meaning to the therapeutic process. Garfield (1994) cited studies that suggest that people who come to therapy have a more specific formulation of their problems and what they want to accomplish than do those who call for an appointment, but who do not show up. Orlinsky et al. (1994), citing the alliance literature, reported that both the clarity of goals and consensus on goals between therapist and client are associated with positive outcome.

Clients' expectancies that therapy will be of help are related to motivation. Following from Jerome Frank's (1974) work, many have assumed that clients' expectations for success should predict therapeutic outcome. Garfield (1994) reported conflicting results in studies examining the role of clients' expectations. Methodological problems have contributed to the lack of clarity. He also notes that expectancies may play an initial role in therapy, but they may be washed out or changed by the experience of therapy itself. In this regard Perotti and Hopewell (1980) have drawn a distinction between initial expectancy, the expectancy the client has at the start of therapy, and ongoing expectancy during therapy. They suggest that initial expectancy may play relatively less of a role compared to ongoing expectancies during therapy. Nonetheless, Garfield's review, which focuses primarily on studies of pretreatment expectancies, cites more positive than negative studies, suggesting some role for the effects of expectancy.

In sum, while the evidence is not uniform, it favors the hypothesis that clients who are motivated, hold expectations that therapy will help and have a clear sense of their goals will be more likely to profit from being in therapy. Beyond this, the client's level of involvement and openness to the process are the most important factors in whether therapy helps.

CLIENT EXPERIENCE IN PSYCHOTHERAPY: WHAT CLIENTS SAY ABOUT THERAPEUTIC CHANGE

Research strongly suggests that what clients find helpful in therapy has little to do with the techniques that therapists find so important. Phillips (1984) interviewed clients who were in a variety of therapy approaches, including cognitive–behavioral therapy, and found that the most helpful factor was having a time and a place to focus on themselves and talk. Other studies typically find that clients emphasize the relationship (having someone listen, care, and understand), and getting encouragement and advice from their therapists. For instance, Elliott and James (1989) reviewed the literature and found that clients reported the most helpful factors across therapies to be facilitative therapist characteristics, unburdening of distress, self-understanding, and encouragement for gradual practice.

As a specific example, Llewelyn, Elliott, Shapiro, and Hardy (1988) found that depressed and anxious clients who received eight sessions of both cognitive–behavioral and psychodynamic–interpersonal therapy rated the following experiences as most helpful: increased awareness, obtaining problem solutions, reassurance, and personal contact. Gold (1980) found that clients in behavior therapy rated the relationship with the therapist as equal to or more important than the specific behavior therapy techniques used. In a study of behavior therapy by Ryan and Gizynski (1971), clients said that the most helpful components were the therapists' faith; calm sympathetic listening; and support, approval, and advice.

Finally, in the now classic study by Sloane et al. (1975, p. 206), in which psychoanalysis was compared with behavior therapy, the items considered most important by clients regardless of therapeutic school were

- The personality of your doctor
- His helping you to understand your problem
- Encouraging you gradually to practice facing the things that bother you
- Being able to talk to an understanding person
- Helping you to understand yourself.

In sum, from the client's perspective, the most important aspects of therapy typically are the "nonspecific" factors—the personality of the therapist; having a time and place to talk; having someone care, listen, and understand; having someone provide encouragement and advice; and having someone help you understand your problems. These are the processes one would expect would be helpful if the primary healing force in therapy comes from the client's own active problem-solving efforts.

Evidence for Client Reflexivity and Agency

An intriguing series of qualitative empirical studies by Rennie (1990, 1994, 1997) provide evidence for client reflexivity and agency in therapy. Rennie conducted a qualitative analyses on interpersonal process recall data (Elliott, 1986) on 14 therapy sessions from 12 therapist–client pairs. Soon after the taped sessions, clients met with

Rennie, listened to the tape, and stopped it whenever they wanted to comment.

Rennie discovered that clients were highly active at a covert level during the sessions. They steered sessions in directions they wanted, deferred to therapists overtly, but then covertly thought about experiences in the way they wanted. They also did not share their covert processing and actively tried to redirect the therapists if they went off course. Clients were anything but passive recipients of therapeutic wisdom.

In a recent report, Rennie (1997) presented the case of a client who answered the therapist's initial question on how things were going by saying things were going well. The client's purpose was to reinforce the therapist's efforts (i.e., the client was deliberately reinforcing the therapist to keep her trying). However, this went awry because the therapist enthusiastically pursued the topic they were discussing when the client actually wanted to talk about something else. The client had to change the topic subtly to get the therapist back on the clients' preferred track. Later, the client deliberately brought up a different topic to deflect the therapist from a potential question about the homework assignment the client did not do. Again, the client was in many ways actively directing the process.

Rennie (1997) also reported on a client who was feeling criticized by his therapist. This client found an indirect way of "putting the therapist" in his place, effectively shutting up the therapist without him catching on to what was happening. Rennie's data provide a rich tapestry of how clients are highly active, thinking, processing, reflective agents during therapy. This research, we believe, paints a more accurate picture of the therapeutic process.

In a therapy analogue study, Tallman, Robinson, Kay, Harvey, and Bohart (1994) compared the effects of "bad" (vapid, superficial) empathy responses with "good" (more richly detailed and deep) empathy responses. Tallman et al. noticed that despite the vapid nature of many bad, empathy responses, some clients found a creative way to make lemonade out of the lemon of the response. In some cases, the client would give a nod to the therapist, as though trying to protect her feelings, by saying something like, "Yes, that is really close . . . " before going off in a different direction. The client would somehow use what the therapist said, but in an innovative way to pursue what he or she wanted to pursue, conduct the analysis he or she wanted to conduct, or achieve the insight for which he or she was searching. Similarly, Elliott (1984) reported finding much sloppiness and slippage in interpretation/insight processes in therapy—therapists make mistakes, but clients ignore mistakes and use what is beneficial to them.

Newfield, Kuehl, Joanning, and Quinn (1991) demonstrated how teenagers in family therapy for drug abuse actively manipulated therapy to their ends. Often in such therapy situations, adolescents are nonresponsive, and are typically labeled as *defensive* and *resistant.* Newfield et al. found that the teens were actually highly active. They were quiet, not because they were being defensive and resistant, but rather were actively trying to figure out what was going on so they could get what they wanted out of the situation. Their aim was to use the information they gathered to placate and maneuver their therapists and parents later. The teens also reported saying what their parents wanted to hear, and trying to talk their parents out of the therapist's interventions during the week.

The lesson of this study is that what may look like a passive or a resistant client is often a highly proactive one, pursuing an agenda other than that of the therapist. Looks can be deceiving. Seeing clients as passive or resistant is not only inaccurate most of the time, but will also be far less helpful than viewing them as active agents, pursuing agendas that make sense within their frame of reference.

Several case reports of client change also support the empirical evidence about client agency and self-healing. Corsini (1989) tells the case of an inmate he tested while working at a prison. Two years after the psychological testing, when the inmate was being released on parole, he came in to see Corsini. He told Corsini he wanted to thank him for what he had done for him. After meeting with Corsini once, the man decided to turn his life around.

This greatly surprised Corsini, as he was not the prisoner's psychotherapist. He asked for elaboration. The man said he had stopped hanging out with the "bad boys' in prison, starting going to the prison high school and church. Now he was planning to go to college. He thanked Corsini for changing his life.

The problem was that Corsini could not remember ever talking to the inmate. Corsini looked up his folder and discovered that he had given the man an IQ-test two years before. He still could not remember having said or done anything to help this man, and so asked him what he had said that was so helpful. The man replied the event that had turned his life around was that Corsini had told him that he had a high IQ.

This story is a clear example of the active, creative, self-changing efforts of the client. Corsini was not even a psychotherapist. Yet his "intervention" was creatively interpreted by the client in a growth-producing way.

Duncan, Hubble, and Miller (1997) reported a study of cases in which they deliberately tried to work with clients who were viewed as "impossible" by other therapists—clients who had repeatedly not been helped by previous therapy. In their book, they describe several clients who were helped primarily by the therapist taking the client's point of view seriously and by relying on client creativity and self-healing. The case of Molly is a particularly good example. Molly was a

10-year-old girl with night terrors who, after a year of therapy with other therapists, came to her own solution to her problems when given the opportunity by the therapist. Similarly, Gold (1994) documented cases where clients spontaneously and creatively generated their own forms of psychotherapy integration.

In summary, several qualitative empirical studies and case histories support the hypothesis of client agency and self-healing in psychotherapy. Clients are proactive directors of the change process, both in and out of therapy.

Evidence for Human Activity and Agency

The idea that the client is an active agent rests on believing that people are active agents. By this we mean that the human being is fundamentally active, constantly in motion, dealing with him- or herself and the environment. A distinction is often made between individuals considered active and those considered passive or apathetic. Yet, even passivity and apathy can be said to be activities, representing a difference in degree rather than in kind. Apathy, for instance, is often very active, as is passivity and dependence. Passivity and dependence should be thought of more as coping styles, embodying a form of survival activity. People are apt to feel apathetic when blocked, thwarted, or frustrated in finding a direction to follow. Apathy, in short, may be the resultant of blocked activity.

Ample support exists for the idea of the human as an active agent. Developmental psychologists believe that humans are active, curious learners from birth. There is also abundant evidence for human resilience. Masten, Best, and Garmazy (1990), researchers on human resilience, have concluded, "studies of psychosocial resilience support the view that human psychological development is highly buffered and self-righting" (p. 438). The recent active learning movement (Cooper, 1995, 1996) in education also provides support for the active, generative nature of the human being.

Finally, there is evidence to show that humans are active, creative transformers of information. Information does not merely affect and change the information-processing system, as some cognitive theories hold. Rychlak (1994) has shown that when subjects learn a fact, they also learn the opposite of the fact, because they can think oppositionally and generate the alternative. People do not merely "process" information, they think. This point is also made by Hayes and Gifford (1997) from a radical-behavioral perspective. They note that "humans have a remarkable ability to derive relations among events" (p. 171).

Closely associated with the human as active thinker and learner is the human capacity for creativity. Epstein (1991), a radical behaviorist, has noted, "The behavior of organisms has many firsts, so many, in fact, that it's not clear that there are any seconds. We continually do new things . . . When you look closely enough, behavior that appears to have been repeated proves to be novel in some fashion" (p. 362). Ward, Finke, and Smith (1995) pointed out the countless ways humans are continually creative in everyday life. These authors note that the idea that people have a set of schemas in the brain, which they then apply to incoming information, is simply wrong. Instead, people continually modify their concepts to fit new information, to the point where it might be more accurate to say that they are continually inventing new concepts, rather than mechanically using old ones.

Summary

The evidence supports our view of the client's active investment in the change process. Clients are not merely conduits or "processors" of information. Instead they are active thinkers who are continually generative and creative in every day life. They modify old concepts and use them, create new concepts, think of alternatives, derive rules and implications. In therapy they are active agents, creatively working to get from the therapist what they want and need, protecting themselves when necessary, and actively supporting the therapist when they think the therapist needs it. Compatible with this view of the client, clients regard therapy as a place where they can focus on themselves, and value relational aspects over technological aspects.

A Model of Client Generativity and Self-Healing

With the above in mind, we shall briefly review our model of how clients self-heal and generate change in therapy (see Bohart & Tallman, 1999, for a full exposition). The ultimate change process, inside and outside of therapy, is one wherein clients actively explore their worlds, both in thought and in behavior, try out new ways of being and behaving, engage in creative variations on old learning, and solve problems as they come up. Life never approaches some ideal smooth "flow" state, but in most cases problems get resolved in an orderly enough fashion for life to go on.

The processes of change in therapy are the same as those outside of therapy. Prochaska and his colleagues have demonstrated that individuals who spontaneously solve major life problems use the same general change strategies used in therapy (see Prochaska, this volume).

Most of the specialized techniques which therapists use occur "naturally" in everyday life (Efran & Blumberg, 1994). For instance, exposure and extinction can be seen as more highly focused and distilled versions of what people naturally know ("if you're thrown off a horse, get right back up on it").

Similarly, an examination of common factors across therapies reveals that many are processes which occur in everyday life. Goldfried and Padawer (1982), for instance, listed the following as common factors in psychotherapy: expectation that therapy will help, therapeutic relationship, obtaining an external perspective on oneself and the world, continued reality testing, and corrective experiences. Grawe (1997), arguing for a common factors approach based on research, identified the following: clarification of meanings, provision of opportunities for mastery/coping experiences, problem actuation (activating the problem in therapy to be worked on), and utilization of client resources (i.e., our client as active self-healer concept).

Goldfried's and Grawe's schemes boil down to therapy being a place where clients can actively experience their problems "live," experience mastery over them, and reflect upon new perspectives in the context of a helpful relationship. With the exception of the helping relationship, these processes are all really client processes that occur in everyday life. Certainly clients experience their problems "live" in everyday life, reflect on and clarify them, gain external feedback from friends, relatives, and the natural occurrence of events, and, if they struggle with a problem and master it, have corrective mastery experiences. *In other words, what therapists do is simply use naturally occurring client change processes.*

The real therapy is living. What we call therapy is a special example of processes that occur outside of therapy. Therapy concentrates or distills the experiential and intellectual contexts of everyday life. Therapy then can be thought of as a prosthetic provision of contexts, experiences, and events which prompt, support, or facilitate clients' self-healing.

A person doesn't always self-heal in everyday life because for some reason, the natural environment has not provided the opportunities. For example, outside of therapy people rarely have a friend who will truly listen to them for more than 20 minutes (Stiles, 1995). Friends do not usually provide the time and space for individuals to think about and explore their problems, gain distance, re-experience them (along with accompanying emotion), and perhaps begin to find the threads of a way out. Instead friends and relatives may jump in with premature advice, and inadvertently, discount their fears. Further, friends and relatives often are involved in the problem and therefore do not provide a "safe outside perspective" which may be required. Nonetheless, as noted above, people often solve their problems by talking to friends, relatives, co-workers, religious leaders, or some other confidant in their lives, or by thinking and exploring themselves.

No matter how problems occur, then, clients resolve them by actively searching and exploring their life space, both in and outside of therapy. This self-healing process is one of exploring through a thinking-experiencing-behaving cycle (modified from Kolb's, 1984, view of experiential learning). These elements are interconnected in a systemic, dialogical, back and forth way. One can enter the cycle at any point. One may first think about one's problems, exploring mentally, and then formulate hypotheses to try out in behavior. Behaving leads to the provision of new experiences, which then feed back in a corrective way to alter conceptions of the problem and strategies.

Or one may enter the cycle experientially by focusing on one's inner experience and trying to articulate it in words, which then leads to thinking and shifts in perception (Watson & Rennie, 1994). These may then lead to behavioral experimentation, providing new experience that then feeds back into the cycle. Or, one may begin by altering behavior first. Strategic and solution-focused therapists, for instance (e.g., de Shazer, 1985) encourage clients to "do something different." Altering behavior brings new experience which may then lead to changes in behavior and new insights. This dialogical back and forth process can happen outside of therapy, inside therapy with a therapist, or in relation to self-help materials.

Change itself is most typically a small, step by step, back and forth effort of trying new things out, changing, trying new things out and so on. Rarely is a problem solved in one "gulp," but instead problem-solving is typically an ongoing process of successive approximations. In some cases, shifts in perspective can create sudden change, as with Corsini's client. However even then the individual must go through the process of making new decisions, setting new goals, developing new strategies, and then pursuing them.

We particularly want to highlight the importance of generative thinking to this self-healing process. Virtually no theory of psychotherapy grants clients the capacity for thinking. In psychoanalysis, insight comes from without, in the form of the analyst's interpretation. In cognitive therapy, thinking is described in dysfunctional terms. There is no model of generative, productive thinking in cognitive therapy. Humanistic therapy has traditionally focused on the process of attending to feelings and emotions and putting them into words, but not to the process of generative thinking. Yet clients and others in everyday life think about their problems just like therapists do: they figure out what is going on, consider alternatives, review experience, generate possible solutions, imagine alternative outcomes if one path is followed versus another, and so forth.

While there is no specific evidence to support our contention that client self-healing occurs through this thinking–experiencing–behaving cycle, there is evidence supporting the usefulness of the various components. For example in the Orlinsky et al. (1994) review, they conclude that "therapeutic realizations" are associated with positive therapeutic change. The category of therapeutic realizations is broad, but includes insight as one of its components.

Some research also supports the importance of an experiential component in therapy. One of us (Bohart, 1993) has argued that experiencing is the basis of change in psychotherapy. Experiencing can be either an internal variable (are clients experientially involved in the self-exploration process?), as in client-centered and psychodynamic therapy, or an external variable (does therapy provide the opportunity for new learning experiences, or for learning through experience?) as in interpersonal psychodynamic, cognitive, behavioral, strategic, or experiential therapies. Defined broadly like this, there is a good deal of evidence that being experientially involved in therapy, and learning through experience are associated with positive therapeutic change (Mathieu-Coughlin & Klein, 1984; Orlinsky et al., 1994). Studies by Martin (1994) and Bucci (1995), while not specifically on experiencing, have found that the degree to which clients connect verbal and nonverbal (experiential) aspects of processing is associated with change. Recently, Drozd and Goldfried (1996) found that psychodynamic-interpersonal therapists tend to focus on in-session corrective experiences (i.e., through the relationship and through experiential exercises), while cognitive–behavioral therapists tend to focus on between-session corrective experiences (i.e., through homework assignments).

Experiencing is important because real change appears to involve shifts in understanding at the bodily level as well as at the intellectual level. We refer to these, after Gendlin (1968), as bodily felt shifts in understanding. If there has been a commonality characterizing all approaches to therapy, it has been the idea that sheer abstract intellectual insight by itself is not therapeutic (Bohart, 1993; Todd & Bohart, 1994). Todd and Bohart have argued that it is precisely because of this that therapy exists—if intellectually knowing what to do or knowing what the causes of one's problems are led to change, most people would not need therapists. They would simply tell themselves what to do, and do it. Yet people come to therapy because this usually does not work (at least for the people who come to therapy).

In essence, there must be a *bodily* shift in "understanding" or in reacting, as well as an intellectual one. There are many paths to the "final common outcome" of a bodily felt shift in psychotherapy: extinction, behavioral practice and rehearsal, engaging in experiential search activities through homework assignments, paradoxical interventions, comparing one's actual experiences to one's dysfunctional cognitions, reviewing the connections between one's childhood experiences and one's present experience, articulating one's experience in words (Gendlin, 1996; Watson & Greenberg, 1996), and so on.

In brief, our model is that clients "make change" through the normal processes by which people make creative discoveries and changes in everyday life. They think about their problems, they explore and experiment, and through experiential feedback from their environment, they develop new perspectives and bodily felt shifts, which in turn lead to further exploration and experience, which further feeds back in a recursive loop. Therapists simply use client generativity and these naturally occurring change processes, the self-healing cycle of thinking–exploring–experiencing–behaving. Therapy refines these ordinary, everyday restorative procedures and provides them in a distilled, highly focused fashion. Therapy is a prosthetic provision of contexts, experiences, and events which prompt, support, or facilitate clients' self-healing.

Psychotherapy

At the level of specific techniques addressing specific outcomes, it does not appear that the dodo bird verdict holds. For instance, with experiential therapy, Greenberg (1984) has shown that the two-chair procedure leads to deeper levels of processing than do empathic reflections. Similarly, an evocative unfolding procedure leads to better resolution of problematic reactions than does traditional empathic reflection (Rice & Saperia, 1984). It is likely that these kinds of effects also occur with cognitive techniques, behavioral techniques and so on.

If this is so, why then at the macro level, does it not matter which particular approach to therapy is used? Our view is that although the specific effects of individual procedures really happen, the actual *therapy* is how the client takes these specific effects and uses them to make changes. Thus there are multiple possible paths to personal change. Challenging dysfunctional cognitions may have the specific effect of modifying dysfunctional cognitions better than, say, receiving a "dose" of empathic reflections. Empathic reflections in turn may lead to more awareness of feelings than say a dose of cognitive restructuring. All such specific effects may be demonstrable.

However, clients are using these specific effects in their own creative ways to resolve their own problems. Thus clients take their insights into cognitive distortions and actively use them to change their life; or take their greater awareness of feelings and change their life. We have already seen that humans are talented at making inferences from what they learn. Thus, their learning does not stop with what they learn from these particular techniques. Instead they actively draw their own conclusions and work them into their lives.

WHY DO CLIENTS COME TO THERAPY?

We have argued that curative processes are found in many individuals' natural environments. In everyday life, people manage to engage in these procedures and make change themselves (Prochaska et al., 1994). Why do they sometimes need to come to therapy? Our answer should be obvious: they come to therapy when they are unable to engage in these procedures to a sufficient extent to generate a restorative function in everyday life.

Why might this be so? First, individuals under stress often get trapped in ruminative thinking cycles which are unproductive in contrast to the generative thinking cycle we have postulated above (Pennebaker, 1995). Second, humans tend to use old knowledge to solve new problems (Ward et al., 1995). This may be counterproductive when creativity is needed. Yet under stress, this is precisely when individuals become more conservative in holding on to their old ways of doing things. Third, if problems are perceived as difficult, and as having resisted numerous attempts at resolution, people exhibit the dysfunctional coping of helpless individuals (Dweck & Leggett, 1988; Tallman, 1996) or individuals low in self-efficacy (Bandura, 1997). They persevere in their strategies even if they are not working, or try new solutions, but in a haphazard, random, or desperate fashion. They may defensively avoid the problem, give up, or blame themselves.

Fourth, all of these things will be exacerbated by a lack of resources in their environment (Hobfall, 1989). Individuals who have good support systems, for instance, are less likely to need therapy. Fifth, to break out of a ruminative cycle, it is helpful to gain some distance and perspective. People are not always able to do this in everyday life. At home or at work the problem stares them in the face. Their life consumes them and they simply do not have the mental or emotional time or "space" to truly stand back. Talking to friends, colleagues, lovers, or relatives might not help because they may themselves be too "close" to the problem. It may help to talk to someone completely outside of the loop.

Sixth, the client may have no one to really listen and "co-think" with them. Instead, the people around the client may be critical, jump to premature conclusions, or give simplistic advice. Finally, some individuals come to therapy because they lack a variety of basic skills and their natural environments have not been successful in providing learning experiences where they could have acquired them.

WHAT THERAPISTS PROVIDE

First, therapists provide an empathically supportive working space in which clients can engage in the generative thinking processes that have been inaccessible for the reasons discussed above. As Jenkins (1996) noted, therapy helps by getting the client's own dialectical thinking capabilities operating again. Therapists provide a safe interpersonal atmosphere where clients can relax, take a deep breath, and begin to look at life's problems from a new, fresh perspective. Therapists empathically listen, are nonjudgmental, and allow clients a place to tell their story. There is evidence to suggest that no matter what the therapeutic orientation, clients feel that this is the most basic and helpful thing therapists have to offer (Phillips, 1984).

The sense of safety may be heightened by therapists' abilities to exude confidence, both in themselves and in clients, thereby helping to overcome demoralization, and helping clients move from a helpless state of mind to a process-focused, mastery-oriented state of mind (Bohart & Tallman, 1999; Tallman, 1996). Basic processes of disclosing one's problems out loud to another allow clients to gain perspective on their problems, and to think them through (Clark, 1993), as well as to engage in the narrative, account-making processes which we have noted previously (Harvey et al., 1991; Pennebaker, 1997).

A second major factor, closely allied to providing a safe working space, is that therapists engage in a co-constructive dialogue with clients, a "meeting of minds," in which it could be said that "two heads are better than one." Clients get to externalize their thoughts, run them by another person, and thereby examine them from a distanced perspective. Therapists and clients can "think together," "explore together," and even "experience together," in ways that facilitate the client's generativity. In this context therapists may offer ideas, advice, interpretations, empathic reflections, ask questions, and so on.

A third thing therapists provide is their interpersonal interactivity. There is direct experiential learning that takes place in therapy through interaction with the therapist. Experiential therapists have traditionally emphasized the learning that occurs through direct experiential feedback. But recently, psychodynamic therapists have also legitimized the "corrective emotional experience" aspect of therapy, and still more recently radical behaviorists have written about the systematic use of the relationship as a curative factor (Kohlenberg & Tsai, 1987).

A fourth thing therapists provide are procedures which focus and distill naturally occurring opportunities for self-healing (Duncan, 1996). These include the whole armamentarium of therapist techniques. From our point of view these techniques do not "operate on" the client, but rather are tools which the client uses to explore, think, have new experiences, and generate self-change. They may also provide new experiences which are corrective in and of themselves, leading to new perceptual/experiential discoveries and shifts in perspective.

Finally, therapists can function as coaches and teachers to help the client acquire new skills. Even here clients only learn what they are actively involved in, actively immerse themselves in, and actively wish to learn.

IMPLICATIONS FOR THERAPY PRACTICE

There are important implications for practice from the idea that therapy is primarily a matter of client self-healing. Like many others (e.g., Duncan et al., 1997; Gold, 1994; Miller, Duncan, & Hubble, 1997), we believe therapists should be much more willing to listen to clients, respect their frame of reference, and genuinely collaborate with them. Collaboration means more than client participation and compliance. It means that therapy must be thought of as the meeting of two minds, each possessing its own expertise and competence, with goals and solutions co-created through mutual dialogue, instead of being chosen and applied to the client by the therapist.

The conclusions we have reached from our review of the empirical literature suggest that recent developments in psychotherapy are headed in the wrong direction. Much of therapy, especially under the influence of managed care, is increasingly adopting a medical model. In the medical model of therapy, the therapist is the expert who diagnoses the nature of the client's problem ("illness") and then "prescribes" the "treatment" for that problem. Client collaboration is limited to client participation and compliance within the expert therapist's agenda.

For instance, the "empirically validated treatments" movement (Task Force on the Promotion and Dissemination of Psychological Procedures, 1995) is based on the medical model of therapy. This document lists therapies which have presumably been "empirically validated" for the treatment of specific disorders. In keeping with the medical model and the assumption that it is the therapist's "treatment" which is responsible for the "cure," treatments must be manualized so they can be "applied to" clients in standardized forms. There is no room in such a model for genuine client choice and collaboration in defining goals of therapy and developing solutions.

The recent development of the "Template" by the American Psychological Association (Task Force On Psychological Intervention Guidelines, 1995) follows along these same lines. This document notes that under certain conditions client choice of treatment may be important, but it is clear that it is up to the expert therapist to decide when clients are allowed to choose. There is nothing in these models which suggests that clients can creatively generate their own unique problem solutions with the aid of the therapist, or that the therapist should truly respect or even access the client's frame of reference (other than to meet the demands of the treatment model). There is nothing genuinely *dialogic* about these models.

On the basis of the wide body of research we have cited, these models disrespect the nature of how humans change as well one of the most robust findings in psychotherapy—the dodo bird verdict. At the same time, many of the therapies on the list of empirically validated treatments include important client self-help aspects, and could be used in ways that are compatible with the idea that the client is the primary healing force in therapy.

We advocate a different direction based upon our interpretation of the data that places the client as the common denominator of change. We see a need to develop more genuinely collaborative models of therapy along the lines of active learning models in education and community psychology models (described below). There have been some movements in this direction. The work of Duncan et al. (1997) is a good example of what can be done when clients and their inherent capabilities are taken seriously. Client-centered therapy, of course, radically respects the generativity of the client, but in its traditional form may detract from the active collaborative potential of the therapist. Recent narrative and constructivist perspectives (Neimeyer & Mahoney, 1995; Rosen & Kuehlwein, 1996) also move in the direction of genuine collaboration.

An alternative to the medical model for doing therapy could be borrowed from the community psychology movement during its heyday in the 1970s. Instead of the community psychologist acting as the authoritative expert "dropping in" on the community, informing it of the diagnosis of its problems, and unilaterally providing the solution, the community psychologist instead acted as a resource to be used by the community. The solutions would be designed in collaboration and dialogue with the community. The community would ultimately be the expert on what would be good for it. The community psychologist was the servant of the community, not the outside expert who fixed the community's problems.

A concrete example of this community psychology model comes from a recent conference on gang problems attended by the second author in the Los Angeles area. He listened to many who worked with gangs, as well as gang members themselves, say that the best way to solve the gang problem would be to consult the gangs themselves, rather than to have outside "experts" design programs and "intervene." Solutions, they asserted, needed to come from the populace being affected: the gang members and the affected communities. Several gang members said that all the programs would not help if the outside agencies did not work collaboratively with the gangs, because that's where the power to change resided.

It is this philosophy which we believe the data support to be most relevant to successful therapy. Thus the idea of preset manualized interventions mechanistically targeted to specific diagnoses is wrong-headed because such a philosophy categorically discounts the dependence of outcome on the client's inherent resources, and his or her participation. If such simpleminded prescriptions are successful, it is only further evidence of the inherent resilience of clients and their abilities to find useful aspects of all approaches.

Finally, our view of the client as an active self-healer is compatible with the increasing emphasis on multicultural counseling as a "fourth force." Therapists need to be sensitive to the meanings of disorders and solutions in culture-specific terms. Solutions need to be collaboratively generated out of the cultural experiences and resources of the client. In many cases it may be meaningful to use "folk" methods (Comas-Diaz, 1992). This is highly compatible with our model in that the therapist helps the client in terms of the client's "language." It suggests that it is the mobilization of client resources which is therapeutic and not the application of a technique to a problem. Certainly this is incompatible with manualization. How does one manualize spontaneously deciding to use a folk method with a client because of how the interaction between therapist and client proceeds?

In sum, we believe that truly taking seriously the active, generative nature of how clients change in therapy would fundamentally restructure how we view the process of therapy. The therapy process would be seen as truly collaborative (not merely "collaborative" in the sense that the client complies with and participates in the therapist's treatment plan). Clients and therapists contribute equally to the final creative outcome, by both contributing to developing solutions in consultation with one another. Therapists as expert consultants would solicit clients' ideas and rely more heavily on client creativity. Clients would equally be expert consultants to the therapist, providing them with their observations on the domain of their expertise—what is working for them in their everyday lives, what is not, and how things might be modified. Finally, researchers would focus their study on clients rather than on therapists.

To conclude, the locus of change resides within clients. Therapists use their process expertise to support clients' natural healing tendencies.

Questions From the Editors

1. Aren't there some clients who are more actively involved in self-healing than others? Are there not some clients who cannot self-heal, especially severely disturbed clients, or who won't self-heal because they resist therapy?

Our premise is not that all clients can entirely self-heal all on their own. Rather, it is that clients have a built in set of self-healing processes that are primarily responsible for change, even if a therapist is needed to assist in their operation. Clients can overcome many problems on their own, but there are some individuals unable to overcome them on their own without assistance. It is then that they come to therapy.

Some individuals have problem behaviors which are very difficult to surmount. They may need considerable assistance. However, they, too, have generative healing processes, and therapists will do well to facilitate those, rather than see themselves as the "golden presence" (G. Goodman, personal communication, February, 1996) who "operates on" clients from outside with potent interventions. Too many therapists effectively disempower clients with severe problems by viewing them as incapable of solving their problems, due to their hypothesized ego or personality defects. Even with clients with severe problems, therapists should still rely on the client's frame of reference, mobilize clients' own thinking–exploring–experiencing process, help clients reinstigate a dialectical thinking process, and support and facilitate client self-healing.

Those who resist are a separate issue. Whether they are child abusers referred by the court or teenagers dragged in by their parents, some clients are typically thought of as being *treatment resistant*. This is an unfortunate metaphor that connotes individuals who have developed immunity to a medication, an unfortunate consequence of a belief in the medical model. The medical model also leads judges to believe that people can be forced to undergo counseling, as if it were a drug that was going to "fix" whatever is wrong, whether they like it or not. Resistance naturally follows and is then itself seen as a manifestation of the client's problem.

The teenager who has abused drugs is there because the parents have made her come. The adult who has abused someone is there because the court has made him come. If therapy worked some kind of medicinal magic on people to alter them against their will, like antipsychotic medication, then one might be able to use one's power to "treat" resistant clients. However, as we have seen, therapy is a set of processes that simply build on and enhance clients' own naturally occurring self-righting processes. For therapy to work, therapists need to be able to join with these self-righting processes. This means therapists must be able to dialogue with clients called resistant, and find some way, over time, of winning their trust. Clients must come to *want* to cooperate with therapists.

So how can therapists get clients to be open to modifying their frame of reference? It will happen more spontaneously and naturally if they support the clients' bringing his or her frame of reference *into dialogue* with the therapist. As people dialogue they are changed. As people begin to bring up their most intimate concerns, they move. As people begin to feel understood, they are mobilized. But we are not "treating" them, we are listening to them, taking them seriously, and engaging in dialogue with them.

2. How do you account for the benign neglect of the client's contributions to change in the formation of psychotherapeutic models of change?

We think "benign neglect" is a good term. Certainly most therapists from Freud on have recognized that clients make a very active contribution to the change process. Yet that recognition has not made it into their formal theories of personality, pathology, or change. When cases are discussed at conferences all one hears about are the expert therapists' "brilliant" moves, and virtually nothing about how clients self-heal. We believe there are many different reasons for this, from the natural tendency to focus on one's own contributions in a situation, to the desire to protect one's special theories and professional status, to a desire to be "like doctors," to economic pressures that are increasingly forcing those in our profession to adopt a medical model view of therapy. To acknowledge that we really have to rely on clients for the thrust in therapy toward healing would be to acknowledge that we aren't "doctors" and to give up considerable power and control. This does not mean we do not provide an important and useful service (we do), but it is not fundamentally the same kind of activity that a "doctor" provides.

3. What are the implications of your model for training?

We believe the principles for training therapists given below follow from our view that the client's self-healing capacity is the primary force which makes therapy work.

- Pave the way for a productive client–therapist relationship with the assumption that the client is reasonable person, but is currently stuck in a difficult situation.
- Deliberately adopt a collaboration metaphor for therapy. It will be more productive than the combat metaphor which sometimes is widely used.
- Teach therapists the process of therapy very early in training. Teach them first to be effective, supportive listeners, instead of teaching diagnosis first. Diagnosis encourages an external perspective on the client, as well as on seeing the client as broken or damaged. Delay the introduction to pathology and diagnosis until the therapist gains some skills relating to clients. Include instruction in the art of dialogue or studies in communication.
- Have beginning therapists practice their listening skills in dyads or triads, acting sometimes as the therapist, sometimes as the

client, and sometimes as the observer. As techniques for exploring are introduced, the trainee learns to evaluate each from the point of view of both the therapist and the client. Firsthand experience is a very effective teaching tool and helps the therapist maintain multiple perspectives.

- Encourage beginning therapists to take seriously the perspective of the problem that the client offers. Encourage them to let clients explain their point of view. There is no one "correct" point of view.

- Encourage them to expect clients will get better. Trainees can convince themselves of this by making notes after each session of the new skills, ideas, goals, and insights clients mention each week.

- The goal of therapy is to support the clients' efforts so they can leave therapy and be effective problem solvers on their own. Allow them to originate some of the solutions.

- New therapists should learn to be comfortable with silence. Silence is very important when the client is thinking effectively, imagining new possibilities, and considering changes.

References

Angus, L. E. (1992). Metaphor and the communication interaction in psychotherapy: A multimethodological approach. In S. G. Toukmanian & D. L. Rennie (Eds.), *Psychotherapy process research: Paradigmatic and narrative approaches* (pp. 187–210). Newbury Park, CA: Sage.

Arkowitz, H. (1992). Integrative theories of therapy. In D. K. Freedheim (Ed.), *History of psychotherapy: A century of change* (pp. 261–303). Washington, DC: American Psychological Association.

Arkowitz, H. (1997, April). *Clients as cognitive therapists for their own depression.* Paper presented as part of the symposium on "The Client's Active Role in Change: Implications for Integration" at the Convention of the Society for the Exploration of Psychotherapy Integration, Toronto, Canada.

Bachelor, A. (1991). Comparison and relationship to outcome of diverse dimensions of the helping alliance as seen by client and therapist. *Psychotherapy, 28,* 534–549.

Bandura, A. (1997). *Self-efficacy.* New York: W. H. Freeman.

Barlow, D. H. (1994). Psychological interventions in the era of managed competition. *Clinical Psychology: Science and Practice, 1,* 109–122.

Barsalou, L. W. (1985). Ideals, central tendency, and frequency of instantiation as determinants of graded structure in categories. *Journal of Experimental Psychology: Learning, Memory, and Cognition, 11,* 629–654.

Bergin, A. E., & Garfield, S. L. (l994). Overview, trends, and future issues. In A. E. Bergin & S. L. Garfield (Eds.), *Handbook of psychotherapy and behavior change* (4th ed., pp. 821–830). New York: Wiley.

Bergin, A. E., & Lambert, M. J. (1978). The evaluation of therapeutic outcomes. In S. L. Garfield & A. E. Bergin (Eds.), *Handbook of psychotherapy and behavior change* (2nd ed., pp. 139–190). New York: Wiley.

Bickman, L., & Salzer, M. S. (1996, August). Dose–response, disciplines, and self help: Policy implications of *Consumer Reports* findings. Paper presented as part of the symposium on *"Consumer Reports* Mental Health Survey Results—Practice and Policy Implications," at the 104th Annual Convention of the American Psychological Association, Toronto, Ontario, Canada.

Bohart, A. (1993). Experiencing: The basis of psychotherapy. *Journal of Psychotherapy Integration, 3,* 51–67.

Bohart, A., & Boyd, G. (1997, December). *Clients' construction of the therapy process: A qualitative analysis.* Paper presented at the meeting of the North American Association of the Society for Psychotherapy Research, Tucson, Arizona.

Bohart, A., & Greenberg, L. (1997). *Empathy reconsidered: New directions in psychotherapy.* Washington, DC: American Psychological Association.

Bohart, A., & Tallman, K. (1996). The active client: Therapy as self-help. *Journal of Humanistic Psychology, 36,* 7–30.

Bohart, A., & Tallman, K. (1999). *How clients make therapy work: The process of active self-healing.* Washington, DC: American Psychological Association.

Bucci, W. (1995). The power of the narrative: A multiple code account. In J. W. Pennebaker (Ed.), *Emotion, disclosure, and health* (pp. 93–124). Washington, DC: American Psychological Association.

Burns, D. D., & Nolen–Hoeksema, S. (1991). Coping styles, homework compliance, and the effectiveness of cognitive behavioral therapy. *Journal of Consulting and Clinical Psychology, 59,* 305–311.

Burton, M. V., Parker, R. W., & Wollner, J. M. (1991). The psychotherapeutic power of a "chat": A verbal response modes study of a placebo attention control with breast cancer patients. *Psychotherapy Research, 1,* 39–61.

Calahan, D. (1987). *Understanding America's drinking problem.* San Francisco: Jossey-Bass.

Cantor, N., & Zirkel, S. (1990). Personality, cognition, and purposive behavior. In L. Pervin (Ed.), *Handbook of personality* (pp. 135–164). New York: Guilford Press.

Castonguay, L. (1993). *Understanding psychotherapy for depression: The role of techniques, relationship, and their interaction.* Unpublished manuscript, Stanford University.

Christensen, A. (1992, April). *The challenge of nonprofessional therapies.* Paper presented at the symposium on "Extending the Integrative Boundaries: What Self-Change Processes Can Teach Us" at the convention of the Society for the Exploration of Psychotherapy Integration, San Diego, CA.

Christensen, A., & Jacobson, N. S. (1994). Who (or what) can do psychotherapy: The status and challenge of nonprofessional therapies. *Psychological Science, 5,* 8–14.

Clark, L. F. (1993). Stress and the cognitive–conversational benefits of social interaction. *Journal of Social and Clinical Psychology, 12,* 25–55.

Comas-Diaz, L. (1992). The future of psychotherapy with ethnic minorities. *Psychotherapy, 29,* 88–94.

Cooper, J. (1995). Cooperative learning "versus" collaborative learning: Should we care? *Cooperative Learning and College Teaching, 6*(1), 1–2.

Cooper, J. (1996). Research in cooperative learning in the mid-1990s: What the experts say. *Cooperative Learning and College Teaching, 6*(2), 2–3.

Corsini, R. J. (1989). Introduction. In R. J. Corsini & D. Wedding (Eds.), *Current psychotherapies* (4th ed., pp. 1–18). Itasca, IL: F. E. Peacock.

Cross, D. G., Sheehan, P. W., & Kahn, J. A. (1980). Alternative advice and counseling psychotherapy. *Journal of Consulting and Clinical Psychology, 48,* 615–625.

De Shazer, S. (1985). *Keys to solution in brief therapy.* New York: Norton.

Drozd, J. F., & Goldfried, M. R. (1996). A critical evaluation of the state-of-the-art in psychotherapy outcome research. *Psychotherapy, 33,* 171–180.

Duncan, B. L. (1996, August). *The client is the only treatment of choice.* Paper presented as part of the symposium on "How Clients Create Change in Psychotherapy—Implications for Understanding," presented at the 104th Annual Convention of the American Psychological Association, Toronto, Ontario, Canada.

Duncan, B. L., Hubble, M. A., & Miller, S. D. (1997). *Psychotherapy with impossible cases: Efficient treatment of therapy veterans.* New York: Norton.

Dweck, C. S., & Leggett, E. L. (1988). A social–cognitive approach to motivation and personality. *Psychological Review, 95,* 256–273.

Efran, J. S., & Blumberg, M. J. (1994). Emotion and family living: The perspective of structure determinism. In S. M. Johnson & L. S. Greenberg (Eds.), *The heart of the matter* (pp. 172–206). New York: Brunner/Mazel.

Elkin, I. (1994). The NIMH treatment of depression collaborative research program: Where we began and where we are. In A. E. Bergin & S. L. Garfield (Eds.), *Handbook of psychotherapy and behavior change* (4th ed., pp. 114–142). New York: Wiley.

Elliott, R. (1984). A discovery-oriented approach to significant change events in psychotherapy: Interpersonal process recall and comprehensive process analysis. In L. S. Greenberg & L. N. Rice (Eds.), *Patterns of change* (pp. 249–286). New York: Guilford Press.

Elliott, R. (1986). Interpersonal process recall as a psychotherapy process research technique. In L. S. Greenberg & W. Pinsof (Eds.), *The psychotherapeutic process* (pp. 503–528). New York: Guilford Press.

Elliott, R. (1996). Are client-centered/experiential therapies effective? A meta-analysis of outcome research. In U. Esser, H. Pbast, G-W. Speierer (Eds.), *The power of the person-centered approach: New challenges–perspectives–answers* (pp. 125–138). Koln, Germany: GwG Verlag.

Elliott, R., & James, E. (1989). Varieties of client experience in psychotherapy: An analysis of the literature. *Clinical Psychology Review, 9,* 443–467.

Epstein, R. (1991). Skinner, creativity, and the problem of spontaneous behavior. *Psychological Science, 2,* 362–370.

Fisher, J. (1995). Uniformity myths in eclectic and integrative psychotherapy. *Journal of Psychotherapy Integration, 5,* 41–56.

Frank, J. D. (1974). Psychotherapy: The restoration of morale. *American Journal of Psychiatry, 131,* 271–274.

Garfield, S. L. (1994). Research on client variables in psychotherapy. In A. E. Bergin & S. L. Garfield (Eds.), *Handbook of psychotherapy and behavior change* (4th ed., pp. 190–228). New York: Wiley.

Gendlin, E. T. (1968). The experiential response. In E. Hammer (Ed.), *Use of interpretation in treatment* (pp. 208–227). New York: Grune & Stratton.

Gendlin, E. T. (1996). *Focusing-oriented psychotherapy.* New York: Guilford Press.

Gold, J. R. (1980). *A retrospective study of the behavior therapy experience.* Unpublished doctoral dissertation, Adelphi University.

Gold, J. R. (1994). When the patient does the integrating: Lessons for theory and practice. *Journal of Psychotherapy Integration, 4,* 133–158.

Goldfried, M. R., & Padawer, W. (1982). Current status and future directions in psychotherapy. In M. R. Goldfried (Ed.), *Converging themes in psychotherapy* (pp. 3–50). New York: Springer.

Gould, R. A., & Clum, G. A. (1993). A meta-analysis of self-help treatment approaches. *Clinical Psychology Review, 13,* 169–186.

Grawe, K. (1997). Research-informed psychotherapy. *Psychotherapy Research, 7,* 1–20.

Grawe, K., Caspar, F., & Ambuhl, H. (1990). The Bernese Comparative Psychotherapy Study. *Zeitschrift fur Klinische Psychologie, 19,* 287–376.

Greenberg, L. S. (1984). A task analysis of intrapersonal conflict resolution. In L. N. Rice & L. S. Greenberg (Eds.), *Patterns of change* (pp. 67–123). New York: Guilford Press.

Greenberg, L. S., Rice, L. N., & Elliott, R. (1993). *Facilitating emotional change: The moment-by-moment process.* New York: Guilford Press.

Greenberg, L. S., & Watson, J. (1998). Experiential therapy of depression: Differential effects of client-centered relationship conditions and process experiential interventions. *Psychotherapy Research, 8,* 210–224.

Grencavage, L. M., & Norcross, J. C. (1990). Where are the commonalities among the therapeutic common factors? *Professional Psychology: Research and Practice, 21,* 372–378.

Gurin, G., Veroff, J., & Feld, S. (1960). *Americans view their mental health.* New York: Basic Books.

Harvey, J. H., Orbuch, T. L., Chwalisz, K. D., & Garwood, G. (1991). Coping with sexual assault: The roles of account-making and confiding. *Journal of Traumatic Stress, 4,* 515–531.

Hayes, S. C., & Gifford, E. V. (1997). The trouble with language: Experiential avoidance, rules, and the nature of verbal events. *Psychological Science, 8,* 170–173.

Hobfall, S. E. (1989). Conservation of resources: A new attempt at conceptualizing stress. *American Psychologist, 44,* 513–524.

Horvath, A. O. (1995). The therapeutic relationship: From transference to alliance. *In Session, 1,* 7–17.

Jacobs, M. J. (Chair). (1995). *Computer psychotherapy: The direction of the future?* Symposium presented at the Western Psychological Association Convention, Los Angeles.

Jacobson, N. (1995). The overselling of therapy. *Family Therapy Networker, 19,* 40–51.

Jenkins, A. H. (1996, August). Enhancing the patient's dialectical abilities in psychotherapy. Paper presented at the 104th Annual symposium on "How Clients Create Change in Psychotherapy: Implications for Understanding Change", Convention of the American Psychological Association, Toronto, Ontario, Canada.

Jordan, J. V. (1997). Relational development through mutual empathy. In A. Bohart & L. S. Greenberg (Eds.), *Empathy reconsidered: New directions in psychotherapy* (pp. 343–352). Washington, DC: American Psychological Association.

Kleinman, A. (1988). *Rethinking psychiatry: From cultural category to personal experience.* New York: Free Press.

Kohlenberg, R. J., & Tsai, M. (1987). Functional analytic psychotherapy. In N. Jacobson (Ed.), *Psychotherapists in clinical practice: Cognitive and behavioral perspectives* (pp. 388–443). New York: Guilford Press.

Kolb, D. A. (1984). *Experiential learning.* Englewood Cliffs, NJ: Prentice-Hall.

Klopfer, B. (1957). Psychological variables in human cancer. *Journal of Projective Techniques, 21,* 331.

Kroll, J. (1988). *The challenge of the borderline patient.* New York: Norton.

Krupnick, J. L., Sotsky, S. M., Simmens, S., Moyher, J., Elkin, I., Watkins, J., & Pilkonis, P. A. (1996). The role of the therapeutic alliance in psychotherapy and pharmacotherapy outcome: Findings in the National Institute of Mental Health Treatment of Depression Collaborative Research Project. *Journal of Consulting and Clinical Psychology, 64,* 532–539.

Lambert, M. (1992). Psychotherapy outcome research. In J. C. Norcross & M. R. Goldfried (Eds.), *Handbook of psychotherapy integration* (pp. 94–129). New York: Basic Books.

Lambert, M. J., & Bergin, A. E. (1994). The effectiveness of psychotherapy. In A. E. Bergin & S. L. Garfield (Eds.), *Handbook of psychotherapy and behavior change* (4th ed., pp. 143–189). New York: Wiley.

Lambert, M. J., Shapiro, D. A., & Bergin, A. E. (1986). The effectiveness of psychotherapy. In S. L. Garfield & A. E. Bergin (Eds.), *Handbook of psychotherapy and behavior change* (3rd ed., pp. 157–212). New York: Wiley.

Lawson, D. (1994). Identifying pretreatment change. *Journal of Counseling and Development, 72,* 244–248.

Llewelyn, S. P., Elliott, R., Shapiro, D. A., & Hardy, G. (1988). Client perceptions of significant events in prescriptive and exploratory periods of individual therapy. *British Journal of Clinical Psychology, 27,* 105–114.

Luborsky, L., McClellan, A. T., Woody, G. E., O'Brien, C. P., & Auerbach, A. (1985). Therapist success and its determinants. *Archives of General Psychiatry, 42,* 602–611.

Luborsky, L., Singer, B., & Luborsky, L. (1975). Comparative studies of psychotherapies: Is it true that "everyone has won and all must have prizes"? *Archives of General Psychiatry, 32,* 995–1008.

Martin, J. (1994). *The construction and understanding of psychotherapeutic change.* New York: Teachers College Press.

Masten, A. S., Best, K. M., & Garmazy, N. (1990). Resilience and development: Contributions from the study of children who overcome adversity. *Development and Psychopathology, 2,* 425–444.

Mathieu-Coughlan, P., & Klein, M. H. (1984). Experiential psychotherapy: Key events in client–therapist interaction. In L. N. Rice & L. S. Greenberg (Eds.), *Patterns of change* (pp. 213–248). New York: Guilford.

Miller, S. D., Duncan, B. L., & Hubble, M. A. (1997). *Escape from Babel: Toward a unifying language for psychotherapy practice.* New York: Norton.

Miller, W. R., Taylor, C. A., & West, J. C. (1980). Focused versus broad-specturm behavior therapy for problem drinkers. *Journal of Consulting and Clinical Psychology, 48,* 590–601.

Neimeyer, R. A., & Mahoney, M. J. (Eds.). (1995). *Constructivism in psychotherapy.* Washington, DC: American Psychological Association.

Newfield, N. A., Kuehl, B. P., Joanning, H. P., & Quinn, W. H. (1991). We can tell you about "psychos" and "shrinks": An ethnography of the family therapy of adolescent drug abuse. In T. C. Todd & M. N. Selekman (Eds.), *Family therapy approaches with adolescent substance abusers* (pp. 277–310). Boston: Allyn & Bacon.

Norcross, J. C. (1986). Eclectic psychotherapy: An introduction and overview. In J. C. Norcross (Ed.), *Handbook of eclectic psychotherapy* (pp. 3–24). New York: Brunner/Mazel.

Norcross, J. C., & Aboyoun, D. C. (1994). Self-change experiences of psychotherapists. In T. M. Brinthaupt & R. P. Lipka (Eds.), *Changing the self* (pp. 253–278). Albany: State University of New York Press.

Orlinsky, D. E., Grawe, K., & Parks, B. K. (1994). Process and outcome in psychotherapy—Noch einmal. In A. E. Bergin & S. L. Garfield (Eds.), *Handbook of psychotherapy and behavior change* (4th ed., pp. 270–378). New York: Wiley.

Orlinsky, D. E., & Howard, K. I. (1980). Gender and psychotherapeutic outcome. In A. M. Brodsky & R. T. Hare-Mustin (Eds.), *Women and psychotherapy* (pp. 3–34). New York: Guilford Press.

Pennebaker, J. W. (1990). *Opening up: The healing power of confiding in others.* New York: Morrow.

Pennebaker, J. W. (1995). Emotion, disclosure, and health: An overview. In J. W. Pennebaker (Ed.), *Emotion, disclosure, and health* (pp. 3–10). Washington, DC: American Psychological Association.

Pennebaker, J. W. (1997). Writing about emotional experiences as a therapeutic process. *Psychological Science, 8,* 162–166.

Perotti, L. P., & Hopewell, C. A. (1980. Expectancy effects in psychotherapy and systematic desensitization: A review. *JSAS: Catalog of Selected Documents in Psychology, 10*(Ms. No. 2052).

Phillips, J. R. (1984). Influences on personal growth as viewed by former psychotherapy patients. *Dissertation Abstracts International, 44,* 441A.

Prochaska, J. O., DiClemente, C. C., & Norcross, J. C. (1992). In search of how people change: Applications to addictive behaviors. *American Psychologist, 47,* 1102–1114.

Prochaska, J. O., Norcross, J. C., & DiClemente, C. C. (1994). *Changing for good.* New York: Morrow.

Project MATCH Research Group. (1997). Matching alcoholism treatments to client heterogeneity: Project MATCH posttreatment drinking outcomes. *Journal of Studies on Alchohol, 58,* 7–29.

Rennie, D. L. (1990). Toward a representation of the client's experience of the psychotherapy hour. In G. Lietaer, J. Rombauts, & R. Van Balen (Eds.), *Client-centered and experiential therapy in the nineties* (pp. 155–172).

Rennie, D. L. (1994). Storytelling in psychotherapy: The client's subjective experience. *Psychotherapy, 31,* 234–243.

Rennie, D. L. (1997, April). *Aspects of the client's control of the therapeutic process.* Paper presented as part of the symposium on "The Client's Active Role in Change: Implications for Integration," at the convention of the Society for the Exploration of Psychotherapy Integration, Toronto, Ontario, Canada.

Rice, L. N., & Saperia, E. P. (1984). Task analysis and the resolution of problematic reactions. In L. N. Rice & L. S. Greenberg (Eds.), *Patterns of change* (pp. 29–66). New York: Guilford Press.

Robbins, L. (1979). Addict careers. In R. Dupont, A. Goldstein, & J. O'Donnell (Eds.), *Handbook on drug abuse.* Rockville, Md: National Institute on Drug Abuse.

Robinson, L. A., Berman, J. S., & Neimeyer, R. A. (1990). Psychotherapy for treatment of depression: A comprehensive review of controlled outcome research. *Psychological Bulletin, 108,* 30–49.

Rosen, H., & Kuehlwein, K. (Eds.). (1996). *Constructing realities.* San Francisco: Jossey-Bass.

Rosenbaum, R. (1994). Single-session therapies: Intrinsic integration? *Journal of Psychotherapy Integration, 4,* 229–252.

Ryan, V. L., & Gizynski, M. N. (1971). Behavior therapy in retrospect: Patients' feelings about their behavior therapies. *Journal of Consulting and Clinical Psychology, 37,* 1–9.

Rychlak, J. F. (1994). *Logical learning theory: A human teleology and its empirical support.* Lincoln: University of Nebraska Press.

Schwitzgabel, R. (1961). *Streetcorner research: An experimental approach to the juvenile delinquent.* Cambridge, MA: Harvard University Press.

Scogin, F., Bynum, J., Stephens, G., & Calhoon, S. (1990). Efficacy of self-administered treatment programs: Meta-analytic review. *Professional Psychology: Research and Practice, 21,* 42–47.

Segal, D. L., & Murray, E. J. (1994). Emotional processing in cognitive therapy and vocal expression of feeling. *Journal of Social and Clinical Psychology, 13,* 189–206.

Seligman, M. E. P. (1995). The effectiveness of psychotherapy: The *Consumer Reports* Survey. *American Psychologist, 50,* 965–974.

Selmi, P. M., Klein, M. H., Greist, J. H., Sorrell, S. P., & Erdman, H. P. (1990). Computer-administered cognitive–behavioral therapy for depression. *American Journal of Psychiatry, 147,* 51–56.

Sloane, R. B., Staples, F. R., Cristol, A. H., Yorkston, N. J., & Whipple, K. (1975). *Psychotherapy versus behavior therapy.* Cambridge, MA: Harvard University Press.

Smith, M. L., Glass, G. V., & Miller, T. I. (1980). *The benefits of psychotherapy.* Baltimore: Johns Hopkins University Press.

Stein, D. M., & Lambert, M. J. (1995). Graduate training in psychotherapy: Are therapy outcomes enhanced? *Journal of Consulting and Clinical Psychology, 63,* 182–196.

Stiles, W. B. (1995). Disclosure as a speech act: Is it psychotherapeutic to disclose? In J. W. Pennebaker (Ed.), *Emotion, disclosure, and health* (pp. 71–92). Washington, DC: American Psychological Association.

Strupp, H. H., & Hadley, S. W. (1979). Specific versus nonspecific factors in psychotherapy: A controlled study of outcome. *Archives of General Psychiatry, 36,* 1125–1136.

Stubbs, J. P., & Bozarth, J. D. (1994). The dodo bird revisited: A qualitative study of psychotherapy efficacy research. *Applied & Preventive Psychology, 3,* 109–120.

Svartberg, M., & Stiles, T. C. (1991). Comparative effects of short-term psychodynamic psychotherapy: A meta-analysis. *Journal of Consulting and Clinical Psychology, 59,* 704–714

Svartberg, M., & Stiles, T. C. (1994). Therapeutic alliance, therapeutic competence, and client change in short-term anxiety-provoking psychotherapy. *Psychotherapy Research, 4,* 20–33.

Tallman, K. (1996). *The state of mind theory: Goal orientation concepts applied to clinical psychology.* Unpublished master's thesis, California State University, Dominguez Hills.

Tallman, K., Robinson, E., Kay, D., Harvey, S., & Bohart, A. (1994, August). *Experiential and non-experiential Rogerian therapy: An analogue study.* Paper presented at the 102nd Annual Convention of the American Psychological Association Convention, Los Angeles.

Task Force on Promotion and Dissemination of Psychological Procedures, Division of Clinical Psychology of the American Psychological Association. (1995). Training and dissemination of empirically-validated psychological treatments: Report and recommendations. *The Clinical Psychologist, 48,* 3–23.

Task Force on Psychological Intervention Guidelines. (1995). *Template for developing guidelines: Interventions for mental disorders and psychosocial aspects of physical disorders.* Washington, DC: American Psychological Association.

Tedeschi, J. T., & Felson, R. B. (1994). *Violence, aggression, and coercive actions.* Washington, DC: American Psychological Association.

Todd, J., & Bohart, A. (1994). *Foundations of clinical and counseling psychology* (2nd ed.). New York: HarperCollins.

Wampold, B. E. (1997). Methodological problems in identifying efficacious psychotherapies. *Psychotherapy Research, 7,* 21–44.

Wampold, B. E., Mondin, G. W., Moody, M., Stich, F., Benson, K., & Ahn, H. (1997). A meta-analysis of outcome studies comparing bona fide psychotherapies: Empirically, "All Must Have Prizes." *Psychological Bulletin, 122,* 203–215.

Ward, T. B., Finke, R. A., & Smith, S. M. (1995). *Creativity and the mind.* New York: Plenum Press.

Watson, J. C., & Greenberg, L. S. (1996). Emotion and cognition in experiential therapy: A dialectical constructivist perspective. In H. Rosen & K. Kuehlwein (Eds.), *Constructing realities* (pp. 253–276). San Francisco: Jossey-Bass.

Watson, J. C., & Rennie, D. L. (1994). Qualitative analysis of clients' subjective experience of significant moments during the exploration of problematic reactions. *Journal of Counseling Psychology, 41,* 500–509.

Weil, A. (1995). *Health and healing.* New York: Houghton Mifflin.

Weiner-Davis, M., de Shazer, S., & Gingerich, W. (1987). Building on pretreatment change to construct the therapeutic solution: An exploratory study. *Journal of Marital and Family Therapy, 13,* 359–364.

Zilbergeld, B., & Lazarus, A. A. (1987). *Mind power.* New York: Ballantine.

Alexandra Bachelor and Adam Horvath

The Therapeutic Relationship | 5

C linicians and researchers alike have acknowledged the central role of the therapist–client relationship in the process of psychotherapy and client change (e.g., Gelso & Carter, 1985; Greenberg & Pinsoff, 1986; Rogers, 1957). The quality of the therapeutic relationship has been shown to be a significant determinant of beneficial outcome across diverse therapy approaches, and it is seen by many to represent a common factor accounting for therapeutic success (e.g., Beutler, Machado, & Allstetter Neufeldt, 1994; Lambert & Bergin, 1994). How has the therapeutic relationship been understood? What are its essential ingredients? What are the characteristics, or personal qualities, of the therapist and of the client that play a crucial role in forging a productive therapeutic relationship? Are there characteristics of the therapy partners that may hinder the development and maintenance of a quality therapy relationship?

In this chapter, we address these questions from the theoretical, empirical, and clinical perspectives. The therapeutic relationship has long been a topic of concern to clinical writers, and our presentation begins with a brief historical account of theories of the relationship and its effective ingredients. We present current research that clarifies what we know about the development, enhancement, and management of the therapeutic relationship, and we identify practical implications of these findings. Finally, we conclude with a summary that highlights the more important features of the therapeutic relationship gleaned from our literature review.

Historical Concepts of the Relationship in Therapy

Freud was one of the first clinical writers to comment explicitly on the importance and impact of the relation between therapist and client (Freud, 1912/1958, 1913/1966). He identified three aspects of the therapeutic relationship: (a) transference, that is, the client's unconscious identification of the therapist with significant figures from the past; (b) countertransference, the therapist's unconscious linking of the client with significant figures or unresolved conflicts from his or her past; and (c) the client's friendly and positive linking of the therapist with benevolent and kind personas from the past (Freud, 1913/1966). This latter aspect, subsequently named the *alliance*, has been the focus of development and elaboration by a number of psychodynamic theorists (e.g., Greenson, 1965; Zetzel, 1956).[1]

The psychodynamic conceptualization of the therapeutic relationship was dominant until a significantly different point of view was introduced by Carl Rogers (Rogers, 1951). He construed the ideal therapeutic relation as more akin to an existential encounter than as a meeting between an expert (therapist) and acolyte (client), and he identified the therapist qualities that would make such a healing relationship possible (i.e., empathy, genuineness, unconditional positive regard). Rogers claimed that a relationship with a person who was able to offer these facilitative conditions was both a necessary and sufficient cause for activating the innate healing and growth potential native to every person.

Other psychologists (e.g., Heppner, Rosenberg, & Hedgespeth, 1992; LaCrosse, 1980; Strong, 1968) noted that Rogers' model dealt exclusively with the therapist's contribution to the relationship; they challenged this focus by developing a theory of the therapeutic relationship that emphasized the client's attributions about the therapist as central to the success of therapy, thus positioning the therapeutic relationship in the framework of social influences. In particular, these writers emphasized clients' beliefs about therapists' perceived expertness, trustworthiness, and attractiveness. The theoretical assumption put forward was, in its most general form, that the degree to which clients believed that therapists had these socially valued qualities, they had "power to influence" the client's thinking, feeling and behavior, and thus to promote therapeutic change.

---

[1]The history and evolution of the concept of the alliance within the psychodynamic framework form a rich and complex tapestry, the review of which is beyond the scope of this chapter, except as they relate to the development of some of the generic concepts about therapeutic relations.

In contrast to the models that emphasized the therapeutic value of the client–therapist relationship, early, classical behaviorists (e.g., Skinner, 1985) challenged the notion that the interpersonal aspects of therapy played a significant role in behavior change. Skinner, who emphasized the relation between the person's behavior and its environmental consequences, viewed successful therapy as a learning process in which the quality of the "teacher or trainer's" interventions (techniques), rather than the relationship between the participants, was the significant factor. The debate between the behavioral and nonbehavioral perspectives on all aspects of therapy came to a focus in the early 1950s. Hans Eysenck published an article comparing the efficacy of behavioral and nonbehavioral therapies, in effect issuing a strong empirical challenge questioning the value of talk (i.e., nonbehavioral) therapies (Eysenck, 1952). Eysenck in particular, and behavior therapists in general, were also highly critical of the quality of therapy research generated outside the behavioral framework. They argued that if psychotherapy was to earn the confidence of the public and respect of the scientific community, it must be able to demonstrate its efficacy using an empirically sound methodology similar to other social sciences.

In retrospect, it appears that these criticisms, as well as the claims for the superior efficacy of behavior therapy, were in large part responsible for a new chapter in psychotherapy research. Investigators on both sides of the Atlantic made a major effort to evaluate the impact of different forms of treatment, using better research designs and evaluating the data with increased statistical sophistication. By the late 1970s, it was possible to summarize the results of hundreds of these studies across a variety of treatment modalities and patient problems (Luborsky, Singer, & Luborsky, 1975; Smith & Glass, 1977). One of the major findings of these research syntheses was the conclusion that, although most therapies were beneficial, there appeared to be no obvious differences, in terms of outcome, among treatments based on broadly diverse theories. This observation led to the logical hypothesis that certain aspects of treatment that were common to all these different therapies might be responsible for a significant portion of the beneficial results of therapy.

In the wake of the rekindled interest in these common or generic variables, there was also a resurgence of interest in the concept of the therapeutic relationship. As a new body of empirical research on the process of therapy began to appear (e.g., Orlinsky & Howard, 1975), a number of important questions about the therapeutic relationship emerged: What proportion of the beneficial results of psychotherapy might be due to the quality of the relationship? What aspects of the relation between client and therapist are most linked to outcome? These questions highlighted the need for a broadly based, generic formulation of the active ingredients of the therapeutic relationship (Bordin, 1975).

Much of the interest, both theoretical and empirical, at this stage shifted to the concept of the alliance. In contrast with both the client-centered focus on the therapist's qualities (Rogers, Gendlin, Kiesler, & Truax, 1967) and social influence theorists' (e.g., Strong, 1968) emphasis on the client as the arbitrator of the qualities of the therapeutic relationship, the new formulation of the alliance concept focused on the collaborative and interactive elements in the relationship. Researchers such as Luborsky (1976) and especially Bordin (1975, 1979, 1980, 1989, 1994), argued that the alliance, viewed as a positive, reality-based component of the therapeutic relation, was ubiquitous and universal in all successful helping endeavors.

Luborsky's concept of the alliance was closer to the original psychodynamic conceptualization (i.e., the alliance is the "glue" that binds the client to the therapist but in itself is not therapeutic). He posited two basic components of the alliance. The first centered around issues of mutual liking and client-perceived support, and the second focused on collaboration and shared responsibilities in therapy. Bordin, extending and broadening Greenson's (1965) concept of the alliance, proposed three essential components: interpersonal bonds, agreement on the goals of therapy, and collaboration on therapeutic tasks (Bordin, 1979). According to Bordin (1994), the positive development and maintenance of the alliance is, in itself, therapeutic curative.

Close on the heels of these theoretical developments, a number of scales were devised to assess the alliance empirically. Four of these instruments (Helping Alliance Questionnaire,[2] Luborsky, 1976; Vanderbilt Psychotherapy Process Scale,[3] Gomes-Schwartz, 1978; Working Alliance Inventory, Horvath, 1981; California Psychotherapy Alliance Scales, Gaston & Marmar, 1994), each based on a slightly different conceptualization of the alliance, are extensively used in current research. The development of these measures opened the door to the empirical investigation of the quality and quantity of the alliance in a variety of therapeutic contexts, as well as the link between the alliance and therapeutic outcome.

The alliance is a vital research topic; to date, well over 100 articles have been published involving this concept, and the list is growing. The results of early investigations of the alliance suggested a reliable relation between a positive alliance during the early phase of therapy

---

[2]The development of this scale was simultaneous with its theoretical development (Luborsky, 1976).

[3]The VPPS was designated to measure a broader range of therapy process variables. However, versions of this scale have been used by some investigators as an alliance measure.

and positive outcome. These findings, in part, were responsible for further stimulating the search for a comprehensive theory of the therapeutic relationship as a whole: If the alliance is a significant component of the therapeutic relationship, how does this construct fit with other variables that play a role in the relationship?

Although definitions of the alliance continue to evolve, there appears to be an agreement that the construct includes those aspects of the relationship that facilitate the collaborative work of therapist and client against a common foe: the client's pain and suffering (Bordin, 1979). Different conceptualizations and measurement approaches, however, have emphasized different components, such as the affective relationship between the participants (e.g., warmth, support), specific activities of client and therapist (e.g., self-observation, exploration), negative contributions (e.g., hostility), the sense of partnership or collaboration, and so on. Some authors use the term *alliance* quite broadly to include various aspects of the therapy relationship, whereas others use a more concise definition. (For the purposes of the present chapter, we will use the term *relationship* in reporting research results that we believe are germane to the therapeutic relationship more inclusively).

The Therapeutic Relationship: Current Viewpoints, Characteristic Features, and Outcome Effects

As Gelso and Carter (1994) pointed out in a recent discussion on the therapy relationship, "It is surprising . . . [given] the centrality of the therapeutic relationship over the years . . . that little effort has been made to define just what that relationship is" (p. 296). These authors proposed that the relationship can be defined as "the feelings and attitudes that counseling participants have toward one another, and the manner in which these are expressed" (Gelso & Carter, 1985, 159; 1994). Other writers have preferred to restrict the notion to the feelings and attitudes of the participants toward each other (as distinct from their respective actions or contributions; Hill, 1994), while still others have emphasized what is specifically therapeutic (i.e., that facilitates progress) about the relationship (Kolden, Howard, & Maling, 1994; Orlinsky & Howard, 1987).

Although consensus has not been achieved on a definition of the therapeutic relationship, nor on its fundamental components for that matter, there is general agreement that the working alliance, emphasizing the collaboration of client and therapist in the work of therapy, is a crucial ingredient. According to Kolden et al. (1994), besides the working alliance, the empathic resonance (i.e., reciprocal understanding) and mutual affirmation (i.e., respect and affective attachment) of the therapy partners are other essential ingredients. In their frequently cited model, Gelso and Carter (1985, 1994) proposed that the relationship includes, in addition to the working alliance, a "real relationship" (i.e., the realistic, undistorted perceptions and reactions of the participants) and a transference (i.e., repetition of past conflicts and feelings with the therapist)–countertransference component. Some authors (e.g., Greenberg, 1994; Hill, 1994) have taken issue with this notion of a "real relationship" on epistemological grounds (e.g., all perceptions are inevitably subjective or biased; Hill, 1994). Also, the role of past relationships (i.e., transference) on the here-and-now client–therapist encounter has been much debated. Some dynamically oriented researchers place such issues at central stage in the therapy relationship (Henry & Strupp, 1994), whereas others view them as external (e.g., existing prior) to the relationship (e.g., Kolden et al., 1994), or ignore them completely (see Watson & Greenberg, 1994). Whether or not past relational experiences should be viewed as a central aspect of the therapeutic relationship, there is evidence (to be discussed later) to support the influence of such factors on the client–therapist interaction.

Notwithstanding these definitional debates, there is strong agreement on the proposition that the therapeutic relationship is an important component in all forms of therapy, and that its overall quality influences the final outcome of therapy. Indeed, major reviews of the psychotherapy literature have documented the significant impact on outcome of the therapeutic relationship, or of related constructs such as the "therapeutic bond," in a variety of treatment environments and across a range of client problems (Beutler et al., 1994; Horvath & Symonds, 1991; Luborsky, Crits-Christoph, Mintz, & Auerbach, 1988; Orlinsky & Howard, 1986)—although the use of the relationship and its salient components may differ (e.g., Callaghan, Naugle, & Follette, 1996; Gomes-Schwartz, 1978; Raue, Castonguay, & Goldfried, 1993). The therapeutic alliance specifically has been found to play a similarly important role across different approaches such as behavioral, eclectic, and dynamically oriented therapies (Gaston, Marmar, Thompson, & Gallagher, 1988; Horvath, 1994). Moreover, the alliance has been shown to be a significant factor not only in individual but also in group therapy and group marital therapy (Bourgeois, Sabourin, & Wright, 1990; Pinsof, 1994). It appears that the therapeutic alliance may also be a factor in helping relations not specifically structured as therapy (e.g., pharmacotherapy combined with minimal supportive contact; Krupnick, Stotsky, Simmens, & Moyer, 1992). Clearly, then, it is important for therapists to attend closely to the relationship developed with their clients, and regularly monitor its quality.

The quality of the relationship in therapy does not appear to be solely a byproduct of incremental therapeutic success, that is, clients do not seem to have a positive relationship in therapy only because therapy is helpful. Insofar as the alliance is concerned, there are data to suggest that its intrinsic quality is an active factor, contributing to the success of therapy over and above concurrent therapeutic gains (Gaston, Marmar, Thompson, & Gallagher, 1991). Thus, the relationship can produce change and is not only a reflection of beneficial results (Lambert & Bergin, 1994).

A number of studies investigating the impact on outcome of the therapeutic alliance early in therapy have clearly established that the early alliance (i.e., the third to the fifth sessions) is a significant predictor of final treatment outcome. Although the relation between the alliance measured at later stages and client change is also significant, it appears to be more modest in magnitude. These findings indicate that the development of a positive therapist–client relationship may be critical from the onset of therapy. There appears to be a "window of opportunity" in the early sessions to establish a viable therapeutic relationship, or else the client may withdraw prematurely (Mohl, Martinez, Ticknor, Huang, & Cordell, 1991; Plotnicov, 1990; Tracey, 1986). Thus, therapists should be particularly attentive to the early relational climate, and work out any apparent difficulties in the client–therapist relationship in these first sessions.

Investigation of the course of the relationship over therapy—that is, whether it increases, remains stable, or perhaps fluctuates—has yielded complex results: When group averages are considered, the alliance shows little change over time, or an increase in specific components (Adler, 1988; Bachelor, 1992; Gaston et al., 1991; Marziali, 1984b). When cases are examined individually however, there is evidence of fluctuation (Horvath & Marx, 1988, 1990; Safran, Crocker, McMain, & Murray, 1990; Safran, Muran, & Wallner Samstag, 1994). Most likely, different patterns of development of the alliance are discernable among clients. In some clients, perceptions of the alliance fluctuate, whereas in others they remain unchanged, improve, or deteriorate (Gaston & Marmar, 1994).

It also appears that clients and therapists differ in their perceptions of the therapeutic relationship. Comparisons of clients' and therapists' ratings of the relationship have consistently indicated low agreement (e.g., Golden & Robbins, 1990; Gurman, 1977; Horvath & Marx, 1990; Tichenor & Hill, 1989). Although the source of this divergence is not entirely clear, it may be that therapists and clients use a different reference base in evaluating the therapy relationship. Perhaps therapists draw primarily on their theoretical perspective in making judgments, whereas clients may evaluate the relationship in comparison to other close personal relationships (Mallinckrodt, 1991) or on the basis of their expectations of the ideal therapist. Therapists, then, cannot assume that their evaluation of the quality of the therapy climate corresponds to their clients' perceptions.

Nor can it be assumed that clients readily perceive therapists' intended attitudes and attempts to forge a positive interrelationship. Clients do not necessarily read the therapist's intentions and messages in the way he or she meant them (Hill, Helms, Spiegel, & Tichenor, 1988; Hill & O'Grady, 1985; Horvath, Marx, & Kamann, 1990). Predisposing factors in clients, which we will examine in a subsequent section, may play an important role in the client's response to the therapist's intended communications. Similar factors that might influence perceptions and misperceptions of the relationship seem operative in therapists (Horvath & Luborsky, 1993). Given the participants' differential evaluation of the therapy relationship, it appears advisable to check with clients their feelings and perceptions about the therapist and the therapeutic interaction, and address and clarify disparate judgments that could threaten the quality of the therapy interaction.

Moreover, it appears that client and therapist differentially emphasize the components of the relationship that contribute most to favorable outcome. Therapists tend to emphasize the role of the clients' contributions (e.g., active participation in the therapy process) in client change—perhaps because they view clients as the agents of their own improvement—whereas clients tend to value therapist characteristics, such as therapist-provided help and demonstrated warmth, caring, and emotional involvement (e.g., Bachelor, 1991, 1995; Lambert & Bergin, 1983; Lazarus, 1971; Murphy, Cramer, & Lillie, 1984). The observed superior value, across numerous studies, of clients' assessment of the relationship in predicting the outcome of therapy, as compared with therapists' appraisal (Horvath & Symonds, 1991; Lambert & Bergin, 1994), underscores the importance of attending to clients' perceptions of the relational climate. Notwithstanding their own sources of bias, clients appear to be good judges of potentially curative factors of the relationship (Bachelor, 1991; Grigg & Goodstein, 1957; Murphy et al., 1984). Thus, it seems advisable to ensure that the characteristics valued by clients are effectively communicated and experienced by the client.

The therapist's experience level does not, in general, appear to ameliorate the strength of the therapeutic relationship. In fact, experienced professional therapists were not found to differ from novice therapists—including helpful college professors and untrained volunteers—on the therapy partners' ratings of therapist attitudes, such as warmth and friendliness or understanding and involvement, or of client contributions such as participation and commitment (e.g., Dunkle & Friedlander, 1996; Gaston, 1991; Gomes-Schwartz &

Schwartz, 1978; Strupp & Hadley, 1979). However, it appears that more experienced therapists' evaluations of the relationship match more closely their clients' ratings (Mallinckrodt & Nelson, 1991). This suggests that, with experience and training, therapists can learn to understand their clients' experience of the therapy relationship better.

Participants' Contributions and Characteristics: An Empirical Review

Several therapist attitudes and behaviors that contribute to the quality of the therapeutic relationship have been empirically identified. However, there is increasing evidence to suggest that clients may respond differentially to these characteristics. It is generally agreed that clients also contribute to the quality of the relational climate, and several studies have addressed the client's role in the therapeutic interaction. In spite of much theoretical interest, characteristics of therapists and clients that could impair the therapy relationship are only beginning to be investigated empirically, and we will look at some recent data. Although the therapeutic relationship is evidently interactive, the interactional process itself has received meager empirical attention. Some recent research has focused on the complementarity of the participants' moment-to-moment communications as it relates to the therapy relationship and to therapy. Finally, various dispositional states of client and therapist (e.g., relational capacity, attachment style) as well as other preexisting characteristics (e.g., clients' psychological functioning, demographic status) are thought to affect the quality of the therapy relationship. In the following section, we review the empirical evidence on these various facets of the client–therapist relationship and draw out some of the implications for practitioners. Our review, which generally covers more recent research, is not intended to offer a comprehensive account of all relationship-relevant variables; rather, it samples some of the important studies in the area.

THERAPIST CONTRIBUTIONS: FACILITATIVE ATTITUDES AND INTERVENTIONS

The therapist attitudes identified by Rogers and colleagues (Barrett-Lennard, 1962; Rogers, 1957; Truax & Carkhuff, 1967) in the 1950s and 1960s remain important ingredients of a positive therapy relationship, especially from the vantage point of clients. Rogers' (1957) contention that accurate empathy, nonpossessive warmth, and genuineness represent the "necessary and sufficient" conditions of beneficial outcome has generated an extensive body of studies that dominated research on the relationship for more than three decades (for reviews of this literature, see Gurman, 1977; Lambert, De Julio, & Stein, 1978; Orlinsky & Howard, 1986; Patterson, 1984). Despite some measurement-related criticisms, most investigators agree that these facilitative qualities (in particular, empathy and warmth) play an important, if not sufficient, role in therapeutic change in most psychotherapies, albeit with varying levels of emphasis (e.g., Beutler, Crago, & Arizmendi, 1986; Beutler et al., 1994). These facilitative variables are among the ones often considered as "common" treatment factors, inherent to most psychotherapy relationships (e.g., Beutler et al., 1994).

With the shift, since the mid-1980s, of research on the relationship to the construct of the alliance, the Rogerian variables have received less empirical attention. Only about a dozen studies have been conducted on one or more of the facilitative conditions over the period 1985 to 1994, most of which have examined the therapist's empathy as it relates to various aspects of the therapy process (Sexton & Whiston, 1994). For example, of several therapist variables, including emotional adjustment, relationship attitudes, and values, empathy was most predictive of being an effective or ineffective therapist (Lafferty, Beutler, & Crago, 1989). Empathy also proved to be robustly associated with clinical improvement in patients who were treated for depression with cognitive–behavioral therapy (Burns & Nolen-Hoeksema, 1992). The therapeutic value of empathy thus continues to receive strong support, although empathy—and probably other facilitative qualities—is evidently a more complex construct than previously thought (see Duan & Hill, 1996; Gladstein, 1977). Related constructs, such as "understanding and involvement" (Gaston & Marmar, 1994), or "warmth and friendliness" (Gomes-Schwartz, 1978), studied in the context of the alliance, have similarly been linked to positive therapy outcome or client satisfaction (e.g., Bachelor, 1991; Gaston, 1991; Windholz & Silberschatz, 1988).

With respect to therapist interventions (i.e., the more technical procedures or strategies used to initiate therapeutic change; Beutler et al., 1994) that contribute to beneficial therapeutic process and outcome, the empirical evidence is less clear-cut. Interventions such as giving advice, directiveness, reflection, open-ended questioning, and support (i.e., encouragement) have generally shown a mixed association with outcome (Beutler et al., 1994). It is possible that different types of clients react differently to these interventions, or that their impact is mediated by various client or therapist factors (e.g., skillfulness). For example, therapist directiveness was found helpful with resistance-prone depressed clients, whereas nondirective therapists were more successful with low-resistance–prone depressives (Beutler et al., 1991). Exploratory actions were found to better suit clients who were highly motivated or had more coherent self-concepts, whereas supportive interventions were better suited to clients who were less motivated and whose self-concepts were less stable (Horowitz, Marmar, Weiss, De Witt, & Rosenbaum, 1984).

With regard to the impact of these types of interventions on the therapy relationship, one recent study reported that support, exploration of thoughts and feelings, and assessment (e.g., obtaining information) negatively influence the early working relationship (Kivlighan, 1990). Too much assessment and global reassurance could detract from the formation of the relationship. Also, clients may not yet be ready, early in therapy, to explore in depth areas that are of concern (Kivlighan, 1990). It also appears that clients who have difficulties with the relationship may benefit more from supportive techniques, whereas those who form positive alliances may profit more from exploratory interventions (Gaston & Ring, 1992; Marziali, 1984a).

The importance of the therapist's self-disclosure in successful process and outcome is difficult to determine. Some studies found that therapist disclosures strengthened involvement in therapy (Elliott, James, Reimschuessel, Cislo, & Sack, 1985) and were favorably viewed by clients (e.g., Peca-Baker & Friedlander, 1987; Watkins & Schneider, 1989), whereas others showed little impact on the relationship (e.g., Cherbosque, 1987; Donley, Horan, & DeShong, 1989). Again, therapist self-disclosure likely contributes to the quality of the relationship for some clients, but may be less productive with others.

Interpretations—that is, explanatory interventions intended to clarify the meaning of an action or experience (Orlinsky & Howard, 1986)—generally appear to be an effective mode of intervention (Beutler et al., 1994). Interpretations have been associated with perceived helpfulness and gains among diverse clinical samples and therapy approaches (Elliott, Barker, Caskey, & Pistrang, 1982; Jacobs & Warner, 1981). It seems that interpretations that specifically focus on the client's "transference"—that is, that link feelings toward the therapist to early childhood figures—are less beneficial than previously thought. Despite earlier findings (e.g., Malan, 1976; Marziali, 1984a), the frequent use of such interpretations has not shown a positive association to outcome in recent, more methodologically sound studies (McCullough et al., 1991; Piper, Azim, Joyce, & McCallum, 1991; Piper, Debbane, Bienvenu, Carufel, & Garant, 1986). One study reported that frequent transference interpretations had a negative affect on the therapeutic alliance—particularly in patients with a high quality of personal relationships (Piper et al., 1991). Too frequent interpretations may cause the client to feel criticized, and could increase defensiveness (Piper et al., 1991).

Transference interpretations, then, should not be overused. Interpretations that are based on broader notions of transference, such as central relationship patterns that characterize the client's relation with others as well as the therapist (Crits-Christoph, Demorest, & Connolly, 1990; Luborsky & Crits-Christoph, 1990; Singer, 1985), or core false and maladaptive beliefs that clients attempt to overcome in therapy (i.e., their particular "plan" for therapy; Norville, Sampson, & Weiss, 1996; Weiss, 1986), generally appear to be more effective. For example, interpretations that accurately addressed the client's "plan formulation," or interpersonal aspects of core conflictual patterns, were associated with the client's increased emotional involvement in therapy and with the positive development of the alliance over therapy, respectively (Crits-Christoph, Barber, & Kurcias, 1993; Silberschatz, Fretter, & Curtis, 1986). Such interpretations may benefit the therapy process for some clients.

The equivocal findings and lack of definitive conclusions that characterize much of the research we have examined on therapist responses could be attributable to a number of factors, including different methods of appraisal or research procedures. However, mixed findings also could reflect the differential responsivity of clients and, consequently, the importance for therapists of matching attitudes and interventions to the individual client.

INDIVIDUALIZING THERAPIST RESPONSES AND THE RELATIONSHIP STANCE

There is some preliminary evidence to suggest that therapist attitudes or behaviors, and the therapeutic relationship in general, may be interpreted differently by individual clients. For example, in a study of clients' perceptions of therapist-offered empathy (Bachelor, 1988), it was found that what was perceived to be a meaningful therapist empathic communication varied among clients. About 44% of clients valued a cognitive-type of empathic response, another 30% valued an affective-toned communication, and the remaining clients viewed empathy to be optimally a sharing of personal information or a nurturant-like therapist response.

More specifically, clients emphasizing the cognitive aspect viewed the empathic therapist as one who accurately recognized their current innermost experience, state, or motivation. With these clients, it was the helper's accurate perception of the client's salient subjective state that resulted in the feeling of being understood (e.g., "She knew very well to discern my emotions and my 'deepest' feelings . . . in such a way that I couldn't deny what was evident"; "The therapist had seen into me, had felt the hidden sense of my thought"; "In the most simple fashion he expressed what I knew how to hide . . . he said exactly what I had felt").

Affective-style clients perceived therapists as empathic when they participated in the client's current feeling state, partaking of the same feeling the client was experiencing (e.g., "He seemed to feel with particular acuteness my reticence to get into my feelings, my difficulties in experiencing my aggressivity"; "I thought I saw her eyes water and I had the impression that she truly understood and felt entirely what I was experiencing"; "I described my feelings and I felt that she felt what I was telling her").

In clients preferring a sharing type of empathy, therapists were perceived as empathic when they readily disclosed personal opinions or experiences bearing on the client's ongoing communication, with spontaneity and naturalness. The therapist–client relationship was seen as a reciprocal exchange or dialogue, or even friendship, between the therapy partners (e.g., "I specified that it wasn't easy to live with one's parents. . . . He then indicated that at the same age as myself . . . he too had to settle things with his parents. . . . I wasn't the only one in this situation"; "There is a step that has been crossed . . . that of two strangers . . . to the stage of two old friends who meet . . . regularly . . . to 'exchange' about the past week"). Finally, clients who were attuned to a nurturant empathic response emphasized the helper's supportive, security-enhancing, or fully attentive and caring presence (e.g., "I find my analyst extremely attentive. . . . She is always very attentive, I find her extremely present").

Thus, it appears that, from the client's perspective, there is no single, invariably facilitative, therapist empathic response. One implication of these findings is that the therapist's reliance on one standard response style to convey empathy, such as reformulation of the client's ongoing communication, may not be equally productive with all clients. Clients respond in an idiosyncratic manner to the therapist's attempts to respond facilitatively, depending on their own unique needs.

A related study (Bachelor, 1995), which examined clients' perceptions of a positive therapy relationship, found that three relatively different types of relationship were viewed as therapeutic, depending on the particular client. Nearly one half of clients described a good relationship in terms of therapist-offered facilitative attributes (in particular, respect and being nonjudgmental, empathic understanding, and attentive listening) including, often, a friendly relationship with the therapist. These characteristics provided the necessary backdrop to the client's self-expression or self-disclosure. For another 40%, a positive relationship was characterized by improved self-understanding, gained through clarification of significant client material. Finally, a smaller proportion of clients viewed the relationship essentially in terms of collaboration. The collaborative-type client acknowledged or recognized that the work of therapy and positive change was not exclusively the therapist's responsibility and that each partner participates in and contributes, although differently, to the therapeutic undertaking. In sum, clients appear to have heterogeneous perceptions of what constitutes a positive therapeutic relationship.

Although many therapists probably adjust their interpersonal style to meet the unique needs of individual clients, the process by which the therapy relationship is tailored to individual clients has not received much systematic attention (Norcross, 1993). A flexible repertoire of relationship stances that suit different clients' needs and expectations seems important in fostering a sound therapeutic alliance and enhancing the efficacy of therapy (Dolan, Arnkoff, & Glass, 1993; Norcross, 1993).

Although some therapist attitudes or behaviors (e.g., respect, receptivity, good listening, not attacking the client's dignity, not minimizing problems) may be considered to be universally applicable, stances that therapists could adjust to specific clients include level of formality (i.e., casual vs. professional stance), self-disclosure, warmth and empathy, supportiveness (vs. directiveness and confrontation), topic focus (i.e., symptomatic vs. conflictual problems), level of focus (i.e., behavioral vs. uncovering), the pace of therapeutic work, and discussion of in-therapy versus extra-therapy material (Beutler & Consoli, 1993; Dolan et al., 1993; Lazarus, 1993).

For example, with an avoidant type of client, attempts on the part of the therapist to further the client's describing and feeling of emotions could lead to less engagement in therapy. Similarly, any expression of warmth could lead to distance and coldness. An appropriate, matching mode of relating to this type of client would be to encourage the client to choose the topics to be addressed but refrain from interpretative or challenging responses, and acting interested but not too supportive or friendly (Dolan et al., 1993). Another example is the oppositional client who may benefit more from a therapeutic relationship with a perceived equal partner and who exerts little direct control, endures the oppositional choices made, and works on establishing a collaborative relationship in which jointly created tasks are developed (Beutler & Consoli, 1993).

In sum, effective responses are attitudes and interventions that are appropriate to the individual client. To develop an effective therapeutic relationship, sensitivity to clients' differential phenomenological worlds as well as to relational needs and expectations seems important. Attitudes or interventions such as warmth, support, self-disclosure, deeper exploration, and so on appear to be highly beneficial to some clients, but more or less inconsequential to others, whereas still other clients may react adversely to such responses. Attentiveness to clients' expressed needs and reactions, as well as seeking confirmation about the perceived helpfulness of specific procedures and behaviors, could assist the therapist in adjusting responses accordingly. Responding in an appropriate manner should also take into account the quality (e.g., affective-toned vs. cognitive-toned empathy, interpretations based on past vs. current relationship patterns), the dosage, and the timing (e.g., phase of therapy, client readiness) of the therapist's attitudes and actions.

CLIENT CONTRIBUTIONS: COLLABORATION AND INVOLVEMENT

The contributions of both therapist and client are viewed as important to maintaining a quality therapeutic relationship. The client's willingness to participate in the therapeutic process and work productively with the therapist in furthering the goals of therapy is essential to the development and maintenance of a sound working alliance. The establishment of a solid alliance enhances the effectiveness of therapy (Horvath & Luborsky, 1993).

A recent major review of the effective ingredients in psychotherapy has documented the importance in therapy outcome of clients' personal involvement or engagement in therapy and cooperative participation (vs. resistance) in therapeutic procedures. Relatedly, the client's level of motivation, viewed as reflecting the desire for therapeutic involvement, has also generally been associated with positive therapy gains (Orlinsky, Grawe, & Parks, 1994). Attitudes such as openness (i.e., ability to assimilate the interventions and relationship offered by the therapist) and specific client activities such as self-exploration and experiencing of affect—which can be viewed as reflecting involvement in therapy—have similarly shown a significant relationship to favorable outcome (Orlinsky et al., 1994). Several studies have in fact demonstrated that the variable of "patient involvement" (reflecting both active participation in the therapy interaction and low distrust and hostility) is a stronger predictor of outcome than are various therapist attitudes or techniques (Gomes-Schwartz, 1978; O'Malley, Suh, & Strupp, 1983; Windholz & Silberschatz, 1988).

In a similar vein, it has been shown that communications on the part of the client that reflected high involvement are more crucial to the therapeutic relationship than are therapist high-involvement messages, and that clients with better alliances, as compared with low-alliance clients, evidence more of such exchanges (Reandeau &

Wampold, 1991). The client's involvement in the therapy process was also found to be of greater importance in outcome than were preexisting traits in the client (Kolb, Beutler, Davis, Crago, & Shanfield, 1985). In sum, research supports the importance of the client's involvement and collaboration in the therapeutic process. Significantly, the client's involvement, whether in terms of participation, commitment, or working capacity, does not appear to be influenced by the therapist's theoretical orientation (Gaston et al., 1988; Gomes-Schwartz, 1978). However, it seems that experienced therapists might be more successful in gaining the cooperation of their clients (as evidenced by greater "coordination" with their therapists' interventions) than would untrained therapists (Westerman & Foote, 1995).

Particular attitudes and behaviors of clients can hinder the development of a cooperative working relationship. Defensiveness (e.g., reluctance to deal with central problems) and hostility, or a hostile-dominant personality type, have been negatively linked to the quality of the client's working relationship (Gaston et al., 1988; Kiesler & Watkins, 1989; Kokotovic & Tracey, 1990; Muran, Segal, Wallner Samstag, & Crawford, 1994; Piper, de Carufel, & Szkrumelak, 1985; Strupp & Hadley, 1979). Some clients, by virtue of their particular "evoking style" (Kiesler, 1982), attempt to pull the therapist into a hostile exchange (Mueller, 1969; Tasca & McMullen, 1992); therapists have difficulty not responding in a counterproductive manner with such clients (Henry, Schacht, & Strupp, 1986; Henry & Strupp, 1994; Strupp, 1980). Clients who present more extreme levels of such hostile interpersonal behaviors most likely misperceive the positive aspects of the therapist's helping behavior and selectively attend and respond to any negative aspects (Kiesler & Watkins, 1989). The establishment of a sound working alliance thus appears to be more difficult with clients who are reluctant to deal with their problems and who express hostility. With such clients, priority should be given primarily to therapeutic work that addresses avoidant or antagonistic behaviors in order to foster the client's active collaboration in the treatment process (Gaston et al., 1988).

However, not all negative feelings and verbalizations during sessions should be taken as indicative of a poor therapeutic relationship. Initially negative affective responses may be relieved and replaced by positive feelings (Orlinsky et al., 1994), or such responses could reflect the client's emerging ability to overtly express sources of dissatisfaction hitherto held private. Also, it should be noted that certain interventions on the part of the therapist appear to undermine the client's collaboration, such as confrontational and transference-type interpretations that elicit defensiveness (Allen, Newsom, Gabbard, & Coyne, 1984).

Given the importance of the client's investment in the therapeutic process, therapists should attempt to enlist and strengthen their clients' active involvement and collaboration if levels of these qualities are found to be less than satisfactory. Acknowledging achievements of the client (e.g., insights) that are a result of the work done together is an example of a strategy that could enhance active collaboration (Adler, 1993).

Many clients may not readily acknowledge the importance of their active participation in the therapeutic process (Bachelor, 1995). They may simply be unaware that their contributions to the therapeutic process are valuable, or they may expect the therapist, as the perceived "expert," to assume full charge of the therapeutic endeavor. A shared view of the goals and methods of treatment is seen as essential to the establishment of a sound working alliance (Bordin, 1979, 1994), and clarifying clients' expectations and understanding of the process of therapy may be necessary.

WHEN THE RELATIONSHIP GOES WRONG: MISUNDERSTANDINGS AND RUPTURES

Minor fluctuations in the client–therapist relationship are a common occurrence, and misunderstandings are probably inevitable (Bordin, 1980; Rhodes, Hill, Thompson, & Elliott, 1994). If frequent and more intense, however, these can occasion serious strains or *ruptures* (Safran et al., 1990) in the relational climate, which in extreme cases can lead to a deadlock or stalemate (*impasse*) resulting in premature termination. Although therapeutic ruptures and impasses have received much theoretical attention (e.g., Bordin, 1994; Elkind, 1992; Grunebaum, 1986), only recently have attempts have been made to investigate these events more systematically within an empirical context. Some innovative work in this area has examined actual therapy sessions or events in which clients and therapists have identified problems in the therapeutic relationship.

Specific behaviors and attitudes of clients have been associated with a greater likelihood of ruptures in the therapeutic relationship. An intensive examination of therapy sessions that were identified by clients and therapists as problematic revealed five common indicators of disruptions attributable to clients: (a) overt and indirect expression of negative sentiments toward the therapist, (b) disagreement about the goals or tasks of therapy (which may be surface manifestations of underlying client issues), (c) compliance and avoidance maneuvers (e.g., ignoring a therapist's remark, arriving late), (d) self-esteem–enhancing communications (e.g., boasting of accomplishments in the face of perceived criticism), and (e) nonresponsiveness to intervention (rejecting, or failing to make use of, particular therapeutic interventions; Safran et al., 1990).

When clients reported, in another study, their own experiences of misunderstandings that resulted in terminating treatment, they typically mentioned that their therapist acted in a way contrary to what they wanted or needed (e.g., the therapist was critical, nonattentive, forgetful), resulting in negative feelings about themselves (e.g., guilt, devastation) and their therapists (e.g., anger, sense of abandonment). Clients also reported that the therapeutic relation had often been poor. Significantly, the clients did not tell their therapists they were upset; in the few cases in which these clients asserted themselves (e.g., shared their negative feelings), the therapists remained rigid in their original view. In contrast, in cases in which misunderstandings were resolved, therapists were often perceived to accommodate the client, for example by apologizing or accepting responsibility for the event (Rhodes et al., 1994).

Therapists' accounts of the therapeutic process with clients who terminated therapy as a result of an impasse are suggestive of several contributing factors. Therapists characterized these impasses in terms of an ongoing general disagreement with the client or a lack of satisfaction on the part of the client about the way in which therapy was conducted, rather than a single major event, and they often involved power struggles over goals and tasks. Therapists also associated four types of events with relationship impasses: (a) mistakes (e.g., the therapist was too pushy or unsupportive, too cautious or nondirective, or changed techniques excessively); (b) triangulation (i.e., person[s] intruding into the therapy relationship, with the client feeling that she or he had to choose between the therapist and the other); (c) clients' transference (i.e., reenacting earlier relationship patterns with the therapist) issues; and (d) therapists' personal issues (e.g., difficulty in dealing with strong negative affect, being drawn into a rescuer-fixer role). Clients had also reacted negatively toward the therapist in response to the impasse, although many therapists became aware of the clients' dissatisfaction only after clients stated they were terminating (Hill, Nutt-Williams, Heaton, Thompson, & Rhodes, 1996).

Taken together, these data provide useful information on misunderstandings in the client–therapist relationship that could eventually lead to premature termination of therapy. Therapists need to be particularly alert to cues that signal problems in the therapy relationship, and, because clients are often reluctant to communicate negative feelings and their dissatisfaction (Hill et al., 1996; Rhodes et al., 1994; Safran et al., 1990), it seems important to monitor carefully the client's level of comfort and satisfaction with the relationship. Therapists are well advised to convey to clients that their perceptions and feelings about therapy and the therapist are welcomed and valued. In the relationship with their clients, therapists should also pay attention to their own feelings (e.g., lack of empathy, frustration), which can be a valuable "barometer" of the therapeutic quality of the relationship and its difficulties (Hill et al., 1996; Safran et al., 1990).

When signs of ruptures and serious misunderstandings are noted, it appears advisable to address these directly (Rhodes et al., 1994; Safran et al., 1990). There is empirical evidence indicating that relationships that were initially poor improved when therapists were challenging, rather than supportive, of clients, and directly addressed problematic feelings in relation to the therapist, linking these to clients' resistances (Foreman & Marmar, 1985; Kivlighan & Schmitz, 1992). The passive acceptance of problematic client behaviors or attitudes (e.g., evasiveness, negativism) and the failure to address deficiencies in the therapeutic relationship have proven to be among the more important negative factors influencing the outcome of therapy (Sachs, 1983). Thus, when the relationship is under stress, focusing on the conflictual situation directly can be relation-enhancing, even though such a course of action could be uncomfortable to the therapist. Because ruptures could reflect failures in empathy and other therapist errors, there may be a natural tendency to avoid addressing them with the client and to respond defensively (Safran et al., 1990). Yet the therapist's sensitivity to the ups and downs of the relationship and her or his ability to attend to relational stresses could directly influence clients' willingness to confront their own dysfunctional relational patterns, as well as increase their confidence in asserting their psychological needs within a relational context.

The data above also suggest that various aspects of therapists' functioning are involved in the occurrence of misunderstandings in, and disruptions of, the therapeutic relationship. Aspects of therapists' behaviors and attitudes contributing to stress in the relationship included errors in technique (e.g., lack of structure, too many techniques), various counterproductive attitudes (e.g., criticism, insensitivity) and personal difficulties (e.g., handling anger). The latter have commonly been studied, in the psychodynamic literature, under the label of "countertransference," designating the influence of personal factors (e.g., unresolved issues and conflicts) that bias the therapist's perceptions and judgments of the client, thus interfering with optimal responsiveness. However labeled, it is commonly agreed that the therapist's personal reactions need to be attended to, understood, and effectively managed (Hayes & Gelso, 1991; Van Wagoner, Gelso, Hayes, & Diemer, 1991).

A large body of studies have investigated such factors and their diverse manifestations, whether in the form of withdrawal, avoidance, hostility, or misperceptions of the client. Various characteristics of clients, as well as factors in therapists themselves, have been linked to the increased likelihood of displaying such reactions. Anger and hostility directed toward the therapist (e.g., Gamsky & Farwell, 1966; Haccoun & Lavigueur, 1979), material impinging on the therapists' own conflict areas (Cutler, 1958), transference (Mueller, 1969), and client–therapist value differences have been shown to precipitate such reactions in the therapist. (For example, one study found that clients who held a political ideology [i.e., liberal vs. conservative] different from their therapist were less liked, less empathized with, and judged as more perturbed; Gartner, Harmatz, Hohmann, & Larson, 1990). In therapists, characteristics such as a strong need for approval (Bandura, Lipsher, & Miller, 1960), high nurturant and affiliative needs (Mills & Abeles, 1965), heightened anxiety (e.g., Milliken & Kirchner, 1971; Yulis & Kiesler, 1968), and strong affect (either positive or negative) toward clients (McClure & Hodge, 1987) have been associated with diverse countertherapeutic reactions, including misperceptions of clients. (For example, therapists with strong positive feelings for their clients viewed these clients as having personalities closer to theirs; when strong negative feelings were present, the client was viewed as more dissimilar from the therapist; McClure & Hodge, 1987).

More appropriate handling of counterproductive reactions has been associated with characteristics such as empathic ability (Peabody & Gelso, 1982), heightened awareness of one's counterproductive feelings—particularly when paired with a viable theoretical framework (Robbins & Jolkowski, 1987)—and reputed excellence and competency as a therapist (e.g., Snyder & Snyder, 1961; Van Wagoner et al., 1991). Excellent therapists, compared with therapists in general and regardless of therapy orientation, possess to a greater extent several attributes held to prevent, or at least moderate, negative reactions; these include self-integration, anxiety management, conceptualizing skills, empathy, and self-insight (Van Wagoner et al., 1991). Two of these attributes, self-integration and self-insight, appeared to be particularly important in managing countertherapeutic behaviors, suggesting that the personality organization of the therapist may be more relevant than therapist skills or focus on others (Hayes, Gelso, Van Wagoner, & Diemer, 1991).

Thus, it seems important for therapists to acknowledge their potential vulnerability to personal tendencies that could interact with particular clients to produce countertherapeutic reactions, so that these can be understood rather than manifested in the therapeutic interaction. Although personal therapy remains a matter of individual choice, and extensive, long-term self-examination does not appear necessary, it seems important that therapists be cognizant of specific counterproductive attitudes and behaviors they may engage in with their clients and of the particular contexts in which these negative responses are likely to occur. Cases in which clients terminate prematurely, consistently show other signs of withdrawal, or otherwise fail to develop a collaborative relationship merit close examination. Access to appropriate feedback and supervision could be helpful in this regard.

THE INTERACTIONAL PROCESS: CLIENT–THERAPIST COMPLEMENTARITY

Relatively few studies have examined the client–therapist interactional process itself—that is, the influence or changes in one partner's behavior as a function of the behavior of the other—rather than separate, unilateral therapist or client contributions. Investigation at this level allows for a more fine-grained understanding of the complex reality of the client–therapist interactional field. One current line of research in this area focuses on the complementarity of the therapy partners' interactions, that is, how well the transactional behaviors of client and therapist fit, or complement, each other (Tracey, 1993). Greater complementarity is assumed to indicate a higher degree of interactional harmony and satisfaction, and therefore the degree of complementarity in a therapeutic interaction should be related to a sound alliance and successful outcome (Kiesler, 1986; Tracey & Ray, 1984).

The complementarity of exchanges is typically assessed in terms of the two characteristics of dominance (or control) and affiliation, seen as basic dimensions of interpersonal behavior (Wiggins, 1982). Complementary interactions are defined as dissimilar responses on the dominance dimension (e.g., dominant communications elicit submissive responses) and similar responses on affiliation (e.g., friendly responses "pull" friendly responses, and hostility elicits hostility).[4] The highest degree of complementarity occurs when an interaction is complementary on both dimensions.

There is some evidence to indicate that the complementarity of client–therapist exchanges discriminates between favorable and unfavorable outcome. For example, a greater number of topics initiated by the therapist and subsequently followed by the client (seen to reflect an absence of disagreement over the tasks and goals of therapy) differentiated among clients continuing in therapy and those who termi-

---

[4]In fact, there are different theoretical models of complementarity (e.g., interpersonal and interactional, the latter focusing on the dominance aspect of communication). Also, these models typically use different methods of operationalizing the construct (e.g., topic initiation vs. a "circumplex coding system" that specifies the different possible combinations of transactions among control and affiliation).

nated prematurely (Tracey, 1986). These findings suggest that a modicum of topic agreement may be required to continue a therapy relationship. Other studies, however, indicate less support for the role of complementary interactions early in therapy or in positive outcome (Dietzel & Abeles, 1975; Friedlander, Thibodeau, & Ward, 1985; Thompson, Hill, & Mahalik, 1991).

Clinically more relevant results have been observed when the distinction is made between the type of complementary reaction, that is, whether the reaction was positive (i.e., friendly and autonomy-enhancing) or negative (i.e., hostile and controlling), as opposed to the overall degree of complementarity. In effect, several studies found that successful, as compared with unsuccessful, dyads were characterized by greater positive (i.e., both participants acting in a friendly manner), and less negative (i.e., at least one member acting in a hostile manner) complementary interactions early in therapy (Henry, Schacht, & Strupp, 1986, 1990; Svartberg & Stiles, 1992; Tasca & McMullen, 1992). For example, in one study, in the positive outcome cases, only 1% of the therapists' and none of the clients' communications were judged to be hostile, whereas in unsuccessful cases, 20% of the clients' (e.g., sulking, less disclosing) and 19% of the therapists' (e.g., belittling, blaming) verbalizations, were hostile (Henry et al., 1986). In a similar vein, and examining specifically the working alliance, it was found that clients with stronger alliances, relative to low-alliance clients, evidenced a greater proportion of high-involvement messages (Reandeau & Wampold, 1991). Thus, even though exchanges may be complementary, all complementary exchanges are not therapeutically equivalent (Henry, 1996).

The complementarity of the participants' interactions has also been investigated with regard to hypothesized stages (i.e., early, middle, and late) of the therapeutic process. Successful cases are expected to be distinguished by a pattern of high complementarity during the early, rapport-building phase, followed by low or noncomplementary therapist responses during the middle ("work") phase, as inappropriate and rigid interpersonal patterns in the client are confronted and destabilized. The later phase of therapy, toward termination, should evidence a return to a high complementarity stance that reinforces the newly acquired, more productive client behaviors (Dietzel & Abeles, 1975; Tracey, 1993). In general, results have not satisfactorily established that a high–low–high pattern of complementarity is characteristic of successful therapeutic process: Some data (Tracey & Ray, 1984) support a high–low–high pattern of complementarity over therapy in successful dyads, but other results indicate a shift from the early to middle stages only, or no consistent patterns over time (Dietzel & Abeles, 1975; Hoyt, Strong, Corcoran, & Robbins, 1993;

Tasca & McMullen, 1992; Thompson et al., 1991). Thus, there is little current support for the notion that different patterns of complementarity or power relations are appropriate for different stages of therapy. It may be premature to dispense with these notions altogether, however. Complementarity is a multidimensional phenomenon, and current attempts at assessing the construct may not fully tap all relevant dimensions of the phenomenon (Thompson et al., 1991).

In conclusion, the most useful results for practioners from this line of research seem to concern the observed relation of negative complementarity to the therapeutic process. Negative complementarity is more frequent in unsuccessful dyads, and virtually absent in successful cases. In other words, negative complementary seems rarely productive in therapy. Instead of meeting a client's hostility with (overt or covert) hostility, a more helpful response would be to encourage the client to explore his or her negative reactions toward the therapist (Friedlander, 1993). Furthermore, there is some evidence that hostility in clients, as well as other negative client or therapist factors (e.g., lack of collaboration, lack of respect) that emerge in the beginning of therapy are pervasive across the entire therapy process, which raises questions about the ability of therapists to deal effectively with such issues (Eaton, Abeles, & Gutfreund, 1993; Tasca & McMullen, 1992). Traditional training methods do not appear to have adequately prepared many therapists to perceive and respond competently to problematic interpersonal processes (Henry et al., 1990). Even well-trained therapists appear to be vulnerable to engage in potentially damaging interpersonal interactions with their clients, which suggests the influence on the interpersonal process of preexisting dispositional characteristics in therapists (Henry et al., 1990; Henry & Strupp, 1994).

Pretherapy Characteristics and the Therapeutic Relationship

SYMPTOMATOLOGY AND PSYCHOLOGICAL ADJUSTMENT

It is commonly believed that clients have varying abilities to form and maintain a therapeutic relationship. The assumption that clients who are under greater psychological distress are more vulnerable and may have more difficulty establishing a sound working relationship has, in general, been supported by research. Ratings of clients' overall psychological health, as assessed from different sources, have been found to correlate negatively with the ability to form a productive relationship in a number of studies.[5] Although there are some exceptions, the majority of results suggest that more severely impaired clients will have greater difficulty in establishing a good working relationship.

CURRENT AND PAST RELATIONSHIPS

Interpersonal qualities such as the ability to invest energy and caring in personal relationships, to have positive attachments, and to trust others are also expected to influence clients' capacity for successful engagement in the therapy relationship (Gelso & Carter, 1985). Various indices of interpersonal functioning, such as social adjustment, the capacity to engage in a stable or intimate relationship, current relationships with friends and family, and social support, have shown a positive, albeit moderate, association with the client's level of participation and collaboration in therapy (Gaston, 1991; Kokotovic & Tracey, 1990; Mallinckrodt, 1991; Marmar, Weiss, & Gaston, 1989; Marziali, 1984b; Moras & Strupp, 1982; Piper et al., 1985). Thus, clients who have difficulty maintaining social relationships or have poor family relationships prior to beginning therapy are less likely to develop strong alliances, whereas those who have experienced positive interactions pretherapy join with the therapist in developing a positive interaction (Horvath, 1994; Marziali, 1984b).

Clients' early relational experiences are also considered to be an important factor that influences their ability to form a productive therapeutic alliance (Gelso & Carter, 1985; Henry & Strupp, 1994; Strupp, 1974). These early interactions are held to give rise to mental schemas that involve representations about oneself and about others' expected behavior and that strongly influence later interpersonal relationships. Variants of these interpersonal dynamics have been investigated from different theoretical perspectives. Researchers in the psychodynamic tradition have demonstrated that the long-term patterns of clients' relationships (*object relations*) are related to the degree of their collaboration in the therapeutic process. The higher the quality of relationships clients tend to establish with others, the stronger the collaboration or working relationship with the therapist (Piper, Azim, Joyce, McCallum, Nixon, & Segal, 1991; Ryan & Cichetti, 1985).

Clinical writers drawing on a developmental perspective have examined the potential influence of clients' early attachment experiences on the therapeutic process. The attachment styles of clients,

---

[5]Allen, Tarnoff, and Coyne (1985); Eaton, Abeles, and Gutfreund (1988); Gaston (1991); Kokotovic and Tracey (1990); Luborsky, Crits-Christoph, Alexander, Margolis, and Cohen (1983); Marziali (1984a); Raue et al. (1993); Sabourin, Coallier, Cournoyer, and Gaston (1990).

developed on the basis of early interactions with caregivers, have been shown to influence clients' perceptions of and reactions to their therapists, as well as the quality of the alliances they develop. Clients whose style of forming close attachments with adults was characterized by a lack of trust in these adults' availability and dependability, were more likely to report a poor working relationship. The extent to which these clients felt they could rely on the therapist's availability and dependability was more important to the formation of the early working alliance than clients' comfort with closeness or fear of being abandoned (Satterfield & Lyddon, 1995).

Different styles of attachment to the therapist have also been identified in clients. "Secure" clients perceive the therapist as responsive, accepting, and providing a secure base; "merger"-type clients desire frequent and intensely personal contact with their therapist; "avoidant" clients distrust the therapist and fear rejection; and, finally, "reluctant"-type clients seem engaged with the therapist, but appear unwilling to participate in the self-revealing tasks of therapy. These attachment styles were also found to be associated with the alliance that clients formed with the therapist. Secure-type clients reported positive working alliances. Clients with a desire to merge were more apt to bond easily with their therapist than they were able to agree on the tasks and goals of therapy. Reluctant–attached clients reported relatively strong alliances, whereas avoidant clients showed the poorest alliances (Mallinckrodt, Gantt, & Coble, 1995). Ingrained patterns of attachment thus appear to predispose clients to respond in particular ways to their therapists, and also seem to influence their capacity to develop a productive alliance.

Other studies have examined the relation of clients' attachment memories to the working alliance. Memories of emotionally warm, responsive, and autonomy-encouraging parenting, seen to promote the child's felt security, worth, and independence, are expected to be positively associated with the therapy relationship (Mallinckrodt, 1991). There is some evidence to indicate that bonds with fathers in particular are relevant to the quality of the alliance. Clients with positive alliances characterized their fathers as emotionally expressive, warm, and nurturing, whereas clients with the poorest alliances tended to characterize their fathers as intrusive, controlling, and unwilling to allow autonomy (Mallinckrodt, 1991; Mallinckrodt, Coble, & Gantt, 1995).

There is also increased interest in how the therapist can function efficaciously as a significant attachment figure for the client (e.g., Dolan et al., 1993; Farber, Lippert, & Nevas, 1995; Pistole & Watkins, 1995). Through a strong alliance, for example, facilitated by the therapist's availability and responsiveness, the therapist can provide a "secure base" (Bowlby, 1988) from which the client can safely explore past and current attachment patterns and experiment with new ways of functioning that can be tried out in the "real world" (Farber et al., 1995). Indeed, as argued by some clinical writers, the therapeutic relationship may play an important role as a corrective experience for the client. Not only can the therapist help clients to understand their limitative relational patterns better, but clients can directly experience, in the therapy relationship, a different mode of relating (including safely trying out new behaviors, such as expressing anger and vulnerability) and being related to. Clients' dysfunctional interpersonal patterns are thus challenged and can be revised. Some authors (e.g., Dolan et al., 1993) have also discussed how the therapist could adapt his or her interpersonal stance and interventions to clients' different attachment styles as a means to foster an effective therapeutic relationship. With an "anxiously–ambivalent" client, for example—who typically shows a desire for closeness with the therapist but appears unable to tolerate expressions of empathy that are welcomed by more securely attached clients—the therapist could consider mirroring back the client's verbalizations, rather than drawing out or reflecting affect. The latter intervention would be experienced as too intense by this type of client (Dolan et al., 1993).

Like clients, therapists bring to the therapy relationship a personal history that affects their rapport with clients (Bordin, 1979; Orlinsky & Howard, 1986). Researchers investigating therapists' past relational experiences have posited that therapists tend to re-create earlier interpersonal patterns in the therapy relationship and treat clients accordingly (Henry, 1996; Henry & Strupp, 1994). Therapists' self-representations based on past relationship experiences (*introjects*) have in fact been shown to exert an important influence on the quality of the alliance developed with some clients. Therapists with negative self-representations—that is, who are self-critical and neglectful toward themselves—were more likely to engage in subtly hostile and controlling interactions with their clients than were therapists with positive self-representations (Henry & Strupp, 1994). These data do not indicate that all therapists with such a personality structure (introject) will display hostility toward all clients; however, some may be more vulnerable to engaging in countertherapeutic exchanges with clients who tend to evoke these negative tendencies (Henry et al., 1990). Furthermore, it appears that therapists' interpersonal schemas influence the way in which clients act toward themselves. Therapists of clients whose hostile (e.g., self-blaming, critical) self-representations remained unchanged during therapy were found to engage in significantly more hostile (e.g., belittling, blaming) conduct as compared with therapists of clients who did change; the latter therapists showed an almost total absence of such conduct (Coady, 1991; Henry et al.,

1990). Thus, therapists' relational schemas not only represent a potential source of vulnerability to problematic interactional processes with their clients, but may also predict differential outcome (Henry & Strupp, 1994).

There has also been emerging interest in therapists' attachment styles and their impact on the therapeutic relationship. For example, compared with insecure clinicians, clinicians with secure attachment models were found to respond more to the dependency needs of clients who dismissed these needs than they did to clients who were preoccupied with such needs, thus challenging clients' existing models of relationships. Clinicians' attachment style was also related to the depth of interventions. Clinicians who were more preoccupied with attachment needs intervened with their clients in greater depth than did helpers who tended to dismiss these needs (Dozier, Cue, & Barnett, 1994). In a similar vein, it was found that therapists with secure attachment styles were more proficient in developing early alliances (McKee, 1992).

Taken together, these data provide evidence for the influence on the therapeutic relationship and process of predispositional factors both in the client and in the therapist. Clients' interpersonal functioning and intrapersonal dynamics in the form of cognitive relational schemas appear to affect their ability to form a therapeutic relationship and engage productively in the work of therapy. It is also likely that clients' particular style of relating to the therapist, including perceptions of and interactions with the therapist (e.g., "pulling for" responses that confirm dysfunctional beliefs about others) are influenced by these factors. Clients' interpersonal histories and issues thus merit consideration. Awareness of these factors could assist clinicians in the early identification and therapeutic management of potential relationship pitfalls, and could also be of benefit to practitioners who do not typically focus on relational issues. To ensure a positive relationship, it may be useful for therapists to adopt an interpersonal stance that is appropriate to the client's specific relational style. It should be noted, however, that on the basis of an earlier review (Horvath, 1991), the impact of clients' antecedent relationship capacities or experiences remains moderate, and thus the therapy relationship is influenced, but not determined, by such characteristics.

Similarly, therapists' predispositional characteristics, in particular when hostile and insecure relational patterns are involved, also ostensibly affect the quality of interactions with clients. As we pointed out earlier, awareness of personal dynamics and vulnerabilities are important in order to minimize countertherapeutic responses. Supervision might be contemplated to assist the practioner in identifying and managing problematic responses.

PARTICIPANTS' SOCIODEMOGRAPHIC CHARACTERISTICS

A few studies have reported a positive association between client characteristics such as education and age, or client–therapist similarity in age, and the helping alliance (Luborsky, Crits-Christoph, Alexander, Margolis, & Cohen, 1983; Marmar et al., 1989). In general, however, there is little evidence to indicate that participants' age, or similarity in age, has a significant impact on the therapeutic process (Atkinson & Schein, 1986; Robiner & Storandt, 1983). Some research suggests that client and therapist gender may influence particular aspects of the relationship process. For example, female clients were found to engage in more self-exploration than were male clients (Hill, 1975) and to respond more favorably to therapist insight, empathy, support, and encouragement of risk taking, whereas male clients indicated greater responsivity to honest feedback (Persons, Persons, & Newmark, 1974).

Female therapists showed greater responsivity to client painful self-exploration (Howard, Orlinsky, & Hill, 1969) and were found to be more direct and address in-session behavior and the therapy relationship in relation to clients' life situations more often (Jones, Krupnick, & Kerig, 1987). Male therapists reported greater degrees of uneasy intimacy (Howard et al., 1969) and appeared to accommodate and alleviate conflict rather than address the source of the conflict (Jones et al., 1987). Female therapists in one study were judged by clients to form more effective therapeutic alliances, although no differences were found with regard to perceived therapy outcome (Jones & Zoppel, 1982). However, while there appear to be some gender differences in both clients and therapists with respect to aspects of the therapeutic process, these findings need greater replication.

Some research has also noted differences in the relationship process as a function of same- or opposite-gender pairing. For example, clients seemed to be able to speak more freely about their feelings with same gender therapists (Hill, 1975), and women clients in same-gender pairing tended to experience greater emotional intensity in therapy (Jones & Zoppel, 1982). On the other hand, some studies have identified greater self-disclosure in opposite-gender dyads (Brooks, 1974; Hill, 1975). Thus far, findings are inconclusive regarding what types of pairings are of greater benefit for clients (Nelson, 1993).

Most cross-cultural psychotherapy research seem to support the notion that a certain amount of similarity in culture and values enhances the likelihood that clients form a good relationship and remain in therapy, although it is not clear whether this finding is equally valid for non–cross-cultural groups (Beutler et al., 1994; Gibbs & Huang, 1989). In sum, although it is possible that similarity of client and therapist on some sociodemographic variables may initially ease the development of a positive relationship, the longer term influence of these matching factors is not clear. In practice as well, matching of therapist and client on demographic variables is seldom practical. It seems that the most important conclusion we can draw for therapists is to alert professionals to the higher risk of misunderstandings or misalignments with clients who come from different sociocultural contexts.

Conclusion

We have addressed, in this chapter, many different facets of the therapeutic relationship. There are a number of conclusions and implications that arise from the rich texture of research findings we have reviewed. To conclude our presentation, we have attempted to highlight some of the more important points that can be gleaned from our discussion of the therapeutic relationship:

- Although the salient components of the therapeutic relationship are viewed differently across theories, it seems beyond doubt that a positive therapeutic relationship is a necessary (but probably not sufficient) component of all forms of effective psychotherapy. Careful attention to, and continued monitoring of, the quality of the therapist–client relationship is advised.
- In general, the therapeutic relationship appears to be formed early in therapy, probably within the first few sessions. Close attention should be paid to the client's early perceptions and reactions and to the establishment of a positive relationship with the client at the beginning of therapy.
- Therapists and clients tend to perceive the therapeutic relationship differently. Clients may not necessarily perceive the therapist's behaviors as meant or intended by the therapist. Moreover, clients and therapists tend to attribute change to different factors. Clients' perceptions of the relationship generally appear to be more relevant to therapy outcome. Attending to clients' perceptions and feelings about the therapeutic process and climate, clarifying divergent perceptions, and establishing agreement on what is helpful and needed are important strategies. It seems advisable to ensure that the elements that clients deem important be communicated to and perceived by the client.
- Both participants' contributions are involved in forging a productive therapeutic relationship. On the part of the therapist, establishing a climate of trust and safety through responsiveness; attentive listening; and the communication of understanding, liking, and respect are generally important characteristics of a

quality relationship. On the part of the client, important contributions include the commitment to participate in the therapeutic endeavor, and collaborate with the therapist in the work involved. If these are found lacking, attempts should be made to clarify with clients the importance of their active engagement to the success of therapy, and to work at a shared view of the therapeutic endeavor.

▪ The specific therapist responses that best foster a strong therapeutic relationship vary from client to client. Attitudes such as warmth, empathy, and so on and interventions and strategies such as support, directiveness, or deeper exploration appear to be differentially productive. Sensitivity to clients' differential responsivity seems important. Verifying with the client his or her expectations and perceptions and the perceived helpfulness of particular responses could aid in adjusting these to the client's individual needs. Factors such as phase of therapy, the client's readiness for change, and interpersonal dynamics also need to be considered.

▪ The therapy relationship itself can represent a therapeutic intervention. The experience of a trusting and safe environment facilitated by the therapist's availability, responsiveness, and constancy, in which clients can explore past and present feelings and interactions, may initiate change (e.g., insight into and reassessment of habitual limitative relationship attitudes and expectations, acquisition of interpersonal skills).

▪ Even in the best of therapies, strains and ruptures of the relationship can occur. Overt or indirect hostile-toned attitudes and behaviors in clients, inappropriate interventions and responses (e.g., criticism) in therapists, and client–therapist interactional dynamics (e.g., power struggles), for example, can create a problematic relational climate that could lead to premature termination. Conveying to clients early in therapy that their perceptions and feelings—including dissatisfactions—about therapy and the therapist are valued, and monitoring the client's level of satisfaction with the relationship seem important. Directly addressing problematic behaviors in the client and troublesome aspects of the relationship is advisable.

▪ Preexisting dispositional characteristics of both client and therapist influence to a certain extent the quality of the therapeutic relationship and the interactional exchanges of the participants. Level of psychological and interpersonal functioning and past relational history are some of the relevant client characteristics. An understanding of the clinical manifestations of clients' underlying relational schemas could be useful to therapists in dealing with their clients. Similar intrapersonal processes appear operative even in highly experienced therapists, and awareness of these seems important in minimizing countertherapeutic responses.

At the conclusion of this chapter, we would like to remind ourselves and our readers that a relationship dedicated to healing involves a commitment of the participants to each other and to the goal of this relationship. In such joining together, the therapist and the client expose themselves to the possibility of profound personal change, of being moved, inspired—and sometimes hurt as well. Science has advanced our understanding of some of the core common features of the good therapeutic relationship and has assisted therapists in understanding the many complexities of this aspect of the healing process. Nonetheless, at its core, the therapeutic relationship remains an intensely human, personal, and essentially unique encounter. Each of us as therapists meets each client with all our theories and past experiences at hand, yet also knowing that every therapeutic engagement entails an encounter with the unknown and demands that the therapist remain open to the uniqueness of the client's world, ready to be surprised and moved at each meeting. Both therapist and client share in this uncertainty, albeit in a different manner, as they face the unknown together and join to labor for the same cause. To us, the development of the therapeutic relationship remains a fascinating area of inquiry because it merges the human and the scientific aspects of the profession.

Questions From the Editors

1. Given the importance of a strong alliance to outcome, what implications do you see in the training of graduate students? Should models still be taught as if they are primarily responsible for client change?

It seems clear that the alliance merits serious attention in the training of graduate students. Students should be provided training not only in developing a strong alliance with their clients, but they should also learn to monitor the alliance, to diagnose difficulties they encounter in building the alliance, and to recognize and repair alliance ruptures. Training efforts should also include teaching students to adapt their relationship stance and their interventions to deal with different clients. Another important focus of training, we believe, should be sensitizing students to the more subtle interpersonal aspects of the client–therapist relationship and interaction. The relational difficulties that trainees may be experiencing with their clients could represent important opportunities to better understand their clients' difficulties and issues about relationships. The notion that these challenges to the development of the alliance often provide a direct clue to the client's source of pain deserves more emphasis. Students should also be encouraged in their training to reflect on their own interpersonal functioning with clients, particularly any tendency to respond negatively or in a hostile manner to certain types of clients.

2. Given the importance of the client's perceptions of the relationship– alliance to outcome, what efforts are being made, or should be made, to incorporate the client's perspective into the therapeutic process?

The emergence of a number of constructivist (sometimes called *post-modern*, *narrative*, or *systemic*) perspectives is an important phenomenon in this respect. Although there are differences among these theorists, they all focus on the importance of the unique inner world of the client. Although we have some reservations about the extreme relativism that some of these writers advocate, we are gratified to see that theorists are paying attention once more to the uniqueness of the person's inner world in contrast to the mechanistic focus of the early years of behaviorism.

We also note the increasing interest of researchers in developing research methods that can adequately capture the natural complexity of the client's experiential reality. Qualitative (also called *descriptive*) methods, based on participants' verbal or written accounts, are increasingly used by psychotherapy researchers to gain a richer understanding of clients' perceptions and experiences of the therapeutic process.

3. How do you account for the benign neglect of the contribution of the alliance to change in the formation of psychotherapeutic models? Or said another way, what do you think accounts for the field's obsession with technique as evidenced by the recent attention to empirically validated treatments?

To some extent, theorizing about therapy has come full-circle: From an emphasis on the interpersonal realm, we moved to create a "mind-less" psychology and tried to reduce human experience to small, finite categories and a few universal "laws" about behavior. Most of our current empirical findings indicate a need to return to the more meaningful understanding of our essential intersubjectivity, of the fundamental importance of relationships and, significantly, of the healing potential of a well-managed therapeutic alliance. In opposition to these findings, there is an effort to reintroduce a reductionist mechanical model of the mind (and therapy) in the name of accountability and efficacy. This move appears to us to stem more from political and perhaps economic motives rather than scientific evidence. In fact, throughout this chapter, as we reviewed a broad cross-section of research evidence, we found little to support such a mechanistic view.

Most reports we read pointed strongly to the importance of the embodied experience of the client.

It may be time for psychotherapists to put some distance between themselves and the classical medical disease model that focuses on the dichotomies of "sickness versus health," or "illness versus cure." We believe that most people seeking help from therapists are not "sick" in the medical sense of the term, but are experiencing mental or emotional pains, or feel that they are functioning below their optimal capacity. In most cases, clients are not "cured," but helped to achieve improved functioning vis-à-vis the difficulties and challenges currently facing them and more productive or meaningful relationships with significant persons in their life. In a similar vein, "scientifically validated" treatments, as the term is used currently, might well encourage therapists to create a Procrustean bed for their clients, where the client has to fit into a preconceived notion of "illness," and a corresponding "cure" mechanically applied. Although we are both committed to rigorous empirical inquiry as a valuable road to more effective treatments, we are equally vocal in rejecting notions that would prescribe narrowly manualized interventions at the expense of ignoring the unique dynamic between therapist and client.

References

Adler, G. (1993). The psychotherapy of core borderline psychopathology. *American Journal of Psychotherapy, 47*, 194–205.

Adler, J. V. (1988). A study of the working alliance in psychotherapy. Unpublished doctoral dissertation, University of British Columbia, Vancouver, Canada.

Allen, J. G., Newsom, G. E., Gabbard, G. O., & Coyne, L. (1984). Scales to assess the therapeutic alliance from a psychoanalytic perspective. *Bulletin of the Menninger Clinic, 48*, 383–400.

Allen, J. G., Tarnoff, G., & Coyne, L. (1985). Therapeutic alliance and long-term hospital treatment outcome. *Comprehensive Psychiatry, 26*, 187–194.

Atkinson, J., & Schein, S. (1986). Similarly in counseling. *The Counseling Psychologist, 14*, 319–354.

Bachelor, A. (1988). How clients perceive therapist empathy: A content analysis of "received" empathy. *Psychotherapy: Theory, Research and Practice, 25*, 227–240.

Bachelor, A. (1991). Comparison and relationship to outcome of diverse dimensions of the helping alliance as seen by client and therapist. *Psychotherapy: Theory, Research and Practice, 28*, 534–549.

Bachelor, A. (1992, June). *Variability in dimensions of the therapeutic alliance*. Paper presented at the annual meeting of the Society for Psychotherapy Research, Berkeley, CA.

Bachelor, A. (1995). Clients' perception of the therapeutic alliance: A qualitative analysis. *Journal of Counseling Psychology, 42,* 323–337.

Bandura, A., Lipsher, D. H., & Miller, P. E. (1960). Psychotherapist's approach—avoidance reactions to patient's expression of hostility. *Journal of Consulting Psychology, 24,* 1–8.

Barrett-Lennard, G. T. (1962). Dimensions of therapist response as causal factor in therapeutic change. *Psychological Monographs, 76* (whole No. 562).

Beutler, L., & Consoli, A. (1993). Matching the therapist's interpersonal stance to clients' characteristics: Contributions from systematic eclectic psychotherapy. *Psychotherapy: Theory, Research, and Practice, 30,* 417–422.

Beutler, L. E., Crago, M., & Arizmendi, T. G. (1986). Research on therapist variables in psychotherapy. In S. L. Garfield & A. E. Bergin (Eds.), *Handbook of psychotherapy and behavior change* (pp. 257–310). New York: Wiley.

Beutler, L. E., Engle, D., Mohr, D., Daldrup, R. J., Bergan, J., Meredith, K., & Merry, W. (1991). Predictors of differential and self-directed psychotherapeutic procedures. *Journal of Consulting and Clinical Psychology, 59,* 333–340.

Beutler, L. E., Machado, P. P. M., & Allstetter Neufeldt, S. A. (1994). Therapist variables. In B. A. & S. L. Garfield (Eds.), *Handbook of psychotherapy and behavior change* (pp. 229–269). New York: Wiley.

Bordin, E. S. (1975, September). *The working alliance: Basis for a general theory of psychotherapy*. Paper presented at the annual meeting of the Society for Psychotherapy Research, Washington, DC.

Bordin, E. S. (1979). The generalizability of the psychoanalytic concept of the working alliance. *Psychotherapy: Theory, Research, and Practice, 16,* 252–260.

Bordin, E. S. (1980, June). *Of human bonds that bind or free*. Presidential address delivered at the annual meeting of the Society for Research in Psychotherapy, Pacific Grove, CA.

Bordin, E. S. (1989, June). *Building therapeutic alliances: The base for integration*. Paper presented at the annual meeting of the Society for Psychotherapy Research, Berkeley, CA.

Bordin, E. S. (1994). Theory and research on the therapeutic working alliance: New directions. In A O. Horvath & L. S. Greenberg (Eds.), *The working alliance: Theory, research, and practice* (pp. 13–37). New York: Wiley.

Bourgeois, L., Sabourin, S., & Wright, J. (1990). Predictive validity of therapeutic alliance in group marital therapy. *Journal of Counseling and Clinical Psychology, 58,* 608–613.

Bowlby, J. (1988). Attachment, communication, and the therapeutic process. In J. Bowlby (Ed.), *A secure base: Parent–child attachment and healthy human development* (pp. 137–157). New York: Basic Books.

Brooks, L. (1974). Interactive effects of sex and status on self-disclosure. *Journal of Counseling Psychology, 21,* 469–474.

Burns, D., & Nolen-Hoeksema, S. (1992). Therapist empathy and recovery from depression in cognitive–behavioral therapy: A structural equation model. *Journal of Consulting and Clinical Psychology, 60,* 441–449.

Callaghan, G. M., Naugle, A. E., & Follette, W. C. (1996). Useful constructions of the client–therapist relationship. *Psychotherapy: Theory, Research, and Practice, 33,* 381–390.

Coady, N. F. (1991). The association between complex types of therapist interventions and outcomes in psychodynamic psychotherapy. *Research on Social Work Practice, 1,* 257–277.

Cherbosque, J. (1987). Differential effects of counselor self-disclosure statements on perception of the counselor and willingness to disclose: A cross cultural study. *Psychotherapy: Theory, Research and Practice, 24,* 434–437.

Crits-Christoph, P., Barber, J., & Kurcias, J. S. (1993). The accuracy of therapists' interpretations and the development of alliance. *Psychotherapy: Theory, Research and Practice, 3,* 25–35.

Crits-Christoph, P., Demorest, A., & Connolly, M. B. (1990). Quantitative assessment of interpersonal themes over the course of psychotherapy. *Psychotherapy, 27,* 513–521.

Cutler, R. L. (1958). Countertransference effects in psychotherapy. *Journal of Consulting Psychology, 22,* 349–356.

Dietzel, C. S., & Abeles, N. (1975). Client–therapist complementarity and therapeutic outcome. *Journal of Counseling Psychology, 22,* 262–272.

Dolan, R., Arnkoff, D., & Glass, C. (1993). Client attachment style and the psychotherapist's interpersonal stance. *Psychotherapy: Theory, Research, and Practice, 30,* 408–412.

Donley, R. J., Horan, J. J., & DeShong, R. L. (1989). The effect of several self-disclosure permutations on counseling process and outcome. *Journal of Counseling and Development, 67,* 408–412.

Dozier, M., Cue, K. L., & Barnett, L. (1994). Clinicians as caregivers: Role of attachment organization in treatment. *Journal of Consulting and Clinical Psychology, 62,* 793–800.

Duan, C., & Hill, C. (1996). The current state of empathy research. *Journal of Counseling Psychology, 43,* 261–274.

Dunkle, J., & Friedlander, M. (1996). Contribution of therapist experience and personal characteristics to the working alliance. *Journal of Counseling Psychology, 43,* 456–460.

Eaton, T. T., Abeles, N., & Gutfreund, M. J. (1993). Negative indicators, therapeutic alliance, and therapy outcome. *Psychotherapy: Theory, Research, and Practice, 3,* 115–123.

Eaton, T. T., Abeles, N., & Gutfreund, M. J. (1988). Therapeutic alliance and outcome: Impact of treatment length and pretreatment symptomology. *Psychotherapy: Theory, Research and Practice, 25,* 536–542.

Elkind, S. N. (1992). *Resolving impasses in therapeutic relationships.* New York: Guilford Press.

Elliot, R., Barker, C. B., Caskey, N., & Pistrang, N. (1982). Differential helpfulness of counselor verbal response modes. *Journal of Counseling Psychology, 29,* 354–361.

Elliot, R., James, E., Reimschuessel, C., Cislo, D., & Sack, N. (1985). Significant events and the analysis of immediate therapeutic impacts. *Psychotherapy: Theory, Research and Practice, 22,* 620–630.

Eysenck, H. J. (1952). The effects of psychotherapy: An evaluation. *Journal of Consulting Psychology, 16,* 319–324.

Farber, B. A., Lippert, R. A., & Nevas, D. B. (1995). The therapist as an attachment figure. *Psychotherapy: Theory Research and Practice, 32,* 204–212.

Foreman, S. A., & Marmar, C. R. (1985). Therapist actions that address initially poor therapeutic alliances in psychotherapy. *American Journal of Psychiatry, 142,* 922–926.

Freud, S. (1958). On the beginning of treatment: Further recommendations on the technique of psychoanalysis. In J. Strachey (Ed. and Trans.), *Standard edition of the complete psychological works of Sigmund Freud* (Vol. 12, pp. 122–144). London: Hogarth Press. (Original work published 1912)

Freud, S. (1966). The dynamics of transference. In J. Strachey (Ed. and Trans.), *Standard edition of the complete psychological works of Sigmund Freud* (Vol. 12, pp. 97–108). London: Hogarth Press. (Original work published 1913)

Friedlander, M. L. (1993). When complimentarity is uncomplementary and other reactions to Tracey. *Journal of Counseling Psychology, 40,* 410–412.

Friedlander, M. L., Thibodeau, J. R., & Ward, L. G. (1985). Discriminating the "good" from the "bad" therapy hour: A study of dynamic interaction: *Psychotherapy: Theory Research and Practice, 22,* 631–641.

Gamsky, N. R., & Farwell, G. F. (1966). Counselor verbal behavior as a function of client hostility. *Journal of Counseling Psychology, 13,* 184–190.

Gartner, J., Harmatz, M., Hohmann, A., & Larson, D. (1990). The effect of patient and clinician ideology on clinical judgment: A study of ideological countertransference. *Psychotherapy: Theory Research and Practice, 27,* 98–106.

Gaston, L. (1991). The reliability and criterion-related validity of the patient version of the California Psychotherapy Alliance Scale.

Psychological Assessment: A Journal of Consulting and Clinical Psychology, 3, 68–74.

Gaston, L., & Marmar, C. (1994). The California Psychotherapy Alliance Scales. In A. O. Horvath & L. S. Greenberg (Eds.), *The working alliance: Theory, research and practice* (pp. 85–108). New York: Wiley.

Gaston, L., Marmar, C. R., Thompson, L. W., & Gallagher, D. (1988). Relation of patient pretreatment characteristics to the therapeutic alliance in diverse psychotherapies. *Journal of Consulting and Clinical Psychology, 56*(4), 483–489.

Gaston, L., Marmar, C. R., Thompson, L. W., & Gallagher, D. (1991). Alliance prediction of outcome: Beyond in-treatment symptomatic change as psychotherapy progresses. *Psychotherapy Research, 1,* 104–112.

Gaston, L., & Ring, J. M. (1992). Preliminary results on the Inventory of Therapeutic Strategies. *Journal of Psychotherapy Practice and Research, 1,* 1–13.

Gelso, C. J., & Carter, J. A. (1985). The relationship in counseling and psychotherapy: Components, consequences, and theoretical antecedents. *The Counseling Psychologist, 13,* 155–243.

Gelso, C. J., & Carter, J. A. (1994). Components of the psychotherapy relationship: Their interaction and unfolding during treatment. *Journal of Counseling Psychology, 41,* 296–306.

Gibbs, J. T., & Huang, L. N. (1989). *Children of color: Psychological interventions with minority youths.* San Francisco: Jossey-Bass.

Gladstein, G. A. (1977). Empathy and counseling outcome: An empirical and conceptual review. *The Counseling Psychologist, 6,* 70–79.

Golden, B. R., & Robbins, S. B. (1990). The working alliance within time-limited therapy: A case analysis. *Professional Psychology: Research and Practice, 21,* 476–481.

Gomes-Schwartz, B. (1978). Effective ingredients in psychotherapy: Prediction of outcome from process variables. *Journal of Consulting and Clinical Psychology, 46,* 1023–1035.

Gomes-Schwartz, B., & Schwartz, J. M. (1978). Psychotherapy process variables distinguishing the "inherently helpful" person from the professional psychotherapist. *Journal of Consulting and Clinical Psychology, 46,* 196–197.

Greenberg, L. S. (1994). What is "real" in the relationship ? Comment on Gelso and Carter. *Journal of Counseling Psychology, 41,* 307–310.

Greenberg, L. S., & Pinsof, W. M. (1986). *The psychotherapeutic process: A research handbook.* New York: Guilford Press.

Greenson, R. R. (1965). The working alliance and the transference neuroses. *Psychoanalysis Quarterly, 34,* 155–181.

Grigg, A., & Goodstein, L. (1957). The use of clients as judges of the counselor's performance. *Journal of Counseling Psychology, 4,* 31–36.

Grunebaum, H. (1986). Harmful psychotherapy experience. *American Journal of Psychotherapy, 40,* 165–176.

Gurman, A. S. (1977). The patient's perceptions of the therapeutic relationship. In A. S. Gurman & A. M. Razin (Eds.), *Effective psychotherapy* (pp. 503–545). Elmsford, NY: Pergamon Press.

Haccoun, C. M., & Lavigueur, H. (1979). Effects of clinical experience and client emotion on therapists' responses. *Journal of Consulting and Clinical Psychology, 47,* 416–418.

Hayes, J. A., & Gelso, C. J. (1991). Effects of therapist-trainees' anxiety and empathy on countertransference behavior. *Journal of Clinical Psychology, 47,* 284–290.

Hayes, J. A., Gelso, C. J., Van Wagoner, S., & Diemer, R. (1991). Managing countertransference: What the experts think. *Psychological Reports, 69,* 139–148.

Henry, W. P. (1996). Structural analysis of social behavior as a common metric for programmatic psychopathology and psychotherapy research. *Journal of Consulting and Clinical Psychology, 64,* 1263–1275.

Henry, W. P., Schacht, T. E., & Strupp, H. H. (1986). Structural analysis of social behavior: Application to a study of interpersonal process in differential psychotherapeutic outcome. *Journal of Consulting and Clinical Psychology, 54,* 27–31.

Henry, W. P., Schacht, T. E., & Strupp, H. H. (1990). Patient and therapist introject, interpersonal process and differential psychotherapy outcome. *Journal of Consulting and Clinical Psychology, 58,* 768–774.

Henry, W. P., & Strupp, H. H. (1994). The therapeutic alliance as interpersonal process. In A. O. Horvath & L. S. Greenberg (Eds.), *The working alliance: Theory, research and practice* (pp. 51–84). New York: Wiley.

Heppner, P., Rosenberg, J., & Hedgespeth, J. (1992). Three methods in measuring the therapeutic process: Clients' and counselors' constructions of the therapeutic process versus actual therapeutic events. *Journal of Counseling Psychology, 39,* 20–31.

Hill, C. E. (1975). Sex of client and sex and experience level of counselor. *Journal of Counseling Psychology, 22,* 6–11.

Hill, C. E. (1994). What is the therapeutic relationship? A reaction to Sexton and Whiston. *The Counseling Psychologist, 22,* 90–97.

Hill, C. E., Helms, J. E., Spiegel, S. B., & Tichenor, V. (1988). Development of a system for categorizing client reactions to therapist interventions. *Journal of Counseling Psychology, 35,* 27–36.

Hill, C. E., Nutt-Williams, E., Heaton, K., Thompson, B., & Rhodes, R. H. (1996). Therapist retrospective recall of impasses in long-term psychotherapy: A qualitative analysis. *Journal of Counseling Psychology, 43,* 207–217.

Hill, C. E., & O'Grady, K. E. (1985). List of therapist intentions illustrated in a case study and with therapists of varying theoretical orientations. *Journal of Counseling Psychology, 32,* 3–22.

Horowitz, M. J., Marmar, C. R., Weiss, D., DeWitt, K. N., & Rosenbaum, R. (1984). Brief psychotherapy of bereavement reactions: The relationship of process to outcome. *Archives of General Psychiatry, 41,* 438–448.

Horvath, A. O. (1981). *An exploratory study of the working alliance: Its measurement and relationship to outcome.* Unpublished doctoral dissertation, University of British Columbia, Vancouver, Canada.

Horvath, A. O. (1991). *What do we know about the alliance and what do we still have to find out?* Paper presented at the annual meeting of the Society for Psychotherapy Research, Lyons, France.

Horvath, A. O. (1994). Research on the alliance. In A. O. Horvath & L. S. Greenberg (Eds.), *The working alliance: Theory, research and practice* (pp. 259–287). New York: Wiley.

Horvath, A. O., & Luborsky, L. (1993). The role of the therapeutic alliance in psychotherapy. *Journal of Consulting and Clinical Psychology, 61,* 561–573.

Horvath, A. O., & Marx, R. W. (1988, April). *Working alliance and counseling outcome: A longitudinal perspective.* New Orleans, LA: The American Educational Research Association.

Horvath, A. O., & Marx, R. W. (1990). The development and decay of the working alliance during time-limited counselling. *The Canadian Journal of Counselling, 24,* 240–259.

Horvath, A. O., Marx, R. W., & Kaman, A. M. (1990). Thinking about thinking in therapy: An examination of clients' understanding of their therapists' intentions. *Journal of Consulting and Clinical Psychology, 58,* 614–621.

Horvath, A. O., & Symonds, B. D. (1991). Relation between working alliance and outcome in psychotherapy: A meta-analysis. *Journal of Counseling Psychology, 38,* 139–149.

Howard, K. I., Orlinsky, D. E., & Hill, J. A. (1969). The therapist's feeling in the therapeutic process. *Journal of Clinical Psychology, 25,* 83–93.

Hoyt, W. T., Strong, S. R., Corcoran, J. L., & Robbins, S. B. (1993). Interpersonal influence in a single case of brief counseling: An analytic strategy and a comparison of two indexes of outcome. *Journal of Counseling Psychology, 40,* 166–181.

Jacobs, M. A., & Warner, B. L. (1981). Interaction of therapeutic attitudes with severity of clinical diagnosis. *Journal of Clinical Psychology, 37,* 75–82.

Jones, E. E., Krupnick, J. L., & Kerig, P. L. (1987). Some gender effects in brief psychotherapy. *Psychotherapy: Theory, Research and Practice, 24,* 336–352.

Jones, E. E., & Zoppel, C. (1982). Impact of client and therapist gender on psychotherapy process and outcome. *Journal of Consulting and Clinical Psychology, 50,* 259–272.

Kiesler, D. J. (1982). Interpersonal theory for personality and psychotherapy. In J. C. Anchin & D. Kiesler (Eds.), *Handbook of interpersonal psychotherapy* (pp. 3–24). Elmsford, NY: Pergamon Press.

Kiesler, D. J. (1986). *Therapeutic metacommunication.* Palo Alto, CA: Consulting Psychologists Press.

Kiesler, D. J., & Watkins, L. M. (1989). Interpersonal complementarity and the therapeutic alliance: A study of relationship in psychotherapy. *Psychotherapy, 26,* 183–194.

Kivlighan, D. M. (1990). Relation between counselors' use of intentions and clients' perception of working alliance. *Journal of Counseling Psychology, 37,* 27–32.

Kivlighan, D. M., & Schmitz, P. J. (1992). Counselor technical activity in cases with improving working alliances and continuing-poor working alliances. *Journal of Counseling Psychology, 39,* 32–38.

Kokotovic, A. M., & Tracey, T. J. (1990). Working alliance in the early phase of counseling. *Journal of Counseling Psychology, 37,* 16–21.

Kolb, D. L., Beutler, L. E., Davis, C. S., Crago, M., & Shanfield, S. (1985). Patient and therapy process variables relating to dropout and change in psychotherapy. *Psychotherapy: Theory Research and Practice, 22,* 702–710.

Kolden, G. G., Howard, K. I., & Maling, M. S. (1994). The counselling relationship and treatment process and outcome. *The Counseling Psychologist, 22,* 82-89.

Krupnick, J., Stotsky, S., Simmens, S., & Moyer, J. (1992, June). *The role of therapeutic alliance in psychotherapy and pharmacotherapy outcome: Findings in the NIMH Treatment of Depression Collaborative Research Program.* Paper presented at the annual meeting of the Society for Psychotherapy Research, Berkeley, CA.

LaCrosse, M. B. (1980). Perceived counselor social influence and counseling outcomes: Validity of the Counselor Rating Form. *Journal of Counseling Psychology, 27,* 320–327.

Lafferty, P., Beutler, L. E., & Crago, M. (1989). Differences between more and less effective psychotherapists: A study of select therapist variables. *Journal of Consulting and Clinical Psychology, 57,* 76–80.

Lambert, M. J., & Bergin, A. E. (1983). Therapist characteristics and their contribution to psychotherapy outcome. In C. E. Walker (Ed.), *The handbook of clinical psychology* (pp. 205–241). Homewood, IL: Dow Jones-Irwin.

Lambert, M. J., & Bergin, A. E. (1994). The effectiveness of psychotherapy. In A. E. Bergin & S. L. Garfield (Eds.), *Handbook of psychotherapy and behavior change* (pp. 143–189). New York: Wiley.

Lambert, M. J., De Julio, S. S., & Stein, D. M. (1978). Therapist interpersonal skills: Process, outcome, methodological considerations and recommendations for future research. *Psychological Bulletin, 85,* 467–489.

Lazarus, A. A. (1971). *Behavior therapy and beyond.* New York: McGraw-Hill.

Lazarus, A. A. (1993). Tailoring the therapeutic relationship, or being an authentic chameleon. *Psychotherapy: Theory, Research, and Practice, 30,* 404–407.

Luborsky, L. (1976). Helping alliances in psychotherapy. In J. L. Cleghhorn (Eds.), *Successful psychotherapy* (pp. 92–116). New York: Brunner/Mazel.

Luborsky, L., & Crits-Christoph, P. (1990). *Understanding transference: The Core Conflictual Relationship Theme Method.* New York: Basic Books.

Luborsky, L., Crits-Christoph, P., Alexander, L., Margolis, M., & Cohen, M. (1983). Two helping alliance methods for predicting outcomes of psychotherapy: A counting signs vs. a global rating method. *Journal of Nervous and Mental Disease, 171,* 480–491.

Luborsky, L., Crits-Christoph, P., Mintz, J., & Auerbach, A. (1988). *Who will benefit from psychotherapy? Predicting therapeutic outcomes.* New York: Basic Books.

Luborsky, L., Singer, B., & Luborsky, L. (1975). Comparative studies of psychotherapies: Is it true that "everyone has won and all must have prizes"? *Archives of General Psychiatry, 32,* 995–1008.

Malan D. H. (1976). *Toward the validation of dynamic psychotherapy.* New York: Plenum.

Mallinckrodt, B. (1991). Clients' representations of childhood emotional bonds with parents, social support, and formation of working alliance. *Journal of Counseling Psychology, 38,* 401–409.

Mallinckrodt, B., Coble, H., & Gantt, G. O. (1995). Working alliance, attachment memories, and social competencies of women in brief therapy. *Journal of Counseling Psychology, 42,* 79–84.

Mallinckrodt, B., Gantt, G. O., & Coble, H. (1995). Attachment patterns in the therapy relationship: Development of the Client Attachment to Therapist Scale. *Journal of Counseling Psychology, 42,* 307–317.

Mallinckrodt, B., & Nelson, M. L. (1991). Counselor training level and the formation of the psychotherapeutic working alliance. *Journal of Counseling Psychology, 38,* 133–138.

Marmar, M. J., Weiss, D. S., & Gaston, L. (1989). Towards the validation of the California Therapeutic Alliance Rating System. *Psychological Assessment, 1,* 46–52.

Marziali, E. (1984a). Prediction of outcome of brief psychotherapy from therapist interpretive interventions. *Archives of General Psychiatry, 41,* 301–305.

Marziali, E. (1984b). Three viewpoints on the therapeutic alliance scales similarities, differences and associations with psychotherapy outcome. *Journal of Nervous & Mental Disease, 172,* 417–423.

McCullough, L., Winston, A., Farber, B. A., Porter, F., Pollack, J., Laikin, M., Vingiano, W., & Trujillo, M. (1991). The relationship of patient–therapist interaction to outcome in brief psychotherapy. *Psychotherapy, 28*, 525–533.

McClure, B. A., & Hodge, R. W. (1987). Measuring countertransference and attitude in therapeutic relationships. *Psychotherapy, 24*, 325–335.

McKee, G. (1992). *Impact of therapist attachment styles on empathic ability and strength of working alliance.* Unpublished master's thesis, University of British Columbia, Vancouver, Canada.

Milliken, R. L., & Kirchner, R. (1971). Counselor's understanding of student's communication as a function of the counselor's perceptual defense. *Journal of Counseling Psychology, 18*, 14–18.

Mills, D. H., & Abeles, N. (1965). Counselor needs for affiliation and nurturance as related to liking for clients and counseling process. *Journal of Counseling Psychology, 12*, 353–359.

Mohl, P. C., Martinez, D., Ticknor, C., Huang, M., & Cordell, M. D. (1991). Early dropouts from psychotherapy. *Journal of Nervous and Mental Disease, 179*, 478–481.

Moras, K., & Strupp, H. (1982). Pretherapy interpersonal relations, patients' alliance, and outcome in brief therapy. *Archives of General Psychiatry, 39*, 405–409.

Mueller, W. J. (1969). Patterns of behavior and their reciprocal impact in the family and in psychotherapy [Monograph]. *Journal of Counseling Psychology, 16*, 1–25.

Muran, C. J., Segal, Z. V., Wallner Samstag, L., & Crawford, C. E. (1994). Patient pretreatment interpersonal problems and therapeutic alliance in short-term cognitive therapy. *Journal of Consulting and Clinical Psychology, 62*, 185–190.

Murphy, P., Cramer, D., & Lillie, F. (1984). The relationship between curative factors perceived by patients in their psychotherapy and treatment outcome: An exploratory study. *British Journal of Medical Psychology, 57*, 187–192.

Nelson, M. L. (1993). A current perspective on gender differences: Implications for research in counseling. *Journal of Counseling Psychology, 40*, 200–209.

Norcross, J. (1993). Tailoring relationship stances to client needs: An introduction. *Psychotherapy: Theory, Research, and Practice, 30*, 402–403.

Norville, R., Sampson, H., & Weiss, J. (1996). Accurate interpretations and brief psychotherapy outcome. *Psychotherapy Research, 6*, 16–29.

O'Malley, S. S., Suh, C. S., & Strupp, H. H. (1983). The Vanderbilt Psychotherapy Process Scale: A report on scale development and a process–outcome study. *Journal of Consulting and Clinical Psychology, 51*, 581–586.

Orlinsky, D. E., Grawe, K., & Parks, B. K. (1994). Process and outcome in psychotherapy—noch einmal. In B. A. Garfield & S. L. Garfield (Eds.), *Handbook of psychotherapy and behavior change* (pp. 270–376). New York: Wiley.

Orlinsky, D. E., & Howard, K. I. (1975). *Varieties of psychotherapeutic experience.* New York: Teachers College Press.

Orlinsky, D. E., & Howard, K. I. (1986). Process and outcome in psychotherapy. In S. L. Garfield & A. E. Bergin (Eds.), *Handbook of psychotherapy and behavior change* (3rd ed., pp. 311–381). New York: Wiley.

Orlinsky, D. E., Howard, K. I. (1987). A generic model of psychotherapy. *Journal of Integrative and Eclectic Psychotherapy, 6,* 6–27.

Patterson, C. H. (1984). Empathy, warmth, and genuineness in psychotherapy: A review of reviews. *Psychotherapy, 21,* 431–438.

Peabody, S. A., & Gelso, C. J. (1982). Countertransference and empathy: The complex relationship between two divergent concepts in counseling. *Journal of Counseling Psychology, 29,* 240–245.

Peca-Baker, T. A., & Friedlander, M. L. (1987). Effects of role expectations on clients' perceptions of disclosing and nondisclosing counselors. *Journal of Counseling and Development, 66,* 78–81.

Persons, R. W., Persons, M. K., & Newmark, I. (1974). Perceived helpful therapist's characteristics, client improvements, and sex of therapist and client. *Psychotherapy: Theory, Research and Practice, 11,* 63–65.

Pinsof, W. M. (1994). Integrative systems perspective on the therapeutic alliance: Theoretical, research and clinical implications. In A. O. Horvath & L. S. Greenberg (Eds.), *The working alliance: Theory, research and practice* (pp. 173–198). New York: Wiley.

Piper, W. E., Azim, F. A., Joyce, S. A., & McCallum, M. (1991). Transference interpretations, therapeutic alliance and outcome in short-term individual psychotherapy. *Archives of General Psychiatry, 48,* 946–953.

Piper, W. E., Azim, F. A., Joyce, S. A., McCallum, M., Nixon, G., & Segal, P. S. (1991). Quality of object relations versus interpersonal functioning as predictors of alliance and outcome. *Journal of Nervous and Mental Disease, 179,* 432–438.

Piper, W. E., de Carufel, F. L., & Szkrumelak, N. (1985). Patient predictors of process and outcome in short-term individual psychotherapy. *The Journal of Nervous and Mental Disease, 173,* 726–733.

Piper, W. E., Debbane, E. G., Bienvenu, J., Carufel, F., & Garant, J. (1986). Relationships between the object focus of therapist interpretations and outcome in short-term individual psychotherapy. *British Journal of Medical Psychology, 59,* 1–11.

Pistole, M. C., & Watkins, C. E. (1995). Attachment theory, counseling process, and supervision. *The Counseling Psychologist, 23,* 457–478.

Plotnicov, K. H. (1990). *Early termination from counseling: The client's perspective.* Unpublished doctoral dissertation, University of Pittsburgh, PA.

Raue, P., Castonguay, L., & Goldfried, M. (1993). The working alliance: a comparison of two therapists. *Psychotherapy Research, 3,* 197–207.

Reandeau, S. G., & Wampold, B. E. (1991). Relationship of power and involvement working alliance: A multiple-case sequential analysis of brief therapy. *Journal of Counseling Psychology, 38,* 107–114.

Rhodes, R. H., Hill, C. E., Thompson, B. J., & Elliot, R. (1994). Client retrospective recall of resolved and unresolved misunderstanding events. *Journal of Counseling Psychology, 41,* 473–483.

Robbins, S. B., & Jolkovski, M. P. (1987). Managing countertransference feelings: An interactional model using awareness of feeling and theoretical framework. *Journal of Counseling Psychology, 34,* 276–282.

Robiner, N. W., & Storandt, M. (1983). Client perceptions of the therapeutic relationship as a function of client and counselor age. *Journal of Counseling Psychology, 30,* 96–99.

Rogers, C. R. (1951). *Client-centered therapy.* Boston: Houghton Mifflin.

Rogers, C. R. (1957). The necessary and sufficient conditions of therapeutic personality change. *Journal of Consulting Psychology, 21,* 95–103.

Rogers, C. R., Gendlin, G. T., Kiesler, D. V., & Truax, L. B. (1967). *The therapeutic relationship and its impact: A study of psychotherapy with schizophrenics.* Madison University of Wisconsin Press.

Ryan, E. R., & Cichetti, D. W. (1985). Predicting quality of alliance in the initial psychotherapy interview. *The Journal of Nervous and Mental Disease, 173,* 717–725.

Sabourin, S., Coallier, J. C., Cournoyer, L. G., & Gaston, L. (1990, June). *Further aspects of the validity of the California Psychotherapy Alliance Scales.* Paper presented at the annual meeting of the Society for Psychotherapy, Wintergreen, VA.

Sachs, J. S. (1983). Negative factors in brief psychotherapy: An empirical assessment. *Journal of Consulting and Clinical Psychology, 51,* 557–564.

Safran, J. D., Crocker, P., McMain, S., & Murray, P. (1990). The therapeutic alliance rupture as a therapy event for empirical investigations. *Psychotherapy: Theory, Research and Practice, 27,* 154–165.

Safran, J. D., Muran, J. C., & Wallner Samstag, I. (1994). Resolving therapeutic ruptures: A task analytic investigation. In A. O. Horvath & L. S. Greenberg (Eds.), *The working alliance: Theory, research and practice* (pp. 335–358). New York: Wiley.

Satterfield, W., & Lyddon, W. (1995). Client attachment and perceptions of the working alliance with counselor trainees. *Journal of Counseling Psychology, 42,* 187–189.

Sexton, T. L., & Whiston, S. C. (1994). The status of the counseling relationship: An empirical review, theoretical implications, and research directions. *The Counseling Psychologist, 22,* 6–78.

Silberschatz, G., Fretter, P. B., & Curtis, J. T. (1986). How do interpretations influence the process of psychotherapy? *Journal of Consulting and Clinical Psychology, 54,* 646–652.

Singer, J. (1985). Transference and the human condition: A cognitive–affective perspective. *Psychoanalytic Psychology, 2,* 189–219.

Skinner, B. F. (1985). *Recent issues in the analysis of behavior.* Englewood, NJ: Prentice-Hall.

Smith, M. L., & Glass, G. V. (1977). Meta-analysis of psychotherapy outcome studies. *American Psychologist, 32,* 752–760.

Snyder, W. U., & Snyder, B. J. (1961). *The psychotherapy relationship.* New York: Macmillan.

Strong, S. R. (1968). Counseling: An interpersonal influence process. *Journal of Counseling Psychology, 15,* 215–224.

Strupp, H. H. (1974). On the basic ingredients of psychotherapy. *Psychotherapy and Psychosomatics, 24,* 249–260.

Strupp., H. H. (1980). Success and failure in time-limited psychotherapy: Further evidence (Comparison 4). *Archives of General Psychiatry, 37,* 947–954.

Strupp, H. H., & Hadley, S. W. (1979). Specific vs. non-specific factors in psychotherapy: A controlled study of outcome. *Archives of General Psychiatry, 36,* 1125–1136.

Svartberg, M., & Stiles, T. C. (1992). Predicting patient change from therapist competence and patient–therapist complementarity in short-term anxiety-provoking psychotherapy: A pilot study. *Journal of Consulting and Clinical Psychology, 60,* 304–307.

Tasca, G. A., & McMullen, L. M. (1992). Interpersonal complementarity and antitheses within a stage model of psychotherapy. *Psychotherapy, 29,* 515–523.

Thompson, B. J., Hill, C. E., & Mahalik, J. R. (1991). A test of the complementarity hypothesis in the interpersonal theory of psychotherapy: Multiple case comparisons. *Psychotherapy, 28,* 572–578.

Tichenor, V., & Hill, C. E. (1989). A comparison of six measures of working alliance. *Psychotherapy, 26,* 195–199.

Tracey, T. J. (1986). Interactional correlates of premature termination. *Journal of Consulting and Clinical Psychology, 54,* 784–788.

Tracey, T. J. (1993). An interpersonal stage model of the therapeutic process. *Journal of Counseling Psychology, 40,* 396–409.

Tracey, T. J., & Ray, P. B. (1984). Stages of successful time-limited counseling: An interactional examination. *Journal of Counseling Psychology, 31,* 13–27.

Truax, C. B., & Carkhuff, R. R. (1967). *Toward effective counseling and psychotherapy.* Chicago: Aldine.

Van Wagoner, S. L., Gelso, C. J., Hayes, J. A., & Diemer, R. A. (1991). Countertransference and the reputedly excellent therapist. *Psychotherapy, 28,* 411–421.

Watkins, C. E., & Schneider, L. J. (1989). Self-involving versus self-disclosing counselor statements during an initial interview. *Journal of Counseling and Development, 67,* 345–349.

Watson, J. C., & Greenberg, L. S. (1994). The alliance in experiential therapy: Enacting the relationship conditions. In A. O. Horvath & L. S. Greenberg (Eds.), *The working alliance: Theory and research* (pp. 153–172). New York: Wiley.

Weiss, J. (1986). Part I: Theory and clinical observations. In J. Weiss, H. Sampson, & The Mount Zion Psychotherapy Research Group (Eds.), *The psychoanalytic process: Theory, clinical observation, and empirical research* (pp. 3–138). New York: Guilford Press.

Westerman, M., & Foote, J. (1995). Patient coordination: Contrasts with other conceptualizations of patients' contribution to the alliance and validity in insight-oriented therapy. *Psychotherapy: Theory, Research and Practice, 32,* 222–232.

Wiggins, J. S. (1982). Circumplex models of interpersonal behavior in clinical psychology. In P. C. Kendall & J. N. Butcher (Eds.), *Handbook of research methods in clinical psychology* (pp. 183–221). New York: Wiley.

Windholz, J. J., & Silberschatz, G. (1988). Vanderbilt psychotherapy process scale: A replication with adult outpatients. *Journal of Consulting and Clinical Psychology, 56,* 56–60.

Yulis, S., & Kiesler, D. J. (1968). Countertransference response as a function of therapist anxiety and content of patient talk. *Journal of Consulting and Clinical Psychology, 32,* 414–419.

Zetzel, E. R. (1956). Current concepts of transference. *International Journal of Psychoanalysis, 37,* 369–376.

C. R. Snyder, Scott T. Michael, and Jennifer S. Cheavens

Hope as a Psychotherapeutic Foundation of Common Factors, Placebos, and Expectancies

6

lthough psychotherapy is no panacea, good evidence exists that it works. Some 20 years ago, the now classic Smith and Glass (1977; also see Smith, Glass, & Miller, 1980) meta-analytic study revealed that the average person treated with psychotherapy (collapsing across various forms of treatment) was better off than 80% of those who did not receive such treatment. The literature that followed also made a compelling case for the effectiveness of psychotherapy (Andrews & Harvey, 1981; Barker, Funk, & Houston, 1988; Lambert, Shapiro, & Bergin, 1986; Landman & Dawes, 1982; Lipsey & Wilson, 1993; Prioleau, Murdock, & Brody, 1983; Shapiro & Shapiro, 1982; VandenBos & Pino, 1980). Likewise, a recent survey in *Consumer Reports* found that readers of the magazine perceived psychotherapy as beneficial (Seligman, 1995).

A fundamental question remains, nevertheless. What makes psychotherapy effective? In response to this question, the proponents of given psychotherapeutic techniques are quick to point to specific aspects of their chosen approaches. The result is a bewildering and often contradictory array of explanations that have defied attempts at integration and maintained the division among the various schools of psychotherapy (Miller, Duncan, & Hubble, 1997). More parsimonious explanations, however, are at hand. The view presented in this chapter, and one championed by the authors of the other chapters in this volume, is that the beneficial effects of psychotherapy largely result from processes shared by the various models and their associated techniques. This latter perspective is supported by 40 years of outcome research showing that most psychotherapy approaches affect change in clients with few differences in effectiveness (Garfield, 1981; Luborsky, Singer, & Luborsky, 1975; Miller et al., 1997; Smith & Glass, 1977; Smith et al., 1980).[1] The uniformity of treatment outcomes is even more pronounced when different approaches share similar foci (Frank & Frank, 1991) and symptom intensity (Ilardi, Craighead, & Evans, 1997). Such findings have led to an examination of processes common across psychotherapies—the so-called nonspecific or common factors (client factors, relationship factors, placebos, and therapeutic techniques [Lambert, 1992]).[2] This chapter explores the role of hope as a key common factor in human change.

We begin with the presentation of a new theory regarding the role of hope in change. Then, we attempt to show how the other nonspecific factors in psychotherapy are related to the common factor of hope. In particular, the similarities among hope, placebo, and expectancy are explored. Throughout the chapter, hope is portrayed as a common part of processes used in varying degrees by most people to cope with daily life. We argue that successful psychotherapy hastens change by enhancing the contribution of this common factor. We conclude the chapter with a case example illustrating the theory and various research findings.

Hope Theory: A Unifying Framework

Hope may be understood in terms of how people think about goals. Thinking about goals is defined in two components. First, there are the thoughts that persons have about their ability to produce one or more workable routes to their goals. And second, there are the thoughts that people have regarding their ability to begin and continue movement on selected pathways toward those goals. These two

---

[1]Karasu (1986) suggested that there are at least 400 differing approaches to psychotherapy. If the number of psychotherapies is akin to a bull market in the ensuing years, the 21st century portends 500 or more psychotherapies.

[2]It is important to note that the term *nonspecific* is not used to connote a vague, unknowable set of factors. As researcher Kazdin (1980) wrote "the term is misleading because it implies that there are nebulous influences in treatment that mysteriously alter client behavior" (p. 325). Rather, *nonspecific* is meant to refer to those factors thought common to all psychotherapy approaches. Throughout the history of the field, the terms *nonspecific* and *common factors* have been used interchangeably. To stay consistent with the language used in this book, the terminology *common factors* is used throughout this chapter.

components are known respectively as *pathways thinking* and *agency thinking* (Snyder, 1994a, 1994b, 1998; Snyder, Harris, et al., 1991; Snyder, Hoza, et al., 1997; Snyder, McDermott, Cook, & Rapoff, 1997; Snyder et al., 1996). Both types of thinking must be present for a person to experience hope. Given the strong emphasis on thought, the theory presented in this chapter is cognitive in nature. It contrasts sharply with most older, emotion-based models of hope (Averill, Catlin, & Chon, 1990; Farran, Herth, & Popovich, 1995; Snyder, 1994a, 1994b; Stotland, 1969).

In this model of hope, stress, negative emotions, and difficulties in coping are considered a result of being unable to envision a pathway or make movement toward a desired goal (Klinger, 1975; Snyder, 1996, 1998). This view is in fact supported by both correlational and causal research showing that people experience negative emotional responses when blocked from achieving their goals (Brunstein, 1993; Diener, 1984; Emmons, 1986; Little, 1983, 1989; Omodei & Wearing, 1990; Palys & Little, 1983; Ruehlman & Wolchik, 1988; Snyder et al., 1996). At the same time, research also shows that people are likely to experience positive emotional responses and maintain hopefulness when they are able to both pursue their goals and generate alternative pathways when needed (Barnum, Snyder, Rapoff, Mani, & Thompson, 1998; Curry, Snyder, Cook, Ruby, & Rehm, 1997; Elliott, Witty, Herrick, & Hoffman, 1991; Hinton-Nelson, Roberts, & Snyder, 1996; Irving, Snyder, & Crowson, 1998; Sherwin et al., 1992; Snyder, 1994a, 1994b, 1996, 1998; Snyder, Cheavens, & Sympson, 1997; Snyder, Harris, et al., 1991; Snyder, Hoza, et al., 1997; Snyder, Irving, & Anderson, 1991; Snyder et al., 1996).[3] In this chapter we use this new model of hope as a conceptual framework for achieving a better understanding of common factors, early improvement in therapy, and placebo and expectancy.

Hope in the Common Factors

More than any other author and researcher in the field, Jerome Frank (1961, 1968, 1971, 1973, 1989; Frank & Frank, 1991; Frank, Hoehn-Saric, Imber, Liberman, & Stone, 1978) has promoted our understanding of the role of the common factors in accounting for treatment outcome. Early on, Frank (1973) argued that people did not seek

---

[3]All of the previous studies are based on the use of various individual differences measures of hope developed and validated for adults (Snyder, Harris, et al., 1991; Snyder et al., 1996) and children (Snyder, Hoza, et al., 1997; Snyder, McDermott, et al., 1997).

psychological help when they developed a problem, but when they became demoralized in their own problem-solving efforts. As Frank and Frank (1991) noted, such individuals are "conscious of having failed to meet their own expectations or those of others, or of being unable to cope with some pressing problem . . . [and] feel powerless to change the situation or themselves" (p. 35).

Frank's (1973) description of the demoralized individual fits nicely with the theory of hope presented in this chapter. Feeling "powerless to change" indicates a lack of agency thinking. That is, the person is lacking thoughts of being able to begin and continue movement successfully on a selected pathway toward his or her goals. As a result, the determination necessary to attempt goals is missing.

Frank and Frank (1991) proposed that four factors work to combat demoralization in all psychotherapy approaches. The four factors area (a) an emotionally charged relationship, (b) a therapeutic setting, (c) a therapeutic myth (or rationale), and (d) a therapeutic ritual. In the case of the first factor, Frank and Frank (1991) argued that the presence of an emotional, confiding relationship with a therapist who is both hopeful and determined to help works to "re-moralize" clients. Therapists must have hope that the client can change (Snyder, 1994b). Indeed, research demonstrates the critical role of helpers' hope in enabling clients to change (Snyder, McDermott, et al., 1997). Therapists who are burned out or otherwise fail to convey hopefulness to their clients implicitly model low agency and pathways thinking. Related theory and research on the role of the therapeutic alliance and clients' views of the therapy process further demonstrates the importance of clients being able to rely on and trust the therapist to guide them on the journey characterizing successful psychotherapy (A. O. Horvath & Greenberg, 1986, 1989; Strupp, Fox, & Lessler, 1969).

The second factor identified by Frank and Frank (1991) encompasses the setting in which therapeutic encounters occur. Frank and Frank argued that settings that reinforce perceptions of the therapist as a helper who is effective in facilitating positive changes strengthen clients' hopes for change. In particular, settings that send the message—implicitly or explicitly—that the client can expect successful change increase the opportunity for critical agency and pathways thinking (see chapter 7, Snyder, 1994b; chapter 3, Snyder, McDermott, et al., 1997). The client must sense that this therapist–helper, working in this particular setting, has helped others to reach their goals.

A compelling "myth," or therapeutic rationale, explaining why the client is experiencing the presenting symptoms and, equally important, how the therapeutic procedure will ameliorate those symptoms is the third common factor Frank and Frank (1991) proposed. Every school of therapy has a clearly defined theory regarding the origin, maintenance, and resolution of difficulties that clients bring to treatment. Research shows that successful treatment depends, at least in part, on the plausibility of a particular school's theory to the client (Duncan, Hubble, & Miller, 1997). Clients who agree with the rationale of a particular therapeutic approach are likely to experience an increase in agency thinking that ultimately translates into increased determination to move toward improvement-related therapy goals. Such thinking further acts to reinforce the resolution to continue trying, thereby decreasing the chances for premature termination from therapy. A compelling theory or therapeutic rationale also invites pathway thinking by providing an explanation for how movement toward desired goals can occur—even in the face of current and future obstacles.

Finally, Frank and Frank (1991) identified therapeutic ritual, or the actual procedures used by therapists, as the fourth common factor. They argued that, in spite of the hundreds of different, and sometimes contradictory, treatment procedures in use today, therapists' confidence in and mastery of a chosen method ultimately works by enhancing the client's belief in the potential for healing. Effective therapists model both agency and pathways thinking through their confidence in and mastery of the techniques they use.

Together, the four factors work to produce cognitions that make the client's therapeutic goals more viable. In general, the therapeutic relationship and setting in which treatment occurs foster agency thinking (e.g., "I *can* do it."), whereas the particular rationale and therapeutic ritual act to enhance pathways thinking (e.g., "Here's *how* I can do it."). The resulting hope, in turn, is predictive of more favorable therapeutic outcomes.

THE ROLE OF HOPE IN EARLY IMPROVEMENT

Research has consistently shown that a substantial portion of client improvement occurs within the first 3 to 4 weeks of treatment (Fennell & Teasdale, 1987; Howard, Kopta, Krause, & Orlinsky, 1986; Howard, Lueger, Maling, & Martinovich, 1993; Ilardi & Craighead, 1994; Rush, Kovacs, Beck, Weissenburger, & Hollon, 1981; Uhlenhuth & Duncan, 1968). Clients have, for example, been observed to experience significant improvement following an initial diagnostic interview or after receiving a promise of treatment (Frank, Nash, Stone, & Imber, 1963; Kellner & Sheffield, 1971; Piper & Wogan, 1970). In a series of studies, researchers have even found that 40% to 66% of clients reported positive, treatment-related improvement before attending their first session (Howard et al., 1986; Lawson, 1994; Weiner-Davis, de Shazer, & Gingerich, 1987).

To date, studies suggest that 56% to 71% of the variance related to total client change can be accounted for by change occurring in the early stages of treatment (Fennell & Teasdale, 1987; Howard et al., 1993). Such dramatic improvement occurring so early in the treatment process can hardly be the result of specific treatment effects (e.g., a particular therapeutic technique [i.e., cognitive mediation, fair fighting, behavioral rehearsal, etc.]). As Ilardi and Craighead (1994) pointed out, clients have usually not even learned the supposedly "active" mechanism for change by the time improvement occurs in these early stages of treatment. Rather, the rapid response of clients must be a product of the common factors—especially hope. On this point, several researchers and authors have highlighted the pivotal role that hope plays in early and subsequent improvement in psychotherapy (e.g., Goldstein, 1962; Ilardi & Craighead, 1994; Peake & Archer, 1984; Peake & Ball, 1987; Wickramasekera, 1985; Wilkins, 1979, 1985).

In terms of the theory presented in this chapter, such early changes in treatment may be viewed as a reflection of increases in agency thinking or a renewed determination to accomplish their goals. Clients are often mired down and seem unable to formulate goals or mobilize themselves toward their goals when they first enter treatment. The very act of deciding to enter psychotherapy, however, represents a new determination to achieve a specific goal of "getting better." As such, a spark in agency thinking propels the new client toward the goal of improvement.

This is not to say that treatment is unimportant or irrelevant. Gains are even more marked when treatment is added to these early improvements. Both agency and pathways thinking are critical in the production and then later maintenance of change. Consider a study by Fennell and Teasdale (1987) on the treatment of depression. Consistent with the findings reviewed earlier, these researchers found that within 2 weeks of beginning treatment in either cognitive-behavioral therapy (CBT) or treatment as usual (TAU), they were able to distinguish between participants in either condition who were rapid (the "steeps") versus slow or nonresponders (the "slights"). Of critical importance, however, is that only members of the steep group who received CBT maintained and enhanced their gains over the course of treatment. The steeps in the TAU condition neither maintained nor enhanced the changes they experienced early in treatment. Such findings indicate that the changes experienced by the CBT steeps were both dependent on the presence of determination to meet goals (agency thinking) and the ability to generate pathways to continue and maintain clinical improvement (pathways thinking).

THE ROLE OF HOPE IN PLACEBO AND EXPECTANCY RESEARCH

Historically, the placebo has played a confusing role in the assessment of psychotherapy outcome (Critelli & Neumann, 1984; White, Tursky, & Schwartz, 1985). From the Latin meaning, "I shall please," the modern use of the term comes to psychological research from the field of medicine. There the word traditionally has been equated in drug studies with a pharmacologically inert substance. In medical research, the use of a placebo in double-blind studies has long been thought to enable researchers to determine the amount of change related to the active ingredients of a drug under study.[4] Specifically, placebos supposedly allow for the differentiation between changes brought about by physiological rather than psychological factors. Greenberg, chapter 10 of this volume, shows that this distinction is much less clear than originally thought in medico-physiological research. The differentiation is considerably murkier in psychological research.

At first, researchers in psychotherapy imported the use of placebo control groups largely unchanged from the field of medicine. As they had in medicine, investigators reasoned that the use of such groups would allow them to distinguish the effectiveness of psychological interventions above and beyond the contribution of placebo factors—perceived at the time as "nuisance" or confounding variables (D. Rosenthal & Frank, 1956; Thorne, 1952; Wilkins, 1984). Unfortunately, this view of placebo factors was tantamount to saying that the nonspecific factors controlled by the placebo control group were "psychologically inert." As Parloff (1986) noted, however, "a clinically meaningful change is not to be dismissed on the presumption that its parent techniques or mechanisms are illegitimate" (p. 82). A significant percentage of participants experienced meaningful change in such groups.

Since then, the view of placebo control groups has considerably evolved. They are now seen as viable means for controlling the effective ingredients common to all psychotherapies. In present research, the use of such groups is thought to allow researchers to ascertain the additional improvement related to a given therapeutic approach. Interestingly, the increase in respect for the concept of placebo corresponds with the emergence of cognitive approaches to understanding the nature of psychotherapy change. Cognitive thinkers expressly rejected the earlier view of placebos as therapeutically inert nuisance

---

[4]In this point, it is interesting to note that the history of medicine up to the 16th century can be described as being the history of placebo effects (see Shapiro, 1971).

variables and instead highlighted their active role in the change process (Kirsch, 1978).

Frank and Frank (1991) argued that the effectiveness of placebos results from their ability to mobilize clients' expectancies for improvement. Research has provided support for this idea. Studies have found, for example, that the degree of improvement treatment correlates positively and significantly with such expectancies (Friedman, 1963; Goldstein, 1960). Other studies have found that a client's expectancies about the effectiveness of coping strategies specific to a therapeutic approach determine whether those strategies are used (Kirsch, Mearns, & Catanzaro, 1990). Together, the expectancy of improvement and expectancies regarding the effectiveness of a particular therapeutic approach are similar to the agency and pathways thinking.

A meta-analysis of the effectiveness of psychological treatment as compared with common factors and no-treatment control conditions provides further evidence for a connection among placebo, expectancy, and the components of hope presented in this chapter. In brief, Barker et al. (1988) found that when positive expectancies were equalized across the three treatment groups, clients in the common factor control condition experienced significantly greater clinical improvement than those in the no-treatment control group (a difference in effect size of approximately 0.5 standard deviation). Obviously, participation in the common factors control group enhanced belief in the capacity to change positively over and above the no-treatment group. Put another way, exposure to the conditions of the common factors group resulted in an increase in agency thinking.

For all that, although common factors control groups produced significantly superior psychotherapy outcomes relative to no-treatment control groups, they were not as successful as the actual treatment groups. Rather, those clients receiving specific treatment profited even further in spite of having equal expectancies (a difference in effect size of approximately 0.5 standard deviation). Again, this finding would be predicted by hope theory as clients benefit by having both their agency and pathways thinking fostered over the course of the psychotherapy sessions. Something beyond expectancies in the treatment groups explains their different outcomes, and in the context of hope theory, we suggest that it is the enhancement of pathway thinking brought about by participation in an active therapeutic approach.

Therapists' expectancies also may play a significant role in therapy outcome. The theory of hope presented in this chapter predicts better outcomes for therapists who have hope both in their clients' abilities to change and in the potential of what they have to offer the client to bring about change. Being motivated to work on helping the client, providing a means to do so, and sharing the common goal of increased psychological functioning are critical to fostering the hope-related processes of agency and pathways thinking.

The research literature shows, for example, that clients model their therapists' patterns of thinking (see Bandura, 1969, for review of modeling). Elsewhere, psychotherapists have been cautioned to monitor their stress and potential burnout (see Pines, 1982; Pines & Aronson, 1988) to avoid projecting their own hopeless feelings onto the people with whom they work (Snyder, 1994b). Related to this point, the National Institute of Mental Health collaborative study on depression (Elkin et al., 1989) produced evidence that supposedly undermines the importance of therapist expectancy regarding the method of treatment. In this study, therapists were purposefully chosen who were not adherents to the therapeutic approaches under study. This was designed to control for the enthusiasm for and expectancies regarding effectiveness of a therapist's preferred brand of treatment. Not surprisingly, few differences between the approaches were found. Given the perspective presented in this chapter, however, the design of the study undermined potential findings by eliminating the agency thinking of the participating therapists. Such thinking is a critical component of therapist hope and is a reality in the actual arenas where psychotherapy is performed. Thus, the external validity of this landmark study is diminished because of the use of persons who were not proponents of the particular techniques. In this regard, which therapists practice approaches they do not expect to foster improvement?

RESEARCH IMPLICATIONS

For the past four decades, psychotherapy researchers have been operating under the assumption that a psychotherapy approach must produce client outcomes superior to nonspecific factors, placebo, or high-expectancy control comparison groups to be considered effective (Eysenck, 1961; Kazdin, 1978; Paul, 1966; Shapiro, 1971). Given the data and perspective shared in this chapter, however, this approach is tantamount to testing the nonsensical question of, Is psychotherapy change superior to psychotherapy change?[5]

In chapter 7 of this volume, Ogles, Anderson, and Lunnen note that psychotherapy outcome research has been conducted with a

---

[5]Horvath (1988) suggested that placebos are more accurately viewed as alternative treatments for purposes of comparison in psychotherapy research. To borrow a distinction previously noted by R. Rosenthal (1985), one can examine placebos as either controls or effects. Clearly, the research and theory presented here suggest that the latter is indicated.

horse race mentality in which treatment approaches are judged in terms of how they perform in relation to each other. The theory of hope presented here suggests that the more important issue is the degree to which given therapeutic approaches derive their effectiveness through teaching people to have productive pathways to reach their goals and fostering the determination or agency to use those pathways. Notably absent in the typical outcome approach is a shared framework for understanding how positive therapeutic changes occur. Instead, the proponents of each approach have spent their time generating support for the unique viability of their preferred theoretical approaches. On this issue, the propensity of psychotherapy researchers to establish the superiority of their particular approaches may be an unfortunate by-product of the American desire to be special or unique (see Snyder & Fromkin, 1980; Wallach & Wallach, 1983).

As psychotherapy undergoes a period which "scientifically validated" treatments are increasingly being advocated and sometimes even mandated (Chambliss, 1996; Crits-Christoph, 1996; Wilson, 1996), researchers in the field still have a relatively meager understanding of the mechanisms by which treatments achieve their beneficial effects (Garfield, 1996). It is time for research energies to be spent on studying the similarities in psychotherapy change processes that produce favorable outcomes in those receiving treatment relative to those who do not. In doing so, the critical question of what works would not be put aside. It would be recast in more cooperative, integrative terms.

The theory presented in this chapter represents just one framework for understanding the role of the common factors in the psychotherapy change process. Although there are many possible frameworks, future research will likely be more fruitful as the most parsimonious, inclusive, and powerful ones are sought.

Clinical Implications of Hope Theory

The theory of hope presented in this chapter applies to ordinary people pursuing the goals of life. Sometimes such goal pursuits go relatively uninterrupted, and, at other times, impediments appear. The people who seek psychotherapy have often experienced difficulties in pursuing their goals. The view guiding this chapter is that the psychological principles that apply to everyday life also apply to the circumstances and participants of psychotherapy (Barone, Maddux, & Snyder, 1997). Accordingly, the present thesis is that agency and pathways thinking about goals are operative in psychotherapy and that these principles can shed some light on the processes that underlie successful psychotherapy change. These ideas are now illustrated with a case example.

Jackie was a 44-year-old woman who sought treatment because she was depressed and "burned out." After completing her undergraduate degree in 1973, she took a job as a secretary in the English Department of the same university from which she had graduated. She described her 20+ years of service and her rise to the position of administrative assistant (the top civil service position in the department). At her first session, her affect was flat and she said that nothing brought her a great deal of pleasure. Much of the visit was spent describing how her "life was racing by," and how tired she was of the same routine. Some professors were reasonable people, but she described many as "big babies who needed taking care of all the time."

In the next few sessions, Jackie expressed the belief that her real problem was a lack of a meaningful relationship with a man. She described how she had endured a string of unfulfilling relationships. Yet, when asked what would happen if she truly did find the "Mr. Right," Jackie decided that a change in this area would not really solve her problems. As a result, she became even more despondent, feeling as though she had no sense of what she really wanted. She described herself as feeling stuck at the bottom of a big hole in the ground—a very vivid and painful image for her.

Instead of asking her to quickly get out of this hole, the therapist suggested that she stay there a while longer. At first, Jackie complied. Nonetheless, over time, her impatience grew and she told the therapist that she was "going to get a ladder and climb out of the hole." She closed her eyes and, after a minute or so, broke into a big smile. On opening her eyes, she said, "I got a ladder. I'm going back to school!" Her burnout, depression, and general boredom lifted over the next three sessions as she plotted a course to obtain a masters degree in social work. All the previous years, though working with professors and graduate students, she had not identified her own longing to go to graduate school. This new goal set off her careful planning to apply to various schools. No longer did she regard herself as unable to chart out her future. The therapist helped her to realize that she did have the capability to find the routes to the things that were really important and pointed out previous instances in her life when she had done this.

People frequently forget their previous skills and success experiences when they are in the throes of depression or struggling with a dilemma. One means of encouraging pathways thinking is to review these previous experiences. In Jackie's case, she saw how she had slowly lost interest in the goals inherent in her secretarial work and that part of remaining interested in the planning process rested on having a new, meaningful goal. Her goal of returning to school also renewed Jackie's sense of energy to pursue this previously hidden desire. In the language of this chapter, she was engaged in agency thinking because of becoming aware of a meaningful life goal. This thinking spilled over into other areas of her life and she soon found herself motivated to consider additional goals not originally on her agenda. In the final phases of treatment, the therapist talked with Jackie about how to prioritize her goals and maintain her mental energy for the most important ones, thus facilitating continued pathways thinking.

Throughout this case, the therapist explained the agency and pathways components and how they work together in the lives of all people. Jackie readily grasped this framework for hope and in the final sessions was using it as a model for how to understand her life. The major role that the therapist played in the remaining sessions was to help Jackie enjoy the process of pursuing her goals, as well as the achieving of the goals (see Snyder, 1994b; Snyder, Cheavens, & Sympson, 1997).

Hope therapy, in many instances, merely involves careful detective work with one's clients into what it is that they really desire. Because of the linkage among goals, pathways, and agency thinking, however, a therapist need not start with a particular component. What the therapist did with Jackie was to track her "down" emotions to get a sense of what was stopping her (recall the earlier theoretical notion that negative emotions reflect important blockages in a person's life). Within hope theory and the related therapeutic endeavors, negative emotions serve as clues about the underlying goal pursuits that are stymied. Little or no attention is paid to labeling the specific nature of the negative emotion, because the action resides in what causes them. In Jackie's case, she created an image of herself trapped at the bottom of a pit. Her therapist helped her discover the nature of the trap and work her way out of it. For all the people like Jackie, however, where the finding of a new goal is the key, there also are other people who merely need to become mobilized. Such agency thinking will find an appropriate goal and the associated pathways thinking to achieve it. Moreover, there are yet other clients for whom the starting component of the hope triad is the acquisition of a new skill (pathway thinking), which quickly finds a target and is fueled by the requisite agency thinking. In all, people in psychotherapy become hopeful by finding any one of the following: a new goal, a new pathway, or a new sense of agency. The thesis developed in this chapter is that a similar process (under the guise of various therapeutic approaches) unfolds in most successful psychotherapeutic relationships.

Questions From the Editors

1. What common therapeutic practices may actually serve to lessen hope?

One answer to this question involves instances in which the therapist does not carefully listen to what the client is saying. This can lead to therapeutic goals that are more for the helper than the helped. Further, therapists at times may lapse into vague goals such as, "Do your best." Goals as these leave clients without a sense of where they are going. It is better to help clients to arrive at specific goals, with concrete markers and substeps. Likewise, if the helper is not listening and attending to the client, the pathways and agency lessons may be more appropriate for the helper than the person being helped. The danger here is that any pathways thinking that is fostered may "work" for the therapist, but not for the client. The same principle applies to agency thought, where it is especially critical to help the client with thoughts that energize him or her and not the therapist.

A related counterproductive circumstance involves those instances in which the therapist rather than the client is doing all of the work of psychotherapy. Here, the helper supplies all the energy (agency) and ideas about what should be done (pathways and goals). Not surprisingly, if the client does not own these therapeutic goals, as well as the pathways to the goals and the energy to use those pathways, then the "hope" that is being promulgated is not for the client. At the same time, however, being overly inactive can undermine the client's hope as much as being overly active. Previously in this chapter and elsewhere (Snyder, 1994b; Snyder, McDermott, et al., 1997), it has been suggested that part of the therapist's effectiveness derives from modeling the components of hope. Similarly, at times there are instances wherein a client truly is stymied and may need ideas about alternative goals, pathways to those goals, as well as how to ignite the agency to use those pathways.

Another potential problem arises with therapists who are wed to a particular paradigm. Specifically, they may conceptualize clients in one way, using only the techniques associated with their favored approach. Thus, driven by one's theoretical and technological predilections, the helper may not entertain other paradigms should the preferred approach fail to facilitate positive change. Hope theory suggests that there are many technologies for helping clients to pursue their goals. To the degree therapists can be flexible in their interventions, then they have a more powerful set of tools.

At length, sometimes because of theoretical and technological chauvinism, psychotherapists may be unwilling to accept the fact that their approaches are not working. This can lead to an unwillingness to refer one's clients to therapists with other sets of intervention skills. From the perspective of hope theory, any and all roads should be explored to find those that are most suited to help clients achieve their goals. Fortunately, surveys show that "integrative" is the most frequent category that practicing clinicians use to describe themselves (Norcross, Karg, & Prochaska, 1997).[6] If this is indeed the case, then such integrative psychotherapists may be quite flexible in sampling differing types of interventions.

2. Given the prominence of hope, expectancy, and placebo, why has psychotherapy theory and research been preoccupied with (a) negative, pathological explanations rather than positive, hope-filled ones and (b) the difficulty of inducing change, rather than a more hope-based premise that such change is quite possible?

Regarding the first part of this question, those involved in either the applied or research psychotherapy arenas may forget the biased nature of their samples (Barone et al., 1997). That is to say, day in and out, we see people who have problems. What this sampling misses, of course, are the numerous people without major problems or those who have problems and are dealing with them through their own resources. There is a related perception-based reason for the focus on the negative, however. As Beatrice Wright (1988, 1991) suggested, there is a fundamental negative bias wherein stimuli that have negative properties (particularly in vague stimulus situations) garner more of our perceptual attention than those with positive properties. People are, in a manner of speaking, coerced to attend to the negative unless they make a conscious effort to counteract this bias. To bring this bias into another realm, there is a saying in the newspaper business—"Bad news sells papers."

The antidote to this approach is to conduct research aimed at understanding how persons who have very high risk factors for maladjustment actually navigate life successfully. The resiliency research paradigm (see Higgins, 1994; Rutter, 1994; Werner & Smith, 1982) offers an excellent example of this latter approach for psychotherapy researchers. Further, hope theory, much like the recent evolution of the field of health psychology, offers a view of not only attending to

---

[6]Norcross, Karg, and Prochaska (1997) found that 27% of practicing clinicians describe themselves as integrative and eclectic in theoretical orientation. To further augment this cohort of clinicians, it is noteworthy that the second highest category regarding self-described theoretical orientation is cognitive, at 24%. Thus, approximately 51% of clinicians are *cognitive/integrative* in theoretical orientation.

the remediation of goals in problem areas of the client's life, but also building on the areas of strength that already are evident. Thus, instead of allowing a negative spread to occur in therapy so the only focus is on client "weaknesses," hope theory and the related therapy focus on what is functional in the client's life.

In regard to the second aspect of this question about the seeming assumed difficulty of change, many of the same points raised in the previous paragraph hold. Because of our sampling of people who have had difficulty changing, as well as the propensity to remember those who have not improved (i.e., the fundamental negative perceptual bias), those of us who labor in the trenches doing psychotherapy may not acquire an overall sense of success. Our failures loom large in our consciousness, but to the degree this pervades our demeanor with subsequent clients, we may be robbing those clients of an important sense of hope. Burnout is a personal diagnosis that should always be considered by psychotherapists as applying to themselves (Snyder, McDermott, et al., 1997). Most effective therapists, much like those people who are effective in coping in other arenas (Taylor & Brown, 1988, 1994), do not let the negative weigh them down and keep, instead, positive, hopeful expectancies about their effectiveness (Snyder, 1994a).

3. What particular therapeutic approaches should promote pathways thinking in clients?

It is tempting to suggest that those cognitive–behavioral approaches, including solution-focused and problem-solving techniques, are most likely to promote effective pathways thinking. On further analysis, it probably is the case that any therapeutic approach, running the gamut from psychodynamic to gestalt, probably inherently teaches and fosters the development of clients' pathway thinking for the desired goals. At times, particular approaches may seem more obvious in their "pull" for pathways thinking, but we believe that a careful content analysis across therapeutic approaches will reveal that all effective interventions beget adaptive pathways thinking in clients. Indeed, this very question presently is being explored in our laboratory. As a vehicle for measuring pathways thought, both the dispositional (Snyder, Harris, et al., 1991) and state (Snyder, Sympson, et al., 1996) hope scales have brief (4-item) subscales that tap self-reported pathways thought. Likewise, there are observer-based means of measuring the pathways components of hope (see Snyder, McDermott, et al., 1997). These self-report and observer measures allow for a quick and valid means of tapping enduring or state pathways thinking.

References

Andrews, G., & Harvey, R. (1981). Does psychotherapy benefit neurotic patients? A re-analysis of the Smith, Glass and Miller data. *Archives of General Psychiatry, 38,* 1203–1208.

Bandura, A. (1969). *Principles of behavior modification.* New York: Holt, Rinehart and Winston.

Barker, S. L., Funk, S. C., & Houston, B. K. (1988). Psychological treatment versus nonspecific factors: A meta-analysis of conditions that engender comparable expectations for improvement. *Clinical Psychology Review, 8,* 579–594.

Barnum, D. D., Snyder, C. R., Rapoff, M. A., Mani, M. M., & Thompson, R. (1998). Hope and social support in the psychological adjustment of children who have survived burn injuries and matched controls. *Children's Health Care.*

Barone, D., Maddux, J., & Snyder, C. R. (1997). *Social cognitive psychology: History and current domains.* New York: Plenum Press.

Brunstein, J. C. (1993). Personal goals and subjective well-being: A longitudinal study. *Journal of Personality and Social Psychology, 65,* 1061–1070.

Chambliss, D. L. (1996). In defense of dissemination of empirically supported psychological interventions. *Clinical Psychology: Science and Practice, 3,* 230–235.

Critelli, J. W., & Neumann, K. F. (1984). The placebo: Conceptual analysis of a construct in transition. *American Psychologist, 39,* 32–39.

Crits-Christoph, P. (1996). The dissemination of efficacious psychological treatments. *Clinical Psychology: Science and Practice, 3,* 260–263.

Curry, L. A., Snyder, C. R., Cook, D. L., Ruby, B. C., & Rehm, M. (1997). The role of hope in student-athlete academic and sport achievement. *Journal of Personality and Social Psychology.*

Diener, E. (1984). Subjective well-being. *Psychological Bulletin, 95,* 542–575.

Duncan, B. L., Hubble, M. A., & Miller, S. D. (1997). *Psychotherapy with impossible cases: Efficient treatment of therapy veterans.* New York. Norton.

Elkin, I., Shea, T., Watkins, J. T., Imber, S. D., Sotsky, S. M., Collins, J. F., Glass, D. R., Pilkonis, P. A., Leber, W. R., Docherty, J. P., Fiester, S. J., & Parloff, M. B. (1989). National Institute of Mental Health treatment of depression collaborative research program: General effectiveness of treatments. *Archives of General Psychiatry, 46,* 971–983.

Elliott, T. R., Witty, S., Herrick, S., & Hoffman, J. T. (1991). Negotiating reality after physical loss: Hope, depression, and disability. *Journal of Personality and Social Psychology, 61,* 608–613.

Emmons, R. A. (1986). Personal strivings: An approach to personality and subjective well-being. *Journal of Personality and Social Psychology, 51,* 1058–1068.

Eysenck, H. J. (1961). The effects of psychotherapy. In H. J. Eysenck (Ed.), *Handbook of abnormal psychology: An experimental approach* (pp. 697–725). New York: Basic Books.

Farran, C. J., Herth, A. K., & Popovich, J. M. (1995). *Hope and hopelessness: Critical clinical constructs.* Thousand Oaks, CA: Sage.

Fennell, M. J., & Teasdale, J. D. (1987). Cognitive therapy for depression: Individual differences and the process of change. *Cognitive Therapy and Research, 11,* 253–271.

Frank, J. D. (1961). *Persuasion and healing.* Baltimore: Johns Hopkins University Press.

Frank, J. D. (1968). The role of hope in psychotherapy. *International Journal of Psychiatry, 5,* 383–395.

Frank, J. D. (1971). Therapeutic factors in psychotherapy. *American Journal of Psychotherapy, 25,* 350–361.

Frank, J. D. (1973). *Persuasion and healing: A comparative study of psychotherapy* (rev. ed.). Baltimore: Johns Hopkins University Press.

Frank, J. D. (1989). Non-specific aspects of treatment: The view of a psychotherapist. In M. Sheppherd & N. Sartorius (Eds.), *Non-specific aspects of treatment* (pp. 95–114). Toronto, Canada: Hans Huber.

Frank, J. D., & Frank, J. B. (1991). *Persuasion and healing* (3rd. ed.). Baltimore: Johns Hopkins University Press.

Frank, J. D., Hoehn-Saric, S., Imber, S., Liberman, B. L., & Stone, A. R. (1978). *Effective ingredients of successful psychotherapy.* New York: Brunner/Mazel.

Frank, J. D., Nash, E. H., Stone, A. R., & Imber, S. D. (1963). Immediate and long-term symptomatic course of psychiatric outpatients. *American Journal of Psychiatry, 120,* 429–439.

Friedman, H. J. (1963). Patient expectancy and symptom reduction. *Archives of General Psychiatry, 8,* 61–67.

Garfield, S. C. (1981). Psychotherapy: A 40-year appraisal. *American Psychologist, 35,* 174–183.

Garfield, S. C. (1996). Some problems associated with "validated" forms of psychotherapy. *Clinical Psychology: Science and Practice, 3,* 218–229.

Goldstein, A. P. (1960). Patients' expectancies and non-specific therapy as a basis for (un)spontaneous remission. *Journal of Clinical Psychology, 16,* 399–403.

Goldstein, A. P. (1962). *Therapist–patient expectancies in psychotherapy.* Elmsford, NY: Pergamon Press.

Higgins, G. O. (1994). *Resilient adults: Overcoming a cruel past.* San Francisco: Jossey-Bass.

Hinton-Nelson, M. D., Roberts, M. C., & Snyder, C. R. (1996). Early adolescents exposed to violence: Hope and vulnerability to victimization. *American Journal of Orthopsychiatry, 66*, 346–353.

Horvath, A. O., & Greenberg, L. S. (1986). The development of the Working Alliance Inventory. In L. S. Greenberg & W. M. Pinsof (Eds.), *The psychotherapeutic process: A research handbook* (pp. 367–390). New York: Guilford Press.

Horvath, A. O., & Greenberg, L. S. (1989). The development of the Working Alliance Inventory. *Journal of Counseling Psychology, 36*, 223–253.

Horvath, P. (1988). Placebos and common factors in two decades of psychotherapy research. *Psychological Bulletin, 104*, 214–215.

Howard, K. I., Kopta, S. M., Krause, M. S., & Orlinsky, D. E. (1986). The dose–effect relationship in psychotherapy. *American Psychologist, 41*, 159–164.

Howard, K. I., Lueger, R. J., Maling, M. S., & Martinovich, Z. (1993). A phase model of psychotherapy outcome: Causal mediation of change. *Journal of Consulting and Clinical Psychology, 61*, 678–685.

Ilardi, S. S., & Craighead, W. E. (1994). The role of nonspecific factors in cognitive–behavior therapy for depression. *Clinical Psychology: Science and Practice, 1*, 138–156.

Ilardi, S. S., Craighead, W. E., & Evans, D. D. (1997). Modeling relapse in unipolar depression: The effects of dysfunctional cognitions and personality disorders. *Journal of Consulting and Clinical Psychology, 65*, 381–391.

Irving, L. M., Snyder, C. R., & Crowson Jr., J. J. (1998). Hope and the negotiation of cancer facts by college students. *Journal of Personality, 66*(2), 195–214.

Karasu, T. B. (1986). The specificity versus nonspecificity dilemma: Toward identifying therapeutic change agents. *American Journal of Psychiatry, 143*, 687–695.

Kazdin, A. E. (1978). Nonspecific treatment factors in psychotherapy outcome research. *Journal of Consulting and Clinical Psychology, 47*, 846–851.

Kazdin, A. E. (1980). *Research design in clinical psychology.* New York: Harper & Row.

Kellner, R., & Sheffield, B. F. (1971). The relief of distress following attendance at a clinic. *British Journal of Psychiatry, 118*, 195–198.

Kirsch, I. (1978). The placebo effect and the cognitive–behavioral revolution. *Cognitive Therapy and Research, 2*, 255–264.

Kirsch, I., Mearns, J., & Catanzaro, S. J. (1990). Mood regulation expectancies as determinants of dysphoria in college students. *Journal of Counseling Psychology, 37*, 306–312.

Klinger, E. (1975). Consequences of commitment to and disengagement from incentives. *Psychological Review, 82*, 223–231.

Lambert, M. J. (1992). Psychotherapy outcome research: Implications for integrative and eclectic therapists. In J. C. Norcross & M. R. Goldfried (Eds.) *Handbook of psychotherapy integration* (pp. 94–129). New York: Basic Books.

Lambert, M. J., Shapiro, D. A., & Bergin, A. E. (1986). The effectiveness of psychotherapy. In S. L. Garfield & A. E. Bergin (Eds.), *Handbook of psychotherapy and behavior change.* (3rd. ed., pp. 157–211). New York: Wiley.

Landman, J. T., & Dawes, R. M. (1982). Psychotherapy outcome: Smith and Glass' conclusions stand up under scrutiny. *American Psychologist, 37*, 504–516.

Lawson, D. (1994). Identifying pretreatment change. *Journal of Counseling and Development, 72*, 244–248.

Lipsey, M. W., & Wilson, D. B. (1993). The efficacy of psychological, educational, and behavioral treatment: Confirmation from meta-analysis. *American Psychologist, 48*, 1181–1209.

Little, B. R. (1983). Personal projects: A rationale and method for investigation. *Environment and Behavior, 15*, 273–309.

Little, B. R. (1989). Personal projects analysis: Trivial pursuits, magnificent obsessions, and the search for coherence. In D. M. Buss & N. Cantor (Eds.), *Personality psychology: Recent trends and emerging directions* (pp. 15–31). New York: Springer-Verlag.

Luborsky, L., Singer, B., & Luborsky, L. (1975). Comparative studies of psychotherapies. Is it true that "everyone has won and all must have prizes"? *Archives of General Psychiatry, 32*, 995–1008.

Miller, S. D., Duncan, B. L., & Hubble, M. A. (1997). *Escape from Babel: Toward a unifying language for psychotherapy practice.* New York: Norton.

Norcross, J. C., Karg, R. S., & Prochaska, J. O. (1997). Clinical psychologists in the 1990s: Part I. *The Clinical Psychologist, 50*, 4–9.

Omodei, M. M., & Wearing, A. J. (1990). Need satisfaction and involvement in personal projects: Toward an integrative model of subjective well-being. *Journal of Personality and Social Psychology, 59*, 762–769.

Palys, T. S., & Little, B. R. (1983). Perceived life satisfaction and organization of personal projects systems. *Journal of Personality and Social Psychology, 44*, 1221–1230.

Parloff, M. B. (1986). Placebo controls in psychotherapy research: A sine qua non or a placebo for research problems? *Journal of Consulting and Clinical Psychology, 54*, 79–87.

Paul, G. L. (1966). *Insight vs. desensitization in psychotherapy.* Stanford, CA: Stanford University Press.

Peake, T. H., & Archer, R. P. (1984). *Clinical training in psychotherapy.* New York: Haworth Press.

Peake, T. H., & Ball, J. D. (1987). Brief psychotherapy: Planned therapeutic change for changing times. *Psychotherapy in Private Practice, 5,* 53–63.

Pines, A. (1982). Helpers' motivation and the burnout syndrome. In T. A. Wills (Ed.), *Basic processes in helping relationships* (pp. 453–475). San Diego, CA: Academic Press.

Pines, A., & Aronson, E. (1988). *Career burnout: Causes and cures* (2nd. ed.). New York: Free Press.

Piper, W. E., & Wogan, M. (1970). Placebo effect in psychotherapy: An extension of earlier findings. *Journal of Consulting and Clinical Psychology, 34,* 447.

Prioleau, L., Murdock, M., & Brody, N. (1983). An analysis of psychotherapy versus placebo studies. *The Behavioral and Brain Sciences, 6,* 275–310.

Rosenthal, D., & Frank, J. D. (1956). Psychotherapy and the placebo effect. *Psychological Bulletin, 53,* 294–302.

Rosenthal, R. (1985). Designing, analyzing, interpreting, and summarizing placebo studies. In L. White, B. Tursky, & G. E. Schwartz (Eds.), *Placebo: Theory, research, and mechanisms* (pp. 110–136). New York: Guilford Press.

Ruehlman, L. S., & Wolchik, S. A. (1988). Personal goals and interpersonal support and hindrance as factors in psychological distress and well-being. *Journal of Personality and Social Psychology, 55,* 293–301.

Rush, A. J., Kovacs, M., Beck, A. T., Weissenburger, J., & Hollon, S. D. (1981). Differential effects of cognitive therapy and pharmacotherapy on depressive symptoms. *Journal of Affective Disorders, 3,* 221–229.

Rutter, M. (1994). Resilience: Some conceptual considerations. *Contemporary Pediatrics, 11,* 36–48.

Seligman, M. E. P. (1995). Effectiveness of psychotherapy: The *Consumer Reports* study. *American Psychologist, 50,* 965–974.

Shapiro, A. K. (1971). Placebo effects in medicine, psychotherapy, and psychoanalysis. In A. E. Bergin & S. C. Garfield (Eds.), *Handbook of psychotherapy and behavior change: Empirical analysis* (pp. 439–473). New York: Wiley.

Shapiro, D. A., & Shapiro, D. (1982). Meta-analysis of comparative therapy outcome studies: A replication and refinement. *Psychological Bulletin, 92,* 581–604.

Sherwin, E. D., Elliott, T. R., Rybarcysk, B. D., Frank, R. G., Hanson, S., & Hoffman, J. (1992). Negotiating the reality of care giving: Hope, burnout, and nursing. *Journal of Social and Clinical Psychology, 11,* 129–139.

Smith, M. L., & Glass, G. V. (1977). Meta-analysis of psychotherapy outcome studies. *American Psychologist, 32,* 752–760.

Smith, M. L., Glass, G. V., & Miller, T. I. (1980). *The benefits of psychotherapy.* Baltimore: Johns Hopkins University Press.

Snyder, C. R. (1994a). Hope and optimism. In V. S. Ramachandren (Ed.), *Encyclopedia of human behavior* (Vol. 2, pp. 535–542). San Diego, CA: Academic Press.

Snyder, C. R. (1994b). *The psychology of hope: You can get there from here.* New York: Free Press.

Snyder, C. R. (1996). To hope, to lose, and hope again. *Journal of Personal and Interpersonal Loss, 1,* 1–16.

Snyder, C. R. (1998). A case for hope in pain, loss, and suffering. In J. H. Harvey, J. Owarzu, & E. Miller (Eds.), *Perspectives on loss: A sourcebook* (pp. 63–79). Washington, DC: Taylor & Francis.

Snyder, C. R., Cheavens, J., & Sympson, S. (1997). Hope: An individual motive for social commerce. *Group Dynamics: Theory, Research, and Practice, 2,* 1–12.

Snyder, C. R., & Fromkin, H. L. (1980). *Uniqueness: The human pursuit of difference.* New York: Plenum Press.

Snyder, C. R., Harris, C., Anderson, J. R., Holleran, S. A., Irving, L. M., Sigmon, S. T., Yoshinobu, L., Gibb, J., Langelle, C., & Harney, P. (1991). The will and the ways: Development and validation of an individual differences measure of hope. *Journal of Personality and Social Psychology, 60,* 570–585.

Snyder, C. R., Hoza, B., Pelham, W. E., Rapoff, M., Ware, L., Danovsky, M., Highberger, L., Rubinstein, H., & Stahl, K. (1997). The development and validation of the Children's Hope Scale. *Journal of Pediatric Psychology, 22,* 399–421.

Snyder, C. R., Irving, L. M., & Anderson, J. R. (1991). Hope and health. In C. R. Snyder & D. R. Forsyth (Eds.), *Handbook of social and clinical psychology: The health perspective* (pp. 285–305). Elmsford, NY: Pergamon Press.

Snyder, C. R., McDermott, D., Cook, W., & Rapoff, M. (1997). *Hope for the journey: Helping children through the good times and the bad.* San Francisco: HarperColllins.

Snyder, C. R., Sympson, S. C., Ybasco, F. C., Borders, T. F., Babyak, M. A., & Higgins, R. L. (1996). Development and validation of the State Hope Scale. *Journal of Personality and Social Psychology, 70,* 321–335.

Stotland, E. (1969). *The psychology of hope.* San Francisco: Jossey-Bass.

Strupp, H. H., Fox, R. E., & Lessler, K. (1969). *Patients view their psychotherapy.* Baltimore: John Hopkins University Press.

Taylor, S. E., & Brown, J. D. (1988). Illusion and well-being: A social psychological perspective on mental health. *Psychological Bulletin, 103,* 193–210.

Taylor, S. E., & Brown, J. D. (1994). Positive illusions and well-being: Separating fact from fiction. *Psychological Bulletin, 116,* 21–27.

Thorne, F. C. (1952). Rules of evidence in the evaluation of the effect of psychotherapy. *Journal of Clinical Psychology, 8,* 38–41.

Uhlenhuth, E. H., & Duncan, D. B. (1968). Subjective change with medical student therapists: Some determinants of change in psychoneurotic outpatients. *Archives of General Psychiatry, 18,* 532–540.

VandenBos, G. R., & Pino, C. D. (1980). Research on outcome of psychotherapy. In G. R. VanderBos (Ed.), *Psychotherapy: Practice, research, policy* (pp. 23–69). Beverly Hills, CA: Sage.

Wallach, M. A., & Wallach, L. (1983). *Psychology's sanction for selfishness: The error of egoism in theory and therapy.* San Francisco: W. H. Freeman.

Weiner-Davis, M., de Shazer, S., & Gingerich, W. (1987). Building on pretreatment change to construct the therapeutic solution: An exploratory study. *Journal of Marital and Family Therapy, 13*(4), 359–364.

Werner, E. E., & Smith, R. S. (1982). *Vulnerable but invincible: A study of resilient children.* New York: McGraw-Hill.

White, L., Tursky, B., & Schwartz, G. E. (1985). Placebo in perspective. In L. White, B. Tursky, & G. E. Schwartz (Eds.), *Placebos: Theory, research, and mechanisms* (pp. 3–8). New York: Guilford Press.

Wickramasekera, I. (1985). A conditioned response model of placebo effect: Predictors form the model. In L. White, B. Tursky, & G. Schwartz (Eds.), *Placebos: Theory, research and mechanisms* (pp. 255–287). New York: Guilford Press.

Wilkins, W. (1979). Expectancies in therapy research: Discriminating among heterogeneous nonspecifics. *Journal of Consulting and Clinical Psychology, 47,* 837–845.

Wilkins, W. (1984). Psychotherapy: The powerful placebo. *Journal of Consulting and Clinical Psychology, 52,* 570–573.

Wilkins, W. (1985). Placebo controls and concepts in chemotherapy and psychotherapy research. In L. White, B. Tursky, & G. Schwartz (Eds.), *Placebos: Theory, research and mechanisms* (pp. 83–109). New York: Guilford Press.

Wilson, G. T. (1996). Empirically validated treatments: Reality and resistance. *Clinical Psychology: Science and Practice, 3,* 241–244.

Wright. B. A. (1988). Attitudes and the fundamental negative bias. In H. E. Yuker (Ed.), *Attitudes toward persons with disabilities* (pp. 3–21). New York: Springer.

Wright, B. A. (1991). Labeling: The need for greater person–environment individuation. In C. R. Snyder & D. R. Forsyth (Eds.), *Handbook of social and clinical psychology: The health perspective* (pp. 469–487). Elmsford, NY: Pergamon.

Benjamin M. Ogles, Timothy Anderson, and Kirk M. Lunnen

The Contribution of Models and Techniques to Therapeutic Efficacy:

7

Contradictions Between Professional Trends and Clinical Research

t first glance, this chapter may seem out of place. Why would a book with a focus on the *common* factors—the "heart and soul" of psychotherapy—include a chapter on factors as *specific* as models and techniques? No understanding of the common factors can be complete, however, without some form of model. This chapter begins, therefore, with a definition of *models* as they have come to be known in psychotherapy. Next, we explore historical and current trends of models within clinical psychology. Whereas treatment models and psychotherapy theories were once considered equivalent, they now imply much more, including the use of treatment manuals, so-called "empirically validated" (or supported) treatments, and, protocol-driven interventions. Various efforts to evaluate the success of models within psychotherapy training and outcome research are presented and discussed. We conclude the chapter with suggestions for reconciling the increasingly disparate positions of professional trends in clinical psychology and psychotherapy research.

Defining Models

Historically, there have been varied and often contradictory definitions for models. Some researchers view them as specific to predicting change in therapy, whereas others consider them highly abstract formulations with applicability to all human behavior. As time has passed, professional interest has shifted from formulating grand unifying theories to identifying groups of effective techniques (Matarazzo & Garner, 1992; Poznanski & McLennan, 1995).

In this chapter, a *model* is defined as a collection of beliefs or unifying theory about what is needed to bring about change with a particular client in a particular treatment context. Models generally include *techniques,* defined here as actions that are local extensions of the beliefs or theory. As researchers Orlinsky, Grawe, and Parks (1994) summarized, "The particular techniques or methods employed by therapists can be thought of as tactical interventions made to implement heuristic goals. These vary according to the treatment model being followed" (p. 306). Models and techniques are therefore related but not identical. This definition implies that all therapists follow some sort of model. In other words, however implicit, all therapists operate according to certain beliefs or assumptions about what facilitates positive outcomes.

EARLY MODELS OF THERAPY: THEORETICAL ORIENTATIONS

The first therapy models were simply extensions of psychological theories. In other words, these early models of treatment were not merely a collection of techniques to be used with people in therapy, but also reflected an overarching world view. Most were rational, quasi-philosophical formulations about individual development and personality that contained implicit assumptions and values about life, mental health, and mental illness. In contrast to the contemporary focus on specificity, these early theories and techniques were thought to be universally applicable. They were thought, in other words, to be useful for *all* psychological problems as well as to have broad applicability to contexts and problems outside of the consulting room. For example, Skinner's (1948) theory of radical behaviorism not only served as the impetus for behavioral treatment, but also as the inspiration for a utopian vision of a society based on the widespread application of behavioral principles. Rogers's (1961) client-centered theory, on the other hand, served as a vision of society based on individual freedom and self-determination as well as the basis for a method of psychotherapy. Finally, and perhaps the most influential of these early theories, the psychoanalytic model was not only applied to personality and psychopathology but also to fields as diverse as religion, art, history, and anthropology (Edelson, 1988).

The effects of such broadly defined models are understandably difficult to assess. Indeed, by definition, the breadth of any particular theory interferes with the empirical need to identify and operationalize central variables. Some research has demonstrated, however, that therapists' behaviors correspond to their theoretical orientation and that therapists of different orientations differ in the way they practice psychotherapy. For example, studies have found that therapists from different theoretical orientations differ in their use of specific therapeutic techniques (e.g., Luborsky, Singer, & Luborsky, 1975) and verbal response behavior (e.g., Stiles, 1979). In spite of these differences, however, early outcome evaluations found little support for the notion that different orientations actually influenced the effectiveness of treatment. Indeed, *studies comparing outcomes of therapists from different theoretical camps consistently found no differences* (Miller, Duncan, & Hubble, 1997). In response, the "do-do bird verdict" was announced: "All have won and all must have prizes" (Luborsky et al., 1975).

THE INCREASING SPECIFICITY OF THERAPY TRAINING AND PRACTICE

In contrast to this early view, recent trends in clinical training and practice favor models of treatment with more narrow applications and precise definitions. Indeed, the delivery of specific technical interventions for identified populations of clients is fast becoming the "standard of care" in the field. One example of this is the dramatic increase in the use of treatment manuals for research and training on psychotherapy. Nowhere, however, is the trend toward specificity more clear than in the development of so-called empirically validated (or supported) treatments by the American Psychological Association (Chambless, 1993) and the focus on protocol-driven intervention within managed mental health care (Shueman & Troy, 1994).

Treatment Manuals

Luborsky and DeRubeis (1984) suggested that the development and use of therapy manuals constituted a minor revolution in psychotherapy. In contrast to the early psychotherapy orientations that broadly described the principles, techniques, and theory of psychotherapy, manuals are characterized by greater *technical* specificity (Lambert & Ogles, 1988). This specificity is evident in several ways: (a) Manuals provide clear descriptions of treatment principles along with operations that are necessary to implement those principles, (b) the operations are detailed for rapid implementation, (c) a clear and orderly sequence of operations are described for session-by-session intervention, and (d) typically, the interventions are sufficiently straight forward so that rating scales can be used to rate the degree of compliance or adherence to the manualized operations.

The earliest manuals were designed for use in behaviorally oriented treatment and research. Typically, these manuals described a specific treatment for a specific problem (e.g., smoking, obesity, or assertiveness [Christensen & Jeffrey, 1977; Hoopes, Fisher, & Barlow, 1982]). Over time, manuals were developed for more complex problems (e.g., depression; Lewinsohn, Munoz, Youngren, & Zeiss, 1978) and treatment approaches (e.g., cognitive behavioral treatment; Beck, Rush, Shaw, & Emery, 1979). Manuals for dynamic, interpersonal, and humanistic approaches (e.g., Luborsky, 1984; Strupp & Binder, 1984) were the last to appear.

Since these early beginnings, a virtual explosion of treatment manuals has occurred. A large number of manuals have been published with highly specific instructions for clinical problems ranging from body image disturbance (Thompson, 1990) to borderline personality disorder (Linehan, 1993). Clearly, treatment manuals are no longer the sole province of researchers. Training workshops, clinicians' conferences, book clubs, and practitioners' libraries all include psychotherapy manuals. Their rising use was one of the first signs of a growing interest in specificity.

Empirically Validated (or Supported) Treatments

In the early 1990s, the Task Force on the Promotion and Dissemination of Psychological Procedures was formed within Division 12 of the American Psychological Association. The mandate of this group was to identify efficacious psychological interventions *and* select strategies for educating therapists in training, practicing clinicians, third-party payers, and the lay public about these "empirically validated (or supported)" treatments (Chambless, 1993). Treatment guidelines for eating disorders, major depression, substance use, and bipolar affective disorder were either in the process of being developed or had already been proposed by a special committee within the American Psychiatric Association (1996).

Such developments provide further evidence of the growing interest in treatment specificity and represent a noticeable shift toward standardizing treatment within the mental health professions. The shift is, of course, based on the belief that models and techniques are among the most important contributors to the success of psychotherapy—an idea heartily disputed by contributors to this volume. In the absence of valid and reliable alternatives, however, demands for accountability and increasing competition for mental health dollars virtually ensure that such guidelines and lists of approved treatments will exert considerable influence over funding and treatment decisions in the future.

Protocol-Driven Intervention

With the rise of managed health care over the past decade, the financing and delivery of mental health services has been undergoing a period of dramatic change. In contrast to private pay or the typical indemnity-style insurance coverage of previous years, managed mental health care involves an intermediary organization that contracts with and is prepaid by a payer or carrier to purchase, authorize, and manage services for the covered beneficiaries (Doty, 1996). Because the managed care organization (MCO) shares the risk for covering all needed services, it has incentives to enhance both efficiency and effectiveness by managing the price, volume, technology, and quality of treatment (Harris, 1994).

One method that MCOs have been using to maximize efficiency and effectiveness is to develop specific protocols for the treatment of the different types of problems that people may present in therapy. To some extent, the delivery of mental health services has always been governed by such guidelines. Shueman and Troy (1994) noted that these *informal* treatment protocols have been manifest in three forms: (a) information in textbooks, (b) the acquired wisdom of experienced professionals who then supervise or consult with students and colleagues, and (c) written criteria intended to provide information to payers and others about what is appropriate care. The development of *formal* guidelines, however, is based on the idea that studied, empirically proven, and expert-approved techniques should be used whenever they are available for particular problems or disorders (Shueman & Troy, 1994). Moreover, when the outcome of available treatment options is equal, the MCO dictates that the least expensive option be used. Similarly, additions to the list of authorized services depend on the balance between the cost and effectiveness of the new service.

As was the case with empirically validated (or supported) treatments, the move to standardize practice with treatment guidelines is based on the assumption that therapist technical operations are responsible for client improvement. In other words, MCOs, and those who develop and implement standardized protocols, assume that better outcomes and lower costs are associated with adherence to the treatment guidelines. At the same time, noncompliance with the protocol is thought to decrease effectiveness and increase costs. Suffice it to say, changes in the management of mental health care services are further evidence of the growing emphasis on therapist technical operations as the key active ingredient in psychotherapy.

Evaluating the Effectiveness of Technique/Model-Oriented Training and Practice

THE EFFECTIVENESS OF TECHNIQUE/MODEL-ORIENTED TRAINING

The history of training therapists has gradually changed from highly abstract, theoretical models learned through close mentoring with a supervisor to more concrete, manual-based models learned through a variety of methods, media, and often with a more collegial relationship with a supervisor. Unfortunately, the nature of the earliest training of therapists did not lend itself to empirical analysis. Such training tended to be psychoanalytic in nature and take place under supervision of a psychiatrist—often in a medical setting (Matarazzo & Garner, 1992). Strict allegiance to a theoretical model was required and supervision tended to resemble the techniques used for treatment. Frequently, therapists in training were required to undergo an extensive "training analysis" aimed, at least in part, at bringing changes in awareness consistent with the assumptions of the model in which they were being trained (e.g., resolving unconscious intrapsychic conflicts).

The earliest training approaches to undergo empirical testing used treatment models that were client centered in nature and focused on helping therapists acquire specific skills thought basic to effective clinical work (e.g., the "necessary and sufficient" conditions of empathy, genuineness, active listening, etc.; Rogers, 1961). A number of training programs developed based on micro-training of these skills (see, e.g., Ivey, 1980, 1983). Interestingly, as Matarazzo and Garner (1992) pointed out, little is known about the effects of this style of training on treatment outcome. The specificity and immediacy of feedback, however, have been shown to be effective in helping therapists acquire the skills they are being taught (e.g., Daniels, Rigazio-DiGilio, & Ivey, 1997; Ivey, 1980).

Training with therapy manuals and protocols was the next approach to be developed. Importantly, this approach had all the specificity of the skill-building approaches but included an organizing framework aimed at helping therapists know when a particular skill or technique would be most effective and how various techniques should interact over the course of treatment. The clear, operational definitions of the various treatment models contained in manuals and protocols make this style of training easier to evaluate with standard research strategies. Such training would provide strong evidence for the contribution of models and techniques to treatment outcome (e.g., if adherence to the manual or protocol led to better treatment outcomes). On the other hand, a finding of few or no differences in outcome would suggest that training in specific models and techniques is relatively pointless (Strupp & Anderson, 1997).

Some evidence has accumulated in favor of this form of training. For example, a few studies have found that strict adherence by therapists to therapy manuals leads to improved treatment outcomes (e.g., Luborsky, McLellan, Woody, O'Brien, & Auerbach, 1985). In addition, training with manuals has also been found to accelerate the pace of therapist training (Rounsaville, O'Malley, Foley, & Weissman, 1988). The news is not all favorable, however. For example, in a study that strongly suggests that factors other than models and techniques are primarily responsible for treatment outcome, Luborsky et al. (1985) found that adherence to a manual or protocol did not prevent widely varying outcomes among therapists. Of even greater concern, however, a series of studies showed that fidelity to treatment manuals may come at the expense of other factors known to impact outcome favorably (e.g., flexibility, acceptability, warmth, therapeutic alliance, etc.; Anderson, Crowley, & Martin, 1997; Henry, Butler, Strupp, Schacht, & Binder, 1993; Henry, Schacht, Strupp, Butler, & Binder, 1993; Lambert & Bergin, 1994). As therapists became more alert to the potential problems in interpersonal process they were also manifesting more disaffiliative communications. Henry and Strupp (1994) suggested that "these results also have important implications for manual-guided treatments in general. In short, technical adherence to a treatment protocol may cause unexpected process changes along other dimensions, particularly those relevant to the alliance. If this is so, then the belief that the treatment variable is truly being specified and controlled with treatment manuals and technical adherence scales may be an illusion" (p. 67). In other words, it is possible that in some cases manuals may have a negative influence on common factors.

The series of studies, known collectively as the Vanderbilt II Psychotherapy Training Project, is particularly enlightening because it was specifically designed to assess the outcome of treatment by comparing therapists before and after training with a manual. A treatment manual based on the principles and techniques of time-limited dynamic psychotherapy (TLDP; Strupp & Binder, 1984) was specifically developed for the study. Briefly, the approach uses frequent and early transference interpretations and is based on the idea that maladaptive interactions with the therapist are representative of similar patterns operating in the client's interpersonal life and history.

Each therapist in the study was monitored for a year prior to being trained with the TLDP manual. During that time, they were each assigned two therapy cases and instructed to use their usual methods and orientation. This initial period was followed by a year of training during which time each therapist worked with a single "training" case, studied the treatment manual, and attended weekly didactic training and supervision with one of two TLDP supervisors. In the final year of the project, the participating therapists were instructed to use the TLDP techniques they had learned with two additional clients.

Evaluation of the training phase found that the therapists *did* learn the manualized protocol as well as improve in their use of some basic clinical skills (Henry, Butler, et al., 1993; Henry, Schacht, et al., 1993). However, the extensive training and supervision *did not* result in improved treatment outcomes. Rather, *clients seen by therapists before their manualized training were as likely to improve as those seen after training* (Bein et al., 1997).

Whatever the cause, the failure to find differences in such a carefully controlled study as this raises serious questions about the utility of training manuals when used in real clinical settings—especially if their adoption assumes that therapists are proficient in basic clinical skills. Consider, for example, that in spite of having successfully completed the manualized training and having at least 2 years of postdoctoral experience, many of the therapists in the study displayed measurable deficits in basic clinical skills. In addition, whereas most learned to dispense the TLDP techniques, only half of the therapists were judged minimally competent in their administration after the year of intensive training, supervision, and monitoring (Bein et al., 1997). One can only speculate about the effectiveness of such training under less optimal conditions (e.g., day-to-day clinical practice). Such results suggest that the goal of isolating specific techniques without greater attention to basic clinical skills (even with professional therapists) is, at least, misguided if not completely illusory.

THE CONTRIBUTION OF MODELS AND TECHNIQUES TO THERAPY OUTCOME

Although training and practice have become increasingly specific, technical, and standardized, 30 years of research suggests that models and techniques have a relatively small influence on treatment outcome. Lambert (1986), for example, concluded that only 15% of the variance in outcome among clients can be attributed to models and techniques. He defined techniques as "those factors unique to specific therapies, such as biofeedback, hypnosis, systematic desensitization" (p. 437). A brief review of two bodies of therapy outcome literature—comparative and dismantling studies—provides compelling evidence of the relatively minor role that specific models and techniques play in producing client change. These and other portions of the therapy outcome literature have consistently been used as evidence for the common factors interpretation of treatment outcome. They are reviewed here because of the overwhelming consistency of the findings.

Comparative Studies

In 1952, Eysenck published his controversial study showing that clients who underwent long-term, expensive psychological therapies improved about as much as those who had no treatment. This unfavorable assessment of psychotherapy outcome generated an enormous debate among practitioners and inspired a generation of reserachers. Within a decade, the general effectiveness of psychological intervention was well established and researchers were taking aim at a new target (Lambert & Bergin, 1994; Miller, Duncan, & Hubble, 1997): which aspects of therapy were helpful?

A variety of questions related to processes, orientations, and client and therapist characteristics was explored in an attempt to identify the active ingredients of therapy. One method used in this effort was the comparison of two or more modalities or treatment orientations. In literally hundreds of studies, researchers conducted (a) naturalistic investigations of uncontrolled psychotherapies among heterogeneous patient groups; (b) controlled studies of well-defined, usually manualized, therapies applied to diagnostically homogeneous samples; and (c) meta-analyses in which one or both types of studies are included (Beutler, 1991). With few exceptions (to be discussed later in this chapter), *the results of these studies failed to find any consistent differences in outcomes among modalities or orientations* (Beutler, 1991; Lambert & Bergin, 1994; Miller, Duncan, & Hubble, 1997; Orlinsky et al., 1994). As just one example, a recent metaanalysis by Wampold et al. (1997), which examined the effect sizes of bona fide treatments compared in the same study once again found in favor of the dodo bird hypothesis. How small were the differences? These researchers estimated that effect sizes of head-to-head comparisons hovered near zero with an approximate range from 0 to .21!

Component Analysis

The robustness of the dodo bird verdict eventually led researchers away from studies in which one treatment was pitted against another—the so-called "horse-race" or "grand prix" designs. Accepting that "all" approaches were equally effective, the researchers began looking for the specific ingredients important to each model. This gave rise to dismantling strategies or component analyses (Cooper et al., 1995; Craske, 1991; Garfield, 1987; Garner, 1987; Jacobson, 1984; Jacobson et al., 1996; Jacobson, Schmaling, & Holtzworth-Munroe, 1987; Labbe, 1995; Millard et al., 1993; Nezu & Perri, 1989).

In these studies, the treatment in question is divided into its major components. A review of the literature reveals that researchers have used at least three primary designs. In one design, participants are randomly assigned to single-component treatment groups. In another common approach, the components are differentially distributed across treatment groups (Jacobson, 1984; Jacobson et al., 1987, 1996; Labbe, 1995). For example, Jacobson (1984) conducted an evaluation of behavioral marriage training (BMT) in which individuals were assigned to one of three conditions: (a) behavior exchange (Com-ponent 1); (b) communication/problem solving (Component 2), or (c) complete BMT (both components). Finally, some researchers have used a type of in-process application/reversal design in which all participants begin with the same treatment conditions, with individual components subsequently being added or removed (Cooper et al., 1995; Milliard et al., 1993). For example, Cooper et al. (1995) evaluated the components of a treatment program for children with feeding disorders by initially starting all participants with the same, complete, treatment until food acceptance improved in all patients. At this point various components were removed from the patients' treatment regimens.

Unfortunately, research designed in this fashion has yielded a mixed bag of results. For example, some studies have found differential effects for specific components of a given treatment (Cooper et al., 1995; Milliard et al., 1993; West, Horan, & Games, 1984), whereas others have not found any appreciable differences (Jacobson, 1984; Jacobson et al., 1987, 1996). Two studies that are representative of the range of results found in the existing literature include West et al. (1984) and Jacobson et al. (1996). In the first study, researchers conducted a component analysis of stress inoculation (SI; Meichenbaum & Turk, 1976). The three components of SI identified in the study were (a) education (ED), (b) coping skills training (CS), and (c) exposure to simulated stressors (EX). The ED component consisted of programmed psychoeducation as well as information on the physiological and psychological effects of stress on the individual. The CS component involved instruction on the application of specific, cognitive–behavioral strategies for managing stress, including relaxation and assertiveness training, cognitive restructuring, and time management. Finally, the EX component consisted of facilitated (through therapist interaction) role play with contrived stress-producing scenarios.

The researchers hypothesized that all three components were important contributors to the overall effectiveness of SI but that the CS and EX were significantly more "active" than ED. To test this hypothesis they randomly assigned 60 nurses to one of five treatment conditions: (a) no-treatment control, (b) education only, (c) education plus coping skills, (d) education plus exposure, and (e) all components (education, coping skills, and exposure). Briefly, the study found that only treatment conditions containing the coping-skills component resulted in significant reductions in participants' levels of stress. As a result, West et al. (1984) concluded,

> The coping skills component of occupational stress inoculation is its major active ingredient. Although the education component provides the logical foundation for coping skills (indeed the coping skills treatment could not be implemented without it), education alone had no beneficial effects whatsoever when compared to no treatment at all. Moreover, the exposure component as operationally defined in this study was similarly impotent. (p. 216)

The same design was less successful in the study of cognitive–behavioral therapy for depression (CT; Beck et al., 1979) conducted by Jacobson et al. (1996). The two primary components of CT identified in this study included (a) behavioral activation (BA) and (b) coping strategies (CS) for automatic thoughts and identification of depressogenic core schema. The BA component involved attempts to make clients become more active and put themselves in contact with available sources of positive reinforcement. The CS provided clients with new strategies for coping with depressing events and depressogenic thinking.

The researchers hypothesized that individuals who received both components would improve more than those receiving only one. They further expected better outcomes for the CS versus the BA condition. To test this hypothesis, they conducted an experiment comparing three treatments for major depression in adults: (a) treatment with BA treatment; (b) treatment including BA and CS; and (c) complete cognitive therapy for depression (CT), including BA and CS, as well a direct focus on identifying and modifying core depressogenic schema. After a lengthy and thorough analysis including examination of mean differences, proportion of clients making clinically significant changes, and theoretically expected changes specific to each component, Jacobson et al. (1996) concluded, "We found no evidence in this study that CT is any more effective than either of its components" (p. 302). These results were particularly surprising to the researchers given that all of the therapists in the study expected the CT component to be the most effective—a finding that runs counter to the allegiance effect commonly observed in outcome research (Robinson, Berman, & Neimeyer, 1990).

Despite the best efforts of countless researchers, the results of both comparative and component-based research designs raise more questions than they answer. Are all treatments really equal? From this data, at least, the answer would appear to be yes and no. Existent literature for the most part supports the idea of equality and strongly suggests that efforts be made to identify the factors common to all approaches. At the same time, however, there are some areas of the literature that appear to contradict this conclusion.

STUDIES OF DISORDER-SPECIFIC TECHNIQUES

Whereas the large majority of grand prix designs and dismantling studies find few differences among the treatments, a few techniques for the treatment of several specific problems have been empirically demonstrated as key to change. Although it is not possible to provide a comprehensive list of all published disorder-specific techniques, a sample of approaches may be useful in illustrating how specific techniques can contribute to treatment outcome.

Exposure for Anxiety Disorders

A number of studies have found exposure techniques to be particularly effective with some anxiety-based disorders, including simple phobia, agoraphobia, and obsessive–compulsive disorder (Beck, Sokol, Clark, Berchick, & Wright, 1992; Chambless, Foa, Groves, & Goldstein, 1978; Emmelkamp, 1982; 1994). Exposure is conducted in two primary ways (a) in the individual's imagination (e.g., the individual imagines himself or herself in the phobic situation) or (b) in vivo, in which the individual is actually exposed to the feared object or situation. In vivo exposure is generally accepted as the more effective of the two approaches. A number of variables moderate the effects of in vivo exposure, such as the severity of anxiety, the duration and frequency of exposure trials, and the level of supervision and support during the exposure trials (e.g., therapist supervised vs. self-directed or unsupervised).

Ost (1989) conducted an evaluation of prolonged in vivo exposure among patients diagnosed with simple phobias that is representative of many other studies. He found that after only a single 2-hour session involving prolonged in vivo exposure, 90% of participants experienced full "recovery." These effects were maintained at a 4-year follow-up evaluation. Likewise, a number of studies have found in vivo exposure superior in the treatment of agoraphobia and obsessive–compulsive disorders (Emmelkamp, 1982, 1992; Emmelkamp, Brilman, Kuipers, & Mersch, 1986; Emmelkamp, Kuipers, & Eggeraat, 1978; Emmelkamp & Mersch, 1982; Rachman & Hodgson, 1980; Steketee & Cleere, 1990).

A review of the comparative treatment literature on anxiety disorders provides a different picture than that described in the previous section where "everyone has won and all must have prizes" (Luborsky et al., 1975). On the basis of this strong research foundation, one can confidently state that exposure is a key technique for successful treatment in several anxiety disorders. Indeed, it would be difficult, and possibly unethical, to argue against the obvious superiority of exposure-based techniques over other treatment modalities for the treatment of these disorders.

Behavioral Treatments of Sexual Dysfunctions

Similarly, among the sexual dysfunctions several techniques have been demonstrated to be more effective than others. Prior to Masters and Johnson's (1970) landmark volume on the treatment of sexual disorders, practitioners used a variety of techniques that were primarily psychodynamic in origin and directed toward treating sexual dysfunction as an individual pathology (Emmelkamp, 1994). Among behaviorists the most common treatment modality was systematic desensitization (Wolpe, 1958), for which there were few controlled studies and consequently little demonstrated efficacy. In contrast to such individualized approaches, Masters and Johnson (1970) advocated the treatment of sexual dysfunction using a dyadic approach (e.g., involvement of a sexual partner). Sexual problems based on performance anxiety (i.e., secondary erectile disorder) were treated with graded exposure in vivo.

Among male patients with disorders in ejaculation (i.e., premature ejaculation), two primary behavioral techniques emerged as the treatments of choice: the "pause technique" (Semans, 1956) and the "squeeze technique" (Masters & Johnson, 1970). In the pause technique the patient is required to masturbate until the point of ejaculation, at which time climax is prevented by a removal of stimulation by the partner (or the patient himself). This sequence is repeated and practiced several times, and eventually the masturbation-induced stimulation is replaced with intercourse. The squeeze technique is similar in procedure to the pause technique. However, at the point of ejaculation, in addition to the removal of stimulation, the partner squeezes the frenulum of the penis, thereby preventing ejaculation. A host of studies have reported positive outcomes as a result of these techniques (Emmelkamp, 1994). Among female patients with orgasmic disorders, a number of studies have highlighted the superiority of masturbation training over other treatment modalities (Barbach, 1974; Ersner-Hershfield, & Kopel, 1979; Wakefield, 1987).

PROCESS RESEARCH FINDINGS

Although comparisons of differing orientations and component analyses typically find few differences among treatment alternatives, research that examines the effect of individual therapist interventions on a session-by-session basis provides some evidence for the usefulness of specific techniques. For example, Orlinsky et al.(1994)

reviewed the huge body of literature examining the relationship between therapeutic processes and outcome. "Therapist interventions" is one category of process variables contained in the massive review and include the following interventions: therapist's focusing on patient problems, therapist's focusing on patient affect, therapist's focusing on here-and-now involvements, therapist's focusing on core personal relationships and transference issues, change strategies, paradoxical intention, experiential confrontation, interpretation, exploration, support, reflection/clarification, and therapist's self-disclosure. In the review, a total of 377 independent relationships (some studies included the examination of several relationships so the actual number of studies may be fewer than 100) between an intervention and outcome were examined. The studies provided evidence both for and against the relationship between therapist interventions and outcome. Some areas of intervention had better evidence for their impact on outcome than others. For example, all 13 studies examining the relationship between paradoxical intervention and therapy outcome found a positive relationship between the use of paradoxical intention and client outcome. Other areas showed little relationship between technique and outcome. For example, there was virtually no evidence for the widely practiced technique of self-disclosure by the therapist.

This type of research, in combination with her own research over the past 2 decades, led Clara Hill (1989) to state, "I believe that therapist techniques are responsible for client change" (p. 1). In spite of her belief, however, *correlations between therapist interventions and client outcome are simply insufficient to rule out common factors as the primary creators of client change.* After all, the success of such interventions may be an artifact of quality relationships, trust, persuasiveness, and other characteristics common to all effective treatment.

DIFFERENCES IN THERAPIST SKILL

Another area of research that may add evidence for the effectiveness of specific techniques includes a set of studies that examine differences among therapists within treatments. Several studies have shown that, when comparing different treatment orientations, few mean differences in treatment effectiveness are identified. When looking within treatments, however, it is not unusual to find dramatic differences among the therapists within a given treatment. In a typical example of such findings, Luborsky et al. (1985) found that some therapists in their study had consistently positive outcomes, whereas others had consistently poor outcomes. Importantly, this occurred in a study where no mean differences were noted among the treatments being compared.

These and other similar findings can be interpreted in several ways. On the one hand, differences among therapists using the same approach may reflect real differences in the use of specific techniques or at least a Skill × Technique interaction. In other words, a therapist may have excellent success with one model and techniques but not with another approach. On the other hand, differences in client outcomes among therapists using the same approach can be interpreted as evidence that common ingredients of psychotherapy are primarily responsible for change. In this latter case, it could be argued that a therapist who has consistently good outcomes using one approach would be effective using any orientation, model, or techniques—a conclusion supported by the other data reviewed in this chapter.

Whether or not differences among therapists support or question the notion that specific techniques lead to better outcome, it is clear that mean comparisons among treatments mask potentially informative data regarding within-treatment variance. Findings in this area have been slow to accrue at least in part because such research requires multiple clients per therapist, so that between-therapist comparisons have sufficient power. Further study of between-therapist differences will help to elucidate the role techniques versus therapist skills might play.

SUMMARY

What is to be concluded from this review of the contribution of models, manuals, and techniques to training and practice? Several points deserve consideration:

- The move toward manualization of treatment is undeniable and relatively pervasive across the field. The results of such attempts are mixed, however, ranging from strong endorsements of improved outcomes as a result of increased manualization to little or no effect on treatment outcome. In the real world of clinical practice, manualization is even more likely to have a negligible impact on treatment effectiveness (Speer & Newman, 1996). In sum, little evidence substantiates the benefit of technique-based training.
- The traditional comparative studies that have pitted therapies against one another, for the most part, have shown no essential differences across modalities. This finding is amazingly consistent across rigorous and controlled studies (Wampold et al., 1997).
- Dismantling strategies have lead to a mixed bag of results, with some studies identifying significant differences in the efficacy of specific identifiable techniques (West et al., 1984) and others

showing no such differences (Jacobson et al., 1996). The preponderance of this data favors the latter rather than the former conclusion. A notable exception is in the area of certain specific behavioral techniques used for the treatment of highly circumscribed problems (e.g., certain anxiety and sexual disorders).

■ Process evaluations provide some limited evidence for the usefulness of specific techniques. However, the collected findings of numerous studies are not entirely conclusive in ruling out the possible effects of common factors as the primary catalysts for change. At the same time, consideration of the specific techniques and models through process-oriented evaluations provides a unique perspective that warrants further investigation.

■ Another area of potential evaluation is within-treatment differences among therapists.Traditional evaluations of this variance have tended to focus on the evidence of common active ingredients rather than differences accrued as the result of differential application of specific techniques, of skill, or of both with specific techniques across therapists. Further study of between-therapist differences will help highlight the impact of specific techniques versus therapist skills.

Reconciling Emerging Clinical Trends With Existing Empirical Research

Psychotherapy is faced with two interesting, contradictory, and potentially divisive facts. First, professional training, theory, and practice are increasingly oriented toward specific techniques and treatment approaches. Second, with few exceptions, existing research evidence on both training and treatment suggests that individual therapist techniques contribute very little to client outcome. A review of the literature finds that three strategies dominate professional attempts to reconcile the conflict between clinical trends and the empirical literature: (a) continuing the search for specificity, (b) searching for common factors, and (c) changing the model.

CONTINUING THE SEARCH FOR SPECIFICITY

The most prevalent strategy for dealing with the discrepancy has been the trumpeter's call to continue the charge. On the basis of findings that suggest some specific techniques are more effective than others for phobias and sex therapies, proponents of this view argue that continued research will eventually discover similar specific techniques that are useful for other common problems and disorders (e.g., depression, personality disorders, etc.). In essence, this strategy dismisses the body of evidence for common factors and argues for continuing the search for evidence regarding specific factors with improvements in research. Beutler (1991) is a good example of this perspective. He suggested that studies used to substantiate the claim of no differences between therapies are methodologically flawed, lacking in theoretical underpinnings, and underrepresentative of the millions of possible Client × Treatment interactions. Consistent with his argument, he stated that "only through coordinated studies that follow a model of prescriptive treatment selection will we be able eventually to specify and prioritize the patient and psychotherapy variables that are most likely to result in positive findings" (p. 231).

THE SEARCH FOR COMMON FACTORS

Another approach to dealing with the contrast between professional directions and the research evidence is reflected in this book. Proponents of this approach attribute the lack of evidence for specific techniques to the lack of specific effects. In their place, they seek factors that cut across treatment modalities, orientations, and components. Although their search is for common factors, the research appears to be focused on specific techniques that are common to therapies (e.g., relationship-enhancement techniques that improve the alliance regardless of the orientation). Given that major portions of this book are dedicated to this approach, no further discussion is needed.

CHANGING THE MODEL

A final strategy for dealing with the discrepancy between clinical practice and research results is to develop new models of therapy. At the beginning of this chapter, models and techniques were carefully defined to sidestep the prevailing tendency to define all models as a collection of specific techniques, which are then starkly held in contrast to common factors shared among all therapies. Recent years have witnessed an explosion of therapy models, most of which have increased in specificity through the use of therapy manuals. In studies comparing these models of treatment it is the unique aspects (both theoretical and technical) that are emphasized. Identifying differences among specific, technique-based models, and nonspecific factors is, however, a relatively meaningless basis for a definition. The distinction between specific or technique-based treatments as models and common or non-technique-based factors as nonmodels may only be meaningful for theoretical purists who operate from the traditional specific-factors perspective. The purist is not likely to see much value in the identification of similarities.

Whereas the vast majority of recent treatments focus on attempts to spell out specific techniques, most also recognize (to varying degrees) various common factors as part and parcel of specific techniques. For example, Strupp (1986) noted that it may be ultimately impossible to tease apart the techniques of a model from its common factors because techniques are inextricably embedded within a complex interpersonal encounter (to which most techniques are directed). That is, as soon as one attempts to harness so-called common factors and apply them in the form of goal-oriented activities (e.g., symptom reduction) they begin to use some sort of model. Thus, the distinction between specific and common factors used to distinguish the crucial components of different therapies is a convenient yet artificial heuristic device.

Models are essential to the advancement of psychotherapy research and practice. Importantly, however, *these models need not necessarily include techniques,* or at least not the variety of routinized verbal strategies that have been linked to therapy models and orientations in the past. Rather, such a model might emphasize the development of a warm and compassionate client–therapist relationship. Research on the therapeutic alliance has, for example, consistently shown the alliance to be related to positive therapeutic outcomes (Luborsky, 1994). This model might also include a description of those personal characteristics of the therapist most frequently associated with client change. Although not exactly new, such constructs, already supported by research, may well be useful in the construction of new, empirically driven models of psychotherapy.

This approach to model construction is more than a collection of common factors. Consider, for example, that the importance of a therapeutic alliance has been emphasized by proponents of the common factors as well as adherents of other therapeutic traditions, most notably interpersonal, psychoanalytic, and humanistic. The idea of the alliance becomes part of a model when it is used intentionally by practitioners of that model and when that usage leads to predictable events (e.g., incremental increases in outcome). Furthermore, once a therapist decides that so-called common factors are the curative agents of the patient–therapist encounter, the therapist has simply switched models.

Clearly, much of future psychotherapy research will aim at the identification of these and other similar "tools" used in interpersonal relationships to relieve psychological distress—most of which have "commonly" been used for thousands of years. Knowledge of how, when, and where to harness these human capacities to an optimal extent is not well understood, however, and is both a scientific problem and a humanitarian concern. The hope is that empiricism will lead to their identification and ultimately their use in a superior therapy model at some point in the future.

Questions From the Editors

1. What factors do you think account for the apparent lack of correspondence between the data and current clinical trends and practices (i.e., empirically validated treatments, emphasis on models and techniques)?

We believe three issues influence the differences between research and practice regarding the role of specific techniques. First, the gap separating research and practice is not a newly created tourist attraction. Researchers' inability to communicate clinically practical findings combined with practitioners' disinterest in research have produced a deeply entrenched schism. Differences observed in this chapter between research and practice are a natural reflection of this long-standing separation.

Second, practitioners focus on accountability and outcome research when outside forces require such a focus. Speer and Newman (1996) suggested the focus on evaluation within the public sector ebbs and flows in a cyclical fashion. Currently, efforts to reduce the costs of health care (and behavioral health care) have lead to increased accountability for practitioners and a resultant focus on finding techniques that produce a specified outcome.

Third, the lack of correspondence between the clinical focus on techniques and research evidence is a reflection of the differences of opinion that are apparent among both researchers and clinicians. Even some who have conducted research that found no differences among competing techniques or dismantled treatments continue to believe that techniques are efficacious and continue to pursue the hunt to discover them.

2. On the basis of your review of the available literature, what suggestions would you make for improving or changing the training of mental health professionals?

We have three recommendations for training mental health professionals. First, to develop more models that emphasize common factors and general relationship-building skills. If, in fact, specific techniques account for only 15% of the variation in outcomes (Lambert, 1986), less time should be used for training in specific techniques. Second, more research is needed to investigate the effects of training with manuals in neophyte therapists. Therapy manuals to date have been studied only as a method of helping trained therapists to adhere to and become competent in a specific therapeutic model. Much less is known about the effects of using manuals when training neophyte therapists. Third, greater emphasis needs to be placed on the evaluation of outcome in clinical practice. Practitioners can and should be more involved in assessing their own effectiveness by using research-based outcome methods in practice (Ogles, Lambert, & Masters, 1996).

3. What does the future portend for psychology if the current trends continue unabated?

Because of the cyclical nature of psychological trends, we believe that it is highly unlikely that current trends will continue unabated. More likely, the move to develop standardized, highly specific protocols within clinical practice will gradually meet a trend that emphasizes more individually tailored, customized therapy that relies more on common factors and relationship skills. If the trend for specification were to continue, however, the practice of psychotherapy may become a highly standardized and technical operation that is practiced by master's level practitioners with narrow areas of expertise. Each client would be greeted by a specified protocol (including expected length of care, anticipated costs, predicted dose–response curves, etc.) that matches the client's "diagnosis."

References

American Psychiatric Association. (1996). *American Psychiatric Association practice guidelines.* Washington, DC: Author.

Anderson, T., Crowley, M. J., & Martin, D. (1997, June). *Educating therapists: The training phase of the Vanderbilt II psychotherapy research project.* Paper presented at the 28th annual meeting of the Society for Psychotherapy Research, Geilo, Norway.

Barbach, L. G. (1974). Group treatment of preorgasmic women. *Journal of Sex and Marital Therapy, 1,* 139–145.

Beck, A. T., Rush, A. J., Shaw, B. F., & Emery, G. (1979). *Cognitive therapy of depression.* New York: Guilford Press.

Bein, E., Anderson, T., Strupp, H. H., Henry, W. P., Schacht, T. E., Binder, J. L., & Butler, S. F. (1997). *The effects of training in time-limited dynamic psychotherapy: Changes in therapeutic outcome.* Unpublished manuscript, Vanderbilt University, Nashville, TN.

Beutler, L. E. (1991). Have all won and must all have prizes? Revisiting Luborsky et al.'s verdict. *Journal of Consulting and Clinical Psychology, 59,* 226–232.

Chambless, D. L. (1993). *Task force on the promotion and dissemination of psychological procedures: A report adopted by the Division 12 board.*

Washington, DC: Division 12 of the American Psychological Association.

Chambless, D. L., Foa, E. B., Groves, G. A., & Goldstein, A. J. (1978). Brevital in flooding with agoraphobics: Countereffective? *Behaviour Research and Therapy, 17,* 243–251.

Christensen, E. R., & Jeffrey, D. B. (1977). Therapist manual for a behavior modification weight reduction program. In E. E. Abramson (Ed.), *Behavioral approaches to weight control.* New York: Springer.

Cooper, L. J., Wacker, D. P., McComas, J. J., Brown, K., et al. (1995). Use of component analysis to identify active variables in treatment packages for children with feeding disorders. *Journal of Applied Behavior Analysis, 28,* 139–153.

Craske, M. G. (1991). Models and treatment of panic: Behavioral therapy for panic. *Journal of Cognitive Psychotherapy: An International Quarterly, 5,* 199–214.

Daniels, T. G., Rigazio-DiGilio, S. A., & Ivey, A. E. (1997). Microcounseling: A training and supervision paradigm for the helping professions. In C. E. Watkins (Ed.), *Handbook of psychotherapy supervision* (pp. 277–297). New York: Wiley.

Doty, D. W. (1996). *The essential children's services planner.* Tiburon, CA: CentraLink Publications.

Edelson, M. (1988). *Psychoanalysis: A theory in crisis.* Chicago: University of Chicago Press.

Emmelkamp, P. M. G. (1982). *Phobic and obsessive–compulsive disorders: Theory, research, and practice.* New York: Plenum Press.

Emmelkamp, P. M. G. (1992). Obsessive–compulsive disorder: The contribution of an experimental clinical approach. In A. Ehlers, W. Fiegenbaum, J. Margraf, & I. Florin (Eds.), *Perspectives and promises of clinical psychology* (pp. 149–156). New York: Plenum Press.

Emmelkamp, P. M. G. (1994). Behavior therapy with adults. In A. E. Bergin & S. L. Garfield (Eds.), *Handbook of psychotherapy and behavior change* (4th ed., pp. 379–427). New York: Wiley.

Emmelkamp, P. M., Brilman, E., Kuipers, H., & Mersch, P. (1986). The treatment of agoraphobia: A comparison of self-insructional training, rational emotive therapy, and exposure in vivo. *Behavior Modification, 10,* 37–53.

Emmelkamp, P. M. G., Kuipers, A., & Eggeraat, J. (1978). Cognitive modification versus prolonged exposure in vivo: A comparison with agoraphobics. *Behavior Research and Therapy, 16,* 33–41.

Emmelkamp, P. M. G., & Mersch, P. P. (1982). Cognition and exposure in vivo in the treatment of agoraphobia: Short-term and delayed effects. *Cognitive Therapy and Research, 6,* 77–90.

Ersner-Hershfield, R., & Kopel, S. (1979). Group treatment of pre-orgasmic women. *Journal of Consulting and Clinical Psychology, 47,* 750–759.

Eysenck, H. J. (1952). The effects of psychotherapy: An evaluation. *Journal of Consulting Psychology, 16,* 319–324.

Garfield, S. L. (1987). Ethical issues in research on psychotherapy. *Counseling and Values, 31,* 115–125.

Garner, D. M. (1987). Psychotherapy outcome research with bulimia nervosa. *Psychotherapy and Psychosomatics, 48,* 129–140.

Harris, J. S. (1994). *Strategic health management.* San Francisco, CA: Jossey-Bass.

Henry, W. P., Butler, S. F., Strupp, H. H., Schacht, T. E., & Binder, J. L. (1993). Effects of training in time-limited dynamic psychotherapy: Changes in therapist behavior. *Journal of Consulting and Clinical Psychology, 61,* 434–440.

Henry, W. P., Schacht, T. E., Strupp, H. H., Butler, S. F., & Binder, J. L. (1993). Effects of training in time-limited dynamic psychotherapy: Mediators of therapists' responses to training. *Journal of Consulting and Clinical Psychology, 61,* 441–447.

Henry, W. P., & Strupp, H. H. (1994). The therapeutic alliance as interpersonal process. In A. O. Horvath & L. S. Greenburg (Eds.), *The working alliance: Theory, research, and practice.* New York: Wiley.

Hill, C. E. (1989). *Therapist techniques and client outcomes.* Newbury Park, CA: Sage.

Hoopes, M., Fisher, B., & Barlow, S. (1982). *Family facilitation programs.* Rockville, MD: Aspen Systems.

Ivey, A. E. (1980). *Counseling and psychotherapy: Skills, theories and practice.* Englewood Cliffs, NJ: Prentice-Hall.

Ivey, A. E. (1983). *Intentional interviewing and counseling.* Monterey, CA: Brooks/Cole.

Jacobson, N. S. (1984). A component analysis of behavioral marital therapy: The relative effectiveness of behavior exchange and communication/problem solving training. *Journal of Consulting and Clinical Psychology, 52,* 295–305.

Jacobson, N. S., Dobson, K. S., Truax, P. A., Addis, M. E., Koerner, K., Gollan, J. K., Gortner, E., & Prince, S. E. (1996). A component analysis of cognitive–behavioral treatment for depression. *Journal of Consulting and Clinical Psychology, 64,* 295–304.

Jacobson, N. S., Schmaling, K. B., & Holzworth-Munroe, A. (1987). Component analysis of behavioral marital therapy: Two year follow-up and prediction of relapse. *Journal of Marital and Family Therapy, 13,* 187–195.

Labbe, E. E. (1995). Treatment of childhood migraine with autogenic training and skin temperature biofeedback: A component analysis. *Headache, 35,* 10–13.

Lambert, M. J. (1986). Some implications of psychotherapy outcome research for eclectic psychotherapy. *International Journal of Ecclectic Psychotherapy, 5,* 16–45.

Lambert, M. J., & Bergin, A. E. (1994). The effectiveness of psychotherapy. In A. E. Bergin & S. L. Garfield (Eds.), *Handbook of psychotherapy and behavior change* (4th ed., pp. 143–189). New York: Wiley.

Lambert, M. J., & Ogles, B. M. (1988). Treatment manuals: Problems and promise. *Journal of Integrative and Eclectic Psychotherapy, 7,* 187–204.

Lewinsohn, P. M., Munoz, R. F., Youngren, M. A., & Zeiss, A. M. (1978). *Control your depression.* Englewood Cliffs, NJ: Prentice-Hall.

Linehan, M. M. (1993). *Skills training manual for treating borderline personality disorder.* New York: Guilford Press.

Luborsky, L. (1984). *Principles of psychoanalytic psychotherapy: A manual for supportive–expressive treatment.* New York: Basic Books.

Luborsky, L. (1994). Therapeutic alliance as predictors of psychotherapy outcomes: Factors explaining the predictive success. In A. O. Horvath & L. S. Greenberg (Eds.), *The working alliance: Theory, research, and practice* (pp. 38–50). New York: Wiley.

Luborsky, L., & DeRubeis, R. J. (1984). The use of psychotherapy treatment manuals—A small revolution in psychotherapy research styles. *Clinical Psychology Review, 4,* 5–14.

Luborsky, L., McLellan, A. T., Woody, G. E., O'Brien, C. P., & Auerbach, A. (1985). Therapist success and its determinants. *Archives of General Psychiatry, 42,* 602–611.

Luborsky, L., Singer, B., & Luborsky, L. (1975). Comparative studies of psychotherapy. *Archives of General Psychiatry, 32,* 995–1008.

Masters, W. H., & Johnson, V. E. (1970). *Human sexual inadequacy.* Boston: Little, Brown.

Matarazzo, R. G., & Garner, A. M. (1992). Research on training for psychotherapy. In D. K. Freedheim, H. J. Freudenberger, J. W. Kessler, S. B. Messer, D. R. Petevsm, H. H. Strupp, & P. L. Wachtel (Eds.), *History of psychotherapy: A century of change* (pp. 850–877). Washington, DC: American Psychological Association.

Meichenbaum, D., & Turk, D. (1976). The cognitive–behavioral management of anxiety, anger, and pain. In P. O. Davidson (Ed.), *The behavioral management of anxiety, depression, and pain* (pp. 1–34). New York: Brunner/Mazel.

Miller, S. D., Duncan, B. L., & Hubble, M. A. (1997). *Escape from Babel: Toward a unifying language for psychotherapy practice.* New York: W. W. Norton.

Milliard, T., Wacker, D. P., Cooper, L. J., Harding, J., Drew, J., Plagmann, L. A., Asmus, J., McComas, J., & Jensen-Kovalan, P. (1993). A brief component analysis of potential treatment packages in an outpatient clinic setting with young children. *Journal of Applied Behavior Analysis, 26,* 475–476.

Nezu, A. M., & Perri, M. G. (1989). Social problem-solving therapy for unipolar depression: An initial dismantling investigation. *Journal of Consulting and Clinical Psychology, 57,* 408–413.

Norcross, J. C. (1985). In defense of theoretical orientations for clinicians. *The Clinical Psychologist, 38,* 13–17.

Ogles, B. M., Lambert, M. J., & Masters, K. S. (1996). *Assessing outcome in clinical practice.* Boston: Allyn & Bacon.

Orlinsky, D. E., Grawe, K., & Parks, B. K. (1994). Process and outcome in psychotherapy—noch einmal. In A. E. Bergin & S. L. Garfield (Eds.), *Handbook of psychotherapy and behavior change* (4th ed., pp. 270–376). New York: Wiley.

Ost, L. G. (1989). One-session treatment for specific phobias. *Behavior Research and Therapy, 27,* 1.

Peterson, C., & Villanova, P. (1988). An expanded attributional style questionnaire. *Journal of Abnormal Psychology, 97,* 87–89.

Poznanski, J. J., & McLennan, J. (1995). Conceputalizing and measuring counselors' theoretical orientation. *Journal of Counseling Psychology, 42,* 411–422.

Rachman, S., & Hodgson, R. J. (1980). *Obsessions and compulsions.* Englewood Cliffs, NJ: Prentice-Hall.

Robinson, L., Berman, J., & Neimeyer, R. (1990). Psychotherapy for treatment of depression: A comprehensive review of controlled outcome research. *Psychological Bulletin, 108,* 30–49.

Rogers, C. R. (1961). *On becoming a person.* Boston: Houghton Mifflin.

Rounsaville, B. J., O'Malley, S., Foley, S., & Weissman, M. M. (1988). Role of manual-guided training in the conduct and efficacy of interpersonal psychotherapy for depression. *Journal of Consulting & Clinical Psychology, 56,* 681–688.

Semans, J. H. (1956). Premature ejaculation: A new approach. *Southern Medical Journal, 49,* 353–357.

Shueman, S. A., & Troy, W. G. (1994). The use of practice guidelines in managed behavioral health programs. In S. A. Shueman, W. G. Troy, & S. L. Mayhugh (Eds.), *Managed health care: An industry perspective* (pp. 149–164). Springfield, IL: Charles C Thomas.

Skinner, B. F. (1948). *Walden two.* New York: Macmillan.

Speer, D. C., & Newman, F. L. (1996). Mental health services outcome evaluation. *Clinical Psychology-Science & Practice, 3,* 105–129.

Steketee, G., & Cleere, L. (1990). Obsessional–compulsive disorders. In A. S. Bellack, M. Hersen, & A. E. Kazdin (Eds.), *International handbook of behavior modification and therapy* (2nd ed., pp. 307–332). New York: Plenum Press.

Stiles, W. B. (1979). Verbal response modes and psychotherapuetic technique. *Psychiatry, 42,* 49–62.

Strupp, H. H. (1986). Psychotherapy: Research, practice, and public policy (how to avoid dead ends). *American Psychologist, 41,* 120–130.

Strupp, H. H., & Anderson, T. (1997). On the limitations of therapy manuals. *Clinical Psychology: Science and Practice, 4,* 76–82.

Strupp, H. H., & Binder, J. L. (1984). *Psychotherapy in a new key: A guide to time-limited dynamic psychotherapy.* New York: Basic Books.

Thompson, J. K. (1990). *Body image disturbance: Assessment and treatment.* New York: Pergamon.

Wakefield, J. C. (1987). The semantics of success: Do masturbation exercises lead to partner orgasm? *Journal of Sex and Marital Therapy, 13,* 3–14.

Wampold, B. E., Mondin, G. W., Moody, M., Stich, F., Benson, K., & Ahn, H. (1997). A meta-analysis of outcome studies comparing bona fide psychotherapies: Empirically, "All must have prizes." *Psychological Bulletin, 122,* 203–215.

West, D. J., Horan, J. J., & Games, P. A. (1984). Component analysis of occupational stress inoculation applied to registered nurses in an acute care hospital setting. *Journal of Counseling Psychology, 31,* 209–218.

Wolpe, J. (1958). *Psychotherapy and reciprocal inhibition.* Stanford: Stanford University Press.

James O. Prochaska

How Do People Change, and How Can We Change to Help Many More People?

8

A fascinating finding in all of psychotherapy science is that very different systems of therapy produce very common outcomes (Smith, Glass, & Miller, 1980). This is a mystery of considerable magnitude that has dogged the field. To treat people affectively, behaviorally, cognitively, psychodynamically, existentially, humanistically, interpersonally, or medicinally and have the results be the same challenges all the leading theories of psychotherapy. After all, these are alternatives created by the best therapy theorists of this century. Are they all right or all wrong? Or does the field not know how therapy works?

The "grand tie" across treatments suggests there are common pathways to change, regardless of how people are treated in therapy. At first I thought there would be common factors in therapy. However, I realized that clients spend less than 1% of their waking hours in therapy sessions. Then I learned that less than 25% of people with *DSM-IV* diagnoses ever participate in psychotherapy. Next, I noted that less than 10% of populations plagued by the major killers of our time (e.g., smoking, sedentary lifestyles, and unhealthy diets) ever seek professional assistance. Given how few people actually participate in treatment, the search shifted from how do people change in therapy to how do people change, period.

What the field now needs most is an adequate theory of behavior change. The field needs a theory that can help explain how people change within and between therapy sessions. The field needs to know how people change before therapy begins, after it ends, and when therapy never occurs. My exploration evolved into one of identifying a more comprehensive theory of change.

This quest began with a comparative analysis of the major systems of psychotherapy (Prochaska, 1979). The transtheoretical approach sought to differentiate common change processes across these leading systems. I found that these systems had much more to say about personality and psychotherapy. That is, they are theories more about why people do not change than how people can change. They emphasize more the content of therapy—such as feelings, fantasies, thoughts, overt behaviors, and relationships—than the process of change.

Nevertheless, 10 processes were identified that are assumed to be among the most powerful approaches to producing change. We then sought to study empirically how much people applied each of these 10 change processes (DiClemente & Prochaska, 1982). We compared people who participated in professional treatments with those who changed on their own. What we discovered was a phenomenon that was not contained within any of the leading theories of therapy. Ordinary people taught us that change involves progress through a series of stages. At different stages, people apply particular processes to progress to the next stage (Prochaska & DiClemente, 1982, 1983).

Since those original findings, it is now possible to predict who signs up, shows up, finishes up, and ends up better off as a result of therapy. Moreover, my colleagues and I have developed professional practices that can produce significant impacts in entire populations of people with problem behaviors. What was learned about how people change and how we can try to help many more people change is the subject of this chapter.

Stages of Change

We discovered that change is a process that unfolds over time. It involves progression through six stages: precontemplation, contemplation, preparation, action, maintenance, and termination.

PRECONTEMPLATION

Precontemplation is the stage in which people are not intending to change or take action in the near future, usually measured in terms of "the next 6 months." People may be in this stage because they are uninformed or underinformed about the consequences of their behavior. They may have tried to change several times and become demoralized about their abilities to do so. They also may be defensive, denying there is a problem. People in this stage avoid reading, talking, or thinking about their high-risk behaviors. They are often characterized in other theories as resistant, unmotivated clients or as not ready for therapy or health promotion programs. Traditional treatment programs were not designed for such individuals and, for that matter, were not especially motivated to match their needs.

People in precontemplation underestimate the benefits of changing and overestimate the costs. They typically are not aware that they are making such mistakes. If they are not conscious of making such mistakes, it will be difficult for them to change. Many remain mired in the precontemplation stage for years, doing considerable damage to their bodies, themselves, and others.

No inherent motivation exists for people to progress from one stage to the next. These are unlike stages of human development, in which children have an innate drive to progress from crawling to walking, although crawling works very well and learning to walk can be both difficult and painful. We have identified two major forces, however, that can motivate people to progress. First are developmental events. For example, in our research the mean age of smokers reaching longer-term maintenance (i.e., consistently maintained abstinence) is 39. At this age, people reevaluate how they have been living. They consider whether they want to die from the way they have been living or enhance the quality and quantity of the second half of their lives.

Environmental events are the other naturally occurring force. A favorite example is a couple we followed who were both heavy smokers. Their dog of many years died of lung cancer. This eventually moved the wife to quit smoking. For his part, the husband bought a new dog. Even the same events can be processed differently by different people.

For many years, a belief circulated among professionals and nonprofessionals alike that people with addictions must hit bottom before they will be motivated to change. As a result, family, friends, and physicians waited helplessly for a crisis to occur. In reality, however, how often does an individual turn 39 or have a dog die? When people show the first signs of a serious physical illness (e.g., cancer or cardiovascular disease), concerned others may rapidly rally to help them seek early intervention. Early interventions are often life-saving, and waiting for such patients to hit bottom is unthinkable. Similarly, a third option now exists to help addicted, precontemplative patients to progress. The third option, a planned intervention, is discussed later in the chapter.

CONTEMPLATION

Contemplation is the stage in which people intend to change in the next 6 months. Although more aware of the pros of changing, they also are acutely aware of the cons. When people begin to contemplate acting seriously, their awareness of the costs of changing can increase. There is no "free change." The balance between the costs and benefits of changing can provoke profound ambivalence. This ambivalence can reflect a type of love–hate relationship, as with an addictive substance or destructive relationship, and it can keep people immobilized in this stage for long periods. We often characterize this phenomenon as chronic contemplation or behavioral procrastination. These individuals, like those in the precontemplation stage, are not ready for traditional action-oriented programs, the prevailing paradigm for treatment.

PREPARATION

In this stage, people intend to take action in the immediate future, usually measured in terms of "the next month." Typically, they have taken some significant action in the past year. Individuals in preparation have a plan for action, such as going to a recovery group, consulting a counselor, talking to their physician, buying a self-help book, or relying on a self-change approach. These are the people best recruited for brief action-oriented treatment programs. They are ready to use them.

ACTION

Action is the stage in which people have made specific, overt modifications in their lifestyles within the past 6 months. Because action is observable, behavior change often has been equated with the action stage. In the transtheoretical model, however, action is only one of six stages. Not all modifications of behavior count as action. Nor does mere statistical improvement count. Rather, there must be real clinical improvement, with recovery being the ideal criterion for action.

Accepting weak criteria for successful action can have serious consequences. For example, in Scotland a colleague carried out an innovative clinical program for controlled drinking. He announced his program in the papers and within a week, was flooded with more than 800 recruits. In time, he was pleased with his completion rates, but not his outcomes: The dramatic reduction in drinking as anticipated did not occur. My wife proposed that his criteria for controlled drinking might be the problem. In response, he considered the suggestion ethnocentric, an instance of imposing U.S. standards on Scottish citizens. As it turns out, the criteria he used for controlled drinking in Scotland was fewer than 50 drinks per week for men and fewer than 35 for women!

The criteria chosen also have consequences for the mental health professions. The finding of common outcomes among diverse therapies is the impetus for this volume. Yet the finding of common out-comes originates, in part, from a reliance on statistical versus actual clinical improvement. Using statistical criteria allowed the field to conclude that a grand tie across therapeutic systems exists. It was then reasonable to say, "All had won, and all must have prizes."

On the other hand, the meta-analyses using such criteria also concluded that such outcomes depended on neither the duration of therapy nor the education or experience of the therapists. Thus, the conclusion that managed care has embraced: They will fund the briefest therapies and cheapest therapists. Some prize we have won!

MAINTENANCE

In maintenance, people are working to prevent relapse, but they do not apply change processes as frequently as do people in action. They are less tempted to relapse and are increasingly more confident that they can continue their changes. Based on clients' reports of self-efficacy and temptation experienced, it is estimated that maintenance lasts from 6 months to about 5 years.

A common reason that people relapse early in action is that they are not well prepared for the prolonged effort needed to progress to maintenance. Many think the worst will be over in a few weeks or a few months. If they ease up on their efforts too early, they are at great risk of relapse.

To prepare people for what is to come, they may be encouraged to compare overcoming chronic problems, like addictions, to running a marathon. They may have wanted to enter the 100th running of the Boston Marathon. Yet if they had little or no preparation, they know they would not succeed and so not enter the race. If they had made some preparation, they might make it for several miles before dropping out. Only those well prepared could sustain their efforts mile after mile.

Continuing with the Boston Marathon metaphor, people know that they have to be well prepared if they are to survive Heartbreak Hill, hitting after 20 miles into the race. We can then ask, what is the behavioral equivalent of Heartbreak Hill? The best evidence we have across problems is that most relapses occur at times of emotional distress. Times of depression, anxiety, anger, boredom, loneliness, stress, and distress are the moments when individuals are at their emotional and psychological weakest.

In the face of emotional pressures, how do Americans cope? The average American routinely drinks, eats, smokes, and takes drugs to manage distress (Mellinger, Balter, Manheimer, Cisin, & Perry, 1978). It is not surprising, therefore, that people struggling to overcome chronic conditions will be at greatest risk of relapse when they face psychological pain and upset. We cannot prevent emotional distress from occurring. Nonetheless, we can help prevent relapse if patients are prepared for coping with distress without reliance on addictive substances or other unhealthy alternatives.

If so many Americans rely on oral consumptive behavior as a way to manage their emotions, what is the healthiest oral behavior they could use? Talking with others about one's distress is a means of seeking support that can help prevent relapse. Therapy is one of the excellent ways of dealing with distress. Another healthy alternative that can used by many people is exercise. Not only does physical activity help manage moods, stress, and distress, but also for 60 minutes per week, a more active client can receive more than 50 health and mental health benefits. Exercise should be prescribed to all sedentary patients. A third healthy alternative is some form of deep relaxation, such as meditation, yoga, prayer, massage, or deep muscle relaxation. Letting the stress and distress drift away from one's muscles and mind helps to advance progress at the most tempting of times.

TERMINATION

In this last stage, individuals experience zero temptation and 100% self-efficacy. No matter whether they are depressed, anxious, bored, lonely, angry, or stressed, they are confident that they will not return to their old unhealthy pattern as a way of coping. It is as though they never acquired the pattern in the first place. In a study of former smokers and alcoholics, we found that less than 20% of each group had reached the criteria of no temptation and total self-efficacy (Snow, Prochaska, & Rossi, 1992). Although the ideal goal is to be cured or recovered, for many people the best that can be accomplished is a lifetime of maintenance.

Phases of Planned Interventions

The stages of change model reviewed above can be applied to help many more people at each phase of therapy, treatment, or other planned intervention. The five phases include: recruitment, retention, progress, process, and outcomes.

RECRUITMENT

Too few studies have paid attention to recruitment—a skeleton long in the closet of professional treatment programs. Historically, these programs recruit or reach too few people. As reported earlier, less than 25% of populations with diagnosable *DSM-IV* disorders will ever enter formal therapy in their lifetimes (Veroff, Douvon, & Kulka, 1981a, 1981b). With smoking, the most deadly of addictions, less than 10% ever participate in professional programs (U.S. Department of Health and Human Services, 1990).

Mental health and behavioral health problems, such as depression and the addictions, are among the most costly of contemporary conditions—costly to the individuals afflicted, their families and friends, their employers, their communities, and their health care systems (Prochaska, 1997). For this reason, traditional case-by-case management as a routine practice policy can no longer be afforded. Instead, programs that recruit people on a population basis are required.

Governments and health care systems are seeking population-wide models to treat such conditions. Notwithstanding their intent, when they turn for guidance to the biggest and best clinical trials ostensibly prepared to treat chronic problems on a population basis, what do they discover? Trial after trial report poor outcomes (e.g., COMMIT Research Group, 1995; Ennett, Tabler, Ringwolt, & Fliwelling, 1994; Glasgow, Terborg, Hollis, Severson, & Boles, 1995; Lucpker et al., 1994). Whether the trials were conducted in work sites, schools, or entire communities, the results are similar. No significant effects compared with the controls are found.

If we examine more closely one of these trials, the Minnesota Heart Health Study, we find hints of what went awry (Lando et al., 1995). Smoking was one of the targeted behaviors. Examining recruitment rates to their most powerful behavior change programs (those employing clinics, classes, and counseling), it was found that only 4% of the smokers in the treatment communities participated over the 5 years of planned interventions. No wonder there were no significant differences between the treatment and control communities. Likewise, if managed care offers free state-of-the-science cessation clinics, only 1% of smokers are recruited (Lichtenstein & Hollis, 1992). If the best treatment programs reach so few people with the deadliest of addictions, little positive impact on the health of the nation's populace will occur.

How then do we motivate many more people with high-cost conditions to seek appropriate help? The answer may be found in changing paradigms and practices. In this regard, two paradigms need revision. The first is the action-oriented paradigm. It construes behavior change as an event that can occur immediately, discretely, and dramatically. That view has dominated clinical practice for the past 50 years. Treatment programs that are designed to have people immediately take action are implicitly or explicitly designed for the portion of the population who are in the preparation stage.

As an example of the problem with the action-based paradigm, consider that across 15 unhealthy behaviors in 20,000 HMO members, typically less than 20% are prepared to take action (Rossi, 1992). The rule of thumb is 40, 40, 20: 40% in precontemplation, 40% in contemplation, and only 20% in preparation. In this light, when brief action-oriented therapies are promoted, they are implicitly recruiting from less than 20% of the population at risk. To meet the needs of entire populations, interventions for the 40% in precontemplation and the 40% in contemplation need to be designed.

The second change requires movement from a passive–reactive to a proactive practice approach. Most professionals have been trained to be passive–reactive: Wait for patients to seek services, and then react. Recalling that the majority of people with high-cost conditions never seek appropriate services, the "wait-till-they-come-to-the-door" method is stacked at the outset against success.

On closer examination, the passive–reactive paradigm is designed to serve populations with acute conditions. The pain, distress, or discomfort of such conditions can motivate people to seek help from health professionals. Sadly, however, the major killers and disablers of our time are conditions caused in large part by *chronic* disorders like the addictions. To treat chronic conditions seriously, we must learn not only to reach out to entire populations, but also to offer stage-appropriate therapies.

What happens if professionals go only halfway—that is, retain an action-oriented paradigm in their programs, but proactively recruit? This experiment has been tried in one of the United States' largest managed care organizations (Lichtenstein & Hollis, 1992). Physicians spent time with every smoker to induce them to sign up for a state-of-the-art, action-oriented clinic. If that failed, nurses spent up to 10 minutes to persuade them to sign up, followed by 12 minutes with health educators, and finally, a counselor's call to home. The result was a base-rate participation of 1%.

Further analysis showed that this most intensive recruitment protocol successfully motivated 35% of smokers in precontemplation to register. Yet only 3% showed, 2% finished, and 0% ended better off. Combining the contemplation and preparation groups, 65% signed, 15% showed, 11% finished, and a negligible percentage ended better off.

In contrast, changing both paradigm and practice yields better results. Offering stage-appropriate interventions and applying proactive or outreach recruitment methods in three large-scale clinical trials, we have been able to recruit 80% to 90% of smokers to our treatment programs (Prochaska, Velicer, Fava, Rossi, & Tsoh, 1997; Prochaska, Velicer, Fava, Ruggiero, et al., 1997). This is a major increase in our ability to reach many more people to start therapy.

With the recommended paradigmatic changes in place, population-wide recruitment programs are now under way. For instance, regional centers of the National Health Service in Great Britain are training health professionals in these new paradigms. More than 4,000 physicians, nurses, counselors, and health educators have been trained to interact proactively at each stage of change with their entire patient populations who abuse alcohol, drugs, food, and tobacco. In the future, we will see similar training for other high-cost conditions such as depression and anxiety disorders.

In summary, what can move a majority of people to start a professional treatment program? Owing to growing evidence to date, an innovative and probably definitive answer may be provided. It is this: Have professionals who are motivated, prepared to reach out proactively to entire populations, and offer interventions that match clients' stage of change. Once health professionals begin to recruit many patients in precontemplation and contemplation stages, will therapists and counselors be prepared to match their needs? This question leads to retention.

RETENTION

The second skeleton in the therapy closet is that therapists do not retain enough people. A meta-analysis of 125 studies found that nearly 50% of clients drop out of treatment (Wierzbicki & Pekarik, 1993). Across studies, there were few consistent predictors of premature termination, except substance abuse, obtained minority status and lower education. Although important, these variables did not account for the highest percentage of dropouts.

Using stages of change as a predictive variable, five studies have been completed on dropouts. Substance abuse, smoking, obesity, and a broad spectrum of psychiatric disorders characterized the problems of the patient groups (e.g., Medeiros & Prochaska, 1997; Prochaska, Norcross, Fowler, Follick, & Abrams, 1992). Results show that stage-related variables outpredicted demographics, type of problem, severity of problem, and other problem-related variables. Figure 1 presents the stage profiles of the three groups of patients with psychiatric problems. In this study, we were able to predict 93% of the three groups: premature terminators, early but appropriate terminators, and continuers in therapy (Medeiros & Prochaska, 1997).

Figure 1 shows the pretherapy profiles of the entire group of people who quickly and prematurely dropped out (40%), all of whom were people in the precontemplation stage. The 20% who finished quickly but appropriately were patients in the action stage when entering therapy. A mixed group, with the majority in the contemplation stage, continued in longer term treatment.

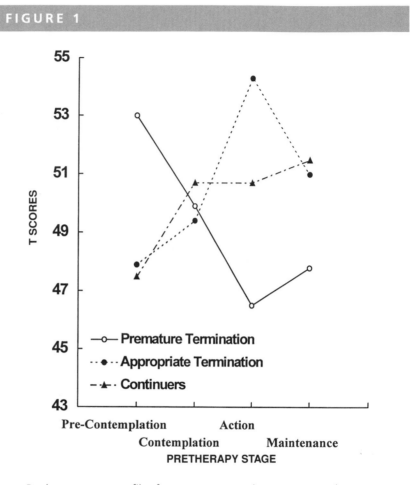

FIGURE 1

Pretherapy stage profiles for premature terminators, appropriate terminators, and continuers.

The implication of these results is clear. People in the precontemplation stage cannot be treated as though they are starting in the same place as those in the action stage and be expected to continue in therapy. If pressured to act when unprepared, should clinicians expect to retain them in therapy? To drive them away and then blame them for being insufficiently motivated or ready for action-oriented interventions are misplaced pursuits.

With patients entering therapy in the action stage for an addiction, an appropriate approach to recommend might be the relapse-prevention strategies developed by Alan Marlatt. Patients in action are likely to be ready to use these methods. In comparison, relapse prevention strategies would make little sense with the 40% of patients who enter in the precontemplation stage. A good match here would be to recommend a dropout prevention approach, because these patients are likely to leave early if not helped to continue (Medeiros & Prochaska, 1997).

With clients starting therapy in precontemplation, a treatment protocol begins with sharing our key concern over their continuation. The therapist might say, "I'm concerned that therapy may not have a chance to make a significant difference in your life, because you may be tempted to leave early." This may lead to an exploration of whether they have been pressured to enter therapy. If so, how do they react when someone tries to pressure or coerce them into taking action when they are not ready? Can they let the therapist know if they feel pressured or coerced? Stage-matched therapists want to help, but will only encourage clients to take steps when they are most ready to succeed.

Four studies with stage-matched interventions examining retention rates of people in precontemplation who enter treatment programs have been completed. When treatment is matched to stage of change, people in precontemplation continue at the same high rates as those who started in preparation. This result held in clinical trials for people recruited proactively (i.e., help was offered) as well as for those participants recruited reactively (i.e., they called for help). So far, these studies have been done only with smokers. If the findings hold up across other conditions, a practical answer to the question of what allows people to continue in therapy can be given. The conclusion would be that it is providing treatments that match patients' stage of change.

PROGRESS

What moves people to progress in therapy and to continue to progress after therapy? Figure 2 presents an example of what is called the *stage effect*. The stage effect predicts that the amount of successful action taken during treatment and after treatment is directly related to the stage that people are in at the start of treatment (Prochaska, DiClemente, & Norcross, 1992). In this example, interventions with smokers end at 6 months. The group of smokers who started in the precontemplation stage show the least amount of effective action as measured by abstinence at each assessment point. Those who started in the contemplation stage made significantly more progress. Finally, patients who entered treatment already prepared to take action were most successful at every assessment.

The stage effect has been found across a variety of problems and populations, including rehabilitative success for brain injury and recovery from anxiety and panic disorders (Beitman et al., 1994; Lam, McMahon, Priddy, & Gehred-Schulz, 1988). In double-blind drug tri-

FIGURE 2

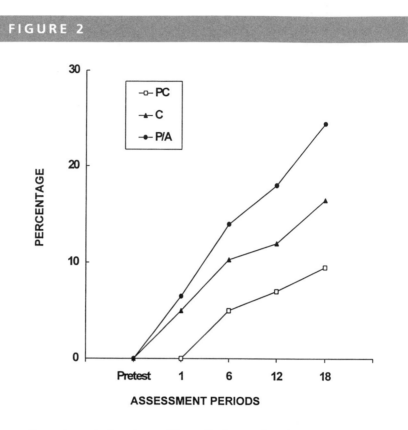

Percentage abstinent over 18 months for smokers in Precontemplation (PC), Contemplation (C), and Preparation (P/A) stages before treatment (N = 570).

als with anxiety and panic disorders, for instance, the best predictor was the subjects' stage of change. The investigator leading this drug trial concluded that patients will need to be assessed for their stage of readiness to benefit from antianxiety medication. They also will need to be assisted through the stages so that they are well prepared for placement on such medication (Beitman et al., 1994).

A strategy for applying the stage effect clinically now suggests itself. Recall that if people are moved to immediate action, the majority will neither show up for therapy nor finish. An alternative is to set realistic goals for brief encounters with clients at each stage of change. In this approach, a realistic goal is to help clients progress one stage during brief therapy. If clients move relatively quickly, they can be helped to progress two stages. The results to date indicate that if clients progress one stage in one month, they double the chances of taking effective action by 6 months. If they progress two stages, they increase their chances of taking effective action by 3 to 4 times (Prochaska, Velicer, Fava, Ruggiero, et al., 1997). Setting realistic goals can enable many more people to enter therapy, remain, progress in therapy, and continue to progress once treatment is completed.

The first results reported back from England, where 4,000 health professionals have been trained in using a stage-based treatment model, show a dramatic increase in the morale of the health professions. They can now see progress with the majority of their patients, whereas before they saw failure when immediate action was the only criteria of success. They are much more confident that they have treatments that can match the stage of all of their patients, rather than the 20% prepared to take immediate action.

It is no overstatement to say that the models of treatment that therapists choose should be good for their own mental health as well as the mental health of clients. After all, clinicians are involved in therapy for a lifetime, whereas most of clients are involved for a brief time.

Unfortunately, as managed care organizations move to briefer and briefer therapies, a danger exists that most health professionals will feel pressured into having to produce immediate action. If this pressure is then transferred to patients who are not prepared for such action, the past will be repeated: Therapists will be neither reaching nor retaining enough patients. A majority of patients can be helped to progress in brief encounters, but only if realistic goals are established for the treatment episode. Otherwise, risk is heightened for demoralizing and demotivating both patients and the therapists who work with them.

PROCESS

To help patients to progress from one stage to the next, the principles and processes of change that can produce such progress need to be applied.

Principle 1. The pros of changing must increase for people to progress from precontemplation. We found that in 12 out of 12 studies the pros were higher in contemplation than in precontemplation (Prochaska, Velicer, et al., 1994). This pattern held true across 12 behaviors: quitting cocaine, smoking, delinquency, obesity, consistent condom use, safer sex, sedentary lifestyles, high-fat diets, sun exposure, radon testing, mammography screening, and even with physicians practicing behavioral medicine.

To initiate movement out of precontemplation, patients may be asked to identify all the benefits or pros of changing, such as starting to exercise. Typically, they list four or five. Then, they can be informed there are 8 to 10 times that amount and challenged to double or triple their list before their next meeting. If their list of pros for exercising starts to indicate many more motives, like a healthier heart, healthier lungs, more energy, healthier immune system, better moods, less stress, better sex life, and enhanced self-esteem, they will be more seriously motivated to begin to contemplate changing.

Principle 2. The cons of changing must decrease for people to progress form contemplation to action. In 12 out of 12 studies, we found that the cons of changing were lower in action than in contemplation (Prochaska, Velicer, et al., 1994).

Principle 3. The pros and cons must "cross over" for people to be prepared to take action. In 12 out of 12 studies, the cons of changing were higher than the pros in precontemplation, but in 11 out of 12, the pros were higher than the cons in the action stage. The one exception to this pattern was with patients quitting cocaine, the only population with a large percentage treated as inpatients. We interpret this exception to mean these individuals' actions may have been influenced more by external controls or constraints than by their own motivation to change. At a minimum, their pattern would not bode well for immediate discharge.

It is noteworthy that if we used raw scores to assess these patterns, we would often find that the pros of changing are higher than the cons, even for people in precontemplation. It is only when we use standardized scores that we find the clear pattern of the cons of changing always being higher than the pros. This means that compared with their peers in other stages, people in precontemplation underestimate the pros and overestimate the cons. (We interpret this to mean that they are not particularly conscious of making these mistakes, because they do not know how they compare with their peers.)

In a more recent study, we found the same pattern for the pros and cons of being in therapy. Heroin and cocaine addicts who were in the precontemplation stage, evaluated the cons of therapy as greater than the pros. The pros increased for those in contemplation. And, there was a crossover between the pros and cons for those in preparation and beyond (Tsoh & Prochaska, 1998). These data indicate that continuing in therapy and progressing in therapy is, in part, related to people's misevaluation of the pros and cons of being in therapy. In this respect, our field has not done a thorough job educating the public on the benefits of therapy beyond help with a particular problem. Such benefits as decreased defensiveness, increased expressiveness, better relationships, increased self-esteem, and increased incomes should be emphasized in preparing patients for completing therapy.

Principle 4. The "strong principle" of progress holds that to progress from precontemplation to effective action, the pros of changing must increase one standard deviation (Prochaska, 1994).

Principle 5. The "weak principle" of progress holds that to progress from contemplation to effective action, the cons of changing must decrease one half standard deviation.

Because the pros of changing must increase twice as much as the cons decrease, therapists should place twice as much emphasis on the benefits of changing than on the costs. What is striking here is the belief that mathematical principles have discovered for how much positive motivations must increase and how much negative motivations must decrease. Such principles can produce much more sensitive assessments for guiding interventions, giving therapists and patients feedback for when therapeutic efforts are producing progress and when they are failing. Together, therapists and clients can modify their methods if they are not seeing as much movement as is needed for becoming adequately prepared for action.

Principle 6. Particular processes of change need to be matched to specific stages of change. Table 1 presents the empirical integration that we have found between processes and stages of change (Prochaska & DiClemente, 1983). Guided by this integration, we would apply the following nine processes with patients in specific stages of change:

1. Consciousness raising involves increased awareness and information about the causes, consequences, and cures for a particular problem. Interventions that can increase awareness include observations, confrontations, interpretations, feedback, and education, such as bibliotherapy. Some techniques, such as confrontation, are high-risk for retention and are not recommended as much as motivational

---

TABLE 1

The Stages of Change in Which Particular Processes of Change Are Emphasized

		Stages of change		
Precontemplation	**Contemplation**	**Preparation**	**Action**	**Maintenance**
Consciousness raising				
Dramatic relief				
Environmental reevaluation				
	Self-reevaluation			
		Self-liberation		
			Contingency management	
			Helping relationships	
			Counterconditioning	
			Stimulus control	

Note. Processes of change are centered between columns to show overlap between stages.

enhancement methods such as personal feedback about the current and long-term consequences of continuing with the chronic pattern. Increasing the cons of not changing is the corollary of raising the pros of changing. So, clearly part of the purpose in applying consciousness raising is to increase the pros of changing.

2. Dramatic relief involves emotional arousal about one's current behavior and relief that can come from changing. Fear, inspiration, guilt, and hope are some of the emotions that can move people to contemplate changing. Psychodrama, role playing, grieving, and personal testimonies are examples of techniques that can move people emotionally.

Earlier behavior-change literature concluded that interventions such as education and fear arousal did not motivate behavior change. Unfortunately, many interventions were evaluated by their ability to move people to immediate action. Processes such as consciousness raising and dramatic relief are intended to move people to contemplation, not immediate action. Therefore, effectiveness of processes should be assessed by whether they produce the progress they are expected to produce for the client's stage of change.

3. Environmental reevaluation combines both emotional and cognitive assessments of how one's behavior affects one's social environment and how changing would affect that environment. Empathy training, value clarification, and family or network interventions can facilitate such reevaluation.

A brief media intervention aimed at smokers in precontemplation is instructive here. A man clearly in grief says, "I always feared that my smoking would lead to an early death. I always worried that my smoking would cause lung cancer. But I never imagined it would happen to my wife." Beneath his grieving face appears this statistic: 50,000 deaths per year are caused by passive smoking, the California Department of Health.

In the 30 seconds that it takes to read and process the message, consciousness raising, dramatic relief, and environmental reevaluation are introduced. It is little surprise that such media interventions have been evaluated as an important part of California's successful initiative to reduce smoking.

4. Self-reevaluation combines both cognitive and affective assessments of one's self-image free from a particular problem. Imagery, healthier role models, and values clarification are techniques that can move people. Clinically, we find people first looking back and reevaluating how they have been as troubled individuals. As they progress into preparation, they begin to develop more of a future focus as they imagine more how their life will be free from the problem.

5. Self-liberation includes both the belief that one can change and the commitment and recommitment to act on that belief. Techniques that can enhance such willpower make greater use of public rather than private commitments. Motivational research also suggests that if people have only one choice, they are not as motivated as if they have two choices (Miller, 1985). Three is even better, but four does not seem to enhance motivation.

Wherever possible, transtheoretical therapists try to provide people with three of the best choices for applying each process. With smoking cessation, for example, we used to believe only one commitment really counted, and that was quitting "cold turkey." We now know there are at least three good choices: cold turkey, nicotine replacement, and nicotine fading. Asking clients to choose which alternative they believe would be most effective for them, and to which they would be most committed, enhances their motivation and self-liberation.

6. Counterconditioning requires the learning of healthier behaviors to replace problem behaviors. Three healthier alternatives to smoking were discussed in the previous section. Earlier, three healthier alternatives for coping with emotional distress and preventing relapse were introduced. Counterconditioning techniques are specific to a particular behavior and include desensitization, assertion, and cognitive counters to irrational, distress-provoking self-statements.

7. Contingency management involves the systematic use of reinforcements and punishments for taking steps in a particular direction. Because we find that successful self-changers rely much more on reinforcement than punishment, we emphasize reinforcements for progressing over punishments for regressing. Contingency contracts, overt and covert reinforcements, and group recognition are procedures for increasing reinforcement. They also provide incentives that increase the probability that healthier responses will be repeated.

To prepare people for the longer term, we teach them to rely more on self-reinforcements than social reinforcements (Prochaska, Norcross, & DiClemente, 1994). We find that many clients expect much more reinforcement and recognition from others than what others actively provide. Too many relatives and friends can take action for granted too quickly, and average acquaintances typically generate only a couple of positive consequences early in action. Self-reinforcements are much more under self-control and can be dispensed more quickly and consistently when temptations to lapse or relapse are resisted.

8. Stimulus control involves modifying the environment to increase cues that prompt healthier responses and decrease cues that are tempting. Avoidance, environmental reengineering (e.g., removing addictive substances and paraphernalia), and attending self-help groups can provide stimuli that elicit healthier responses and reduce risks for relapse.

9. Helping relationships combine caring, openness, trust, and acceptance as well as support for changing. Rapport building, a therapeutic alliance, counselor calls, buddy systems, sponsors, and self-help groups can be excellent resources. If people become dependent on social support for maintaining change, care is needed in fading out that support lest the termination of therapy becomes an unwelcome condition for relapse.

Integrating the Processes of Change With Common Factors

Competing theories of therapy have implicitly or explicitly advocated alternative processes for producing change. Are cognitions what move people or emotions? Are values, decisions, or dedication? Are contingencies what motivate us, or are we controlled by environmental conditions or conditioned habits? Is it the therapeutic relationship that is the common healer across all therapeutic modalities?

An "eclectic" answer to each of these questions is yes. An integrative answer is that therapeutic processes originating from competing theories can be compatible when they are matched to the client's stage of change. With patients in earlier stages of change, therapists can enhance progress through more experiential processes that produce healthier cognitions, emotions, evaluations, decisions, and commitments. In later stages, we seek to build on such solid preparation and motivation by emphasizing more behavioral processes that can help condition healthier habits, reinforce these habits, and provide physical and social environments supportive of healthier lifestyles.

One of the qualities I value most about the transtheoretical model is that it can provide an integration of some of the best change processes derived from theories that are usually seen as competing and incompatible. So, too, I believe that this model can provide an integration of common factors derived from empirical comparisons across competing therapies and medical and social services. Weinberger (1995) has identified five common factors that he believes have adequate empirical support: expectations, therapeutic alliance, confronting strategies, mastery techniques, and attributions.

Hypotheses of how the common factors delineated by Weinberger are likely to be related to and integrated within the stage dimension of the transtheoretical model follow (Prochaska, 1995). People in precontemplation are likely to have the poorest expectations for change and for therapy. We know that individuals in this stage will show the poorest outcomes following therapy. These patients are least aware of the benefits of changing and the benefits of therapy and are likely to be in particular need of interventions that help them understand that particular patterns are self-defeating and self-destructive. Patients in precontemplation are also likely to have the most problems forming a therapeutic alliance early in therapy. They are most at risk of dropping out quickly and inappropriately unless therapists are trained to match strategies to their stage, such as dropout prevention strategies.

Confronting strategies, such as exposure and flooding techniques, that help patients actively face their fears are likely to be tolerated most by patients who are prepared for such action-oriented approaches. People not prepared for such intensive treatments are likely not to show up for therapy nor finish such therapy. Mastery techniques also are likely to be most effective with patients who are prepared to take action or are already in the action stage. As for attributions, psychotherapies that are designed to maximize self-change processes are likely to attribute progress through the stages as due first to the client's efforts and only secondarily to the therapist's efforts. Exhibit 1 presents a conceptual integration between stages and these five common factors.

OUTCOMES AND IMPACTS

What happens when the six principles and nine processes of change discussed earlier are combined to help patients and entire populations move toward action? Below, a series of clinical trials applying stage-matched interventions are examined to see what lessons we might learn about the future of therapy, behavioral medicine, and social services.

In our first large-scale clinical trial, we compared four treatments for smoking cessation: (a) one of the best home-based, action-oriented

---

EXHIBIT 1

Integration of Stages of Change and Five Common Factors

Precontemplation	◊	Contemplation	◊	Preparation	◊	Action	◊	Maintenance

Low expectations
Poor therapeutic alliance
Confronting strategies
Mastery strategies
Self-change attributions
for progressing

Note. Stages of change are centered between columns to show overlap between factors.

cessation programs (Standardized); (b) stage-matched manuals (Individualized); (c) expert system computer reports plus manuals (Interactive); and (d) counselors plus computers and manuals (Personalized). We randomly assigned by stage 739 smokers to one of the four treatments (Prochaska, DiClemente, Velicer & Rossi, 1993).

In the computer or Interactive condition, participants completed by mail or telephone 40 questions that were entered into our central computers and generated feedback reports. These reports informed participants about their stage of change, their pros and cons of changing, and their use of change processes appropriate to their stages. At baseline, participants were given positive feedback on what they were doing correctly and guidance on which principles and processes they needed to apply more to progress. In two progress reports delivered over the next 6 months, participants also received positive feedback on any improvement they made on any of the variables relevant to progressing. As a result, demoralized and defensive smokers could begin progressing without having to quit and without having to work too hard. Smokers in the contemplation stage could begin taking small steps, like delaying their first cigarette in the morning for an extra 30 minutes. They could choose small steps that would increase their self-efficacy and help them become better prepared for quitting.

In the Personalized condition, smokers received four proactive counselor calls over the 6 month intervention period. Three of the calls were based on the computer reports. Counselors reported much more difficulty in interacting with participants without any progress data. Without scientific assessments, it was much harder for both clients and counselors to tell whether any significant progress had occurred since their last interaction.

Figure 3 presents point prevalence abstinence rates for each of the four treatment groups over 18 months, with treatment ending at 6 months. The two self-help manual conditions paralleled each other for 12 months. At 18 months, the stage matched manuals moved ahead. This is an example of a *delayed action effect,* often observed with stage-matched programs specifically and self-help programs generally. It takes time for participants in early stages to progress to action. Therefore, some treatment effects as measured by action will be observed only after considerable delay. However, it is encouraging to find treatments producing therapeutic effects months and even years after treatment ended.

The computer alone (Interactive) and computer plus counselor conditions (Personalized) paralleled each other for 12 months. Then, the effects of the counselor condition flattened out, while the computer condition effects continued to increase. We can only speculate about delayed differences between these two conditions. Participants

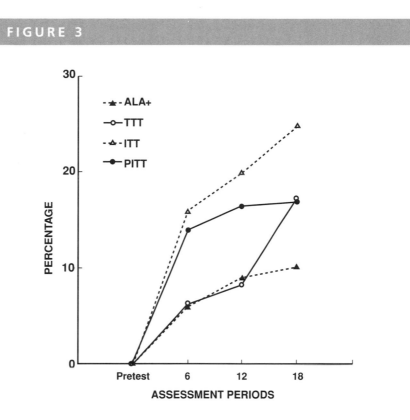

FIGURE 3

Point prevalence abstinence (%) for four treatment groups at pretest and at 6, 12, and 18 months. ALA+ = standardized manuals; TTT = individualized stage-matched manuals; ITT = interactive computer reports; PITT = personalized counselor calls.

in the personalized condition may have become somewhat dependent on the social support and social control of the counselor calling. The last call was after the 6 months assessment and benefits would be observed at 12 months. Termination of the counselors could result in no further progress because of the loss of social support and control. The classic pattern in smoking cessation clinics is rapid relapse beginning as soon as the treatment is terminated. Some of this rapid relapse could well be due to the sudden loss of social support or social control provided by the counselors and other participants in the clinic.

The next test was to demonstrate the efficacy of the expert system (Interactive) when applied to an entire population recruited proactively. With more than 80% of 5,170 smokers participating and fewer that 20% in the preparation stage, we demonstrated significant benefit of the expert system at each 6 month follow-up (Prochaska, Velicer,

Fava, Rossi, & Tsoh, 1997). Further, the advantages over proactive assessment alone increased at each follow-up for the full 2 years assessed. The implications here are that expert system interventions in a population can continue to demonstrate benefits long after the intervention has ended.

We then showed remarkable replication of the expert or Interactive system's efficacy in an HMO population of 4,000 smokers with 85% participation (Prochaska, Velicer, Fava, Ruggiero, 1997). In the first population-based study, the expert system was 34% more effective than assessment alone. In the second, it was 31% more effective. These replicated differences were clinically significant as well. While working on a population basis, we were able to produce the level of success normally found only in intense clinic-based programs with low participation rates of much more selected samples of smokers. The implication is that once expert systems are developed and show effectiveness with one population, they can be transferred at much lower cost and produce replicable changes in new populations.

Enhancing Interactive Interventions

In recent benchmarking research, we have been trying to create enhancements to our expert system to produce even greater outcomes. In the first enhancement in our HMO population, we added a personal hand-held computer designed to bring the behavior under stimulus control (Prochaska, Velicer, Fava, Ruggiero, 1997). This commercially successful innovation was an action-oriented intervention, yet it did not enhance our expert system program on a population basis. In fact, our expert system alone was twice as effective as the system plus the enhancement. There are two major implications here: (a) More is not necessarily better, and (b) providing interventions that are mismatched to stage can make outcomes markedly worse.

Counselor Enhancements

In our HMO population, counselors plus expert system computers (Personalized) were outperforming expert systems alone at 12 months. But at 18 months, the counselor enhancement had declined, while the computers alone had increased. Both interventions were producing identical outcomes of 23.2% abstinence—excellent for an entire population. Why did the effect of the counselor condition drop after the intervention? Again, our leading hypothesis is that people can become dependent on counselors for the social support and social monitoring they provide. Once these social influences are withdrawn, people may do worse. The expert system computers on the other hand may maximize self-reliance. In a current clinical trial, we are fading out counselors over time as a method for dealing with dependency on the counselor. If fading is effective, it will have implications for how counseling should be terminated: gradually over time rather than suddenly.

We believe that the most powerful change programs will combine the personalized benefits of counselors and consultants with the individualized, interactive and data-based benefits of expert system computers. Nevertheless, to date we have not been able to demonstrate that the more costly counselors, who had been our most powerful change agents, can actually add value over computers alone. These findings have clear implications for cost-effectiveness of expert systems for entire populations needing health promotion programs.

Interactive Versus Noninteractive Interventions

Another important aim of the HMO project was to assess whether interactive interventions (i.e., computer-generated expert systems) are more effective than noninteractive communications (i.e., self-help manuals) when controlling for number of intervention contacts (Velicer, Prochaska, Fava, Laforge, & Rossi, 1997). At 6, 12, and 18 months for groups of smokers receiving a series of 1, 2, 3, or 6 interactive versus noninteractive contacts, the interactive interventions (i.e., expert systems) outperformed the noninteractive manuals in all four comparisons. In three of the comparisons (1, 2, and 3), the differences at 18 months were at least five percentage points, a difference between treatment conditions assumed to be clinically significant. These results clearly support the hypothesis that interactive interventions will outperform the same number of noninteractive interventions.

In all, these results support the assumption that the most powerful behavior change programs for entire populations will be interactive. In the "reactive" clinical literature, interactive interventions, like behavioral counseling, produce greater long-term abstinence rates (20 to 30%) than do noninteractive interventions such as self-help manuals (10 to 20%). It should be kept in mind that these traditional action-oriented programs were implicitly or explicitly recruiting for populations in the preparation stage. Our results indicate that even with proactively recruited smokers with less than 20% in the preparation stage, the long-term abstinence rates are in the 20% to 30% range for the interactive interventions and in the 10% to 20% range for the noninteractive interventions. The implications are clear.

Providing interactive interventions via computers is likely to produce greater outcomes than relying on noninteractive communications, such as newsletters, media, or self-help manuals.

Proactive Versus Reactive Results

I believe that the future of behavioral and mental health programs lies with stage-matched, proactive, and interactive interventions. Much greater impacts can be generated by proactive programs because of much higher participation rates, even if efficacy rates are lower. I also believe that proactive programs can produce comparable outcomes to traditional reactive ("wait-till-they-come") programs. It is counterintuitive to believe that comparable outcomes can be produced with people who we reach out to help as with people who call us for help. Yet that is what informal comparisons strongly suggest. Comparing 18 month follow-ups for all participants who received our three expert system reports in our previous reactive study and in our current proactive study, the abstinence curves are remarkably similar (Prochaska et al., 1993; Prochaska, Velicer, Fava, Ruggiero, et al., 1997).

The results with counseling plus computer conditions were even more impressive. Proactively recruited smokers working with counselors and computers had higher abstinence rates at each follow-up than did the smokers who had called for help. One of the differences is that the proactive counseling protocol had been revised and, we hope, improved on the basis of previous data and experience. The point is, however, if professionals reach out and offer people improved behavior change programs that are appropriate for their stage, we probably can produce efficacy or abstinence rates at least equal to those we produce with people who contact us for help. Unfortunately, there is no experimental design that could permit researchers to randomly assign people to proactive versus reactive recruitment programs. We are left with these informal but provocative comparisons.

If these results continue to be replicated, therapeutic programs will be able to produce significant impacts on entire populations. Once more, I believe that such impacts require scientific and professional shifts from (a) an action paradigm to a stage paradigm, (b) reactive to proactive recruitment, (c) expecting participants to match the needs of therapeutic programs to having these programs match their needs, (d) clinic-based to population-based programs that still apply the field's most powerful individualized and interactive intervention strategies, and (e) specific strategies varying from therapy to therapy to common pathways and processes integrated from across competing theories that were once thought to be incompatible.

Questions From the Editors

1. With your current research findings in mind, what implications do you see for the training of the next generation of mental health professionals?

Our findings have profound implications for training the next generation of mental health professionals. What will *not* be needed are more therapists who are trained only in case management. Once mental health falls under managed care, there will be two to three times as many mental health specialists as managed care needs. Although this is troubling, it is true of most health specialists.

What will be needed instead are mental health specialists who can manage entire populations presenting with costly conditions such as alcohol abuse, anxiety disorders, depression and smoking. Creating, providing, and managing services on a population basis is something very few mental health specialists are prepared to do.

Our research indicates that mental health care providers will need to be trained in proactive outreach approaches to entire populations with such conditions. They will also need to know how to match intervention strategies to the stages of change. For example, with the important portion of populations in precontemplation, they will need to know dropout prevention strategies. For those in action, they will need to provide relapse prevention approaches.

In summary, future mental health specialists will need to know how to prescribe and provide interactive technologies to entire populations. I am convinced that such technologies will be to behavior change what medications have been to biological medicine: the most cost-effective way to bring the maximum amount of science to bear on important problems in entire populations. More costly professional therapists will be reserved for the most complicated cases that cannot be helped by the more cost-effective computers.

2. How in day-to-day clinical practice can the individual practitioner apply the lessons learned in your population-wide studies with the transtheoretical model?

The first lesson is assess the stage of change for each of your clients. Mismatching change processes can produce resistance, for example, pressuring patients in precontemplation or contemplation to take action when they are not ready. Premature dropouts with patients in precontemplation can be prevented by matching the client's stage rather than expecting clients to match the therapist's preferred processes. Further, helping patients appreciate the many benefits that can come from completing therapy, besides solving their presenting problem, is recommended.

Several practical suggestions can also be made. For instance, when therapy must be brief, set realistic goals. Assisting clients to break out of a "stuck place," like precontemplation or contemplation, can make a difference in helping them to take effective action soon. Unfortunately, therapists may assume that brief therapy must be an action oriented. Such a mistake will mismatch the needs of most patients except those prepared to act. Once patients break out of a stuck place, encourage them to take their progress and run with it to see if they can keep changing on their own. If they get stuck again in the future, encourage them to return for another brief course of therapy to help resume change. It is helpful to remember that change is a process that typically occurs outside therapy but can be prepared and accelerated with brief therapy.

3. What state of change would you say the field of mental health (psychology, psychiatry, social work) is in regarding moving beyond the schoolism of traditional therapeutic thinking and toward the transtheoretical approach? What might facilitate transition to the next stage?

Michael O'Donnell, the editor of the *American Journal of Health Promotion* has said that by the year 2000, all health promotion programs in the United States will be based on the stage model. Counselors and therapists who focus on behavior health are readily adopting the transtheoretical model for working with many patient populations.

Ironically, although the model began in mental health, specialists in this field have been slower to change. My speculation is that because "all had won and all must get prizes," why would any therapist need to change? Nevertheless, I do see the younger generation recognizing that the golden days of practicing any form of therapy leading to a successful private practice have disappeared. These therapists have many more pros for changing. As they seek better opportunities for themselves and those troubled by self-defeating or self-destructive lifestyles, many are turning to more innovative alternatives. The transtheoretical approach provides innovative programs that can reach more people, retain more people, and affect a much greater percentage of troubled populations. This is one of the alternatives that can help the next generation create a better future for mental health.

References

Beitman, B. D., Beck, N. C., Deuser, W., Carter, C., Davidson, J., & Maddock, R. (1994). Patient stages of change predicts outcome in a panic disorder medication trial. *Anxiety, 1,* 64–69.

COMMIT Research Group. (1995). Community intervention trial for smoking cessation: II. Changes in adult cigarette smoking prevalence. *American Journal of Public Health, 85,* 193–202.

DiClemente, C. C., & Prochaska, J. O. (1982). Self-change and therapy change of smoking behavior: A comparison of processes of change of cessation and maintenance. *Addictive Behaviors, 7,* 133–142.

Ennett, S. T., Tabler, N. S., Ringwolt, C. L., & Fliwelling, R. L. (1994). How effective is drug abuse resistance education? A meta-analysis of Project DARE outcome evaluations. *American Journal of Public Health, 84,* 1394–1401.

Glasgow, R. E., Terborg, J. R., Hollis, J. F., Severson, H. H., & Boles, S. M. (1995). Take heart: Results from the initial phase of a worksite wellness program. *American Journal of Public Health, 85,* 209–216.

Lam, C. S., McMahon, B. T., Priddy, D. A., & Gehred-Schultz, A. (1988). Deficit awareness and treatment performance among traumatic head injury adults. *Brain Injury, 2,* 235–242.

Lando, H. A., Pechacek, T. F., Pirie, P. L., Murray, D. M., Mittelmark, M. B., Lichtenstein, E., Nothwehyr, F., & Gray, C. (1995). Changes in adult cigarette smoking in the Minnesota Heart Health Program. *American Journal of Public Health, 85,* 201–208.

Lichtenstein, E., & Hollis, J. (1992). Patient referral to smoking cessation programs: Who follows through? *The Journal of Family Practice, 34,* 739–744.

Luepker, R. V., Murray, D. M., Jacobs, D. R., Mittelmark, M. B., Bracht, N., Carlaw, R., Crow, R., Elmer, P., Finnegan, J., Folsom, A. R., Grimm, P. J., Hannan, R., Jeffrey, R., Lando, H., McGovern, P., Mullis, R., Perry, L., Pechacek, P., Pirie, J. M., Sprafka, R., Wiesbrod, R., & Blackburn, H. (1994). Community education for cardiovascular disease prevention: Risk factor changes in the Minnesota Heart Health Program. *American Journal of Public Health, 84,* 1383–1393.

Medeiros, M. E., & Prochaska, J. O. (1997). *Predicting termination and continuation status in psychotherapy using the Transtheoretical Model.* Manuscript submitted for publication.

Mellinger, G. D., Balter, M. B., Manheimer, D. I., Cisin, I. H., & Perry, H. C. (1978). Psychic distress, life crisis, and use of psychotherapeutic medications: National household survey data. *Archives of General Psychiatry, 35,* 1045–1052.

Miller, W. R. (1985). Motivation for treatment: A review with special emphasis on alcoholism. *Psychological Bulletin, 98,* 84–107.

Prochaska, J. O. (1979). *Systems of psychotherapy: A transtheoretical analyses.* Chicago: Dorsey Press.

Prochaska, J. O. (1994). Strong and weak principles for progressing from precontemplation to action based on twelve problem behaviors. *Health Psychology, 13,* 47–51.

Prochaska, J. O. (1995). Common problems: Common solutions. *Clinical Psychology: Science and Practice, 1,* 101–105.

Prochaska, J. O. (1997). A revolution in health promotion: Smoking cessation as a case study. In R. J. Resnick & R. H. Rozensky (Eds.), *Health psychology through the lifespan: Practice and research opportunities*. Washington, DC: American Psychological Association.

Prochaska, J. O., & DiClemente, C. C. (1982). Transtheoretical therapy: Toward a more integrative model of change. *Psychotherapy: Theory, Research and Practice, 19,* 276–288.

Prochaska, J. O., & DiClemente, C. C. (1983). Stages and processes of self-change of smoking: Toward an integrative model of change. *Journal of Consulting and Clinical Psychology, 51,* 390–395.

Prochaska, J. O., DiClemente, C. C., & Norcross, J. C. (1992). In search of how people change: Applications to the addictive behaviors. *American Psychologist, 47,* 1102–1114.

Prochaska, J. O., DiClemente, C. C., Velicer, W. F., & Rossi, J. S. (1993). Standardized, individualized, interactive and personalized self-help programs for smoking cessation. *Health Psychology, 12,* 399–405.

Prochaska, J. O., Norcross, J. C., & DiClemente, C. C. (1994). *Changing for good.* New York: William Morrow.

Prochaska, J. O., Norcross, J. C., Fowler, J. Follick, M., & Abrams, D. B. (1992). Attendance and outcome in a work-site weight control program: Processes and stages of change as process and predictor variables. *Addictive Behavior, 17,* 35–45.

Prochaska, J. O., Velicer, W. F., Fava, J., Rossi, J., & Tsoh, J. (1997). *A stage matched expert system intervention with a total population of smokers.* Manuscript submitted for publication.

Prochaska, J. O., Velicer, W. F., Fava, J., Ruggiero, L., Laforge, R., & Rossi, J. (1997). *Counselor and stimulus control enhancements of a sage matched expert system for smokers in a managed care setting.* Manuscript submitted for publication.

Prochaska, J. O., Velicer, W. F., Rossi, J. S., Goldstein, M. G., Marcus, B. H., Rakowski, W., Fiore, C., Harlow, L., Redding, C. A., Rosenbloom, D., & Rossi, S. R. (1994). Stages of change and decisional balance for twelve problem behaviors. *Health Psychology, 13,* 39–46.

Rossi, J. S. (1992). *Stages of change for 15 health risk behaviors in an HMO population.* Paper presented at the 13th meeting of the Society for Behavioral Medicine, New York, NY.

Smith, M. L., Glass, G. V., & Miller, T. I. (1980). *The benefits of psychotherapy.* Baltimore: Johns Hopkins University Press.

Snow, M. G., Prochaska, J. O., & Rossi, J. S. (1992). Stages of change for smoking cessation among former problem drinkers: A cross-sectional analysis. *Journal of Substance Abuse, 4,* 107–116.

Tsoh, J., & Prochaska, J.O. (1998). *Stages of change, drop-outs and outcomes in substance abuse treatment.* Manuscript submitted for publication.

U.S. Department of Health and Human Services. (1990). *The health benefits of smoking cessation: A report of the Surgeon General* (DHHS Publication No. CDC 90-8416). Washington, DC: U.S. Government Printing Office.

Veroff, J., Douvan, E., & Kulka, R. A. (1981a). *The inner America.* New York: Basic Books.

Veroff, J., Douvan, E., & Kulka, R. A. (1981b). *Mental health in America.* New York: Basic Books.

Velicer, W. F., Prochaska, J. O., Fava, J. L., Laforge, R. G., & Rossi, J. S. (1997). *Interactive and non-interactive interventions and dose-response relationships for stage matched smoking cessation programs in a managed care setting.* Manuscript submitted for publication.

Weinberger, J. (1995). Common factors aren't so common: The common factors dilemma. *Clinical Psychology: Science and Practice, 2,* 45–69.

Wierzbicki, M., & Pekarik, G. (1993). A meta-analysis of psychotherapy dropout. *Professional Psychology: Research and Practice, 29,* 190–195.

III | SPECIAL APPLICATIONS OF THE COMMON FACTORS

Albert W. Scovern

From Placebo to Alliance:
The Role of Common Factors in Medicine

9

n the summer of 1901 A. E. MacDonald, superintendent of Manhattan State Hospital, confronted a logistics problem quite unfamiliar to hospital administrators today—too many patients and too few beds. To alleviate cramped conditions created by an influx of tuberculosis admissions, about 40 patients with this disease were transferred from the main wards to two large tents that had been set up on the hospital grounds. The novelty of this arrangement generated excitement among the staff and created a desire to provide the tent residents the very best of care, nutrition, and attention. Before long, staff began to observe symptomatic improvement in many of these patients, gains that were lost in the winter when the patients were returned to quarters within the main hospital. Positive treatment outcomes were attributed to the effects of fresh air and physical environment, leading to enthusiastic efforts to construct camplike treatment settings for tuberculosis patients elsewhere, including outdoor or "tent" wards. Eventually, when the novelty of the experiment wore off and life within the tents began to mimic the monotony of the regular wards, the new environments lost their curative power (Caplan, 1969).

Nearly one hundred years later, the May 12, 1997, issue of *Time* magazine featured a discussion of Andrew Weil's holistic medicine approach, a combination of conventional prescriptions for healthy living—exercise, diet, vitamins, stress reduction—and more controversial herbal, hypnotic, and chiropractic remedies for a variety of physical ailments and diseases (Kluger, 1997). Inside the magazine, Weil, with bald pate and full gray beard, photographed against the backdrop of his new age, southern Arizona surroundings, looked every bit the guru that he claims not to be. The article cited earnest testimonials from patients and anecdotes from Weil about the curative powers of such treatments as cranial manipulation for ulcerative colitis and the ingestion of garlic to reduce blood pressure. Other physicians weighed in, expressing their concern that Weil is touting treatments that have no proven effectiveness, and criticized his reliance on emotional self-report as unscientific and subject to bias. Still, the article boldly headlined the conclusion that "the rub for Weil's critics is that so many of his followers and patients do seem to improve" (pp. 74–75).

Are Weil's remedies different in their actions and effects from the long abandoned tent therapy, or the crocodile dung, frog sperm, human perspiration, animal blood, purgings, blisterings, and bleedings that were administered to patients throughout medicine's pre-scientific history? Time and research will tell. But even these primitive treatments, now known to be useless at best and dangerous at worst, were apparently quite helpful to many patients. Shapiro and Morris (1978) argued that the honor and respect accorded to physicians historically, and the dedicated reliance of patients on their superstitious remedies, leads to this conclusion.

"THE POWERFUL PLACEBO"

Research now shows that medical treatments subsequently found to be ineffective in controlled studies, or treatments for which there is little rational basis for their use considering their known mechanism of action on specific physiologic states, can, for some period of time during their life cycle, be either curative or ameliorative. Such treatments are especially potent early in their life cycle, when there is new hope for their effectiveness and when their purported benefits are publicized by prestigious, enthusiastic, or charismatic physicians (Beecher, 1955). The initial success of tent wards as a treatment for tuberculosis is a good example of the effects of novelty, hope, enthusiasm, and proselytizing. The power of these treatments, of course, has come to be summarized under the concept of *placebo effects*.

Since the publication in 1955 of Beecher's article "The Powerful Placebo," physicians have understood that aspects of the patient–doctor relationship, the patient's belief that he or she is receiving helpful treatment, and psychological qualities already present in the patient are factors that strongly influence recovery and healing. These factors, which exert their influence through psychological and psychophysiological pathways, are responsible for the initial success of treatments subsequently judged useless and then discarded. More important, because they operate in every medical procedure, these factors also account for some portion of therapeutic response in treatments with proven medical efficacy and where the treatment's action is known, precise, and *specific* to a given pathophysiology. For this reason such placebo effects are increasingly referred to as *nonspecific effects*, which are conceptualized as deriving from the operation of psychological and psychophysiological factors present in all medical treatment—the *common factors*.

HOW POWERFUL IS THE POWERFUL PLACEBO?

From his review of 15 single or double-blind studies that assessed the effects of placebos on a variety of conditions including postoperative pain, cough, and headache, Beecher (1955) concluded that, on average across studies, placebos produced "satisfactory relief" in 35% of the patients. Though Beecher's review lacked methodological rigor, it was nonetheless ground-breaking, and his figures have been cited often as the average placebo effect size. In fact, placebo effects vary widely depending on disease, treatment, type of placebo, and experimental design. Estimates of placebo strength drawn from double-blind studies have been suspected of erring on the low side as true blindness frequently is impossible (S. Fisher & Greenberg, 1989) and because the optimism and strong belief in the treatment being administered, the *sine qua non* of the placebo effect, may be diminished under these conditions.[1]

---

[1]To Beecher we largely owe the double-blind design, which attempts to control for experimenter bias and nonspecific effects in medical outcome research. The idea is to establish the therapeutic power of a specific treatment over and above the healing effects of the common factors. One of the most underappreciated findings from the thousands of published double-blind studies that today exist in the medical literature is the fact that attention, placebo, and sham-treatment control conditions consistently show some therapeutic response. Every double-blind study using placebo controls, therefore, provides support for the presence of powerful nonspecific effects in medicine. Benson and McCallie (1979) examined data regarding the effectiveness of methyl xanthines and khellin (vasodilators), vitamin-E, surgical ligation of the internal mammary artery, and the Vineberg operation, which involved the implantation of the internal mammary artery into the myocardium. Despite the fact that controlled studies found each to be no better than strict placebo, early investigations demonstrated high rates of improvement in angina patients on measures of pain intensity. The authors indicated that these "ineffective" treatments also produced long lasting change on objective measures of exercise tolerance, nitroglycerin usage, and electrocardiogram results. Unfortunately, they did not provide data from which one could estimate average improvement rates on these more objective indexes of outcome.

Two studies tackled this problem in a novel way by analyzing outcome data from medical treatments that are now known to be ineffective. Specifically, each study examined efficacy estimates obtained during a period when the treatments were believed to be highly effective, thus maximizing the effects of heightened expectations and enthusiasm in both doctors and patients. In all cases, later controlled studies found these treatments to have success rates indistinguishable from those produced by a strict placebo condition. The earlier data are assumed to be a purer estimate of placebo or common factors effect size because later controlled studies, by skeptics, may actually diminish positive expectations in patients and physicians. In evaluating five discarded treatments for angina pectoris, Benson and McCallie (1979) found that early assessments of their outcome yielded average subjective improvement rates of over 80%, changes that in some cases lasted for a year or more.[2] In a similar but more rigorous investigation, Roberts, Kewman, Mercier, and Hovell (1993) randomly chose for study five currently abandoned treatments once thought effective for asthma, herpes simplex lesions, and duodenal ulcer.[3] Uncontrolled clinical trials, when patients ($N = 6,931$) and doctors had high expectations for success, reported an *excellent* response in 40% of treated patients, a *good* response in 30%, and a *poor* outcome in the remaining 30%.

These estimates of the power of nonspecific effects, obtained under conditions that more closely approximate real-life clinical situations in which doctor and patient have confidence in the procedure, indicate that common factors play a stronger role in medicine than previously believed. To understand them and their mechanism of action fully, however, is equivalent to understanding the mind–body connection—a daunting task indeed! The past 15 years have seen an explosion of

---

[2]Roberts et al. (1993) compiled a list of medical treatments that were thought to be highly effective at the time of their initial reporting but that later were determined to be ineffective. Treatments were included if they met the following criteria: strong positive reports by at least two investigators; at least one well-controlled negative report; abandoned by the medical profession as ineffective; and outcome data from the studies could be classified as excellent, good, or poor. The treatments that met these criteria included glomectomy for asthma, levamisole, photodynamic inactivation, and organic solvents in the treatment of lesions caused by herpes simplex virus and gastric freezing for duodenal ulcer. The 70% rate of good or excellent response to these treatments suggests that nonspecific effects are much stronger than previously thought. These findings should be interpreted cautiously, however, because the uncontrolled trials on which they are based are subject to rater bias, a fairly potent influence on outcome assessments in nonblind experiments.

[3]From the standpoint of causal attribution theory, attributing negative events to stable factors would lead to a belief that such events will occur reliably, whereas attributing such events to global factors would lead to a belief that they will occur across situations. This is a devastatingly pessimistic style of thinking.

research findings from the fields of behavioral medicine and psychoneuroimmunology demonstrating the effects of attitude, behavior, cognitive set, and unpleasant states of mind on physiology and illness. It is now accepted that such variables play a role in the course of diseases such as diabetes, heart disease, asthma, and cancer. Similarly, it is well established that these psychological factors can influence the pain experience, affect immune response, and have a demonstrable impact on health care variables like length of hospitalization, compliance with treatment, and response to surgery. Companion research also has shown, sometimes in dramatic and moving ways, how modifications of attitude, behavior, cognitive set, and unpleasant states of mind can promote healing.

A comprehensive survey of this literature, of course, is beyond the scope of a book chapter. Our task here is to address questions that are more narrow and modest. What is it about the doctor–patient interaction, independent of medical technique or procedure, that is ameliorative? What psychological factors do physician and patient bring to this interaction that affect treatment outcome? And what can we as researchers draw, from what is now a huge literature examining the effects of psychological variables on disease and recovery, that would help us to conceptualize the mechanisms by which the common factors promote healing?

THE DOCTOR– PATIENT ALLIANCE: AN ORGANIZING CONCEPT

As part of his PBS series "Healing and the Mind," Bill Moyers interviewed Thomas Delbanco, MD, Director of General Medicine and Primary Care at Beth Israel Hospital in Boston. Speaking about the roles and functions of the physician in the context of the patient–doctor relationship, Delbanco (1993) had this to say:

> First of all, a good doctor listens to you and then addresses what you're feeling . . . I want to know what they [patients] bring to the table. I want to know what they want from me. I want to know what kind of person they are, so I'd know how they filter what I say. I think doctors are actually chameleon-like. I find myself a very different person with different patients . . . It's my sense of what that patient wants from me, what kind of doctor he or she wants me to be . . . I've got to know what makes you tick. I may know a lot about your disease, but I don't know how you experience your illness. (pp. 8–10)

Intuitively, perhaps, Delbanco is describing healing aspects of the doctor-patient relationship that are remarkably similar to concepts in the psychotherapy literature having to do with the importance of rapport; fostering a collaborative partnership; empathy; and adopting the client's language, problem conceptualization, and frame of reference. These concepts are related to and often subsumed under the broader category of *therapeutic alliance*, which has been shown to be a significant predictor of outcome in psychotherapy (Frieswyk et al., 1986; Hartley & Strupp, 1983).

Now, with the latest report from the National Institute of Mental Health Treatment of Depression Collaborative Research Program (Krupnick et al., 1996), it appears that the therapeutic alliance is equally powerful as a predictor of outcome in medical/pharmacological treatment (see chapter 10 by Greenberg). In a comparison of cognitive–behavior therapy, interpersonal psychotherapy, imipramine plus clinical management, and drug placebo plus clinical management, therapeutic alliance assessed by independent raters accounted for 21% of the outcome variance across all treatment conditions, accounting for more of the variance than treatment method. Two aspects of these findings are worth underscoring here: (a) alliance related to the effectiveness of drug treatment—the higher the alliance between patient and managing physician, the better the outcome, and (b) alliance related to the effectiveness of the drug placebo—*the higher the alliance with the managing physician the more powerful the placebo effect.*

These are compelling findings. They corroborate earlier studies that have found a strong association between the quality of the doctor–patient relationship and such factors as patient compliance with prescribed medical regimens. The fact that alliance predicted outcome in the imipramine group might be due to increased adherence to the drug protocol in patients with better relationships with the managing physician. However, that alliance also predicted outcome in the placebo group indicates that something else is going on—that the doctor–patient relationship has, as a nonspecific factor in the treatment, some direct bearing on outcome in medicine. But what is it, in this complex interaction between doctor and patient, that is taking place? What are the ingredients of the "alliance," and what do patient and physician contribute to it?

"I WANT TO KNOW WHAT THEY BRING TO THE TABLE": PATIENT CONTRIBUTIONS TO THE COMMON FACTORS

Miller, Duncan, and Hubble (1997) reported that as much as 40% of the variance in psychotherapy outcome can be attributed to factors relating to client characteristics (i.e., skills and problem-solving competencies) and aspects of the client's life situation. This finding has intuitive appeal, insofar as most psychotherapy is a collaborative effort to produce change and the psychotherapy literature is rich in studies of client variables that predict outcome. The notion that patient qualities can significantly influence outcome in medicine lacks intuitive appeal, however, to the extent that *modern* medical treatment has come to be construed as an interaction between a physician and a disease rather than between a physician and an ill person striving to get well. Fortunately, in the past two decades a reawakening of appreciation for the patient's role in recovery has been seen.

Patient Optimism, Expectancy, and Hope

It has been conventional wisdom that patients' attitudes play a role in their response to medical and surgical procedures. Empirical evidence is now gathering to substantiate some important pieces of this medical folklore. Using causal attribution theory as a springboard, Peterson has defined *optimism* as the tendency to attribute negative events to external, unstable, and specific factors, and *pessimism* as the tendency to attribute such events to internal, stable, and global factors. He found that an optimistic attribution style in college students is associated with fewer days of illness and fewer health center visits (Dykema, Bergbower, & Peterson, 1995; Lin & Peterson, 1990; Peterson, 1988). And, using data from the Harvard Study of Adult Development, he determined that retrospective ratings of attribution style among men at age 25 predicted physical status from age 45 to 60, with an especially strong correlation between pessimism and poor health at age 45 (Peterson, Seligman, & Vaillant, 1988). This correlation held even when physical and emotional health at age 25 were controlled, leading the investigators to recommend that pessimism in early adulthood be considered a risk factor for poor health in middle and late adulthood.

To the extent that negative events are attributed to stable and global factors in particular, a person would be predisposed to form rather gloomy expectations about the future.[4] It should not be surprising to find that positive and negative expectations, including beliefs about health and treatment efficacy, about one's capacity to cope effectively, and about the extent to which one has personal control over illness have all been associated with various indices of treatment response. In fact, the patient's belief in the efficacy of the treatment, the so-called "placebo belief," is thought by some to be at the heart of placebo effects (Lundh, 1987).

The evidence for the power of patient expectancy comes from many sources, but perhaps none more convincing than the repeated finding that patients who believe that they will have complications following surgery typically have longer recovery times, more medical complications, and report greater pain experience than patients with less negative expectations (e.g., George, Scott, Turner, & Gregg, 1980). A study by Jamison, Parris, and Maxson (1987) is illustrative. Fifty female patients scheduled to have elective laparoscopic surgery for infertility investigation were given a series of measures assessing mood and outcome expectancy. Psychological and physical aspects of response to surgery were obtained 3 days and 1 month after surgery. Women who expected to have a long recovery period and to have high degrees of pain reported more postoperative difficulties than patients with more favorable expectations. Using data obtained from 121 patients undergoing the same laparoscopic procedure, Wallace (1985) found similar results: Women who expected to have more pain in fact reported more pain, distress, and upset following surgery. In other words, expectations seem to serve as a "self-fulfilling prophesy" for surgery outcome.

A number of studies have borrowed on Bandura's (1977) self-efficacy theory and the locus of control construct to assess the impact of beliefs on pain tolerance and pain management. *Self-efficacy expectancy* is defined as a belief that one can successfully perform a required behavior in a given situation. Women with higher self-efficacy expectancy regarding their ability to cope with birthing pain have been shown to spend more time in labor without pain medications and to use fewer pain medications overall (Manning & Wright, 1983). Similarly, thoracic surgery patients with stronger "self-control" expectancy experienced lower pain intensity (as measured by both analgesic use and subjective report) and a shorter duration of postsurgical pain (Bachiocco, Morselli, & Garli, 1993). When the assessment of expectations on pain tolerance was done under laboratory conditions using the cold pressor test, the relationship was the same: Higher self-efficacy expectations predicted greater pain tolerance (Dolce et al., 1986).

A concept closely related to self-efficacy expectations is that of health locus of control, which refers to a person's belief in his or her control over illness. As measured by the Health Locus of Control Scale and its adaptations, chronic pain patients with a greater internal locus of control have been shown to experience lower pain levels and lower pain frequency (Toomey, Mann, & Thompson-Pope, 1991) and to respond more favorably to pain management programs. Patients with an internal health locus of control learned their rehabilitation exercises better, practiced the exercises more frequently, and were rated as less disabled after treatment (Harkapaa, Jarvikoski, Mellin, Hurri, & Luoma, 1991).

Optimistic attitude, positive expectancy, belief in one's own power to promote recovery—these are "what the patient brings to the table" that can influence treatment response. These "common factors" are all aspects of an old-fashioned concept that recently has been the focus of renewed research interest—that concept is *hope*. As a state of mind, hopefulness embodies optimism and expectations for positive outcomes and for goal attainment. Efforts to assess the effects of hope have been furthered considerably by Snyder (see chapter 6 by Snyder, Michael, and Cheavens in this volume), who defines hope as derived from a sense of being able to create plans to attain goals (*pathways*) and to energetically initiate actions in the pursuit of them (*agency*). Having developed a questionnaire to assess the strength of these components of hope, Snyder and his colleagues have shown that hope is positively associated with success on a number of coping, work, and achievement tasks. One such coping challenge is posed by physical trauma. Using Snyder's construct, Elliott, Witty, Herrick, and Hoffman (1991) studied the relationship between hope and response to traumatically acquired severe physical disability in patients undergoing rehabilitation. These researchers found that a sense of being able to devise plans to meet goals (pathways), an experience similar to self-efficacy expectancy, was predictive of better psychosocial and emotional adjustment in this patient group.

Conversely, the loss of hope—hopelessness—has been associated with health complications and poor treatment outcomes. For example, hopelessness has been related to greater tumor progression and earlier death among cancer patients (Pettingale, Morris, Greer, & Haybittle, 1985), and to increased morbidity and mortality from ischemic heart disease (Anda, Williamson, & Jones, 1993). In a related study, Oxman, Freeman, and Manheimer (1995) examined the relationship between response to cardiac surgery and religious conviction, recognizing the powerful experience of hope and optimism that religious faith affords patients confronting serious illness. Even after controlling for the effects of prior surgical history, presurgical functional impairment, and age, Oxman et al. found that the absence of strength and comfort in religion was related to risk for death during the 6 months postsurgery. Recently, these findings were dramatically confirmed by a prospective, longitudinal study of 2,428 men, ages 42 to 60, who were part of the Kuopio Ischemic Heart Disease (KIHD) project (Everson et al., 1996). The KIHD project was designed to assess risk factors for heart disease and other illnesses among men in the Kuopio region of Finland who have been found to have unusually high coronary morbidity.

Two cohorts of these men were given a variety of measures, including two questionnaire items measuring hopelessness, and then were followed over several years. Responses to the following were rated on a 5-point Likert scale: "I feel that it is impossible to reach the goals I would like to strive for" and "The future seems to me to be hopeless, and I can't believe that things are changing for the better." Participants were divided into groups low, moderate, and high in hopelessness on the basis of their responses, with 11% of the sample scoring in the highly hopeless range. Data analyses revealed a dramatic dose–response relationship between hopelessness and mortality: Compared with low scorers, moderately hopeless men were at more than *twice* the risk and highly hopeless men more than *three times* the risk of death, primarily due to cardiovascular disease and cancer. High levels of hopelessness also predicted incidence of first heart attack in men with no history of angina, and moderate and high hopelessness significantly predicted incident cancer. Strikingly, these relationships held even when adjustments were made for other medical, demographic, and behavioral risk factors, including depression and availability of social supports. Everson et al. (1996) provided a convincing argument that hopelessness is an independent and powerful predictor of morbidity and mortality, that it is a distinct psychological construct from depression, and, consequently, that hopelessness should be distinguished from depression when considering it's impact on health. Old-fashioned, perhaps, but the concept of hope has regained center stage as a patient variable influencing treatment outcome in medicine.

Patient Affect States and Stress Arousal

Another set of "patient variables" that affect health status and treatment response includes emotional states and the personality organizations within which they are embedded. For many decades, researchers in the field of psychosomatic medicine have attempted to find personality types, unconscious need states, and particular impulse–defense configurations that are associated with specific diseases. For the most part, these attempts have failed (Surwit, Feinglos, & Scovern, 1983). After reviewing the literature in this area, however, H. S. Friedman and Booth-Kewley (1987) concluded that there is some evidence for a general "disease prone" personality with high levels of anxiety, depression, and anger/hostility. Although this area of research has produced controversial and equivocal findings, there is fairly clear evidence that high levels of affective and stress arousal can influence the onset and course of certain illnesses as well as recovery.

In 1991, Sheldon Cohen and his colleagues published findings that settled the debate about whether psychological "stress" is a risk factor for disease (Cohen, Tyrrell, & Smith, 1991). In fact, they demonstrated convincingly that psychological variables can alter functioning of the immune system in such a way as to increase susceptibility to infectious illness. Three hundred ninety-four healthy adults agreed to be quarantined for 9 days as part of a study conducted at the Medical Research Council's Common Cold Unit in England. During the first 2 days they were assessed physically and psychologically. Three measures of psychological stress were administered: a stressful life events scale measuring stressful events over the past year, a scale assessing the degree to which participants felt that current stresses were exceeding their coping resources, and a measure of current negative affects like anger, irritation, anxiety, sadness, and guilt. Highly correlated, these indexes of stress were combined to form an overall psychological stress score.

Volunteers were then given nasal drops containing a low infectious dose of one of five respiratory viruses and were examined daily for signs and symptoms of respiratory infection. Clinical colds were defined as clinical symptoms with infection verified by the isolation of virus or increase in the virus-specific antibody titer. Impressively, there was a significant dose–response relationship between degree of psychological stress and rates of both infections and clinical colds. These relationships were the same for each of the five challenge viruses, and they held even after adjustments were made for variables such as baseline virus-specific antibody status and possible stress-illness mediators like smoking, alcohol consumption, exercise, diet, white cell counts, and total immunoglobulin levels! Degree of stress and negative affect predicted susceptibility to infection and illness. This positive relationship between negative life events and perceived stress and susceptibility to colds and respiratory infection has been confirmed by Cohen (Cohen, Tyrrell, & Smith, 1993) as well as others. Recent research suggests that this relationship may be mediated by other psychological variables, such as coping style and family structure, which either limit or enhance adaptability. Cobb and Steptoe (1996), for example, found risk of upper respiratory infection greatest in "high stress" groups that were low in the capacity to manage stress by distraction or cognitive avoidance, and in highly stressed individuals who came from families with a strict, rule-bound organization.

The extent to which stress and unpleasant affects contribute to the onset of more serious illnesses is now the subject of research at major medical centers around the world. At Duke University Medical Center, Williams (Barefoot, Dahlstrom, & Williams, 1983; Barefoot, Dodge, Peterson, Dahlstrom, & Williams, 1989) conducted pioneering work examining the relationship between hostility and cynicism and coronary heart disease. In several studies, he and his colleagues found that ratings of cynicism, experience of anger, and expression of anger predicted incidence of heart disease in doctors and lawyers at a 25-year follow-up. Professionals with high hostility scores were *four to five times more likely* than low scorers to develop coronary disease. A complementary finding

is that intervention programs designed to help patients in cardiac rehabilitation to reduce their hostility and anger have been shown to significantly reduce the incidence of a second heart attack and death
(M. Friedman et al., 1986). Depression, similarly, has a debilitating
effect on cardiac functioning, particularly after the occurrence of a
heart attack. Cameron (1996) summarized this literature succinctly in
stating that depression increases morbidity and mortality from heart
attack at 1 month, increases the risk of cardiac death and arrhythmic
events at 6 months, and, in those with coronary artery disease,
increases 12-month post-heart attack morbidity and mortality.

Richard Surwit at Duke University Medical Center and Daniel Cox
at the University of Virginia Health Sciences Center have taken the
lead in investigating the role of behavioral factors, including stress, in
diabetes mellitus and its treatment. Although psychological stress cannot "cause" diabetes, it does appear to play a role in the onset of diabetes in patient's genetically or physiologically predisposed, and in the
course of the disease. A number of studies have found an increased
incidence of stressful life events before the onset of insulin-dependent
diabetes (Cox & Gonder-Frederick, 1992), and some studies have
shown that relaxation training enhances the metabolic control of non-
insulin-dependent diabetics who report significant anxiety in their
lives (Surwit, Schneider, & Feinglos, 1992).

As with diabetes, there is no compelling evidence to support the
idea that stress or other states of mind cause cancer. There is probably
only a weak relationship at this point between depressive symptoms
and bereavement and the onset of cancer, despite the popular notion
that such an association exists. As of yet, the hypothesis that depression
suppresses or alters immune system functioning has been tested insufficiently to draw firm conclusions (Stein, Miller, & Trestman, 1991).

On the other hand, Everson et al.'s (1996) data from the KIHD
project described earlier suggest that hopelessness, a construct independent from depression, may be a risk factor for cancer. Studies that
have examined factors predicting survivability in patients who have
already developed cancer have given some support to this notion.
Working out of the Pittsburgh Cancer Institute at the University of
Pittsburgh School of Medicine, Sandra Levy has built a solid program
of research exploring risk factors, stress, and immune functioning as
they relate to cancer. She found that a factor she termed *listless apathy*
is associated with poor prognosis in women with early stage breast
cancer (Levy, Herberman, Maluish, Schlien, & Lippman, 1985). More
recently, her research team examined variables that predicted survival
time in women with first recurrent breast cancer. Of four predictor
variables, the most powerful was a biological one: The longer the
interval between primary treatment and recurrence the longer the

survival time after recurrence. Surprisingly, the second most powerful predictor was a psychological one: *joy* as measured by the Affect Balance Scale. That is, women with higher scores on the Joy subscale, who endorsed items indicating that they felt "glad," "cheerful," and so on lived significantly longer after recurrence than low scorers, who endorsed items such as "hopeless," "worthless," and "unhappy" (Levy, Lee, Bagley, & Lippman, 1988). The authors felt that the positive affect state that characterized women who lived longer was very much related to attitudes of hope and optimism.

Kiecolt-Glaser and Glaser (1995) summarized some very recent data pertaining to the impact of depressed affect and bereavement on the course of human immunodeficiency virus (HIV). There is some indication that depressed HIV-infected men show faster rates of decline in CD4 (help/inducer cell) counts than those nondepressed, a relationship that is strongest in men with higher baseline CD4 cells. Depression caused by object loss (grief) apparently does not produce this effect, suggesting that bereavement and non-bereavement-related depression have different immunological correlates and different effects on disease progression. Intervention programs, including exercise and cognitive–behavioral stress management techniques, have successfully reduced depression caused by notifying patients about their HIV serostatus, with corresponding positive changes in CD4 and natural killer cell counts. These very exciting and promising findings should be regarded with caution, although several efforts at replication have been successful. Recent longitudinal data obtained from a sample of HIV-infected men show a positive relationship between severe stress and depressive symptoms, and declines in CD8 T-cells and CD56 and CD16 NK cell subsets (Leserman et al., 1997).

If stress arousal and negative affect states play a role in the onset and natural course of some diseases, do they also influence patients' response to treatment? Once again I return to the surgery outcome literature, where this question can be answered confidently in the affirmative. The anticipation of surgery precipitates high levels of anxiety in most patients (Johnston, 1980), having to do with fear of pain, anesthesia, bodily intrusion, disfigurement, and death. Janis (1958) is typically credited with initiating inquiry into the relationship between preoperative fear and anxiety and response to surgery. On the basis of limited data he suggested that there was a curvilinear relationship between preoperative fear and surgery outcome, such that "moderately" anxious patients, motivated to engage in active coping efforts, demonstrated the best treatment outcomes. This model has not been confirmed by subsequent studies. Rather, a simpler linear relationship between preoperative fear and trait anxiety, and postoperative indices of recovery have been repeatedly described in the literature

(Auerbach, 1989). Patients who are most fearful and anxious tend to have the greatest postoperative pain and longer hospital stays.

In 1964, Egbert, Battit, Welch, and Bartless published an interesting observation in the *New England Journal of Medicine*: When physicians visited patients before surgery and related to them in a supportive way, providing information about the upcoming procedure, patients showed improved postoperative recovery. Since then, behavioral interventions designed to reduce preoperative anxiety and fear have been studied fairly extensively, and these have included relaxation techniques and the provision of realistic information about surgery to promote coping and cognitive mastery. Wilson (1981) compared preoperative relaxation therapy, information about procedures and sensations likely to be experienced, and a combination of the two with respect to their effect on length of stay, use of analgesics, and postoperative pain and recovery. Patients in all three treatment groups were discharged from the hospital 1 day sooner than control patients. Relaxation training proved to be the more powerful intervention, producing significantly greater in-hospital recovery, reduced use of pain medications, and decreased pain report. These findings are consistent with a meta-analysis of the effects of various psychoeducational interventions on length of postsurgery hospital stay, which found that such interventions reduce hospital stay an average of 1.25 days (Devine & Cook, 1983). Although questions remain about which interventions are most helpful for which patients, the general thrust of this literature is clear: (a) Patient anxiety and fear complicate response to surgery, and (b) behavioral interventions structured to reduce fear and foster coping counteract this effect.

Patient Social Support

Some very exciting contemporary research examining the association between patient factors and disease has shifted focus from intrapersonal to extrapersonal variables. The patient brings to the table not only character attitudes, beliefs, and levels of stress arousal, but also particular living environments. Among these, a powerful element is the quality of the patient's social matrix. Epidemiological studies (Berkman & Syme, 1979; House, Landis, & Umberson, 1988) have revealed a fairly strong link between various measures of social relatedness and mortality. People who are more connected socially by way of marriage, having close contact with extended family, or through group membership are two to three times less likely to die over 10- to 12-year follow-ups than those less socially involved. Divorce is particularly devastating to health and a risk factor for premature death.

But is social relatedness associated with alterations in the course of an existing illness? Again, the answer is yes. Cancer patients (e.g., Goodwin, Hunt, Key, & Sarnct, 1987) who are married and those with more frequent social contacts seem to respond better to treatment and live longer. Williams and his associates have reported a similar trend among patients with coronary artery disease. Those patients who were unmarried and socially isolated had a 50% mortality rate after 5 years as compared with a 17% rate for those who had a close relationship. Even when degree of illness was controlled for, socially isolated coronary patients were three times as likely to die (Williams et al., 1992). For patients undergoing cardiac surgery, the relationship is the same—lack of participation in social and community groups is associated with increased risk of death during the 6 months after surgery (Oxman et al., 1995). Finally, social relatedness appears to be related to disease progression among patients with HIV. In an investigation of the disease course in 49 HIV-infected men, Theorell et al. (1995) found that men rated low in their "availability of attachments" when told of their serostatus around 1985 showed in subsequent years more rapid and progressive deterioration in CD4 counts than men with high social support.

These chilling findings raise the question whether the effects of social isolation are reversible. An answer to this question comes from one of the most widely cited studies in the medical literature over the past 10 years. In an article published in *Lancet* in 1989, David Spiegel and his colleagues presented data that shook many long cherished notions about cancer and its treatment (Spiegel, Bloom, Kraemer, & Gottheil, 1989). In this study 50 women with metastatic breast cancer were enrolled in weekly group therapy that encouraged the expression of feelings about disease and loss, the development of strong group connectedness, and increased assertiveness with doctors and treatment staff. Self-hypnosis techniques also were taught. Over a 10-year follow-up these women were compared with 36 patients who did not participate in the group experience but who received comparable medical treatment. The most noteworthy finding was that patients who obtained social support from the group lived twice as long as the controls (36.6 months vs. 18.9 months from entry into the study). After 4 years, none of the control patients were alive, yet one third of the group treated patients were still living. Fawzy et al. (1993) reported similar increases in survivability at a 6-year follow-up for patients with malignant melanoma who received group therapy.

The data are converging in this area. Social relatedness is associated with health and mortality, is a factor influencing outcome in patients with cancer and coronary artery disease, and can affect the course of cancer if provided after the onset of the disease. Social support and connectedness, therefore, are aspects of the patient's life situation that play a role in recovery and, as such, are important members of the family of common factors in medicine.

"FIRST OF ALL, A GOOD DOCTOR LISTENS TO YOU AND THEN ADDRESSES WHAT YOU'RE FEELING": PHYSICIAN CONTRIBUTIONS TO THE COMMON FACTORS

The capacity of the physician to create a relationship with the patient that is characterized by support, negotiation, mutual agreement, and partnership has a great impact on the patient's willingness to cooperate and to be an active participant in the treatment. There is reason to believe that the same core attitudes of the psychotherapist that create a facilitative environment in psychological treatments—those being empathy, warmth, and genuineness among others—are attitudes of the physician necessary to create a healing climate in medicine. In saying that "first of all a good doctor listens to you," Delbanco is saying that he understands the importance of entering into patients' subjective worlds to grasp their experience and the personal meaning of their symptoms. This is the posture of the physician that provides a context or "holding environment" within which the technical aspects of diagnosis and treatment take place.

Physician Communication

The effect of the physician's style of communication on patient satisfaction, compliance with treatment, and treatment outcome has been the subject of intensive study over the past several years. This is a dense literature that has produced findings that are difficult to summarize succinctly owing to the lack of a uniform methodology for measuring patient and physician communication and because measures of satisfaction, compliance, and outcome are imperfectly related (Kaplan, Greenfield, & Ware, 1989). Nonetheless, some tentative conclusions can be drawn, and several research efforts stand out as holding promise for the future.

It makes intuitive sense that empathic communication by the physician is essential to establishing rapport and that the quality of rapport will influence patient satisfaction with treatment. In a recent review of the literature, Frankel (1995) drew just that conclusion—the physician's sensitivity to the patient's emotional state and efforts to facilitate a clarification of problems, he argued, are positively associated with patient satisfaction and negatively associated with suits alleging malpractice. Several studies have now shown that interpersonal skills, including empathic communication, can be taught to physicians with a predictable effect on patient satisfaction. Smith, Lyles, Mettler, and Marshall (1995), for example, trained internal medicine and family practice residents in a 1-month experiential program that emphasized physician empathy. Compared with patients of residents who had participated in a control condition, the patients of trained physicians rated themselves as more confident in their doctor and more generally satisfied with their treatment. Efforts are now underway to develop training programs that teach even more complicated interpersonal and empathic skills, such as those necessary to relate to the kinds of seriously ill patients who often produce emotional blunting or defensive distancing and objectification in treatment staff (e.g., Parle, Maguire, & Heaven, 1997).

Clear, concise, empathic communication by the physician also is necessary to elicit accurate information from the patient and foster compliance with treatment. A study by Hulka, Cassel, Kupper, and Burdette (1976), for example, found a relationship between physician communication and drug error rates among congestive heart failure patients. As one might expect, the poorer the communication the more frequently the patients took the wrong amount of medicine or took the medicine on an incorrect schedule. Using hypertensive patients, Stanton (1987) replicated these findings. Compliance with the medication regimen was associated with clear doctor–patient communication, patient knowledge about the treatment, and patient satisfaction with the doctor. This correlation between satisfaction and compliance has been reported fairly frequently in the literature (Frankel, 1995) and is a finding with common sense appeal. In a study of the effects of doctor–patient communication on a wide range of outcome variables, Winefield, Murrell, and Clifford (1995) found that poor compliers were more dissatisfied with their treatment, and they rated their doctors as disinterested and condescending. In other words, rapport, satisfaction, and compliance were interrelated.

Unfortunately, the relationship between physician communication and health status after treatment is not yet well understood. Kaplan et al. (1989) audiotaped physician consultations with 252 patients presenting with ulcer disease, hypertension, diabetes, and breast cancer. The tapes were rated according to categories of physician and patient communication, and these ratings were then examined with respect to their relationship to various measures of treatment outcome, including patient ratings of improvement and physiologic markers of change. Greater communicative control by the physician, in the form of asking questions, giving directions, and interrupting, was associated with poorer treatment outcomes. Whereas the expression of positive affect by the physician was unrelated to outcome, physician expression of negative affects such as frustration or tension was *positively* associated with treatment response. Kaplan et al. speculated that this counterintuitive finding might be explained by patients interpreting the doctor's expression of negative affect as a sign of caring, but this explanation is not compelling given that positive emotional expressions had no effect on outcome.

Even the finding of Kaplan et al. (1989) that more patient and less physician control are associated with better treatment outcomes is not uniformly supported in the literature. When and in what manner the physician asserts control during the consultation appears to matter a great deal. Winefield et al. (1995) examined physician communication during the diagnostic (beginning) phase of the consultation and during the prescriptive phase when the diagnosis and treatment plan were explained. Patients who talked less about their illness during the prescriptive phase while their physician talked more improved the most. Similarly, from a sample of 400 taped consultations in an outpatient clinic in Mexico City (Finkler & Correa, 1996), these simple aspects of physician communication and patient–physician interaction were found to be most highly associated with patients' *perceived* recovery: The physician explained what was wrong and gave a diagnosis (even if it was not correct), the patient agreed with the physician, and the patient asked questions regarding his or her illness. The physician asserting control in an authoritative way, while leaving room for patient participation, was the important aspect of the communication process that related to outcome.

Contradictory and confusing findings in this literature primarily spring from the lack of a clinically relevant way to conceptualize and measure physician communication. Interruptions and response latencies are measurable, but they are not especially interesting variables from which to construct understandings of the effect of doctor–patient interactions on outcome. Such research has shown that physician communication leaves much to be desired—for example, a general practitioner will spend only 7 minutes with each patient and will interrupt the patient within 18 seconds of the start of the consultation (Beckman & Frankel, 1984)—but it has not provided the basis for a conceptual framework. The work of Doherty and his colleagues promises to fill in this void. Borrowing on a framework for assessing levels of physician involvement with families (Doherty & Baird, 1986), Marvel, Schilling, Doherty, and Baird (1994) developed a five-level model for conceptualizing and measuring the cognitive and emotional involvement of physicians with individual patients during the medical interview. Each successive level requires more complicated communicative skills by the physician, moving the process away from fact gathering toward the establishment of a collaboration, the identification and clarification of emotional conflicts and important psychological contributions to illness, and finally to interventions designed to intervene with these issues. Marvel et al. (1994) showed that their model can reliably code and measure levels of physician involvement with patients. It breaks down information gathering, empathic listening, and communication skills into concrete segments that can be taught, and it is conceptually relevant to the question of what kind and depth of physician communication facilitates healing. Doherty and his colleagues are now focusing on just that question.

Physician Expectations

Recall that the strength of the placebo effect depends not only on the patient's belief in the efficacy of the treatment, but the doctor's as well. New treatments with great promise, prescribed by enthusiastic practitioners, often produce high success rates until the bubble of belief is burst by controlled investigations. More important, does physician expectancy and belief influence the effectiveness of established treatments?

The available evidence, from various sources, suggests that the answer is yes, at least sometimes. For example, the effectiveness of certain drug treatments with known efficacy has been found to depend on the belief, interest, and enthusiasm of the physician prescribing the drug. In one of the first studies of this kind Feldman (1956) compared the effectiveness of chlorpromazine prescribed by psychiatrists who were enthusiastic about the drug to the effectiveness of chlorpromazine prescribed by psychodynamic psychiatrists who did not believe in drug treatment. Enthusiastic physicians obtained a 77% success rate; antagonistic physicians only 10%! The finding that drug efficacy relates to prescribing physician attitudes has been replicated repeatedly (e.g., Uhlenhuth, Canter, Neustadt, & Payson, 1959).

If physician belief in the treatment is important, belief in the patient may be as well. Liking and interest in the patient have been found to influence various drug treatments (Shapiro & Morris, 1978). And, nursing home residents whose staff were led to believe were a "special" group who could be expected to do better than average, were found after 3 months to have fewer depressive symptoms and hospital admissions than residents for whom expectations were not favorably manipulated (Learman, Avorn, Everitt, & Rosenthal, 1990).

The words of the physician are powerful. Through them, the physician conveys not only her or his confidence in the treatment, but also she or he imparts specific expectations about how the treatment will feel to the patient and what its therapeutic effects will be. These words create an expectancy that has a psychological impact and induces measurable physiological effects. A clever study by Luparello, Leist, Lourie, and Sweet (1970) illustrates this beautifully. Twenty asthmatic patients were enlisted to participate in a study assessing the effects of two drugs on airway reactivity as measured by airway resistance and thoracic gas volume. Each patient participated in four trials on successive days, under the following conditions: The patient was (a) told that he or she would be given a bronchodilator that "will open up your airways and make it easier for you to breathe" and was given a bronchodilator, (b) told that he would be given a bronchodilator but instead was given a bronchoconstrictor, (c) told he would be given a bronchoconstrictor that "will tighten up your airways and make it harder for you to breathe" and was given a bronchoconstrictor, and (d) told that he would be given a bronchoconstrictor but instead was given a bronchodilator. The order of conditions was randomized, and the drugs were administered by technicians blind to condition. Results showed that the physiologic effect of the bronchodilator was twice as great when the patient was told it was a dilator than when told it was a constrictor, and, conversely, the effect of the bronchoconstrictor was almost twice as great when the patient was told it was a constrictor rather than a dilator. Even more startling, in some patients the expectancy created by the instructions produced an effect "of sufficient magnitude to completely reverse the airway response so that it was opposite in direction from that expected on the basis of the pharmacological action of the drug alone" (p. 512). Through words the physician conveys belief in the treatment and belief in the patient, and shapes expectancies that have real effects. Words and expectations are powerful.

Physician Efforts to Empower the Patient

Patients' beliefs in their ability to cope and to exert control over illness have already been shown to influence their response to medical treatments. The opportunity for patients to actually take control of aspects of the treatment may be even more important. Sharing responsibility requires a willingness on the part of the physician to see treatment as a partnership, a relationship in which there is a division of labor and shared control.

Suzanne Miller (1979), in her exhaustive review of the data on controllability and stress, cited a number of studies showing that control over aversive stimuli increases pain tolerance—that is, having control of a painful stimulus makes it hurt less. Her theory about this has interesting implications for medicine. It is her contention that personal control is preferred because it is attributed to internal and especially stable factors: the person's own responding. This attribution provides a reliable predictor that future danger can be responded to, that maximum future danger can be kept low. According to Miller, people will prefer to control painful stimuli, but only if they believe that their controlling response is more stable than someone else's. People should yield control to someone else, Miller predicts, when they believe that the other's controlling response is more stable (reliable). This speaks directly to the division of labor in medicine. Patients' control over treatment should be encouraged, but patient confidence in the stability of the physician's skills should also be maximized in those treatment domains that require expert control by the physician.

Clinical evidence for the value of empowering patients comes from various sources. Two studies from very different settings demonstrate this effect. Nursing home residents frequently deteriorate in an environment that gives them little opportunity to make decisions and to take personal responsibility in their daily lives. Langer and Rodin (1976) gave one group of nursing home residents instructions emphasizing their responsibility for themselves. They were allowed freedom to make choices and were given responsibility for taking care of a plant. To another group it was emphasized that staff had responsibility for them, decision making was minimized, and their plant was cared for by staff. This very ordinary intervention produced a significant effect: Residents given control were rated as more alert, more active, and as having a greater sense of well-being. At 18 months, importantly, they also were more likely to be alive (Rodin & Langer, 1977).

Patient control of postsurgical pain has been enhanced by analgesic pumps, which dispense medications by the push of a button. There has been some concern that this technology might lead to overmedication and drug dependence, but several studies show otherwise. Thomas, Rose, Heath, and Flory (1993) compared patient-controlled opioid analgesia to nurse-administered analgesia in 55 adults postsurgically. Patients who were given control over the administration of pain medicine had significantly less pain, used less pain medicine overall, and had shorter hospital stays than patients who were given the drug by the nurse.

Finally, evidence for the value of enhancing patient control over some aspects of treatment comes from studies examining patient and physician communications during medical consultations and their effects on treatment outcome. A fairly robust finding is that patient involvement in the medical interview, even in the simple form of question asking, is associated with more positive treatment outcomes (Finkler & Correa, 1996). Kaplan et al. (1989) actually trained patients to take a more active role in the medical consultation by coaching them in behavioral strategies for asking questions, negotiating with their physician, focusing the interview in relevant directions, and reducing their embarrassment in discussing difficult issues. Trained patients, in contrast to controls, assumed more control during the interview. They were more successful in obtaining information from their doctors, limited "controlling" communications from their physicians, and showed greater improvement in response to treatment. As a group, these studies examing the effects of patient control over treatment are compelling, and they present a strong challenge to medicine: Find ways to maximize patient participation by making them genuine members of the treatment team.

THE ALLIANCE REVISITED

Patients bring to their encounter with the physician a set of potentialities. They are more or less hopeful, shaky or confident in their own coping capacities, and socially isolated or engaged with others in a supportive way. They are most assuredly anxious, uncertain about what is wrong and what is to be done to and for them, and at least minimally expectant of meeting up with a helpful and skillful person. Whether or not these potentialities will be actualized, whether or not the common factors will be brought to bear on recovery, depends in large part on the physician. Will the physician instill confidence and hope, allay fear and anxiety, communicate clearly and convey belief in himself or herself, the treatment, and the patient, and extend an invitation to engage in a collaboration in which responsibility for the outcome is shared appropriately? If she or he does, then a certain kind of "magic" is possible, in which nontechnical aspects of the doctor–patient encounter can increase treatment efficacy and alleviate suffering.

Jerome Frank (1982) has described this process in a unique way. By virtue of the physician's role, confidence, and status she or he has the opportunity to evoke in the patient a state of mind Frank termed *expectant faith*. Expectant faith is a complex mental state having cognitive, affective, and object–relational components. Perhaps foremost, expectant faith involves *belief* in the efficacy of the treatment. The patient is instilled with a heightened *expectancy* for relief from suffering and for specific kinds of physical change. By his or her enthusiasm, warmth, and confidence the physician promotes *hope*, which increases motivation and a perceived *sense of control*. Finally, expectant faith involves the patient's (partly transferential) sense of being in an important human relationship with a person who can be trusted. The patient views the physician as someone who is competent and who wishes to help, and who therefore can be counted on as *stable* and *predictable*. All of these elements involved in expectant faith produce affects such as relief and optimism that are incompatible with anxiety and dread.

Whether this connection between doctor and patient is referred to as a *positive alliance*, a dry clinical term, or Frank's more spiritual phrase "expectant faith," the phenomenon is the same. The physician engages the patient in a way that maximizes the curative power of the common factors. It is my contention that it is this particular "magic" that is responsible for placebo effects, for whatever value many "alternative" treatments possess and for nonspecific effects seen even in medical procedures with proven efficacy.

Having established that factors in the patient, in the physician, and in their interaction potentiate the curative effects of conventional medical treatment, however, does not explain how this occurs. The truly difficult question is, By what mechanisms do the common factors exert their influence? Given the state of the current knowledge, three general pathways are proposed.

INCREASED COMPLIANCE

Noncompliance with prescribed treatment is a significant problem in medicine, one that diminishes the efficacy of many interventions. Estimates are that about half of patients fail to follow referral advice, 75% miss follow-up appointments, and half with chronic illnesses drop out of treatment within 1 year (Sackett & Snow, 1979). And as has been shown, effective physician communication and positive alliance between patient and physician (Berg, 1987) improve compliance and may promote more healthy behaviors in general, such as exercise, proper diet, cessation of smoking, and regulation of alcohol use. In intervention studies with long follow-up assessments of patient improvement, increases in patient compliance, and pro-health behavior are always possible explanations for improvements among patients in the intervention group unless these effects are partialed out. For example, one mechanism by which group therapy may have increased longevity in Spiegel et al.'s (1989) breast cancer patients was by increasing treatment compliance, knowledge about health and behavior, and shifts toward more healthy lifestyles. Although there is reason to believe that other factors were at play, as I show next, Spiegel et al.'s data do not allow for an assessment of mechanism.

IMPROVED SUBJECTIVE SENSE OF WELL-BEING

Insofar as the doctor–patient interaction increases hope and confidence and decreases social isolation, it almost certainly alters the patient's affect state, diminishing anxiety and depression. Subjectively, the patient feels better and now, with expectations for improvement, begins to selectively attend to signs, including bodily sensations, of improved health (Lundh, 1987). This simple process may be sufficient in that percentage of cases presented to the internist or family doctor in which anxiety and depression, expressed somatically, are at the heart of what ails the patient. These processes also may account for some of the improvement of patients with chronic diseases and pain syndromes in which affect arousal, attitude, and attention to bodily states play a large part. This mechanism is a relatively straightforward, psychological one. The alliance makes people feel better. Feeling better alters the sick role and sick role behavior. This mechanism may account for the fact that strict placebos appear to produce their largest effects in patients with the highest levels of anxiety and depression (Gallimore & Turner, 1977).

DIRECT PSYCHOPHYSIOLOGICAL EFFECTS

There is mounting evidence that alterations in state of mind produce not only attentional, behavioral, and self-image shifts, but also physiological changes that may affect disease. Although we still do not know with precision, for example, how decreasing hostility aids in cardiac rehabilitation or how relaxation improves metabolism in some non-insulin-dependent diabetics, it is likely that a decrease in levels of stress hormones plays a role. Almost 100 years ago Walter Cannon described the body's fight or flight response, which he regarded as a psychophysiological adaptation to threat. As part of this response, the body secretes "stress hormones" like adrenalin and cortisol that prepare a person for action. These hormones raise blood pressure, heart rate, respiration, and blood sugar level. Under conditions of chronic threat, stress hormones can trigger a range of bodily reactions that can foster the development of atherosclerotic plaques that clog coronary arteries and may elevate blood glucose levels in some patients with diabetes. The logic that stress exacerbates some circulatory and endocrine disorders through the autonomic nervous system's fight–flight response and that reducing emotional arousal will help is seductive, but probably too simple. The relationship between the stress response and circulatory processes and glucose metabolism are quite complex and just now being understood. Until future research delineates the precise mechanisms whereby stress affects these systems, however, we can be fairly confident that decreasing anxiety and hostility in some patients with coronary artery disease and diabetes helps through psychophysiological as well as strictly psychological pathways.

By far, the most exciting and dynamic research in psychophysiology is occurring in the new field of psychoneuroimmunology. In a story that has now been told many times, a fortuitous observation by psychologist Robert Ader in the 1970s that rats that he was using in classical conditioning studies appeared to show conditioned suppression of their immune response led to experiments with Nicholas Cohen that proved just that. Shattering notions about the autonomy of the immune system, Ader and Cohen (1975) demonstrated a link between the nervous system and the immune system: Immune suppression could be learned! They had, in fact, discovered the possibility that a physiological mechanism could be established to explain the apparent effects of stress and other states of mind on cancer and infectious disease and their treatment.

Janice Kiecolt-Glaser, a psychologist, and Ronald Glaser, an immunologist, have produced an elegant and systematic program of research that has literally shaped and defined much of this new field. Recall that Cohen et al.'s (1991) landmark study had demonstrated a relationship between susceptibility to cold virus and stress. Kiecolt-Glaser and Glaser (1992) showed that this effect may be mediated by stress-induced immune suppression. Using medical students undergoing the relatively ordinary stress of academic exams, they found that such stress caused significant declines in natural killer cell activity and in gamma interferon production, as well as other important markers of immune functioning. More important, these changes appear to have clinical relevance. In a separate study, on the last day of exams medical students were given three hepatitis B inoculations. The speed and strength with which students produced an antibody response to the vaccine was related to stress, anxiety, and social support: Lower anxiety and stress and higher social support predicted faster and stronger immune responses to the virus (Glaser et al., 1992).

Because social isolation is a risk factor for disease, these researchers also have been interested in understanding the effects of social relationships on the immune response. Here they have found that lonelier medical students have poorer immune functioning and that divorce and spousal loss through death decrease immune response. Even among married individuals, the quality of their social interaction appears to make a difference in immune functioning. Laboratory studies of marital interactions in young (Kiecolt-Glaser et al., 1993; Malarkey, Kiecolt-Glaser, Pearl, & Glaser, 1994) and older couples (Kiecolt-Glaser et al., 1997) have shown that hostile, negative, and conflictual interactions produce poorer immune responses. The findings of the Kiecolt-Glaser and Glaser team dovetail nicely with those of Levy et al. (1990) who found that significant variance in natural killer cell activity in women with breast cancer could be accounted for by the extent of high-quality support by an intimate partner and by perceived social support from their doctor. Again, these researchers have begun to establish a physiological link between epidemiological findings and disease processes.

Is there evidence that immune functioning can be enhanced with psychological interventions designed to decrease stress and anxiety and to promote social connectedness? Kiecolt-Glaser and Glaser (1986) found that relaxation training, when practiced frequently, was associated with higher helper T-lymphocyte percentages in medical students undergoing exams. In a separate study, Pennebaker, Kiecolt-Glaser, and Glaser (1988) examined the effects of a very low intensity, ordinary intervention on immune functioning. Twenty-five college students were asked to keep a journal for 4 days in which they were instructed to write about traumatic events that had occurred in their lives, and they were compared with 25 students who made trivial journal entries. After only 4 days of this self-disclosure, the students who wrote about relevant, painful experiences showed better immune functioning and, during the subsequent 6 weeks, had fewer health clinic visits (Pennebaker et al., 1988). Pennebaker and Francis (1996) showed that confronting and processing emotions associated with negative life events can produce improvements in mood, immune functioning, and health. In a more serious context, melanoma patients who had increased survivability after group therapy also showed increased natural killer cell activity and a small increase in the percentage of helper/inducer T-cells at a 6-month follow-up (Fawzy et al., 1990; Fawzy et al., 1993).

Kiecolt-Glaser and Glaser as well as others in this field caution against an overly zealous response to current findings because there is still not solid evidence that laboratory-induced changes in immune functioning are sufficient to cause disease susceptibility or whether treatment-produced positive changes in immune functioning will prove to have true clinical significance. But there is reason to be hopeful. An especially interesting aspect of this research is that ordinary stresses and very mild, nonintrusive interventions produced measurable effects on immune functioning. This suggests that the kind of routine contact between patient and physician, out of which an alliance develops, may be of sufficient strength to create psychophysiological shifts in immune response. This would, of course, depend on the quality of this interaction, the extent to which it decreases anxiety, fosters hope, establishes as environment for meaningful self-disclosure, and creates a subjective experience of support for the patient. Levy et al.'s (1990) findings are worth repeating here. Natural killer cell activity in breast cancer patients was highest in those patients with social support, including the *perception of social support from their physician.*

Clinical Implications

A model is proposed here in which an optimal treatment alliance between doctor and patient actualizes common factors in such a way that they potentiate medical outcome. Increased adherence, enhanced subjective experience, and therapeutic shifts in psychophysiological functioning are three mechanisms that can account for the impact of the common factors on disease course and treatment efficacy.

We live in an age of rapid and exciting technological advancement in medicine. Developments in the brain sciences and immunology show promise in providing powerful pharmacological cures for devastating and fatal diseases like cancer and HIV, and we are all grateful for these discoveries. Yet the research covered in this chapter, more than anything else, emphasizes that medicine is far from a technological enterprise. It remains a distinctly human process, an often ambiguous encounter between two people who hope to achieve healing. Diagnosis is far from simple and straightforward, and how cure occurs is not always very clear.

Current health care models often overobjectify medical practice and disregard the "art" of cultivating and maximizing the patient–doctor relationship. In many delivery systems the patient is reduced to diagnosis X for which treatment Y is mechanically prescribed to obtain dollar amount Z from the third party. In some settings an assembly line approach to medicine has been fostered in which the physician spends less time with each patient and in which doctors, now called "providers," are regarded as interchangeable. The objectification of patients and treatment often results in decreased patient compliance, poorer outcomes, increased cost, fear of litigation, and loss of morale among doctors (F. D. Fisher & Leigh, 1990). Moreover, the idealization of drug and procedure over the power of the physician–healer overlooks what are potent sources of cure—the common factors that operate through the medium of a personal relationship between doctor and patient.

The literature on nonspecific effects points to a number of strategies with respect to the arrangement of health care systems and the conduct of individual medical practice that can optimize treatment outcomes:

- *Maximize patient control in choice of physician.* Patient choice is the first step in assuring that the treater is not just any doctor but this particular patient's doctor. This establishes the relationship as a personal one, imbued from the beginning with optimism and trust, and fosters an opportunity for a relationship that has consistency and continuity, providing opportunity for a stable alliance.
- *Develop third-party reimbursement schedules that reward, not discourage, thoroughness and patience in the clinical exam.* Empathic listening, assessment of patient attitudes, and alliance building take time. The medical interview must be thought of as more than an opportunity to review systems. It is the forum for establishing a

relationship that can enhance treatment. Somehow, we can do better than 7 minutes.

- *Preserve the physician's autonomy and status.* Current health care systems have dethroned the physician, stripping him or her of their aura and in so doing diminishing that part of healing power that comes from patient confidence, or "expectant faith." Demoralized, physicians believe less in themselves and their profession, which inhibits treatment outcomes.

- *Invite patients to be partners in the diagnostic and treatment process.* Although the physician must remain the confident leader of the treatment team, patients should be offered membership on it by being given real opportunities to understand their treatment and to take control of some of its aspects. Whenever possible, patients should be given choices about timing and form of treatment, should be actively involved in preparing for surgery or aversive diagnostic procedures, and should be encouraged to assume responsibility for pain management.

- *Assessment of affect state, life stress, and social support should occur routinely but especially in illnesses such as cancer and heart disease where the link between these factors and outcome is clear.* Anxiety and hopelessness are states of mind that the physician can begin to modify from the first moment of contact. Chronic and severe life stresses and social isolation may require referral to treatments such as psychotherapy or group therapy, which can potentiate the effects of the doctor–patient relationship.

- *Physicians should believe in the treatment, should explain it confidently, and should maximize the patient's hope and expectation of cure.* Physician belief in the treatment and the patient, and patient hope and positive expectancy, all influence outcome. In our increasingly litigious society many physicians adopt the self-protective stance, under the guise of obtaining informed consent, of explaining every possible negative outcome and side effect, and of giving the patient statistical odds of recovery, no matter how bleak. These anxious tactics can have unfortunate consequences, creating in the patient anxiety, pessimism, and fatalistic expectations. A particular patient is not a statistical average. His or her response to treatment, or even survival, may depend on maximizing rather that minimizing the effects of the common factors.

Questions From the Editors

1. Common factors clearly account for a good portion of the variance in medical treatment outcome. What are the implications of this finding for the way that we educate young physicians in medical schools and residency training programs?

Distinct from the field of psychotherapy, medicine has moved toward specific, empirically supported treatments that are based on precise knowledge of underlying disease mechanisms. The administration of insulin for diabetes is a prototypic example. And, of course, the education of physicians must be primarily concerned with these matters. Who would want a physician without the very best training in the sciences, pharmacology, neurology, and so on?

Yet family practitioners and internists all know that patient care is seldom a simple matter of prescribing precise treatments for distinct disease states. Patients present as polysymptomatic; complaints are often vague and emotional; and neat, clearly identifiable syndromes and diseases often fail to emerge from the review of systems. For example, Sobel (1995) summarized data that showed that when patients present with 1 of the 14 most common symptoms reported in outpatient clinics (e.g., headache, chest pain, fatigue), in less than 16% of the cases is a probable cause established. In these situations the physician uses intuition, follows a hunch, prescribes a "little of this and a little of that," and waits to see what happens over time. Frequently, time, reassurance, and confidence is enough, as all experienced physicians routinely see in their practices. They understand that for large numbers of their patients, particularly those whose physical complaints reveal and express emotional pain, treatment involves creating a healing, containing environment through the doctor–patient relationship.

Unfortunately, this common wisdom is poorly transmitted in formal training programs where virtually the whole of education focuses on physiology and disease, drug and procedure. Findings such as those summarized in this chapter must be a part of the basic medical school curriculum. The idea is to shape, as early as possible in the training process, the student's identity as a scientist–healer rather than as a scientist–technician. The most powerful way of doing this is through encouraging identification with a mentor. Students and residents need to watch attending and supervising physicians do doctoring, and watch this over time. What is the best way to talk to a patient? How does one reduce anxiety and instill confidence and hope? These are learned, if at all, by watching a teacher in action, not by memorizing journal findings. The practice of having students rotate through services, where they have many supervisors and where the emphasis is on technique, neglects the importance of mentoring and misses completely the importance of healing factors that are common across treatments, diseases, and subspecialties.

2. Given that common factors in medicine are largely psychological/behavioral factors, what role should psychologists play in health care?

Psychology has already established itself in its contributions to medical research and health care delivery. We are already a part of the medical research/health care team and have been for a long time. But it is my view that we still have not found our identity there, nor have we yet contributed in a way that has earned us sufficient status and influence. We remain ancillary or adjunctive and, I must say, we have ourselves to blame. By and large psychologists come into medical settings unprepared, with a limited view of their role, and with outdated models through which to shape their understanding of the mind–body interaction. Given the depth and richness of the research surveyed in this chapter, one would bet that psychologists had moved well beyond interpreting Minnesota Multiphasic Personality Inventory profiles of patients who treaters find to be "odd," unduly distraught, or grossly noncompliant. Nonetheless, in many settings we have not. We still view our role as confined to diagnosing and treating psychological problems in medical patients, rather than having a role to play in treating the primary medical complaints themselves. And this is true despite the fact that behavioral medicine as a subspecialty of clinical psychology has been around for more than 20 years.

Too often we are still viewed as being soft and simplistic in our thinking about medical matters and a little foolish in our claims about the "psychological" basis of this or that ailment and disease. We simply cannot afford any longer to behave and speak in ways that confirm that image. If we enter the health care system, then we have to be conversant. We have to be familiar with anatomy, physiology, and neurology, and we must be able to speak with authority about psychophysiology. It is no longer an interesting question to ask whether there are psychological aspects to disease and its treatment. We know that the answer is, to varying degrees, yes—the important question now is *how*. By what mechanisms do psychological factors affect biology and by what mechanisms do they affect cure? Richard Surwit's research on the psychophysiology of diabetes and Kiecolt-Glaser's work in the area of stress and immune functioning are two of the best models for psychology in the medical arena. Both are interested in questions about mechanism and therefore both speak articulately about physiology.

3. How can health care delivery systems attend to what we now know about the power of common factors in medical treatment?

Obviously, this is a difficult and complicated problem. Forces both within medicine (increasing specialization) and outside of it (the increasing control of health care delivery by third-party payers) have created an overemphasis on the technical or procedural aspects of medicine. Diagnostic related groupings (DRGs) are one example. Unlike the situation in psychology, where we are far from defining specific treatments for specific disorders, there are many standard treatment protocols in medicine. However, and this is the important point, much of patient response even to these standard treatments depends on *nonspecific* as opposed to specific effects. DRGs and managed care systems underestimate or ignore this. Nonspecific effects are maximized by the *way* the treatment is administered and by how the patient is treated in the general sense. These effects are produced by that combination of science and art that constitutes the doctor's establishment and maintenance of the treatment relationship. Therefore, we need health care systems that acknowledge that much of outcome is mediated by the common factors and that are structured accordingly. Managed care systems or preferred provider organizations, for example, would seek out members who are less compliant technicians than they are mature healers. These systems would recognize the long-term health and economic benefits of allowing for variability in the administration of treatments, maximizing physician autonomy in decision making, and increasing patient freedom in choice of their physician.

REFERENCES

Ader, R. & Cohen, N. (1975). Behaviorally conditioned immunosuppression. *Psychosomatic Medicine, 37,* 333–340.

Anda, R., Williamson, D., & Jones, D (1993). Depressed affect, hopelessness, and the risk of ischemic heart disease in a cohort of US adults. *Epidemiology, 4,* 285–294.

Auerbach, S. M. (1989). Stress management and coping research in the health care setting: A review and methodological commentary. *Journal of Consulting and Clinical Psychology, 57,* 388–395.

Bachiocco, V., Morselli, A. M., & Garli, G. (1993). Self-control expectancy and post-surgical pain: Relationships to previous pain, behavior in past pain, familial pain tolerance models, and personality. *Journal of Pain and Symptom Management, 8,* 205–214.

Bandura, A. (1977). Self-efficacy: Toward a unifying theory of behavior change. *Psychological Review, 84,* 191–215.

Barefoot, J. C., Dahlstrom, G., & Williams, R. D. (1983). Hostility, CHD incidence, and total mortality: A 25 year follow-up study of 225 physicians. *Psychosomatic Medicine, 45,* 59–63.

Barefoot, J. C., Dodge, K. A., Peterson, B. L., Dahlstrom, G., & Williams, R. B. (1989). The Cook–Medley Hostility Scale: Item content and ability to predict survival. *Psychosomatic Medicine, 51,* 46–57.

Beckman, H. B., & Frankel, R. M. (1984). The effect of physician behavior on the collection of data. *Annals of Internal Medicine, 101,* 692–696.

Beecher, H. K. (1955). The powerful placebo. *Journal of the American Medical Association, 159,* 1602–1606.

Benson, H., & McCallie, D. P. (1979). Angina pectoris and the placebo effect. *New England Journal of Medicine, 300,* 1225–1227.

Berg, M. (1987). Patient education and the physician–patient relationship. *Journal of Family Practice, 24,* 169–172.

Berkman, L. F., & Syme, S. L. (1979). Social networks, host resistance, and mortality: A nine-year follow-up study of Alameda County residents. *American Journal of Epidemiology, 109,* 186–204.

Cameron, O. (1996). Depression increases post MI mortality: How? *Psychosomatic Medicine, 58,* 111–112.

Caplan, R. B. (1969). *Psychiatry and the community in nineteenth century America: The recurring concern with the environment in the prevention and treatment of mental illness.* New York: Basic Books.

Cobb, J. M. T., & Steptoe, A. (1996). Psychological stress and susceptibility to upper respiratory tract illnesses in an adult population sample. *Psychosomatic Medicine, 58,* 404–412.

Cohen, S., Tyrrell, D. A. J., & Smith, A. P. (1991). Psychological stress and susceptibility to the common cold. *New England Journal of Medicine, 325,* 606–612.

Cohen, S., Tyrrell, D. A. J., Smith, A. P. (1993). Life events, perceived stress, negative affect, and susceptibility to the common cold. *Journal of Personality and Social Psychology, 64,* 131–140.

Cox, D. J., & Gonder-Frederick, L. (1992). Major developments in behavioral diabetes research. *Journal of Consulting and Clinical Psychology, 60,* 628–638.

Delbanco, T. (1993). The healing roles of doctor and patient. In B. Moyers (Ed.), *Healing and the mind* (pp. 7–23). New York: Doubleday.

Devine, E. C., & Cook, T. D. (1983). A meta-analysis of effects of psychoeducational interventions on length of post-surgical hospital stay. *Nursing Research, 32,* 267–274.

Doherty, W. J., & Baird, M. A. (1986). Developmental levels in family centered medical care. *Family Medicine, 25,* 337–342.

Dolce, J. J., Doleys, D. M., Raczynski, J. M., et. al. (1986). The role of self-efficacy expectancies in the prediction of pain tolerance. *Pain, 27,* 261–272.

Dykema, J., Bergbower, K., & Peterson, C. (1995). Pessimistic explanatory style, stress, and illness. *Journal of Social and Clinical Psychology, 14,* 357–371.

Egbert, L. D., Battit, E. W., Welch, C. E., & Bartless, J. K. (1964). Reduction of postoperative pain by encouragement and instruction of patients. *New England Journal of Medicine, 270,* 825–827.

Elliott, T. R., Witty, T. E., Herrick, S. M., & Hoffman, J. T. (1991). Negotiating reality after physical loss: Hope, depression, and disability. *Journal of Personality and Social Psychology, 61,* 608–613.

Everson, S. A., Goldberg, D. E., Kaplan, G. A., Cohen, R. D., Pukkala, E., Tuomilehto, J., & Salonen, J. T. (1996). Hopelessness and risk of mortality and incidence of myocardial infarction and cancer. *Psychosomatic Medicine, 58,* 113–121.

Fawzy, F. I., Kemeny, M. E., Fawzy, N. W., Elashoff, R., Morton, D., Cousins, N., & Fahey, J. L. (1990). A structured psychiatric intervention for cancer patients: Changes over time in immunological measures. *Archives of General Psychiatry, 47,* 729–735.

Fawzy, F. I., Kemeny, M. E., Fawzy, N. W., Hyun, C. S., Elashoff, R., Guthrie, D., Fahey, J. L., & Morton, D. L. (1993). Malignant melanoma: Effects of an early structured psychiatric intervention, coping, and affective state on recurrence and survival 6 years later. *Archives of General Psychiatry, 50,* 681–689.

Feldman, P. E. (1956). The personal element in psychiatric research. *American Journal of Psychology, 113,* 52–59.

Finkler, K., & Correa, M. (1996). Factors influencing patient perceived recovery in Mexico. *Social Science Medicine, 42,* 199–207.

Fisher, F. D., & Leigh, H. (1990). Models of the doctor–patient relationship. In R. Michels (Ed.), *Psychiatry, Volume 2.* Philadelphia: J. B. Lippincott.

Fisher, S., & Greenberg, R. P. (1989). A second opinion: Rethinking the claims of biological psychiatry. In S. Fisher & R.P. Greenberg (Eds.), *The limits of biological treatments for psychological distress: Comparisons with psychotherapy and placebo.* Hillsdale, NJ: Erlbaum.

Frank, J. (1982). Biofeedback and the placebo effect. *Biofeedback and Self Regulation, 7,* 449–460.

Frankel, R. M. (1995). Emotion and the physician–patient relationship. *Motivation and Emotion, 19,* 163–173.

Friedman, H. S., & Booth-Kewley, S. (1987). The disease-prone personality. *American Psychologist, 42,* 539–555.

Friedman, M., Thoreson, C. E., Gill, J. J., Ulmer, D., Powell, L. H., Price, V. A., Brown, B., Thompson, L., Rabin, D. D., Breall, W. S., Bourg, E., Levy, R., & Dixon, T. (1986). Alteration of Type A behavior and its effect on cardiac recurrences in post-myocardial infarction patients: Summary results of the Recurrent Coronary Prevention Project. *American Heart Journal, 112,* 653–665.

Frieswyk, S. H., Allen, J. G., Colson, D. B., Coyne, L., Gabbard, G. O., Horwitz, L., & Newsom, G. (1986). Therapeutic alliance: its place as process and outcome variable in dynamic psychotherapy research. *Journal of Consulting and Clinical Psychology, 54,* 32–39.

Gallimore, R. G., & Turner, J. L. (1977). Contemporary studies of placebo phenomenon. In M. E. Jarvik (Ed.), *Psychopharmacology in the practice of medicine.* New York: Appleton-Century-Crofts.

George, J. M., Scott, D. S., Turner, S. P., & Gregg, J. M. (1980). The effects of psychological factors and physical trauma on recovery from oral surgery. *Journal of Behavioral Medicine, 3,* 291–309.

Glaser, R., Kiecolt-Glaser, J. K., Bonneau, R., Malarkey, W., Kennedy, S., & Hughes, J. (1992). Stress induced modulation of the immune response to recombinant hepatitis B vaccine. *Psychosomatic Medicine, 54,* 22–29.

Goodwin, J. S., Hunt, W. C., Key, C. R., & Sarnet, J. M. (1987). The effect of marital status on stage, treatment, and survival of cancer patients. *Journal of the American Medical Association, 258,* 3125–3130.

Harkapaa, K., Jarvikoski, A., Mellin, G., Hurri, H., & Luoma, J. (1991). Health locus of control beliefs and psychological distress as predictors for treatment outcome in low-back pain patients: Results of a 3-month follow-up of a controlled intervention study. *Pain, 46,* 35–41.

Hartley, D. E., & Strupp, H. H. (1983). The therapeutic alliance: Its relationship to outcome in brief psychotherapy. In J. Masling (Ed.), *Empirical studies of psychoanalytic theories* (Vol. 1). Hillsdale, NJ: Erlbaum.

House, J. S., Landis, K. R., & Umberson, D. (1988). Social relationships and health. *Science, 241,* 540–545.

Hulka, B. S., Cassel, J. C., Kupper, L. L., & Burdette, J. A. (1976). Communication, compliance, and concordance between physicians and patients with prescribed medications. *American Journal of Public Health, 66,* 847–853.

Jamison, R. N., Parris, W. C. V., & Maxson, W. S. (1987). Psychological factors influencing recovery from outpatient surgery. *Behaviour Research and Therapy, 25,* 31–37.

Janis, I. L. (1958). *Psychological stress: Psychoanalytic and behavioral studies of surgical patients.* New York: Wiley.

Johnston, M. (1980). Anxiety in surgical patients. *Psychosomatic Medicine, 10,* 145–152.

Kaplan, S. H., Greenfield, S., & Ware, J. E. (1989). Assessing the effects of physican-patient interactions on the outcomes of chronic disease. *Medical Care, 27,* S110–S125.

Kiecolt-Glaser, J. K., & Glaser, R. (1986). Modulation of cellular immunity in medical students. *Journal of Behavioral Medicine, 9,* 5–21.

Kiecolt-Glaser, J. K., & Glaser, R. (1992). Psychoneuroimmunology: Can psychological interventions modulate immunity. *Journal of Consulting and Clinical Psychology, 60,* 569–575.

Kiecolt-Glaser, J. K., & Glaser, R. (1995). Psychoneuroimmunology and health consequences: Data and shared mechanisms. *Psychosomatic Medicine, 57,* 269–274.

Kiecolt-Glaser, J. K., Glaser, R., Cacioppo, J. T., MacCallum, R. C., Snydersmith, M. A., Cheongtag, K., & Malarkey, W. B. (1997). Marital conflict in older adults: Endocrinological and immunological correlates. *Psychosomatic Medicine, 59,* 339–349.

Kiecolt-Glaser, J. K., Malarkey, W. B., Chee, M. A., Newton, T., Cacioppo, J. T., Mao, H. Y., & Glaser, R. (1993). Negative behavior during marital conflict is associated with immunological down-regulation. *Psychosomatic Medicine, 55,* 395–409.

Kluger, J. (1997, May 12). Mr. Natural: Millions of Americans swear by the alternative medicine of Dr. Andrew Weil. But is anybody really getting better? *Time,* pp. 68–75.

Krupnick, J. L., Sotsky, S. M., Simmens, S., Moyer, J., Elkin, I., Watkins, J., & Pilkonis, P. A. (1996). The role of the therapeutic alliance in psychotherapy and pharmacotherapy outcome: Findings from the National Institute of Mental Health Treatment of Depression Collaborative Research Program. *Journal of Consulting and Clinical Psychology, 64,* 532–539.

Langer, E. J., & Rodin, J. (1976). The effects of choice and enhanced personal responsibility for the aged: A field experiment in an institutional setting. *Journal of Personality and Social Psychology, 34,* 191–198.

Learman, L. A., Avorn, J., Everitt, D. E., & Rosenthal, R. (1990). Pygmalion in the nursing home: The effects of caregiver expectations on patient outcomes. *Journal of the American Geriatrics Society, 38,* 797–803.

Leserman, J., Petitto, J. M., Perkins, D. O., Folds, J. D., Golden, R. N., & Evans, D. L. (1997). Severe stress, depressive symptoms, and changes in lymphocyte subsets in human immunodeficiency virus-infected men. *American Journal of Psychiatry, 54,* 279–285.

Levy, S. M., Herberman, R. B., Maluish, A., et. al. (1985). Prognostic risk assessments in primary breast cancer by behavioral and immunological parameters. *Health Psychology, 4,* 99–113.

Levy, S. M., Herberman, R. B., Whiteside, T., Schlien, B., & Lippman, M. (1990). Perceived social support and tumor estrogen/progesterone receptor status as predictors of natural killer cell activity in breast cancer patients. *Psychosomatic Medicine, 52,* 73–85.

Levy, S. M., Lee, J., Bagley, C., & Lippman, M. (1988). Survival hazards analysis in first recurrent breast cancer patients: Seven year follow-up. *Psychosomatic Medicine, 50,* 520–528.

Lin, E. H., & Peterson, C. (1990). Pessimistic explanatory style and response to illness. *Behaviour Research and Therapy, 28,* 243–248.

Lundh, L.-G. (1987). Placebo, belief, and health: A cognitive–emotional model. Scandinavian *Journal of Psychology, 28,* 128–143.

Luparello, T. J., Leist, N., Lourie, C. H., & Sweet, P. (1970). The interaction of physiologic stimuli and pharmacologic agents on airway reactivity in asthmatic subjects. *Psychosomatic Medicine, 32,* 509–513.

Malarkey, W., Kiecolt-Glaser, J. K., Pearl, D., & Glaser, R. (1994). Hostile behavior during marital conflict alters pituitary and adrenal hormones. *Psychosomatic Medicine, 56,* 41–51.

Manning, M. M., & Wright, T. L. (1983). Self-efficacy expectations, outcome expectancies, and the persistence of pain control in childbirth. *Journal of Personality and Social Psychology, 45,* 421–431.

Marvel, M. K., Schilling, R., Doherty, W. J., & Baird, M. A. (1994). Levels of physician involvement with patients and their families: A model for teaching and research. *Journal of Family Practice, 39,* 535–541.

Miller, S. D. (1979). Controllability and human stress: Method, evidence, and theory. *Behaviour Research and Therapy, 17,* 287–304.

Miller, S. D., Duncan, B. L., & Hubble, M. A. (1997). *Escape from Babel: Toward a unifying language for psychotherapy practice.* New York: W. W. Norton & Company.

Oxman, T. E., Freeman, D. H., & Manheimer, E. D. (1995). Lack of social participation or religious strength and comfort as risk factors for death after cardiac surgery in the elderly. *Psychosomatic Medicine, 57,* 5–15.

Parle, M., Maguire, P., & Heaven, C. (1997). The development of a training model to improve health professionals' skills, self-efficacy and outcome expectancies when communicating with cancer patients. *Social Science Medicine, 44,* 231–240.

Pennebaker, J. W., & Francis, M. E. (1996). Cognitive, emotional, and language processes in disclosure. *Cognition and Emotion, 10,* 601–626.

Pennebaker, J. W., Kiecolt-Glaser, J. K., & Glaser, R. (1988). Disclosure of trauma and immune function: Health implications for psychotherapy. *Journal of Consulting and Clinical Psychology, 56,* 239–245.

Peterson, C. (1988). Explanatory style as a risk factor for illness. *Cognitive Therapy and Research, 12,* 119–132.

Peterson, C., Seligman, M. E. P., & Vaillant, G. E. (1988). Pessimistic explanatory style as a risk factor for physical illness: A thirty-five year longitudinal study. *Journal of Personality and Social Psychology, 55,* 23–27.

Pettingale, K. W., Morris, T., Greer, S., & Haybittle, J. L. (1985). Mental attitudes to cancer: An additional prognostic factor. *Lancet, 3,* 750.

Roberts, A. H., Kewman, D. G., Mercier, L., & Hovell, M. (1993). The power of nonspecific effects in healing: Implications for psychosocial and biological treatments. *Clinical Psychology Review, 13,* 375–391.

Rodin, J., & Langer, E. J. (1977). Long term effects of a control-relevant intervention with the institutionalized aged. *Journal of Personality and Social Psychology, 35,* 897–902.

Sackett, D. L., & Snow, J. C. (1979). The magnitude of compliance and noncompliance. In R. B. Haynes, D. W. Taylor, & D. L. Sackett (Eds.), *Compliance for health care.* Baltimore: Johns Hopkins University Press.

Shapiro, A. K., & Morris, L. A. (1978). Placebo effects in medical and psychological therapies. In S. L. Garfield & A. E. Bergin (Eds.), *Handbook of psychotherapy and behavior change: An empirical analysis* (pp. 369–410). New York: Wiley.

Smith, R. C., Lyles, J. S., Mettler, J. A., & Marshall, A. A. (1995). A strategy for improving patient satisfaction by the intensive training of residents in psychosocial medicine: A controlled, randomized study. *Academic Medicine, 70,* 729–732.

Sobel, D. S. (1995). Rethinking medicine: Improving health outcomes with cost-effective psychosocial interventions. *Psychosomatic Medicine, 57,* 234–244.

Spiegel, D., Bloom, J. R., Kraemer, H. C., & Gottheil, E. (1989). Effect of psychosocial treatment on the survival of patients with metastatic breast cancer. *Lancet, 2,* 888–891.

Stanton, A. L. (1987). Determinants of adherence to medical regimens by hypertensive patients. *Journal of Behavioral Medicine, 4,* 377–394.

Stein, M., Miller, A. H., & Trestman, R. L. (1991). Depression, the immune system, and health and illness. *Archives of General Psychiatry, 48,* 171–177.

Surwit, R. S., Feinglos, M. N., & Scovern, A. W. (1983). Diabetes and behavior: A paradigm for health psychology. *American Psychologist, 38,* 255–262.

Surwit, R. S., Schneider, M. S., & Feinglos, M. N. (1992). Stress and diabetes mellitus. *Diabetes Care, 15,* 1413–1422.

Theorell, T., Blomkvist, V., Johsson, H., Schulman, S., Berntop, E., & Stigindal, L. (1995). Social support and the development of immune functions in human immunodeficiency virus infection. *Psychosomatic Medicine, 57,* 32–36.

Thomas, V. J., Rose, F. D., Heath, M. L., & Flory, P. (1993). A multidimensional comparison of nurse and patient controlled analgesia in the management of acute post-surgical pain. *Medical Science Research, 21,* 379–381.

Toomey, T. C., Mann, J. D., & Thompson-Pope, S. (1991). Relationship between perceived self-control of pain, pain description and functioning. *Pain, 45,* 129–133.

Uhlenhuth, E. H., Canter, A., Neustadt, J. O., & Payson, H. E. (1959). The relief of anxiety with meprobamate, phenobarbital, and placebo. *American Journal of Psychiatry, 115,* 905–910.

Wallace, L. M. (1985). Surgical patients' expectations of pain and discomfort: Does accuracy of expectations minimize post-surgical pain and distress? *Pain, 22,* 363–373.

Williams, R. D., Barefoot, J. C., Califf, R. M., Haney, T. L., Saunders, W. B., Pryor, D. B., Hlatky, M. A., Siegler, I. C., & Mark, D. B. (1992). Prognostic importance of social and economic resources among medically treated patients with angio-graphically documented coronary heart disease. *Journal of the American Medical Association, 267,* 520–524.

Wilson, J. F. (1981). Behavioral preparations for surgery: Benefit or harm. *Journal of Behavioral Medicine, 4,* 79–102.

Winefield, H. R., Murrell, T. G., & Clifford, J. (1995). Process and outcomes in general practice consultations: Problems in defining high quality care. *Social Science Medicine, 41,* 969–975.

Roger P. Greenberg

Common Psychosocial Factors in Psychiatric Drug Therapy | 10

One should treat as many patients as possible with
a new drug while it still has the power to heal.

—SIR WILLIAM OSLER (1849–1919)

T he history of medicine is marked by a shift from treatments
directed at the patient as a whole person to a quest for
focused cures tied to specific organs. Before the 19th century, prescribed remedies were often based on frightening,
even assaultive attempts to restore health by bringing supposed body systems into better balance. In this vein, global
techniques such as bloodletting and purging were used, as
physicians tried to reinstate equilibrium in the postulated
body humors (i.e., yellow bile, black bile, blood, and
phlegm). Hoped-for gains were assumed to result from the
pain inflicted, and solutions to medical problems had all the
sophistication of kicking a television set to bring back a clear
picture.

Initially, medication treatments also lacked specificity.
Not until the end of the 19th century, with the advent of
the germ theory of disease, did drugs aimed at circumscribed illnesses arrive. Tenner (1996) described the trends
(and associated problems) in the development of medical
technology. Regarding drugs, he stated

> In the early nineteenth century, doctors classified
> drugs by their effect on the whole body. Terms like
> "cathartic," "diuretic," and "narcotic" survive from
> this vocabulary. Dosage depended not only on the
> drug's usual effects but on the patient's constitution

and even the local climate. Prescribing a single drug uniquely for a certain condition was the mark of a quack. Specific drugs were slow to arrive. (Tenner, 1996, pp. 33–34)

Psychological distress has, of course, fostered a parallel search to match precisely delineated categories of psychiatric disorder with exact therapies. Within the treatment arsenal for emotional problems, drugs have perhaps emerged as the approach most thought of as having pinpointed effects. Each drug, because of its specific chemical components, is designed to produce a unique and predictable effect on the target symptoms. Specificity of biological action is the underlying treatment tenet. Psychosocial factors that might explain the results across different treatments are largely ignored. From a strict biological perspective, potential common factors, such as the nature of the therapeutic relationship or the patient's dominant personality traits, are considered nuisance variables that only hamper the study of the "presumed real treatments," the drugs.

For all that, how successful and devoid of common factors are biological approaches to psychological distress? This is a question that I, along with my colleague Seymour Fisher[1] and others, have considered in two books and a series of articles published over more than a decade (e.g., Fisher & Greenberg, 1989, 1993, 1997b; R. P. Greenberg, Bornstein, Greenberg, & Fisher, 1992; R. P. Greenberg, Bornstein, Zborowski, Fisher, & Greenberg, 1994; R. P. Greenberg & Fisher, 1994). Our examination of the research has been eye-opening for us. Time and again we have been struck by how important common factors are, even with psychoactive drug treatment. We have been impressed by the inevitability of psychosocial influences on biological outcomes. This chapter reviews much of what we have uncovered and highlights why we have come to see common factors (i.e., those not directly deriving from chemical composition) as important for psychoactive drug treatments.

Research Designs and Placebo Effects

Claims regarding the unique potency of psychoactive (and other) drugs rest on the ability to show that chemically active agents produce

---

[1]In memory of Seymour Fisher for his inspiration and dedication to knowledge based on research evidence.

outcomes that are significantly better than those produced by chemically inert substances (i.e., placebos). The core hypothesis for all drug trials is that the active substance will demonstrate therapeutic power superior to the placebo. If this result appears, it is concluded to be due to the potency of the active biological ingredients that cannot be matched by the placebo. The benefits of active drugs are attributed to biochemical components, whereas any curative potential shown by the placebo is credited to nonbiological, psychological factors, such as expectancy or suggestibility.

From a biological vantage point, change arising from psychological common factors represents noise in the system that needs to be separated from the more biologically specific treatment—medication, "the brew that is true." Practitioners have long debated the need to separate specific from nonspecific (i.e., drug-induced from psychological) sources of treatment gain. Shepherd (1993) placed the debate in historical perspective and noted that medicine's obsession with specificity can be traced back to ancient Greece. Two different views of disease emerge. First is the Platonic or "ontological," in which disease is seen as an independent, self-sufficient entity (e.g., a diagnostic category) possessing a natural history of its own. The second is the Hippocratic, which emphasizes the patient's individual history. The ontological viewpoint is associated with the use of mechanistic explanations for illness, with the body viewed as a machine. The contrasting perspective looks at disease (and treatment outcomes) more broadly as evolving from the overall conditions existing in a person's life. These disparate frames of reference have waxed and waned in their ascendancy, with interpretive disputes revolving around whether the body (e.g., bacteriological specificity) or the mind (e.g., psychosomatics) is most responsible for the patient's condition. The forced dichotomous perspective prompts a question sometimes attributed to the noted observer of the human condition Woody Allen: If the body is separate from the mind, which one should I want?

In any case, because of a strong interest in establishing the effectiveness of pure biological therapies, unblemished by psychological factors, outcomes with active drugs are routinely compared with outcomes attained by biochemically inert substances, placebos. As a result, a sizable literature on the placebo effect has arisen and has been analyzed by a host of investigators (e.g., Beecher, 1955; Brody, 1977; Dinnerstein, Lowenthal, & Blitz, 1966–1967; Evans, 1974; Fisher & Greenberg, 1997a; Frank, 1973; Grunbaum, 1981, 1985; Jospe, 1978; Ross & Buckalew, 1983; A.K. Shapiro, 1968; White, Tursky, & Schwartz, 1985). On the surface, these discussions have focused on the nature of the placebo and factors that might augment or diminish its powers. Frequently, the real motivation for investigating placebos in psychiatric research has been to create an experimental design that guarantees only specific biological factors will account for the cures. In reading this literature, however, it is hard not to be impressed with the power of the placebo and the continuing struggle to disentangle psychoactive drug from placebo effects. Placebos have been shown to have wide-ranging and surprising potency. Moreover, for conditions such as depression, the therapeutic impact of placebos approaches the level reached by psychoactive drugs (e.g., R. P. Greenberg & Fisher, 1989, 1997). Despite lengthy debates about what makes each work, investigators have yet to reach a consensus about how to differentiate cleanly active drug from placebo effects at a theoretical level (Brody, 1977, 1985; Grunbaum, 1981, 1985; A.P. Shapiro & Morris, 1978).

Even the idea that psychoactive drugs produce their effects through biological mechanisms while psychological approaches do not is found wanting. As Fisher and Greenberg (1997b) noted, all effects occur in tissue, and one type is no more biologically real than the other. Thus, one can point to evidence that placebo effects are physiologically mediated (e.g., by changes in endorphin levels; Evans, 1985) or that successful psychotherapeutic treatment produces biochemical changes just as drugs do. For example, Baxter and his colleagues (1992) demonstrated equivalent brain imagery changes in successful psychotherapeutic and drug treatments for obsessive–compulsive disorder. Talking treatment proved to be as facilitative of biological alteration (on brain imagery changes) as did the specific drug therapy. In short, although medications provide specificity of ingredients that cannot be matched by psychosocial approaches, treatment outcomes may overlap to the point of being indistinguishable, even on biological measures.

Psychoactive Drug Malleability

The scientific literature often reflects an overstated certainty about the unique value of psychoactive drugs. This is accompanied by the belief that a pill's intrinsic potency lies essentially in its chemical makeup. Elsewhere we have detailed many ways in which psychoactive drug effects can be influenced by factors wholly unrelated to a medication's biochemical ingredients (Fisher & Greenberg, 1997a). Largely forgotten is a sizable body of research published in the 1950s and 1960s, before the appropriately heightened concern about informed consent, demonstrating a relatively easy manipulation of chemical compound influence on human feelings and behaviors by a variety of situational and state variables. More recent literature reaffirms that response to psychoactive agents can be modified by an array of (frequently psychosocial) factors. These results suggest that rather than being solely, or even predominantly, biochemically determined, a drug's impact can be restructured in many ways. Medication response can be readily altered by who delivers the drug, how its properties arc described, the degree of familiarity with the setting in which it is presented, and the ethnic identity or socioeconomic status of the person ingesting it.

Anecdotal reports suggesting that various psychosocial factors can change response to psychoactive drugs began appearing in the 1950s as these drugs were introduced in a variety of treatment settings (e.g., Leveton, 1958; Linn, 1959; Sabshin & Ramot, 1956). For example, drug response could be influenced by the attitudes of the health care professionals working with the patients, the differences in atmospheres of the wards on which patients were housed, the patient's personality features, and the patient's previous drug experience. Considerable doubt was voiced about the true potency of psychoactive drugs during this initial introductory period. Psychodynamic clinicians were particularly skeptical about the merits of drug treatments and offered a challenge by drawing attention to the psychosocial forces that might affect the drug experience. Their resistance is represented in the provocative comments of Leveton (1958):

> The study of mood-changing drugs and their effect on human beings, embraces, in its complexity, all that is known about man in health and sickness, as an individual, a species, and a social being. He is not a preparation suspended in isotonic saline that awaits the careful variation of a single determinant, and then responds in simple fashion to drugs introduced into the system. A group of chronic mental patients from a relatively isolated ward with little professional supervision who are brought to a research ward staffed by interested, enthusiastic, and hopeful investigators and given a mood-changing drug, will be influenced by many factors in addition to the specific pharmacodynamic effects of the medication. (p. 232)

Presently, the suspicious attitude of the 1950s and 1960s has been largely replaced by widespread and uncritical acceptance of psychiatric drugs as simple, direct solutions to emotional discomfort. Notwithstanding, research continues to confirm that psychosocial conditions significantly affect responsivity to psychiatric drugs. Simply put, drug treatment success is not as insulated from psychosocial factors as many have assumed. In the following sections, I provide general and specific findings to illustrate this point.

Site Effects

Studies routinely differ in reporting the apparent level of effectiveness of the same drug. This observation frequently occurs in drug trials taking place in multiple centers, although the differences are sometimes obscured when data are pooled. It is common, however, to discover that the same drug prescribed to patients defined in the same way produces much better outcomes at some locales than it does at others. I will briefly describe just three of the numerous examples of outcome variability as a consequence of locale.

Greenblatt, Grosser, and Wechsler (1964) assessed the improvement rates achieved by three antidepressant drugs and a placebo at three different hospitals. No matter which treatment was monitored, the rank order of effectiveness remained the same. One hospital consistently delivered the highest levels of effectiveness, whereas another delivered the lowest. Imipramine proved to be more than twice as effective in promoting improvement at the most successful site as it was at the least effective hospital (67% vs. 31%).

A parallel set of results comes from a study comparing imipramine, alprazolam, and placebo as treatments for depression at five different centers (Feighner, Aden, Fabre, Rickels, & Smith, 1983). When the data were pooled, the drugs were declared to be more effective than placebos. Even so, examining the results for each center individually revealed marked variability. Following 6 weeks of treatment, differences emerged from the centers on six outcome measures. Each of the measures of outcome showed imipramine to be equivalent to placebo in at least two of the five centers. Two centers found a difference favoring imipramine on only 1 of 12 comparisons. A comparable 1 out of 12 comparisons favored placebos.

Another example of site variability is presented by Uhlenhuth, Rickels, Fisher, Park, Lipman, and Mock (1966), who contrasted the effects of meprobamate on symptom relief in "psychoneurotic outpatients" at three different clinical settings. Again, outcome was related to site, not medication usage. Struck by this result, Uhlenhuth et al. stated, "It is important to recognize that variations in results among the three clinics in this study came about in spite of painstaking effort to assure uniform experimental conditions" (p. 413).

Although the reported differences among sites is clear, rarely is it possible to account for the specific source of the discrepancies. Investigators conjecture about possible variations in personnel attitudes or selectivity of samples but are typically unable to muster data permitting exact explanations. For our purposes, the most that can be said is that the same drug delivered in comparable dosages to ostensibly similar patients produces diverse levels of effect as a consequence of conditions peculiar to each treatment center.

Course differences in medication potency have been attributed to variables like "ward atmosphere," "social settings," and "situational familiarity." In a study of schizophrenic patients treated with phenothiazines and hospitalized on 12 wards in four hospitals, improvements were significantly related to measures of ward attributes (e.g., patient-to-staff ratios and level of social contact; Kellam, Goldberg, Schooler, Berman, & Shmelzer, 1967). Similar drug effect variations associated with ward differences are documented in an array of studies reviewed by Honigfeld (1964). He also pointed to evidence that drug power might be different in clinical and research settings as well as in situations where medications are administered individually instead of in groups. A related type of finding showed differential success of phenothiazine treatments for patients with schizophrenia tied to whether they were given the chance to describe body complaints arising from the drugs they were taking (Freedman, Engelhardt, Mann, Margolis, & London, 1965).

Context has also proved to influence how drugs like morphine, alcohol, LSD, and cocaine are experienced. Reports show morphine controls pain more effectively in a "real life" than in a research setting (Beecher, 1960), alcohol promotes more sexual fantasies at a party than in a classroom (McClelland, 1985), and drinking in a group is more likely to promote feelings of happiness than drinking alone (Pliner & Cappell, 1974). Similarly, feelings associated with LSD (Goldstein, Searle, & Schmike, 1960) and cocaine (Van Dyke, Ungerer, Jatlow, Barash, & Byck, 1982) seem more intense in a naturalistic social scene than in a laboratory.

This section has presented evidence of a global connection between settings and drug effects. I provide greater specificity in tracing the connection between psychosocial factors and outcome in the material that follows.

The Treatment Relationship

The relationship factor has garnered major attention in discussions of verbal treatments for emotional problems. Until recently, though, it has not been the primary object of much systematic research with psychoactive drug treatments. It is informative to highlight the evidence associating therapeutic relationship and psychotherapy outcome as an introduction to the issue of relationship effects on psychoactive drug response.

The empirical literature dealing with psychotherapy outcome reveals general benefits from treatment. Yet differences in outcome among specific brands of psychotherapy have typically not emerged. The finding of psychotherapy outcome equivalence among approaches was anticipated as early as 1936, by Rosenzweig, and later empirically documented in a review by Luborsky, Singer, and Luborsky (1975). Their classic works were subtitled with the Dodo bird's pronouncement in *Alice's Adventures in Wonderland* (Carroll, 1865/1962), "Everybody has won and all must have prizes." Several subsequent reviews of the research evidence have also struggled with the finding of seeming parity of benefits accruing from a variety of techniques (e.g., M. L. Smith, Glass, & Miller, 1980; Stiles, Shapiro, & Elliot, 1986; Stubbs & Bozarth, 1994).

Probably the most prominent explanation presented for similar outcomes has been the notion that common therapeutic factors cut across the different approaches (e.g., Luborsky et al., 1993; Stiles et al., 1986; Stubbs & Bozarth, 1994). Such factors are believed to be potent enough to override components specific to any individual approach. The common ingredient most often addressed in psychotherapy studies has been the nature of the therapist–patient relationship. Research on different types of verbal psychotherapy documents that the level of collaboration developed between clinician and patient usually predicts how successful the treatment will turn out to be (e.g., Castonguay, Wiser, Raue, Hayes, & Goldfried, 1993; Fisher & Greenberg, 1996; Friewsyck et al., 1986; Horvath & Symonds, 1991; Luborsky & Auerbach, 1985; Safran & Wallner, 1991). Thus, the therapeutic alliance, broadly defined as the collaborative bond between patient and therapist, has been described by psychotherapy researchers as "the most promising of the common elements for future investigation" (Bordin, 1976) and "the quintessential, integrative variable" (Wolfe & Goldfried, 1988) because of its influence across an array of different talking treatments.

By contrast, researchers interested in psychiatric drugs seem to have tried to eradicate or minimize the possible influence of interpersonal factors as explanations for drug results. Although some investigators have suggested that factors other than a drug's biochemical properties, such as the doctor–patient bond, might sway outcomes with either active medications or placebos (e.g., Downing & Rickels, 1978), the therapeutic relationship has usually been viewed by drug researchers more as an instrument affecting compliance than as a principal cause of change (Docherty & Feister, 1985).

During the 1990s, data coming from the Treatment of Depression Collaborative Research Program (TDCRP), sponsored by the National Institute of Mental Health, have revealed that interpersonal factors can be important for securing a positive result, even when drugs are the primary treatment. The design of the TDCRP involved the random assignment at three different sites of 250 unipolar depressed patients to four treatment conditions: cognitive–behavioral therapy, interpersonal psychotherapy, imipramine plus clinical management, and a pill-placebo plus clinical management control condition. After 16 weeks, all the study treatment conditions, including placebo plus clinical management, led to significant and equivalent benefits for patients (Elkin et al., 1989; Ogles, Lambert, & Sawyer, 1995). There was some suggestion, as a result of secondary analyses, that the drug-treated and interpersonal psychotherapy groups attained better outcomes than did the placebo-treated group, but only with the most severely depressed patients.

With the finding of minimal outcome differences among treatment groups as background, investigators turned their attention to variables that might account for some patients' doing better than others in this elaborate and complex project. The doctor–patient relationship became the special focus for several studies because of its previously discovered significance for psychotherapy outcome. For this chapter, however, the impact of the relationship on the antidepressant (imipramine) group is of special import. In brief, the pertinent questions are: Did the doctor–patient relationship turn out to play a significant role in the improvement of depressed patients assigned to the various treatment groups? Was the quality of the doctor–patient relationship any less important when the treatment was antidepressant drugs than when it was psychotherapy?

It turns out that the interpersonal aspect of the doctor–patient relationship was indeed a very important factor in determining outcome. It was just as important for patients treated with drugs as it was for those receiving psychotherapy. Blatt, Zuroff, Quinlan, and Pilkonis (1996) analyzed patient responses to a questionnaire designed to measure their perception of the therapeutic relationship. Ratings obtained at the end of the second session were predictive of outcome. The more the clinician was perceived as empathic, caring, open, and sincere, the better the outcome at termination. Previously, it had been shown that patients fared worse as their level of perfectionism increased (Sotsky et al., 1991). Blatt and his colleagues demonstrated that a positive treatment relationship significantly reduced the negative effects of perfectionism, particularly at moderate levels of perfectionism. Overall, the authors concluded that clinical improvement was minimally related to the type of treatment received, but substantially determined by the quality of therapeutic relationship that patients experienced.

Another study examining the importance of the doctor–patient relationship for treatment outcomes of depressed patients in the TDCRP is presented by Krupnick et al. (1996). Data on the relationship were derived from ratings made on a standardized scale of therapeutic alliance (defined broadly as the collaborative bond between therapist and patient). Four independent clinical raters scored videotapes of the early, middle, and late complete therapy sessions for 225 cases. Ratings were then related to standard measures of treatment outcome. This investigation is the largest study of therapeutic alliance and outcome ever conducted.

Results showed that the alliance had a significant and "very large effect" on outcome. The effect was equally visible across both drug and nondrug treatment modalities with no differences among treatments in the association between doctor–patient relationship and outcome. That the results applied as much to treatment with drugs as to psychotherapy treatment surprised the researchers. They had originally hypothesized that the therapeutic alliance would be significantly more important for psychotherapy than pharmacotherapy groups. Reflecting on the discovery of a powerful association between alliance and outcome in pharmacotherapy in both the antidepressant and placebo conditions, the authors commented:

> What this finding suggests is that the therapeutic alliance may strongly influence the placebo response embedded in pharmacotherapy as a nonspecific factor above and beyond the specific pharmacologic action of the drug. The therapeutic alliance may help to create a "holding" environment in which the acceptance of taking a drug may be enhanced and permit concerns to be addressed and worked through within the context of a supportive and collaborative relationship. . . . The variability of the doctor–patient relationship may account for the considerable variability in placebo and active drug response rates across studies of tricyclic antidepressants. . . . Thus, the role that the therapeutic alliance plays in affecting outcome extends not only beyond psychodynamic psychotherapy to cognitive behavior therapy, but also beyond psychotherapy itself, with implications for the way in which pharmacotherapy is conceptualized and practiced. (Krupnick et al., 1996, p. 537)

An additional set of important results stemming from the TDCRP comes from the work of Blatt, Sanislow, Zuroff, and Pilkonis (1996). These researchers were interested in trying to identify characteristics of more effective therapists in the project. This was accomplished by dividing the 28 participating clinicians into three levels of therapeutic effectiveness on the basis of how well their patients did. Efficacy was defined by the average therapeutic gain achieved by patients over five measures of outcome.

The salient findings were that the most effective clinicians had a psychological rather than a biological orientation to the treatment of depressed outpatients, they placed less emphasis on medication per se in their usual clinical practices, and they expected outpatient treatment for depression to take longer than did moderately and less effective clinicians. These features identified the most successful clinicians in the TDCRP, no matter which of the therapy modalities they were assigned to deliver. Thus, they were as characteristic of clinicians who successfully used drugs as of treaters providing successful psychody-namic, cognitive–behavioral, or even placebo therapies.

Again, as with the other results described in this section, thera-peutic outcome appears to be most influenced by the interpersonal dimensions of the treatment process. No specific factors associated with either drug or psychotherapy treatments proved to be more important than the patient and practitioner personal qualities that interact to establish an effective therapeutic relationship. As Rickels (1968) suggested decades ago, there is more to practicing effective pharmacotherapy than simply choosing an appropriate drug and dosage level.

The Drug Advocacy Stance of the Provider

Researchers have been interested in the degree to which psychoactive drug response might be influenced by the clinician's feelings about the treatment being provided. Some of the studies addressing this issue have employed a double-blind design (in which neither patient nor clinician is informed about whether an active drug or placebo is being delivered), whereas others have not. Research has shown that biasing of results increases as blindness decreases (Fisher & Greenberg, 1989). Therefore, only studies employing double-blind controls will be cited in this section.

Do positive or negative clinician attitudes toward the supplied psychoactive drug make a difference for outcome? Research addressing this issue has generally taken one or two forms: either measuring the clinician's attitudes during treatment and calculating their relationship with effectiveness, or having clinicians playact divergent attitudes and assessing the impact on outcome.

Several studies concentrating on the drug administrator's natural attitudes have shown such attitudes can affect therapeutic outcome. Findings reveal, for instance, that physicians who were more invested in and favorable toward treating "neurotic outpatients" with pheno-barbital or diazepam obtained significantly better symptomatic improvements when treating patients with these substances than those who were less positively inclined (Downing, Rickels, & Dreesman, 1973). Conversely, drug-administering nurses achieved less improvement with patients on tranquilizers when they had negative attitudes about treating them with drugs (Baker & Thorpe, 1957). Similarly, Wheatley (1967) demonstrated that antianxiety medications worked better when physicians had positive expectations about the outcome of the treatment. He was not able to show such a relationship between efficacy and attitude in a couple of samples of depressed patients. Another report examined results with antianxiety agents delivered by two psychiatrists who had divergent attitudes about the merits of these drugs (Uhlenhuth, Canter, Neustadt, & Payson, 1957). The active drugs were superior to placebo, but only when administered by the psychiatrist with a favorable drug attitude.

The few double-blind studies employing drug administrators who role-played their attitudes produced results grossly consistent with the reports based on naturally occurring feelings. In one investigation, antianxiety drugs delivered to anxious patients were more potent when physicians acted enthusiastically. In fact, when they acted skeptically, drugs were no more effective than placebo (Fisher et al., 1964). In another study conducted at three sites, physicians acting enthusiastically again achieved better results with antianxiety agents than placebo (Uhlenhuth et al., 1966). This finding, however, appeared at only one of the sites. At the other two, it was not replicated. There was even a tendency for the results to be reversed. The authors speculated that socioeconomic differences in the samples at the various centers might have led to the discrepancy.

In reviewing studies such as those described, Downing and Rickels (1978) acknowledged that physician attitudes can often influence outcome. However, the direction and stability of the impact are not always predictable. Complexities arise because other variables, besides the orientation of the person administering drugs, also exert an impact. These may include patient characteristics, the nature of the clinical site, or even, as von Kerekjarto (1966) reported, the gender of the examiner. Another potentially complicating factor is suggested by the finding that positive physician attitudes toward drugs may translate into prescribing larger doses (e.g., Downing & Rickels, 1978; Haefner, Sacks, & Mason, 1960). Therefore, in situations where the dosage level is not controlled, the apparent relationship between psychiatric enthusiasm and therapeutic outcome might be a direct function of differences in dosage and only an indirect result of attitude. Overall, granting the possibility that several psychosocial factors may interact to modify drug response in any particular case, it is reasonable to conclude from the evidence that efficacy can be augmented by an enthusiastic drug provider.

The placebo literature also affirms that healing effectiveness is increased by clinician-radiated confidence. Several relevant findings are summarized by A. K. Shapiro (1964) with the following statement: "Placebo effectiveness may decrease from 70 to 25 percent when attitudes toward treatment change from positive to negative" (p. 78). An analogous comment is provided by Gryll and Katahn (1978) following a description of various ways to present placebos as pain-relieving drugs: "The results agree with and extend previous findings . . . that a physician's warm, supportive attitude can potentiate the occurrence of placebo effects" (p. 259).

Interesting examples of the therapeutic potency that enthusiasm can generate are provided by the work of Roberts (1994, 1995). He conjectured that the real power of unbridled zeal might be muted in studies using a double-blind, placebo controlled design. In such experimental contexts, he reasoned, patients and clinicians might have more modest expectations about the success of any particular therapy because of their awareness that the treatment being delivered could be a placebo. By contrast, the impact of enthusiasm is likely to be amplified in the typical real-life clinical situation in which there is less reason to doubt that the treatment will be successful. Roberts assembled a list of eventually discarded treatments that had initially shown high levels of success, approximately 70% improvement. Only later when these treatments (such as "glomectomy" for asthma or "gastric freezing" for duodenal ulcers) were subjected to more rigorous double-blind appraisals did it become apparent that effectiveness was no greater than with placebo. Roberts concluded that early exuberance about new treatments provides a glimpse of maximum placebo potential.

Studies by Kirsch and Weixel (1988) and Kirsch and Rosadino (1993) support the idea that the double-blind dilutes the placebo effect. In these studies, placebos were presented to participants as caffeine under one of two different conditions: a double-blind design (where participants believed they might receive a placebo instead of caffeine) and a condition where participants were led to believe they could only receive caffeine (with no possibility of a placebo). All participants received placebo. As anticipated, placebo effects were greater when the expectation was that caffeine delivery was the only possibility.

The implications of the results cited in this section are

- Enthusiastic fervor for a medical treatment, drug, or placebo can enhance its effect.
- Enhancement is likely to be greater in the real world than in carefully controlled drug trials because of heightened assurance that an active agent is actually being ingested.

Labels and Psychological Sets

Over the years, a variety of studies have shown that both drugs and placebos may have their effects enhanced, diminished, or sometimes even reversed either by the way in which they are labeled or by the instructions accompanying their presentation. Manipulations have induced changes in mood, body experiences, and measures of physiological change. Many of the studies, which sometimes involved significant participant deception, could probably not be conducted today because of stricter standards for conducting human participant testing with informed consent. Nonetheless, the results are revealing and clearly show that a drug's chemical makeup is not the only factor determining how it will be experienced. A few illustrative examples follow.

Wolf (1950) provided a dramatic account of how a drug's expected effects might be reversed by means of suggestion. He treated with ipecac (a drug normally producing nausea) a woman who had been suffering from unremitting nausea for several days. He presented the medication with the message that it would relieve her nausea. Within 20 minutes it had. A similar result was achieved with a second female patient. This apparent ability to transform a drug's usual effect into its opposite is, if true, an extraordinary result. Several other reports of effects obtained under controlled research conditions support this possibility.

Luparello, Leist, Lourie, and Sweet (1970) wondered if by verbal labeling they could change the usual bronchodilating or bronchoconstricting properties of two aerosol medications administered to asthmatic participants. Using measures of airway resistance, they found that they could indeed influence the drugs' actions. Airway reactions to the drug were greater when instructions were consistent with the medications' usual pharmacological actions than when they were not. In some cases they completely reversed a medication's pharmacological action simply by presenting instructions discordant with the properties of the inhalant.

Schachter and Singer (1962) and later Penick and Fisher (1965) showed that the effects of a dose of epinephrine could be predictably altered with the proper instructions. Describing the drug as a stimulant that could cause anxiety, tremor, palpitation, or alertness, versus a sedative that could result in slowed-down or sleepy feelings, produced results consistent with the instructions on both physiological and subjective measures (Penick & Fisher, 1965). Conditions suggesting anger or euphoria also changed how the drug was experienced (Schachter & Singer, 1962).

In another experiment, Pentobarbitone (normally a sedative) was more sedating when it was preceded by the suggestion that it would make subjects feel "sleepy" and "slow" then when it was ingested without any priming instructions (Frankenhaueser, Post, Hagdahl, & Wrangsjo, 1964). In this instance, the natural biochemical effects were amplified by the verbal message.

A similar magnifying effect occurred in a study of an appetite-depressing drug (Phenmetrazine). Caloric intake after taking this drug was only lowered when participants were informed that they were receiving an agent that would depress appetite. The same suggestion did not reduce caloric intake after ingesting a placebo. When participants received no instructions about the active drug or placebo, they did not differ in subsequent eating behavior. Thus, the drug became effective only when labeled as an "appetite-depressing" substance (Penick & Hinkle, 1964).

Others have also presented data gathered from elderly participants showing that the alerting and sedating effects of amphetamines and chloral hydrate could be maneuvered by consistent or discordant information about the drugs' properties (Lyerly, Ross, Krugman, & Clyde, 1964; S. Ross, Krugman, Lyerly, & Clyde, 1962). Wilson and Huby (1960), after examining responses to caffeine, secobarbital, thiopropazate, and placebo, concluded

> If a drug is administered and a description of its effect is given to the recipient, it can be anticipated that the effect will be more pronounced than if the description is not given. Similarly, some degree of inhibition or variation in the drug's action can be anticipated if a false description of its action is given. (p. 596)

A particularly creative dissertation project was reported by Guy (1967). Unfortunately, this study and its intriguing results are available only in abstract form. In this work, the antipsychotic drug Thorazine was presented to participants either as the agent it was or as a less potent medication (the placebo condition). Effects on both behavioral and autonomic measures (such as heart rate and blood pressure) were significantly lower when Thorazine was deceptively presented as a relatively innocuous substance. Here, an active agent was made less active simply by lowering expectations about its potency.

Only a few studies have attempted to manipulate active drug reactions through labeling or presenting instructions. Therefore, we do not have a clear idea about the limits of such manipulations or how generalizable the impacts might turn out to be over a wider range of medications. Demonstrations, however, have been dramatic in showing that both behavioral and physiological outcomes can be profoundly affected in active drugs just as they have been in investigations of response to placebos (e.g., Fisher & Greenberg, 1997a; Jospe, 1978; White et al., 1985). In all, there is ample reason to surmise that reactions to psychoactive medications may be skewed by the manner in which they are presented.

The Double-Blind

Psychiatric drugs available to the public are usually assumed to be effective. It is also assumed that common interpersonal factors will not play a central role in determining results because they have presumably been controlled in the drug-testing process. The ability to claim that drug effectiveness stems solely from medication ingredients rests with the objectivity of the double-blind research design. It is reasoned that opportunities for selective interpersonal influence are reduced by randomly assigning patients to active medication or pharmacologically inert placebo groups. Participant blindness is a critical element in the research design. Neither patients nor clinicians are supposed to be aware of which treatment is being delivered. The double-blind design was created because it had become obvious that drug outcome could not be objectively determined without constraining psychosocial influence arising from the natural desire to see treatment succeed (e.g., Lasagna, 1955). The problem of influencing results may be of special importance in tests of psychiatric drugs because outcome is typically measured by easily swayed judgments about how patients are feeling and behaving. Research design has been found to have substantial influence over how trials will turn out with the level of effectiveness of psychiatric drugs beyond placebo declining as blindness increases (e.g., Fisher & Greenberg, 1989; M. Ross & Olson, 1981; Smith, Traganza & Harrison, 1969). In brief, assurance that blindness prevails in tests of efficacy is crucial if outcome is to be attributed to specific drug composition.

Are psychiatric drug trials effectively preserving the double-blind and filtering out psychosocial influences? Our attempt (Fisher & Greenberg, 1993) to answer this question led to the conclusion that the double-blind research strategy is much more fragile than is commonly believed. The vast majority of studies in the psychiatric drug literature simply assume that the double-blind schema is effective and do not try to verify that participants are actually blind to study conditions. When checks are made, they almost always reveal that blindness has not been preserved. Over time, we have uncovered more than 30 studies addressing this issue—most often by asking participants to guess whether a drug or placebo was administered—and more than 90% of them show the double-blind was penetrated (Fisher & Greenberg, 1993; R. P. Greenberg & Fisher, 1989, 1994, 1997). This finding indicates that outcome results are tainted to an unknown degree. It is likely, therefore, that the superiority of active drug to placebo may often be less than is claimed.

How is the double-blind unmasked? One positive possibility is that the active drugs are identified by their ability to produce more helpful changes than the placebo (e.g., Henker, Whalen, & Collins, 1979; Rickels, Raab, & Carranza, 1965). Differential responsivity patterns might make visible what is supposed to remain concealed. However, an array of studies has pointed to side effects (which occur more frequently and predictably with active drugs than with placebo) as a major source of unmasking information (e.g., Engelhardt & Margolis, 1967; Letemendia & Harris, 1959; Marini, Sheard, Bridges, & Wagner, 1976; Oxtoby, Joncs, & Robinson, 1989; Rabkin et al., 1986; Rickels et al., 1966).

Side effects or body sensations may also serve as a signal that a potent treatment is being provided. This reassurance itself may be enough to generate therapeutic effects. What would happen then if patients could be provided with placebos that create body sensations? Would the outcome differences between active drug and active placebo wane? On the basis of the relatively small number of studies that have used active placebos, the answer to this question may be yes. Thomson (1982) reviewed all the double-blind placebo controlled studies conducted on tricyclic antidepressants between 1958 and 1972. He found that 7 of the 75 studies had used an active placebo (atropine, which produces body sensations) rather than an inactive one. Comparisons of the two types of studies revealed antidepressants were more effective than inactive placebo 59% of the time, where they were more effective than active placebo in only one study (about 14% of the reports). The difference was statistically significant. Using an active placebo dissipated the antidepressant advantage. Moreover, the equalization of effectiveness was achieved not by lowering the rates of improvement with antidepressants, but through elevation of improvement rates for patients receiving active placebos. A few other reports have shown similar results (R. P. Greenberg & Fisher, 1989).

The idea that the appearance of side effects may help to boost therapeutic efficacy by convincing study participants of an agent's potency is consistent with a few studies in the literature. In one, a meta-analysis was performed on all the double-blind placebo controlled outcome trials of fluoxetine (Prozac; R. P. Greenberg et al., 1994). The overall results showed that the drug produced a relatively modest but positive effect size, comparable to studies of other types of antidepressants. However, investigating whether side effects might have influenced the ratings by unblinding the participants revealed an interesting relationship. Side effects and outcome were indeed significantly related. The greater the number of drug-treated patients who experienced side effects, the better the antidepressant results were judged to be. These findings heightened concerns that biasing psychosocial factors might well be leaking into drug trials and influencing outcome. It is also striking that a drug being marketed in part for its benign side effects would be perceived as more effective when side effects are experienced. A similar result appeared in a meta-analytic review of drug treatments for obsessive–compulsive disorder (Abramowitz, 1997). Again, judgements of therapeutic benefit rose as the percentage of patients experiencing side effects increased.

In contrast to the studies of drug amplification reported above, R. P. Greenberg, et al. (1992) demonstrated a decrease in antidepressant effectiveness relative to placebo in research designs that were more complex and seemingly blinder. This work calculated effectiveness in double-blind studies that compared newer antidepressants with both established antidepressants and placebos. It was anticipated that the presence of two active drugs, each producing its own array of body sensations, would make it more difficult to mobilize bias or prejudge outcome. It was also assumed there would be less motivation for amplifying the effectiveness of the old standard drug in such a design, because researchers' primary interest would be on establishing a new drug. Overall, it was expected that using two active drugs rather than one in a comparison with placebo would decrease differences in ratings of effectiveness by introducing both more complexity and greater blindness into the design. The prediction was borne out as efficacy measures revealed effect sizes for the older antidepressants to be only one half to one quarter the size of those attained in earlier, simpler studies that compared placebo with only the older antidepressants. Again, suspicions were raised that psychosocial factors can compromise blindness and contaminate the biochemical purity of drug outcome.

Conclusion

My aim in this chapter has been to demonstrate that responsivity to psychoactive drugs can be shaped by a variety of psychosocial factors. Responsivity does not rest uniquely on a medication's chemical composition. To support this assertion, many investigations were highlighted showing significant impact of such diverse variables as the treatment relationship, site-specific effects, the beliefs and attitudes of drug providers, and the labels or descriptions attached to medication presentation. Evidence was also supplied for the conclusion that drug testing is not as protected from psychosocial influence as many believe. This is because the double-blind design, as typically used, turns out to be more science fiction than science fact.

Elsewhere we have reviewed additional nonbiochemical influences on reactions to psychiatric drugs that have received periodic research support (Fisher & Greenberg, 1997c). These include patient personality dimensions such as acquiescence, sociability, and anxiety level. Patient personality constellations may also come into play through resistance to the pharmacologic actions of drugs that challenge characteristic systems of defense or methods for dealing with the world. Thus, a sedative might be especially resisted by an individual who prizes vigor, or a drug producing disinhibition might lead to antithetical responses in a patient wedded to maintaining control. Finally, the simple physical appearance of a medication may affect its potency. For example, one study found that phobic patients improved more when their pills (oxazepam) were green rather than red (Schapira, McClelland, Griffiths, & Newell, 1970).

The material in this chapter documents that effects of psychiatric drugs are inextricably bound up with psychosocial forces. There is great overlap in the power of the placebo and that of psychiatric drugs, with both types of substances displaying an influence over biochemical, behavioral, and psychological states. Furthermore, with proper controls, differences in outcome between active drug and placebo have been shown to recede in treatments of depression, anxiety, and even schizophrenia (Fisher & Greenberg, 1989, 1997b). In fact, psychosocial factors are arguably the largest therapeutic component in most effective psychiatric medication treatments—more critical than dosage or blood levels of the ingested drug (which usually show small associations with outcome at best; Fisher & Greenberg, 1989, 1997b). For example, on the basis of a meta-analysis of antidepressant drug studies, Kirsch and Saperstein (1998) concluded that at least 75% of drug effectiveness could be due to placebo effects. Similarly, it has been estimated that 80% to 90% of the effectiveness in antidepressant treatments of mild to moderate depressions can be attributed to "nonspecific factors" such as clinical support (Thase & Kupfer, 1996).

The impression that psychoactive drug treatments have great specificity is fostered by labeling classes of drugs as antidepressant, antianxiety, antipsychotic, and so forth. Each label is supposed to designate a clearly defined category of disorder based on the system created for providing diagnoses, the latest edition of the *Diagnostic and Statistical Manual for Mental Disorders* (*DSM–IV*; American Psychiatric Association, 1994). Yet investigators who have carefully analyzed the construction and application of the *DSM* have been sharply critical of its ability to provide pinpointed targets at which one could aim medication magic bullets (e.g., Carson, 1997; Kirk & Kutchins, 1992). They note, quite accurately, that the system for diagnosing mental disorders has gone through periodic and significant changes (i.e., *DSM-I, DSM-II, DSM-III, DSM-III–R,* and *DSM-IV*). With each alteration, new specification criteria have been introduced while categories have shuffled and proliferated. Most telling are (a) findings of lower reliabilities than had been hoped for in pigeonholing disorders and (b) questionable validity in making predictions based on the diagnostic labels. Furthermore, the system has been accused of being more the product of sociopolitical forces than of research evidence (e.g., Carson, 1997;

Kirk & Kutchins, 1992). Adding to the obstacles impeding the production of successful disorder-specific drug treatments is the revelation that most individuals with emotional problems do not fit neatly into only one disorder category (e.g., M. D. Greenberg, 1997). Typically, problem patterns are diverse with individuals meeting criteria for multiple classifications. Comorbidity is the rule, not the exception, and drug trials have largely ignored this reality in attempts to validate treatments on supposedly pure forms of the various disorders.

Not surprisingly, considering the fluidity and interpenetration of diagnoses, classes of psychiatric medications themselves have been observed to lack therapeutic specificity. Hudson and Pope (1990), for instance, provided data showing that antidepressants may be helpful for the following: major depression, bulimia, panic disorder, obsessive–compulsive disorder, attention deficit hyperactivitiy disorder, cataplexy, migraine, and irritable bowel syndrome. Likewise, it is not unusual for antipsychotics to be used not only for treating schizophrenia, but also for such conditions as autism, uncontrolled aggressive behavior, and manic–depressive symptoms. Further, it turns out that antidepressants have been found to be more effective for the treatment of anxiety than are drugs specifically designed as antianxiety agents (e.g., Danton & Antonuccio, 1997; Lipman, 1989). In general, the argument for the importance of common factors in treating emotional problems is bolstered by evidence of spongy specificity in psychiatric diagnostic categories and the medications designed to treat them.

Some readers may interpret the material covered in this chapter as providing a rationale for eliminating drug usage in treating emotional disorders. This is not the intent of the present review. Although it is true that research shows a strong common factor component in medication therapies, fragility in the scientific evidence used to validate many biological treatments, and an undervaluing of the comparative merits of psychotherapy (e.g., Fisher & Greenberg, 1989, 1997b), there are several reasons to be circumspect. On the practical side, by responding to the implicit demand to do something concrete quickly, drug treatments, for all their potential problems, attract and maintain some patients who would otherwise be reluctant to address their discomforts. Drug treatments are also less threatening to some because they are blame-free. Problems may be attributed to body chemistry rather than to faulty relationships, personal deficiencies, or other stressors.

Regardless of practical considerations, research findings have not invalidated the usefulness of psychiatric drugs. Findings have, however, raised questions about the magnitude of effectiveness beyond appropriately constructed placebo comparison groups. Because the integrity of the double-blind design is suspect, the level of effectiveness attributable to psychoactive drugs cannot be accurately assessed.

In consequence, what drugs add over and above other treatment components is currently uncertain.

In any event, numerous testimonials of successful treatment make it doubtful that the empirical evidence reviewed here will roll back the current fascination with drug therapy. Many of these findings—in the literature for decades—have been dismissed or ignored. The seduction to apply simple, specific, and biologically based solutions to psychological distress remains strong. Yet those practitioners who choose to endorse and prescribe drugs will need to attend to the inescapable influence of common factors.

The clinical implications of the research evidence are clear. Practitioners need to be sensitive to the interpersonal aspects of their transactions with patients, even if they are ostensibly relying on treatment with psychoactive medication. Effectiveness is optimized when patients are truly convinced that they are receiving a potent agent (one producing body sensations) from a confident practitioner who expects a successful outcome. The presentation should include an outline of the benefits to be expected, along with a description of potential side effects framed as routine indicators of the drug's power. Instructions to the patient should include not only explanations of the expected drug efficacy, but also the strong suggestion that they will be expected to play an active collaborative role in problem resolution with their clinician. The objective in therapy is to alleviate patient distress, not to prove that relief must come about only from direct manipulation of body chemistry. Conducting a treatment that is unaffected by interpersonal events and influences is neither necessary nor possible. Thankfully, Woody Allen's dilemma, presented at the beginning of this chapter, about having to choose between mind and body does not need to be addressed in real-world clinical encounters.

Questions From the Editors

1. *That common psychosocial factors significantly affect the drug therapy of patients with anxiety or depressive complaints is understandable, almost commonsensical. But what of drug interventions with patients ultimately diagnosed as severely mentally ill (e.g., the schizophrenias, bipolar disorders)? Does the research not support that the psychoactivity of neuroleptics is far more influential in the treatment of such patients than any psychosocial factors you identify in your chapter?*

The conventional view, adopted on faith by most clinicians, accepts the idea that drug treatments are especially beneficial when applied to severe disorders. A reasonable case can be made for the usefulness of drugs with severe emotional conditions. However, benefits are often overstated and drawbacks downplayed. Detailed reviews of research evidence, as presented in books I have edited with Seymour Fisher, add perspective to prevailing clinical impressions. Chapters by Cohen (1997), R. P. Greenberg and Fisher (1989, 1997), and Karon (1989) all suggest that things may not be what many have been led to believe. All indicate that long-term unique benefits of drugs for conditions such as schizophrenia, bipolar disorder, and severe depression have been exaggerated. Furthermore, consistent with material in the present chapter, all raise questions about potential bias in the data gathered to date, as a result of transparency in the double-blind design and research participant samples that may differ in important ways from typical patients seen in everyday practice.

Regarding schizophrenia, in the short run, medications do seem to exert a subduing, tranquilizing effect on disturbing and disturbed behavior. Overall, however, positive initial treatment response may occur for only a minority of patients. Reported relapse rates are high, and over time, medication effects are frequently achieved at a price of significant behavioral symptoms and toxicity induced by the drugs themselves. Furthermore, shortcomings of medication treatments become more glaring if outcome is assessed by measures of interpersonal or social functioning and quality of life. Recent reviews of lithium treatments for bipolar disorder also reveal lower benefits relative to placebos than initial enthusiastic reports indicated. It is an open question at this point whether highly touted newer generation medications will produce fewer problems for those suffering with schizophrenia or bipolar disorder.

Surprisingly, current data on effectiveness of psychotherapy and interpersonal treatment approaches in structured living settings have demonstrated comparatively positive results and lower relapse rates for schizophrenia, without the side effect problems caused by drug treatments. Similarly, several studies indicate psychotherapy approaches are a viable alternative to medications with severe depressions, and possibly even more protective against relapse than antidepressants.

2. Biological psychiatry has advocated the use of drug therapy with a growing number of so-called disorders of childhood. What special evidence is available to justify this practice? Or, would the conclusions you draw about drug therapy with adults be equally applicable with children?

Actually, the case for using psychoactive medications with children is weaker than the justification for their use with adults. Overall, the literature is sparse when looked at in terms of controlled double-blind studies, and outcome studies that do exist are not encouraging. For example, Fisher and Fisher (1997) were able to locate only 13 appropriately controlled trials evaluating the power of antidepressants for children and adolescents. Results were uniformly discouraging with placebos proving the equal of drugs. Other investigators have concurred with this conclusion, and the reviews have sparked debates about whether it is ethical to prescribe treatments that are not supported by empirical evidence. Uneasiness was fueled further by the appearance of serious side effects (including death) for a small percentage of children taking antidepressants. There is also a dearth of studies and no consistent scientific evidence showing that drugs are of greater value than placebos in treating children with anxiety, psychosis, or bipolar disorder.

Attention deficit hyperactivity disorder (ADHD) is a diagnostic classification that has received a good deal of research attention. Interestingly, reviewers looking at essentially the same outcome studies have not always agreed about the value of treating this disorder with medications. For example, Whalen and Henker (1997) advocated the use of stimulant drugs for this condition, whereas McGuinness (1989) noted that the data consistently fail to support their usefulness. Like drug research in general, there is room for disagreement in interpretation of the same material. In the case of these reviewers, however, there is considerable overlap in their observations, despite disagreement about a bottom-line recommendation. For instance, they agreed the syndrome is vaguely defined, various side effects accompany the use of the medications, long-term efficacy has not been shown, and "improvements" have been largely limited to problems with conduct and oppositionality, not gains in social relationships or academic achievement. Disagreement about treatment recommendations is in part a product of differences in value systems and uncertainty about what to make of drug trial results.

3. The stakes in the development, production, and promotion of drugs are high, not only in the billions of dollars involved, but also, and more important, in the lives of patients. What methods could be used in future clinical trials to ensure that psychiatric drug treatments deliver as marketed?

Elsewhere, my colleague Seymour Fisher and I addressed the topic of improving clinical trials in some detail (Fisher & Greenberg, 1997b). The following comments highlight some of the issues we addressed.

Perhaps the biggest deficiency in current research trials is vulnerability of the double-blind design. Because of differences in body sensations (side effects) created by active medications and inactive placebos, patients and researchers are tipped off as to who is receiving which treatment. This opens the door to differential responsivity and biased outcome ratings that may not be tied directly to a drug's specific chemical composition. To reduce this design flaw; we (see Fisher & Greenberg, 1997b) have advocated replacing inert placebos with active placebos that arouse body sensations, simulating at least some of the body experiences caused by active drugs. In addition, it would be useful to systematically gather data from patients and research staff reflecting their accuracy in guessing whether active medications or placebos are being ingested. Failure to establish blindness could be used to invalidate study results and to determine the degree to which awareness of study conditions sways outcome.

Another interesting way to try to assess the level of nonspecific influence is to present all patients the same active drug treatments, but with half the group led to believe that they are receiving drugs inert for their particular condition (possibly in preparation for the "real" treatment to be delivered later). Delivering only treatments believed to be effective by the researchers, with varying instructions, offers another avenue for shedding light on the degree of psychological influence on outcome.

In order to increase generalizability, trials also need to pay more attention to representativeness of participant samples. Typically, patients in the real world display comorbidity, with problems fitting into more than one diagnostic category (M. D. Greenberg, 1997). Drug trials are usually conducted with diagnostically purified samples of patients. This may make results look better than they are likely to turn out for many practitioners and their patients. Research with comorbid samples is needed to address this issue.

Finally, there needs to be a good deal more study of side effects. Too often, discomforts caused by drugs are minimized or dismissed by clinicians as an expected price of taking medications. More needs to be learned about the duration and impact of these untoward reactions on the patients experiencing them.

References

Abramowitz, J. S. (1997). Effectiveness of psychological and pharmacological treatments for obsessive–compulsive disorders: A quantitative review. *Journal of Consulting and Clinical Psychology, 65,* 44–52.

American Psychiatric Association. (1994). *Diagnostic and statistical manual of mental disorders* (4th ed). Washington, DC: Author.

Baker, A., & Thorpe, J. (1957). Placebo responses. *American Medical Association Archives of Neurology and Psychiatry, 78,* 57–60.

Baxter, L. R., Schwartz, J. M., Bergman, K. S., Szuba, M. P., Guze, B. H., Mazziotta, J. C., Akazraju, A., Selin, C. E., Ferng, H. K., Munford, P., & Phelps, M. E. (1992). Caudate glucose metabolic rate changes with both drug and behavior therapy for obsessive–compulsive disorder. *Archives of General Psychiatry, 49,* 681–689.

Beecher, H. K. (1955). The powerful placebo. *Journal of the American Medical Association, 159,* 1602–1606.

Beecher, H. K. (1960, July 8). Stress and effectiveness of placebos and "active" drugs. *Science, 132,* 91–92.

Blatt, S. J., Sanislow, C. A., Zuroff, D. C., & Pilkonis, P. A. (1996). Characteristics of effective therapists: Further analyses of data from the National Institute of Mental Health Treatment of Depression Collaborative Research Program. *Journal of Consulting and Clinical Psychology, 64,* 1276–1284.

Blatt, S. J., Zuroff, D. C., Quinlan, D. M., & Pilkonis, P. (1996). Interpersonal factors in brief treatment of depression: Further analyses of the NIMH Treatment of Depression Collaborative Research Program. *Journal of Consulting and Clinical Psychology, 64,* 162–171.

Bordin, E. (1976, September). *The working alliance: Basis for a general theory of psychotherapy.* Paper presented at the 84th Annual Convention of the American Psychological Association, Washington, DC.

Brody, H. (1977). *Placebos and the philosophy of medicine.* Chicago: University of Chicago Press.

Brody, H. (1985). Placebo effect: An examination of Grunbaum's definition. In L. White, B. Tursky, & G.E. Schwartz (Eds.), *Placebo: Theory, research, and mechanisms* (pp. 37–57). New York: Guilford Press.

Carroll, L. (1962). *Alice's adventures in Wonderland.* Harmondsworth, England: Penguin. (Original work published 1865)

Carson, R. C. (1997). Costly compromises: A critique of the *Diagnostic and Statistical Manual of Mental Disorders.* In S. Fisher & R. P. Greenberg (Eds.), *From placebo to panacea: Putting psychiatric drugs to the test* (pp. 98–114). New York: Wiley.

Castonguay, L. G., Wiser, S., Raue, P., Hayes, A. M., & Goldfried, M. R. (1993, June). *Predicting change in cognitive therapy for depression: The role of the client's experience, the therapist's focus of intervention, and the working alliance.* Paper presented at the annual meeting of the Society for Psychotherapy Research, Pittsburgh, PA.

Cohen, D. (1997). A critique of the use of neuroleptic drugs in psychiatry. In S. Fisher & R. P. Greenberg (Eds.), *From placebo to panacea: Putting psychiatric drugs to the test* (pp. 173–228). New York: Wiley.

Danton, W. G., & Antonuccio, D. O. (1997). A focused empirical analysis of treatments for panic and anxiety. In S. Fisher & R. P. Greenberg (Eds.), *From placebo to panacea: Putting psychiatric drugs to the test* (pp. 229–280). New York: Wiley.

Dinnerstein, A. J., Lowenthal, M., & Blitz, B. (1966–1967). The interaction of drugs with placebos in the control of pain and anxiety. *Perspectives in Biology and Medicine, 10,* 103–117.

Docherty, J. P., & Feister, S. J. (1985). The therapeutic alliance and compliance with psychopharmacology. In American Psychiatric Association (Ed.), *Psychiatry update* (Vol. 4, pp. 607–632). Washington, DC: American Psychiatric Press.

Downing, R. W., & Rickels, K. (1978). Nonspecific factors and their interaction with psychological treatment in pharmacotherapy. In M. A. Lipton, A. DiMascio, & K. F. Killam (Eds.), *Psychopharmacology: A generation of progress* (pp. 1419–1428). New York: Raven Press.

Downing, R. W., Rickels, K., & Dreesmann, H. (1973). Orthogonal factors vs. interdependent variables as predictors of drug treatment response in anxious outpatients. *Psychopharmacologia, 32,* 93–111.

Elkin, I., Shea, T., Watkins, J. T., Imber, S. D., Sotsky, S. M., Collins, J. F., Glass, D. R., Pilkonis, P. A., Leber, W. R., Docherty, J. P., Fiester, S. J., & Parloff, M. B. (1989). National Institute of Mental Health Treatment of Depression Collaborative Research Program: General effectiveness of treatments. *Archives of General Psychiatry, 46,* 971–982.

Engelhardt, D. M., & Margolis, R. (1967). Drug identity, doctor conviction & outcome. In H. Brill, J. Cole, P. Deniker, H. Hippius, & P. B. Bradley (Eds.), *Neuropsychopharmacology* (pp. 543–544). Amsterdam: Excerpta Medica Foundation.

Evans, F. J. (1974). The placebo response in pain reduction. *Advances in Neurology, 4,* 289–296.

Evans, F. J. (1985). Expectancy, therapeutic instructions, and the placebo response. In L. White, B. Tursky, & G. E. Schwartz (Eds.), *Placebo: Theory, research, and mechanisms* (pp. 215–234). New York: Guilford Press.

Feighner, J. P., Aden, G. C., Fabre, L. F., Rickels, K., & Smith, W. T. (1983). Comparison of alprazolam, imipramine, and placebo in the treatment of depression. *Journal of the American Medical Association, 249,* 3057–3064.

Fisher, R. L., & Fisher, S. (1997). Are we justified in treating children with psychotropic drugs? In S. Fisher & R. P. Greenberg (Eds.), *From placebo to panacea: Putting psychiatric drugs to the test* (pp. 307–322). New York: Wiley.

Fisher, S., Cole, J. O., Rickels, K., & Uhlenhuth, E. H. (1964). Drug-set interaction: The effect of expectations on drug response in outpatients. *Neuropsychopharmacology, 3,* 149–156.

Fisher, S., & Greenberg, R. P. (Eds.). (1989). *The limits of biological treatments for psychological distress: Comparisons with psychotherapy and placebo.* Hillsdale, NJ: Erlbaum.

Fisher, S., & Greenberg, R. P. (1993). How sound is the double-blind design for evaluating psychotropic drugs? *Journal of Nervous and Mental Disease, 181,* 345–350.

Fisher, S., & Greenberg, R. P. (1996). *Freud scientifically reappraised: Testing the theories and therapy.* New York: Wiley.

Fisher, S., & Greenberg, R. P. (1997a). The curse of the placebo: Fanciful pursuit of a pure biological therapy. In S. Fisher & R. P. Greenberg (Eds.), *From placebo to panacea: Putting psychiatric drugs to the test* (pp. 3–56). New York: Wiley.

Fisher, S., & Greenberg, R. P. (1997b). What are we to conclude about psychoactive drugs? Scanning the major findings. In S. Fisher & R. P. Greenberg (Eds.), *From placebo to panacea: Putting psychiatric drugs to the test* (pp. 359–384). New York: Wiley.

Fisher, S., & Greenberg, R. P. (Eds.) (1997c). *From placebo to panacea: Putting psychiatric drugs to the test.* New York: Wiley.

Frank, J. D. (1973). *Persuasion and healing.* Baltimore: Johns Hopkins University Press.

Frankenhaueser, M., Post, B., Hagdahl, R., & Wrangsjo, B. (1964). Effects of a depressant drug as modified by experimentally-induced expectation. *Perceptual and Motor Skills, 18,* 513–522.

Freedman, N., Engelhardt, D., Mann, D., Margolis, R., & London, S. (1965). Communication of body complaints and paranoid symptom change under conditions of phenothiazine treatment. *Journal of Personality and Social Psychology, 1,* 310–318.

Frieswyk, S. H., Allen, J. G., Colson, D. B., Coyne, L., Gabbard, G. O., Horwitz, L., & Newsom, G. (1986). Therapeutic alliance: Its place as process and outcome variable in dynamic psychotherapy research. *Journal of Consulting and Clinical Psychology, 1,* 32–39.

Goldstein, A., Searle, B. W., & Schmike, R. T. (1960). Effects of secobarbital and of D-Amphetamine on psychomotor performance of normal subjects. *Journal of Pharmacology and Experimental Therapeutics, 130,* 55–58.

Greenberg, M. D. (1997). Treatment implications of psychiatric comorbidity. In S. Fisher & R. P. Greenberg (Eds.), *From placebo to panacea: Putting psychiatric drugs to the test* (pp. 57–97). New York: Wiley.

Greenberg, R. P., Bornstein, R. F., Greenberg, M. D., & Fisher, S. (1992). A meta-analysis of antidepressant outcome under "blinder" conditions. *Journal of Consulting and Clinical Psychology, 60,* 664–669.

Greenberg, R. P., Bornstein, R. F., Zborowski, M. J., Fisher, S., & Greenberg, M. D. (1994). A meta-analysis of fluoxetine outcome in the treatment of depression. *Journal of Nervous and Mental Disease, 182,* 547–551.

Greenberg, R. P., & Fisher, S. (1989). Examining antidepressant effectiveness: Findings, ambiguities, and some vexing puzzles. In S. Fisher & R. P. Greenberg (Eds.), *The limits of biological treatments for psychological distress: Comparisons with psychotherapy and placebo* (pp. 1–37). Hillsdale, NJ: Erlbaum.

Greenberg, R. P., & Fisher, S. (1994). Seeing through the double-masked design: A commentary. *Controlled Clinical Trials, 15,* 244–246.

Greenberg, R. P., & Fisher, S. (1997). Mood-mending medicines: Probing drug, psychotherapy, and placebo solutions. In S. Fisher & R. P. Greenberg (Eds.), *From placebo to panacea: Putting psychiatric drugs to the test* (pp. 115–172). New York: Wiley.

Greenblatt, M., Grosser, G. H., & Wechsler, H. (1964). Differential response of hospitalized depressed patients to somatic therapy. *American Journal of Psychiatry, 120,* 935–943.

Grunbaum, A. (1981). The placebo concept. *Behavior Research and Therapy, 19,* 157–167.

Grunbaum, A. (1985). Explication and implications of the placebo concept. In L. White, B. Tursky, & G. E. Schwartz (Eds.), *Placebo: Theory, research and mechanisms* (pp. 9–36). New York: Guilford Press.

Gryll, S. L., & Katahn, M. (1978). Situational factors contributing to the placebo effect. *Psychopharmacology, 57,* 253–261.

Guy, W. H. (1967). Placebo proneness: Its relationship to environmental influences and personality traits. *Dissertation Abstracts, 28*(5-B), 2137–2138.

Haefner, D. P., Sacks, J. M., & Mason, A. S. (1960). Physicians' attitudes toward chemotherapy as a factor in psychiatric patients' responses to medication. *Journal of Nervous and Mental Disease, 131,* 64–69.

Henker, B., Whalen, C. K., & Collins, B. E. (1979). Double-blind and triple-blind assessments of medication and placebo responses in hyperactive children. *Journal of Abnormal Child Psychiatry, 7,* 1–13.

Honigfeld, G. (1964, April). Non-specific factors in treatment. *Diseases of the Nervous System, 25,* 225–239.

Horvath, A. O., & Symonds, B. D. (1991). Relation between working alliance and outcome in psychotherapy: A meta-analysis. *Journal of Counseling Psychology, 38,* 139–149.

Hudson, J. I., & Pope, H. G., Jr. (1990). Affective spectrum disorder: Does antidepressant response identify a family of disorders with a common pathophysiology? *American Journal of Psychiatry, 5,* 552–564.

Jospe, M. (1978). *The placebo effect in healing.* Lexington, MA: Heath.

Karon, B. P. (1989). Psychotherapy versus medication for schizophrenia: Empirical comparisons. In S. Fisher & R. P. Greenberg (Eds.), *The limits of biological treatments for psychological distress: Comparison with psychotherapy and placebo* (pp. 105–150). Hillsdale, NJ: Erlbaum.

Kellam, S. G., Goldberg, S. C., Schooler, N. R., Berman, A., & Shmelzer, J. L. (1967). Ward atmosphere and outcome of treatment of acute schizophrenia. *Journal of Psychiatric Research, 5,* 145–163.

Kirk, S. A., & Kutchins, H. (1992). *The selling of DSM: The rhetoric of science in psychiatry.* New York: Aldine de Gruyter.

Kirsch, I., & Rosadino, M. J. (1993). Do double-blind studies with informed consent yield externally valid results? *Psychopharmacology, 110,* 437–442.

Kirsch, I., & Sapirstein, G. (1998). Listening to Prozac but hearing placebo: A meta-analysis of antidepressant medication. *Prevention and Treatment, 1,* Article 0002a. Available at www.http://journals.apa.org/treatment/volume1/pre0010002a.html.

Kirsch, I., & Weixel, L. J. (1988). Double-blind versus deceptive administration of a placebo. *Behavioral Neuroscience, 102,* 319–323.

Krupnick, J. L., Sotsky, S. M., Simmens, S., Moyer, J., Elkin, I., Watkins, J., & Pilkonis, P. A. (1996). The role of the therapeutic alliance in psychotherapy and pharmacotherapy outcome: Findings in the National Institute of Mental Health Treatment of Depression Collaborative Research Program. *Journal of Consulting and Clinical Psychology, 64,* 532–539.

Lasagna, L. (1955). The controlled clinical trial: Theory and practice. *Journal of Chronic Disease, 1,* 353–367.

Letemendia, F. J. J., & Harris, A. D. (1959). The influence of side effects on the reporting of symptoms. *Psychopharmacologia, 1,* 39–47.

Leveton, A. F. (1958). The evaluation and testing of psychopharmaceutic drugs. *American Journal of Psychiatry, 116,* 97–103.

Linn, E. L. (1959). Sources of uncertainty in studies of drugs affecting mood, mentation, or activity. *American Journal of Psychiatry, 116,* 97–103.

Lipman, R. S. (1989). Pharmacotherapy of the anxiety disorders. In S. Fisher & R. P. Greenberg (Eds.), *The limits of biological treatments for psychological distress: Comparisons wtih psychotherapy and placebo* (pp. 69–103). Hillsdale, NJ: Erlbaum.

Luborsky, L. L., & Auerbach, A. H. (1985). The therapeutic relationship in psychodynamic psychotherapy: The research evidence and its meaning for practice. In R. E. Hales & A. J. Frances (Eds.), *Psychiatric update annual review* (Vol. 4, pp. 550–561). Washington, DC: American Psychiatric Press.

Luborsky, L., Diguer, L., Luborsky, E., Singer, B., Dickter, D., & Schmidt, K. A. (1993). The efficacy of dynamic psychotherapies: Is it true that "Everyone has won and all must have prizes?" In N. E. Miller, L. Luborsky, J. P. Barber, & J. P. Docherty (Eds.), *Psychodynamic treatment research* (pp. 497–516). New York: Basic Books.

Luborsky, L., Singer, B., & Luborsky, E. (1975). Comparative studies of psychotherapies: Is is true that "Everybody has won and all must have prizes?" *Archives of General Psychiatry, 32,* 995–1008.

Luparello, T. J., Leist, N., Lourie, C. H., & Sweet, P. (1970). The interaction of psychologic stimuli and pharmacologic agents on airway reactivity in asthmatic subjects. *Psychosomatic Medicine, 32,* 509–513.

Lyerly, S. B., Ross, S., Krugman, A. D., & Clyde, D. (1964). Drugs and placebos: The effects of instructions upon performance and mood under amphetamine sulphate and chloral hydrate. *Journal of Abnormal and Social Psychology, 68,* 321–327.

Marini, J. L., Sheard, M. H., Bridges, C. I., & Wagner, E., Jr. (1976). An evaluation of the double-blind design in a study comparing lithium carbonate with placebo. *Acta Psychiatrica Scandinavica, 53,* 343–354.

McClelland, D. C. (1985). The social mandate of health psychology. *American Behavioral Scientist, 28,* 451–467.

McGuinness, D. (1989). Attention deficit disorder: The emperor's clothes, animal "pharm," and other fiction. In S. Fisher & R. P. Greenberg (Eds.), *The limits of biological treatments for psychological distress: Comparisons with psychotherapy and placebo* (pp. 151–188). Hillsdale, NJ: Erlbaum.

Ogles, B. M., Lambert, M. J., & Sawyer, J. D. (1995). Clinical significance of the National Institute of Mental Health Treatment and Depression Collaborative Research Program data. *Journal of Consulting and Clinical Psychology, 63,* 321–326.

Oxtoby, A., Jones, A., & Robinson, M. (1989). Is your "double-blind" design truly double-blind? *British Journal of Psychiatry, 155,* 700–701.

Penick, S. B., & Fisher, S. (1965). Drug-set interaction: Psychological and physiological effects of epinephrine under differential expectations. *Psychosomatic Medicine, 27,* 177–182.

Penick, S. B., & Hinkle, L. E., Jr. (1964). The effect of expectation on response to Phenmetrazine. *Psychosomatic Medicine, 26,* 369–373.

Pliner, P., & Cappell, H. (1974). Modification of affective consequences of alcohol. *Journal of Abnormal Psychology, 83,* 418–425.

Rabkin, J. G., Markowitz, J. S., Stewart, J., McGrath, P., Harrison, W., Quitkin, F. M., & Klein, D. S. (1986). How blind is blind? Assessment of patient and doctor medication guesses in a placebo-controlled trial of imipramine and phenelzine. *Psychiatric Research, 19,* 75–86.

Rickels, K. (Ed.) (1968). *Non-specific factors in drug therapy.* Springfield, IL: Thomas.

Rickels, K., Cattell, R. B., Weiss, C., Gray, B., Yee, R., Mallin, A., & Aaron, H. G. (1966). Controlled psychopharmacological research in private psychiatric practice. *Psychopharmacologia, 9,* 288–306.

Rickels, K., Raab, E., & Carranza, J. (1965). Doctor medication guesses: An indication of clinical improvement in double-blind studies. *Journal of New Drugs, 5,* 67–71.

Roberts, A. H. (1994). "The powerful placebo" revisited: Implications for headache treatment and management. *Headache Quarterly: Current Treatment and Research, 5,* 208–213.

Roberts, A. H. (1995). The powerful placebo revisited: Magnitude of nonspecific effects. *Mind–Body Medicine, 1,* 35–43.

Rosenzweig, S. (1936). Some implicit common factors in diverse methods of psychotherapy. *American Journal of Orthopsychiatry, 6,* 412–415.

Ross, M., & Olson, J. M. (1981). An expectancy-attribution model of the effects of placebos. *Psychology Review, 88,* 408–437.

Ross, S., & Buckalew, L. W. (1983). The placebo as an agent in behavioral manipulations: A review of problems, issues, and affected measures. *Clinical Psychology Review, 3,* 457–471.

Ross, S., Krugman, A. D., Lyerly, S. B., & Clyde, D. J. (1962). Drugs and placebos: A model design. *Psychological Reports, 10,* 383–392.

Sabshin, M., & Ramot, J. (1956). Pharmacotherapeutic evaluation and the psychiatric setting. *Archives of Neurology and Psychiatry, 75,* 363–370.

Safran, J. D., & Wallner, L. K. (1991). The relative predictive validity of two therapeutic alliance measures in cognitive therapy. *Psychological Assessment, 3*(2), 188–195.

Schachter, S., & Singer, J. (1962). Cognitive, social and physiological determinants of emotional state. *Psychological Review, 69,* 379–399.

Schapira, K., McClelland, H., Griffiths, M., & Newell, D. (1970). Study on the effects of tablet colour in the treatment of anxiety states. *British Medical Journal, 2,* 446–449.

Shapiro, A. K. (1964). Factors contributing to the placebo effect. *American Journal of Psychotherapy, 18,* 73–88.

Shapiro, A. K. (1968). Semantics of the placebo. *Psychiatric Quarterly, 42,* 653–695.

Shapiro, A. P., & Morris, L. A. (1978). The placebo effect in medical and psychological therapies. In S. L. Garfield & A. E. Bergin (Eds.), *Handbook of psychotherapy and behavior change* (pp. 369–410). New York: Wiley.

Shepherd, M. (1993). The placebo: From specificity to the non-specific and back. *Psychological Medicine, 23,* 569–578.

Smith, A., Traganza, E., & Harrison, G. (1969). Studies on the effectiveness of antidepressant drugs. *Psychopharmacology Bulletin, 5,* 1–53.

Smith, M. L., Glass, G. V., & Miller, T. I. (1980). *The benefits of psychotherapy.* Baltimore: Johns Hopkins Press.

Sotsky, S. M., Glass, D. R., Shea, M. T., Pilkonis, P. A., Collins, J. R., Elkin, I., Watkins, J. T., Imber, S. D., Leber, W. R., Moyer, J., & Oliveri, M. E. (1991). Patient predictors of response to psychotherapy and pharmacotherapy: Findings in the NIMH Treatment of Depression Collaborative Research Program. *American Journal of Psychiatry, 148,* 997–1008.

Stiles, W. B., Shapiro, D. A., & Elliot, R. (1986). "Are all psychothera- pies equivalent?" *American Psychologist, 41,* 165–180.

Stubbs, J. P., & Bozarth, J. D. (1994). The Dodo bird revisited: A qual- itative study of psychotherapy efficacy research. *Applied and Preventive Psychology, 3,* 109–120.

Tenner, E. (1996). *Why things bite back: Technology and the revenge of unin- tended consequences.* New York: Knopf.

Thase, M. E., & Kupfer, D. J. (1996). Recent developments in the phar- macotherapy of mood disorders. *Journal of Consulting and Clinical Psychology, 64,* 646–659.

Thomson, R. (1982). Side effects and placebo amplification. *British Journal of Psychiatry, 140,* 64–68.

Uhlenhuth, E. H., Carter, A., Neustadt, J. D., & Payson, H. E. (1957). The symptomatic relief of anxiety with meprobamate, phenobarbi- tal, and placebo. *American Journal of Psychiatry, 115,* 905–910.

Uhlenhuth, E. H., Rickels, K., Fisher, S., Park, L. C., Lipman, R. S., & Mock, J. (1966). Drug, doctor's verbal attitude and clinic setting in the symptomatic response to pharmacotherapy. *Psychopharmacologia, 9,* 392–418.

Van Dyke, C., Ungerer, J., Jatlow, P., Barash, P., & Byck, R. (1982). Intranasal cocaine: Dose relationships of psychological effects and plasma levels. *International Journal of Psychiatry in Medicine, 12,* 1–13.

von Kerekjarto, M. (1966). Studies on the influence of examiner's sex on the effects of drugs. In H. Brill (Ed.), *Neuropsychopharmacology: Proceedings of the Fifth International Congress of the Collegium Internationale Neuropsychopharmacologicum* (pp. 552–556). New York: Exerpta Medica Foundation.

Whalen, C. K., & Henker, B. (1997). Stimulant pharmacotherapy for attention deficit/hyperactivity disorders: An analysis of progress, problems, and prospects. In S. Fisher & R. P. Greenberg (Eds.), *From placebo to panacea: Putting psychiatric drugs to the test* (pp. 323–358). New York: Wiley.

Wheatley, D. (1967, November). Influence of doctors' and patients' attitudes in the treatment of neurotic illness. *Lancet, 2,* 1133–1135.

White, L., Tursky, B., & Schwartz, G. E. (Eds.) (1985). *Placebo: Theory, research, and mechanisms.* New York: Guilford Press.

Wilson, C. W. M., & Huby, P. M. (1960). An assessment of the responses to drugs acting on the central nervous system. *Clinical Pharmacology and Therapeutics, 2,* 587–598.

Wolf, S. (1950). Effects of suggestion and conditioning on the action of chemical agents in human subjects—The pharmacology of place- bos. *Journal of Clinical Investigation, 29,* 100–109.

Wolfe, B. E., & Goldfried, M. R. (1988). Research on psychotherapy integration: Recommendations and conclusions from an NIMH workshop. *Journal of Consulting and Clinical Psychology, 56,* 448–451.

Douglas H. Sprenkle, Adrian J. Blow, and Mitchell H. Dickey

Common Factors and Other Nontechnique Variables in Marriage and Family Therapy

11

The field of marriage and family therapy (MFT) has been slow to consider the common factors. This is ironic as most of these important factors for change are highly relational in nature. While keeping in mind a few exceptions—the work of Duncan and his colleagues (Duncan, 1992; Duncan, Hubble, & Miller, 1997; Duncan, Solovey, & Rusk, 1992) and the attention given within MFT research to the therapeutic alliance—we agree with Wampler's (1997) conclusion: "Outcome research in marriage and family therapy has largely ignored the research literature on common factors underlying effective psychotherapy" (p. 10).

The neglect of the common factors becomes understandable once the history of the profession is examined. In the first three decades of MFT's existence, distinctiveness was strongly emphasized over commonality. Family therapy began as a maverick discipline. It was oppositional, even defiant to the prevailing psychotherapy *zeitgeist.* In addition, perhaps because they were rebels of a sort, many of the discipline's founders were feisty and dynamic. They drew attention to their uniqueness and created theories matching their personalities. Carl Whitaker's experiential family therapy, for example, stressing spontaneity, creativity, and the benefits of "craziness," flowed from his "right-brained," iconoclastic style. Minuchin's structural family therapy, positing family problems as flaws in family organization, fit his preferred role as a forceful director or choreographer of change. It hardly occurred to many people in the field (notwithstanding the contributions of Framo, 1996) to focus on the similarities of the work of the founders.

Indeed, family practitioners would have been surprised by Friedlander, Ellis, Raymond, Siegel, and Milford's (1987) later finding. On the basis of an analysis of the language and communication patterns of six videotapes each of Whitaker and Minuchin, the researchers showed that convergence was far more evident than divergence. Both therapists took a highly active, here-and-now educational approach. Friedlander et al. (1987) noted, for instance, that 51% of all their responses could be "categorized as providing information, interpretation, or direct guidance and advice" (p. 580).

As schools of family therapy consolidated around the emerging "cults of personality," not only did pressure increase for family therapy to separate from mainstream psychotherapy, but also for the various camps to accentuate their differences (and alleged superiority). It did not help that most practicing family therapists were not particularly influenced by research (Sprenkle & Moon, 1996). The growth of the field depended far more on its intuitive or emotional appeal than solid research evidence (Nichols & Schwartz, 1995). At least until the early to mid-1980s, MFT could be described fairly as a coterie of competing religions. It was possible (and regrettably still is) for a highly charismatic individual to create a model of family therapy, find success on the workshop circuit, and obtain book contracts with reputable publishers to promulgate the model, without offering an iota of evidence for its efficacy beyond personal testimony.

For all that, change is in the air. Influential forces are now leading family therapy to consider more its similarities and connections. These same forces are moving the profession in the direction of greater attention to the common factors.

In this regard, Jay Lebow (1997a) has written about the quiet revolution occurring in the profession favoring the ascendance of integrative theory and practice. Most of the reasons Lebow cites for the field's entry into an era of integration can be used to support the case for the common factors. Lebow notes that the trend toward integration parallels the movement away from the modernist belief in the limitless possibilities of single models to a postmodern understanding of the limits of unitary perspectives. He also argues that MFT is more broadly accepted among more mental health disciplines. As a result, less need to distinguish any differences with other approaches is experienced. He maintains, too, that the field's overarching meta-theory (i.e., systems theory), "invites examination of what lies within and outside the system, opening up a world of multiple inputs and possible actions" (p. 3). At length, he believes, and we concur, a stronger ideological commitment to the diversity of ideas within the community of family therapists can be found today. Leading journals and organizations now promote discourse "that transcends scholastic boundaries" (p. 3).

We add that the watershed article by Shields, Wynne, McDaniel, and Gawinski (1994) supports Lebow's position. These authors argue that family therapy has overemphasized its distinctiveness. So much so it is in danger of marginalizing itself and becoming irrelevant.

Besides the reasons just cited, the realities of clinical practice are compelling therapists to renounce their devotion to a pure approach. As family therapy trainers, we frequently hear students say that the "classic" methods do not fit as well for the clients they see as those in the so-called master therapists' videotapes and live demonstrations. In addition, the pressures of managed care and therapists' own felt need to integrate diverse theoretical perspectives are factors (Lebow, 1997a). Greater awareness of the research findings regarding the lack of evidence for the superiority of any one theoretical orientation and the importance of "generic dimensions" like the therapeutic alliance is also surfacing (Lebow, 1997a). Finally, interest is growing in the common threads that characterize the best of today's integrative MFT approaches. For his part, Lebow (1997a) made a clear appeal to common factors—whereas each of the best integrative approaches "suggests specific methods for conceptualizing and intervening . . . each also underscores the importance of core, generic factors in effective psychotherapy" (p. 13).

Organization of This Chapter

Similar to individual psychotherapy, far too much credit for therapeutic change has been accorded to model-based techniques in family therapy. It is time to consider the full range of variables that influence client change. To create a context for examining the common factors in MFT treatment, the four-part typology developed by Lambert (1992) is used (see chapters 1 and 2, this volume). For each of these dimensions, the contributions of MFT research are then reviewed. In ending, an attempt is made to delineate those common factors that may be unique to MFT. Our hope is that this discussion will contribute to the growing conversations about MFT integration and will help spur clinicians' and researchers' interest in the common factors.

Lambert's Four-Factor Model as Applied to MFT Research

EXTRATHERAPEUTIC CHANGE

Client Factors

Lambert (1992) suggested that 40% (the largest percentage of his four categories) of the improvement in therapy is due to factors that are part of the client (e.g., ego strength) or of the environment (e.g., fortuitous events and social support) that aid in recovery regardless of whatever benefits there may be to participating in psychotherapy itself. Although we cannot currently delineate what percentage of the outcome variance in MFT treatment is attributable to these extratherapeutic factors, we surmise that it is also high. Client factors (especially nonstatic and motivational characteristics) probably have more to do with successful outcomes in MFT and, in most cases, overpower techniques. Client factors in MFT fall into three major groups.

Static characteristics of individuals

The first category of client factors refers to variables like age, gender, race, and sexual orientation. In this vein, Bischoff and Sprenkle's (1993) reviewed client variables associated with dropping out of MFT treatment. They found that dropout rates are higher for lower socio-economic status (SES) clients. Dropout rates are also higher when the ethnic background of the client diverges from that of the therapist.

Another example is Jacobson's finding, based on a review of the behavioral marital therapy (BMT) research, that traditional BMT is more effective with younger than older clients (Jacobson & Christiansen, 1996). Probably because this category of client factors is easier to study (data can be gathered retrospectively from intake reports), we have more research on it than the two that follow. However, despite all the recent attention given to static client variables, not as much research on these variables has been performed as might be expected (Clark & Serovich, 1997; Gregory & Leslie, 1996; Leslie & Clossick, 1996). It is particularly telling that no research exists on client strengths and resources.

Nonstatic characteristics of individuals, couples, and families

These variables (e.g., individual learning style, level of couple commitment, family cohesion, family expressed emotion) are potentially malleable in therapy. Nevertheless, they probably bias, if not determine the outcome from the onset of intervention. To illustrate, Jacobson and Christiansen (1996) concluded that traditional BMT is most successful for couples with high (to each other) commitment and emotional engagement, low "traditionality," and convergent goals for the marriage. Although several of these variables have been included in MFT research, still many remain unexamined (e.g., the role of social and emotional intelligence and the role of different learning styles).

Motivational characteristics

These are individual, couple, or family/system characteristics that relate to clients' motivation to engage in treatment. They include variables such as perseverance, willingness to cooperate and do homework assignments. Naturally, a fine line exists between client characteristics in this category and the nonstatic characteristics just reviewed; sometimes the two categories become blurred (e.g., a person may not be motivated because she or he is not committed).

In all, very little research on motivational characteristics is found in MFT. One of the few is Holtzworth-Munroe, Jacobson, DeKlyen, and Whisman's (1989) investigation of client factors associated with a positive response to behavioral marital therapy. Holtzworth-Munroe et al. reported that a high degree of client collaboration, active participation, and homework compliance were associated with treatment success. That we do not know more about the impact of client motivational variables in MFT is unfortunate. They are probably quite potent.

Until the more recent emphasis on collaboration, a strong tradition arose within MFT to hold the therapist responsible for outcome. This was particularly evident in the writings of Jay Haley (1976). Yet, in assessing the importance of the client factors in MFT, the conclusions of Smith, Glass, and Miller's (1980) meta-analysis of 475 controlled studies of psychotherapy bear remembering.

> The possibility ought to be considered more seriously that the locus of those forces that restore and ameliorate the client in psychotherapy resides more within the client himself and less within the therapist and his actions. What the client brings to psychotherapy—the will to solve a problem or be rid of it, the intelligence to comprehend contingencies and relationships, the strength to face weakness, the confidence to trust another person—may contribute more to the success of therapy than whether it lasts twenty sessions or ten . . . or whether the therapist pays obeisance to Fritz Perls or to Joseph Wolpe. (p. 188)

Fortuitous Events

These variables also may be more salient than our cherished theories. During the review for this chapter, only one MFT investigation examining chance events was found. Even so, the results were quite telling.

In a 2-year follow-up study of BMT, Jacobson, Schmaling, and Holtzworth-Munroe (1987) conducted telephone interviews with 19 couples to detect any differences between the "relapsers" and "maintainers" from their treatment programs. Neither therapist-attributed nor treatment-related skills had any predictive value. Instead, relapsers experienced more stressful external events in their lives than did maintainers. That is, fortuitous events, versus anything associated with the actual BMT, predicted relapse.

Social Support

Although seldom directly measured in MFT outcome research, social support is a major variable in the literatures ancillary to MFT. The divorce adjustment literature, for instance, clearly notes that social participation is one of the major factors contributing to divorce recovery (Everett & Volgy, 1991). The family stress literature emphasizes social support as both a major buffer and healing force (McCubbin & Figley, 1983). Further, within the medical family therapy literature, social support stands out as one (if not the most powerful) of the dimensions in the treatment and management of illness (McDaniel, Hepworth, & Doherty, 1992). No matter their theoretical orientation, wise family therapists use social support as a backbone of their treatment of severely depressed and suicidal clients. Clients' abilities to mobilize social support may, like fortuitous events, have more to do with outcome than we now recognize.

After combining the "extratherapeutic factors" (client factors, fortuitous events, and social support), it is not surprising that Lambert believes they account for the largest percentage of improvement. We would not be surprised if this eventually holds true for MFT outcome as well.

RELATIONSHIP FACTORS

Lambert (1992) reported that relationship variables account for 30% of improvement in psychotherapy. For MFT, this figure likely represents a very conservative estimate. The relationship in psychotherapy is the common factor most emphasized in the individual literature and most clearly addressed in the MFT research. If there could be said to be a "gold standard" finding in the MFT research literature, it would be that the quality of the client–therapist relationship is the *sine qua non* of successful therapy.

In an early investigation (with 3,956 cases, still the largest single MFT outcome study), Beck and Jones (1973) used regression techniques to determine which of 11 factors contribute most to positive therapy outcome. Their own words vividly capture the potency of this variable:

> Of the findings with specific implications for practice, probably the most important in the present study is that of the marked association of the counselor–client relationship with outcomes . . . This factor was found to be twice as powerful a predictor of outcomes as any other client or service characteristic covered by the study and more powerful than all client characteristics combined. An unsatisfactory relationship was found to be highly associated with client-initiated disengagement and with negative explanations by the client of his reason for terminating. (p. 8)

Further, in the first major review of the marriage and family therapy outcome literature, Gurman and Kniskern (1978) wrote: "The ability of the therapist to establish a positive relationship with his or her clients, long a central issue of individual therapy, receives the most consistent support as an important outcome-related factor in marital-family therapy" (p. 875). Several other research reports, both early and recent, support this conclusion.

The often cited study by Alexander, Barton, Schiavo, and Parsons (1977), for example, found relationship skills (warmth, affect–behavior integration, humor) accounted for 44.6% of outcome variance in a study of systems–behavioral intervention with families of delinquents. Investigating a systemic/strategic team approach, Green and Herget (1991) also found that therapist warmth was a major predictor of outcome.

In another telling study, Stolk and Perlesz (1990) took ratings of client satisfaction during a two year strategic therapy training program. They actually found clients to be less satisfied with therapy from second year students than first. They interpreted the decline in scores to the diminishing of the students' relationship skills as they focused more on strategic techniques. The authors wrote: "Feedback from the families acts as a poignant reminder that our clients require respect, understanding, warmth, and positive regard, not merely thought provoking and systematically correct hypotheses and interventions" (p. 56). Similarly, Kuehl, Newfield, and Joanning (1990) found therapist "caring" to be the most important contributor to success (along with relevant therapist suggestions) from the client's perspective.

The importance of relationship issues is further reflected in the MFT supervision literature. Frankel and Piercy (1990), for instance, coded supervisor "support" (a relationship variable) and "teach" behaviors and looked at their impact on therapist and client behaviors. Although both support and teach behaviors influenced trainee behavior, the supervisor's supportive behavior was more influential. In turn, it facilitated effective supportive behavior on the part of the therapists. Finally, they found the family was significantly more cooperative when the supervisor and trainee were effective at performing support behaviors.

Pinsof and Catherall (1986) were the first MFTs to look at relationship skills in the context of a variable imported from the individual psychotherapy literature—namely, the therapeutic alliance. They based their Family and Couple Therapy Alliance scales on the work of Bordin (1979). Bordin suggested that the alliance breaks into three dimensions: tasks, or the clinical processes and techniques used by the therapist and their acceptability to clients; goals, the agreement on desired outcomes in the implicit and explicit therapeutic contract; and bonds, or the affective feeling of relatedness and connection between client and therapist). Heatherington and Friedlander (1990) affirmed the basic factor structure and other psychometric properties of the scales.

To date, studies have shown somewhat mixed results. Catherall (1984) found that a high overall appraisal of the alliance had a strong positive association with progress ratings by therapists. On the other hand, Bourgeois, Sabourin, and Wright (1990) showed, in a study of group marital therapy, that the overall Couple Alliance Scale accounted for 5% to 8% of the variance on three out of four outcome measures for men, but only one out of four measures for women.

Johnson and Talitman (1997), researching emotionally focused marital therapy, found that couple alliance scores accounted for 22% of the variance in posttreatment satisfaction and 29% of the variance at follow-up. The Task subscale, a measure of whether the tasks within therapy were pertinent to clients' presenting concerns, accounted for most of the variance in both posttreatment and follow-up assessments of satisfaction (similar to the findings of Crane, Griffin, & Hill, 1986, and Kuehl et al. 1990). Addressing predictors of success, Johnson and Talitman noted that couples most likely to be satisfied after 12 sessions and at follow-up, made a positive alliance with the therapist and saw the tasks of emotionally focused marital therapy as promoting emotional engagement.

Sorting out what contributed to the dissimilar results observed between Bourgeois et al. (1990) and Johnson and Talitman (1997) is difficult. Differences in the mode of treatment and clinical population may account for the conflicting findings. In particular, the Bourgeois et al. study was done in group marital therapy with French speaking participants.

Two unpublished manuscripts have also shown a relationship between the therapeutic alliance and outcome. Tolan and his colleagues studied phases of therapy in a large-scale project aimed at preventing aggression in urban youth (Hanish, Tolan, McKay, & Dickey, 1997). The therapeutic alliance was associated with improvements in mothers' child management practices, which, in turn, were associated with improvements in child cooperation and aggression. Howard Liddle (personal communication October 20, 1997) adapted the Vanderbilt Psychotherapy Process Scale (O'Malley, Suh, & Strupp, 1983), an alliance measure from the individual literature. Scores predict outcome in the family treatment of drug-abusing adolescents. The positive results in these two investigations may be related to tailoring the alliance questions to a specific treatment population using a specific treatment protocol.

In summary, the extant literature supports the conclusion that relationship factors exert a potent influence on MFT outcome. Fewer answers are available for this question: "What specific aspects of the relationship are crucial and why?" Even without greater precision, it is still useful to (a) wonder how MFT practitioners can be helped to improve their relationships with clients and (b) reflect on the personal or interpersonal qualities that should be considered for recruiting people to become MFTs (Beck & Jones, 1973).

Few family therapists will go as far as to say that relationship skills are sufficient for doing effective therapy. Indeed, Gurman and Kniskern (1978) explicitly stated that they are not. Most family therapists continue to focus on other skills and see the therapy relationship as a vehicle for carrying out their craft. Again however, the vehicle may be more important than is often credited or recognized.

EXPECTANCY (PLACEBO EFFECTS)

Lambert (1992) wrote that expectancy and placebo factors refer to the portion of improvement that results from the client's knowledge of being in treatment and the differential credibility of specific techniques. He believes that this accounts for approximately 15% of improvement in psychotherapy. For the present discussion, *expectancy* "refers to the anticipation of a systematic relationship between events or objects and some upcoming situation" (Goldman, Brown, & Christiansen, 1987, p. 183).

Expectancy

Most MFTs try to enhance expectancy through engendering optimism and self-efficacy in their clients. This is especially true for practitioners of what O'Hanlon (1994) described as the "third wave" (i.e., competency based) therapies—narrative, solution-focused, or collaborative language systems. Unfortunately, few systematic discussions of expectancy in the MFT literature and very little research are found.

When clients come to treatment, they hold expectations about one or more of the following: (a) what they hope to get out of therapy, (b) whether therapy is likely to help, (c) what they hope the therapist will do, and (d) whether they have the strength or capacity to change. No doubt, expectations are ever present; however, owing to its complexity and mutability, the actual role of expectancy may be one of the least understood variables. A client may entertain one set of expectations before therapy begins, but these may change radically later.

Two studies in the MFT literature that specifically relate client expectancy to outcome were found. The results about expectation turned out to be "contrary to expectation!" Adams, Piercy, and Jurich (1991) investigated the impact of a solution-focused versus a problem-focused approach. They studied their effect in initial treatment and the effect of the two approaches on both client and family optimism of whether therapy was likely to help. The authors found no differences in client or therapist optimism—a finding at odds with the belief that a solution-focused orientation would enhance optimism. In addition, no relationship obtained between client optimism and outcome at the end of ten sessions. Because measurements were only made in the early stages of therapy, the Adams et al. note that it is possible that optimism may be stable initially, but become more variable later.

Dumka, Sprenkle, and Martin (1995) developed several brief scales to measure client expectancy in family therapy. They defined *outcome optimism* as the degree to which clients estimate that therapy will result in desired improvement. They also studied "self-efficacy," the degree to which clients believe that they can do what is necessary to alleviate the problematic situation. The results: The scales made for these constructs did not relate to progress in therapy three sessions postmeasurement.

Different explanations may account for these negative results. As both studies measured expectancy only at the beginning of therapy, it may need to be assessed more frequently, especially in later sessions. Second, perhaps the measures were invalid or did not tap the expectancy created in successful family therapy. Less likely, but possible, is that client expectancy, at least in MFT, has little relation to outcome in spite of logical arguments that it should.

Besides clients, therapists harbor expectancies. Beck and Jones (1973), in a nationwide study of family service agencies, found that when therapists (at intake) predicted that clients would not improve or get worse, on average clients' perceptions of outcome significantly exceeded the therapists' predictions. The research did not address how well these same clients would have fared if their therapists had been more optimistic in their assessment.

Patterson and Forgatch (1985) reported that family therapy failures are due in some cases to the therapist giving up on the family after they resist suggestions. In their paradigm, the child defeats the parents in their attempts to manage the child. The parents, in turn, defeat the therapist in his or her attempts to manage them (through teaching and confronting interventions). Thus, the parents' expectation of failure is conveyed to the therapist who then feels defeated, blames the parents for being nonresponsive, and lets the family drop out. Shapiro (1974) in an earlier study, found that premature termination in MFT is associated with therapists' initial negative feelings toward their clients, which may constitute a dimension of negative expectancy.

Credibility

Lambert's (1992) position that the differential credibility of specific treatment techniques is a dimension of expectancy relates to the first type of client expectancy discussed above—what clients hope to get out of therapy. Crane et al. (1986) surveyed clients in two MFT clinics and found that how well the treatment "fit" the clients' view of their problems accounted for 35% of outcome variance. That is, the therapists' ability to present therapy as consistent and congruent with client expectations is important to clients. Similarly, Kuehl et al. (1990), using a qualitative ethnographic interview methodology, found that clients with successful outcomes emphasized the relevancy of therapist suggestions.

Although the factor of expectancy is important theoretically to many MFTs, empirical support is mixed. Some evidence suggests that outcome is affected negatively when client expectations regarding the fit of therapy are not met. Also, results indicate that difficult clients may demoralize therapists, which then contributes to dropout. To date, the MFT research performed has not found a relationship between initial client optimism or initial perception of self-efficacy and positive outcome.

TECHNIQUES

Here Lambert (1992) refers to factors unique to specific treatments. Applied to MFT, this refers to the percentage of improvement related to using the model specific techniques of Bowenian, structural, strategic, narrative, solution-focused, or other family therapies. As noted throughout this volume, Lambert suggests that only 15% of outcome variance in individual psychotherapy is attributable to model specific techniques. With the empirical literature in mind, no convincing reason can be found to believe that the percentage would be much higher for MFT.

Below the family literature regarding technique in general is reviewed. In addition, the MFT research bearing on several well-known methods or generic techniques often described in individual psychotherapy is sampled.

Model-Specific Effects in MFT

As Shadish, Ragsdale, Glaser, and Montgomery (1995) put it, from the most comprehensive meta-analysis of marital and family therapy completed to date: "Despite some superficial evidence apparently favoring some orientations over others, no orientation is yet demonstrably superior to any other. This finding parallels the psychotherapy literature generally" (p. 348).

Shadish et al. (1995) also submit that what modest theoretical orientation differences do appear may result from the confounding influence of other variables (e.g., client characteristics, lack of uniformity in outcome measures across studies, reactivity of outcome measures). When they entered potential methodologic confounding variables into a regression analysis, all orientation differences disappeared. Naturally, the failure to reject the "null hypothesis" does not negate the possibility that real differences do exist across different treatment approaches. Nevertheless, current knowledge calls for a much higher measure of modesty from the proponents of different therapies than now observed.

Increased constraint or humility makes sense for additional reasons. First, only two of the major schools within MFT sponsor programmatic research—BMT and emotionally focused therapy. Gurman, Kniskern, and Pinsof's (1986) earlier finding that most schools of family therapy had completed no studies with most major presenting problems still holds true today!

Second, the best studies of treatment efficacy are randomized, controlled trials, using treatment manuals and strict adherence to treatment protocols. Such studies are also completed on highly specified populations. Although the rigor is laudable, the results obtained only have a modest relationship with what takes place in actual clinical settings.

Third, with much MFT research, disentangling treatment effects from therapist effects is impossible (Gurman & Kniskern, 1981). Sprenkle is aware of one outcome study in which the effectiveness of the two treatment approaches was based entirely on the results of one therapist. If his cases were included, the first treatment looked worse. If his data were omitted, the first treatment looked best! Because most MFT research has not used a treatment manual or provided even a detailed description of the treatment, what techniques were actually employed cannot be determined.

So we are not seen as only critical of MFT outcome research, we acknowledge that impressive strides have been made in the past decade. The body of research literature presented in a special issue of the *Journal of Marital and Family Therapy* (October, 1995), for instance, on the efficacy of MFT is quite impressive. A quick examination reveals, however, that the majority of the most effective treatment programs, such as those used in the family management of schizophrenia (Goldstein & Miklowitz, 1995), represent multidisciplinary or integrative models and not school specific approaches. In all, the extant literature shows that techniques that are the province of any one model have never been proven superior. They probably contribute far less to the success of therapy than model proponents prefer to believe.

MFT Research Related to Generic Techniques Described in Individual Therapy

Surveying the individual psychotherapy literature, Garfield (1992) identified several generic techniques that cut across most models. In this section, MFT research bearing on these commonly used techniques is briefly examined.

Reattribution

Garfield (1992) and Frank (1973) suggested that therapies give the client an explanation of his or her difficulties and a healing ritual to overcome them. The particular explanations or interpretations are not as important as whether the client finds them credible or acceptable. Acknowledged or not, all orientations within MFT have behavioral, affective, *and* cognitive components. Relevant to technique factors is how their clients "make meanings," and attribute expectations of change to the therapist's actions. Hoffman (1990) argued that with the emergence of the social constructionist family therapies, MFT has shifted more to a focus on meaning rather than the earlier emphasis on behavior.

It is noteworthy that even earlier therapies that principally emphasized behavior (e.g., strategic therapy's focus on interrupting dysfunctional behavioral sequences) also contained strong cognitive elements, exampled in the interventions of "normalizing" and "reframing." These are sometimes called "reattributional" techniques because they influence clients to modify their beliefs and premises. Morris, Alexander, and Turner (1991) stated that family therapy models, particularly the functional, structural, and strategic "claim that reattributional techniques are central to therapeutic change" (p. 200).

The only empirical research to come out on reattribution techniques was a series of investigations completed by Alexander and his colleagues (Alexander, Waldron, Barton, & Mas, 1989; Morris et al., 1991; Robbins, Alexander, Newell, & Turner, 1996). The first two studies consisted of experimental simulations that laid the groundwork for the Robbins et al.'s (1996) investigation of functional family therapy with delinquent adolescents. Therapists' interventions were coded and assessed for their impact on adolescent negativity. The researchers found that only following reframes did client attitude scores move out of the negative range. They conclude: "This effort supports the clinical use of reframing with adolescent patients in family therapy" (p. 32). They caution, however, that this finding may not generalize to other treatments or contexts.

Several investigators have also explored adding a cognitive component to BMT (Baucom, Sayers, & Sher, 1990; Behrens, Sanders, & Halford, 1990). The results of these efforts were largely disappointing. Specifically, the studies did not demonstrate the effectiveness of cognitive marital therapy over wait-list control groups or the standard behavioral treatment (Alexander, Holtzworth-Munroe, & Jameson, 1994).

In accounting for the results, Alexander et al. (1994) indicated that these problems may be attributable to limited statistical power, problems in measuring cognitive shifts, and a simplistic understanding of the role of cognition in marriage. They also speculated that these treatments may not have been a good fit for the clients, recalling Garfield's (1992) position that particular explanations or interpretations may not be as important as whether the client finds them to be credible or acceptable.

Many family therapies place a strong emphasis on client "meaning." This is especially true in some newer social constructionist approaches like narrative therapy and the collaborative language systems approaches. Their proponents have yet to substantiate their claims empirically. For now, we have modest evidence in support of reframing, limited evidence for the value of cognitive marital therapy, and growing evidence for the importance of designing treatments which match client needs.

Reinforcement

Garfield (1992) noted that reinforcement is a commonly used therapeutic technique. All psychotherapists respond positively to verbal reports or to positive behaviors through nodding, smiling, and verbal responses. It is self-evident that all marriage and family therapists use reinforcement in this way. Although reinforcement is often viewed as a behavioral strategy, when solution-focused family therapists discover an "exception" to a problem situation and encourage its repetition, this could be seen as a type of reinforcement strategy. The same could be said for a narrative therapist who finds a "unique outcome" in a "problem saturated story" and helps the client to embellish this subplot.

There is a shortage of MFT research specifically studying therapist reinforcement of clients. Of the few studies completed, Bandler and Grinder (1975) performed a qualitative analysis of the videotapes of well-known therapists like Virginia Satir and Milton Erickson. They found that Satir frequently "anchored" therapeutic gains by facial expressions, body postures, or by touch. Erickson also did the same by manipulating voice tone and pace. Most family therapists engage in these behaviors, even if not deliberately or consciously.

Some family therapies have explicitly emphasized reinforcement between clients—for example, behavioral exchange models within BMT (Jacobson & Margolin, 1979). Communication training approaches, incorporated into several MFT models, also promote "reinforcement" when they encourage clients to "validate" each other (Guerney, 1977; Hendrix, 1988).

Desensitization

Another technique frequently used in individual therapy is desensitization. The clinical and research tradition within MFT that most openly acknowledges the role of desensitization is sex therapy. One of its major leaders, Helen Kaplan (1979) maintained that at one level all nonorganically based sex dysfunctions were caused by anxiety, whether rooted in intrapsychic or interpersonal processes. Incorporating Masters and Johnson's (1970) "sensate focus" exercises, most of her treatment protocols used a desensitization paradigm. That is, the client was gradually exposed to the feared stimulus (a specific activity like intercourse or any form of sex for those with sexual aversions). Other sex therapy techniques like the "stop–start" technique for premature ejaculation or the use of dilators in the treatment of vaginismus are examples of desensitization procedures. This is not to say, of course, that desensitization is all there is to sex therapy. In fact, sex therapy, like MFT in general, has moved in the direction of acknowledging the importance of both meaning and affect as well as behavior in the treatment process (Leiblum & Rosen, 1989).

Information and skills training

Garfield (1992) suggested that providing information and facilitating skill development are common techniques across forms of therapy.

Many MFT practitioners, however, are reluctant to see themselves in this role. Especially within the social constructionist school, some therapists believe the "expert" role should be avoided. They might also be reluctant to see what they do as teaching or training. Still, helping clients, for example, to "re-author" their life stores, contains an instructional element. We believe that the imparting of information is probably a larger part of what most MFTs do than is customarily recognized.

Earlier Friedlander et al.'s (1987) study was introduced. Analyzing tapes of Minuchin and Whitaker, these researchers showed that most of the therapists' responses could be categorized as providing information, interpretation, and guidance.

Several MFT approaches openly acknowledge their educational thrust. The psychoeducational approaches to the family management of schizophrenia (Goldstein & Miklowitz, 1995) involve considerable didactic instruction and have produced some of the most impressive outcome studies in all the MFT literature. Many family therapies for child behavioral disorders (Chamberlain & Rosicky, 1995; Estrada & Pinsof, 1995) also entail education. Medical family therapists (McDaniel et al., 1992) are encouraged to become familiar with up-to-date information about the illnesses of their patients and to share it when appropriate.

BMT is the MFT approach most overtly emphasizing skills training. Training packages have been developed in behavioral exchange techniques (i.e., couples are taught how to increase positive behaviors and decrease negative ones in the home) and in communication/problem-solving skills. The short-term effects of these programs are among the most well documented findings in MFT. Long-term follow-up studies also have been completed (Jacobson & Addis, 1993; Jacobson et al., 1987) suggesting that combining both training packages may be necessary for gains to be maintained beyond 1 year. Looking at the longer term picture, as many as 50% of couples who participate in BMT may not remain above the clinically distressed threshold (Jacobson & Christiansen, 1996). These authors report that the long term outcomes for other non-BMT marital therapies are probably not much better.

Several other MFT approaches incorporate skills training (e.g., Imago couples therapy; Hendrix, 1988), but these packages have yet to be researched. Though outside the scope of this review, as they are not strictly therapy, many marriage and family enrichment programs, highly skills training in nature, have produced impressive results (Lebow, 1997b; Stanley, Markman, & St. Peters, 1995).

The dodo bird verdict applies to MFT as much as it does to individual therapy. Some specific techniques show promise and yet, many do not. In the next and final section of this chapter we address the question, "Are there common factors unique to MFT?" We also broach how a common factor approach to MFT might bring greater coherence to the field and enhance its research agenda.

Unique Common Factors in MFT

RELATIONAL CONCEPTUALIZATION

A common factor, perhaps unique to the field of MFT is the translation of human/family difficulties into relational terms. Most family therapists re-conceptualize, for example, many *Diagnostic and Statistical Manual of Mental Disorders* (*DSM*) diagnoses in relational terms. This is so despite the claim in the *DSM* stating that mental disorders are conditions that occur "within a person."

To illustrate, while not ignoring the role of biology, most MFTs would view a "depressed" man's malady within the context of his social network, staying alert to the complex web of reciprocal influences involved in the complaint. Furthermore, this translation leads MFTs to keep the whole system (or systems) in view when interacting with any part of a system (Wampler, 1997). While focusing on the depressed man's relationship with his employer, for instance, the therapist might also be attending to patterns or expectations from his family of origin. MFTs, moreover, typically attempt to relate in a positive way to all parts of the system(s) regardless of who happens to be in the treatment room (Wampler, 1997). If the depressed man's wife refused treatment, she still would be very much "present" in the session as would the man's colleagues at work. These inferences hold true for most MFT orientations and may be a common explanation for some of the efficacy of MFT.

EXPANDED DIRECT TREATMENT SYSTEM

Family therapists differ in the extent to which they push to involve more people than the identified patient (or in some cases the willing participant) directly in treatment. Pinsof (1995) distinguishes between direct patient systems (persons physically in treatment) and indirect patient systems (persons not physically in treatment, but who affect in important ways the problem being treated and are, in turn, significantly affected the therapy.) Although probably all MFTs pay attention to indirect systems, therapists who take pains to expand the direct system (even in the face of resistance) believe that the power, at the heart of family treatment, resides in the therapy of "live" systems. At the 1997 Annual Conference of the American Association for Marriage and Family Therapy, Augustus Napier questioned whether the new social constructionist therapies (such as narrative and collaborative language systems) were truly "family therapy." He asserted that the postmodern movement within family therapy places too much emphasis on changing individual internal meaning systems. They fail to capitalize on the immediacy only made possible by in-the-room interaction among family members.

This debate will probably continue as it is rooted in theoretical assumptions regarding how family problems originate, are maintained, and best ameliorated. Naturally, there are individual differences on this issue among MFTs of all theoretical orientations. Further, practical, life cycle, and ethical considerations abound. Even the most ardent believers in conjoint treatment choose to see family members individually under certain circumstances (e.g., active violence, sexual abuse), or simply because all attempts by the client and the therapist to involve others has been unsuccessful.

Regrettably, little research is available to shed light on whether conjoint direct participation adds to relational conceptualization. Though there has been much research comparing conjoint therapy with (nonsystemic) individual therapy (Gurman & Kniskern, 1978, focused on these comparisons in the first major review of family therapy research), there is almost none comparing systemically conceptualized individual therapy with conjoint therapy.

We could find only two studies, both completed by Jose Szapocznik and his colleagues (Szapocznik, Kurtines, Foote, Perez-Vidal, & Hervis, 1983, 1986) that compared "individual" family therapy with a conjoint method (similar assumptions, but a different unit of treatment). In particular, these investigators compared a conjoint version of structural family therapy with a single person (typically the adolescent) version. While both significantly (but not differentially) reduced adolescent drug use and improved family functioning among Hispanic families, the single person version had better long-term results. The generalizability of the results is limited, however, because of small sample sizes, ethnic homogeneity, the use of a single theoretical orientation, and one presenting complaint.

The superiority of conjoint treatment of marital difficulties is well established in the research literature (Gurman & Kniskern, 1978, 1981). Such treatment also has wide intuitive and theoretical appeal. However, how many of the comparison (individual) treatments utilized a systemic conceptualization of the marital problem is unclear. Because most MFTs have had some success treating marriages with an absent partner, it is probable the issue is complex and not all the pertinent variables have been researched.

Pinsof (1995) offered several reasons for the value of expanding the direct client system. These benefits may constitute common factors in all conjoint approaches. His five "interpersonal premises" follow.

1. "Therapists will generally learn more about patient systems if they meet as many of the key patients as possible" (Pinsof,

1995, p. 98). The therapist obtains a clearer snapshot of the interpersonal dimensions of the patient system.

2. "The therapist usually will establish a stronger therapeutic alliance with the patient system if that alliance is based on face-to-face contact" (Pinsof, 1995, p. 98).

3. "Doing as much of the work as possible in front of the key patients maximizes the likelihood of creating a wider, more stable, and more empathic collective observing ego" (Pinsof, 1995, p. 98). This means that more people understand what is going on and why. If one person loses perspective, another can help him or her regain it.

4. "The transforming impact of major breakthroughs is usually greater when they occur in the presence of key patients" (Pinsof, 1995, p. 99).

5. "The therapist will have a more accurate understanding of the problem maintenance structure if key patients are directly involved in ongoing treatment" (Pinsof, 1995, p. 99). By "problem maintenance structure," Pinsof referred to all of the constraints (be they organizational, biological, emotional, cognitive, family of origin, object relations, or issues of the self) that prevent family members from resolving their problems.

Pinsof qualified these propositions depending on several factors, including the stage of treatment, the type of family, the presenting problems, and life cycle. He calls for a flexible approach that emphasizes the presence of different subsystems (and individuals alone) at certain times in treatment. Nonetheless, the general maxim is to include the "key players" at least some of the time.

Mindful of these qualifications, Pinsof's propositions have intuitive appeal. Probably MFTs from most orientations can recount instances where the "common factor" of including more people in the direct client system led to salutary results. Sadly, however, no research evidence was offered by Pinsof for these "interpersonal premise" propositions. Future research on the unit of treatment hopefully will be forthcoming.

THE EXPANDED THERAPEUTIC ALLIANCE IN MFT

When more than one person is involved in the direct client system, the expanded therapeutic alliance may be a common factor unique to MFT. If, for example, a husband and wife and two teenage children participate in therapy, each of the four individuals will have an alliance with the therapist. In addition, each subsystem (parents, marriage partners, siblings) will also have a subsystem alliance with the therapist which is more than the individual alliances. Further, the entire client system will have an alliance with the therapist that may be more than the individual and subsystem alliances (Pinsof, 1995) combined.

As noted earlier in this chapter, the therapeutic alliance is composed of bonds, tasks, and goals. The bonds component refers to the quality of the therapeutic relationship. If the key players in the family experience the therapist as warm, empathic, and genuine, and they experience this bonding not only as individuals, but also as members of the various subsystems—parents (the therapist genuinely supports their efforts at parenting), married couple (the therapist warmly affirms their caring for each other), and siblings (the therapist reinforces their sticking up for each other)—then the therapy should receive a powerful boost. This kind of positive synergy is also possible for the goals and tasks dimensions of the alliance.

Of course, inclusion is a two-edged sword. If a split develops in the alliance (e.g., parents bond well with the therapist, but the teenagers poorly), then broadening the direct system may turn into a liability. Because not all alliances are equally important, the extent of the damage would depend on the centrality of the teenagers to the problem for which the family sought treatment and their power to sabotage therapy.

Before concluding this section, MFTs, by virtue of their systemic conceptualization, may sometimes also have a unique "alliance" with the indirect treatment system. If an MFT, for example, treats a school phobic child and his parents, and sees the school as part of the indirect treatment system (school representatives never attend sessions), this therapist may establish an alliance with the school either indirectly through the clients or through telephone calls or correspondence. Feeling valued by the therapist, even indirectly, might motivate school personnel. Presumably, a nonsystemic therapist who conceptualized the child's problem intrapsychically, would not have such an alliance and lose out on its potential salutary effect.

Research on the alliance in MFT is in its infancy. We hope, however, that the field will devote careful attention to alliance issues and their impact on outcome.

BEHAVIORAL, COGNITIVE, AND AFFECTIVE COMMON FACTORS IN MFT

Beyond what has been said about understanding problems relationally, expanding the "direct" patient system, and capitalizing on the special qualities of the alliance, the case for other "unique" factors in MFT becomes less compelling. Within the individual therapy literature, Karasu (1986) argued that besides the relationship variables, common factors can be classified as falling into three major groups: behavioral regulation, cognitive mastery, and affective experiencing. He believes that these change factors can be activated in diverse ways through techniques used by the different schools. Although different therapies use different interventions, they bring about change through one of these three final common pathways (Norcross, 1995).

We also believe most, if not all, MFT interventions work through the common pathways of behavioral regulation, cognitive mastery, and affective experiencing. These interventions are only distinctive when they work through the unique MFT common factors of systemic conceptualization, the expanded direct treatment system, and the expanded therapeutic alliance. Below, we list our candidates for behavioral, cognitive, and affective common factors, highlighting several emphasized in MFT to illustrate how they are employed across different schools.

Behavioral regulation occurs in MFT when therapists facilitate clients' changing interactional patterns or dysfunctional sequences, modifying boundaries and changing family structures, learning new skills, becoming more supportive of each other, and learning to empower self (self-agency) and others. An example of a primarily behavioral common factor emphasized in many current MFT models (but is not unique to MFT) is developing a sense of personal "agency." Narrative therapy helps clients experience a sense of agency by exploring alternate life-empowering stories. Solution-focused therapy asks clients to attend to exceptions to their problems and encourages clients to find ways to expand these exceptions. Clients access forgotten resources and become aware of their abilities to solve their own problems (Walter & Peller, 1992). Feminist family therapists support clients' agency by helping them to challenge sexist institutions and practices. Medical family therapists (McDaniel et al., 1992) help clients to find alternative ways to cope with life's physical challenges and to develop alternatives (Blow & Piercy, 1997).

Cognitive mastery takes place in MFT when therapists facilitate clients' gaining insight (understanding, new meaning) about interactional processes within themselves and the family, between the family and other systems, and across generations (Wampler, 1997). An example of a leading cognitive common factor emphasized in MFT models (but is not unique to MFT) is "separating the individual from the problem or symptom." Although narrative therapy is probably the most explicit in stressing that people are not the problem (the problem is the problem), virtually all MFT models "externalize" problems. From its earliest days, MFTs labeled symptoms as problems of the family system as a whole, not simply the individual. By noticing and tracking exceptions to problems, solution-focused therapists focus on client competencies. The internal family systems model (Schwartz, 1995) regards symptoms as the result of extreme "parts" and the individual as having a core healthy "self."

Another example of a cognitive common factor emphasized within MFT is self-differentiation. Coined by Bowen (1978) to refer to the process by which individuals come to guide their lives by intellectual functioning as opposed to emotional reactivity, many models of MFT try to achieve similar ends.

In this respect, Minuchin's boundary-setting techniques, can be recast as differentiation strategies as clients, by setting boundaries, think of themselves as more in control of their lives. In the sexual crucible approach of Schnarch (1991), differentiation of self is a key component of healthy sexual functioning. Highly differentiated partners have a strong sense of personal identity enabling them to become emotionally involved without depending on others as primarily sources of validation. Napier and Whitaker (1978) encouraged clients to turn inward and focus on their own growth as opposed to thinking of others as the source of their problems. What they call individuation equals personal growth, which equals marital and family growth. In narrative and collaborative language systems models, therapists "deconstruct" emotionally charged situations so clients are free to make calmer and more self-directed choices.

Emotional experiencing occurs in MFT when therapists facilitate clients making emotional connections with themselves, the therapist, and most important, with each other. We believe that the greater attention being given to the role of emotions in therapy rests in the growing realization that much of what MFTs do is (to borrow the title of Susan Johnson's, 1996, book) "creating connection." Human beings (according to attachment theory, the basis for emotion focused MFT) are "hard wired" to want closeness and intimacy. Their failure to experience connection is what impels them into therapy. When they feel they have achieved it, the end of therapy is often near.

We also recognize that saying what is a behavioral, cognitive, or affective intervention is arbitrary. If a therapist successfully teaches a couple new communication skills (a behavioral intervention), the partners will probably have new thoughts about each other (e.g., "There is hope for this relationship") and new feelings about each other (e.g., greater warmth). The classic MFT schools have varied in the extent to which they give each of these three domains priority. For example, traditional BMT has emphasized behavior, the social constructionist approaches have stressed cognitions (meaning), and EFT, emotions. Again, however, all effective approaches affect these three final common pathways in salutary ways.

We also believe models gradually evolve in ways that emphasize the common pathways initially downplayed or neglected in their theoretical base. For example, BMT started as a "pure" behavioral approach. Yet, as family therapy began to give more attention to meaning, BMT added more intentional cognitive elements (Alexander et al., 1994). The most current version of BMT (Jacobson & Christiansen, 1996), with its strong emphasis on "acceptance," includes an intentional component related to affect. There is greater awareness that all three pathways are needed for successful treatment.

PRIVILEGING OF CLIENTS' EXPERIENCES

A final common factor, though not unique to MFT, has been strongly emphasized in the social constructionist approaches and writings of Duncan and his colleagues (Duncan et al., 1997). It is the privileging of client experience (whether cognitive, behavioral, or affective). This movement to incorporate more the client's perspective into the therapist's work has influenced all schools of MFT. Although there remains considerable debate concerning the nature of therapist "expertise" and how to use it, family therapists are much less commanding and controlling than twenty years ago. Moving away from a "father/mother knows best" stance, MFTs today are apt to pay close attention to the clients' own "theories" about the problem and their wisdom concerning what would be helpful and unhelpful. We consider this a welcome trend within the field.

Conclusion

This chapter has gone "against the grain" of most MFT literature. Here change variables not unique to the field's cherished theories were explored and emphasized. We began by stating the reasons the field has emphasized differences and why a shift toward commonalties is long overdue. Building on Lambert's (1992) schema, extratherapeutic factors, relationship factors, expectancy variables, and technique were examined. In our view, many nontechnique variables that are potent in individual psychotherapy probably also account for most of the success in MFT. We also identified several unique MFT common factors (e.g., systemic conceptualization) and several common factors which, although not unique to MFT, have been strongly emphasized in MFT literature.

We hope that this chapter will contribute to diminishing the bombast and hubris of MFT theorists. Indeed, a mellowing of the field would be most desirable. Less attention needs to be paid to charismatic claims of uniqueness and more credence given to those common variables from which most change springs.

Questions From the Editors

1. How do you account for the neglect given to common factors in the MFT literature?

As we mentioned earlier, the history of MFT has been a history of emphasizing differences. This may have been necessary for a time for the discipline to "differentiate" itself from mainstream psychotherapy. However, the ongoing competition within MFT among the various schools reflects the forceful personalities of their founders and the field's general indifference to research. As long as the field continues to reward model developers who come up with techniques that get clinicians excited, and that seem to produce better short-term results than what the clinicians believe they are already achieving (research is not required), a common factors approach is likely to take a back seat.

In fact, we believe that the "worship" of technique is so ingrained in the MFT culture that it would produce considerable cognitive dissonance for most MFTs to be persuaded that their cherished techniques are not primarily responsible for change. This would be like convincing a cult follower, who had given his or her possessions and allegiance to the charismatic founder, that this figure is only an ordinary mortal. It can be done, but it entails considerable "deprogramming." Sprenkle discovered that even after teaching his students about common factors, they seemed to "drift" back into taking advocacy stances for their cherished models without acknowledging the "religious" dimensions of their positions. This is a fascinating and powerful witness to the power of the culture of technique. The MFT "industry" also supports this culture. Books about new models are published only on the basis of their ability to sell (evidence for differential efficacy is not required). These will probably continue to be more marketable (and sexy) than research-based treatises about "dull" topics like common factors. Charismatic model developers are also the ones who fill workshop seats and enable organizations to have "successful" conferences. In short, acceptance of a common factors approach within MFT will require a change in the whole MFT culture, something that will require the discipline to mature and take decades to achieve.

2. How should common factors impact the training of MFTs?

Common factors should be given much more attention in the training of MFTs. This should be done both by exposing students to the common factors literature and incorporating a common factors approach into MFT clinical training. Hopefully, this chapter will be an aid to the first objective because, Duncan and his colleagues previously had been among the few voices within MFT pushing for a common factors emphasis.

Teaching MFT models as though they are primarily responsible for client change verges on professional scandal. Although certain models are probably the best "match" for certain clients under certain circumstances (particularly when a good match occurs between the model and the particular therapist), there is not a scintilla of evidence for the general superiority of "unique" models. Because most evidence we have centers on the quality of the therapeutic relationship/alliance, we think that the heart of training should be on how to develop mutually satisfying and empowering bonds, goals, and tasks with clients. We are not saying that the relationship variables are sufficient for therapeutic change in most cases (although they undoubtedly are in some). Instead, we are saying there is little evidence for the *differential* effect of what MFTs do beyond establishing strong bonds and credible goals and tasks with their clients. As noted earlier, all of the models rely on a systemic conceptualization of family problems and (whether directly or indirectly) have some salutary impact on clients' cognitions, behaviors, and feelings.

Our current state of knowledge suggests that it is less crucial what therapists do (beyond establishing strong alliances) than it is that the "what" is perceived as credible and helpful by the clients. Because this relates to the "tasks" and "goals" dimensions of the alliance, we are willing to say that the heart of MFT training should be teaching therapists to establish strong alliances (broadly conceived to include goals and tasks as well as bonds) with their clients. As noted above, however, because this runs against the grain of the MFT culture, instructors will probably need to talk explicitly about the MFT culture and the "subversive" nature of the common factors approach. Perhaps this can be made more attractive by reframing the "culture of technique" as the "old school" and the common factors approach as the latest development within MFTs maverick tradition.

3. What are MFTs doing, and what should they do, to incorporate more of the clients' perspective into their work?

One of the greatest strengths of the social constructionist (e.g., narrative, collaborative language systems) approaches to MFT has been the emphasis on a more collaborative approach to working with clients. We think this thrust seems to have "rubbed off" on the field in general so that MFTs of most stripes seem less likely simply to "lay" goals and solutions on clients (as in the 1970s heyday of strategic therapy). Adopting a common factor approach will entail an even stronger emphasis (as Duncan and his colleagues have been saying for years) on listening more carefully to the clients' beliefs about why they have their problems and what they think should be done (and not done) about them. This should lead to a greater flexibility in treatment and less rigidity in adhering to "orthodox" or therapists' favorite approaches. Such listening (and not just to the clients' words) should provide clues as to the relative emphasis that should be placed on cognitive, affective, and behavior approaches and (more important) what is likely to be perceived as both helpful and credible by the client.

Therapists should not forget there is more than one road to Rome (what the client wants from therapy). One can get there by way of Paris or London or even Bombay. The most important route, however, is the way the clients would choose for the journey as they themselves are the ones who must make it.

References

Adams, J. F., Piercy, F. P., & Jurich, J. A. (1991). Effects of solution focused therapy's "formula first session task" on compliance and outcome in family therapy. *Journal of Marital and Family Therapy, 17,* 277–290.

Alexander, J. F., Barton, C., Schiavo, R. S., & Parsons, B. V. (1977). Systems–behavioral intervention with families of delinquents: Therapist characteristics, family behavior, and outcome. *Journal of Consulting and Clinical Psychology, 44,* 656–664.

Alexander, J. F., Holtzworth-Munroe, A., & Jameson, P. B. (1994). In A. E. Bergin & S. L. Garfield (Eds.), *Handbook of psychotherapy and behavior change* (4th ed., pp. 595–630). New York: Wiley.

Alexander, J. F., Waldron, H. B., Barton, C., & Mas, C. H. (1989). The minimizing of blaming attributions and behaviors in delinquent families. *Journal of Consulting and Clinical Psychology, 57,* 19–24.

Bandler, R., & Grinder, J. (1975). *The structure of magic, I.* Palo Alto, CA: Science and Behavior Books.

Baucom, D. H., Sayers, S. L., & Sher, T. G. (1990). Supplementing behavioral marital therapy with cognitive restructuring and emotional expressiveness training: An outcome investigation. *Journal of Consulting and Clinical Psychology, 58,* 636–645.

Beck, D. F., & Jones, M. A. (1973). *Progress on family problems: A nationwide study of clients' and counselors' views on family agency services.* New York: Family Service Association of America.

Behrens, B. C., Sanders, M. R., & Halford, W. K. (1990). Behavioral marital therapy: An evaluation of treatment effects across high and low risk settings. *Behavior Therapy, 21,* 423–433.

Bischoff, R. J., & Sprenkle, D. H. (1993). Dropping out of marriage and family therapy: A critical view of research. *Family Process, 32,* 353–375.

Blow, A. J., & Piercy, F. P. (1997). Teaching personal agency in family therapy training programs. *Journal of Systemic Therapies, 16,* 274–283.

Bordin, E. S. (1979). The generalizability of the psychoanalytic concept of the working alliance. *Psychotherapy: Theory, Research, and Practice, 16,* 252–260.

Bourgeois, L., Sabourin, S., & Wright, J. (1990). Predictive validity of therapeutic alliance in group marital therapy. *Journal of Consulting and Clinical Psychology, 58,* 608–613.

Bowen, M. (1978). *Family therapy in clinical practice.* New York: Aronson.

Catherall, D. R. (1984). *The therapeutic alliance in individual, couple, and family therapy.* Unpublished doctoral dissertation, Northwestern University, Evanston, IL.

Chamberlain, P., & Rosicky, J. G. (1995). The effectiveness of family therapy in the treatment of adolescents with conduct disorders and delinquency. *Journal of Marital and Family Therapy, 21,* 441–460.

Clark, W. M., & Serovich, J. M. (1997). Twenty years and still in the dark?: Content analysis of articles pertaining to gay, lesbian, and bisexual issues in marriage and family therapy journals. *Journal of Marital and Family Therapy, 23,* 239–270.

Crane, R. D., Griffin, W., & Hill, R. D. (1986). Influence of therapist skills on client perceptions of marriage and family therapy outcome: Implications for supervision. *Journal of Marital and Family Therapy, 12,* 91–96.

Dumka, L. E., Sprenkle, D. H., & Martin, P. (1995). Development of brief scales to monitor clients' constructions of change. *Journal of Family Psychology, 9,* 385–401.

Duncan, B. (1992). Strategic therapy, eclecticism, and the therapeutic relationship. *Journal of Marital and Family Therapy, 18,* 17–24.

Duncan, B. L., Hubble, M., & Miller, S. (1997, July/August). Stepping off the throne. *The Family Therapy Networker, 21,* 22–33.

Duncan, B. L., Solovey, A. D., & Rusk, G. S. (1992). *Changing the rules: A client directed approach to therapy.* New York: Guilford Press.

Estrada, A. U., & Pinsof, W. M. (1995). The effectiveness of family therapies for selected behavioral disorders of childhood. *Journal of Marital and Family Therapy, 21,* 403–440.

Everett, C., & Volgy, S. (1991). Treating divorce in family therapy practice. In A. S. Gurman & D. P. Kniskern. *Handbook of family therapy* (Vol. 2, pp. 508–524). New York: Brunner/Mazel.

Framo, J. L. (1996). A personal retrospective of the family therapy field: Then and now. *Journal of Marital and Family Therapy, 22,* 289–316.

Frank, J. D. (1973). *Persuasion and healing: A comparative study of psychotherapy.* Baltimore: Johns Hopkins University Press.

Frankel, B. R., & Piercy, F. P. (1990). The relationship among selected supervisor, therapist, and client behaviors. *Journal of Marital and Family Therapy, 16,* 407–421.

Friedlander, M. L., Ellis, M. V., Raymond, L., Siegel, S. M., & Milford, D. (1987). Convergence and divergence in the process of interviewing families. *Psychotherapy, 24,* 570–583.

Garfield, S. L. (1992). Eclectic psychotherapy: A common factors approach. In J. C. Norcross & M. R. Goldfried (Eds.), *Handbook of psychotherapy integration* (pp. 169–201). New York: Basic Books.

Goldman, M. S., Brown, S. A., & Christiansen, B. A. (1987). *Alcohol Expectancy Questionnaire.* Odessa, FL: Psychological Assessment, Resources, Inc.

Goldstein, M. J., & Miklowitz, D. J. (1995). The effectiveness of psychoeducational family therapy in the treatment of schizophrenic disorders. *Journal of Marital and Family Therapy, 21,* 361–376.

Green, R. J., & Herget, M. (1991). Outcomes of systemic/strategic team consultation: III. The importance of therapist warmth and active structuring. *Family Process, 30,* 321–336.

Gregory, M., & Leslie, L. (1996). Different lenses: Variation in clients' perception of family therapy by race and gender. *Journal of Marital and Family Therapy, 20,* 239–252.

Guerney, B. (1977). *Relationship enhancement.* San Francisco: Jossey Bass.

Gurman, A. S., & Kniskern, D. P. (1978). Research on marital and family therapy: Progress, perspective, and prospect. In S. L. Garfield & A. E. Bergin (Eds.), *Handbook of psychotherapy and behavior change: An empirical analysis* (2nd ed., pp. 817–901). New York: Wiley.

Gurman, A. S., & Kniskern, D. P. (1981). Family therapy outcome research: Knowns and unknowns. In A. S. Gurman & D. P. Kniskern (Eds.), *Handbook of family therapy* (Vol. 1, pp. 742–776). New York: Brunner/Mazel.

Gurman, A. S., Kniskern, D. P., & Pinsof, W. M. (1986). Research on the process and outcome of marital and family therapy. In S. L. Garfield & A. E. Bergin (Eds.), *Handbook of psychotherapy and behavior change* (3rd ed., pp. 565–624). New York: Wiley.

Haley, J. (1976). *Problem-solving therapy: New strategies for effective family therapy.* San Francisco: Jossey Bass.

Hanish, L., Tolan, P. H., McKay, M., & Dickey, M. H. (1997). *Process measures for child and family interventions.* Paper presented at the 105th Annual Convention of the American Psychological Association, Chicago, IL.

Heatherington, L., & Friedlander, M. L. (1990). Couple and family therapy alliance scales: Empirical considerations. *Journal of Marital and Family Therapy, 16,* 299–306.

Hendrix, H. (1988). *Getting the love you want.* New York: Holt.

Hoffman, L. (1990). Constructing realities: An art of lenses. *Family Process, 29,* 1–12.

Holtzworth-Munroe, A., Jacobson, N. S., DeKlyen, M., & Whisman, M. A. (1989). Relationship between behavioral marital therapy outcome and process variables. *Journal of Consulting and Clinical Psychology, 57,* 658–662.

Jacobson, N. S., & Addis, M. E. (1993). Research on couple therapy: What do we know? Where are we going? *Journal of Consulting and Clinical Psychology, 61,* 85–93.

Jacobson, N. S., & Christiansen, A. (1996). *Integrative couple therapy.* New York: Norton.

Jacobson, N. S., & Margolin, G. (1979). *Marital therapy: Strategies based on social learning and behavior exchange principles.* New York: Brunner/Mazel.

Jacobson, N. S., Schmaling, K. B., & Holtzworth-Munroe, A. (1987). Component analysis of behavioral marital therapy: Two-year follow up and prediction of relapse. *Journal of Marital and Family Therapy, 13,* 187–195.

Johnson, S. M., & Talitman, E. (1997). Predictors of success in emotionally focused marital therapy. *Journal of Marital and Family Therapy, 23,* 135–152.

Kaplan, H. S. (1979). *Disorders of sexual desire and other new concepts and techniques in sex therapy.* New York: Brunner/Mazel.

Karasu, T. B. (1986). Specificity versus nonspecificity. *American Journal of Psychiatry, 143,* 687–695.

Kuehl, B. P., Newfield, N. A., & Joanning, H. (1990). A client based description of family therapy. *Journal of Family Psychology, 3,* 310–321.

Lambert, M. J. (1992). Psychotherapy outcome research: Implications for integrative and eclectic therapists. In J. C. Norcross & M. R. Goldfried (Eds.), *Handbook of psychotherapy integration* (pp. 94–129). New York: Basic Books.

Lebow, J. (1997a). The integrative revolution in couple and family therapy. *Family Process, 36,* 1–18.

Lebow, J. (1997b, September/October). Is couples therapy obsolete? *Family Therapy Networker, 21,* 81–88.

Leiblum, S. R., & Rosen, R. C. (Eds.). (1989). *Principles and practice of sex therapy: Update for the 1990s (2nd ed.).* New York: Guilford Press.

Leslie, L., & Clossick, M. (1996). Sexism in family therapy: Does training in gender make a difference? *Journal of Marital and Family Therapy, 22,* 253–265.

Masters, W. H., & Johnson, V. E. (1970). *Human sexual inadequacy.* Boston: Little, Brown.

McCubbin, H. I., & Figley, C. R. (1983). *Stress and the family: Coping with transitions* (Vol. 1). New York: Brunner/Mazel.

McDaniel, S. H., Hepworth, J., & Doherty, W. J. (1992). *Medical family therapy: A Biopsychosocial approach to families with health problems.* New York: Basic Books.

Morris, S. B., Alexander, J. F., & Turner, C. W. (1991). Do reattributions of delinquent behavior reduce blame? *Journal of Family Psychology, 5,* 192–203.

Napier, A. Y., & Whitaker, C. (1978). *The family crucible: The intense experience of family therapy.* New York: Harper.

Nichols, M. P., & Schwartz, R. C. (1995). *Family therapy: Concepts and methods (3rd ed.).* Boston: Allyn & Bacon.

Norcross, J. C. (1995). A roundtable on psychotherapy integration: Common factors, technical eclecticism, and psychotherapy research. *Journal of Psychotherapy Practice and Research, 4,* 248–270.

O'Hanlon, W. (1994, November/December). The third wave. *The Family Therapy Networker, 18,* 18–29.

O'Malley, S. S., Suh, C. S., & Strupp, H. H. (1983). The Vanderbilt Psychotherapy Process Scale: A report on the scale development and a process–outcome study. *Journal of Consulting and Clinical Psychology, 51,* 581–586.

Patterson, G. R., & Forgatch, M. S. (1985). Therapist behavior as a determinant for client noncompliance: A paradox for the behavior modifier. *Journal of Consulting and Clinical Psychology, 53,* 846–851.

Pinsof, W. M. (1995). *Integrative problem centered therapy.* New York: Basic Books.

Pinsof, W., & Catherall, D. R. (1986). The integrative psychotherapy alliance: Family, couple, and individual scale. *Journal of Marital and Family Therapy, 12,* 137–151.

Robbins, M. S., Alexander, J. F., Newell, R. M., & Turner, C. W. (1996). The immediate effect of reframing on client attitude in family therapy. *Journal of Family Psychology, 10,* 28–34.

Schnarch, D. M. (1991). *Constructing the sexual crucible.* New York: Norton.

Schwartz, R. C. (1995). *Internal family systems therapy.* New York: Guilford Press.

Shadish, W. R., Ragsdale, K., Glaser, R. R., Montgomery, L. M. (1995). The efficacy and effectiveness of marital and family therapy: A perspective from meta-analysis. *Journal of Marital and Family Therapy, 21,* 345–360.

Shapiro, R. J. (1974). Therapist attitudes and premature termination in family and individual therapy. *The Journal of Nervous and Mental Disease, 159,* 101–107.

Shields, G. C., Wynne, L. C., McDaniel, S. H., & Gawinski, B. A. (1994). The marginalization of family therapy: A historical and continuing problem. *Journal of Marital and Family Therapy, 20,* 117–138.

Smith, M., Glass, G., & Miller, T. (1980). *Benefits of psychotherapy.* Baltimore: Johns Hopkins University Press.

Sprenkle, D. H., & Moon, S. M. (1996). Toward pluralism in family therapy research. In D. H. Sprenkle & S. M. Moon (Eds.), *Research methods in family therapy* (pp. 3–24). New York: Guilford Press.

Stanley, S. M., Markman, H. J., & St. Peters, M. (1995). Strengthening marriages and preventing divorce: New directions in prevention research. *Family Relations, 44,* 392–401.

Stolk, Y., & Perlesz, A. J. (1990). Do better trainees make worse family therapists? A follow-up study of client families. *Family Process, 29,* 45–58.

Szapocznik, J., Kurtines, W. M., Foote, F. H., Perez-Vidal, A, & Hervis, O. (1983). Conjoint versus one-person family therapy: Some evidence for the effectiveness of conducting family therapy through one person. *Journal of Consulting and Clinical Psychology, 51,* 881–899.

Szapocznik, J., Kurtines, W. M., Foote, F. H., Perez-Vidal, A, & Hervis, O. (1986). Conjoint versus one-person family therapy: Further evidence for the effectiveness of conducting family therapy through one person through drug-abusing adolescents. *Journal of Consulting and Clinical Psychology, 54,* 395–397.

Walter, J. L., & Peller, J. E. (1992). *Becoming solution focused in brief therapy.* New York: Brunner/Mazel.

Wampler, K. (1997). *Systems theory and outpatient mental health treatment.* Paper presented at the Inaugural American Association for Marriage and Family Therapy Research Conference, Santa Fe, NM.

John J. Murphy

Common Factors of School-Based Change | 12

C hange is the heart of psychotherapy and the goal of almost all school interventions. The success of school practitioners rests largely on their ability to encourage and manage change. Drawing from research on common factors of psychotherapy, this chapter explores key elements of school-based change across a variety of contexts.

The Quest for the Best

During graduate school, I decided that the road to effective practice was paved by finding the best treatment model and perfecting its use. My quest for the best was mirrored in the psychotherapy literature, where clinicians and researchers vied for top billing by both arguing the merits of their favored model and criticizing all the rest. Just when it appeared that one treatment model was pulling away as a winner, another would nose ahead and claim victory. Not coincidentally, the winner was usually the model with which the writer or researcher was affiliated.

My search for the holy grail of treatment models became even more muddled when I began working as a school psychologist in an urban public school district. Equipped with the model that I was most comfortable with, I quickly discovered that interventions that "should" have worked according to the model failed. Equally baffling were cases in which students quickly improved without the aid of any discernible treatment on my part.

As with most practitioners, the usefulness of doing what worked took precedent over theoretical purity. I began to borrow techniques from a variety of models to fit the student and situation with favorable results. These real-world experiences, combined with the futile search for the best model from the literature, convinced me that no single model is adequate in explaining and treating the wide variety of people and problems encountered by practitioners. One nagging question remained: How can treatment models that appear very different in theoretical orientation and technique yield similar outcomes? Enter common factors.

Common Factors: The Lion's Share of Change in Psychotherapy

A cumulative body of research encompassing a diverse range of practitioners, clients, and problems suggests that successful outcomes may be enhanced by a set of common factors that are operative across different theoretical models and techniques (Frank & Frank, 1991; Frank & Gunderson, 1990; Garfield, 1994; Garfield & Bergin, 1994; Goldfried, 1980; Highlen & Hill, 1984; Kottler, 1991; Lambert, 1992; Lambert, Shapiro, & Bergin, 1986; Morgan, Luborsky, Crits-Christoph, Curtis, & Solomon, 1982; Orlinsky, Grawe, & Parks, 1994; Patterson, 1989; Sexton, Whiston, Bleuer, & Walz, 1997; Smith, Glass, & Miller, 1980). Common or "nonspecific" factors refer to elements of change that are operable in any model of therapy. In a comprehensive synthesis of psychotherapy research, Lambert (1992) proposed that favorable outcomes result primarily from the operation of four interrelated components. Adapted from Lambert, these factors and their percentage of contribution to successful change are as follows:

- client (40%; personal strengths, talents, resources, beliefs, social supports, spontaneous remission, and fortuitous events in the client's life),
- relationship (30%; perceived empathy, acceptance, and warmth),
- expectancy (15%; the client's hope and expectancy of change as a result of participating in therapy), and

▪ model/technique (15%; theoretical orientation and intervention techniques used by the practitioner).

This chapter combines client, relationship, and expectancy components into the broad category of common factors, which account for a substantial 85% of the contribution to therapeutic change (Lambert, 1992).

Client factors are the most potent source of therapeutic change (Garfield, 1994; Lambert, 1992). They comprise what clients bring to therapy, including their unique strengths, beliefs, values, skills, experiences, ability to enlist the help and support of others, potential for change, and desired changes that are already happening in the client's life.

Mobilization of client resources is essential to successful outcomes. These factors have been sorely underused in traditional diagnostic–prescriptive approaches to change. Client factors are empowered when practitioners (a) assess the client's unique strengths and resources relevant to the problem, (b) ask clients about their beliefs regarding the problem and its potential solution, and (c) select interventions that are compatible with the client's beliefs and values.

Relationship factors, the second most important ingredient of effective therapy, include variables such as empathy, warmth, caring, genuineness, acceptance, and encouragement. In a comprehensive review of psychotherapy literature, Patterson (1984) stated that "there are few things . . . for which the evidence is so strong as that supporting the necessity, if not sufficiency, of . . . accurate empathy, respect or warmth, and therapeutic genuineness" (p. 437). Relationship factors are enhanced when the client perceives a strong alliance with the therapist. The client–therapist alliance has been studied extensively by Bachelor (1988, 1991), who reported that client perceptions of the alliance are much better predictors of outcomes than therapist perceptions (Bachelor, 1991). The therapeutic alliance is enhanced by (a) accepting the client's goals at face value instead of challenging them or altering them to fit a specific theoretical model, (b) tailoring therapeutic tasks and suggestions to the client instead of requiring the client to conform to the therapist's chosen model and beliefs, (c) collaborating with clients instead of dictating to them, and (d) exploring material that is relevant to the client.

Expectancy factors consist primarily of the client's expectations and hope regarding the possibility of change (Lambert, 1992). The client's expectation of change counteracts demoralization and improves outcomes (Frank & Frank, 1991). Expectancy factors are empowered when therapists (a) convey an attitude of hope and possibility without minimizing the problem or the pain that accompanies it and

(b) encourage clients to focus on present and future possibilities instead of past problems.

A growing body of research challenges model-driven therapies and suggests that the success of therapy results largely from a set of common factors that are operable across different theoretical models and techniques. Outcomes improve when practitioners instill hope and accommodate therapy to clients instead of requiring clients to conform to the therapist's favorite model or technique. Change is enhanced when practitioners prioritize client beliefs, resources, and preferences throughout the course of therapy. Specific strategies for utilizing common factors in psychotherapy are described elsewhere (Miller, Duncan, & Hubble, 1997; Sexton et al., 1997). Psychotherapy research on common factors serves as a catalyst for the next section, which explores the key ingredients of change in schools.

Common Factors of School-Based Change

School literature offers fertile ground for the exploration of change. Change is part of the daily fabric of schools. Parents ask the school counselor to meet with their daughter in order to improve her school attendance and grades. A teacher decides to alter his approach to classroom management in an effort to improve the behavior and academic achievement of his students. A school district is required to develop a new language arts curriculum to meet the needs of an increasingly multicultural population. Each of these represents a request or desire for change.

An effective approach to change is essential to the success of schools and school practitioners. It is much more difficult to pinpoint common factors of school change as compared with common factors of psychotherapy. The context of psychotherapy and therapeutic change is more narrow than that of schools and school-based change. Psychotherapy typically occurs in a one-to-one context involving a therapist and client, whereas requests for school-related change come in various shapes and sizes and encompass a wide range of services, service providers, and contexts. As a result, the empirical literature on school-based change is much broader than the psychotherapy literature. A comprehensive review of change in schools is beyond the scope of this chapter. However, a sampling of the literature is provided as a way to explore the operation of common factors across various school services and contexts.

CLASSROOM MANAGEMENT AND TEACHING

Change is a routine aspect of teaching and classroom management. This section highlights a few salient features of the literature that are particularly relevant to the exploration of common factors in the classroom.

Many studies have linked effective classroom teaching and management with a *democratic leadership style* (Beyer, 1996; Rodero, 1995; Thayer-Bacon & Bacon, 1998). Democratic leadership is evidenced by the following characteristics:

- respecting the integrity of students and expecting them to act responsibly (Nelson, 1996; Rodero, 1995);
- encouraging and teaching students to examine and resolve their own problems (Kohn, 1993); and
- actively involving students in classroom discussions, activities, and decisions (Stewart, 1985).

Just as effective psychotherapy requires the client's active participation, the success of teaching rests largely on the student's involvement in the learning process. Democratic teachers do not simply let students run the class (Ensign, 1994) but actively manage the process and structure of classrooms while encouraging student input and participation. The democratic teacher connects instructional topics and activities to the experiences of students and provides ample opportunity for students to share their opinions and experiences (Nelson, 1996; Rodero, 1995). For example, in presenting a geography lesson, the teacher might encourage students to read and write about a place they have actually visited. Researchers have linked a democratic leadership style with a positive classroom climate conducive to active learning and fewer behavior problems (Shectman, 1993).

In terms of preventing and managing problem behavior in the classroom, research supports the effectiveness of a *proactive, positive approach* in which teachers clearly communicate classroom expectations and requirements (Jensen, Rhode, & Reavis, 1994). Effective teachers explicitly encourage and recognize student success instead of attending exclusively to mistakes and problems (Brooks, 1991; Nelson, 1996).

PARENT AND TEACHER CONSULTATION

Mental health practitioners working within and outside schools consult regularly with parents and teachers for the purpose of changing school problems. School psychologists have made substantial contributions to the empirical research on school consultation (Bramlett & Murphy, 1998). The term *consultation* is defined in school psychology as a problem-solving approach in which the practitioner works collaboratively with teachers, parents, or other caregivers to assist children with problems involving learning, adjustment, or behavior (Gutkin & Curtis, 1990; Meyers, Parsons, & Martin, 1979). For instance, a school psychologist (consultant) works with a teacher (consultee) to develop behavioral interventions for a particular student. Consultation is considered an "indirect service" because it allows practitioners to serve a larger number of students than would be possible if they worked directly with every student referred. The following features have been linked with successful outcomes of parent and teacher consultation.

1. *A behavioral consultation approach is more preferable and effective than medical–model or insight-oriented approaches* (Gresham & Kendell, 1987; Medway & Forman, 1980; Medway & Updyke, 1985; Slesser, Fine, & Tracey, 1990). Behavioral consultation is an efficient, ecological approach to problem solving involving (a) problem/goal definition (specific, concrete definition of the problem and goal), (b) problem analysis (delineation of factors that increase or decrease the problem), (c) intervention, and (d) outcome evaluation. One reason that may account for the effectiveness of behavioral consultation over other approaches is that the focus on resolving specific problems matches parents' and teachers' desire for concrete assistance. Another reason may pertain to its focus on accessible and modifiable factors of a problem situation such as teaching or parenting strategies as compared with less accessible and changeable features such as a student's ability level or family background. The ecological conceptualization of problems and solutions also promotes a wider range of intervention options than medical–model and insight-oriented approaches that focus primarily on internal traits and deficits of students, parents, and teachers. The explicit attention to evaluating outcomes is another appealing feature of behavioral consultation (Bramlett & Murphy, 1998; Busse, Kratochwill, & Elliott, 1995; Sheridan, Kratochwill, & Bergan, 1996).

2. *Consultation is more effective when it is voluntary rather than coerced* (Gutkin & Curtis, 1990). Consultation with the parents of a truant student is more likely to be successful when the parents are willing participants than when they are coerced into consulting by school personnel or the court system. Although it is ideal for parents and teachers to initiate consultation on their own, they are sometimes persuaded to do so by others. Even in these situations, consultants can enhance effectiveness by focusing their efforts on what the parent or teacher sees as important instead of imposing ideas and interventions on them.

3. *Outcomes are enhanced when the consultant and consultee assume co-equal versus hierarchical status* (Gutkin & Curtis, 1990). Effective consultants relate to teachers and parents as equal partners in the change

process. Consultees who perceive themselves as active and able participants in the problem-solving process are likely to assume ownership of desired changes and to sustain such changes on their own after consultation is terminated (Reinking, Livesay, & Kohl, 1978).

4. *Consultation is more effective when consultants "collaborate with" instead of "dictate to" consultees* (Babcock & Pryzwansky, 1983; Pryzwansky & White, 1983; Wenger, 1979). Collaborative relationships are generally more effective in promoting change than authoritative relationships. Effective consultants emphasize the parent's or teacher's freedom to accept or reject intervention suggestions on the basis of the notion that consultees are in the best position to judge the feasibility and appropriateness of interventions that they are expected to implement.

Collaboration: The Heart of Effective Consultation

The importance of collaboration is woven throughout the school consultation literature (Babcock & Pryzwansky, 1983; Pryzwansky & White, 1983; Wenger, 1979). Collaboration does not imply a nondirective or inactive role on the part of the consultant. Teachers and parents tend to follow the lead of consultants (Erchul, 1987; Martens, Erchul, & Witt, 1992). Therefore, it is important for practitioners to manage the process actively in ways that encourage parent and teacher input. "Managing the process" does not imply dictating the specific goals and content of consultation sessions. Erchul and Chewning (1990) reported that effectiveness was enhanced when consultants took the lead in managing the consultation process by establishing a cooperative relationship with consultees. When the practitioners establish a cooperative relationship in which the consultee's ideas and expertise are acknowledged and taken seriously, the consultee is more likely to take ownership in and implement the interventions that are developed (Reinking et al., 1978).

ORGANIZATIONAL CHANGE

In the current era of educational reform, organizational change is crucial to school effectiveness. Although school reform has been a long-standing topic in American education, discussions over the past decade convey an unparalleled level of urgency. For example, several national studies have clarified the dramatic need for system-level change to meet the needs of an increasingly diverse and at-risk student population effectively (Annie E. Casey Foundation, 1996; National Commission on Excellence in Education, 1983; National Education Goals Panel, 1995).

Research on organizational change includes a diversity of efforts ranging from a local school's attempt to improve staff morale to sweeping federal changes in school curriculum. Regardless of the specific type of change, the literature suggests that the following steps or tasks are essential to success (Curtis & Stollar; 1996; Schmuck & Runkel, 1985):

- Task 1: Needs/goals assessment (comprehensive identification of major organizational needs and goals of those who are expected to implement the change and those who will be affected by the change),
- Task 2: Force–field analysis (analysis of organizational strengths and barriers, referred to as *helping* and *hindering forces,* relevant to stated needs and goals),
- Task 3: Program planning and implementation (the planning and implementation of organizational interventions on the basis of information from the previous two steps), and
- Task 4: Program evaluation (the systematic evaluation of intervention outcomes on the basis of the stated goals of the change program).

The features of effective organizational change in schools are very consistent across different research and applications, and they bear a close resemblance to those noted in the business literature on organizational change (Hersey, Blanchard, & Johnson, 1996). Once again, collaboration is at the top of the list.

COLLABORATION, STRENGTHS, AND ORGANIZATIONAL CHANGE

Anyone who has worked in an agency that has pursued organizational change is aware of the crucial importance of staff "buy-in." As noted by Henning-Stout and Conoley (1988), "for real change to occur, the vehicles for change must be presented in a manner consistent with the values of the people within the system" (p. 472). As with interventions in consultation and psychotherapy, the effectiveness of organizational interventions depends largely on the input and approval of those who are expected to implement them (Hersey et al., 1996; Ponti, Zins, & Graden, 1988). A collaborative approach to organizational change is essential to gaining such commitment and assuring that interventions will be implemented as intended (Schmuck & Runkel, 1985).

In the midst of organizational problems, it is easy to become overwhelmed by the magnitude and scope of the problem. For this reason, Curtis and Stollar (1996) emphasized "the importance of acknowledging and building upon the existing strengths, resources, and successes of the organization" (p. 412). The empowerment of personal resources is a long-standing recommendation in the literature on organizational development in business (Hersey et al., 1996) and education (Schmuck & Runkel, 1985). In addition to capitalizing on strengths within the school, the goal-focused steps of organizational change help people shift their focus from past problems to future possibilities.

ACCEPTABILITY AND EMPOWERMENT: INTEGRATIVE CONCEPTS OF SCHOOL-BASED CHANGE

This section explores two concepts, acceptability and empowerment, that link the various levels and types of school-based change. These factors, along with collaboration, can be considered common factors of school-based change.

Acceptability

Treatment acceptability is the degree to which people accept an intervention model or technique that is presented to them. Research on acceptability originated in clinical contexts (Kazdin, 1980). However, much of the subsequent literature has been provided by school psychologists who have examined factors influencing the outcomes of school interventions (Elliott, Witt, Galvin, & Peterson, 1984; Elliott, Witt, & Kratochwill, 1991). Researchers have consistently reported that interventions rated by parents and teachers as more acceptable are implemented more often than interventions rated as less acceptable (Elliott et al., 1984; Reimers, Wacker, Cooper, & De Raad, 1992). The obvious and crucial fact regarding acceptability is that "a treatment that is not used is no treatment at all" (Witt & Elliott, 1985, p. 253).

The acceptability of an intervention often depends on the amount of time, expense, and other resources required to implement it (Elliott et al., 1991; Witt & Elliott, 1985). Interventions that require excessive amounts of time, money, and materials are less likely to be implemented than those that are more practical and inexpensive.

Another factor that influences the acceptability of an intervention is the rationale in which it is presented. In one study, the rationale used to present an intervention significantly influenced its acceptability to teachers (Conoley, Ivey, Conoley, Scheel, & Bishop, 1992). An intervention presented with a rationale that closely matched the teacher's perception of the causes and severity of a school problem were significantly more acceptable than the same intervention presented with a rationale that mismatched the teacher's perception. For example, a teacher who believed that a misbehaving student was "troubled and in need of support" was more amenable to a strategy that was presented as a way to teach and support the student versus the same strategy presented as a way of "gaining control and getting the student to shape up." Practitioners often view people as resistant when they do not implement interventions. Conoley et al. (1992) cautioned against labeling people as resistant to change when, in fact, they may be responding to discrepancies between their views of the problem and those of the practitioner.

The notion of acceptability reflects good common sense: People tend to do what makes sense to them and what they believe will work. It is hardly profound to suggest that the best way to determine what is appealing and feasible for people is to ask them. A collaborative alliance between practitioners and clients ensures acceptability by providing ongoing opportunities for client input and contributions to the change process. This point is underscored by a study of instructional interventions (de Mesquita & Zollman, 1995), in which the authors recommend that "before allowing a theoretical orientation to limit the range of intervention possibilities, consultants should consider the values and attitudes of the teachers with whom they consult" (p. 168). Acceptability research alerts practitioners to the importance of selecting and presenting change strategies in a manner that accommodates people's view of the problem, instead of requiring people to conform to one's own preferred model. After all, the clients are the ones expected to implement interventions, not us.

Empowerment

Many educators and researchers recommend an empowerment approach to school-related change (Carlson, Hickman, & Horton, 1992; Dunst & Trivette, 1987; Webster-Stratton & Herbert, 1994). Carlson et al. (1992) described this approach as one in which the practitioner "may be of assistance in creating opportunities for competencies to be acquired or displayed by the help seeker, but the client is the essential agent of change and is expected to play a major role in deciding actions and solutions" (p. 197). An empowerment philosophy shifts the focus of helping from the diagnosis and treatment of problems to the collaborative discovery of existing strengths and resources relevant to the client's goals. Inherent in this philosophy is the assumption that people possess various capabilities that can be applied to bring about changes and solutions.

Dunst and Trivette (1987) proposed that the manner in which school practitioners relate to the people they are helping strongly affects the outcomes of such efforts, and they made the following recommendations to school personnel:

- offer suggestions in a way that fits with the individual's or family's own culture and with their own appraisal of the problem;
- promote the family's use of natural support networks and neither replace nor supplant them with professional services;
- convey a sense of cooperation and joint responsibility for solving problems; and
- help family members not only see that the problem has been solved, but also that they functioned as active, significant change agents in the problem-solving process.

In their work with school behavior problems, Webster-Stratton and Herbert (1994) stressed the importance of empowering parents instead of viewing them as deficient: "The essential goal of our collaborative therapy is to empower parents by building on their strengths and experience so that they feel confident about their parenting skills and about their ability to respond to new situations that may arise when the therapist is not there to help them" (p. 118). They recommend that practitioners (a) explore and validate parents' ideas and opinions regarding potential solutions, (b) acknowledge and validate parents' frustration and anger regarding the problem, and (c) help parents focus on the times in which they were successful in managing their child's behavior.

The connection between collaboration and empowerment has also been noted in other contexts of schooling. Collaborative leadership styles on the part of district-level and building-level school administrators have been associated with teacher empowerment (Blase & Anderson, 1995), which in turn has been linked with student achievement (Etheridge & Hall, 1995). Empowerment-based leadership differs markedly from the bureaucratic style of leadership that has prevailed in schools and classrooms. Kreisberg (1992) suggested that "bureaucratic management of schools proceeds from the view that teachers lack the talent or motivation to think for themselves" (p. 10). The same could be said of "bureaucratic interventions" that minimize the client's contribution to change.

The key ingredients of school-based change examined in this chapter—empowerment, acceptability, and collaboration—are very compatible with the common factors of effective psychotherapy. The notion of empowerment echoes Lambert's (1992) findings regarding the potency of the client's contribution to successful outcomes in therapy. The significance of treatment acceptability and collaboration in school-based intervention complements psychotherapy research on the therapeutic alliance and the importance of a collaborative client–therapist relationship in promoting change.

Although different in many respects, psychotherapy and school-based intervention share some important common threads when it comes to the issue of change. Next, these common elements are integrated into a five-step model of school-based change.

The 5-E Method:
A Common Factors Approach
to School-Based Change

This section describes a five-step approach to change that builds directly on client resources to promote solutions to school problems. The five *E*s refer to five specific tasks in the problem-solving process—*eliciting* or identifying relevant client resources, *elaborating* or clarifying the details of such resources, *expanding* or applying resources to the problem at hand, *evaluating* the effectiveness of such applications, and *empowering* desired changes. Before describing the 5-E Method in more detail, a brief discussion of its conceptual and empirical foundation is presented.

In dealing with a school problem involving a student or an entire school staff, efforts usually focus on reducing or eliminating the problem. Assessment clarifies various features of the problem such as its history and presumed causes. Intervention is practitioner directed. Strategies are prescribed to clients on the basis of the counselor's chosen treatment model. These methods imply that there is something defective about the client or client system and that the problem will be resolved only when the deficits are corrected.

The deficit-based perspective is strongly embedded in a range of human service contexts including schools. However, this perspective flies in the face of what works to promote change. Empirical findings on common factors in psychotherapy (Garfield, 1994; Lambert, 1992) and school-based intervention (Carlson et al., 1992; Conoley et al., 1992; Shechtman, 1993; Witt & Elliott, 1985) indicate that change is enhanced when practitioners persistently recognize and use the client's strengths, beliefs, resources, experiences, ideas, and hope throughout the change process. Respect for the client's contribution to change is paramount to effective outcomes.

In contrast to deficit-based approaches, the 5-E Method (Murphy, 1994) adopts a competency orientation grounded in the following common factors notions:

- change is enhanced when people are viewed as resourceful and capable of improving their lives,
- cooperation and collaboration promote change,
- change efforts that focus on future possibilities instead of past problems promote hope and solutions, and
- change is enhanced when practitioner techniques are flexibly selected to fit the client instead of expecting the client to conform to the invariant and favorite techniques of the practitioner.

DESCRIPTION OF THE 5-E METHOD

The 5-E Method was originally applied to school behavior problems (Murphy, 1994) but is expanded here to include any type of school-based change. The 5-E Method is a systematic approach to using exceptions to problems and other client resources to bring about change. *Exceptions* are nonproblem aspects of the client and his or her circumstances, including (a) times and situations in which the problem is absent or less noticeable (e.g., in the case of a student referred for a behavior problem, the classes or times at school during which the student is well behaved) and (b) strengths and resources of the client that are antithetical to the problem or that could be applied toward the goal of change (e.g., in the case of a school staff that wishes to improve its image in the community, the staff members who are already well-respected in the community). The 5-E Method involves five steps or tasks that are implemented within a collaborative framework. Collaboration is ensured when practitioners accept, acknowledge, and accommodate the unique ideas and resources of the people expected to implement a change (Murphy & Duncan, 1997).

Step 1: Eliciting

Once practitioners obtain a clear sense of the client's goal at the outset of intervention, they can empower "client factors" by identifying exceptions to the problem and other client resources. This is not as easy as it sounds. Students and others who are involved in a school problem often view it as constant and unchanging. As de Shazer (1991) observed, "times when the complaint is absent are dismissed as trivial by the client or even remain completely unseen, hidden from the client's view" (p. 58).

Other resources include the client's hobbies, talents, interests, family, friends, and ideas about potential solutions. Similar to exceptions, these resources often go unnoticed in the face of serious school problems. For example, it is easy to overlook a student's strong interests in music when responding to an urgent request to alter the student's undesirable classroom behavior. However, the student's musical interest might be used in an important and powerful way in addressing the classroom problem. Because students and others typically do not volunteer information regarding exceptions and other important resources, it is necessary to elicit such information with the following types of questions:

- Of all your classes, which one is the most tolerable? Which class do you do best in?
- When is this problem absent or less noticeable?
- What do you enjoy doing in your spare time?
- How might someone finish this sentence about you: "This person is really good at . . .?
- How have you managed to keep things from getting worse?
- Of all the things you've already tried in dealing with this, which strategy worked best, if only just a little better than the others?
- How have you handled similar situations in the past?
- Are you or your family connected with any places or groups that might help you with this problem?
- If you were the counselor/consultant in this situation, what would you say to someone who is struggling with this type of situation?

Students, teachers, parents, and other clients can provide essential information and ideas toward intervention goals if they are asked. Problem solving is impeded when clients are viewed merely as "keepers" of the problem with little or nothing to offer toward its solution (Murphy, 1997). Eliciting exceptions and other resources serves not only to empower client factors, but also mobilizes relationship and expectancy factors. Asking about the clients' previous successes, coping strategies, social supports, and other competencies establishes a collaborative relationship and sets an optimistic tone of hope and expectancy.

Step 2: Elaborating

Once an exception or other resource is discovered, practitioners can encourage people to elaborate on it by inquiring about related circumstances. The same kinds of questions used to clarify problem-related factors are helpful in clarifying information related to exceptions and other resources. For example, a student who misbehaves frequently in every class except math class might be asked the following questions to clarify this exception:

- What is different about your math class than your other classes? What else?
- What is different about your math teacher than your other teachers? What else?
- Where do you sit in math class?
- How would you rate your interest in math as compared with your other classes?
- How do you resist the urge to mess around more in math class?

Consider the school principal who complained that it was "like pulling teeth" to get help from the faculty. Following the discovery of an exception to the problem in which several faculty members responded more favorably to one particular request for help, she was asked the following questions:

- What were you asking for in this case?
- How did you communicate this request?
- What else was different about this request than most of the other requests you have made of faculty members?

The exception was more fully elaborated with similar questions, and it was discovered that the "exceptional" request was different from most others in the following ways: (a) It was presented "in person" instead of by memorandum, (b) to small groups of faculty members instead of to the entire faculty, and (c) as part of an overall school goal, not an isolated, discrete task.

Other client resources can be explored in similar ways. For example, in consulting with a high school staff seeking to revise its curriculum, the consultant can inquire about the details and circumstances of other school-wide changes that have been successfully implemented.

Step 3: Expanding

This is the heart of the 5-E Method in which clients are encouraged to expand exceptions and other resources in ways that affect intervention goals. Consider the student who behaves better in history than in any other class. On discovering that history was the only class in which the student sat close to the teacher and the chalkboard, the counselor encourages the student to sit closer to the teacher in another class or two. Improvements in school problems frequently result from expanding "what works" in one context to another, then another, and so on.

In addition to expanding successes and resources to other situations, people can be encouraged to "do the exception" more frequently. Recall the principal who discovered important distinctions between circumstances related to successful and unsuccessful requests for faculty assistance. In this case, she decided to make the exception the rule in communicating future requests to faculty. The results were quite favorable.

As another example, consider a case of a 9th-grade biology teacher requesting help in managing the behavior of his entire class. When asked about times or activities when things went a little smoother in class, he reported fewer behavior problems (the exception) during small group activities and experiments (the exception context). I suggested that he consider doing more activities and experiments in class, providing that course objectives could still be met while doing so. When I saw the teacher the next month, he commented that the class was much better and that he was doing some type of special activity almost every day. As we talked, it became evident that he had modified my suggestion in two creative ways. First, whenever possible, he scheduled group activities and experiments during the last half of the class because students' behavior was usually worse during the latter portion of class. Second, he offered certain "special activities" as rewards contingent on acceptable classroom behavior during the entire week. That is, he modified the intervention to make it more acceptable. The collaborative aspect of the 5-E approach encourages people to adapt interventions to their own unique style and circumstances. They know better than we do what will work (and not work) for them.

Step 4: Evaluating

In traditional intervention approaches, effectiveness is evaluated by practitioner-selected measures. Client judgments, if solicited at all, play a minor role in gauging the success of intervention. In contrast, the 5-E Method regards client judgments as central in evaluating interventions. The following evaluation methods are responsive to the client-directed nature of this approach as well as the time constraints and other practical realities of practitioners.

Scaling is a quick way to assess progress on an ongoing basis. People can be asked variations of the following scaling question on a regular basis throughout the intervention process: "On a scale of 1 to 10, with 1 being 'the worst' and 10 'the best,' how would you rate the problem during the past week?" Refer to Kowalski and Kral (1989) for additional discussion of scaling techniques.

Paper-and-pencil methods can also be used to assess change by asking people to complete rating scales, checklists, inventories, or questionnaires. If available rating scales do not sufficiently address the goals of change, practitioners can design simple checklists and forms that address the goals of intervention.

Another method of evaluating the effectiveness of intervention is by examining data from *permanent products* such as report cards, test scores, and discipline records. For example, comparison of a school district's overall achievement scores and discipline records before, during, and following a staff development project could be used to evaluate the project's effectiveness.

Step 5: Empowering

When desired changes occur, the emphasis shifts toward empowering these changes and helping people maintain them. The maintenance of treatment gains has been extensively covered in the literature (Lambert & Bergin, 1994; Nicholson & Berman, 1983; Stokes & Baer, 1977), and this section highlights those strategies that are particularly compatible with the notion of utilizing client resources. The 5-E Method "begins with the end in mind" by routinely using maintenance strategies throughout the change process.

Collaborating with clients throughout the change process is one of the surest methods for promoting ownership and maintenance of desired changes. One way to do this is by "offering" suggestions instead of telling people what to do. People who perceive their role in the change process as active and important are more likely to continue applying interventions on their own (Reinking et al., 1978).

Another way to empower positive changes is to *blame the client* for such changes (Kral, 1986). This strategy is based on the notion that people are more likely to maintain improvements when they attribute the result to something they did and can do again in the future (Murphy, 1997). The following questions help people clarify their role and contribution to successful changes:

- How did you make it through math class for a whole week without getting kicked out?
- What are you doing differently now to create this type of positive learning atmosphere in your class?
- How did you manage to get your daughter to school on time for the past three days?
- What does this tell you about yourself? What do you think this tells your parents and teachers about you?
- How did you get this to happen? What did you do differently?
- How did you get faculty to volunteer more for projects?

Practitioners can also encourage people to *clarify their plans* for maintaining progress by asking variations of the question, "How are you going to maintain these changes?" In addition to helping people clarify their intentions to maintain progress, the following questions convey the practitioner's expectation and confidence in their ability to do so:

- Do you plan to continue these changes? Why is it important for you to do so?
- What can you do to continue the progress you have made so far?
- How are you going to stick with this plan in the future?

These questions apply to any context of school-based change, including counseling, teaching, consultation, and organizational development. In terms of common factors, these questions convey a positive expectancy regarding clients' ability to maintain changes successfully. Next, the 5-E Method is illustrated by a short case example involving a group of high school students.

ILLUSTRATION OF THE 5-E METHOD: THE TEST ANXIETY GROUP

Five female students in Grades 10 and 11 were referred to the school psychologist by their counselor for test anxiety problems. They participated in six group counseling sessions in which the strategy of using exceptions and other resources was combined with educational and skill-building activities in the areas of study skills, test taking, and relaxation.

During the first meeting, students completed basic information forms and responded to questions about what they hoped to gain from the group. Their goals included improved test performance, better study habits, and less worry and tension before important tests. In the beginning of the second session, each student was asked to think of one or two recent testing situations in which they studied more effectively, were a little more relaxed than usual, or received a higher grade. This question was designed to *elicit* exceptions and was directly tied to the stated goals of the group. After the students listed their exceptions, they were asked to *elaborate* on them by way of the following types of questions:

- What subject area was the test in? What was different about this test compared with other tests?
- What was different about the way you prepared for the test?
- What did you do differently right before the test? During the test?
- How did you study for the test? What was different about the way you studied?
- How did you manage to relax more?

Students expressed appreciation for the opportunity to discuss what they were already doing to help themselves. One student commented, "I thought I was doing everything wrong." The students were urged to continue paying attention to those times and circumstances in which they studied more effectively, performed better, and were more relaxed during a test. They were also encouraged to *expand* the successes and coping resources during the following week. For example, a student who said she relaxed more effectively during a math test by taking a few 10-second breaks was invited to take similar breaks during her upcoming history test.

In addition to the educational material presented throughout the next four sessions, the practitioner continued exploring exceptions, resources, and related circumstances. Educational and skill-building material on test taking, relaxing, and studying was integrated with student-generated ideas and strategies.

The collaborative style of group leadership enhanced the acceptability of the counselor's suggestions and increased students' ownership of the ideas and strategies presented during the group. When students reported improvements, these changes were *empowered* by asking them how they managed to bring them about and how they intended to maintain them. Students developed several creative strategies for maintaining desired changes. For example, one student carried a small card containing test-taking tips that she could conveniently review immediately before a test. Another student taught her younger sister many of the study and test-taking strategies covered by the group, adding that this greatly improved her own understanding and application of these strategies.

In terms of *evaluating* the effectiveness of the group, it was agreed during the first meeting that grades were the best indicators of progress. Four of the five students increased their overall grade point average, and all five students reported improvements in test-taking skills on a self-report questionnaire. The comments that students made following the group's termination were indicative of the collaborative and empowering nature of the 5-E process:

- I realized that I had good ideas, even if I wasn't using them all the time.
- It was cool when we rattled off all those ideas, and I used some of them.
- It was good to get ideas from other students for a change, instead of teachers.
- I started doing better on tests when I did the stuff I said I needed to do. It was a lot simpler than I thought.

Although space limitations preclude other examples of the 5-E Method, this approach is applicable to any type of school-based change ranging from behavior problems of an individual student to organizational changes involving an entire school or school district. Additional examples of the 5-E approach in schools are described elsewhere (Murphy, 1997; Murphy & Duncan, 1997).

Conclusion

There is an oft-told story about a man who was walking down the street when he spotted his friend searching for something under the street lamp. When the man asked what he was doing, his friend explained that he was looking for his lost keys. The man joined his friend in the search, and they continued looking for several minutes without success. Finally, he asked his friend where he dropped the keys. "Way over there," his friend replied, pointing to a field across the road. "Then why, might I ask, are you looking here?" Without hesitation, his friend stated, "Because the light is so much better here than over there."

Practitioners have traditionally searched for the keys of change on the familiar road of client deficiencies and weaknesses. Research on common factors suggests that solutions are more plentiful on the less familiar road of strengths and resources. The empowerment of client resources and hope within a collaborative framework is the central theme of the 5-E Method and of empirical findings regarding change in psychotherapy and schools. This chapter invites practitioners to "do what works" instead of merely doing what is familiar. Finding the keys is always more important than looking under the light.

Questions From the Editors

1. *How do you deal with students who don't want to be in counseling?*
Most students are referred for services by teachers or parents. Therefore, they may enter counseling as "reluctant clients." Teachers, parents, and counselors often try to convince students that they have a problem. This usually makes matters worse because it establishes an adversarial relationship in which the counselor ends up working much harder than the student to bring about change.

I try to avoid power struggles of any sort by accepting the student's opinion and working within it to bring about change. For example, with a high school student who expresses minimal interest in becoming "a better, more responsible student" in line with the wishes of parents and teachers, I might offer another goal that is more compatible with the student's position ("Would you be interested in working on ways to get your teachers and parents off your case?"). The behavioral changes required to get people off the student's back are typically the same behaviors required for the student to become "more responsible." This is one way to accommodate each person's language and goals without taking sides. There are also times when the student is unwilling to work on any goals. In these cases, counselors can work with parents, teachers, or others who are willing to do something about the problem, while maintaining an ongoing invitation for the student to participate more actively.

2. *You advocate accepting the client's beliefs and views. How do you accept a student's beliefs when these beliefs differ markedly from your own?*

I frequently hear this question when conducting training workshops, and I have wrestled with it myself. Two key distinctions are useful here. The first is the distinction between *acceptance* and *agreement*. Differences between the values and views of clients and their counselors are inevitable. However, counselors can accept and accommodate the client's views without "personally" agreeing with or ascribing to them.

A related distinction pertains to the relative impact of practitioner opinions and client opinions on therapeutic outcomes. The potency of client and relationship factors makes it clear that client opinions are always more important than those of the practitioner or anyone else. This should not surprise anyone, because it is the client who is expected to implement suggestions and interventions. Placing the client's views at center stage is the surest and quickest way to promote change. The purpose of school-based intervention is to help people change specific problems and reach specific goals, not to convert them to the counselor's belief system.

3. *What are the implications of a common factors approach for training graduate students who will work with children and adolescents in schools and other settings?*

As evidenced throughout this volume, research on common factors in psychotherapy has existed for many years. One interesting question is, "Why hasn't this research had a stronger impact on the practice of therapy?" Part of the answer pertains to training. Some graduate students may not be exposed to such research in their training program. When empirical information on common factors is included in graduate training, its practical applications may not be sufficiently addressed. For example, the empirical evidence on the potency of client factors and therapeutic alliance in the process of change has profound implications for the manner in which practitioners approach clients of any age in any setting. Establishing productive, empowering relationships with parents, teachers, and students of a variety of backgrounds is a crucial skill for current and future graduate students.

Training programs must go beyond the abstract presentation of research to emphasize the direct and practical significance of these findings in the real world of clinical practice. This can be done by considering the practical implications of research and encouraging students to do the same. I present case studies and anecdotes from my own experience to illustrate the operation of common factors, and I invite students to reflect on specific ways to apply a common factors approach in their current or future work. As research findings continue to be translated into practical ideas and procedures, graduate students will become better equipped to use a common factors approach in their work with children, adolescents, and schools.

References

Annie E. Casey Foundation. (1996). *Kids count data book.* Baltimore, MD: Author.

Babcock, N. L., & Pryzwansky, W. B. (1983). Models of consultation: Preferences of educational professionals at five stages of service. *Journal of School Psychology, 21,* 359–366.

Bachelor, A. (1988). How clients perceive therapist empathy. *Psychotherapy, 25,* 227–240.

Bachelor, A. (1991). Comparison and relationship to outcome of diverse dimensions of the helping alliance as seen by client and therapist. *Psychotherapy, 28,* 534–549.

Beyer, L. E. (1996). *Creating democratic classrooms: The struggle to integrate theory and practice.* New York: Teacher's College Press.

Blase, J., & Anderson, G. (1995). *The micropolitics of educational leadership: From control to empowerment.* New York: Teacher's College Press.

Bramlett, R. K., & Murphy, J. J. (1998). School psychology perspectives on consultation: Key contributions to the field. *Journal of Educational and Psychological Consultation, 9,* 29–55.

Brooks, R. (1991). *The self-esteem teacher.* Circle Pines, MN: American Guidance Service.

Busse, R. T., Kratochwill, T. R., & Elliott, S. N. (1995). Meta-analysis for single-case consultation outcomes: Applications to research and practice. *Journal of School Psychology, 33,* 269–285.

Carlson, C. I. , Hickman, J., & Horton, C. B. (1992). From blame to solution: Solution-oriented family school consultation. In S. L. Christenson & J. C. Conoley (Eds.), *Home-school collaboration: Enhancing children's academic and social competence* (pp. 193–214). Silver Spring, MD: National Association of School Psychologists.

Conoley, C. W., Ivey, D., Conoley, J. C., Scheel, M., & Bishop, R. (1992). Enhancing consultation by matching the consultee's perspectives. *Journal of Counseling Development, 69,* 546–549.

Curtis, M. J., & Stollar, S. A. (1996). Applying principles and practice of organizational change to school reform. *School Psychology Review, 25,* 409–417.

de Mesquita, P. B., & Zollman, A. (1995). Teacher's preferences for academic intervention strategies in mathematics: Implications for instructional consultation. *Journal of educational and psychological consultation, 6,* 159–174.

de Shazer, S. (1991). *Putting difference to work.* New York: Norton.

Dunst, C. J., & Trivette, C. M. (1987). Enabling and empowering families: Conceptual and intervention issues. *School Psychology Review, 16,* 443–456.

Elliott, S. N., Witt, J. C., Galvin, G., & Peterson, R. (1984). Acceptability of behavior interventions: Factors that influence teachers' decisions. *Journal of School Psychology, 22,* 353–360.

Elliott, S. N., Witt, J. C., & Kratochwill, T. R. (1991). Selecting, implementing and evaluating classroom interventions. In G. Stoner, M. Shinn, & H. Walker (Eds.), *Interventions for achievement and behavior problems* (pp. 99–136). Silver Spring, MD: National Association of School Psychologists.

Ensign, J. (1994). *Changing roles in the classroom: An attempt that didn't work.*

Erchul, W. (1987). A relational communication analysis of control in school consultation. *Professional School Psychology, 2,* 113–124.

Erchul, W., & Chewning, T. G. (1990). Behavioral consultation from a request-centered relational communication perspective. *School Psychology Quarterly, 5,* 1–20.

Etheridge, C. P., & Hall, M. L. A. (1995, April). *Challenge to change: The Memphis experience with school-based decision making revisited. Interrupted continuity.* Paper presented at the Annual Meeting of the American Educational Research Association, San Francisco, CA.

Frank, J. D., & Frank, J. B. (1991). *Persuasion and healing* (3rd ed.). Baltimore: Johns Hopkins University Press.

Frank, A. F., & Gunderson, J. G. (1990). The role of the therapeutic alliance in the treatment of schizophrenia: Relationship to course and outcome. *Archives of general psychiatry, 47,* 228–236.

Garfield, S. L. (1994). Research on client variables in psychotherapy. In A. E. Bergin, & S. L. Garfield (Eds.), *Handbook of psychotherapy and behavior change* (pp. 190–228). New York: Wiley.

Garfield, S. L., & Bergin, A. E. (1994). Introduction and historical overview. In A. E. Bergin, & S. L. Garfield (Eds.), *Handbook of psychotherapy and behavior change* (pp. 3–18). New York: Wiley.

Goldfried, M. R. (1980). Toward the delineation of therapeutic change principles. *American psychologist, 28,* 7–10.

Gresham, F., & Kendell, G. K. (1987). School consultation research: Methodological critique and future research directions. *School Psychology Review, 16,* 306–316.

Gutkin, T. B., & Curtis, M. J. (1990). School-based consultation: Theory and techniques. In T. B. Gutkin & C. R. Reynolds (Eds.), *The handbook of school psychology* (2nd ed.). New York: Wiley.

Henning-Stout, M., & Conoley, J. C. (1988). Influencing program change at the district level. In J. L. Graden, J. E. Zins, & M. J. Curtis (Eds.), *Alternative educational delivery systems: Enhancing instructional options for all students* (pp. 471–490). Washington, DC: National Association of School Psychologists.

Hersey, P., Blanchard, K. H., & Johnson, D. E. (1996). *Management of organizational behavior: Utilizing human resources.* Upper Saddle River, NJ: Prentice Hall, Inc.

Highlen, P. S., & Hill, C. E. (1984). Factors affecting client change in individual counseling: Current status and theoretical speculations. In S. D. Brown & R. W. Lent (Eds.), *Handbook of counseling psychology* (pp. 334–396). New York: Wiley.

Jensen, W. R., Rhode, G., & Reavis, K. (1994). *The tough kid book: Practical classroom management strategies.* Longmont, CO: Sopris West.

Kazdin, A. E. (1980). Acceptability of alternative treatments for deviant child behavior. *Journal of Applied Behavior Analysis, 13,* 259–273.

Kohn, A. (1993). Choices for children: Why and how to let students decide. *Phi Delta Kappan, 75,* 8–16, 18–21.

Kottler, J. A., (1991). *The complete therapist.* San Francisco, CA: Jossey-Bass.

Kowalski, K., & Kral, R. (1989). The geometry of solution: Using scaling techniques. *Family Therapy Case Studies, 4,* 59–66.

Kral, R. (1986). Indirect therapy in the schools. In de Shazer, S. & Kral, R. (Eds.), *Indirect approaches in therapy.* Rockville, MD: Aspen.

Kreisberg, S. (1992). *Transforming power: Domination, empowerment, and education.* New York: State University of New York.

Lambert, M. J. (1992). Implications of outcome research for psychotherapy integration. In J. C. Norcross & M. R. Goldfried (Eds.), *Handbook of psychotherapy integration* (pp. 94–129). New York: Basic.

Lambert, M. J., & Bergin, A. E. (1994). The effectiveness of psychotherapy. In A. E. Bergin, & S. L. Garfield (Eds.), *Handbook of psychotherapy and behavior change* (pp. 143–189). New York: Wiley.

Lambert, M. J., Shapiro, D. A., & Bergin, A. E. (1986). The effectiveness of psychotherapy. In S. L. Garfield & A. E. Bergin (Eds.), *Handbook of psychotherapy and behavior change* (pp. 157–211). New York: Wiley.

Martens, B. K., Erchul, W. P., & Witt, J. C. (1992). Quantifying verbal interaction in school-based consultation: A comparison of four coding schemes. *School Psychology Review, 21,* 109–124.

Medway, F. J., & Forman, S. G. (1980). Psychologists and teachers reactions to mental health and behavioral school consultation. *Journal of School Psychology, 18,* 338–348.

Medway, F. J., & Updyke, J. F. (1985). Meta-analysis of consultation outcome studies. *American Journal of Community Psychology, 13,* 489–505.

Meyers, J., Parsons, R. D., & Martin, R. (1979). *Mental health consultations in the schools.* San Francisco: Jossey-Bass.

Miller, S. D., Duncan, B. L., & Hubble, M. A. (1997). *Escape from Babel: Toward a more unifying language of change.* New York: Norton.

Morgan, R., Luborsky, L., Crits-Christoph, P., Curtis, H., & Solomon, J. (1982). Predicting the outcomes of psychotherapy by the Penn Helping Alliance Rating Method. *Archives of general psychiatry, 39,* 397–402.

Murphy, J. J. (1994). Working with what works: A solution-focused approach to school behavior problems. *The School Counselor, 42,* 59–65.

Murphy, J. J. (1997). *Solution-focused counseling in middle and high schools.* Alexandria, VA: American Counseling Association.

Murphy, J. J., & Duncan, B. L. (1997). *Brief intervention for school problems.* New York: Guilford Press.

National Commission on Excellence in Education. (1983). *A nation at risk: The imperatives for educational reform.* Washington, DC: U.S. Government Printing Office.

National Education Goals Panel. (1995). *The national education goals report. Volume one: National data.* Washington, DC: Author.

Nelson, J. (1996). *Positive discipline.* New York: Ballantine Books.

Nicholson, R. A., & Berman, J. S. (1983). Is follow-up necessary in evaluating psychotherapy? *Psychological Bulletin, 93,* 261–278.

Orlinsky, D. E., Grawe, K., & Parks, B. K. (1994). Process and outcome in psychotherapy—Noch einmal. In A. E. Bergin, & S. L. Garfield (Eds.), *Handbook of psychotherapy and behavior change* (pp. 270–376). New York: Wiley.

Patterson, C. H. (1984). Empathy, warmth, and genuineness in psychotherapy: A review of reviews. *Psychotherapy, 21,* 431–438.

Patterson, C. H. (1989). Foundations for an eclectic psychotherapy. *Psychotherapy, 26,* 427–435.

Ponti, C. R., Zins, J. E. & Graden, J. L. (1988). Implementing a consultation-based service delivery system to decrease referrals for special education: A case study of organizational considerations. *School Psychology Review, 17,* 89–100.

Pryzwansky, W. B., & White, G. W. (1983). The influence of consultee characteristics on preferences for consultation approaches. *Professional psychology: Research and practice, 14,* 457–461.

Reimers, T. M., Wacker, D. P., Cooper, L. J., & De Raad, A. O. (1992). Acceptability of behavioral treatments for children: Analog and naturalistic evaluations by parents. *School Psychology Review, 21,* 628–643.

Reinking, R. H., Livesay, G., & Kohl, M. (1978). The effects of consultation style on consultee productivity. *American Journal of Community Psychology, 6,* 283–290.

Rodero, M. L. (1995). Active learning in a democratic classroom: The pedagogical invariants of Celestin Freinet. *The Reading Teacher, 49,* 164–167.

Schmuck, R. A., & Runkel, P. J. (1985). *The handbook of organization development in schools (third edition).* Palo Alto, CA: Mayfield.

Sexton, T. L., Whiston, S. C., Bleuer, J. C., & Walz, G. R. (1997). *Integrating outcome research into counseling practice and training.* Alexandria, VA: American Counseling Association.

Shechtman, Z. (1993). Education for democracy: Assessment of an intervention that integrates political psychosocial aims. *Youth and Society, 25,* 126–139.

Sheridan, S. M., Kratochwill, T. R., & Bergan, J. R. (1996). *Conjoint behavioral consultation: A procedural manual.* New York: Plenum Press.

Slesser, R. A., Fine, M. J., & Tracey, D. B. (1990). Teacher reactions to two approaches to school-based psychological consultation. *Journal of Educational and Psychological Consultation, 1,* 243–258.

Smith, M. L., Glass, G. V., & Miller, T. I. (1980). *The benefits of psychotherapy.* Baltimore: Johns Hopkins.

Stewart, W. J. (1985). *How to involve the student in classroom decision making.* Saratoga, CA: R & E Publishers.

Stokes, T. F., & Baer, D. M. (1977). An implicit technology of generalization. *Journal of Applied Behavior Analysis, 10,* 349–367.

Thayer-Bacon, B. J., & Bacon, C. S. (1998). *Philosophy applied to education.* Columbus, OH: Prentice Hall.

Webster-Stratton, C., & Herbert, M. (1994). *Troubled families: Problem children.* New York: Wiley.

Wenger, R. D. (1979). Teacher response to collaborative consultation. *Psychology in the Schools, 16,* 127–131.

Witt, J. C., & Elliott, S. N. (1985). Acceptability of classroom interventions strategies. In T. Kratochwill (Ed.), *Advances in school psychology* (pp. 251–288). Hillsdale, NJ: Erlbaum.

IV | IMPLICATIONS OF THE COMMON FACTORS FOR REIMBURSEMENT POLICY AND PRACTICE

Jeb Brown, Sandra Dreis, and David K. Nace

What Really Makes a Difference in Psychotherapy Outcome?

Why Does Managed Care Want to Know?

13

The managed behavioral health care industry is the broker of behavioral health services. It functions as the middleman between providers and the wholesale purchasers of behavioral health care services (e.g., insurance companies, employers, and government). This industry responds to the market rather than to any particular psychotherapy theory, model, or treatment ideology. Historically, managed behavioral health care has been an intensively competitive business in which purchase decisions have often appeared to be driven chiefly by price. Improving quality of care remained an ideal to which all parties paid tribute. Until recently, this was more an abstraction than a tangible reality based on sound data.

The nature of the market is changing, however. The purchasers of managed behavioral health care services are asking managed behavioral health care organizations (MBHOs) to make good on their claims that costs can be reduced without sacrificing outcomes. In this chapter, we discuss the efforts of MBHOs to meet the demand for cost-effective, high-quality treatment. In addition, we present preliminary findings from one company's efforts to use outcome information to improve both the effectiveness and efficiency of psychotherapeutic treatment.

Human Affairs International (HAI) is one of the largest MBHOs in the nation and is part of the larger Magellan Health Services family of companies, which provide managed mental health and employee assistance services for more than 60,000,000 covered enrollees. Over the past several years, HAI has devoted considerable time and resources to the development of a system for collecting and assessing individual clients' responses to treatment. By comparing the response of an individual case to the normative expectation for improvement in similar cases, this system enables an MBHO such as HAI to determine which cases are proceeding toward success and which are at risk for a poor outcome.

Clearly, the era of such data-based outcome management is in its infancy. However, the data collected from thousands of patients in treatment with hundreds of different therapists living and practicing in areas across the country have already resulted in some startling findings:

- *The outcome of therapy is highly variable.* The standard deviation of the change score tends to be approximately twice as large as the mean average change score for a large sample of clients.
- *Ensuring the application of specific guidelines and approved or "empirically validated" psychotherapy methods does not lead to improved treatment outcome.* Differences in treatment methods, diagnoses, and even length of treatment account for less than 5% of the variance in outcome.
- *There are significant differences in effectiveness between individual providers and even entire clinical delivery systems.* Such differences cannot be explained by the nature of the cases being seen or the treatment methods being used.
- *Response to treatment in the first few sessions is highly predictive of the eventual outcome.* This phenomenon makes it feasible to monitor cases and predict cases at risk of a poor outcome early in the treatment process.

Such preliminary findings have broad implications for the practicing psychotherapist and managed behavioral health care industry. Obviously, the MBHO is most likely to increase effectiveness and efficiency by actively managing those cases at highest risk for negative outcome and by identifying providers with the best treatment record. At the same time, clinicians able to use outcome information to monitor and improve their services will not only have healthier clients but better relationships with MBHOs. The chapter concludes with a discussion of these and other implications for data-based outcome management in clinical practice.

Making Good on Their Claims: MBHOs Search for Quality and Value

From the outset, the managed behavioral health care industry has professed a dual purpose: (a) to contain the cost of treatment and

(b) to improve the quality of care provided. Some critics have argued that MBHOs and purchasers of managed care products make decisions based solely on the cost rather than on quality of care (Ackley, 1993; Schoenholtz, 1988). This was more likely to be true in the early days of managed care. As the industry has matured, however, the savings accrued by switching from indemnity style insurance to managed health care products have been wrung out of the system. Now, purchasers of managed care services see fewer differences in cost between competing plans. As a result, the role of "quality" has become increasingly important in the acquisition and retention of customers for the MBHOs.

Indeed, the pursuit of quality has emerged as *the* major factor in the evolving health care marketplace. Consider, for example, that over half of all HMOs either have gone or will shortly go through a certification process conducted by the National Committee for Quality Assurance (NCQA), an independent nonprofit organization dedicated to assessing the quality of managed care plans. Although voluntary, quality has become so important that health plans cannot compete effectively for business in major markets without the NCQA "seal of approval." Among the stringent requirements for approval are guidelines for appropriate care and an ongoing research program aimed at improving treatment outcome.

One method MBHOs have used to ensure quality and manage costs has been the development of treatment guidelines. The federal government has likewise sponsored the development of treatment guidelines for Depression in Primary Care (U.S. Department of Health and Human Services, 1993) as has the American Psychiatric Association (1996). Such guidelines have typically been based on evidence from placebo-controlled and double blind studies gleaned from the available outcome literature. Evidence from other sources, including case histories, expert opinion, and poorly controlled studies has been used but is typically given proportionately less weight.

There are several serious problems with this approach to quality improvement, however. First and foremost, little controlled research exists for the majority of conditions listed in the fourth edition of the *Diagnostic and Statistical Manual of Mental Disorders* (*DSM-IV*; American Psychiatric Association, 1994). The result is that a substantial percentage of the outpatient treatment population presents with problems for which even the best treatment guidelines offer limited specific guidance for psychotherapeutic approach. Even where a consensus exists for using a specific treatment for a particular disorder (e.g., cognitive and behavioral for certain anxiety disorders and depression), there continues to be considerable controversy among researchers about the interpretation of supporting data (see chap. 14 in this volume, as well as Duncan, Hubble, & Miller, 1997; S. D. Miller, Duncan, & Hubble,

1997; Wampold, 1997). Finally, there is the problem of generalizing from the controlled studies on which the guidelines are based to the largely uncontrolled and unstructured practice of outpatient therapy in an MBHO. Until the results of naturalistic field studies with large samples can be conducted, the actual differential response of clients to specific treatment interventions outside of the research settings must be considered speculative.

Obviously, all quality improvement efforts require sound data. Indeed, part of the problem in the early days of the industry was that "quality" was much more difficult to quantify than the cost of care. If something cannot be measured, however, it cannot be improved in a measurable way. For this reason, the behavioral health care industry has started to develop systems for collecting and evaluating clinical outcomes and then using the data to inform the routine provision of treatment services (Bartlett & Cohen, 1993; Brown, Fraser, & Bendoraitis, 1995). Such systems, it is hoped, will enable MBHOs and treatment professionals to demonstrate the value of their services. In health care economics, *value* is understood as the ratio of the benefit to the client to the cost of the treatment (with benefit to the client being determined by self-reported reduction in distress and recovery of well-being).

Psychotherapy as a Commodity in the Health Care Marketplace

Over the past several decades, third-party payers (e.g., insurance companies, MBHOs) rather than individual consumers have become the primary purchasers of psychotherapy services. In the absence of evidence for superior outcomes from more expensive providers and treatments, business has naturally flowed toward those who could deliver care at less cost (S. D. Miller et al., 1997; S. D. Miller, Hubble, & Duncan, 1995). In short, psychotherapy services became a commodity.

The downward pressure on reimbursement has only been exacerbated by the rapid proliferation of psychotherapists able to bill third-party payers for treatment services. A simple calculation reveals the magnitude of the oversupply of psychotherapists (Hurst, 1997). Consider, for example, that there are approximately 400,000 providers currently licensed to serve a population of 260,000,000 in the United States. If 10% of the total population seek services at any time in a given year—a very generous assumption—there would be a total of 26,000,000 cases, or 65 cases per practitioner per year. If full-time clinical practice consists of 30 billable hours per week, 48 weeks out of the year, then each provider has the capacity to provide 1,440 hours of psychotherapy per year. Making the generous assumption that treatment averages 12 billable hours per case—the average figure is actually much closer to 6 (Garfield, 1989)—then each provider has the capacity to treat 120 cases per year ($1440 \div 12 = 120$). Dividing the actual number of cases available annually per therapist (65) by the annual capacity of each therapist (120) indicates that only 54% percent of provider capacity would be utilized. With nearly twice the number of therapists than are needed to fill current demand, the marketplace ends up favoring the buyers rather than the sellers of psychotherapy services.

Surprisingly, MBHOs are caught in the same market forces as providers. As contradictory as it may sound, the downward pressure on reimbursement actually restricts opportunities for sustained profit by the MBHOs. Additionally, there are a large number of MBHOs—a problem that makes it difficult for any single organization to differentiate their products from others available in the marketplace solely on the basis of quality or perceived value. As with providers, cost often ends up being the key factor in acquiring and retaining clients. In addition to this, providers have become increasingly proficient at containing costs and are willing to assume some of the financial risk for an insured population through capitation or other risk-sharing arrangements.

Historically, providers and third-party payers have tended to view psychotherapy as a service. The qualifications for reimbursement were the level of training (e.g., PhD, MSW), professional certification or licensure, and years of experience of the provider. In a commodity market, however, such credentials will only result in reimbursement if they can be shown to result in better outcomes. In a real and radical way, then, the very nature of the psychotherapy business is shifting from simple reimbursement for services to compensation for the clinical outcome. In the emerging environment, the outcome of the service rather than the service itself is the product that providers and payers have to market and sell. Those unable to systematically evaluate the outcome of treatment will have nothing to sell to purchasers of health care services.

The focus on outcomes has several advantages for MBHOs, providers, and clients. For example, such research could potentially answer critics who have long contended that MBHOs care little about client welfare and sacrifice clinical outcomes (I. J. Miller, 1996). The same focus would ensure that those being served receive the best and most effective care possible. At the same time, providers would be able to prove to third-party payers that their services are indeed effective.

Given their size and capital, MBHOs are in a unique position to develop systems for tracking and evaluating treatment outcomes. The unmanaged fee for the service system of care is, given its emphasis on provider autonomy, unable to mount such a coordinated effort. Rather, MBHOs can provide the structure and motivation for providers to participate in the systematic collection of standardized clinical data on those under their care. Only MBHOs have access to potential data on the quality of care from a population of clients large enough to make strong empirical inferences. Such data could be used to establish national and regional norms for treatment outcomes and to evaluate individual providers, group practices, and integrated systems of care. The same data could also be used to show whether substantial undertreatment is occurring. After all, an MBHO is not going to be harmed by an employer's increasing spending on behavioral health if doing so provides compelling evidence of improved outcomes. In any event, few employers or other payers would be willing to increase spending without such evidence.

Toward the Development of a Comprehensive System: A Real-World Example

In late 1994, HAI embarked on a project to develop a comprehensive system for tracking and evaluating treatment outcomes.[1] After a year, the pilot project involving 150 therapists practicing in Texas was expanded to over 2,000 providers practicing in different parts of the country. The resulting Clinical Information System (CIS) embodies most if not all of the features of a new generation of information systems and serves as an example of what is possible. Basically, the goals of system include

- enhancing provider effectiveness through information and performance feedback;
- determining the factors contributing to superior outcomes;
- reducing time spent requesting additional care and completing paperwork;

---

[1]The authors of this chapter have been active participants in this project from the outset.

■ automating utilization review; and

■ targeting cases in need of review, based on empirical criteria.

Data enter the CIS from simple paper-and-pencil forms ("bubble sheets") that can be scanned or faxed for automated data entry. As the project has expanded, the number of cases included in the CIS has grown rapidly. Continuous analysis of the data from these cases drives ongoing refinement of the system—especially the computer-generated algorithms used for automatically certifying continuing care and highlighting cases at risk for poor outcome. Data presented later in this chapter are drawn primarily from this sample of clients treated by a broad cross-section of geographically dispersed providers.

GATHERING OUTCOME DATA

Outcome data can be gathered from a variety of sources: (a) the person in treatment, (b) a significant other (e.g., spouse, parent, the courts, independent observer), (c) the payer, and (d) the treatment professional. Each source has advantages and disadvantages. In a typical outpatient setting, routinely gathering data from significant others would often be impractical, with some exceptions (e.g., parents bringing children to treatment). Among other things, there are problems with confidentiality and conflicting views about the focus of treatment. At first glance, the therapist would seem to be a logical source for outcome information. Such data can be difficult to interpret, however. For example, there could be a tendency to distort information that might negatively affect a provider's performance evaluation or threaten his or her financial security. Clients' ratings of satisfaction have also been used as a measure of outcome. Given that such measures are often inflated (e.g., "90% report being satisfied or highly satisfied"), however, they are also difficult to interpret. Moreover, there is no reason to believe that a high degree of satisfaction is necessarily a sign of a successful outcome.

Given these and other problems, the HAI system is based on psychometrically sound, client self-report measures of improvement in functioning, symptom severity, emotional well-being, and general quality of life. An average of 5 minutes is needed to collect the data that include (a) a 45-item patient self-report measure for adults (OQ-45.2; Burlingame, Lambert, Reisinger, & Neff, 1995; Wells, Burlingame, Lambert, & Hoag, 1996); (b) *DSM* diagnosis, (c) Global Assessment of Functioning (GAF), (d) history of prior treatment, (e) nature of family environment (e.g., supportive, hostile), and (f) treatment already delivered. The CIS uses a repeated-measures design with data collected at the first, third, and fifth visits and then every fifth session thereafter.[2] This schedule was based on data indicating that nearly 50% of the clients attend five sessions or fewer and was intended to result in at least two data points on half of all clients.

Broadly speaking, behavioral health outcomes can be described in terms of the percentage of clients who meet a predetermined criterion (e.g. "improved" or "recovered") or expressed as a continuous variable in the form of a change score. The latter represents the difference between the score on an outcome measure taken at intake and at the completion of treatment or at follow-up. The average change for a group of clients is known as *effect size,* which is simply the change scores expressed as a standard score. It is calculated by dividing the average change score by the standard deviation of the outcome instrument. The system at HAI uses effect size as the metric for reporting treatment outcomes, because this statistic

- conveys information about the magnitude of improvement;
- permits comparisons across multiple instruments;
- is more sensitive to detecting subtle differences in the patient–treatment–provider interaction; and
- permits comparison with a substantial body of behavioral health outcome research reporting effect sizes for various treatments.

ESTABLISHING OUTCOME NORMS

There is ample research to demonstrate that some psychotherapy is better than no treatment for most common problems (Lambert & Bergin, 1994). Indeed, in most studies the average treated client is better off that 80% of those in an untreated sample (S. D. Miller et al., 1997). However, the goal of a system for managing outcomes is not simply to prove the overall value of treatment but rather to improve the overall effectiveness of treatment for a given population of clients. The first step in this process is to develop norms for expected outcomes. In turn, these norms become the standards against which the effectiveness of therapists and quality improvement efforts can be judged and compared.

---

[2]Data collected in this manner can result in an underestimation of the length of treatment and effect size. For example, if data are collected at the fifth session and the client actually utilized nine sessions, the last data point will be for the fifth session only. If this session number is used to estimate the length of treatment, the estimate will be low by four sessions. Likewise, using this data point to estimate the effectiveness of treatment will fail to capture any improvement experienced beyond this session. Collecting data at every session is impractical for most providers and clients, however, so the problem is difficult to avoid.

HAI has approached the development of norms through use of "patient profiles." A patient profile is a set of specifications used to cluster similar patients into groups for which normative expectations for improvement can be established. Typically, a patient profile will include a specification of diagnoses (or diagnostic clusters) as well as severity of illness at intake. Other factors such as socioeconomic status, gender, or duration of illness can be included as the data warrant.

Table 1 provides normative information on expected improvement for patients with the most common AXIS I disorders falling into one of four severity ranges as determined by the OQ-45.2 score at intake.

Using this information, it becomes possible to evaluate the outcome for a specific patient with a mood disorder by referencing it to the normative data on improvement for patients in a similar severity range. HAI provides this sort of normative information on patient profiles to its providers in order to enhance the value to the outcome measures and to permit them to evaluate the effectiveness of their own treatment.

CONTROLLING FOR CLIENT DIFFERENCES THROUGH CASE MIX ADJUSTMENT

In 1995, researchers Hiatt and Hargrave conducted a study at the Foundation Health Plan in an effort to determine the qualities of effective therapists. Using client self-report data and peer ratings, the researchers were able to distinguish between therapists in their sample who were the most and least effective (as determined by clinical outcome). Interestingly, therapists in the high-effectiveness group were disproportionately female (82%). By contrast, only 47% of those in the low-effectiveness group were female. Therapists in the low-effectiveness group also tended to have been in practice for more years than those in the high-effectiveness group (18.2 vs. 12.9; $X = 13.6$). Tellingly, the most effective and least effective therapists had identical outcomes when judged from the their assessments alone.

TABLE 1

Patient Profiles: Adults (Mood, Anxiety, and Adjustment Disorders)

Severity range	OQ-45.2 score at intake	Effect size
Mild	0–55	−.08
Moderate	56–79	.16
Moderately severe	80–104	.48
Severe	105 and higher	.84

Although highly experienced male therapists reading this chapter may be hoping that this research is neither replicated nor widely disseminated, the study actually contains several methodological weaknesses that limit any straightforward interpretation of the results. For example, were there differences in therapeutic techniques or other treatment variables that might explain the differences? Were the clients treated by the "effective" and "ineffective" therapists equivalent, or was there some selection bias that resulted in older, more experienced male therapists getting more difficult cases? This latter question in particular highlights the difficulty of drawing conclusions regarding the effectiveness of providers without first controlling for the severity or difficulty of the cases being seen. Such "case mix adjustment" ensures that providers treating more difficult patients are not unduly penalized.

Included as variables for case mix adjustment in the CIS at HAI are (a) severity of distress as measured by client self-report, (b) severity of functional impairment using clinician administered standardized scales; (c) *DSM* diagnosis, (d) standardized list of problems that are the focus of treatment, (e) prior treatment history, (f) level of family support, and (g) client demographics (e.g., gender, age). One very interesting result of the HAI system is that when case mix is adjusted for severity, there are no statistically significant differences in outcomes (as measured by reduction in patient distress) between the broad diagnostic clusters of anxiety disorders, mood disorders, or adjustment disorders. In other words, in spite of their widespread use, diagnosis as recorded by the treatment professional added nothing to the predictive validity of case mix adjusted treatment outcomes. Clients entering treatment in a high level of distress (regardless of diagnosis) did tend to stay in treatment about 30% longer, but overall length of treatment was not correlated with improvement.

The previously cited patient profiles become a simple and easily understood means of case mix adjustment. When evaluating the outcomes for a sample of patients, each patient is compared only with other patients in the database with the same profile.

HAI uses an Outcome Index when reporting comparisons on outcomes between providers. An Outcome Index score is calculated for each patient and represents the difference between that patient's change score and the average change for all patients with a similar profile. An Outcome Index score of 0 represents average improvement. Positive scores represent above-average improvement. By averaging the Outcome Index scores for all patients seen by that provider, a global Outcome Index score is obtained for that provider. This score provides the case mix adjusted estimate of that provider's effectiveness.

PROVIDER PROFILING

The contributors to this book make a compelling case for common rather than specific factors' being responsible for most of the effects associated with psychotherapy. For example, based on reviews of research spanning decades, Asay and Lambert (see chap. 2) identify four factors common to all therapies including (a) client factors (e.g., ego strength, environmental events and resources [40%]); (b) relationship factors (e.g., empathy, warmth, acceptance, encouragement of risk taking [30%]); (c) placebo factors (e.g., hope and expectancy [15%]); and (d) models and technique factors (e.g., the elements believed unique to specific to a given therapeutic approach [15%]).

According to this view, relationship factors are twice as important as technique in successful outcome. Moreover, 70% of the total outcome variance is accounted for when a strong therapeutic relationship is combined with a successful incorporation of client factors in the treatment process. Such data strongly suggest that the interests of MBHOs would be better served by focusing on how well providers facilitate client change rather than on managing or dictating the treatment approaches they use—in other words, shifting the emphasis in management of behavioral health care away from identifying the "correct" treatment and toward the personal attributes and abilities of the individual provider. Given the pioneering role that MBHOs have played in the development of treatment guidelines, however, such a shift would represent a significant departure from traditional methods for managing behavioral health care.

Interestingly, available data from the CIS at HAI supports this shift. Consider, for example, that practitioners in the HAI system identified with a variety of different therapeutic orientations, such as (a) cognitive–behavioral (51%); (b) medication management; (13%); (c) solution-focused (11%); (d) mind–body; behavioral, client-centered, supportive, and crisis intervention (each with 3%); and (e) psychodynamic, family, marital, and other (each with 2%). After controlling for case mix (e.g., severity), however, no significant differences were found in treatment outcome based on the theoretical orientation of the therapist. Even when the various treatment orientations were combined into four larger clusters in order to increase statistical power—Behavioral (behavioral and cognitive–behavioral), Brief (solution-focused, crisis intervention), Insight/awareness-oriented (mind–body, client-centered, supportive, psychodynamic), and Family (family and marital)—no statistically significant differences in effect size were observed.

Significantly, the same findings applied to medically oriented treatment. In contrast to widely held beliefs, the use of medication did not result in demonstrably superior outcomes either when used alone or in combination with other therapeutic approaches, even for patients with OQ-45.2 scores above 105, which placed them in the upper 15% of our clinical sample in terms of self-reported distress.

In short, the theoretical orientation of the therapist was unrelated to the outcome of treatment. Nor were any differences found in the length of treatment for the various therapies. Indeed, all psychotherapies were of relatively equal cost without any statistically significant differences in effectiveness.

Clearly, questions can and should be raised about quality of the data collected in this study. After all, there is no way to determine whether a particular therapist actually delivered a treatment consistent with the theoretical orientation they had endorsed. One could conceivably argue, for example, that managed care's proclivity for cognitive–behavioral and solution-focused therapies led some practitioners to endorse a treatment orientation that they actually did not practice. Neither is there any way to determine the quality of the treatment that was offered by providers practicing a particular brand of therapy.

Likewise, the data on use of medications are relatively crude at this point. We have no way of knowing the dosing of the medication, nor the patient compliance. Also, the patient may be receiving a medication from a primary care physician, and the treating mental health professional may have neglected to provide us with this information. In the future, as the size of the sample grows, we plan to match our outcomes data to pharmacy data to gain a more accurate picture of the impact of medications.

Whatever the reason for the results, however, it is clear from our data that there is no relationship between the treatment methods endorsed by providers and differences in outcomes as reported by clients. For this reason, it is safe to say that MBHOs would be better off using their resources to manage something other than provider compliance with preferred psychotherapy methods. In particular, MBHOs could help therapists improve effectiveness and efficiency by providing them with reliable and empirically valid feedback about the outcome of their work.

Unfortunately, the present reality is that MBHOs cannot gain sufficient data on individual providers in their network to provide each with reliable and valid feedback about their work. For most therapists, a single MBHO accounts for only a fraction of their practice. The problem is that by the time a given MBHO could amass a sample of cases large enough to make meaningful inferences, a therapist might already have altered his or her treatment methods.

The alternative to a focus on individual therapists is to gather data and provide feedback to groups of practitioners. For example, HAI has entered into a number of contractual relationships with group practices in key markets. In exchange for increased referrals and autonomy in treatment planning and delivery, the group agrees to systematically collect outcome data according the HAI's requirements.

Assessing outcomes at the group practice enables HAI to provide feedback on how effectively a clinical organization as a whole provides multidisciplinary services to a large and diverse population of clients. At the same time, it shifts responsibility for the performance of individual therapists to the group in which they practice.

HAI produces a monthly Outcome Report for the group practices that serve a large volume of patients. As an example of how such data might be used to improve outcome, consider information gathered on 12 different provider groups practicing within the HAI system (see Figure 1). In each instance, the results reflect data for at least 100 cases that have been adjusted statistically to control for severity so that differences in case mix do not skew the findings. The upper and lower 95% confidence intervals have been included to aid in interpreting the significance of the differences. As can be seen in the figure, sizable variability exists in the average amount of improvement achieved by the various groups.

Although perhaps surprising, the data from HAI are consistent with previous findings that have documented a large amount of variability between practitioners using the same treatment methods and treating the same types of clients (Wampold, 1997). The variability in outcomes across group practices may in the future provide clues to factors contributing to this variability. For example, factors such as wait time for the first appointment, time between appointments, use of group treatment, or other variables within a group's control may ultimately be found to make a difference in outcome.

FIGURE 1

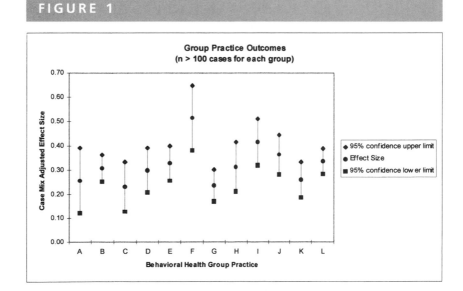

Relative Effectiveness of Five Group Practices.

In the example above, Groups C, G, and K have outcomes that place them below the 15th percentile of all group practices in HAI's sample. Falling below this threshold triggers a process of consultation and collaboration with the practice to formulate hypotheses and implement an action plan to improve outcomes. Although this process is still in its infancy at HAI, our initial experience with this process of collaboration has been encouraging.

In fact, over the course of a year, the outcomes for group practices participating in the outcomes management process improved significantly compared with those of solo practitioners. During the 12-month period prior to completion of this chapter, the monitored groups achieved an average effect size of .36 compared with .29 for solo practitioners who did not have the benefit of continuous feedback and coaching ($p < .01$). Perhaps more significantly, the groups used an average of less than five sessions per case, whereas solo providers averaged almost seven sessions.

As the MBHO's understanding of clinical outcomes grows, so will its ability to provide normative feedback to providers regarding the role of such factors in effective care. The providers of the future will then be able to engage in a continuous process of monitoring, measuring, and applying such outcome and normative information to systematically improve their practice. Clearly, clients will be better served by such efforts.

OUTCOME MANAGEMENT

Results from the research reviewed thus far indicate that such widely used and popular criteria as *DSM* diagnosis, treatment orientation or method, and even length of treatment contact are neither reliable nor valid determinants of psychotherapy outcome. Although little may be known about what makes the treatment of a given client successful or unsuccessful, the likely outcome is often revealed in the first few sessions (Lambert & Bergin, 1994). This is due to the fact that the trajectory of change is highly predictable.

Consider, for example, that data from the CIS at HAI revealed that the response of clients to the first few treatment contacts was highly predictive of eventual treatment outcome. In this regard, clients who improved quickly were likely to continue to improve and vice versa. In fact, clients reporting no improvement by the third session on average showed no improvement over the entire course of treatment. Actual worsening by the third session was a very poor sign, with such clients being twice as likely as those who fared better to drop out of treatment early. This data allowed HAI to identify cases at risk for a negative outcome and inform the practitioner of the need to take constructive action. Those cases proceeding in the expected manner are automatically authorized for continued treatment.

Conclusion

In this chapter, we have sought to provide information regarding the interest of the managed care industry in evaluating and managing psychotherapy outcome. Both managed care companies and providers have a strong need to understand which factors do make a difference in psychotherapy. Those therapists who can most effectively exploit these factors and demonstrate the greatest value should have their practices flourish. In this regard, if there were one lesson for practicing therapists to learn from this chapter, it is, "Pay attention to individual outcomes!" This is the demand of the evolving marketplace for behavioral health care services.

Credentials, professional discipline, and preferred theoretical models mean nothing if they cannot be translated into measurable improvement in the quality of clients' lives. In other words, the outcome rather than the service of psychotherapy is the product that therapists have to offer in the behavioral health care marketplace. Psychotherapists who fail to measure their outcomes in a reliable and empirically sound manner have no means to evaluate their own skills against those of their peers. More importantly, they are limited to relying on their own clinical judgment to assess the client progress. In a very real sense, use of self-report measures gives the client the means to speak directly to the MBHO about his or her experience in treatment. Mental health professionals need to pay attention to the voices of those they serve—their clients.

The findings we reviewed in this chapter also point to the importance of paying attention to the individual's response to treatment as the process unfolds. In this regard, the data indicate that however expertly a specific psychotherapy may be delivered, a client's failure to respond early in the treatment process decreases the chances of a favorable outcome. Collecting outcome data for later analysis misses the opportunity to use the information dynamically as the treatment progresses (as well as devalues the client's effort to provide the information). By completing an outcome measure, the client is communicating very specific information to the therapist. Therapists who ignore this information do so at their own risk.

Questions From the Editors

1. How can the field balance the outcome focus of future clinical practice with the need for experimentation and innovation?

There need not be a conflict between the focus on outcomes and innovation. The key is to collect outcome data in the course of routine delivery of clinical services. As normative data on the expected improvement for different patient types become available, providers can evaluate any innovation in treatment as the care is delivered, constantly comparing their results against the norms.

For example, the clinical algorithms HAI uses to manage care do not attempt to assign certain patients to specific treatments. Rather, we simply monitor the patient's progress. Only if the patient has failed to progress as expected do we actually look at the treatment being delivered. Using this method of outcome management, providers are free to innovate and provide any legal and ethical treatment they deem appropriate so long as outcomes do not suffer.

2. What are the implications of your research for the training of mental health professionals (e.g., therapists)?

Our research indicates that there is a high degree of variability in outcomes, even between cases that have been matched for diagnosis, severity, level of family support, and so on. This variability does not appear to be a factor of the specific type of psychotherapy used. Also, the change in the first few sessions of treatment is the best predictor of the eventual outcome. In others words, providing the "correct" treatment may not be as important as knowing whether or not the treatment being provided is actually working.

In order to provide optimal treatment and to make changes to the treatment plan in a timely manner, the mental health provider needs to be assessing the response to treatment on a session-by-session basis, continuously evaluating the patient's progress against the expected rate of recovery. A standardized patient self-report measure is the most reliable and valid method of assessing this response. A physician would never try to take a patient's temperature by feeling his or her forehead and using his or her "clinical judgment." Training of mental health professionals needs to emphasize the importance of assessing response to treatment using reliable and valid measures, just as other health care providers are trained to routinely monitor vital signs and lab results.

3. What can the average clinician do to begin monitoring and using outcome information to inform and improve his or her clinical practice?

The first step is to begin to systematically administer simple patient self-report measures such as the OQ-45.2. The measure need not take more than 5 minutes to complete or a couple of minutes to score. The measures need to be administered and scored routinely so that the information is immediately available to the provider and patient.

Managed care companies such as HAI are beginning to make available to their providers normative information regarding the average improvement for various patient types. More information of this type will become available to practitioners as the number and size of the outcome databases increase. This normative information will permit providers to begin to evaluate their results immediately against those obtained by thousands of their peers.

References

Ackley, D. C. (1993). Managed care and self esteem. *The independent practitioner, 13,* 49–53.

American Psychiatric Association. (1994). *Diagnostic and statistical manual of mental disorders* (4th ed.). Washington, DC: Author.

American Psychiatric Association. (1996). *Practice guidelines,* Washington, DC: Author.

Bartlett, J., & Cohen, J. (1993) Building an accountable, improvable delivery system. *Administration and Policy in Mental Health, 21,* 51–58.

Brown G. S., Fraser, J. B., & Bendoraitis, T. M. (1995). Transforming the future—the coming impact of CIS. *Behavioral Health Management, 14,* 8–12.

Burlingame, G. M., Lambert, M. J., Reisinger, C. W., & Neff, W. M. (1995). Pragmatics of tracking mental health outcomes in a managed care setting. *Journal of Mental Health Administration, 23,* 226–236.

Duncan, B. L., Hubble, M. A., & Miller, S. D. (1997). *Psychotherapy with impossible cases: Efficient treatment of therapy veterans.* New York: Norton.

Garfield, S. (1989). *The practice of brief therapy.* New York: Pergamon Press.

Hiatt, D., & Hargrave, G. E. (1995). The characteristics of highly effective therapists in managed behavioral providers networks. *Behavioral Healthcare Tomorrow, 4,* 19–22.

Hurst, M. W. (1997). *How to use emerging communication technologies to streamline and improve care management and delivery.* Paper presented at the 1997 Behavioral Informatics Tomorrow conference.

Lambert, M. J. (1992). Psychotherapy outcome research: Implications for integrative and eclectic therapists. In J. Norcross & M. Goldfried (Eds.), *Handbook of psychotherapy integration* (pp. 94–129). New York: Basic Books.

Miller, I. J. (1996). Managed care is harmful to outpatient mental health services: A call for accountability. *Professional Psychology: Research and Practice, 27,* 349–363.

Miller, S. D., Duncan, B. L., & Hubble, M. A. (1997). *Escape from Babel: Toward a unifying language for psychotherapy practice.* New York: Norton.

Miller, S. D., Hubble, M. A., & Duncan, B. L. (1995). No more bells and whistles. *Family Therapy Networker 19*(2), 53–58, 62–63.

Schoenholtz, J. C. (1988). *Managed care or managed cost.* Rey, NY: Rey Psychiatric Center.

U.S. Department of Health and Human Services. (1993). *Depression in primary care* (Publication No. 93-0550). Washington, DC: Author.

Wampold, B. (1997). Methodological problems in identifying efficacious psychotherapies. *Psychotherapy Research, 7,* 1–20.

Wells, M. G., Burlingame, G. M., Lambert, M. J., & Hoag, M. J. (1996). Conceptualization and measurement of patient change during psychotherapy: Development of the Outcome Questionnaire and Youth Outcome Questionnaire. *Psychotherapy 33,* 275–238.

Mark A. Hubble, Barry L. Duncan, and Scott D. Miller

Directing Attention to What Works

14

P utting a final touch on this book is in no small way daunting. Discussions of common factors, with even the intimation that traditional models of therapy and their associated technical procedures do not open the royal road to change, often trigger impassioned opposition and criticism. Yet, despite the many arguments raised against the findings of equivalent outcomes of treatments, "massive evidence" (Bergin & Garfield, 1994, p. 822) exists affirming these results. To ignore the research literature—to pretend much as the proverbial ostrich that if one does see it, it will go away—keeps therapy trapped in a mythological world.

As suggested at the outset, the customary rejection of the common factors is an indulgence the field can ill afford. If the profession will not come to terms with the knowledge it now possesses and continues to promote assertions rich in bombast but bereft of fact, others will surely define a reality for us. All signs indicate that the emerging reality in "behavioral health care" is an unpleasant one for many.

Though this may be equally subject to criticism, payers and consumers deserve to know what works. Should the profession not tell them, they will decide for themselves. On a moment's reflection, asking whether therapists can deliver the goods as promised is hardly presumptuous. If transference interpretations, finger waving, desensitization hierarchies, miracle questions, cognitive restructuring, narrative re-storying, and all of the other methods available are said to have special curative properties, then they should show it convincingly. This is equally true of the theories underlying such interventions.

Fortunately, that therapy advances change is no longer at issue. That we need to understand more fully how it works is what this book attempts to do. Besides reviews of the principal common factors, various practice domains where beneficial change occurs and is fostered are examined and recommendations provided. The task established for this final chapter is threefold. First, further distillation of the implications for clinical work is offered. To say that common factors largely account for change is not enough. What may be done to promote their therapeutic action merits additional emphasis. Second, the part clients play in therapy is revisited. Long cast in a supporting role to the main action of therapists and their theories, clients' contributions to therapy need to be reinterpreted. Here, the case is made that working within and empowering the clients' "theory of change" is integral to their participation and the formation of the all-important alliance. Finally, speculation into what the future may hold for therapy is made.

Clinical Implications

Bergin and Garfield (1994) said the following in the last chapter of the last edition of the *Handbook of Psychotherapy and Behavior Change:* "One of the most difficult findings . . . to use practically is the continuing and frequent lack of difference in the outcomes of various techniques" (p. 822). Their observation aptly sums up the dilemma many practitioners experience when they appreciate that pantheoretical factors are the chief drivers of therapeutic outcome. Accepting that common factors account for much of the change does not mean, however, that suddenly a "model *less*" or "technique*less*" therapy is being advocated. As part of the family of curative factors shared by all therapies, models and techniques have something to offer. A therapy informed by an understanding of common factors, therefore, incorporates and actively uses all of the elements or ingredients that have been found to facilitate change.

In what follows, more suggestions are presented for supporting the action of the four major therapeutic factors examined in this book. By no means do these recommendations constitute an exhaustive formulary for the conduct of therapy. Indeed, there are likely to be many approaches for doing treatment that capitalize on the contribution of the common factors. In the end, their usefulness will depend on their performance—do they achieve the desired results or not? Theoretical correctness, the alleged uniqueness of an intervention, or the political standing of a therapy's advocates are no longer adequate criteria for judging what works.

CLIENT OR EXTRATHERAPEUTIC FACTORS

Sad to say, clients have not been highly regarded in most therapeutic systems. Called the maladjusted, disturbed, regressed, neurotic, psychotic, and character-disordered (to name just a few), a reasonable person might conclude that therapists have nothing good to recount about the very people who support their livelihoods. This is no fault of therapists, but it does strongly speak to the professions' traditions. As Held (1991) pointedly observed, most theories of therapy are, in reality, theories of psychopathology.

No matter how many unfavorable ways clients are classified in professional discourse, the practice of therapy is not about nosology. It is about change. Change rules. Because, as Brown, Dreis, and Nace report in chapter 13, we are in a time in which payers increasingly track outcomes (change for better or worse), the question arises how can clinicians become more change focused in their day-to-day work.

Becoming Change Focused

Heraclitis, the Greek philosopher (fl. c. 500 B.C.), is known for saying, "Nothing is permanent but change." Unlike diagnoses—static characterizations connoting a measure of constancy, even permanence, in clients' presenting complaints—the magnitude, severity, and frequency of problems are in flux, constantly changing. In this regard, clients will report better and worse days, times free of symptoms, and moments when their problems seem to get the best of them. Without or with a little prompting, they can describe these changes—the ebb and flow of the problem's presence and ascendancy in their daily affairs. From this standpoint, it might be said that change itself is a powerful extratherapeutic factor, affecting the lives of clients before, during, and after therapy.

To develop a change focus, a therapist can listen for and validate change for the better, whenever and for whatever reason it occurs (Hubble, Miller, & Duncan, 1998). A change focus also requires that the therapist believe, like Heraclites, in the certainty of change and to create a context in which new or different perspectives, behaviors, or experiences are welcomed and explored. As Tallman and Bohart note in chapter 4 of this volume, of special interest is what the client has done or is doing to bring about or take advantage of change. Tallman and Bohart fervently argue that therapists attend to clients' self-healing and to any competencies used in service of positive change.

Inquiry into change can proceed along two lines. First, clients can be asked about pretreatment change. Discussed by Tallman and Bohart, pretreatment change is any change taking place in the direction of the client's goal before the first session. It can be welcomed in several ways. For instance, during the opening moments of a first session the therapist may inquire about what, if any, changes the clients have noticed since the time they scheduled their appointment for therapy and the first meeting (S. D. Miller, Duncan, & Hubble, 1997a).

> *Many people notice that, between the time they called for the appointment and the actual first session, things already seem different (already have improved). What have you noticed about your situation?* (Lawson 1994; Weiner-Davis, de Shazer, & Gingerich, 1987)

When clients report goal-directed, pretreatment changes, questions can then be asked to elaborate the change and the client's contribution to it. In effect, this helps to link directly the positive change to the client's own behavior, thus highlighting it as an instance of self-healing.

> *What was happening at those times? [obtain a detailed description] What do you think you were doing to help that along? What would you need to do (or what would need to happen) for you to experience more of that? As you continue to do these good things for yourself (or take advantage of what is helping), what difference will that make to you tomorrow? How will your day go better? The day after that?* (Hubble et al., 1998).

Similarly, should the client return for additional visits, attention can be directed to changes taking place between sessions. For example, therapists can heed and then amplify any references the client makes during the session to between-session improvement. Also, in the opening moments of the session, therapists can directly ask clients about what, if any, changes have occurred since their last visit (S. D. Miller et al., 1997a). The simplest question comes in this form, "What is different?" or "What is better?" Inquiry, as in the example, when used judiciously and with sensitivity to the client's acceptance, focuses both on change and the client's contribution in bringing about change. In this way, clinicians may assist the client in attributing any change to their own efforts. The 5-E Method, described by Murphy in chapter 12, represents a change focus in action.

Potentiating Change for the Future

Whether change begins before or during treatment, whether it results from the client's own actions or by happenstance, a crucial step in enhancing the effect of extratherapeutic factors is helping clients see any changes—as well as the maintenance of those changes—as a consequence of their own efforts (S. D. Miller et al., 1997a). Naturally, a cardinal consideration is perception: specifically, the clients' perception of the relationship between their own efforts and the occurrence of change. It is important that clients come to view the change as resulting, at least in part, from something they did and can repeat in the future. Therapists, moreover, can support changes resulting from extratherapeutic factors in several ways. As illustrated above, the therapist can express curiosity about the client's role in changes that occur during treatment. In addition, the therapist can ask questions or make direct statements that presuppose client involvement in the resulting change (Berg & Miller, 1992; Imber, Pilkonis, Harway, Klein, & Rubinsky, 1982; Walter & Peller, 1992).

> *Wait a second. You did what? Tell me more about that. How did you know to do what you did? That was thoughtful. What is it about you that helped you to do what you did?*

As part of ending therapy, therapists may also summarize the changes that occurred during therapy and invite clients to review their own role in the change. Even if clients resolutely attribute change to luck, fate, the acumen of the therapist, or a medication they can still be asked to consider in detail (a) how they adopted the change in their lives, (b) what they did to use the changes to their benefit, and (c) what they will do in the future to ensure their gains remain in place.

Minding the Client's Competence

As suggested, therapists can begin to cast their clients in the role as the primary agents of change by listening for and being curious about their competencies (i.e., their part in bringing about and maintaining positive change). This approach requires a balance between listening empathically to their difficulties with a mindfulness to their strengths and resources. The key here is the attitude the practitioner assumes with regard to the client's ability. This attitude involves treating clients as though they are capable and have the strengths and resources necessary to solve their problems (Watzlawick, 1987). It is perhaps best summarized by Alfred Adler when he said he approached all clients, "fully convinced that no matter what I might be able to say . . . the patient can learn nothing from me that he, as the sufferer, does not understand better" (cited in Ansbacher & Ansbacher, 1956, p. 336). Approaching clients in this manner not only helps to combat discouragement and instill hope but, as Adler also noted, "make[s] it clear that the responsibility for . . . cure is the patient's business" (cited in Ansbacher & Ansbacher, 1956, p. 336).

Tapping the Client's World Outside Therapy

Clinicians are also mindful of clients' contribution to change by incorporating resources from their world outside therapy. Whether seeking out a trusted friend or family member, purchasing a book or tape, attending church or a mutual-help group, clients find support outside the formal therapy relationship (S. D. Miller et al., 1997a). To attend to the client's world outside therapy, the therapist, for example, can listen for and express curiosity about what happens in the client's life that is helpful. Several questions are useful to bear in mind:

- Whom does the client refer to as helpful in his or her day-to-day life?
- How or what does the client do to get these persons to help him or her?
- What persons, places, or things does the client seek out between treatment sessions for even a small measure of comfort or aid?
- What persons, places, or things has the client sought out in the past that were useful?
- What was different about those times that enabled the client to use those resources?

The therapist also may want to ask direct questions about these same elements. In particular, the therapist may inquire about the helpful aspects of the client's existing social support network, activities that provide relief, even if temporary, and circumstances outside therapy in which the client feels most capable, successful, and composed. Sometimes, the therapist may wish to be even more direct by inviting someone from the client's existing social support network (e.g., parent, partner, employer, friend) to participate in the therapy or by referring the client to resources in the community (e.g., self-help groups, support lines, social clubs). Whatever path the therapist takes, it is important to remember that the purpose is to identify not what clients need, but what they already have in their lives that can be put to use in reaching their goals (S. D. Miller et al., 1997a).

RELATIONSHIP FACTORS

Relationship factors make up the second largest contributor to change in psychotherapy. The client's view of the relationship is the "trump card" in therapy outcome, second only to the winning hand of the client's strengths. Clients who rate the relationship highly are very likely to be successful in achieving their goals. Despite how chronic, intractable, or "impossible" a case may appear, if the client's view of the relationship is favorable, change is more likely to occur (Duncan,

Hubble, & Miller, 1997a). Perhaps, the art of therapy comes most into play with those clients, who, owing to past trauma or disillusionment, have problems in establishing meaningful interpersonal bonds. Following are a few additional suggestions for insuring a positive view of the therapeutic relationship. These include (a) accommodating treatment to the client's motivational level or readiness for change and (b) accommodating the client's view of the therapeutic alliance.

Accommodating the Client's Motivational Readiness or Stage of Change

Bachelor and Horvath note in chapter 5 of this volume that to forge a strong relationship with clients, their readiness for change needs to be taken into account. Readiness for change is inseparably tied to motivation or what might be called *motivational readiness.* Nevertheless, for decades, clients' motivation has been dichotomized—either they were motivated or not.

As it turns out, the idea of an unmotivated client is not true. All people, all clients have motivation; only the dead are plausibly unmotivated. It is more correct to say the motivation of "unmotivated" clients may not match the therapist's goals and expectations (Duncan et al., 1997a). Further, no longer is motivation for change understood strictly as some trait, or stable personality characteristic, that passively tags along with clients. Instead, it is a dynamic process strongly influenced by others' contribution to the interaction. In short, motivation is as much or even more contextually as it is personally determined.

With the recognition that motivation for change is partly a product of what people do together, clinicians can work in harmony with their clients to increase their participation in treatment. As reviewed by Prochaska in his chapter, a central consideration in increasing motivation and an eventual positive outcome is to take into account the client's stage of change.

The Stages of Change

Change begins in the stage called *precontemplation.* Clients in this phase "haven't a clue" that a problem exists. They have not, as of yet, made a connection between a problem in their lives and their contribution to its formation or continuation. Because they do not think they have a problem, these clients are usually not in the mood either to participate in or establish an alliance with a helping professional (Prochaska, 1995).

To help clients in precontemplation take that first step, a "light touch" is recommended. Having a light touch means first and foremost that the therapist is courteous to the client and willing to listen to his or her point of view (S. D. Miller et al., 1997a). The goal is not to make the client do something. Rather, in accommodating a client in precontemplation, the therapist's job is to create a climate in which the client can consider, explore, and appreciate the benefits of changing. This could include, for example, providing information or helping the client become aware of the causes, consequences (positive and negative), and cures of their problems or concerns (Prochaska & DiClemente, 1992, p. 304).

In all, as the word *stage* implies, accommodating motivational readiness requires us to be "in phase" with the client. In the earliest stage, if the client expresses an inkling that some action may be necessary, an important step forward has been made.

The second stage of change is *contemplation*. Clients in contemplation are renown for their use of two words, "Yes, but." Frequently, these clients recognize that a change is needed. They may also have a sense of a goal and even know what they need to do to reach it. Even so, they are unsure whether the change is worth the cost in time, effort, and energy. In addition, they are frequently unsure or ambivalent about the losses attendant to any change they might make (S. D. Miller et al., 1997a).

Accommodating clients in contemplation takes considerable patience given their tendency to vacillate and be indecisive. An effective approach entails creating a supportive environment in which the client can carefully consider changing without feeling the pressure or need to take action (Duncan, 1989). In certain cases, the therapist might even actively discourage the client from taking action and, instead, simply encourage thinking or observation.

A classic example of accommodating clients who are contemplating change can be found in the "go slow" injunction from the brief strategic therapy tradition (Duncan, 1989; Fisch, Weakland, & Segal, 1982). The advice to go slow (i.e., not change too quickly, postpone, consider how much change is optimal) is not some piece of paradoxical subterfuge. When clients are contemplating change, allying with their ambivalence is perhaps the most empathic stance a therapist can assume. After all, by the time most of these clients see a therapist, they have been exposed to all sorts of exhortations to do something—both from others and their own conscience. Also from the strategic tradition is a variation of the go slow suggestion known as the "dangers of improvement" (Fisch et al., 1982). This approach is helpful in accommodating clients who have stayed in contemplation for a protracted period—clients whose lengthy inaction, multiple false starts or failures have led them to be labeled "difficult" or "chronic." In raising the dangers of improvement, it is suggested that change be set aside for some period. The client is then asked to consider carefully any risks that might be associated with improvement. No danger is too small to contemplate. By taking this very conservative position about progress, the therapist provides an opportunity for the client to explore and express the risks associated with change (Duncan, 1989). Overall, showing the understanding that change requires time, thoughtfulness, and sometimes radical accommodation is respectful, helps to take off pressure, and gives the client the space and support to commit to change.

No matter the particular therapeutic tradition followed or applied in accommodating the client in contemplation, it helps to keep one's finger off the hot button of change. Should therapists attempt to push clients in contemplation to change, they will, instead of moving them forward, likely cause them to dig in their heels. As such, it is better to listen, agree, provide a small encouraging nudge when invited, and engage the client in an exploration of what they stand to both gain and lose from changing (S. D. Miller et al., 1997a).

The third stage is *preparation*. By the time clients reach this stage they have crossed the Rubicon of change. Now, the focus turns to identifying the criteria and strategies for success. Preparation is also characterized by the clients' experimenting with the desired change—trying it on for size, noticing how it feels, and then experiencing the effects. Therapists accommodate such clients when they encourage rather than downplay (as has been characteristic of traditional drug and alcohol treatment approaches) the significance of such early problem-solving efforts (i.e., "too little, too late").

Clinicians accommodate clients in preparation when they help them sort through and select their treatment goals, as well as explore and map out potential paths that might be taken to reach those goals (S. D. Miller et al., 1997a). At this point, the therapist can assume a more active role in raising possibilities, presenting treatment options or change strategies, and constructively challenging the client's problem-solving abilities. As during all of the stages, however, choice is important (W. R. Miller, 1986). Clients in preparation need to be active in choosing and designing their own strategy for change. Therapists are most likely to be helpful when they present alternatives or different methods that clients can use to achieve their goals. Implying there is only one way invites resistance and increases the risk of the client terminating treatment prematurely.

Following preparation, the *action* stage commences. Clients in the action phase present with both a firm commitment and plan for the future. When clients reach action it is almost as though the therapist need not even meet with the client. In contemporary parlance, the client in action is "cookin." During this stage, therapists can stand by, offer measured emotional support, and help the client monitor, modify, or fine tune the plan of action.

In the *maintenance* stage, change continues. Now, however, stress is placed on what the client needs to do to maintain or consolidate the gains. In this stage, providers can accommodate the client's motivational level by helping him or her anticipate the challenges that might provoke regression or relapse (S. D. Miller et al., 1997a). As they are identified, prevention plans are developed. For instance, if, in the past, driving down a certain street increased the risk of a stop at a certain bar, a prevention plan might specify a new route for the recovering drinker to take until the street no longer served as a cue for alcohol consumption.

Therapists also accommodate clients in maintenance by helping them design retention plans for the inevitable lapses that accompany any change. Should the client find themselves sliding down the slippery slope of relapse, the retention plan provides handholds for the client to grab onto so the slide to the bottom need not continue. For example, if the drinker drives down the street, goes into a bar, and has the first drink or two, a prearranged retention plan might kick in that defines specific actions for the client to take to stop further drinking. The plan might identify a person for the drinker to call or another predetermined alternative.

In the final stage, *termination*, "there is zero temptation to engage in the problem behavior, and there is a 100 percent confidence (self-efficacy) that one will not engage in the old behavior regardless of the situation" (Prochaska, 1993, p. 253). So defined, termination may be more of an ideal than an achievable stage. For many, maintenance is where they will stay. That is, they continue to be mindful of possible threats to their desired change and monitor what they need to do to keep the change in place.

In all, stages of change offer a way for therapists to design a treatment that will increase the likelihood of the client's participation and positive assessment of the therapy. Clients will more likely engage in change projects when their therapists and other interested parties "assess the stage of a client's readiness for change and tailor their interventions accordingly" (Prochaska, DiClemente, & Norcross, 1992, p. 1110).

Treatment Should Accommodate the Client's View of the Alliance

Closely related to accommodating clients' readiness for change is tailoring treatment to fit with their view of the therapeutic alliance or relationship. First, to increase the chances that the client becomes involved in the therapy and experiences the relationship positively, practitioners need to ensure they are working on what the client deems important. From this perspective, treatment is best understood as a partnership for change. It is a process that client and therapist do together, rather than something done to the client (e.g., fill out a genogram, take this medication, go into trance) because the therapist happens to think it is best. In a well-functioning alliance, therapists and clients jointly work to construct interventions that are in accordance with clients' preferred outcomes. In this light, interventions represent an instance of the alliance in action. They cannot be separated from the client's goals or the relationship in which they occur. They have no meaning or power separate—on their own—from the alliance.

Therapists can accommodate therapy to the client's goals by listening and then amplifying the stories and experiences that clients offer about their problems, including their thoughts, feelings, and ideas about "where they want to go and the best way to get there." The therapist can also directly inquire about the client's goals. For instance, the therapist might ask the following questions:

- What is your goal in coming here?
- What did you (hope/wish/think) would be different because of our meeting together?
- What did you want to change about your (life/problem/etc.)?
- What would have to be minimally different in your life to consider our work together a success?
- What will be the first sign to you that you have taken a solid step on the road to improvement even though you might not yet be out of the woods?

Research from several fields indicates that goals specified in small, concrete, specific, and behavioral terms and that clients perceive as both desirable and attainable are more likely to influence their behavior in the desired direction (Bandura & Schunk, 1981; Berg & Miller, 1992; Locke, Shaw, Saari, & Latham, 1981; W. R. Miller, 1987). For this reason, therapists will want to help their clients describe their goals whenever possible in terms that match these considerations.

To foster a positive alliance, attention to the client's goals is but one step. Another is to attend to the client's perceptions of the therapist and the relationship the therapist is offering. As Bachelor and Horvath report in chapter 5, clients have been found to vary widely in their experience of the core conditions that distinguish good therapeutic relationships. They suggest, too, that successful therapeutic relationships are those in which the definition of the therapist-provided variables is extended to fit with the client's own unique experience of those variables—the client's definition of therapist-provided warmth, empathy, respect, and genuineness. For practice, therefore, clinicians stand the greatest chance of enabling the contribution of relationship factors to outcome when they purposefully tailor their provision of the core conditions to the client's definition.

To do this on a day-to-day basis requires careful monitoring of the client's reaction to comments, explanations, interpretations, questions, and suggestions. It also demands a higher measure of flexibility on the part of the therapist and a willingness to change one's relational stance to fit with the client's perceptions of what is most helpful. Some clients, for instance, will prefer a formal or professional manner over a casual or warmer one. Others might prefer more self-disclosure from their therapist, greater directiveness, a focus on their symptoms or a focus on the possible meanings beneath them, and a faster or perhaps a more laid back pace for therapeutic work (Bachelor & Horvath, chap. 5, this volume). Clearly, the one-approach-fits-all strategy is guaranteed to undermine alliance formation.

Combining the findings on both client/extratherapeutic and relationship factors, this conclusion follows. Therapeutic success depends on enabling and confirming the client's resources in a partnership informed by the client's goals and perceptions.

PLACEBO, HOPE, AND EXPECTANCY

Research confirms the importance of hope and expectation in psychotherapy (see chap. 6 by Snyder, Michael, and Cheavens). Already potent ways for therapists to facilitate hope and positive expectations for change have been presented (i.e., forming strong therapeutic relationships, identifying goals, and incorporating clients' strengths into the treatment). The suggestions and "techniques" now sampled possess no special curative powers on their own. Instead, their value resides in the extent to which they facilitate hope and a positive expectation for change.

Having a Healing Ritual

Rituals are a shared characteristic of healing procedures in most cultures and date back to the earliest origins of human society (Frank & Frank, 1991; Frazer, 1920; Van Gennep, 1960). Their use inspires hope and a positive expectation for change by conveying that the user—shaman, astrologer, or therapist—possesses a special set of skills for healing. That the procedures are not in and of themselves the causal agents of change matters little (Kottler, 1991). What does matter is that the participants have a structured, concrete method for mobilizing the placebo factors.

When viewed as a healing ritual, even the latest therapies (e.g., eye movement desensitization and reprocessing) offer nothing new. Healing rituals have been a part of psychotherapy dating back to the modern origins of the field (Wolberg, 1954, 1977). Whether instructing clients to lie on a couch, talk to an empty chair, or chart negative self-talk, mental health professionals are engaging in healing rituals. Because comparisons of therapy techniques have found little differential efficacy, they may all be understood as healing rituals—technically inert, but nonetheless powerful, organized methods for enhancing the effects of placebo factors (S. D. Miller et al., 1997a).

The perennial question facing therapists is what particular ritual to use when working with an individual client. Some guidelines for making a selection follow.

The therapist should believe in the procedure or therapeutic orientation.

Therapists enhance the placebo component of the procedures they use when they believe in and are confident that the procedures will be therapeutic. As Benson and Epstein noted, treatment professionals "who have faith in the efficacy of their treatments . . . are the most successful in producing positive placebo effects" (cited in O'Regan, 1985, p. 17).

The therapist should show interest in the results of the procedure or orientation.

Placebo effects are heightened when therapists show interest in the results of whatever technique or orientation they use. It has long been known that people participating in research studies are more likely to respond in the predicted direction when they know the purpose of the experiment (Matheson, Bruce, & Beauchamp, 1978; Smith & Glass, 1987). Clinicians can put the same phenomenon to work by engaging in activities that convey a positive expectation of and hope for client change (S. D. Miller et al., 1997a). For example, as Asay and Lambert suggest in chapter 2, therapists can make a practice of asking about the beneficial effects of the therapy at some point during each session. A more proactive approach is to ask clients to notice and record any changes for the better that occur between sessions (Kral & Kowalski, 1989). Such a homework assignment conveys the therapist's hope for and expectation of improvement, which may in turn create an observational bias on the part of the client favoring therapeutic change.

Have a Possibility Focus

Clients are best served by helping them believe in possibilities—of change, of accomplishing or getting what they want, of starting over, of succeeding or of controlling their life. There are a variety of ways for therapists to be more "possibility focused" in their clinical work.

Treatment should be oriented toward the future.

Traditionally, psychotherapy has focused more on the past. The idea has been that, for clients to have better tomorrows, therapists must first help them create better yesterdays. As Frank and Frank (1991) suggested, however, it is not revisiting or "working through" the past that matters. What does count in facilitating hope and positive expectations for change is challenging or modifying the pessimistic assumptions clients have about the future.

Several questions follow that can be used to assist clients in envisioning a better future:

- What will be different when (e.g., anxiety, drinking, feuding with your spouse, etc.) is behind you?
- What will be the smallest sign that the (_____) is getting better?
- What will be the first sign?
- When you are no longer (e.g., fighting, in trouble with the law, drinking, etc.) what will you be doing more of instead?
- Who will be the first person to notice that you have achieved a victory over this? What will that person notice different about you that will tell him or her that the victory is achieved?
- Where do you suppose you will be when you first notice the changes? What will have taken place just before the changes that will have helped them to happen? What will happen later that will help maintain them?

When engaging in future-oriented work, assisting clients to describe the future they want tends to make that future more salient to the present (de Shazer et al., 1986). The detail lends, too, an aura of reality, implying that the future the client is describing is possible to achieve in the present. In many instances, possibility even becomes connected with reality when the increasingly detailed description elicits recollections of having experienced all or at least part of what is being described (S. D. Miller & Berg, 1995). It should be mentioned that therapists need not use direct questions to bring a future orientation to treatment. Clients frequently provide opportunities for the therapist to join them in a discussion of their hopes for the future. When such opportunities arise, therapists can follow the client's lead and amplify the discussion (S. D. Miller et al., 1997a).

Treatment should enhance or highlight the client's felt sense of personal control.

People who believe they can influence or modify the course of life events cope better and adjust more successfully when meeting adversity. This holds true regardless of whether the belief in personal control is accurate. As Taylor, Wayment, and Collins (1993) pointed out, simply *believing* one "has the means to influence, terminate, or modify a noxious event [helps people] cope better with those events" (p. 329). At the same time, research has established a link between a successful treatment outcome and clients' general belief in their ability to influence the course of life events (e.g., Beyebach, Morejon, Palenzuela, & Rodriguez-Arias, 1996).

With this in mind, therapists can work to enhance clients' feelings of personal control. Several approaches suggest themselves. Again, the therapist can listen for and then amplify any references clients make to their actions having an impact on the outcome of daily events. The therapist can also be more direct by asking questions or making direct statements that presuppose the client's influence over events occurring in his/her life.

> *It is impressive that you took that step on your own to let the depression know who's boss. When did it occur to you that was the right thing to do? Now that you have done this, what else will you do to keep the depression on a short leash?*

MODELS AND TECHNIQUES

In contrast with the tradition of separating models and techniques from the common factors (or so-called specific factors from nonspecific factors), theoretical models and their related techniques are included here as part of the family of common factors. Though the research reviewed in this volume suggests a much more modest appraisal of the differential effects of theory-driven models and methods, they still have value. For this reason, and because they are used in all forms of therapy, recommendations are offered for how they can be incorporated into practice.

As a start, it is helpful to stand back from the squabbles over whose is best and consider what it means to regard models and techniques as part of the pantheoretical factors shared by all effective therapies. When viewed from this vantage point, models and techniques no longer reflect a particular theoretical doctrine or school. Instead, as Simon (1996) suggested, they become "a practice which teaches *the therapist*, through naming, enactment, and talking to colleagues, the attitudes and values from which [therapeutic] work is generated" (p. 53, emphasis added; see also Fancher, 1995). Therefore, models and techniques help provide therapists with replicable and structured ways for developing and practicing the values, attitudes, and behaviors consistent with the core ingredients of effective therapy. This nontraditional role for models and techniques suggests that their principal contribution to therapy comes about by enhancing the potency of the other common factors—client/extratherapeutic, relationship, placebo, hope, and expectancy. Possibilities for how that occurs are discussed next.

Structure and Focus

In any therapy session, one sees a clinician either asking questions, listening and reflecting, dispensing reassurance, confronting, providing information, offering explanations (interpretations, reframes, and rationales), making suggestions, self-disclosing, or assigning tasks for both within and outside a session (Garfield, 1989). The content of the talk or question differs depending on the therapist's preferred orientation. Yet, at the root, all of these procedures are intended to prepare clients to take or continue some action to help themselves. As noted in the first chapter, across all models, therapists expect their clients to change, to do something different—be it developing new understandings, feeling emotion, facing fears, taking risks, or altering old patterns of behavior.

A way to view techniques is to see them as something akin to a magnifying glass. They bring together, focus, and concentrate the forces of change, narrow them to a point in place and time, and cause them to ignite into action (S. D. Miller et al., 1997a). Not surprising, the literature indicates that focus and structure are essential elements of effective psychotherapy. In fact, one of the best predictors of negative outcome in psychotherapy is a lack of focus and structure. Failure to provide a structure or focus in therapeutic sessions can have a greater impact on treatment outcome than the personal qualities of either the therapist or client (Mohl, 1995).

The challenging question, because of the large number of choices available, is which structure or focus the therapist should adopt when working with a particular client. In this regard, the data indicate that the particular orientation or technique is less important than the degree to which an orientation or technique helps the therapist develop and practice attitudes and behaviors that are consistent with the common curative factors and fit both with the client's world view (discussed further in the next section of this chapter) and expectations for treatment.

As an aid to selecting a particular model or technique, one that will empower the common therapeutic factors, the following questions are proposed:

- Does the orientation or strategy fit with, support, or complement the client's world view? If so, how?
- Does the theory or intervention fit with, or can it be tailored to complement, the client's expectations for treatment? How so?

- Can it be tailored?
- Does the particular strategy capitalize on client strengths, resources, abilities? How?
- To what extent does the orientation/intervention take into account and use the client's environment and existing support network?
- Does the method identify or build on the spontaneous changes that clients experience while in therapy? How?
- To what degree does the orientation/technique identify, fit with, or build on the client's goals for therapy?
- Would the client describe the therapeutic interaction resulting from the adoption of the particular strategy or orientation as empathic, respectful, and genuine?
- How does the orientation or intervention increase the client's sense of hope, expectancy, or personal control?
- How does the method or orientation contribute to the client's sense of self-esteem, self-efficacy, and self-mastery? (S. D. Miller et al., 1997a, p. 190)

Models and Techniques as Novelty

Another way models and techniques can be useful is through giving clinicians different options for case conceptualizing and intervening, especially when little progress is occurring. Historically, treatment failures were attributed to the client or the therapist. Clients were labeled either resistant to change or inappropriate for psychotherapy. For their part, therapists were considered inadequately trained or countertransferentially impaired. Once the fault was found, the integrity of the model or technique could be maintained.

Nowadays, with over 400 therapy models and techniques to choose from, little reason exists for continued allegiance to a particular theoretical orientation when that way of thinking about or conducting treatment falters or fails. Instead, another model or technique can be considered. No blame need be assigned; therapists and clients can simply change their minds and make another selection. In this light, the different schools of therapy may be most helpful when they provide therapists with novel ways of looking at old situations, when they empower therapists to change rather than make up their minds about clients. This is not to say that therapists should capriciously switch orientations every time progress is not immediate. On the other hand, theoretical or technical orthodoxy should be considered secondary to whether progress is being made (S. D. Miller et al., 1997a).

One way for therapists to determine whether a change of mind is called for is to be, as presented earlier, more change focused in their clinical work, namely, to be mindful of—to listen for or inquire about—any changes that the client experiences before, during, or between treatment sessions. All large-scale, meta-analytic studies of client change indicate that the most frequent improvement occurs early in the treatment process (Howard, Kopta, Krause, & Orlinsky, 1986; Smith, Glass, & Miller, 1980; Steenbarger, 1992, 1994; Talmon, 1988, 1990). Moreover, these same data, as Orlinsky and Howard (1986) pointed out, "suggest a course of diminishing returns with more and more effort required to achieve just noticeable differences in patient improvement" (p. 361). As far as timing is concerned, the data indicate therapists should consider doing something different when they fail to hear or elicit reports of progress from clients within a few hours rather than months of therapy (S. D. Miller et al., 1997a).

Whether switching from passive to active, intrapsychic to interpersonal, individual to interactional, clinicians can use the common factors as a guide in choosing alternative therapies. In this regard, orientations that help the therapist adopt a different way to identify or approach the client's goals, establish a better match with the client's stage of change, foster hope, capitalize on chance events and clients' strengths, and to make use of or become aware of environmental supports are likely to prove the most beneficial in promoting progress.

In the next section, one "last call" for the client is made. Specifically, the benefits of exploring and working within the client's world view or frame of reference are presented. In addition, the practical applications of this stance in clinical work are explored. Adopting the client's frame of reference as the defining "theory" for the therapy is posited as a catalyst to the empowerment of the common factors.

Dinosaurs, Common Factors, and the Client's Frame of Reference

In 1964, Yale paleontologists John Ostrom and Grant Meyer discovered the fossil remains of an animal that Ostrom would later name, Deinonychus (Terrible Claw). The finding of Deinonychus shook the very foundation of paleontological thought and fueled the flames of a major revolution in the way dinosaurs were viewed. Before, dinosaurs were seen as ponderous, cold-blooded, shuffling monsters. Yet Deinonychus, by its skeletal anatomy, pointed to the existence of an agile, swift, larger-brained, and perhaps even a warm-blooded hunter that was anything but slow, sprawling, and stupid (Hubble & Hanlon, 1992). Consequently, the earlier orthodoxy, solidly in place in paleontology, was doomed, soon to be as extinct as the animals it presumed to explain (Wilford, 1986).

Just as the discovery of Deinonychus dramatically changed how dinosaurs were viewed, converging empirical evidence—regarding the importance of clients and their perceptions to positive outcome—is transforming how clients are treated and therapy is conducted. Specifically, the shift is encompassing changes in perspective from (a) clients as slow-witted plodders (or pathological monsters) to resourceful, motivated hunters of more satisfying lives; (b) the clinician as the leading character in the drama of therapy to the client as the star of the therapeutic stage; and (c) the omnipotence of the therapist's theory of therapy to the prominence of the client's theory of change.

We have come to understand the empirical findings on the common factors as largely explainable under the concept of the client's frame of reference (Duncan et al., 1997a; Duncan & Moynihan, 1994). The client's resources, skills, and agency in and outside therapy (see Tallman & Bohart, this volume), and the client's perceptions and experience of the therapeutic relationship (see Bachelor & Horvath, this volume) comprise two components of the client's frame of reference. These two parts combine to account for a hypothesized 70% of outcome variance (see Asay & Lambert, this volume). The third aspect of the client's frame of reference is the client's perceptions of the presenting complaint, its causes, and how therapy may best address the client's goals and expectations for therapy, that is, the client's theory of change.

The Client's Theory of Change

A BRIEF HISTORICAL REVIEW

The idea that client perceptions of problem formation and resolution have important implications for outcome has a rich but largely overlooked heritage in the therapy literature. As early as 1955, Hoch proposed,

> There are some patients who would like to submit to a
> psychotherapeutic procedure whose theoretical foundations are
> in agreement with their own ideas about psychic functioning.
> We feel that it would be fruitful to explain patient's own ideas
> about psychotherapy and what they expect from it. (p. 322)

Later, Torrey (1972) asserted that sharing similar beliefs with clients about the causes and treatment of mental disorders is a prerequisite to successful psychotherapy. He suggested that when confronted with differences between themselves and their clients, therapists have a choice of adjusting their own beliefs or convincing clients that the therapist's point of view will lead to the desired therapeutic effect. The former suggestion (see below) has far more empirical support.

Wile (1977), too, believed that clients enter therapy with their own theories about their problems, how they developed, and how they are to be solved. "Many of the classic disputes which arise between clients and therapists can be attributed to differences in their theories of [etiology and] cure" (Wile, 1977, p. 437). Similarly, Brickman et al. (1982) hypothesized that many of the problems characterizing relationships between help givers and help recipients arise from the fact that the two parties are applying models that are out of phase with one another (p. 375).

Building on the work of Milton Erickson and the tradition of accepting what the client brings to therapy, the Mental Research Institute (MRI; Watzlawick, Weakland, & Fisch, 1974) developed the idea of position. This refers to the client's beliefs, values, and attitudes that specifically influence the nature of the presenting problem and the client's participation (Fisch et al., 1982). The MRI argued for a rapid assessment of the client's position so the therapist can accept the client's statements, recognize the values they represent, avoid inflammatory therapeutic moves, and tailor all intervention to be consistent with the client's position. Likewise, Frank and Frank (1991) suggested that "ideally therapists should select for each patient the therapy that accords, or can be brought to accord, with the patient's personal characteristics and view of the problem" (p. xv).

Held (1986, 1991), influenced by the work of Prochaska and DiClemente (1982), defined *process* as the activities in which the therapist engages to promote change. *Content* is the object of the change, involving those aspects of the client that focus the therapist's interventional efforts (Held, 1991). Content is defined at both formal and informal theoretical levels. *Formal theory*, held by therapists, consists of predetermined explanatory schemes (e.g., fixated psychosexual development, triangulation) addressed across cases to solve problems (Held, 1986). *Informal theory*, held by clients, involves their specific beliefs about the causes of their particular complaints. With these ideas in mind, Held (1991) argued for a shift in focus from the content-oriented goals prescribed by formal theories. She suggests that intervention strategies may be selected from any of the available models, which at the content level, are congruent with the informal theory of the client. Duncan, Solovey, and Rusk (1992) clinically demonstrated such a selection process in their "client-directed" approach.

Duncan and Moynihan (1994) asserted, moreover, that adopting the client's perceptions of the presenting complaint, it's causes, and potential solutions facilitates a favorable relationship, increases client participation, and therefore enhances positive outcome. They advocate the intentional use of the client's theory of change throughout all phases of the therapeutic process. Similarly, Jerome Frank (1995) concluded, "I'm inclined to entertain the notion that the relative efficacy of most psychotherapeutic methods depends almost exclusively on how successfully the therapist is able to make the methods fit the patient's expectations" (p. 91).

Building on and applying the wisdom of therapy's most influential scholars, Duncan et al. (1997a) view the client's theory as containing most, if not all of the trappings of any psychological theory. It encompasses etiology, treatment, and prognosis and includes clients' thoughts, attitudes, and feelings about their problems and how therapy may best address their goals. They view the client's theory of change as not only having the values that most affect the client's participation in therapy but also as holding the keys to success despite the method or technique used by the therapist.

Besides the specific theoretical discussions cited above, constructivist (Neimeyer & Mahoney, 1995), social constructionist (Flemons & Green, 1998; Gergen, 1985), narrative (Eron & Lund, 1996; Goolishian & Anderson, 1987), and solution-focused approaches (Shilts, Fillippino, & Nau, 1994; Walters & Peller, 1996) privilege the client's "voice" (Conran & Love, 1993) as the source of insight and solution (see Hoyt, 1998, for a broad sample of these approaches). Although not specifically highlighting the client's theory of change, the collaborative and egalitarian therapeutic stance of these approaches enables the client's perceptions and ideas to form an integral part of the therapeutic process.

Many practitioners and scholars, past and present, and from many clinical orientations, agree that client perceptions about problem etiology and resolution are likely to affect the process and outcome of therapy. Do these hypothesized effects have an empirical support? To answer that question, we survey findings from a variety of research areas: attribution, expectancy, acceptability, and the alliance.

ATTRIBUTION RESEARCH: A BRIEF REVIEW

Attribution research bears on the issues just raised. Psychologists have increasingly investigated the role causal attributions play in therapy. Martin (1988) proposed the following question to identify the relationship between the theories of therapists and clients: "Does the degree of similarity in client and counselor theories predict success in counseling?" (p. 263). A growing number of studies address this question.

Claiborn, Ward, and Strong (1981), for instance, placed clients in conditions that were discrepant and congruent with the therapist's beliefs about problem causality. Clients in the congruent condition showed greater expectations for change, achieved more change, and rated higher levels of satisfaction than those in the discrepant condition. Tracey (1988) investigated attributional congruence about responsibility for the cause of the problem and found that agreement between the therapist and client was significantly related to client satisfaction, client change, and inversely related to premature termination.

O'Brien and Murdock (1993) studied shelter worker perceptions of battered women as related to the causal attributions made by those women. They found that the staff perceived clients more favorably when clients' attributions were consistent with the staff's opinions about client change. For example, women who believed the abuse was not their fault and the abuser would never change were perceived by shelter workers to be easier to work with than women believing their abuser would change. In short, perceptions of attributional congruence on the part of the shelter workers influenced their judgments about clients.

Finally, two studies (Atkinson, Worthington, Dana, & Good, 1991; Worthington & Atkinson, 1996) found that clients' perceptions about the similarity of causal beliefs with their therapists were related to ratings of therapist credibility, how well they felt understood by the therapist, and their satisfaction with therapy. Worthington and Atkinson (1996) concluded that therapists whom clients perceive to hold similar attributions of etiology are judged to be more credible and approachable than therapists holding disparate beliefs.

These studies support the theoretical and clinical argument that therapist–client attributional similarity is beneficial to outcome. A clinician's awareness of clients' attributions of problem etiology and resolution may not only help prevent ruptures of the alliance, but also, by explicitly adopting the client's theory of change, positive treatment outcomes may be enhanced.

EXPECTANCY AND ACCEPTABILITY: SELECTED FINDINGS

Client expectancies and beliefs about the credibility of specific therapeutic procedures is also an important factor to address in predicting who will benefit from therapy (Frank & Frank, 1991; Lambert, 1992). For example, Safran, Heimberg, and Juster (1997) examined the expectancies of socially phobic clients regarding their prospects for improving in cognitive–behavioral group treatment. They found that initial expectancy ratings accounted for a modest but significant portion of the variance in posttreatment severity of social phobia and depression. On the basis of these results, Safran et al. (1997) suggested that early detection of low expectancies for treatment outcome should be a priority, even when that treatment has established efficacy in other cases.

Another similar study (Hester, Miller, Delaney, & Meyers, 1990) compared the effectiveness of traditional alcohol treatment with a learning-based approach. Predictably, both approaches were initially equally effective. What was surprising was the difference that emerged 6 months later related to the beliefs and expectations the clients held about alcohol problems before treatment. Clients who believed that alcohol problems were caused by a disease were much more likely to be sober at 6-months if they had received the traditional alcoholic treatment. In contrast, clients who believed that alcohol problems were a bad habit were more likely to be successful if they had participated in the learning-based therapy. It was the match between client beliefs, expectations, and therapeutic approach that proved crucial.

At length, Crane, Griffin, and Hill (1986) found that how well treatment seemed to "fit" clients' views of their problems accounted for 35% of outcome variance. They concluded that the therapist's ability to present therapy as consistent and congruent with client expectations was critical. The credibility of a given procedure, and therefore the positive expectancy effects, is enhanced when complementary to clients' preexisting beliefs about their problems and the change process. Of course this is nothing new. As the renowned French philosopher and mathematician Blaise Pascal (1623–1662) once said, "People are generally better persuaded by the reasons which they have themselves discovered than by those which have come into the minds of others."

A construct related to expectancy, arising from the school and behavioral consultation literature, is acceptability. Kazdin (1980) asserted that although a treatment may have demonstrated its efficacy, it may still be viewed as inappropriate, unfair, unreasonable, or too intrusive to the client. Acceptability to the client of a particular procedure is a major determinant of its use and ultimate success (Elliott, Witt, Galvin, & Peterson, 1984; Murphy & Duncan, 1997; Reimers, Wacker, Cooper, & De Raad, 1992; Witt & Elliott, 1985). For example, Conoley, Ivey, Conoley, Scheel, and Bishop (1992) compared matched and unmatched intervention rationales in a study of consultation with teachers. They found a greater acceptance of and compliance with treatment when rationales were congruent with clients' perceptions about themselves, the target problem, and their theory of change.

The expectancy and acceptability research points to a similar conclusion reached from the review of the attribution literature. It is a recurring finding that the credibility of the intervention and how well it fits with client's theory of change is a variable worthy of attention. Literature on the alliance provides further support.

THE ALLIANCE

Contrast the position of matching or accommodating the client's theory with the stance of applying the therapist's treatment orientation across cases. In theory-driven approaches to psychotherapy, the orientation of the therapist takes priority over the client's views. This formal theory structures problem definition and outcome criteria. The more theory-driven the approach, the more theory-directed the goals become.

The client presents with a complaint, and the therapist recasts the complaint within the language of the therapist's theory. The therapist's reformulation of the complaint into a specific preconceived content enables treatment to proceed down a particular path prescribed by the formal theory. A clinician's loyalty to that formal theory and its later impact on the ways events are understood and handled in therapy can be understood as "theory countertransference" (Hubble & O'Hanlon, 1992).

Two of the first to call attention to the existence of theory countertransference (TC) were Salvador Ferenczi and Otto Rank, members of Freud's inner circle of followers. In 1925, they questioned certain tenets of the theoretical orthodoxy in Freud's writing and recommended practice. Ferenczi and Rank criticized how their colleagues placed more importance on proving the correctness of their theory than helping their analysands efficiently (Flegenheimer, 1982).

Milton Erickson (cited in Zeig & Gilligan, 1990) also pointedly spoke about the hazards of TC. For him, theoretical loyalty could lead to oversimplifications about people, close off possibilities for change, and promote technical inflexibility. His now famous quote summarizes his position on the role of theory in therapy:

> Each person is an individual. Hence, psychotherapy should be formulated to meet the uniqueness of the individual's needs, rather than tailoring the person to fit the Procrustean bed of a hypothetical theory of human behavior. (cited in Zeig & Gilligan, 1990, p. xix)

Rather than squeezing the client's complaint into the language and theoretic bias of the therapist's, the data suggest the exact opposite. Therapists should consider elevating the client's perceptions above theory and allow the client to direct therapeutic choices. Such a process all but guarantees the security of a strong alliance.

Gaston (1990) partitioned the alliance into four components: (a) the client's affective relationship with the therapist, (b) the client's capacity to work in therapy purposefully, (c) the therapist's empathic understanding and involvement, and (d) client–therapist agreement in the goals and tasks of therapy. Although components a and c capture the importance of the relationship and the therapist-provided variables, the client's participation and agreement on goals and tasks refer to the congruence between the client's and the therapist's beliefs about how people change in therapy (Gaston, 1990).

Accommodating the client's theory, therefore, builds a strong alliance by promoting therapist agreement with client beliefs about change as well as the goals and tasks of therapy. The therapist attends to what the client considers important, addresses what the client indicates as relevant, and tailors both in- and out-of-session intervention to accomplish goals specified by the client. The therapist and client work to construct interventions that fit with the client's experience and interpretation of the problem. Relevancy to the client is therefore all but guaranteed and relevancy of therapeutic procedures is crucial to client ratings of the alliance (see Bachelor & Horvath, and Sprenkle, Blow, & Dickey, this volume).

LEARNING AND HONORING THE CLIENT'S THEORY: PRACTICAL GUIDELINES

Within the client is a theory of change waiting for discovery, a framework for intervention to be unfolded and accommodated for a successful outcome. Each client presents the therapist with a new theory to learn, a new language to practice, and new interventions to suggest. Psychotherapy, then, is an idiosyncratic, process-determined synthesis of ideas that culminates in a new theory with explanatory and predictive validity for the client's specific circumstance.

To learn the client's theory, therapists may be best served by viewing themselves as "aliens" or visitors seeking a pristine understanding of a close encounter with the clients' unique interpretations and cultural experiences. To learn clients' theories, clinicians must adopt clients' views in their terms with a very strong bias in their favor. The process begins by listening closely to the client's language (Duncan, Hubble, Miller, & Coleman, 1998).

Beyond simply a joining tactic to enhance compliance, using clients' language privileges their particular understandings and conveys to clients the importance of their ideas and participation. It represents another way for therapists to keep clients center stage, respect their contribution to change, and build on what clients already know (S. D. Miller et al., 1997a). Speaking the client's language prevents the client from being trapped in and influenced by a particular theoretical view and increases the chances that any change will generalize outside therapy. In addition, speaking and working within the client's language provides the container for learning the client's theory.

Next, after direct inquiries about the client's goals (discussed earlier) for treatment are made, questions regarding his or her ideas about intervention are asked. What the client wants from treatment and how those goals can be accomplished may be the most important pieces of information that can be obtained. Client responses to this next series of questions provide a snapshot of the client's theory and a pathway to a successful conclusion.

- What ideas do you have about what needs to happen for improvement to occur?
- Many times people have a pretty good hunch about not only what is causing a problem, but also what will resolve it. Do you have a theory of how change is going to happen here?
- In what ways do you see me and this process being helpful to attaining your goals?

It is also helpful simply to listen for or ask about the client's usual method of or experience with change. The credibility of a procedure is further enhanced when it is based on, paired with, or elicits a previously successful experience of the client. For example,

- How does change usually happen in the client's life?
- What does the client and others do to initiate change?

Finally, a discussion of the prior solution efforts regarding the current complaint (Watzlawick et al., 1974) provides an excellent way for learning the client's theory of change and preferred modus operandi. Exploring solution attempts enables the therapist to hear the client's frank evaluation of previous efforts and their fit with what the client believes to be helpful.

- What have you tried to help the problem/situation so far? Did it help? How did it help? Why didn't it help?

Honoring the client's theory occurs when a given therapeutic procedure is complementary to clients' preexisting beliefs about their problems and the change process. Therefore, we listen and then amplify the stories, experiences, and interpretations that clients offer about their problems and their thoughts, feelings, and ideas about how those problems might best be addressed. Honoring the client's theory of change is a process-determined synthesis of ideas that evolves from listening and engaging the client's participation. We are also not saying that we never offer ideas or suggestions or that we do not contribute to the construction of the client's theory of change. Exploration for and discovery of the client's theory is a co-evolutionary process; a crisscrossing of ideas that generates a seamless connection of socially constructed meanings. The degree and intensity of our input vary and are driven by the client's expectations of our role. The client's theory of change is an "emergent reality" that unfolds from a conversation structured by the therapist's curiosity about the client's ideas, attitudes, and speculations about change. As the client's theory evolves, we implement the client's identified solutions or seek an approach that both fits the client's theory and provides possibilities for change.

SUMMARY

Setting aside the intellectual appeal of diverse models of psychotherapy, the allure of quick psychotropic fixes, and the seductiveness of so-called "treatments of choice," the common factors research suggests that successful outcome occurs largely by (a) creating a space for clients to use their resources and (b) ensuring clients' positive experience of the alliance. In this section, we proposed a third aspect of what we called "the client's frame of reference," namely the client's theory of change. A brief historical review revealed the broad base of orientations woven together by their consistent agreement about the importance of matching the client's ideas about problem formation and resolution. This section also briefly sampled the attribution, expectancy, acceptability, and alliance literatures and asserted that these diverse literatures provide empirical support for accommodating (matching, fitting, sharing attributions with, being credible to, being acceptable to) the client's theory of change. Such a process may also enhance placebo and technique factors by raising the credibility and persuasiveness of the therapist and the methods he or she uses.

Again, therapy selection must go beyond the mere prescriptive matching of client problems with empirically validated treatments (EVTs), toward a more individualized tailoring of treatment options accomplished through open and collaborative negotiation with clients. What matters, according to outcome data, is the client: the client's resources, participation, evaluation of the alliance, and perceptions of the problem and its resolution. Our techniques, it turns out, are only helpful if the client sees them as relevant and credible. Therapy models are merely potentially helpful "lenses" to be shared as they fit the client's "frame" and "prescription."

Historically, mental health professions have relegated clients to playing nameless, faceless parts in therapeutic change. This is giving way. No longer interchangeable cardboard cutouts, identified only by diagnosis or problem, clients emerge as a source of wisdom and solution. They are the true heroes and heroines of the therapeutic stage.

This book presents a strong empirical case for recasting the client as the star of a new psychotherapy drama. Because of the level playing field of models and the significance of the client's "voice" to successful outcome, we are left with trusting our clients to show us the way on their own map of the therapeutic territory. Unfolding the client's map reveals not only the destination wanted from the therapeutic journey, but also what paths may be followed to get there. We explore the landscape and cross the terrain of the client's theory of change, finding vantage points along the way that reveal the client's own routes to restoration. In that endeavor, our clients have shown us trails we never thought existed.

Science, Politics, and the Future of Psychotherapy

Speech is a mirror of the soul: As a man speaks, so is he.

—PUBLILIUS SYRUS (100 B.C.)

A recent flyer from the Behavioral Science Book Service offered to send three books deemed "The *Essential* Clinician's Reference Set" to any therapist who joined the club. What were these three books the ad claimed all mental health professionals needed and would "refer to over and over" throughout their career? In the order they appeared on the 8½ by 11 inch, multicolor brochure: *The Clinicians Thesaurus* (Zuckerman, 1995), updated to match the language of the *Diagnostic and Statistical Manual of Mental Disorders DSM–IV*, (4th ed.; APA, 1994); the second edition of *Psychotropic Drugs: Fast Facts* (Maxmen & Ward, 1995a); and *Essential Psychopathology and Its Treatment* (Maxmen & Ward, 1995b), revised to reflect new and changing diagnostic classifications contained in the *DSM–IV.* Inside the envelope, a personalized letter urged the recipient to take advantage of a superb offer—all three books could be had for just under $6. All one needed to do was fill out the membership application and agree to purchase at least one additional book over the next 12 months. The "'must read' references you'll use every day" would arrive in just a few weeks.

However hyperbolic the copy might appear, the ad provides an interesting glimpse into how others view the mental health professions. In the estimation of advertising and marketing types, at least, members of the *helping* profession define their work in terms of pathology, psychoactive drugs, and a changing professional language. These three areas of discourse are in fact, "essential" to day-to-day clinical practice. Interestingly enough, a cursory review of one of the most prestigious research and practice journals published by the American Psychological Association strongly suggests that those plying their trade on Madison Avenue are not far off the mark. For example, of all the articles appearing in the *Journal of Consulting and Clinical Psychology* during 1997, nearly 66 % were organized around a psychiatric diagnosis. More than 25% reported on specific treatments for specific disorders as defined in the *DSM*. Clearly, therapists are interested in psychopathology and specific methods for its treatment.

The same themes figure prominently in the interaction between the helping professions as a whole and the broader lay community. Take, for example, the self-help and psychology sections of most bookstores. The shelves are usually brimming with titles about the latest psychological disorder to afflict the nation. Attention-deficit disorder, posttraumatic stress, obsessive–compulsive disorder, codependency, sex addiction, and ritual satanic abuse are but a few in recent years to provoke public anxiety about their own, or their children's, mental status. Located nearby are books touting the most recent treatment developed by mental health experts for these disorders. Consider the best-selling book, *Listening to Prozac.* In this book, psychiatrist Peter Kramer explores the wide-ranging ethical and social ramifications of a drug presumed to be powerful enough to transform the personalities of its users. On a national level, mental health professional organizations, drug manufacturers, and hospital corporations design and support campaigns aimed at informing the public about the nature of psychiatric illness and benefits of professional treatment. National Depression Awareness Day, sponsored by the National Institute of Mental Health, is a good example of one such effort. The radio, television, and print media broadcast the signs and symptoms of depression and then tell people where they can go to be evaluated and speak with a professional therapist.

What is alarming about these common beliefs and practices is their serious lack of scientific support. As the contributors to this volume clearly and carefully spell out, data from more than 40 years of increasingly sophisticated outcome research evince little empirical support for

- the differential effectiveness of competing therapeutic approaches,
- the superiority of psychopharmacological over psychological intervention, or
- the utility of psychiatric classifications in either determining the appropriate course or predicting the outcome of treatment.

This alarm turns into confusion when one considers that reliable and empirically valid alternatives exist to these three traditional means for defining and organizing professional activity that have been and continue to be overlooked (S. D. Miller et al., 1997a). This is no doubt due to the radical implications their adoption would have for almost every aspect of professional training, practice, and identity.

CASE IN POINT: WEDDING APA TO THE EVTS

When money speaks, the truth keeps silent.

—Russian Proverb

In 1993, a special task force was created within Division 12 of the American Psychological Association (APA) "at the request" of one of the leading figures in the cognitive–behavior therapy movement. The purpose of the group was to promote and "disseminate important findings about innovations in psychological procedures" (Chambless, 1996; *Task Force Report on Promotion and Dissemination of Psychological Procedures,* 1993, p. 1). Prominent figures within APA argued passionately that "patients . . . have a right to safe and effective treatment" and that failing to develop a list of approved treatments was unethical" (Wilson, 1995, p. 163). In the end, the committee gave the APA "seal of approval" to 22 approaches for the treatment of 21 *DSM* disorders.

There is a certain seductive appeal to the idea of having a specific psychological intervention for a given type of problem. That therapists might possess the psychological equivalent of a "pill" for emotional distress is one that resonates strongly with the public and government policy makers. In addition, no one can argue with the success of the idea of problem-specific interventions in the field of medicine. Recent publications suggest that this point is not lost on movers and shakers within APA. In his 1996 article in the *American Psychologist,* the official house organ of the APA, researcher and cognitive–behavior therapist David Barlow argued persuasively that

> The evidence is now incontrovertible that there are effective psychological interventions for a large number of (but by no means all) psychological disorders . . . Numerous studies and subsequent meta-analyses have demonstrated that any number of specific psychotherapeutic approaches . . . are more effective than credible alternative psychological interventions. (p. 1051)

Barlow's assessment is, however, a bit like men's and women's bikini wear: interesting for what it reveals, but essential for what it conceals.

The observation that psychotherapy is, in general, effective is not particularly newsworthy. For some time now, researchers have known that the average treated person is better off than approximately 80% of those who go untreated in any particular study (Asay & Lambert, chap. 2, this volume; Lambert & Bergin, 1994). However, what Barlow means when he said, "the evidence is now incontrovertible that there are effective psychological interventions for a large number of . . . disorders" is less clear. His subsequent citation of studies on specific treatment approaches (e.g., cognitive–behavior therapy, dialectical behavior therapy) for specific problems (e.g., panic, depression, borderline personality disorder) might lead the casual reader to conclude that specific brands of therapy exist that are differentially more effective than others. However, in light of the overwhelming evidence of equivalence for competing therapeutic approaches, Barlow's statements can only be taken to mean that some treatment approaches have had the privilege of being investigated and others have not—a conclusion that hardly seems worth noting.

Statements by other leaders in APA suggest that factors unrelated to science are responsible for the drive to wed psychology to the so-called empirically validated (or supported) treatments. For example, in the June 1997 issue of *Register Report*, Peter Nathan, secretary and treasurer of the National Register of Psychologists, argued that failing to develop a list of "approved" therapies would allow competing mental health professionals to dominate and control the future of mental health practice. He pointed out that the American Psychiatric Association had already put together a list of scientifically flawed, but nonetheless comprehensive, treatment guidelines for most of the major psychiatric disorders. Nathan urged psychologists to put any "differences aside . . . and join together to confront a greater threat"—according to him, "the specter of psychiatry's [treatment] guidelines becoming psychology's" (p. 5).

What Nathan and others do not realize, however, is that attempting to "beat psychiatry to the punch" by developing a competing list of approved treatments is a de facto endorsement of the concept of treatment guidelines as defined by the American Psychiatric Association. Rather than leading, the pursuit of empirically validated treatments actually puts professional psychology in a position subservient to psychiatry: They define the game, they define the rules, and psychology simply plays along. To compete successfully psychology must stop following in the footsteps of its much envied and economically more successful half-sibling and, instead, promote reliable and empirically valid methods for enhancing effectiveness and ensuring accountability. Treatment guidelines for specific diagnostic categories accomplish neither of these objectives (S. D. Miller et al., 1997b; see also Brown et al., chap. 13, and Ogles et al., chap. 7, this volume).

The development of valid and reliable alternatives to the empirically bankrupt approaches sponsored by the American Psychiatric Association is possible using the very same body of research that psychologists have been instrumental in creating. For example, on the basis of the research discussed by Brown et al. (see chap. 13), the time of professional organizations would be better spent promoting an approved method for the routine, systematic, and empirical assessment of outcome rather than dictating which treatment approaches their members use. Going one step further, actually collecting outcome data from their members would make professional associations active participants in the development of national norms for clinical practice. Norms that could, in turn, be used to help third-party payers and other funding agencies determine appropriateness for psychological treatment based more on ability to benefit rather than psychiatric diagnosis.

This is not, however, the direction in which the various professional organizations look to be heading. For example, the *DSM*, in spite of continuing to be plagued by poor reliability and validity and having absolutely no predictive power in terms of treatment outcome (Kirk & Kutchins, 1992; Kutchins & Kirk, 1997), is now a fixed part of most graduate training programs and a prominent feature of the whole empirically validated treatment movement (Hayes & Heiby, 1996; Riley, Elliot, & Thomas, 1992). In another game of "follow the leader," the APA is attempting to wrestle prescription privileges away from the field of medicine (DeLeon & Wiggins, 1996; Klein, 1996; Lorion, 1996; *Report of the Ad Hoc Task Force on Psychopharmacology*, 1992). This is particularly perplexing given that the data reviewed in chapter 10 by Greenberg so clearly shows that being able to prescribe will not necessarily make psychologists one bit more effective or accountable. The data continues to accumulate. For example, a recent meta-analytic study of antidepressant medication published in APA's first electronic journal *Prevention and Treatment* found that virtually all of the variation in drug effect size was due to placebo factors. Such research, in combination with the data cited throughout this book, leaves little question that the organizational push for prescription privileges is motivated more by politics than concern for increasing the effectiveness of treatment (Kirsch & Sapirstein, 1998).

Believe it or not, the existing ethical codes of the three largest nonmedically oriented mental health provider organizations (National Association of Social Workers [NASW], APA, and the American Association for Marriage and Family Therapy [AAMFT]) mandate that therapists neither practice effectively nor even subject their practices to any systematic or ongoing assessment of outcome. Instead, all that is required is that therapists practice, "within the boundaries of their *competence* and experience" (APA, 1997 [Principle A], p. 1600, emphasis added; NASW, 1997 [Principle 1.04]; AAMFT, 1991 [Principle 3.4]). Historically, the assumption has been that competence engenders effectiveness. As strange as it may sound, however, a therapy can be administered competently and still be ineffective.

Several simple, straightforward methods for evaluating the progress and overall effectiveness in treatment exist besides the one proposed by Brown et al. (cf. Howard, Moras, Brill, Martinovich, & Lutz, 1996; Johnson & Shaha, 1996). These approaches take advantage of the fact, despite theoretical orientation, that the trajectory of change in successful treatment is highly predictable. Therefore, rather than repeating the failures of the past and attempting to determine a priori "what approach works for which problem" these methods focus on whether or not a given treatment is working for an individual client at a given point in time. As such, they abandon the "search for the winner" mind set that has characterized the first 100 years of psychotherapy practice and instead focus on the factors that research has shown really do make a significant contribution to outcome (e.g., incorporation of client strengths, the development of a strong therapeutic alliance, the creation of hope and expectancy, etc. [S. D. Miller et al., 1997a]).

These same factors suggest that the effectiveness of psychotherapy could also be improved by overhauling the methods used to train and credential mental health practitioners. In this regard, consider the sizable body of research that shows that the personal qualities of individual therapists contribute as much as three times more to the variance of psychotherapy outcome than the model or theoretical orientation that is used (Luborsky et al., 1986). Even adherence to a carefully designed manual or treatment protocol has failed to prevent widely varying outcomes among therapists (Luborsky, McLellan, Woody, O'Brien, & Auerbach, 1985)! These results, in combination with others showing a weak correlation between amount of training and clinical outcome, strongly suggest that admission to training and eventual credentialing be based on the ability to perform rather than the mastery of various theories or techniques. The survival of the mental health professions, in other words, will be better ensured by identifying empirically validated trea*ters* rather than empirically validated trea*tments*.

A good place to start would be the current system of continuing education for licensed professionals. In theory, the continuing education requirement is designed to ensure that clinicians stay abreast of developments that enhance treatment outcome. In reality, however, there is absolutely no evidence that participation either informs or improves clinical work. How could it? A perusal of a recent issue of *The Family Therapy Networker*, for example, will reveal ads for continuing education training that focus almost exclusively on specific therapeutic modalities—EMDR, thought field therapy™, divorce mediation, biofeedback, solution-focused therapy, advanced energy therapy, light therapy, systematic applied kinesiology, and neurolinguistic programming, to name a few. None of the methods taught in these fully accredited continuing education programs has ever proven to be reliably more effective than any other. Nor do these workshops teach therapists practical, systematic methods for either evaluating the effectiveness of or making informed modifications of the approach they learn. Rather, sole emphasis is placed on mastering the skills or techniques associated with a particular version of treatment.

In contrast, an accountable system of continuing education would be truly continuous. For example, therapists could routinely receive feedback about their work resulting from the outcome data systematically gathered and analyzed by the professional organization to which they belong. Existing technology virtually ensures that such a system is possible. Currently, therapists are free to choose the training they want—a process that likely serves to reinforce rather than correct ineffective therapy practices.

In tracking actual outcomes, moreover, the cost to the mental health provider cannot be much more than the present system, which often includes flying to a distant location, staying in a hotel, buying meals, and paying exorbitant workshop fees one or more times a year. Furthermore, and more important, such a system, dependent as it would be on client self-report data, will finally give the users of therapy the voice that 40 years of data say they deserve in the treatment process. They are, after all, the real heart and soul of change.

References

Ansbacher, H., & Ansbacher, R. (1956). *The individual psychology of Alfred Adler.* New York: Basic Books.

Atkinson, D., Worthington, R., Dana, D., & Good, G. (1991). Etiology beliefs, preferences for counseling orientations, and counseling effectiveness. *Journal of Counseling Psychology, 38,* 258–264.

Bandura, A., & Schunk, D. H. (1981). Cultivating competence, self-efficacy, and intrinsic interest through proximal self-motivation. *Journal of Personality and Social Psychology, 41,* 586–598.

Barlow, D. H. (1996). Health care policy, psychotherapy research, and the future of psychotherapy. *American Psychologist, 51,* 1050–1058.

Berg, I. K., & Miller, S. D. (1992). *Working with the problem drinker: A solution-focused approach.* New York: Norton.

Bergin, A.E., & Garfield, S. L. (Eds.). (1994). *Handbook of psychotherapy and behavior change* (4th ed.). New York: Wiley.

Beyebach, M., Morejon, A. R., Palenzuela, D. L., & Rodriguez-Arias, J. L. (1996). Research on the process of solution-focused therapy.

In S. D. Miller, M. A. Hubble, & B. L. Duncan (Eds.), *Handbook of solution-focused brief therapy* (pp. 299–334). San Francisco: Jossey-Bass.

Brickman, P., Rabinowitz, V., Karuza, J., Coates, D., Cohn, E., & Kidder, L. (1982). Models of helping and coping. *American Psychologist, 37,* 368–384.

Chambless, D. L. (1996). Identification of empirically supported psychological interventions. *Clinicians Research Digest, 14*(6), 1–2.

Claiborn, C., Ward, S., & Strong, S. (1981). Effects of congruence between counselor interpretations and client beliefs. *Journal of Counseling Psychology, 28,* 101–109.

Conoley, C. W., Ivey, D., Conoley, J. C., Scheel, M., & Bishop, R. (1992). Enhancing consultation by matching the consultee's perspectives. *Journal of Counseling Development, 69,* 546–549.

Conran, T., & Love, J. (1993). Client voices: Unspeakable theories and unknowable experiences. *Journal of Systemic Therapies, 12,* 1–19.

Crane, R. D., Griffin, W., & Hill, R. D. (1986). Influence of therapist skills on client perceptions of marriage and family therapy outcome: Implications for supervision. *Journal of Marital and Family Therapy, 12,* 91–96.

de Shazer, S., Berg, I., Lipchik, E., Nunnally, E., Molnar, A., & Gingerich, W. (1986). Brief therapy: Focused solution development. *Family Process, 25,* 207–222.

DeLeon, P. H., & Wiggins, J. G. (1996). Prescription privileges for psychologists. *American Psychologist, 51,* 225–229.

Duncan, B. L. (1989). Paradoxical procedures in family therapy. In M. Ascher (Ed.), *Therapeutic paradox* (pp. 310–348). New York: Guilford Press.

Duncan, B. L., Hubble, M. A., Miller, S. D., & Coleman, S. (1998). Escaping the lost world of impossibility: Honoring clients' language, motivations, and theories of change. In M. A. Hoyt (Ed.), *The handbook of constructive therapies* (pp. 293–313). San Francisco: Jossey-Bass.

Duncan, B. L., Hubble, M. A., & Miller, S. D. (1997a). *Psychotherapy with "impossible" cases: The efficient treatment of therapy veterans.* New York: Norton.

Duncan, B. L. Hubble, M. A., & Miller, S. D. (1997b). Stepping off the throne. *The Family Therapy Networker, 21*(4), 22–31, 33.

Duncan, B. L., Miller, S. D., & Hubble, M. A. (1998). Some therapies are more equal than others. In W. Matthews & J. Edgette (Eds.), *Current thinking and research in brief therapy: Solutions, strategies, narratives* (pp. 231–235). New York: Brunner/Mazel.

Duncan, B. L., & Moynihan, D. (1994). Applying outcome research: Intentional utilization of the client's frame of reference. *Psychotherapy, 31,* 294–301.

Duncan, B., Solovey, A., & Rusk, G. (1992). *Changing the rules: A client-directed approach.* New York: Guilford Press.

Elliott, S. N., Witt, J. C., Galvin, G., & Peterson, R. (1984). Acceptability of behavior interventions: Factors that influence teachers' decisions. *Journal of School Psychology, 22,* 353–360.

Eron, J., & Lund, T. (1996). *Narrative solutions in brief therapy.* New York: Guilford Press.

Ethical Principles for Marriage and Family Therapists. (1991). Washington, DC: American Association for Marriage and Family Therapy.

Ethical Principles for Psychologists. (1997). Washington, DC: American Psychological Association.

Ethical Principles for Social Workers. (1997). Washington, DC: National Association of Social Workers.

Fancher, R. (1995). *Cultures of healing: Correcting the image of American mental health care.* New York: Freeman.

Fisch, R., Weakland, J., & Segal, L. (1982). *The tactics of change.* San Francisco: Jossey-Bass.

Flegenheimer, W. V. (1982). *Techniques of brief psychotherapy.* New York: Aronson.

Flemons, D., & Green, S. (1998). Hanging on to letting go: A relational approach to sex therapy. In W. Matthews & J. Edgette (Eds.), *Current thinking and research in brief therapy: Solution, strategies, narratives* (pp. 29–56). New York: Brunner/Mazel.

Frank, J. D. (1995). Psychotherapy as rhetoric: Some implications. *Clinical Psychology: Science and Practice, 2,* 90–93.

Frank, J. D., & Frank, J. B. (1991). *Persuasion and healing: A comparative study of psychotherapy* (3rd ed.). Baltimore: Johns Hopkins University Press.

Frazer, J. G. (1920). *The golden bough.* New York: Collier Books.

Garfield, S. L. (1989). *The practice of brief psychotherapy.* New York: Pergamon.

Gaston, L. (1990). The concept of the alliance and its role in psychotherapy: Theoretical and empirical considerations. *Psychotherapy, 27,* 143–152.

Gergen, K. J. (1985). The social constructionist movement in modern psychology. *American Psychologist, 40,* 266–275.

Goolishian, H., & Anderson, H. (1987). Language systems and therapy: An evolving idea. *Psychotherapy, 24,* 529–538.

Hayes, S. C., & Heiby, E. (1996). Psychology's drug problem: Do we need a fix or should we just say no? *American Psychologist, 51,* 198–206.

Held, B. S. (1986). The relationship between individual psychologies and strategic/systemic therapies reconsidered. In D. E. Efron (Ed.), *Journeys: Expansion of the strategic systemic therapies* (pp. 222–260). New York: Brunner/Mazel.

Held, B. S. (1991). The process/content distinction revisited. *Psychotherapy, 28,* 207–218.

Hester, R., Miller, W., & Delaney, H., & Meyers, R. (1990, November). *Effectiveness of the community reinforcement approach.* Paper presented at the 24th annual meeting of the Association for the Advancement of Behavior Therapy, San Francisco, CA.

Hoch, P. (1955). Aims and limitations of psychotherapy. *American Journal of Psychiatry, 112,* 321–327.

Howard, K. I., Koptea, S. M., Krause, M. S., & Orlinsky, D. E. (1986). The dose–effect relationship in psychotherapy. *American Psychologist, 41,* 159–164.

Howard, K. I., Moras, K., Brill, P. L. Martinovich, Z., & Lutz, W. (1996). Evaluation of psychotherapy: Efficacy, effectiveness, and patient progress. *American Psychologist, 51,* 1059–1065.

Hoyt, M. F. (1998). *The handbook of the constructive therapies.* San Francisco: Jossey-Bass.

Hubble, M. A., Miller, S. D., & Duncan, B. L. (1998). S.W.A.T.: "Special" words and tactics for critical situations. *Crisis Intervention and Time-Limited Treatment, 4,* 179–195.

Hubble, M. A., & O'Hanlon, W. H. (1992). Theory countertransference. *Dulwich Centre Newsletter,* (1), 25–30.

Imber, S. D., Pilkonis, P. A., Harway, N. I., Klein, R. H., & Rubinsky, P. A. (1982). Maintenance of change in the psychotherapies. *Journal of Psychiatric Treatment and Evaluation, 4,* 1–5.

Johnson, L., & Shaha, S. (1996). Improving quality in psychotherapy. *Psychotherapy, 35,* 225–236.

Kazdin, A. E. (1980). Acceptability of alternative treatments for deviant child behavior. *Journal of Applied Behavior Analysis, 13,* 259–273.

Kirk, S. A., & Kutchins, H. (1992). *The selling of DSM: The rhetoric of science in psychiatry.* New York: Aldine.

Kirsch, I., & Sapirstein, G. (1998). Listening to prozac but hearing placebo: A meta-analysis of antidepressant medication. *Prevention and Treatment, 1,* Article 0002a.

Klein, R. G. (1996). Comments on expanding the clinical role of psychologists. *American Psychologist, 51,* 216–218.

Kottler, J. (1991). *The complete therapist.* San Francisco: Jossey-Bass.

Kral, R., & Kowalski, K. (1989). After the miracle: The second stage in solution-focused brief therapy. *Journal of Strategic and Systemic Therapies, 8*(2–3), 73–76.

Kramer, P. (1997). *Listening to prozac.* New York: Penguin.

Kutchins, H., & Kirk, S. A. (1997). *Making us crazy.* New York: Free Press.

Lambert, M. J. (1992). Implications of outcome research for psychotherapy integration. In J. C. Norcross & M. R. Goldfried (Eds.), *Handbook of psychotherapy integration* (pp. 94–129). New York: Basic Books.

Lambert, M. J., & Bergin, A. E. (1994). The effectiveness of psychotherapy. In A. E. Bergin & S. L. Garfield (Eds.), *Handbook of psychotherapy and behavior change* (pp. 143–189). New York: Wiley.

Lawson, D. (1994). Identifying pretreatment change. *Journal of Counseling and Development, 72,* 244–248.

Locke, E. A., Shaw, K. N., Saari, L. M., & Latham, G. P. (1981). Goal setting and task performance: 1969–1980. *Psychological Bulletin, 90,* 125–152.

Lorion, R. P. (1996). Applying our medicine to the psychopharmacology debate. *American Psychologist, 51,* 219–224.

Luborsky, L., Crits-Cristoph, P., McLellan, T., Woody, G., Piper, W., Liberman, B., Imber, S., & Pilkonis, P. (1986). Do therapists vary much in their success? Findings from four outcome studies. *American Journal of Orthopsychiatry, 56,* 501–512.

Luborsky, L., McLellan, A. T., Woody, G. E., O'Brien, C. P., & Auerbach, A. (1985). Therapist success and its determinants. *Archives of General Psychiatry, 42,* 602–611.

Martin, J. (1988). A proposal for researching possible relationships between scientific theories and the personal theories of counselors and clients. *Journal of Counseling and Development, 66,* 261–265.

Matheson, D., Bruce, R., & Beauchamp, K. (1978). *Experimental psychology: Research design and analysis.* New York: Holt, Rhinehart and Winston.

Maxmen, J. S., & Ward, N. G. (1995a). *Essential psychopathology and it's treatment.* New York: Norton.

Maxmen, J. S., & Ward, N. G. (1995b). *Psychotropic drugs: Fast facts.* New York: Norton.

Miller, S. D. & Berg, I. K. (1995). *The miracle method: A radically new approach to problem drinking.* New York: Norton.

Miller, S. D., Duncan, M. A., & Hubble, M. A. (1997a). *Escape from Babel: Toward a unifying language for psychotherapy practice.* New York: Norton.

Miller, S. D., Duncan, B. L., & Hubble, M. A. (1997b). Why the E.V.T. movement is dead wrong [letter to the editor]. *Social Work, 42*(6), 619.

Miller, W. R. (1986). Increasing motivation for change. In W. R. Miller & N. H. Heather (Eds.). *Addictive behaviors: Processes of change* (pp. 67–80). New York: Plenum Press.

Miller, W. R. (1987). Motivation and treatment goals. *Drugs and Society, 1,* 131–151.

Mohl, D. C. (1995). Negative outcome in psychotherapy: A critical review. *Clinical Psychology: Science and Practice, 2,* 1–27.

Murphy, J. J., & Duncan, B. L.(1997). *Brief intervention for school problems.* New York: Guilford Press.

Nathan, P. E. (1997). Fiddling while psychology burns? *Register Report, 23*(2), 1, 4–5, 10.

Neimeyer, R. A., & Mahoney, M. J. (Eds.). (1995). *Constructivism in psychotherapy.* Washington, DC: American Psychological Association.

O'Brien, D., & Murdock, N. (1993). Shelter workers' perceptions of battered women. *Sex Roles, 29,* 183–194.

O'Regan, B. (1985). Placebo: The hidden asset in healing. *Investigations: A Research Bulletin, 2*(1), 1–3.

Orlinsky, D. E., & Howard, K. I. (1986). Process and outcome in psychotherapy. In S. L. Garfield & A. E. Bergin (Eds.), *Handbook of psychotherapy and behavior change* (3rd ed.). New York: Wiley.

Prochaska, J. O. (1993). Working in harmony with how people change naturally. *The Weight Control Digest, 3,* 249, 252–255.

Prochaska, J. O. (1995). Common problems: Common solutions. *Clinical Psychology: Science and Practice, 2,* 101–105.

Prochaska, J. O., & DiClemente, C. C. (1982). Transtheoretical therapy: Toward a more integrative model of change. *Psychotherapy, 19,* 276–288.

Prochaska, J. O., & DiClemente, C. C. (1992). The transtheoretical approach. In J. D. Norcross & M. R. Goldfried (Eds.), *Handbook of psychotherapy integration* (pp. 300–334). New York: Basic Books.

Prochaska, J. O., DiClemente, C. C., & Norcross, J. C. (1992). In search of how people change. *American Psychologist, 47,* 1102–1114.

Reimers, T. M., Wacker, D. P., Cooper, L. J., & De Raad, A. O. (1992). Acceptability of behavioral treatments for children: Analog and naturalistic evaluations by parents. *School Psychology Review, 21,* 628–643.

Report of the Ad Hoc Task Force on Psychopharmacology. (1992). Washington, DC: American Psychological Association.

Riley, W. T., Elliot, R. L., & Thomas, J. R. (1992). Impact of prescription privileging on psychology training: Training director's survey. *The Clinical Psychologist, 45,* 63–70.

Safran, S., Heimberg, R., & Juster, H. (1997). Clients' expectancies and their relationship to pretreatment symptomatology and outcome of cognitive–behavioral group treatment for social phobia. *Journal of Consulting and Clinical Psychology, 65,* 694–698.

Shilts, L., Fillippino, C., & Nau, D. (1994). Client-informed therapy. *Journal of Systemic Therapies, 13,* 39–52.

Simon, D. (1996). Crafting consciousness through form: Solution-focused therapy as a spiritual path. In S. D. Miller, M. A. Hubble, & B. L. Duncan (Eds.), *Handbook of solution-focused brief therapy* (pp. 44–62). San Francisco: Jossey-Bass.

Smith, M. L., & Glass, G. V. (1987). *Research and evaluation in education and the social sciences.* Englewood Cliffs, NJ: Prentice-Hall.

Smith, M. L., Glass, G. V., & Miller, T. I. (1980). *The benefits of psychotherapy.* Baltimore: Johns Hopkins University Press.

Steenbarger, B. N. (1992). Toward science–practice integration in brief counseling and therapy. *The Counseling Psychologist, 20,* 403–450.

Steenbarger, B. N. (1994). Duration and outcome in psychotherapy: An integrative review. *Professional Psychology, 25,* 111–119.

Talmon, M. (1988, December). *When the first session is the last: A map for rapid therapeutic change.* Paper presented at the Fourth International Congress on Ericksonian Approaches to Hypnosis and Psychotherapy, San Francisco, CA.

Talmon, M. (1990). *Single session therapy.* San Francisco: Jossey-Bass.

Task Force Report on Promotion and Dissemination of Psychological Practices. (1993). Washington, DC: American Psychological Association.

Taylor, S. E., Wayment, H. A., & Collins, M. A. (1993). Positive illusions and affect regulation. In D. M. Wegner & J. W. Pennebaker (Eds.), *Handbook of mental control* (pp. 325–343). Englewood Cliffs, NJ: Prentice-Hall.

Torrey, E. (1972). *The mind game: Witchdoctors and psychiatrists.* New York: Emerson Hall.

Tracey, T. (1988). Relationship of responsibility attribution congruence to psychotherapy outcome. *Journal of Social and Clinical Psychology, 7,* 131–146.

Van Gennep, A. (1960). *The rites of passage.* Chicago: Chicago University Press.

Walter, J., & Peller, J. (1992). *Becoming solution-focused in brief therapy.* New York: Brunner-Mazel.

Walters, J., & Peller, J. (1996). Rethinking our assumptions: Assuming anew in a postmodern world. In S. D. Miller, M. A. Hubble, & B. L. Duncan (Eds.), *Handbook of solution-focused brief therapy* (pp. 9–26). San Francisco: Jossey-Bass.

Watzlawick, P. (1986). If you desire to see, learn how to act. In J. Zeig, (Ed.), *The evolution of psychotherapy* (pp. 91–104). New York: Brunner/Mazel.

Watzlawick, P., Weakland, J., & Fisch, R. (1974). *Change: Problem formation and problem resolution.* New York: Norton.

Weiner-Davis, M., de Shazer, S., & Gingerich, W. (1987). Building on pretreatment change to construct the therapeutic solution: An exploratory study. *Journal of Marital and Family Therapy, 13,* 359–364.

Wile, D. (1977). Ideological conflicts between clients and psychotherapists. *American Journal of Psychotherapy, 37,* 437–449.

Wilford, J. (1986). *The riddle of the dinosaur.* New York: Knopf.

Wilson, G. T. (1995). Empirically validated treatments as a basis for clinical practice: Problems and prospects. In S. C. Hayes, V. M. Follette, R. M. Dawes & K. E. Grady (Eds.), *Scientific standards of psychological practice: Issues and recommendations* (pp. 163–196). Reno, NV: Context Press.

Witt, J. C., & Elliott, S. N. (1985). Acceptability of classroom intervention strategies. In T. Kratochwill (Ed.), *Advances in school psychology* (pp. 251–288). Hillsdale, NJ: Erlbaum.

Wolberg, L. (1954). *The technique of psychotherapy.* New York: Grune & Stratton.

Wolberg, L. (1977). *The technique of psychotherapy* (3rd ed.). New York: Grune & Stratton.

Worthington, R., & Atkinson, D. (1996). Effects of perceived etiology attribution similarity on client ratings of counselor credibility. *Journal of Counseling Psychology, 43,* 423–429.

Zeig, J. K., & Gilligan, S. G. (Eds.). (1990). *Brief therapy: Myths, methods, and metaphors.* New York: Brunner/Mazel.

Zuckerman, E. L. (1995). *Clinician's thesaurus* (4th ed.). New York: Guilford Press.

Index

About the Editors

Mark A. Hubble, PhD, is a national trainer, author, and consultant. Dr. Hubble is a graduate of the postdoctoral fellowship in clinical psychology at Menninger and is a member of the Editorial Advisory Board of the *Journal of Systemic Therapies*. Dr. Hubble founded and directed the Brief Therapy Clinic at the University of Missouri, Kansas City. He has also served as a contributing editor of *The Family Therapy Networker*. Currently, he is a member of the senior faculty for the Family Therapy Institute of Columbus, Ohio.

Barry L. Duncan, PsyD, is an educator, trainer, and therapist with more than 40 publications and 14,000 hours of clinical experience. An approved supervisor of the American Association for Marriage and Family Therapy, Dr. Duncan also holds an associate professorship in the Department of Family Therapy at Nova Southeastern University. In addition to the books he has authored with Mark A. Hubble and Scott D. Miller, Dr. Duncan has co-authored *Overcoming Relationship Impasses: Ways to Initiate Change When Your Partner Won't Help* (Insight Books, 1991), *Changing the Rules: A Client-Directed Approach to Therapy* (Guilford, 1992), and *Brief Intervention for School Problems* (Guilford, 1997).

Scott D. Miller, PhD, is a therapist and trainer both in the United States and abroad. Dr. Miller is also a member of the Editorial Advisory Board of the *Journal of Systemic Therapies*. An author of numerous publications, Dr. Miller has presented to the American Psychological Association, the International Congress on Ericksonian Approaches to Hypnosis, the International Society for the Study of Multiple Personality and Dissociation, and the National Association of Social Workers, among many other organizations. He is coauthor of *Working With the Problem Drinker: A Solution-Focused Approach* (Norton, 1992), *Finding the Adult Within: A Solution-Focused Self-Help Guide* (Brief Therapy Center, 1994), and *The "Miracle" Method: A Radically New Method for Finding Solutions to Problem Drinking* (Norton, 1995).

Dr. Hubble, Dr. Duncan, and Dr. Miller are founders of the Institute for the Study of Therapeutic Change. Their collaboration has culminated in three books: *The Handbook of Solution-Focused Brief Therapy* (Jossey-Bass, 1996), *Escape From Babel: Toward a Unifying Language for Psychotherapy Practice* (Norton, 1997), and *Psychotherapy With "Impossible" Cases: The Efficient Treatment of Therapy Veterans* (Norton, 1997).